BLOOM'S PERIOD STUDIES

BLOOM'S PERIOD STUDIES

Elizabethan Drama

Edited and with an introduction by
Harold Bloom
Sterling Professor of the Humanities
Yale University

CHELSEA HOUSE
PUBLISHERS
A Haights Cross Communications Company
Philadelphia

©2004 by Chelsea House Publishers, a subsidiary of
Haights Cross Communications.

A Haights Cross Communications Company

Introduction © 2004 by Harold Bloom.

Printed and bound in the United States of America.
10 9 8 7 6 5 4 3 2 1

Library of Congress Cataloging-in-Publication Data
Applied for.
ISBN: 0-7910-7675-X

Chelsea House Publishers
1974 Sproul Road, Suite 400
Broomall, PA 19008-0914

http://www.chelseahouse.com

Contributing Editors: Brett Foster and Camille-Yvette Welsch

Cover designed by Keith Trego

Layout by EJB Publishing Services

Contents

Editor's Note

My Introduction begins with a general overview of the Jacobean hero-villain in Marlowe's Barabas, the Jew of Malta and Jonson's *Volpone*, before returning to John Webster's Basola in *The Duchess of Malfi*.

Theatrical contexts are provided by Peter Happé, while Martin Wiggins shows the minting of new plays out of old, and Eugene Waith introduces us to Marlowe and his *Tamburlaine* plays. Marlowe's *Doctor Faustus* and *Edward II* are analyzed by Martha Tuck Rozett and Patrick Cheney, respectively.

Muriel Bradbrook traces Shakespeare's inheritance from the highly mannered John Lyly and from the roustabouts Peele, Greene, and Nashe.

Henry of Navarre, who turned Catholic so as to enter Paris as Henry IV in 1593, makes appearances in Marlowe, Shakespeare, and Spenser, as is chronicled here by Paul Voss.

Alvin Kernan perceptively contrasts the attitudes of Shakespeare and Ben Jonson to their audiences, after which Richard Dutton finds in Robert Armin's replacement of Will Kempe as Shakespeare's principal comedian an effect of the Privy Council's meddling with the stage during 1598-1610.

The "Poets' War" between Jonson, and Shakespeare with his allies, is splendidly recounted in two extracts from James P. Bednarz's book on the subject, and then is taken up again by Matthew Steggle.

Jonathan Dollimore expounds Cyril Tourneur's parodistic *The Revenger's Tragedy* and George Chapman's heroic *Bussy D'Ambois*, while Gail Kern Paster examines the city comedies of Jonson and Thomas Middleton.

Jonson's exuberant *Bartholomew Fair* is acutely analyzed by Leah S. Marcus, after which Stephen Orgel learnedly describes the Court masques.

G.K. Hunter provides fresh insights into Shakespeare's *The Winter's Tale* and *Cymbeline* as instances of tragicomedy, while Anthony B. Dawson confronts the language of Thomas Middleton's *The Changeling* in this volume's final essay.

HAROLD BLOOM

Introduction

The Jacobean Hero-Villain

I

Why, I, in this weak piping time of peace,
Have no delight to pass away the time,
Unless to see my shadow in the sun
And descant on mine own deformity.
And therefore, since I cannot prove a lover
To entertain these fair well-spoken days,
I am determined to prove a villain
And hate the idle pleasures of these days.

The opening ferocity of Richard, still Duke of Gloucester, in *The Tragedy of Richard the Third*, is hardly more than a fresh starting-point for the development of the Elizabethan and Jacobean hero-villain after Marlowe, and yet it seems to transform Tamburlaine and Barabas utterly. Richard's peculiarly self-conscious pleasure in his own audacity is crossed by the sense of what it means to see one's own deformed shadow in the sun. We are closer already not only to Edmund and Iago than to Barabas, but especially closer to Webster's Lodovico who so sublimely says: "I limn'd this nightpiece and it was my best." Except for Iago, nothing seems farther advanced in this desperate mode than Webster's Bosola:

O direful misprision!
I will not imitate things glorious,
No more than base: I'll be mine own example.—
On, on, and look thou represent, for silence,
The thing thou bear'st.

Iago is beyond even this denial of representation, because he does will silence:

1

Demand me nothing; what you know, you know;
From this time forth I never will speak word.

Iago is no hero-villain, and no shift of perspective will make him into one.
Pragmatically, the authentic hero-villain in Shakespeare might be judged to be
Hamlet, but no audience would agree. Macbeth could justify the description,
except that the cosmos of his drama is too estranged from any normative
representation for the term hero-villain to have its oxymoronic coherence.
Richard and Edmund would appear to be the models, beyond Marlowe, that
could have inspired Webster and his fellows, but Edmund is too uncanny and
superb a representation to provoke emulation. That returns us to Richard:

Was ever woman in this humor woo'd?
Was ever woman in this humor won?
I'll have her, but I will not keep her long.
What? I, that kill'd her husband and his father,
To take her in her heart's extremest hate,
With curses in her mouth, tears in her eyes,
The bleeding witness of my hatred by,
Having God, her conscience, and these bars against me,
And I no friends to back my suit [at all]
And the plain devil and dissembling looks?
And yet to win her! All the world to nothing!
Hah!
Hath she forgot already that brave prince,
Edward, her lord, whom I, some three months since,
Stabb'd in my angry mood at Tewksbury?
A sweeter and a lovelier gentleman,
Fram'd in the prodigality of nature
Young, valiant, wise, and (no doubt) right royal—
The spacious world cannot again afford.
And will she yet abase her on me,
That cropp'd the golden prime of this sweet prince
And made her widow to a woeful bed?
On me, whose all not equals Edward's moi'ty?
On me, that halts and am misshapen thus?
My dukedom to a beggarly denier,
I do mistake my person all this while!
Upon my life, she finds (although I cannot)
Myself to be a marv'llous proper man.
I'll be at charges for a looking-glass,
And entertain a score or two of tailors
To study fashions to adorn my body:

Since I am crept in favor with myself,
I will maintain it with some little cost.
But first I'll turn yon fellow in his grave,
And then return lamenting to my love.
Shine out, fair sun, till I have bought a glass,
That I may see my shadow as I pass.

Richard's only earlier delight was "to see my shadow in the sun / And descant on mine own deformity." His savage delight in the success of his own manipulative rhetoric now transforms his earlier trope into the exultant command: "Shine out, fair sun, till I have bought a glass, / That I may see my shadow as I pass." That transformation is the formula for interpreting the Jacobean hero-villain and his varied progeny: Milton's Satan, the Poet in Shelley's *Alastor*, Wordsworth's Oswald in *The Borderers*, Byron's Manfred and Cain, Browning's Childe Roland, Tennyson's Ulysses, Melville's Captain Ahab, Hawthorne's Chillingworth, down to Nathanael West's Shrike in *Miss Lonelyhearts*, who perhaps ends the tradition. The manipulative, highly self-conscious, obsessed hero-villain, whether Machiavellian plotter or later, idealistic quester, ruined or not, moves himself from being the passive sufferer of his own moral and/or physical deformity to becoming a highly active melodramatist. Instead of standing in the light of nature to observe his own shadow, and then have to take his own deformity as subject, he rather commands nature to throw its light upon his own glass of representation, so that his own shadow will be visible only for an instant as he passes on to the triumph of his will over others.

II

No figure in this tradition delights me personally more than Barabas, Marlowe's Jew of Malta, who so fittingly is introduced by Machiavel himself:

Albeit the world think Machiavel is dead,
Yet was his soul but flown beyond the Alps,
And now the Guise is dead, is come from France,
To view this land, and frolic with his friends.
To some perhaps my name is odious,
But such as love me guard me from their tongues;
And let them know that I am Machiavel,
And weigh not men, and therefore not men's words.
Admired I am of those that hate me most.
Though some speak openly against my books,
Yet will they read me, and thereby attain
To Peter's chair: and when they cast me off,
Are poisoned by my climbing followers.

I count religion but a childish toy,
And hold there is no sin but ignorance.
Birds of the air will tell murders past!
I am ashamed to hear such fooleries.
Many will talk of title to a crown:
What right had Caesar to the empire?
Might first made kings, and laws were then most sure
When, like the Draco's they were writ in blood.
Hence comes it that a strong-built citadel
Commands much more than letters can import;
Which maxim had but Phalaris observed,
H'had never bellowed, in a brazen bull,
Of great ones' envy. Of the poor petty wights
Let me be envied and not pitied!
But whither am I bound? I come not, I,
To read a lecture here in Britain,
But to present the tragedy of a Jew,
Who smiles to see how full his bags are crammed,
Which money was not got without my means.
I crave but this—grace him as he deserves,
And let him not be entertained the worse
Because he favors me.

From Shakespeare's Richard III and Macbeth through Webster's Bosola and Flamineo on to Melville's Ahab and, finally, to West's Shrike, the descendants of Marlowe's Machiavel have held there is no sin but ignorance, and have become involuntary parodies of what ancient heresy called gnosis, a knowing in which the knower seeks the knowledge of the abyss. Nihilism, uncanny even to Nietzsche, is the atmosphere breathed cannily by the Jacobean hero-villain, who invariably domesticates the abyss. Barabas, Machiavel's favorite, wins our zestful regard because of the Groucho Marxian vitalism of his deliciously evil self-knowings:

As for myself, I walk abroad a'nights
And kill sick people groaning under walls:
Sometimes I go about and poison wells;
And now and then, to cherish Christian thieves,
I am content to lose some of my crowns,
That I may, walking in my gallery,
See 'em go pinioned along by my door.
Being young, I studied physic, and began
To practice first upon the Italian;
There I enriched the priests with burials,

And always kept the sexton's arms in ure
With digging graves and ringing dead men's knells:
And after that was I an engineer,
And in the wars 'twixt France and Germany,
Under pretense of helping Charles the Fifth,
Slew friends and enemy with my strategems.
Then after that was I an usurer,
And with extorting, cozening, forfeiting,
And tricks belonging unto brokery,
I filled the jails with bankrupts in a year,
And with young orphans planted hospitals,
And every moon made some or other mad,
And now and then one hang himself for grief,
Pinning upon his breast a long great scroll
How I with interest tormented him.
But mark how I am blessed for plaguing them;
I have as much coin as will buy the town.
But tell me now, how hast thou spent thy time?

The hyperboles here are so outrageous that Marlowe's insouciant identification with Barabas becomes palpable, and we begin to feel that this is how Tamburlaine the Great would sound and act if he had to adjust his overreachings to the limits of being a Jew in Christian Malta. Barabas is too splendidly grotesque a mockery to set a pattern for dramatic poets like Webster, Tourneur, Ford, and Middleton. They found their model for revenge tragedy in Kyd rather than Shakespeare, for many of the same reasons that they based their dark knowers upon Marston's Malevole in *The Malcontent* rather than upon Barabas. We begin to hear in Malevole what will culminate in Tourneur's *The Revenger's Tragedy* and in Webster's *The White Devil* and *The Duchess of Malfi*. Disdaining to take revenge upon his craven enemy, Mendoza, Malevole expresses a contempt so intense and so universal as to open up the abyss of nihilism:

O I have seene strange accidents of state,
The flatterer like the Ivy clip the Oke,
And wast it to the hart: lust so confirm'd
That the black act of sinne it selfe not shamd
To be termde Courtship.
O they that are as great as be their sinnes,
Let them remember that th'inconstant people,
Love many Princes meerely for their faces,
And outward shewes: and they do covet more
To have a sight of these then of their vertues,
Yet thus much let the great ones still conceale,

When they observe not Heavens imposd conditions,
They are no Kings, but forfeit their commissions.

That, for a Jacobean, leaves not much, and is the prelude to the hysterical
eloquence of Tourneur's Vindice the revenger:

And now methinks I could e'en chide myself
For doting on her beauty, though her death
Shall be revenged after no common action.
Does the silkworm expend her yellow labors
For thee? For thee does she undo herself?
Are lordships sold to maintain ladyships
For the poor benefit of a bewitching minute?
Why does yon fellow falsify highways
And put his life between the judge's lips
To refine such a thing, keeps horse and men
To beat their valors for her?
Surely we're all mad people and they,
Whom we think are, are not: we mistake those.
'Tis we are mad in sense, they but in clothes.

Does every proud and self-affecting dame
Camphor her face for this, and grieve her maker
In sinful baths of milk, when many an infant starves
For her superfluous outside—all for this?
Who now bids twenty pound a night, prepares
Music, perfumes and sweetmeats? All are hushed,
Thou may'st lie chaste now! It were fine, methinks,
To have thee seen at revels, forgetful feasts
And unclean brothels; sure 'twould fright the sinner
And make him a good coward, put a reveler
Out of his antic amble,
And cloy an epicure with empty dishes.
Here might a scornful and ambitious woman
Look through and through herself; see, ladies, with false forms
You deceive men but cannot deceive worms.
Now to my tragic business. Look you, brother,
I have not fashioned this only for show
And useless property, no—it shall bear a part
E'en in its own revenge. This very skull,
Whose mistress the duke poisoned with this drug,
The mortal curse of the earth, shall be revenged
In the like strain and kiss his lips to death.

As much as the dumb thing can, he shall feel;
What fails in poison we'll supply in steel.

It takes some considerable effort to recall that Vindice is addressing the skull of his martyred mistress, and that he considers her, or any woman whatsoever, worth revenging. These remarkable lines were much admired by T.S. Eliot, and one sees why; they are close to his ideal for dramatic poetry, and their intense aversion to female sexuality suited his own difficult marital circumstances during one bad phase of his life. What the passage clearly evidences is that Vindice is a true Jacobean hero-villain; he is more than skeptical as to the value of his own motivations, or of anyone else's as well. But this is hardly the historical skepticism that scholars delight in tracing; it has little to do with the pragmatism of Machiavelli, the naturalism of Montaigne, or the Hermeticism of Bruno. The horror of nature involved, whatever Tourneur's personal pathology, amounts to a kind of Gnostic asceticism, akin to the difficult stance of Macbeth and Lady Macbeth. Perhaps the hero-villain, like Milton's Satan, is truly in rebellion against the God of the Jews and the Christians, the God of this world.

III

Though the central tradition of the hero-villain goes directly from Shakespeare through Milton on to the High Romantics and their heirs, we might be puzzled at certain strains in Browning, Tennyson, Hawthorne, and Melville, if we had not read John Webster's two astonishing plays, *The White Devil* and *The Duchess of Malfi*. Russell Fraser memorably caught Webster's curious link to Marlowe, whom he otherwise scarcely resembles:

> His violent protagonists are memorable as they are endowed with the same amoral energy with which Barabas and Tamburlaine and Mortimer are endowed. Unlike these Marlovian heroes or hero-villains, they do not speak to us—quoting from Michael Drayton's tribute to Marlowe—of "brave translunary things," rather of the charnel house and the grisly business appurtenant to it.

Here is the death scene of Flamineo, and of his sister, Vittoria Corombona, in *The White Devil*:

VIT. COR. Oh, my greatest sin lay in my blood!
   Now my blood pays for't.
FLAM.   Thou'rt a noble sister!
   I love thee now. If woman do breed man,
   She ought to teach him manhood. Fare thee well.

Know, many glorious women that are famed
For masculine virtue have been vicious,
Only a happier silence did betide them.
She hath no faults who hath the art to hide them.
VIT. COR. My soul, like to a ship in a black storm,
Is driven I know not whither.
FLAM.   Then cast anchor.
Prosperity doth bewitch men, seeming clear,
But seas do laugh, show white, when rocks are near.
We cease to grieve, cease to be fortune's slaves,
Nay, cease to die, by dying. Art thou gone?
And thou so near the bottom? False report,
Which says that women vie with the nine Muses
For nine tough durable lives! I do not look
Who went before, nor who shall follow me;
No, at myself I will begin and end.
While we look up to heaven, we confound
Knowledge with knowledge. Oh, I am in a mist!
VIT. COR. Oh, happy they that never saw the court,
Nor ever knew great men but by report!
                        VITTORIA dies.
FLAM. I recover like a spent taper, for a flash,
                And instantly go out.
Let all that belong to great men remember the
old wives' tradition, to be like the lions i' the
Tower on Candlemas-day: to mourn if the sun
shine, for fear of the pitiful remainder of
winter to come.
'Tis well yet there's some goodness in my death;
My life was a black charnel. I have caught
An everlasting cold; I have lost my voice
Most irrecoverably. Farewell, glorious villains!
This busy trade of life appears most vain,
Since rest breeds rest where all seek pain by pain.
Let no harsh flattering bells resound my knell;
Strike, thunder, and strike loud, to my farewell!
                                        Dies.

Vittoria Corombona rides her black ship to Hell without final knowledge, but Flamineo is a knower, a Machiavel in the high Marlovian sense, which has its Gnostic aspect. By beginning and ending "at myself," Flaminio seeks to avoid a final agon between his self-knowledge and a rival Christian knowledge: "While we look up to heaven, we confound / Knowledge with knowledge." And yet,

Flamineo cries out: "Oh, I am in a mist!", which is what it is to the confounded, and perhaps leads to the self-epitaph: "My life was a black charnel." The mist appears also in the death speech of a greater hero-villain than Flamineo, Bosola in *The Duchess of Malfi*:

> In a mist; I know not how;
> Such a mistake as I have often seen
> In a play. Oh, I am gone.
> We are only like dead walls, or vaulted graves
> That ruined, yields no echo. Fare you well;
> It may be pain, but no harm to me to die
> In so good a quarrel. Oh, this gloomy world,
> In what shadow, or deep pit of darkness
> Doth womanish and fearful mankind live?
> Let worthy minds ne'er stagger in distrust
> To suffer death or shame for what is just.
> Mine is another voyage.
>
> *Dies.*

Bosola's final vision is of the cosmic emptiness, what the Gnostics called the *kenoma*, into which we have been thrown: "a shadow, or deep pit of darkness." When Bosola dies, saying: "Mine is another voyage," he may mean simply that he is not suffering death for what is just, unlike those who have "worthy minds." But this is Bosola, master of direful misprision, whose motto is: "I will not imitate things glorious, / No more than base; I'll be mine own example." This repudiation of any just representation of essential nature is also a Gnostic repudiation of nature, in favor of an antithetical quest: "On, on: and look thou represent, for silence, / The thing thou bearest." What Bosola both carries and endures, and so represents, by a kind of super-mimesis, is that dark quest, whose admonition, "on, on" summons one to the final phrase: "Mine is another voyage." As antithetical quester, Bosola prophesies Milton's Satan voyaging through Chaos towards the New World of Eden, and all those destructive intensities of wandering self-consciousness from Wordsworth's Solitary through the Poet of Alastor on to their culmination in the hero-villain who recites the great dramatic monologue, "Childe Roland to the Dark Tower Came":

> Burningly it came on me all at once,
>   This was the place! those two hills on the right,
>   Crouched like two bulls locked horn in horn in fight;
> While to the left, a tall scalped mountain ... Dunce,
> Dotard, a-dozing at the very nonce,
>   After a life spent training for the sight!

What in the midst lay but the Tower itself?
>The round squat turret, blind as the fool's heart,
>>Built of brown stone, without a counterpart
In the whole world. The tempest's mocking elf
Points to the shipman thus the unseen shelf
>He strikes on, only when the timbers start.

Not see? because of night perhaps?—why, day
>Came back again for that! before it left,
>>The dying sunset kindled through a cleft:
The hills, like giants at a hunting, lay,
Chin upon hand, to see the game at bay,—
>'Now stab and end the creature—to the heft!'

The Machiavel spends a life training for the sight, and yet is self-betrayed, because he is self-condemned to be "blind as the fool's heart." He will see, at the last, and he will know, and yet all that he will see and know are the lost adventurers his peers, who like him have come upon the Dark Tower unaware. The Jacobean hero-villain, at the end, touches the limit of manipulative self-knowledge, and in touching that limit gives birth to the High Romantic self-consciousness which we cannot evade, and which remains the affliction of our Post-modernism, so-called, as it was of every Modernism, from Milton to our present moment.

MARLOWE'S BARABAS

I

Like Shakespeare, born only a few months after him, Marlowe began as an Ovidian poet. Killed at twenty-nine, in what may have been a mere tavern brawl, or possibly a political intrigue (fitter end for a double agent), Marlowe had the unhappy poetic fate of being swallowed up by Shakespeare's unprecedented powers of dramatic representation. We read Marlowe now as Shakespeare's precursor, remembering that Shakespeare also began as a poet of Ovidian eros. Read against Shakespeare, Marlowe all but vanishes. Nor can anyone prophesy usefully how Marlowe might have developed if he had lived another quarter century. There seems little enough development between *Tamburlaine* (1587) and *Doctor Faustus* (1593), and perhaps Marlowe was incapable of that process we name by the critical trope of "poetic development," which seems to imply a kind of turning about or even a wrapping up.

There has been a fashion, in modern scholarly criticism, to baptize Marlowe's imagination, so that a writer of tragic caricatures has been converted into an orthodox moralist. The vanity of scholarship has few more curious monuments than this Christianized Marlowe. What the common reader finds in

Marlowe is precisely what his contemporaries found: impiety, audacity, worship of power, ambiguous sexuality, occult aspirations, defiance of moral order, and above all else a sheer exaltation of the possibilities of rhetoric, of the persuasive force of heroic poetry. The subtlest statement of the scholar's case is made by Frank Kermode:

> Thus Marlowe displays his heroes reacting to most of the temptations that Satan can contrive; and the culminating temptation ... is the scholar's temptation, forbidden knowledge ... [Marlowe's] heroes do not resist the temptations, and he provides us, not with a negative proof of virtue and obedience to divine law, but with positive examples of what happens in their absence. Thus, whatever his intentions may have been, and however much he flouted conventions, Marlowe's themes are finally reducible to the powerful formulae of contemporary religion and morality.

"Finally reducible" is the crucial phrase here; is final reduction the aim of reading or of play-going? As for "Marlowe's themes," they count surely rather less than Marlowe's rhetoric does, and, like most themes or topics, indubitably do ensue ultimately from religion and morality. But Marlowe is not Spenser or Milton, and there is one originality he possesses that is not subsumed by Shakespeare. Call that originality by the name of Barabas, Marlowe's grandest character, who dominates what is certainly Marlowe's most vital and original play, *The Jew of Malta*. Barabas defies reduction, and his gusto represents Marlowe's severest defiance of all moral and religious convention.

II

Barabas (or Barabbas, as in the Gospels) means "son of the Father" and so "son of God," and may have begun as an alternate name for Jesus. As the anti-Jewish tenor of the Gospels intensified from Mark to John, Barabbas declined from a patriotic insurrectionist to a thief, and as either was preferred by "the Jews" to Jesus. This is a quite Marlovian irony that the scholar Hyam Maccoby puts forward, and Marlowe might have rejoiced at the notion that Jesus and Barabbas were historically the same person. One Richard Baines, a police informer, insisted that Marlowe said of Jesus: "If the Jews among whom he was born did crucify him they best knew him and whence he came." The playwright Thomas Kyd, arrested after his friend Marlowe's death, testified that the author of *The Jew of Malta* tended to "jest at the divine Scriptures, gibe at prayers, and strive in argument to frustrate and confute what hath been spoke or writ by prophets and such holy men." Are we to credit Baines and Kyd, or Kermode and a bevy of less subtle scholars?

Marlowe, who was as sublimely disreputable as Rimbaud or Hart Crane, is more of their visionary company than he is at home with T.S. Eliot or with academic moralists. *The Jew of Malta* contrasts sharply with *The Merchant of Venice*, which may have been composed so as to overgo it on the stage. It cannot be too much emphasized that Marlowe's Barabas is a savage original, while Shakespeare's Shylock, despite his supposed humanization, is essentially the timeless anti-Semitic stock figure, devil and usurer, of Christian tradition. Stating it more plainly, Shakespeare indeed is as anti-Semitic as the Gospels or T.S. Eliot, whereas Marlowe employs his Barabas as a truer surrogate for himself than are Tamburlaine, Edward II, and Dr. Faustus. Barabas is Marlowe the satirist:

> It's no sin to deceive a Christian;
> For they themselves hold it a principle,
> Faith is not to be held with heretics.
> But all are heretics that are not Jews;
> This follows well ...

And so indeed it does. The art of Barabas is to better Christian instruction, unlike Shylock, who has persistence but who lacks art. Shylock is obsessive-compulsive; Barabas delights because he is a free man, or if you would prefer, a free fiend, at once a monstrous caricature and a superb image of Marlowe's sly revenge upon society. What Hazlitt gave us as a marvelous critical concept, gusto, is superbly manifested by Barabas, but not by poor Shylock. "Gusto in art is power or passion defining any object." Hazlitt accurately placed Shakespeare first among writers in this quality:

> The infinite quantity of dramatic invention in Shakespeare takes
> from his gusto. The power he delights to show is not intense, but
> discursive. He never insists on anything he might, except a quibble.

But Shylock is the one great exception in Shakespeare, and surprisingly lacks invention. Marlowe's superior gusto, in just this one instance, emerges as we contrast two crucial speeches. Barabas is outrageous, a parody of the stage-Jew, and Shylock speaks with something like Shakespeare's full resources, so that the power of language is overwhelmingly Shakespeare's, and yet Barabas becomes an original representation, while Shylock becomes even more the nightmare bogey of Christian superstition and hatred:

> SALERIO: Why, I am sure if he forfeit thou wilt not take his flesh.
>   What's that good for?
> SHYLOCK: To bait fish withal. If it will feed nothing else, it will
>   feed my revenge. He hath disgraced me, and hind'red

> me half a million, laughed at my losses, mocked at my gains, scorned my nation, thwarted my bargains, cooled my friends, heated mine enemies—and what's his reason? I am a Jew. Hath not a Jew eyes? Hath not a Jew hands, organs, dimensions, senses, affections, passions?—fed with the same food, hurt with the same weapons, subject to the same diseases, healed by the same means, warmed and cooled by the same winter and summer as a Christian is? If you prick us, do we not bleed? If you tickle us, do we not laugh? If you poison us, do we not die? And if you wrong us, shall we not revenge? If we are like you in the rest, we will resemble you in that. If a Jew wrong a Christian, what is his humility? Revenge! If a Christian wrong a Jew, what should his sufferance be by Christian example? Why revenge! The villainy you teach me I will execute, and it shall go hard but I will better the instruction.

"If you prick us, do we not bleed? If you tickle us, do we not laugh?" Shylock himself is not changed by listening to these, his own words, and neither are the audience's prejudices changed one jot. No one in that audience had seen a Jew, nor had Shakespeare, unless they or he had watched the execution of the unfortunate Dr. Lopez, the Queen's physician, condemned on a false charge of poisoning, or had glimpsed one of the handful of other converts resident in London. Shylock is rendered more frightening by the startling reminders that this dangerous usurer is flesh and blood, a man as well as a devil. Jews after all, Shakespeare's language forcefully teaches his audience, are not merely mythological murderers of Christ and of his beloved children, but literal seekers after the flesh of the good and gentle Antonio.

Can we imagine Barabas saying: "If you prick us, do we not bleed? If you tickle us, do we not laugh?" Or can we imagine Shylock intoning this wonderful and parodistic outburst of the exuberant Barabas?

> As for myself, I walk abroad a-nights,
> And kill sick people groaning under walls.
> Sometimes I go about and poison wells;
> And now and then, to cherish Christian thieves,
> I am content to lose some of my crowns,
> That I may, walking in my gallery,
> See 'em go pinion'd along by my door.
> Being young, I studied physic, and began
> To practise first upon the Italian;
> There I enrich'd the priests with burials,

And always kept the sexton's arms in ure
With digging graves and ringing dead men's knells.
And, after that, was I an engineer,
And in the wars 'twixt France and Germany,
Under the pretence of helping Charles the Fifth,
Slew friend and enemy with my stratagems:
Then after that was I an usurer,
And with extorting, cozening, forfeiting,
And tricks belonging unto brokery,
I fill'd the gaols with bankrupts in a year,
And with young orphans planted hospitals;
And every moon made some or other mad,
And now and then one hang himself for grief,
Pinning upon his breast a long great scroll
How I with interest tormented him.
But mark how I am blest for plaguing them:
I have as much coin as will buy the town.
But tell me now, how has thou spent thy time?

This would do admirably in a Gilbert and Sullivan opera, had the anti-Semitic Gilbert (see *The Bab Ballads*) been willing to mock his own prejudices. We do not know how the more sophisticated among Marlowe's audience received this, but properly delivered it has the tang and bite of great satire. A more fascinating surmise is: How did Shakespeare receive this? And how did he react to Barabas in what we can call the mode of Hemingway, sparring with his holy friars?

FRIAR BARNARDINE: Barabas, thou has—
FRIAR JACOMO: Ay, not what thou hast—
BARABAS: True, I have money; what though I have?
FRIAR BARNARDINE: Thou art a—
FRIAR JACOMO: Ay, that thou art, a—
BARABAS: What needs all this? I know I am a Jew.
FRIAR BARNARDINE: Thy daughter—
FRIAR JACOMO: Ay, thy daughter—
BARABAS: O, speak not of her! Then I die with grief.
FRIAR BARNARDINE: Remember that—
FRIAR JACOMO: Ay, remember that—
BARABAS: I must needs say that I have been a great usurer.
FRIAR BARNARDINE: Thou hast committed—
BARABAS: Fornication: but that was in another country,
        And besides the wench is dead.

We can say that Shakespeare refused the hint. Shylock's grim repetitions ("I will have my bond") come out of a different universe, the crimes of Christendom that Shakespeare had no thought of rejecting. This is hardly to say that Marlowe was in any sense humane. *The Jew of Malta* is bloody farce, more than worthy of Jarry or Artaud. Barabas emerges from the world of Thomas Nashe and Thomas Kyd, Marlowe's half-world of espionage and betrayal, of extravagant wit and antithetical lusts, which was the experiential scene that must have taught Shakespeare to go and live otherwise, and write otherwise as well.

III

The Australian poet Alec Hope, in a remarkable essay upon Marlowe, ascribes to *Tamburlaine* "a thorough-going morality of power, aesthetics of power and logic of power." Hope is clearly right about *Tamburlaine*. I would go further and suggest that there is no other morality, aesthetics or logic anywhere in Marlowe's writings. Where Hope usefully quotes Hazlitt on the congruence between the language of power and the language of poetry, I would cite also the great American theoretician of power and poetry, the Emerson of *The Conduct of Life*:

> A belief in causality, or strict connection between every trifle and the principle of being, and, in consequence, belief in compensation, or, that nothing is got for nothing,—characterizes all valuable minds, and must control every effort that is made by an industrious one. The most valiant men are the best believers in the tension of the laws ...
>
> All power is of one kind, a sharing of the nature of the world. The mind that is parallel with the laws of nature will be in the current of events, and strong with their strength.

Like Marlowe, Hazlitt and Emerson are agonists who understand that there are no accidents. In Marlowe, the implicit metaphysics of this understanding are Epicurean-Lucretian. Barabas and Tamburlaine seek their own freedom, and ultimately fail, but only because they touch the ultimate limits at the flaming ramparts of the world. Edward II and Dr. Faustus fail, but they are weak, and their fate does not grieve Marlowe. Indeed, the aesthetic satisfaction Marlowe hints at is not free from a sadistic pleasure the poet and his audience share at observing the dreadful ends of Edward and Faustus. Marlowe's heroes, Tamburlaine and Barabas, die defiantly, with Tamburlaine still naming himself "the scourge of God," and Barabas, boiling in a cauldron, nevertheless cursing his enemies with his customary vehemence:

And, villains, know you cannot help me now.
Then, Barabas, breathe forth thy latest fate,
And in the fury of thy torments strive
To end thy life with resolution.
Know, Governor, 'twas I that slew thy son,
I fram'd the challenge that did make them meet.
Know, Calymath, I aim'd thy overthrow:
And, had I escap'd this stratagem,
I would have brought confusion on you all,
Damn'd Christians, dogs, and Turkish infidels!
But now begins the extremity of heat
To pinch me with intolerable pangs.
Die, life! fly, soul! tongue, curse thy fill, and die!

Shylock, alas, ends wholly broken, "content" to become a Christian, a resolution that is surely the most unsatisfactory in all of Shakespeare. I cannot envision the late Groucho Marx playing Shylock, but I sometimes read through *The Jew of Malta*, mentally casting Groucho as Barabas. T.S. Eliot, whose admiration for *The Jew of Malta* was strong, was also a fan of the sublime Groucho. I rejoice, for once, to share two of Eliot's enthusiasms, and enjoy the thought that he too might have wished to see Groucho play Barabas.

VOLPONE, OR THE FOX

I

In his conversations with (or harangues at) the Spenserian poet Drummond of Hawthornden in 1619, Ben Jonson repeated a joke of Sir Francis Bacon's:

At his hither coming, Sir Francis Bacon said to him, He loved
not to see poesy go on other feet than poetical dactyls and
spondees.

Jonson, burly Laureate, portly Master Poet, rather grandly had marched into Scotland on foot, and greatly appreciated the Baconian compliment that poesy and Ben were identical. If Bacon presumably preferred Jonson, The Ancient, over Shakespeare, the Modern, this extraordinary evaluation was as remarkably reciprocated when Jonson gave Bacon the accolade as essayist and wisdom writer over Montaigne:

One, though he be excellent and the chief, is not to be imitated
alone; for never no imitator ever grew up to his author; likeness is
always on this side truth. Yet there happened in my time one noble
speaker who was full of gravity in his speaking; his language, where

he could spare or pass by a jest, was nobly censorious. No man ever spake more neatly, more pressly, more weightily, or suffered less emptiness, less idleness, in what he uttered. No member of his speech but consisted of his own graces. His hearers could not cough, or look aside from him, without loss. He commanded where he spoke, and had his judges angry and pleased at his devotion. No man had their affections more in his power. The fear of every man that heard him was lest he should make an end.

The art of this generous overpraise is that it is an elegant, if perhaps too neat, cento of commonplaces from Seneca, common precursor of Bacon and Montaigne. Jonson would have expected us to juxtapose this passage of *Timber, or Discoveries* with another, in which Montaigne, Shakespeare of essayists, is somewhat warily deprecated.

Such are all the essayists, even their master Montaigne. These, in all they write, confess still what books they have read last, and therein their own folly so much, that they bring it to the stake raw and undigested; not that the place did need it neither, but that they thought themselves furnished and would vent it.

That is vigorous, nasty, and about as effective against Montaigne as were Jonson's ambivalent remarks against Shakespeare. Bacon himself, Jonson's authority, more cunningly said that the word "essay" was "late but the thing is ancient," which is shrewdly translated by Charles Whitney as: "Montaigne, the so-called first essayist, isn't as original as everyone thinks; *my* essays in fact represent the authentic continuity with a long tradition of skeptical, probing inquiry." But to take sides with Montaigne and Shakespaeare against Bacon and Jonson, both too subtle and dialectical for mere paraphrase, were fighting on the side neither of Ancients nor Moderns. Modernity, as we always insist upon forgetting, is an Alexandrian concept, formulated by our grand precursor, Aristarchus, in defense of the first great Modernist poet, Callimachus. Doubtless, we cannot call Sir Francis Bacon the Nietzsche of his age, but we might begin to think of Nietzsche as the Bacon shadowing the threshold of our own era. Bacon too is concerned for the use and abuse of history for life, though he means by "life" something like civil society, the state, the future prospects of a people. Nietzsche, heroic vitalist, urged us to think of the earth, hardly a Baconian injunction, thought Bacon has his own version of the Nietzschean admonition: "Try to live as though it were morning." Bacon and Nietzsche share the same resolution: do not live, work, or think as though you were a latecomer.

The heirs of Spenser in the earlier seventeenth century suffered a most acute sense of imaginative belatedness, typified by the Kabbalistic Henry Reynolds at the opening of his *Mythomystes*:

> I have thought upon the times we live in, and am forced to affirm the world is decrepit, and, out of its age & doating estate, subject to all the imperfections that are inseparable from that wrack and maim of Nature.

That is to replace history by poetry, or to read history as a Spenserian romance. Aristotle had placed poetry between philosophy and history, a stationing that Sir Philip Sidney had modified, perhaps slyly, by his apothegm that poetry took place between the precept and the example, and so could fulfill moral purposes that neither philosophy nor history could hope to serve. Bacon, in contrast, judged poetry to be a mere imitation of history, made to no end except the giving of pleasure. Spenser and Bacon were antipodes of thought and feeling, and their visions of history were almost irreconcilable. Their heirs necessarily possessed almost nothing in common. Ben Jonson and his school were divided from the Spenserians by multiple considerations, reflecting cultural choices that intricately fused religion, politics, and aesthetics.

Angus Fletcher, our great contemporary Spenserian, observes that Spenser "subordinates the insights of cyclical and scientific history to the Christian revelation of prophetic historicism," though Fletcher shrewdly adds that this kind of poetic prophecy is as Orphic as it is Christian. I would add to Fletcher that such Orphic historicism is anti-Baconian in consequences, rather than as policy. Another major contemporary Spenserian, the late and much missed Isabel G. MacCaffrey, caught the precise agon between Spenser and the involuntary latecomer Bacon with admirable economy: "Bacon was later to disparage poets for submitting 'the shows of things to the desires of the mind,' but as both Sidney and Spenser affirm, those desires themselves bear witness to the presence of a realm of being inadequately figured by the shows of things."

Bacon's polemic against the poets presumably resulted from his desperate ambition to substitute his own historicism for the orphic prophecies of the great poets. He too was a prophet, perhaps the most optimistic of British prophets before the young John Milton, and is rightly named as a counter-apocalyptic by Achsah Guibbory: "Like many of his contemporaries, Bacon believes that he is living in the 'autumn of the world,' that the end of time is approaching. But his sense that the end is not far off leads to a vision of progress, not an obsession with decay."

Charles Whitney, seeking to define Bacon's concept of modernity, notes the revision by misquotation that Bacon carries out in his use of the prophet Jeremiah:

> Bacon's spectacular misquotation of Jeremiah in *The Advancement of Learning*'s best-known pronouncement on tradition and innovation

reveals the problematic relationship of his instauration to the religious models. (The misquotation is repeated in the *De Dignitate et Augmentis Scientiarum* and in the essay "Of Innovations.") Failure to appreciate that complex relationship (or to note misreading) has led commentators, among them Harold Bloom and Renato Poggioli to construe the passage either as a bellwether of Enlightenment faith in free reason (Bloom) or as a defense of traditionalism (Poggioli).

In criticizing the "extreme affection" of either "Antiquity" or "Novelty" in learned men, Bacon says:

> Antiquity envieth there should be new additions, and novelty cannot be content to add but it must deface: surely the advice of the prophet is the true direction in this matter, *State super vias antiquas, et videte quaenam sit via recta at bona et ambulate in eas.* Antiquity deserveth that reverence, that men should make a stand thereupon and discover what is the best way; but when the discovery is well taken, then to make progression. And to speak truly, *Antiquitas saeculi juventus mundi.* These times are the ancient times, when the world is ancient, and not those which we account ancient *ordine retrogrado*, by a computation backward from ourselves.

Bacon's apparently moderate view of tradition and innovation here—the reversal of ancient and modern times being a sentiment found in several earlier contemporaries—reflects the generally reconciliatory attitude about the past assumed in the *Advancement*.

The present is "old," clearly, because there has been cumulative development, fruitful imitation, and emulation. Even so, it has become necessary for Bacon to distort Jeremiah considerably. The Vulgate renders him thus:

> State super vias, et videte
> Et interrogate de semitis antiques quae sit via bona,
> Et ambulate in ea,
> Et invenietis refrigirium animabus vestris
>
> (Stand in the ways, and look, and ask for the old
> paths, where the good way is, and walk in it, and
> find rest for your soul.)

Whitney interprets Jeremiah as meaning that "the right way is the old way," but that is to misread the prophet more weakly than Bacon did. Bacon's *Stand in the old ways, and see which is the straight and good path, and walk in that,* omits asking for the old paths, because Jeremiah himself appears to mean that the good way is only one of the old paths, and the prophet's crucial emphasis is: "walk in it," which is the entire burden of normative Judaism. Bacon indeed is battling against contemporary cultural undervaluation, including the Spenserians, with their study of the nostalgias, and his polemical insistence is that the ancients were the true moderns, and the moderns the true ancients, since those who arrived later knew more, and Bacon himself knew most of all.

II

The contemporary critic-scholar Thomas M. Greene, who may be our very last Renaissance Humanist, battles his own profound sense of belatedness in a splendid essay on "Ben Jonson and the Centered Self":

> The equilibrated energy of the centered self is most amply demonstrated by Jonson's *Timber*. The stress in that work falls on the faculty of judgment, and in fact it demonstrates this faculty at work, choosing among authors and passages, discriminating conduct and style.
>
>> Opinion is a light, vain, crude, and imperfect thing, settled in the imagination, but never arriving at the understanding, there to obtain the tincture of reason.
>
> The passages gathered in *Timber* are exercises of the reasonable understanding. A sentence like the one quoted seems to place the imagination in an outer layer of consciousness, where the centrifugal "opinion" can momentarily alight. The understanding is further within, at the psychic center of gravity, impervious to the flights of the butterfly-caprice. All of *Timber*, whether or not "original" in the vulgar sense, seems to issue from this center of gravity.

Greene, a well-tempered Humanist, powerful and crafty, but in the last ditch, centers upon *Timber* as a gathering of "exercises of the reasonable understanding." Thirty years ago, the great Humanist William K. Wimsatt, Jr., Greene's mentor as well as mine, asserted rather more for *Timber*.

> Jonson's stout and craftsmanly common sense about imitation, shown even more convincingly in his practice than in his precepts, may be taken as the key to a theory of poetry which stressed hard work—imitation, practice, study, art (and with these but one poor pennyworth of *ingenium*)—a theory too which stressed poems squared off by the norm of reality. This theory celebrated the mobility and power of poetry, but it included no hymn to spontaneity

or to what today we think of as creative imagination. It included no statement even remotely parallel to that of Sidney about the free range of wit within its zodiac or that of Bacon about poetry submitting the shows of reality to the desires of the mind. Some deviation or wavering from the classic norm may appear in Jonson's treatment of such a minor article as that prescribing the unity of place—and we have seen that he is guilty of defying the authority of the antique critics. But he is the first English man of letters to exhibit a nearly complete and consistent neo–classicism. His historical importance is that he throws out a vigorous announcement of the rule from which in the next generation Dryden is to be engaged in politely rationalized recessions. One basic problem which Jonson leaves us pondering (the same as that posed implicitly once before, by a strong appreciator of poetic inspiration, Longinus) might be formulated as follows: Does an aesthetic norm of objective reality entail a *genetic* theory of conscious and strenuous artistic effort? If a poet is to give us a truthful account of general human nature, does this poet have to be a learned consumer of midnight oil, a graduate in grammar, logic, and rhetoric, and in the higher liberal disciplines? Or on the other hand: Does an aesthetic norm of personal expression entail a genetic theory of untrammeled and unstudied inspiration? If a poet is to tell the truth as he himself most really and deeply experiences it, does he have to be a rebel against tradition and conventional education, a Bohemian, long-haired, and unwashed, a defiler of ancestral ashes?

On this view, Jonson is more on the side of Ancients against Moderns than his master Bacon was, and that must be right. But how could Jonson have inaugurated English neoclassicism, when he seems to have held a Stoic or cyclical theory of history? His identification with Horace, I suspect, was not truly founded upon some supposed and rather dubious parallel between Roman and English history, despite the persuasive arguments of Achsah Guibbory in *The Map of Time*. Whatever Horace's actual temperament may have been, we know that the fierce and violent Jonson, burly Ben indeed, was not exactly a Stoic. Can we not surmise that Jonson's preference for the Ancients was antithetical, against the grain, a correction of the most vehement sensibility ever possessed by a major English poet? History, including the events of his own time, disgusted the passionate moralist Jonson, who turned to Stoicism and the Ancients so as to withdraw from what might have provoked him to madness of no use to literature.

There is a great passage in *Timber* in praise of Bacon, "the late Lord Saint Albans," that can serve to sum up both of these great minds on the virtues of the Ancients, and on the possibility of becoming an Ancient in your own time:

It was well noted by the late Lord Saint Albans, that the study of words is the first distemper of learning; vain matter the second; and third distemper is deceit, or the likeness of truth, imposture held up by credulity. All these are the cobwebs of learning, and to let them grow in us is either sluttish or foolish. Nothing is more ridiculous than to make an author a dictator, as the schools have done Aristotle. The damage is infinite knowledge receives by it; for to many things a man should owe but a temporary belief, and a suspension of his own judgment, not an absolute resignation of himself, or a perpetual captivity. Let Aristotle and others have their dues; but if we can make farther discoveries of truth and fitness than they, why are we envied? Let us beware, while we strive to add, we do not diminish or deface; we may improve, but not augment. By discrediting falsehood, truth grows in request. We must not go about, like men anguished and perplexed for vicious affectation of praise, but calmly study the separation of opinions, find the errors have intervened, awake antiquity, call former times into question; but make no parties with the present, not follow any fierce undertakers, mingle no matter of doubtful credit with the simplicity of truth; but gently stir the mould about the root of the question, and avoid all digladiations, facility of credit, or superstitious simplicity, seek the consonancy and concatenation of truth; stoop only to point of necessity, and what leads to convenience. Then make exact animadversion where style hath degenerated, where flourished and thrived in choiceness of phrase, round and clean composition of sentence, sweet falling of the clause, varying an illustration by tropes and figures, weight of matter, worth of subject, soundness of argument, life of invention, and depth of judgment. This is *monte potiri*, to get the hill; for no perfect discovery can be made upon a flat or a level.

To discover the errors that have intervened is to awaken antiquity while making no alliances with the present, yet also is to call all former times into question. Here, at least, Jonson admirably joins himself to Bacon, and prepares the way for Milton's much more drastic transumption of the tradition.

III

Jonson's magnificent vehemence carries him over to Volpone's side, in defiance of Jonsonian moral theory. Not that Volpone (and the plebeian Mosca even more so) is not hideously punished. He—like Mosca—is outrageously overpunished, which may be Jonson's self-punishment for the imaginative introjection of his greatest creation. Perhaps Jonson is chastising us also, knowing that we too would delight in Volpone. The representation of gusto, when worked with

Jonson's power, becomes a gusto that captivates us, so that it scarcely matters if we remember how wicked Volpone is supposed to be. Massively aware of this paradox, distrusting the theatrical while creating Volpone as a genius of theatricality, Jonson takes moral revenge upon Volpone, the audience, and even himself. The imagination wishes to be indulged, and delights in being deceived. No playgoer or reader wishes to see Volpone's deceptions fail, and our delight is surely Jonson's delight also.

Robert M. Adams has some shrewd comments upon what I suppose we might want to call Jonson's ambivalences towards the theater:

> The tone of punishment and correction runs through a lot of Jonson's dramatic work; there are passages which don't come far short of suggesting that he thought the work itself a form of correction, if not punishment, for the audience: "physic of the mind" was one of his terms.

Jonson might have observed that he was following Aristotle's precepts, yet a "physic of the mind" does seem stronger than a catharsis. You tend to receive worse than you (badly) merit in Jonson, and that hardly purges you to fear. It is something of a mystery anyway why Jonson believed Volpone and Mosca needed to be so severely punished. Except for his exasperated attempt to rape Celia, Volpone preys only upon those who deserve to be fleeced, and thus defrauds only the fraudulent. Nor does Jonson represent Volpone's failed lust for Celia as being without its own imaginative opulence. As with Sir Epicure Mammom in *The Alchemist*, we hear in Volpone's mad eloquence the equivocal splendor of a depraved will corrupting imagination to its own purposes:

CELIA: Some sérene blast me, or dire lightning strike
   This my offending face!
VOLPONE: Why droops my Celia?
   Thou hast, in place of a base husband, found
   A worthy lover: use thy fortune well,
   With secrecy and pleasure. See, behold,
   What thou art queen of; not in expectation,
   As I feed others: but possessed and crowned.
   See here a rope of pearl; and each, more orient
   Than that brave Egyptian queen caroused:
   Dissolve and drink them. See, a carbuncle
   May put out both the eyes of our St. Mark;
   A diamond, would have bought Lollia Paulina,
   When she came in like star-light, hid with the jewels,
   That were the spoils of provinces; take these,

And wear, and lose them: yet remains an earring
To purchase them again, and this whole state.
A gem but worth a private patrimony,
Is nothing: we will eat such at a meal.
The heads of parrots, tongues of nightingales,
The brains of peacocks, and of ostriches,
Shall be our food: and, could we get the phoenix,
Though nature lost her kind, she were our dish.
CELIA: Good sir, these things might move a mind affected
With such delights; but I, whose innocence
Is all I can think wealthy, or worth th' enjoying,
And which, once lost, I have nought to lose beyond it,
Cannot be taken with these sensual baits:
If you have conscience—
VOLPONE: 'Tis the beggar's virtue;
If thou hast wisdom, hear me, Celia.
Thy baths shall be the juice of July-flowers,
Spirit of roses, and of violets,
The milk of unicorns, and panthers' breath
Gathered in bags, and mixed with Cretan wines.
Our drink shall be preparéd gold and amber;
Which we will take, until my roof whirl around
With the vertigo: and my dwarf shall dance,
My eunuch sing, my fool make up the antic,
Whilst we, in changèd shapes, act Ovid's tales,
Thou, like Europa now, and I like Jove,
Then I like Mars, and thou like Erycine:
So, of the rest, till we have quite run through,
And wearied all the fables of the gods.
Then will I have thee in more modern forms,
Attiréd like some sprightly dame of France,
Brave Tuscan lady, or proud Spanish beauty;
Sometimes, unto the Persian Sophy's wife;
Or the Grand Signior's mistress; and, for change,
To one of our most artful courtesans,
Or some quick Negro, or cold Russian;
And I will meet thee in as many shapes:
Where we may so transfuse our wandering souls
Out at our lips, and score up sums of pleasures.

It is difficult to believe that Jonson did not admire the superb audacity of
Volpone's hyperboles, which out-Marlowe Marlowe. "Could we get the phoenix,
/ Though nature lost her kind, she were our dish," is particularly fine, as that

firebird, mythical and immortal, is always present only in one incarnation at any single moment. Heroic in the bravura of his lust, the Ovidian Volpone charms us by the delicious zeal with which he envisions Celia's changes of costume. Sir Epicure Mammon holds on always in my memory for his energetic "here's the Rich Peru," but Volpone is positively endearing as he gets carried away in transports of voluptuousness, and bursts into strains of Catullus in his exuberance:

> Come, my Celia, let us prove,
> While we can, the sports of love,
> Time will not be ours for ever,
> He at length, our good will sever;
> Spend not then his gifts in vain:
> Suns that set may rise again;
> But if once we lose this light,
> 'Tis, with us, perpetual night.
> Why should we defer our joys?
> Fame and rumour are but toys.
> Cannot we delude the eyes
> Of a few poor household spies?
> Or his easier ears beguile,
> Thus removéd by our wile?—
> 'Tis no sin love's fruit to steal,
> But the sweet thefts to reveal;
> To be taken, to be seen,
> These have crimes accounted been.

Jonas Barish moved by his depth of Jonsonian scholarship to a Jonsonian moralizing, reads Volpone's Ovidian and Cattulan allusions as evidence that: "Folly, vanity, lust, have been, are, will be. At any given moment their practioners are legion, and often interchangeable." Yes, and doubtless Jonson would have been gratified, but what about the verve, wit, lyric force, and intoxicating eloquence with which Jonson has endowed Volpone? Foolish and vain lusters may be interchangeable, but whom would you get if you gave up Volpone? We are again in the paradox of Jonson's theatrical art at its most extraordinary, which brings Volpone back to delight us after he has been so cruelly sentenced:

> [VOLPONE comes forward.]
> The seasoning of a play is the applause.
> Now, though the Fox be punished by the laws,
> He yet doth hope, there is no suffering due,
> For any fact which he hath done 'gainst you;
> If there be, censure him; here he doubtful stands:
> If not, fare jovially, and clap your hands. [Exit.]
> THE END

Where can we find the Jonsonian ambivalence in this? Volpone indeed has done nothing except entertain us, richly beyond most rivals. Barish strongly remarks that when Jonson imposes a terrible punishment upon Volpone, we feel betrayed. I would use a darker word, and say that we are outraged, though we grant that Volpone is outrageous. Jonson's moral aesthetic was not quite what he thought it to be. His savage relish in Volpone's tricks is also a savage relish for the stage, and so also a savage appreciation for the savagery of his audience.

PETER HAPPÉ

Theatres and Companies:
The Context of the Professional Stage—
James Burbage and John Lyly

When James Burbage began the construction of the Theatre in 1576, he inaugurated a new era in the history of English drama. From his establishment of a specially built theatre there developed a way of life on the stage which comprised a much greater concentration of resources, human and financial, than had existed before. From now on, whatever the difficulties, it was possible for an increasing number of actors, writers and entrepreneurs to hope to make a livelihood from the theatre, and this meant ultimately an enhancement in the quantity and quality of what could be presented and what audiences could expect. It also meant that the stage might become more influential, or, as some might consider, more dangerous in ideological terms.

But there is another underlying factor against which such developments should be considered. However enormous the changes inaugurated by Burbage, there was also a continuity in many traditions of entertainment, and of the skills of performers and playwrights alike. The art of theatre may have been rejuvenated as a result of Burbage's new building, but the rich and complex achievement described in the earlier parts of this book did not suddenly disappear. It is not possible to evaluate properly the changes which now came about without being conscious that many inherited aspects of the nature of plays and their performance helped in the development of the new drama. Indeed, as has already been suggested, it is one of the features of this particular study that it can give a sense of the continuities between medieval and Renaissance drama.

From *English Drama before Shakespeare*. © 1999 by Addison Wesley Longman Limited.

The years following the building of the Theatre yield far more information about theatrical activities, and more London plays are recorded than ever before. It is perhaps worth recalling that, just as this expansion was about to begin, the old art of the mystery cycles was being brought to an end, largely by government intervention. The last performance at Chester was in 1575, the last in York was 1569, with further unsuccessful attempts up to 1580.

In this chapter we shall look at the buildings, the companies, the audiences and some conditions of performance which make up the context of the theatre in the years immediately preceding the arrival of Shakespeare in London in the early 1590s. This includes some of the physical changes which arose, and also a look at the ways in which the profession of acting developed as a result of having permanent theatres which could be the centres for many new undertakings. It is significant that this third section of our study is as long as the two previous ones even though it is centred on only fourteen well-packed years. In essence it is an account of ways in which thinking about drama were renewed.

THEATRES

Burbage's Theatre was not the only kind of place for performance open in London in 1576. There were amateur companies having various degrees of continuity performing at the Inns of Court, and in private houses of the nobility. There were productions at court which could draw upon extensive financial support. These might be by the Children of St Paul's or of the Chapel Royal under the control of the Master of the Revels, who began operating on a permanent basis from 1545. These two companies each had their own regular place of performance within the precinct of St Paul's cathedral and at Blackfriars respectively. It was also customary for the court to reward adult companies for putting on special performances of plays which had been written for other contexts. At different times the great halls at Hampton Court, Greenwich and Whitehall were used for such occasions. It is apparent that performances at court took place annually at certain seasons. Most of these ways of presenting plays had been going on for years.

The adult companies at work before 1576 may have been professional, in the sense that some of the successful members earned most of their living from acting, but it is apparent that the organisation was intermittent and that the groups were too unstable to last very long. The instability was a feature of the necessity to be itinerant. Such groups would have been responsible for less prestigious performances at inns, some of which were within the City of London. By 1576 players had performed at the Boar's Head in Aldgate, the Saracen's Head in Islington, the Bel Savage on Ludgate Hill, the Red Lion in Stepney and the Bell Inn in Gracechurch Street. Of these the Red Lion is most noteworthy, since John Brayne, a grocer, paid in 1567 for a 'wooden scaffold or stage for interludes or plays'. The legal document in which this is mentioned gives the dimensions as

40 feet by 30 feet, and 5 feet high. Brayne was the brother-in-law of James Burbage, and later he helped with the financing of the Theatre.[1]

Such performances may well have been quite frequent, though it seems likely that the boothed stages they employed were movable. One feature of these inns was that the open-air courtyards where performances took place could accommodate spectators looking down from galleries and upper windows. These performing spaces were shared with other forms of entertainment such as displays of fencing or prize-fighting. The multiple use of buildings could also have operated in reverse: it is possible that on the south bank of the Thames the pits used for bull- and bear-baiting were used for plays, hired out to the company for the occasion.

Burbage built his Theatre about a mile to the north of the City of London in Holywell Lane, off Shoreditch, no doubt because he wanted to be free of the jurisdiction of the City authorities which often bore heavily on players. It was an open-air building, polygonal in shape, made largely of wood (Burbage was trained as a carpenter), with three layers of galleries of seats surrounding the paved central area where many stood to watch the play. Part of one of these layers was designated a lords' room for wealthy patrons. To one side of the central space was the fixed stage, which was itself partly roofed by the 'heavens' supported on pillars, and at the back of this was the tiring house for the players. The stage was raised above the level of the courtyard and its back wall had doors into the tiring house which were thus the primary means of entry on to the stage. The 'heavens' could accommodate lifting gear, and there was probably a trap in the stage floor.

From these details it is apparent that the Theatre was an imaginative combination of features previously found in inn-yards, pits for animal baiting, the screens of great halls, and the commonplace demountable booth stage. The arena structure whereby an audience in a circular configuration looked down into a performing area, as in an amphitheatre, is virtually too ancient and too widespread to be attributed to any particular precedent. Burbage's originality lies in this very combination of preexisting elements: it proved so effective that the Theatre became a model for other playhouses which were built in London in succeeding years. They all followed the Theatre in being located outside the City limits: most of them were on Bankside, which was accessible via London Bridge or by boat across the Thames. Initially, and falling within the scope of this volume, they were:

1577   The Curtain in Moorfields, south of the Theatre, and used in close collaboration with it;

1587   The Rose on Bankside, built by the entrepreneur Philip Henslowe and enlarged and refurbished by him in 1594.

Later, as both the business and the art took greater hold, there came a second phase of construction. These theatres were similarly outside the City and showed some variations derived from the experience of a generation of playing, but still substantially they followed Burbage's combination:

1595   The Swan on Bankside;

1599   The Globe on Bankside, built by Cuthbert and Richard Burbage from the timbers of the Theatre—burnt down in 1613, and rebuilt;

1600   The Fortune at Cripplegate, built by Henslowe and Edward Alleyn, the actor;

1614   The Hope on Bankside, built by Henslowe on the model of the Swan, with a movable stage to accommodate bear-baiting.

From a financial point of view, the Theatre had the enormous advantage that access could be controlled and indeed graded according to entrance charges. This method was much preferable to the traditional but uncertain collection from the crowd, and it no doubt played a part in stabilising the companies. The performance advantages, on the other hand, centred on a number of features which undoubtedly left their mark upon how plays were to be written. There was virtually no scenery, though furniture and properties could be brought on stage. This helped rapid transitions between scenes. The location of scenes could be very flexible, ranging from the virtually unspecified to the highly atmospheric, conjured up chiefly by language. In this respect the plays at the Theatre followed the practice of many earlier performances. The details given above about doors, the heavens, and the trap indicate that entrances and exits remained a major resource making possible such things as surprise, or indeed its opposite, as comment could be made on characters approaching or leaving the action. It was also possible to play on two levels, giving an important vertical dimension—one found also in the use of pageant carts for mystery cycles—and this facility contributed much to the convention which we shall consider in the two following chapters of framing the action with fictionalised onlookers. The open stage encouraged processions, marches and battles, including sieges: theatrical devices going back as far as *The Castle of Perseverance*. One of the characteristics of the Theatre which has emerged at the New Globe in recent months is that the actors seem very close to the audience. This is made very plain if one stands on the stage and looks up at ranks of spectators banked in the facing and surrounding galleries. From such a position it is plain why soliloquies were so favoured.

Because of the entrance charges and the fact that the Theatre and its progeny took in a socially diverse audience—whoever wished to pay—they have come to be known as the public theatres. By contrast, the private theatres were more selective in that they charged more. They were also roofed, and had smaller audiences, who were all seated. Since they were inside it was also possible to use scenery and to make the most of unexpected revelations and changes. That they were under the control of the Master of the Revels may also have meant that there was money for scenic effects, especially when productions were translated to court.

Essentially, these private theatres were used by boys who were amateurs, but since both the Children of the Chapel Royal and the Paul's Boys came together for the purposes of education as well as to sing at services, the role of the schoolmasters who led them was very important. As these men tended to serve for many years, their professional status gave continuity in management and expertise. At St Paul's the work of John Redford, author of *Wit and Science* and associate of John Heywood, was continued by his successor Sebastian Westcott, who was Master from 1547 until 1582. Working with the Chapel Children, Richard Farrant took over the Blackfriars in 1576, where were presented some of the plays of his associate, John Lyly, whose work we shall consider later in this chapter.

Although the Paul's Boys were well known and certainly attracted an audience within the City, the exact location and nature of their playhouse is somewhat obscure. In an accusation against Westcott in 1575 it is alleged that he 'kepethe playes' as though he had been doing so for some time. The playhouse was somewhere in the precinct of old St Paul's, probably in the cloister, partially in the undercroft ('the shrouds') of the chapterhouse: almost certainly it was completely roofed. In such a place, access could be fully controlled as in the public theatres.[2]

The Children of the Chapel, together with their associate company, the Children of the Windsor Chapel, performed in the Blackfriars: an upper storey in the old Dominican priory within the west wall of the City. Richard Farrant took this over in 1576 for the purpose of public performances by the Children. He used it until his death in 1580, and his successor continued until trouble arose over the lease in 1584. It was at this period that some of Lyly's plays were done at the Blackfriars. The Children of the Chapel were sometimes joined by the Paul's Boys and together they took performances of Lyly's *Campaspe* and *Sappho and Phao* to court. As the difficulties over the lease at the Blackfriars continued, performances were stopped. For this brief period, 1576–84, this so-called First Blackfriars offered entertainment to audiences drawn from within the City in parallel with the Paul's playhouse. Many years later, in 1609, the King's Men, Shakespeare's company, under Richard Burbage gained access to a different part of Blackfriars and used it as a seasonal alternative for their Globe: this is known as the Second Blackfriars, but its history is beyond our scope here. The impact of these private theatres must have been an important complement to that of new public playhouses, even though the First Blackfriars, and presumably Paul's, were both quite small, accommodating up to 200 spectators. By contrast, the Rose is thought to have had room for up to 2,000, and the Globe for 3,000.

The plays done at the First Blackfriars suggest that there was a raised platform for the stage and that there were two doors at the back into the tiring house. There was probably an inner stage, as used for *Sappho and Phao*, and a trap is required so that a tree can be raised in Peele's *The Arraignment of Paris*.[3] The performances could take place after dark and in the winter, and the theatre had the added advantage of being within the City. The private theatre arrangements no doubt contributed a great deal to the development of drama at court, and especially to the evolution of the court masque which was to be so successful after the accession of James I.[4]

To return to Burbage, however, his creation at the Theatre was the central act in a remarkable period of expansion: but the physical characteristics of these buildings were not the only innovations. Because they concentrated players together it became possible and necessary to develop new ways of operating the financial business of acting; and there were also influential extraneous factors.

COMPANIES

On 6 December 1574 an Act of Common Council was promulgated by the City of London severely restraining the activities of players. It is an elaborate document, which in its first part dwells upon perceived abuses encouraged by the performing of plays in inns and public places.[5] The hostility to acting exhibited there may have been based upon some genuine difficulties, such as the undesirability of allowing gatherings during times of plague, or even the possibility that acting plays might encourage people not to go to work or not to go to church; but there are also indications of further prejudice against acting on moral grounds, a theme which, as we have seen elsewhere, can be traced far back in Christian thinking. It was now re- surfacing in the developing Protestant, or even Puritan, ethos. There is no doubt that the city housed many people who were chronically circumspect if not hostile towards performing plays. The prejudice was expressed, for example, by Stephen Gosson in *The School of Abuse* (1579) and *Plays Confuted in Five Actions* (1582), and Philip Stubbes in *The Anatomy of Abuses* (1583). Stubbes says, 'Plays were first invented by the Devil, practised by heathen gentiles, and dedicate to their false idols, gods and goddesses.'[6]

Against this, it is manifest that there was a huge amount of dramatic activity of many types all over the country, as the REED volumes indicate. One of the chief means by which this was delivered was by the well-established activities of itinerant companies of actors working under the patronage of the nobility. Such patronage was a function of power and thus it served the political ambitions of individual nobles as well as offering protection for the players against criticism and interference. This meant that to preserve troupe solidarity was desirable and necessary, and that patrons would continue to support it if possible. The arrival of the Theatre implied the idea of a physical base for such groups, and from then onwards the London-based acting companies carried out a major role in the presentation of plays.

In the years immediately preceding the opening of the Theatre, there was action by the government on a national scale which militated against the activities of itinerant players. This manifested itself in the Statute against Unlawful Retainers (3 January 1572), and the Act for the Punishment of Vagabonds (29 June 1572) directed against Rogues and Sturdy Beggars, in which the prescribed punishments for not having a proper licence to be on the roads were gruesome, and ultimately capital. However, on 10 May 1574 the Patent issued to Leicester's Men enabling them to perform plays allowed by the Master of the Revels in London and elsewhere may have helped to create an opportunity for Burbage.[7] Presumably it was the political influence of Leicester which enabled him to go against the palpable trend towards suppression.

For some companies, like the Queen's Men, established in 1583, or the Admiral's Men, first known to be active as Lord Howard's at court at Christmas 1576, continuity over a long period was possible, but there were plenty of others which came and went as patronage or business competence wavered. The records show that the most successful companies performed at court regularly, had opportunities to perform in the new public theatres, and were occasionally licensed by the authorities to perform within limits of the City itself in spite of the 1574 Act. They had many long and complicated itineraries throughout the country taking in the houses of the nobility and gentry as well as being rewarded for performances at inns and other public places. As time went by, there were plenty of changes in the configuration of the companies, and they seem sometimes to have co-operated and sometimes to have been rivals. For example, the Admiral's Men played at the Theatre at times, but after a quarrel with James Burbage, Alleyn and others moved into the Rose in 1591, where they worked in close association with Henslowe.[8] So successful were these companies that by 1599 Thomas Platter reported:

> Thus daily at two in the afternoon London has two,
> sometimes three plays running in different places,
> competing with each other, and those which play best
> obtain most spectators.[9]

The consumption of plays was enormous and the repertory was built up very rapidly in the 1580s. Some popular plays were repeated, but by the 1590s Henslowe was financing thirty-five new plays a year.[10]

The financial organisation of the companies depended upon a hierarchy in which the 'sharers' formed the core and derived the largest financial benefit. They hired journeymen for individual performances on a specific wage and made arrangements for apprentices. The journeymen moved from company to company and some of them had other employment, while the sharers' investments kept them in the home company. The profits had to be shared with the entrepreneur who leased the theatre to the company. This meant that he might take a large part in management, and it does appear that over the years Henslowe became more and more involved in specifics. The evolution of such a financial system was an indispensable part of the development of the professional stage. Significantly, it is a direct development of the medieval guild structure. It systematised the need to please audiences and in doing so it helped to set up a remarkable feature of the Elizabethan stage: the sustaining of certain well-tried plays, such as the anonymous *Mucedorus* and Kyd's *Spanish Tragedy*, which came to be favourites over a long period.

The main income of the companies was taken at the door of the theatres, which were vulnerable to closure by the City authorities, usually on grounds of the danger from plague. There is a formidable list of such interventions: plays were restrained seven times between 1572 and 1583, and almost continuously from August 1592 to the end of 1593.[11] On such occasions there were two ways of filling the income gap: by taking the company on tour, and by marketing play texts. The long plague closure of 1592–93 was followed by a flurry of publication in 1594 of plays many of which had been performed several years earlier, and might otherwise have now been lost to us. For an extra attraction it was a frequent recommendation on title pages to refer to performance by an eminent company. It is apparent, however, that the plays as printed texts were given much less recognition than the plays when performed, and sometimes the printed versions were truncated and ill-prepared. As to the travelling, the details given by E.K. Chambers (*ES* 3.1–261) show that the companies went up and down the country in complicated journeys. Unfortunately we do not usually know how many players went on each journey, and it is unwise to assume that the number was consistent. This naturally would mean that texts were often cut or enlarged in order to adapt them for local performance, a process which makes for intriguing problems about the consistency of texts.

Before 1576, many plays had been printed with doubling schemes, the number of players required varying from four to nine. After 1576, the companies grew in size, presumably as a result of the settled base and the more sophisticated organisation and finance. Doubling schemes appeared less frequently as a recommendation for purchase. But the practice did continue in the new companies even with their greater resources. The Queen's Men comprised twelve members in 1583, and T.J. King has shown that the average number of players in the performance of Shakespeare's plays was just under ten adults with three or four boys (apprentices, not sharers) for the women's parts.[12] The number of sharers and the number of players in a specific play need not necessarily be the same, but it is clear that the new arrangements offered much greater freedom to playwrights.

Audiences

Even though the theatres were placed outside the City of London, Burbage's intention must have been to attract city-dwellers, who formed his main constituency. As far as the public theatres were concerned, the Bankside gradually became a centre for a variety of amusements including the plays, and the price of entry remained low enough to enable even apprentices to afford it. The lowest charge for standing entry in the pit was one penny, and the galleries could be entered for twopence or threepence. There was more expensive provision for eminent or affluent spectators in the lords' room. Though there was much contemporary criticism of the behaviour of audiences, much of it comes from groups hostile to the stage, and therefore it cannot be assumed that the audiences consisted entirely of low-class rowdies. There are certainly legal cases about disorder, mostly after 1600. The presence of women cannot be doubted. In spite of the efforts of those interested in denigrating all females at plays, it is clear that respectable citizens' wives attended throughout the period.

The private theatres do seem to have admitted all comers, though there must have been a tendency to exclude the socially undesirable. Several times Lyly shows uneasiness about audience reaction. He asks that the players 'may enjoy by your wonted courtesies a general silence' (Campaspe, Prologue at the Blackfriars, 1. 35). In Sappho and Phao he asks for 'soft smiling, not loud laughing' (Prologue at the Blackfriars, 1. 9). Higher entrance fees might have been a deterrent. The experience of being present in a small audience, and in an indoor auditorium must have been remarkably different from that at the Theatre, and it is most likely that performance in these theatres would have required a different style of acting. Because of their educational and humanist inheritance the subject matter was also different. One special feature was that in these theatres the cheapest places were furthest away from the stage, in direct contrast to the practice in the public playhouses.

If audiences at both kinds of theatre came from different social classes, the expectations of the playwrights and the actors must have been that the spectators would be prepared to take in a fairly sophisticated diet. We shall note in some individual plays that there was knockabout fooling and often a good deal of fighting including prolonged swordplay. But in contrast there is much language which is fascinating in its complexity and which reflects rhetorical skills of a high order. Playwrights consciously assailed ears as well as eyes.[13] Most of the audience must have been educated enough to enjoy what they heard. Many of them would be literate, London having a higher rate of literacy than elsewhere.[14] It is clear, however, that the aural culture of sermons and public speaking presumed that even those who could not read would still be able to respond to the complex material they were accustomed to listening to. The palpable pressure from Marlowe and other dramatists about the nature of the language they were using indicates that expectations were high. As most of the audience were city-dwellers, the success of the stage derived in part from the concentration of wealth and expertise in a thriving city. Gosson contemptuously stigmatised the playgoers as 'the common people which resort to theatres being but an assembly of tailors, tinkers, cordwainers, sailors, old men, young men, women, boys, girls and such like'. Take away his prejudice and this seems a very varied audience.

Alongside the developing interest in drama there was naturally a variety of other forms of entertainment. Many of these activities had a long ancestry, and they were drawn into the city by the same concentration of people, wealth and opportunity we have been considering for the plays. The Bankside housed bull- and bear-baiting. There were frequent displays of warlike arts, including fencing and archery. Magic, usually known as conjuring, and other demonstrations of skills attracted attention. There was music in taverns and on the streets. Dancing was popular, and perhaps one of the most interesting forms of entertainment was the jig. Its origins lay in popular folk festivals before the middle of the sixteenth century. It was a combination of song, in ballad form, with an accompanying dance. It was much developed by Richard Tarlton, who included a variety of popular entertainments in his performances as a clown. Many early plays contain dances which are forms of jig, such as the dancing Devil and Vice in *Like Will to Like*. In the 1590s, after Tarlton's death, jigs were entered increasingly in the Stationers' Register. Sometimes they were performed as an after-piece of plays. The following is a refrain from the dialogue between a lady and her lover in *A New Northern Jig called Dainty come thou to me*, registered in 1591:

> Cast no care to thy heart
> From thee I will not flee
> Let them all say what they will
> Dainty come thou to me.[15]

The activities of clowns and fools had been encouraged in the houses of the nobility for generations. The Tudor monarchs had court fools, including the famous Will Summers (d. 1560).[16] No doubt these different forms of entertainment were all available to playwrights. Indeed, all the ones mentioned found their way into plays in some form or other.

Most of what has been said here concentrates upon the City of London. The vigorous drama away from the capital must have been fed and stimulated by the performances of the London companies on tour. Unfortunately, we do not usually know exactly what the itinerant players brought to provincial towns, but there are indications that the popular *Mucedorus*, for example, was performed outside London. According to Nashe, Tarlton went on tour with the Queen's Men.[17] Such performances were done under the auspices of the local civic authorities, or in the houses of the affluent. It barely needs saying, however, that there is hardly a watershed comparable with that in London to be found in the provinces. Away from the capital the presentation of plays had for centuries depended upon either local amateurs or travelling companies, and we have no reason to suppose that these practices changed very much, except that the companies from London now could bring richer and more varied fare. The May games and the church ales continued, and Robin Hood was still popular. Some of these para-dramatic activities, indeed, fed back into the popular plays of the London stage, and we find traces of them in the repertory to be considered in the next two chapters. Before turning to these, however, we shall consider the plays of John Lyly, who made a significant individual contribution before 1590.

JOHN LYLY

In many ways Lyly's plays are a continuation of the work of playwrights like John Heywood and John Redford, for all his surviving dramatic work is closely directed towards court performance. Like these predecessors a generation earlier, he worked with the boys' companies, and it is probable that the performances were given by boys with some adults in key roles—a practice which Heywood is thought to have adopted. Only with *Mother Bombie* (printed 1594) is evidence lacking of presentation at court: *Campaspe* and *Sappho and Phao* were given there in 1584, *Love's Metamorphosis* in 1586, *Gallathea* and *Endymion* in 1588, *Midas* in 1590, and *The Woman in the Moon* in 1593.[18] As we have seen, Lyly had the special advantage of being able to prepare some of his plays by showing them beforehand to audiences at the Blackfriars. His response to the circumstance of court performance followed the others in the sense of propriety which governs all his writing. He was prepared to open up topical or delicate issues, but his handling of them suggests that he was aware of the need to be circumspect. In this he showed a courtier's judgement comparable to Heywood's, though Lyly was not as successful at surviving in court circles as Heywood had been.

The subjects of his plays revolve around characters and episodes drawn from classical myth, and in this he shows his preoccupation with humanist education such as was desirable for young men. Indeed, he is master of managing events, topics, plots and language which were appropriate to this end. But his interest in myth reveals one of its great strengths: its potential for use as allegory. In this Lyly manifests his medieval inheritance, and shows that allegorical modes could still be used successfully to expose philosophical issues, and as a means of presenting and analysing characters or situations. There are places where his use of allegory also has political dimensions, though it is not apparent that all his plays, or that everything in any one of them, should necessarily be read in this way.

The classical influence can be found in several aspects. All his plays are comedies: though the endings are not necessarily smooth resolutions of all difficulties, they are chiefly concerned with love, and often involve Cynthia, Cupid and Venus. At times, as in *Mother Bombie*, the intrigue shows distinctly classical motifs. Here, there are two wealthy fathers, one with a foolish son and the other a foolish daughter, who wish their children to marry. There are also two other not so wealthy fathers of an intelligent son and daughter who wish to marry their offspring to the wealthy but foolish heiress and heir. The sorting out of this elegantly balanced plot is the result of the activities of the four pages who work for each of the four fathers. Mother Bombie herself is a very wise English woman who tells fortunes, but her predictions are given the authority of a classical oracle.

In other plays, however, the classical setting shows itself in the interaction of gods and goddesses in human affairs, and the familiar device of the impact of dissension between them upon human affairs is the substance of the plots. This is found in the even more elegant balances of the plot of *Love's Metamorphosis*, which turns on the conflict between Cupid and Ceres. This plot is thought to be largely original, but its nature suggests the complexities and attractions of classical myths. The setting is a pastoral one in which Erisichthon (*Gk*: angry and earthy), a farmer, furious with Ceres, cuts down a tree sheltering her nymph Fidelia whom he kills. He is punished by Famine, who gives him an insatiable appetite. Nisa, Celia and Niobe, three other nymphs devoted to Ceres, anger Cupid in disdaining their rural lovers, Ramis, Montanus and Silvestris. This rejection is a material part of the play, giving scope for witty and ingenious speeches explaining the grounds for rejection. But the inventive ingenuity is situational as well as linguistic. Nisa is cruel, Celia coy and Niobe inconstant. Cupid transforms them into symbols of these Petrarchan dispositions as a stone, a rose (which fades), and a bird of paradise (which, according to contemporary belief, lives only by air and dies if it touches the ground). In doing this Cupid is moved by the faithful love exhibited by Protea, daughter of Erisichthon, for her beloved Petulius. When Ceres begs Cupid to relent, a bargain is struck whereby Erisichthon is pardoned in return for the acceptance of their lovers by Ceres' three nymphs. But at the last moment the nymphs themselves resist the deal, and they are only persuaded to relent when each of their lovers in turn accepts the respective natural flaws as part of what he has to enjoy and love. Thus the psychology of love is cleverly entangled with the quasi-mythic framework. For example, Celia and Montanus finally agree to love in spite of difficulties:

> *Celia*   I consent so as Montanus when in the midst of his sweet
>   delight shall find some bitter overthwarts [*frustrations*]
>   impute it to his folly in that he suffered me to be a rose
>   that hath prickles with her pleasantness as he is like to
>   have with my love shrewdness.
> *Montanus* Let me bleed every minute with the prickles of the rose so
>   I may enjoy but one hour the savour.
>
> (5.4.140–5)

These complexities of love, so carefully balanced and so neatly interactive, are well within the capabilities of young male actors. The emotional range is limited, and yet the powerful expression which relies heavily but dazzlingly upon carefully modulated sentence structure is well suited to youngsters carefully schooled in speaking as well as in singing. At the same time, it is obvious that here and elsewhere Lyly is able to exploit the physical presence and attributes of these young men. The overall effect, therefore, is that the ideas about love and its discomforts are intellectually well explained, while the appearance of the young actors in costume exhibit elegance and attractiveness. It must have been a very effective dramatic mixture. No doubt the sexual aspects of these characterisations were played up, and, though it is always difficult to be certain about matters of taste, it would seem that this was a much enjoyed combination since the plays were done so frequently at court.

At the same time, there is a political dimension which does much to explain both their success and Lyly's motivation. In several plays there are powerful authoritarian figures, either monarchs, gods or goddesses, who dominate the action. There have been attempts to identify Cynthia in *Endymion* and Sappho in *Sappho and Phao* with Queen Elizabeth and other figures, in consequence with courtiers interacting with her, but these have not proved convincing. The only real exception is Midas, whose ambition to conquer the islands north of his kingdom, whose lust for gold and whose folly can be identified with Philip II of Spain. *Midas* was performed at court not long after the Armada of 1588.

Nevertheless, the plays are often concerned with the relationships between the superior and powerful and those of lesser stature as with Cynthia, the goddess who is loved by Endymion, and Sappho who is presented as a princess loved by Phao, a humble ferryman. In such cases the social distance between the two lovers is material: Endymion is rescued from his sleep by a kiss from Cynthia, but she does not love him in return, and Sappho, though she did return the love of Phao, cannot respond to it fully and she lets him go:

> for destiny calleth thee as well from Sicily as from love.
> Other things hang over thy head which I must neither tell
> no thou inquire.
>
> (*Sappho and Phao*, 5.3.27–9)

Alexander the Great does love Campaspe, one of his Theban captives, and the action of the play shows how the great conqueror pauses briefly in his military campaigns to show how she has impressed him. But when she, in her turn, falls in love with Apelles, whom Alexander has commissioned to paint her portrait, Alexander withdraws and continues with his conquests, finally seeing love as beneath him:

> Well enjoy one another. I give her thee frankly, Apelles.
> Thou shalt see that Alexander maketh but a toy of love and

> leadeth affection in fetters, using fancy as a fool to make
> him sport or as a minstrel to make him merry. ... Alexander
> is cloyed with looking on that which thou wonderest at.
>
> (*Campaspe*, 5.4.145–57)

That Lyly took plays dealing with such situations to court is an indication that he is concerned with more than trifles. The politics there were still intimately involved with Elizabeth's political and psychological exploitation of her femininity, even though the possibility of marriage receded during the 1580s on the grounds of her age. There was still flirtation in her affairs, and there was also the question of how those seeking to influence her—mostly men—could manage a situation dominated by a woman. To entertain such a person with elegant fictions about love and to show the pains and perhaps the rewards of amorous relationships between those of unequal rank was more than titillating. It must have been an attempt to use such material to win influence for Lyly himself, or perhaps for his patron the Earl of Oxford who supported the court performances.

The plays exploited the imagery surrounding the Queen, especially by their humanist tone, with the discussion of such philosophical issues as chastity versus true love. They show characters, human as well as divine, struggling with virtue and honour in their love affairs. These are accompanied by a discourse of power, but the interesting dramatic aspect of this is that the Queen herself was expected to be present at performances and to see an image of herself both as monarch and woman in the business of the plays. She is to be complimented by the action, though her direct involvement in it, as in Peele's *Arraignment of Paris*, is avoided.

Lyly goes near to idealism. He presents a partly magic and partly supernatural world which is simplified. There are a few touches of earthy realism, but in general he portrays a rarefied society concerned with honour and perfection. Much of the action of the plays is verbal exploitation of ideas in highly decorative ways, often using repetitive devices which turn ideas inside out and upside down. Yet the flaws in this world, the love affairs uncompleted, the rage and frustration, the disappointed affections, suggest that the superficial gloss is a deliberate artifice—attractive in itself no doubt—aimed at hinting or reflecting an underlying disturbance.

One of these is the failure of court life to meet the real aspirations of Lyly himself. It has been rightly noted that his exploitation of it was ultimately unsuccessful and that some of the plays show a disenchantment in spite of the apparent elegance. The elaboration of the plays betrays a high intelligence, one which might be expected to see through the worship of the chaste Queen, to perceive the power struggle underneath in the court intrigues. He was not the only court poet to have played with idealism and to have presented grim authority. He may even have been partly concerned to support such a structured hierarchy even though he was conscious of flaws within it.

Disturbance shows itself at another level, however: in the presentation of women in the plays. Here the rather stereotyped masculine view is offered that women are fickle, changeable, corrupt even, and the contrast between female failings and the unsullied devotion which men offer is much emphasised. On the one hand, this may lead to the loving embrace of human weakness noted above in *Love's Metamorphosis*, but it may also be an index of apprehension about the power of women and be the result of a need to portray unfavourable feminine characteristics. To this we should add that the image of woman in authority recurs again and again in the plays. Sometimes she is endowed with insight, but more often figures like Sappho and Endymion's Cynthia are a threat to masculinity. One intriguing detail, for example, is that ferrymen such as Phao were noted in London for the way in which their powerful and attractive physiques were sexually attractive to the noble ladies they served. Lyly's plays undoubtedly reflect a conflation of sexual and political attraction and power.

If this is so, it can be seen that the dramatic forms he employs are effective as ways of embodying these preoccupations, even if Lyly is working partially at an unconscious level. We have already noted the particular effect of using boys as performers. The impersonation of women of various ages by young males is sexually challenging. This is most striking in *Gallathea*, in which the two daughters of shepherds disguise themselves as males, and each in her disguise falls in love with the apparent masculinity of the other.

The reason for the disguise of Gallathea and Phyllida as young men is a version of the beast-from-the-sea myth. Although the setting is the English River Humber, it is an offence to Neptune by the locals which has led to the imposition of the obligation to sacrifice annually the most beautiful virgin to Agar, Neptune's sea-monster. The disguises are an attempt to deceive Neptune, but early in the play the theme that destiny overrules everything and cannot be deceived is firmly stated. These disguises have counterparts in the disguise taken by Cupid in order to catch Diana's nymphs, and the disguise of Neptune that seeks to uncover the trickery which is being played against him.

The conflict between Venus and Diana, which is really another debate between love and chastity, is made sharper by the activities of the disguised Cupid. He brings tormenting pleasures:

A heat full of coldness, a sweet full of bitterness, a pain full
of pleasantness, which maketh thoughts have eyes and
hearts ears, bred by desire, nursed by delight, weaned by
jealousy, killed by dissembling, buried by ingratitude, and
this is love.

(1.2.16–19)

Such passages illustrate how skilfully Lyly adapted the decorative prose style he had used in his *Euphues* novels (1578–80) to dramatic speech. Though Cupid is disgraced by the power of Diana, in the end she herself is matched by Venus who represents true love, differentiated from lust. This philosophical framework is presented wittily and ironically in the play, so that the idea of love is at least ambivalent. The same may be said for the love between the two girl-men: they approach each other warily and distrust their own feelings. Here Lyly makes the audience fully aware of the circumstances so that their hesitancy is appealingly comic, but he is careful to keep the tone light, and here he avoids the bawdy suggestiveness which is found elsewhere in the play among the male characters.[19] Part of the dramatic effectiveness lies in the way each mirrors the other, giving a typical balance to their dialogue:

Phyllida	Suppose I were a virgin (I blush in supposing myself one), and that under the habit of a boy were the person of a maid: if I should utter my affection with sighs, manifest my sweet love by my salt tears, and prove my loyalty unspotted and my griefs intolerable, would not then that fair face pity this true heart?
Gallathea	Admit that I were as you, would you have me suppose that you are, and that I should with entreaties, prayers, oaths, bribes, and whatever can be invented in love, desire your favour, would you not yield?
Phyllida	Tush, you come in with 'admit'.
Gallathea	And you with 'suppose'.
Phyllida	(*aside*) What doubtful speeches be these! I fear me he is as I am, a maiden.
Gallathea	(*aside*) What dread riseth in my mind! I fear the boy to be as I am, a maiden.
Phyllida	(*aside*) Tush, it cannot be; his voice shows the contrary.
Gallathea	(*aside*) Yet I do not think it, for he would then have blushed.

(3.2.17–34)

The audience is hardly likely to be deeply involved emotionally in such an exchange, but the closeness of the dialogue and its stylistic ingenuity encourage the appreciation of wit. The experience of a play by Lyly is thus more a matter of intellectual engagement set up by his interest in structural parallels and contrasts. No doubt the classical humanist subject matter and the ideological approach implied in this also helps. The fact that he used the Boys' Companies also meant that he could use larger casts than had been the case with the interludes acted by adult companies, and this facility broadened the range of his structures.

These considerations suggest that Lyly was a dramatist of skill and experience. Modern criticism has tended to stress his small stature and limited achievement, but in fact his approach to the subject matter of love and authority shows that he is not merely a decorative dramatist. His treatment of both is extensive and it brings out conflicting elements. Although there are similarities between the plays and we have found themes and techniques which link them, there is a notable variety in the way he sets about his dramatisations, and his approach to each play has a strong element of originality in both design and execution. He may have been conscious of the limitation of writing plays for boys, but in fact he seems to have made this into an opportunity for exploring the differing possibilities of comedy. He was sufficiently aware of the traditions of classical comedy to realise the importance of decorum and this may have been of considerable help to him in preparing his work for court performance.

The printing of Lyly's plays in his lifetime suggests that he was held in high esteem. The texts give us enough evidence about their staging to indicate that he had an imaginative grasp of how his plays were to be performed. As far as we know, the First Blackfriars was used for public performances which were in effect rehearsals for subsequent court production, and the assumption must be that the acting spaces were comparable in size and configuration. We must also assume that the performances at the Blackfriars and at court were very much alike, even if the latter was in the great hall at Greenwich on one occasion, and Whitehall on another. For the later plays, however, the Blackfriars was not available for rehearsal, and Lyly may have moved into the Paul's acting area which, as we have seen, is less easy to identify and describe. At court, the Queen's presence is often implied, as in the Court Epilogue of *Campaspe*, which refers to 'your Highness' (l. 7).

Whatever the difficulty in specifying details now, his general concept of the stage is a combination of the Terentian street and the medieval unlocalised central playing space. The former used a series of doors, each leading into an unseen interior which was identified as the house or base of one of the characters.[20] Lyly chose two or perhaps three such locations as in those identified as Sappho's or Cynthia's palaces. However, the Revels documents show that payments were made quite frequently for the construction of houses, presumably three-dimensional, in preparing court entertainments. This tradition of erecting such free-standing structures was well established: it could have been appropriate for both *Apius and Virginia* (c. 1559) and *Horestes* (1567). In this way the Terentian street would be modified because it becomes undetermined and unidentified.

This space is much used by Lyly in the action, as for the boasting of Sir Tophas in *Endymion* (2.2), which could be demonstrated anywhere. It is also the place for enacting movement between one house and another, during the course of which journeys, dialogues could take place, as when Cynthia wishes to visit the bank where the sleeping Endymion lies (4.3.57). During such movement there is also the possibility of the passing of time. Lyly owes much to medieval precedents in this feature, particularly as it was applied to indoor staging in great halls. The principle behind it is not realistic but symbolic or allegorical: it does not really matter how far Cynthia has to walk. The effect, however, may be to change the perspective and in this way to enhance the balance between parts of the play, which was so important in Lyly's dramatic style. In *Love's Metamorphosis*, *Gallathea*, and *Endymion* Lyly makes various uses of a tree so as to suggest that it was the same property which could be invested in different but appropriate meanings from play to play. The contrast in *Campaspe* between Alexander's palace and the studio of Apelles on either side of the stage has an imaginative significance. As to the houses themselves, some of them had interiors, as is implied in the stage direction—*Sappho in her bed* (3.3.1)—from which she speaks. Endymion needed to disappear within the bank on which he fell asleep, for he had to age before being 'discovered' in order to be awakened.

The plays are rich in musical elements, and no doubt the boys would be adept in singing. The Master of the Chapel had the right to recruit boys from anywhere in the kingdom, a bit like a press-ganging. In Act 5 of *Campaspe* there is provision for one character to do some tumbling and for another to dance. This variety of activities suggests that Lyly realised the importance of entertainment in commanding attention at court. It is a striking enhancement of the intellectual pleasure of debate and the emotional ones which would arise from seeing boys evoke the conduct and experiences of women.

Notes

1. The legal plea is given in full by J.S. Leongard, 'An Elizabethan Lawsuit: John Brayne, his Carpenter, and the Building of the Red Lion Theatre', *Shakespeare Quarterly* 34 (1983), 298–310.

2. R. Gair, *The Children of Paul's: The Story of a Theatre Company, 1553–1608* (Cambridge, 1982), pp. 44–9.

3. I. Smith, *Shakespeare's Blackfriars Playhouse* (London, 1964), pp. 137–43.

4. D. Lindley, *Court Masques* (Oxford, 1995).

5. The Act is printed in full in *ES* 4.273–6.

6. Substantial passages from these works are in *ES* 4.203–5, 213–9, and 221–3; see also p. 223. For the link between theatre-going and the perceived and dangerous loss of social identity, see J.E. Howard, *The Stage and Social Struggle in Early Modern England* (London, 1994), pp. 26–40.

7. Details of this legislation are in *ES* 4.268–72.

8. *ES* 2.138. In fact Alleyn was married to Henslowe's step-daughter.

9. *Travels in England*, pp. 166–75, quoted in A. Gurr, *Playgoing in Shakespeare's London* (Cambridge, 1987), p. 213. For afternoon performances, see *ES* 2.543.

10. Gurr, p. 118.

11. *ES* 4.346–9.

12. *ES* 2.106; and for later years T.J. King, *Casting Shakespeare's Plays: London Actors and their Roles*, 1590–1642 (Cambridge, 1992), pp. 254–5.

13. On hearing as opposed to seeing, see Gurr, pp. 85–97.

14. Gurr, p. 54.

15. C.R. Baskervill, *The Elizabethan Jig* (Chicago, 1929), pp. 107, 377–8; for further information, see pp. 12 (origins), 81 (types) and 85 (plays).

16. E. Welsford, *The Fool: His Social and Literary History* (London, 1935), pp. 159–70.

17. A. Gurr, *The Shakespearean Stage* 1574–1642 (Cambridge, 1980), p. 86.

18. References are to *Campaspe* and *Sappho and Phao*, edited by G.K. Hunter and D. Bevington (Manchester, 1991); *Endymion*, edited by D. Bevington (Manchester, 1996), and for the remainder, *The Complete Works of John Lyly*, edited by R.W. Bond, 3 vols (Oxford, 1902).

19. The playing of women's parts by boys attracted unfavourable comment from Puritans: 'When I see ... young boys, inclining of themselves unto wickedness, trained up in filthy speeches, unnatural and unseemly gestures, to be brought up by these schoolmasters in bawdry and idleness, I cannot choose but with tears and grief of heart lament', Antony Munday; *A Second and Third Blast of Retreat from Plays and Theatres* (1580), *ES* 4.212.

20. See the edition of a slightly earlier English version of Terence's *Andria: Terence in English: That Girl from Andros*, ed. M. Twycross (Lancaster, 1987), pp. 1–5.

MARTIN WIGGINS

New Tragedies for Old

'Modern drama' began late for the Elizabethans. The time of Stephen Gosson may have bequeathed the theatrical institutions within which it took place, but it was not until the second half of the 1580s that the playhouses achieved their first durable popular successes, plays which not only defined audience taste for years afterwards, but were also individually memorable in their own right. The earliest to appear was probably Thomas Kyd's *The Spanish Tragedy* (c. 1586), which dealt with crime, politics, and imperialism in a fictitious modern court of Spain, the mightiest of the secular states of sixteenth-century Europe. *Tamburlaine the Great* soon followed in 1587, dramatizing the rise to power of a Tartar bandit turned would-be world conqueror; and its author, Christopher Marlowe, went on to co-write (with an unknown collaborator) another major success in *Doctor Faustus*, a tragic morality play in which, for once, the magic-fixated protagonist is not saved at the end but goes to hell. Conjuring Faustus, mighty Tamburlaine, and *The Spanish Tragedy's* grieving, vengeful Hieronimo, were to become part of the period's common cultural discourse, as familiar in casual allusion as figures like Hercules and Aeneas, Adam and Jesus, from England's inherited mythologies.

These are plays on the cusp of a seismic shift in drama which was more or less complete by the time Shakespeare began his writing career in about 1590. In some respects they look back to the theatre of the recent past. This is most obvious in *Doctor Faustus*, which not only inhabits the conceptual world of the old allegorical drama but also uses many of its stage devices, like the Good and Evil Angels that prompt the devil-ridden hero towards sin and repentance. But *The*

From *Shakespeare and the Drama of His Time*. © 2000 by Martin Wiggins.

Spanish Tragedy and *Tamburlaine the Great* too were inheritors of the age of Gosson, at least in their subject matter: Kyd was not the first English dramatist to write about murder and revenge, and the lost play *The Sultan* (anonymous, 1580) testifies to an interest in eastern potentates even before Marlowe made them a subject of fashionable fascination. Yet these were also plays which seemed to their first audiences so radically, excitingly new that they all but erased the memory of Stephen Gosson and his colleagues.

At the most superficial level, one reason for this sense of novelty was simply that the writing of Marlowe and Kyd *sounded* new. The plays of the late 1570s which their work displaced would seem comically crude to ears that are accustomed to the mellifluous dramatic verse of Shakespeare and his contemporaries. They were usually written in rhyming couplets, as Gosson avers: 'the poets send their verses to the stage upon such feet as continually are rolled up in rhyme at the fingers' ends, which is plausible [pleasing] to the barbarous'. A few were written in prose (Gosson mentions the exceptional case of 'two prose books [i.e. scripts] ... where you shall find never a word without wit, never a line without pith, never a letter placed in vain'),' but the surviving texts show most playwrights using a hodge-podge of often irregular verse forms, especially 'fourteeners': 'I was so troubled in my mind with fright of sudden fear | That yet I feel my sinews shake and tremble everywhere.' (*Fedele and Fortunio*, 647–8) Less than four years after those lines were written, Marlowe sneeringly dismissed this sort of thing, in the prologue to *Tamburlaine the Great*, as 'jigging veins of rhyming mother wits'.

Though a skilful rhymer in his non-dramatic poetry, Marlowe wrote for the stage in blank verse, using stately, five-beat iambic pentameter lines like these from his first play, *Dido, Queen of Carthage*: 'Now, Dido, with these relics burn thyself, / And make Aeneas famous through the world / For perjury and slaughter of a queen.' (5. 1. 292–4) This was avant-garde writing when Lyly's boys first presented the play in 1586. For all Marlowe's condescension in *Tamburlaine*, rhymed fourteeners had, only five years before, been considered good enough for the standard Elizabethan translation of Seneca. Blank verse was a minority literary form, little used and less understood; yet its simplicity and economy made it an ideal medium for serious dramatic writing compared with the clunky over-elaboration that fourteeners can encourage. To the Elizabethans, Marlowe's plays must have had all the aural impact of a symphony orchestra taking over from a barrel-organ. And not only did this new verse form sound excellent, it also offered the ideal rhythm to suit the acoustic conditions of the London amphitheatres, as modern performances at the reconstructed Globe have shown. By the end of the 1580s, it had become the usual metre for plays, whatever their venue and audience: the lush referentiality of Marlowe's writing and the powerful emotion of Kyd's set a new standard of artful, thrilling rhetoric which other playwrights strove to rival; even Lyly, who had previously written his comedies exclusively in an polished, filigree prose, turned to blank verse for his last play, *The Woman in the Moon* (c. 1592). The sound of drama had changed forever.

If their subject matter was old, moreover, Kyd and Marlowe breathed into it a new commercial life. The impact of *Tamburlaine the Great* in particular was immediate and awesome, and the first to exploit it was Marlowe himself: 'The general welcomes Tamburlaine received / When he arrived last upon our stage / Have made our poet pen his second part,' begins the prologue to the sequel, *The Second Part of Tamburlaine*, written only months after the original was first performed. A slew of lesser imitations followed, evoking the glamour of conquest in far-off lands, while others addressed the guilty fascination of magic, after *Doctor Faustus*, or the social, ethical, and political dilemmas of revenge, after *The Spanish Tragedy*; in the last years of its existence even Lyly's boy company, better suited to a less robust repertory, attempted to climb the conqueror bandwagon with *The Wars of Cyrus* (anonymous, 1588). Just as they had to learn to write in blank verse, older playwrights, left over from the London theatre's first decade, had to extend their range to satisfy the new fashions: George Peele, the Oxford dramatist who had begun his professional career writing witty pastorals for the boy actors, ended it with blood-and-thunder tragedy in the style of Christopher Marlowe.

MORAL ENDS AND AMORAL ENDINGS

Beneath the shift of taste they generated, and beyond their technical innovations, Marlowe and Kyd were important for the new ethical and political sophistication of their plays, which initiated a fundamental artistic change in drama, and particularly in tragedy. Conventional justifications of the stage in the late sixteenth century, surveyed in the previous chapter, emphasized above all that it was politically safe. The purpose of drama was a moral one, it was asserted, and the morality was conservative: plays offered no challenge to the notions of degree and decorum which were central to Elizabethan social theory. On the contrary, they reinforced the existing order by showing the proper subordination of subject to ruler and the miserable end of traitors, and vindicated the inequalities of rank at all levels—placing old over young, master over servant, man over woman—by portraying members of the subjugated groups as errant, undisciplined figures in need of control by their superiors: youths were foolish and servants corrupt, and the warnings offered to fair women admonished them to obey their husbands and avoid adultery. In contrast, *The Spanish Tragedy*, *Tamburlaine the Great*, and *Doctor Faustus* all covered dangerous territory in their shared concern with the appropriation of power beyond the normal limits prescribed by society or by God, and their handling of the theme denied such stultifying moral simplicity.

Tamburlaine was the most obviously original play of the three, and the most intellectually perverse. Several elements of its imaginative appeal are evident in its poetic treatment of landscape, as in the words with which Tamburlaine woos his prisoner and future wife, the Egyptian princess Zenocrate:

> A hundred Tartars shall attend on thee,
> Mounted on steeds swifter than Pegasus;
> Thy garments shall be made of Median silk,
> Enchased with precious jewels of mine own,
> More rich and valurous than Zenocrate's;
> With milk-white harts upon an ivory sled
> Thou shalt be drawn amidst the frozen pools
> And scale the icy mountains' lofty tops,
> Which with thy beauty will be soon resolved [melted].
>
> (1. 2. 93–101)

This kind of soaring set-piece celebration of an unfamiliar environment, with its distinctive use of proper names and adjectives, was among the most imitable features of Marlowe's writing, and many another dramatist sought to reproduce the effect. Here is another wooing speech, from an anonymous comedy of the early 1590s, *The Taming of a Shrew* (not to be confused with its Shakespearian cousin), which offers the same heady compound of classical allusion, exotic scenery, and glittering physical luxury:

> when I crossed the bubbling Canibey
> And sailed along the crystal Hellespont,
> I filled my coffers of the wealthy mines
> Where I did cause millions of labouring Moors
> To undermine the caverns of the earth
> To seek for strange and new found precious stones
> And dive into the sea to gather pearl
> As fair as Juno offered Priam's son,
> And you shall take your liberal choice of all.
>
> (4.74–82)

Both the weakness and the strength of the imitation can be seen in those millions of Moors: compared with Tamburlaine's hundred Tartars, the numerical exaggeration offers only crude overstatement; yet the playwright has also homed in astutely on another level of appeal beyond opulence and vicarious tourism. Just as Tamburlaine offers Zenocrate not only sight but ownership, so here the jewels of the earth are not only seen and enjoyed as part of a rich, exotic vista: they are mined. And in the image of Moors forced to slave in their millions to find them, we become uneasily aware of the fantasy's baser aspect.

In Marlowe's sequel, *The Second Part of Tamburlaine*, one of the subject kings, vassals and emulators of Tamburlaine himself, revealingly describes his adventures in Africa, which have included a trip to Zanzibar,

The western part of Afric, where I viewed
The Ethiopian sea, rivers, and lakes,
But neither man nor child in all the land.
Therefore I took my course to Manico.
                    (1. 3. 195–8)

This is no travelogue fired by the thrill of discovery: the new geography of the region seems incidental, and the absence of any population moves the explorer on. He conquers the rest of the dark continent; Zanzibar escapes only because there is not a human soul there for him to subjugate. It is relevant that some of the most memorable and most copied images in the two plays focus on acts of humiliation against defeated potentates: Bajazeth, once Emperor of the Turks, now confined to an iron cage and fed with scraps on the end of his master's sword, and, in the sequel, Tamburlaine's entrance onto the stage in a chariot drawn by conquered kings instead of horses. Both landscape and people are figured as things to be dominated, and the audience is imaginatively aligned with the hero who grasps so eagerly for dominion: part of the play's appeal is that of a fantasy of power.

Tamburlaine presents his ambition as a given fact: nature, he says, 'Doth teach us all to have aspiring minds' (2. 7. 20). This was the more challenging in coming from a protagonist of humble origins. Tamburlaine is a shepherd by birth and a bandit by inclination, but he refuses to accept the lowly status imposed in those roles: 'I am a lord, for so my deeds shall prove, / And yet a shepherd by my parentage.' (1. 2. 34–5) This must have been a startling assertion in 1587. An Elizabethan shepherd could not normally expect to become a gentleman, let alone a lord: the rigidly stratified society of contemporary orthodoxy was organized as an ascending hierarchy of allegiance and responsibility, culminating in the immense and centralized might of the crown; peasants and aristocrats each had their place and were expected to remain in it, their lofty or lowly status defining the nature of their actions. This is the principle by which Tamburlaine's enemies always calculate: they construe him as an ignorant peasant and his Tartar army as 'greedy-minded slaves' (2. 2. 67), who will, for instance, easily be distracted by treasure strategically scattered across the battlefield. In the event, however, his soldiers are not, as planned, cut to pieces while stooping for riches, and in consequence Tamburlaine wins his first major victory. The action consistently validates his position as he goes on to defeat progressively mightier opponents: his success comes through refusing to act true to type, through disdaining the base behaviour that is presumed to go with base birth; in that sense, his deeds do indeed prove his lordliness.

The plot of *Tamburlaine the Great*, showing the hero's ruthless ascent to power, has a simplicity which seems to be belied by the closing words of the prologue: 'View but his picture in this tragic glass / And then applaud his fortunes as you please.' Before the action begins, the audience is told the play's genre, tragedy, and its subject matter, Tamburlaine's fortunes. Tragedy, in the definition which the Elizabethans had inherited from the middle ages, dealt with the fall of great men, sometimes destroyed by the heavens in retribution for their overweening arrogance, and sometimes overthrown by the capricious and uncontrollable actions of Fortune: whether it emphasized the randomness of fate or the purposive working-out of providential history, it was a highly moral genre within the terms of contemporary dramatic criticism. So in its statement that the play is tragic, the prologue initiates an unseen context which ironizes the hero: Tamburlaine's career can be read as an exemplary illustration of pride, with the expectation that he will himself be the last of the story's great men to fall, his own fate foreshadowed in the treatment he metes out to his vanquished enemies. Such a conclusion would have enfolded the play safely back into contemporary social orthodoxy by showing the eventual punishment of excessive ambition. The play was most radically, shockingly new in withholding that expected moral ending: though his destruction is insistently telegraphed throughout, Tamburlaine finishes the play as the undefeated master of Asia. If the prologue seems to invite an interpretation according to the period's moralistic theories of drama, the conclusion calculatedly frustrates this—and the more you thought you knew about how tragedies worked, the more you would be wrong-footed by this one.

Marlowe faced several problems when box-office imperatives required a sequel. One was that he had already dramatized almost every significant element in the Tamburlaine story: all that was left was the conqueror's eventual demise. Accordingly the action is a long march to death, with the usual violence and victory *enroute*. These elements were necessary because the appeal of commercially driven sequels is that they reproduce, with minor variations, the exciting experience of the original: audience demand traps their action within the parameters of the work which created that demand. That was the other problem: it might be easy enough to overturn the peaceful conclusion of *Tamburlaine the Great* and give playgoers the conquering hero they were paying to see, but the genre-shattering surprise of the first play's conclusion was obviously not directly reproducible; indeed, ending the sequel with the central character's death could all too easily reopen the whole story to the moralistic, exemplary reading so deliberately excluded from the available responses to the first play.

The Second Part of Tamburlaine is, accordingly, much more aggressive than its predecessor in unsettling the conventional moral positions which can inform an audience's casual reaction. Such pieties are exposed as mere expedient hypocrisy: the play's Christian characters are dishonourable and corrupt, anticipating Marlowe's fuller treatment of Christian perfidy in *The Jew of Malta* (1589); and though Tamburlaine's son refuses to fight on conscientious grounds—'I take no pleasure to be murderous' (4. 1. 29), he says—he is shown really to be just a coward and voluptuary. The conclusion builds on this disruption by giving Tamburlaine a death that is temptingly legible as an act of nemesis: he burns a holy book, provocatively invites supernatural reprisals, and minutes later is struck by the sickness which kills him. Marlowe would have known from his studies at Cambridge the logical principle usually expressed in Latin as *post hoc non est propter hoc* (subsequently doesn't mean consequently), and in Tamburlaine's death he taunts the kind of literary interpretation which supposes otherwise; for the holy book the conqueror profanes is the Koran, and it is Muhammad whom he invites to take vengeance. Tamburlaine is guilty of sacrilege only in Islamic terms alien to playgoers who were Christian by law and habit even if not by zealous personal conviction, and so there can be no easy moral reading to guide the audience: it must, in the words of the previous play's prologue, applaud his fortunes as it pleases. It is the first attempt at an openness in the tragic conclusion which Marlowe was soon to push to its farthest extreme.

THE METAPHYSICS OF CALAMITY

The Spanish Tragedy can also look like a story of exciting human empowerment, albeit with a more reluctant hero than Tamburlaine. Its central character, Hieronimo, is presented as a victim of the unequal power relations in his society: he has no legal redress for his son's murder because, though he is himself a senior judge, the murderer, Lorenzo, is a member of the royal family, unassailable by public indictment; for him as later for Hamlet, the only available satisfaction is a private revenge. The narrative structure is accordingly very different from that of *Tamburlaine*, which develops through successive acts of military power constituting the stages of the ambitious hero's ascent to ultimate supremacy. The focus of Kyd's play is on a single, climatic act of destruction when Hieronimo irrevocably steps outside the law and takes a revenge that results in five deaths and destabilizes the kingdoms of Spain and Portugal by leaving them without an heir: the action leads towards a subordinate man's cataclysmic appropriation of power beyond his station.

What complicates this interpretation is the existence of another level to the action, continuously present but invisible to the characters: the main events are watched by an on-stage audience who 'serve for chorus' (1. 1. 91) and discuss the plot at the end of the play's acts. These are supernatural figures: the allegorical personification of Revenge has brought the ghost of Don Andrea to earth to witness the destruction of his killer, the Portuguese prince Balthazar. But what is perplexing, for the theatre audience as much as for the ghost, is that this declared plot seems not to match the actual events: the play seems more centrally concerned with the bereaved Hieronimo's vengeance than it is with Andrea's grievances, and Balthazar is at best a secondary character. Perhaps understandably, the ghost spends much of the entr'acte dialogue complaining that events are not following the course he expected, but diverting into a further, independent murder and its own separate revenge action. Revenge's consistent response is to demand patience—'Thou talkest of harvest when the corn is green' (2. 5. 7)—and ultimately the action does indeed reach the desired outcome; as one character says, 'The heavens are just, murder cannot be hid. / Time is the author both of truth and right.' (2. 4. 119–20) But the route by which that truth is revealed and that right achieved is obscure to human eyes, including those of the play's audience. Because Revenge lives in eternity, the whole action is already synoptically present to him as it cannot be to the human characters, including the ghost, who exist in time and can only see the events in sequence as they happen.

What Revenge necessarily underestimates is the temporary experience which, for him, is subsumed in the overall pattern: it is ironic that he should tell the ghost, 'imagine thou / What 'tis to be subject to destiny' (3. 15. 25–6), because that is precisely what he cannot imagine himself. Unlike *Tamburlaine*, whose hero proclaims his own mastery of fate—

> I hold the Fates bound fast in iron chains,
> And with my hand turn Fortune's wheel about,
> And sooner shall the sun fall from his sphere
> Than Tamburlaine be slain or overcome.
>   (1. 2. 174–7)

—the central dynamic of *The Spanish Tragedy* is human submission to fate. Its poetry also includes set-piece landscapes, but these are not, as in Marlowe, invigorating vistas, nor can they be possessed: they feature in narratives of a journey to hell, first told by Don Andrea (1. 1. 18–85) and later by Hieronimo (3. 13. 108–21), and their focus is on a human figure who is alienated and powerless in his uncanny environment. The central experience which the play dramatizes is the frustration and psychic suffering that arise from the characters' absolute dependence on mechanisms of justice which seem not to be operating. Hieronimo knows intellectually that he has two avenues of redress, first the King and then providence, and though his access to the former is blocked, he can still rely on the biblical assurance of God's justice:

> Ay, heaven will be revenged of every ill,
> Nor will they suffer murder unrepaid.
> Then stay, Hieronimo, attend their will,
> For mortal men may not appoint their time.
>   (3.13.2–5)

Yet such patience is stressful beyond mortality's tolerance: it drives him over the edge into a madness which alienates him from his public identity as the state's principal executive officer of justice, but which also makes him, as a private revenger, the agent of a higher, super-natural justice. His vengeance destroys not only Lorenzo but Balthazar: it is the medium through which unseen powers have executed their very different purposes. The pity of it is that this process had, as it were, to go the long way round: it took a second murder to raise up an unwitting instrument of Don Andrea's revenge. The conclusion is just, with Revenge accompanying the ghost to the underworld, 'To place thy friends in ease, the rest in woes' (4. 5. 46); but we can never forget the cost of that justice in human pain and innocent life.

The Spanish Tragedy was the most widely quoted, copied, and, later, parodied play of its time. This material helps us to assess its impact on early audiences, because it shows which elements they found most memorable. Hieronimo figures largely, of course, but it is telling that he does not seem to have been associated with the Marlovian self-empowerment of his revenge: in fact, the most widely quoted of all his lines was the one with which he prudently restrains himself from overstepping the mark, 'Hieronimo, beware! Go by, go by!' (3. 12. 31) He seems to have been most compelling as an articulate but passive figure, a man to whom things are done: he was remembered as a character roused from sleep who demands, 'What outcries pluck me from my naked bed?' (2. 4. 63), just before discovering his dead son's body hanging in the garden, and who utters the manic poetry of grief—'O eyes, no eyes, but fountains fraught with tears' (3. 2. 1)—that Kyd's successors found so powerful and imitable. The central experience of the play for sixteenth-century audiences was his suffering.

Pain is an inevitable concomitant of tragedy, but in Kyd's play there is a distinct shift of emphasis from the genre's conventional tales of the fall of princes. Part of the response which such tragedies evoked was a grim, objective satisfaction at the humbling of the mighty, much as audiences tend to feel towards Tamburlaine's victims or the surviving royals at the end of The Spanish Tragedy. In contrast, the treatment of Hieronimo, a man of relatively lower rank, invites engagement and sympathy. Subsequent revenge plays followed suit: their heroes were known not as awesome angels of death sent to scourge the living, but for their almost insupportable burdens of human responsibility to the dead. It is no arbitrary chance that there survives from the first English tragedy based on the Hamlet story, written more than a decade before Shakespeare's version, only a single line of dialogue: it was the ghost's terrible injunction, 'Hamlet, revenge!' that playgoers most remembered and quoted.[1] Tragedy had begun to ask its audiences to respond with humane subjectivity; the essence of the experience was now a relationship with another human being.

This was as radical as Tamburlaine the Great's refusal to supply the expected tragic catastrophe. If the genre's moral purpose was to show the mutability of fortune and the punishment of vice, then a degree of audience detachment was a necessary element: any pity which might be felt for the suffering hero served primarily to enhance the terror which made his destruction an effective moral example. In the new tragedy, the process was reversed: the terror of events now became the basis for pity, and this in turn made it impossible to represent the tragic outcome as transcendently right and just. Where conventional tragedy promoted an unquestioning acceptance of the order of things, these plays evoked a sense of regret that political and metaphysical circumstances should be such as to make suffering inevitable: as Shakespeare's Hamlet expresses it, 'The time is out of joint. O cursed spite / That ever I was born to set it right!' (1. 5. 189–90) Often this works through a tension between our ethical sense of a moral ending and our humane sense of an unhappy ending. In *The Spanish Tragedy*, such feelings remain relatively unfocused; but in *Doctor Faustus* Marlowe and his collaborator made their object dangerously precise.

A play whose protagonist sells his soul, practises the forbidden arts of magic, and ends up damned cannot avoid the punitive dynamic: with angels and devils and, ultimately, the inescapable certainty of divine judgement, the action of *Doctor Faustus* literally depicts the Christian metaphysics which underpin and guarantee conventional moral thinking. Almost any seminar on the play will contain someone who wants to argue that the scholar hero gets his just deserts, and indeed when the discussion is framed in those terms it is difficult to disagree: the closing lines (quoted in the last chapter) expressly invite an exemplary reading of his 'hellish fall', and the action repeatedly emphasizes his more than suicidal folly. There is something ineluctably crass about a man who knows that the reward of sin is death, as it says in the biblical text that provokes him to reject theology, yet who chooses sin anyway; who declares that 'A sound magician is a mighty god' (1. 1. 64) when all his academic studies should have told him that there is a mightier; who conjures up the devil and then tells him that hell's fable. Yet the epilogue also contains a simple, human statement which opens the play to a response beyond the merely judgemental: 'Faustus is gone.'

John Faustus is without doubt a failure. It is difficult to make a convincing case for a sense of tragic loss based on his appeal as a character, because that appeal lies more in desire than in act. There is a poetic magnificence in his initial fantasies about spirits that will fetch him gold from India and pearls from the deep, but they remain fantasies, unfulfilled even once he has the magical power to realize them: Germany is not given a defensive wall of brass, the university's poor students do not receive silken clothes, and he does not make himself the world's most powerful secular ruler. In his case, the waste of human potential has happened long before he goes to hell: though it is amusing and spectacular for him to give an insolent knight a pair of horns or fetch out-of-season fruit to satisfy a Duchess's pregnancy craving, such legerdemain is also imaginatively trivial.

It is important to recognize, however, that there is more than one kind of failure in the play. Faustus' greatest desire is for a knowledge that goes beyond the frustrating limits of the traditional academic disciplines, yet even with magic he learns nothing that he did not already know: his demonic factotum Mephistopheles will not, or cannot, enter into theological discussion, and when, in the revised version of the play produced nine years after Marlowe's death, Faustus explores the heavens to find out the secrets of astronomy, all he discovers are the enclosing concentric spheres of medieval cosmology which he could have read about in his own study. It is not Faustus' imagination that is at fault here, but the created world in which he exists: there is no new learning available to him because scholastic writers have told the truth about human existence, and he has already mastered their works. Both his folly and his desire spring from a conviction that there must be more to life than there really is: in a sense, he goes to hell because he is mistaken. This is the point at which we have to choose between orthodox and radical readings, between the old tragedy and the new. If the play reinforces conventional, conservative morality by condemning Faustus absolutely, then by implication it also condemns wishing for a better world. But if it does not condemn him, it must perforce call into question the world that is, and the presiding godhead that decrees damnation: if there is no justice, there can only be tyranny. It is sixteenth-century drama's most challenging dilemma.

THE LURE OF THE CROWN

Between them, Marlowe and Kyd reinvented tragedy for the English Renaissance, but of the three plays it was the least fundamentally tragic, *Tamburlaine the Great*, which exerted the most immediate and quantifiable influence. This extended well beyond the derivative and short-lived conqueror play genre: for nearly a decade afterwards, drama engaged widely with Marlowe's themes of ambition and social mobility. In the later 1590s, it was said that the typical story of a tragedy told 'How some damned tyrant, to obtain a crown, / Stabs, hangs, empoisons, smothers, cutteth throats.' (*A Warning for Fair Women*, induction, 50-1) Not the fall of princes now, but the rise of usurpers: aspirant characters like Shakespeare's Richard III and Marlowe's Duke of Guise in *The Massacre at Paris*, who are not born to supreme power but who seek it through crime and stratagem. If the insistent beat of that list of atrocities expresses severe criticism of the stage tyrant, the passage also evokes, in spite of itself, the new drama's tendency to depict the fascination of ambition as much as its hazards. The use of the word *crown* is distinctive, highlighted in end-stopped magnificence as the culmination not only of the usurper's aspirations but also of the pentameter line. This echoes the thrilling poetry of political desire first spoken by Tamburlaine:

> The thirst of reign and sweetness of a crown,
> That caused the eldest son of heavenly Ops
> To thrust his doting father from his chair
> And place himself in th' empyreal heaven
> Moved me to manage arms against thy state.
>   (2.7. 12–16)

In the ensuing years, the crown was a subject of obsessive interest among stage villains: Stukely the ambitious Englishman can think of nothing else in *The Battle of Alcazar* (Peele, 1589), and in the anonymous *Edmond Ironside* (c. 1592) the

Machiavellian schemer Edricus even claims to value it above his own life. Shakespeare's reworking of Marlowe's lines, spoken by Richard of Gloucester in *Henry VI, Part 3* (1591), is especially interesting in the way it develops their mythological apparatus: 'How sweet a thing it is to wear a crown, / Within whose circuit is Elysium / And all that poets feign of bliss and joy.' (1. 2. 29–31) Tamburlaine, who cites the rise of Jove to the throne of the gods as an analogue for his own aspiration to an earthly crown, seems oddly respectful in comparison with Richard's assertion that bliss, the condition of the soul in heaven, is only a poetical fiction whose equivalent in reality is the satisfaction of kingship. This independence of supernatural sanction must have been shocking to early audiences; and it is an important part of the dynamic of ambition in these plays.

Richard's immediate problem as a would-be king is the existence of his elder brothers and their male issue, who stand between him and the throne according to the usual laws of succession. In *Richard III* (1592–3) he expresses this in terms of physical restriction: their deaths will 'leave the world for me to bustle in' (1. 1. 152), as if selective depopulation will give him more elbow-room. Atheism does much the same in existential terms. The title character of Robert Greene's Turkish conqueror play, *Selimus* (1592), who determines 'to arm myself with irreligion' (304), is even more explicit than Richard in his denial of hell: 'I think the cave of damned ghosts / Is but a tale to terrify young babes, / Like devil's faces scored on painted posts.' (424–6) Without the prospect of eternal punishment, there is no check on transgressive human action, and with no God there can be no purposeful providence but only the haphazard arbitrariness that a character in *Henry VI, Part 2* (1591) calls 'Fortune's pageant' (1. 2. 67). Moreover, if there is no higher power to which humanity is necessarily subject, a man can be the maker of his own destiny. Selimus articulates the point in metaphorically describing himself as a cardsharp:

> Will Fortune favour me yet once again,
> And will she thrust the cards into my hands?
> Well, if I chance but once to get the deck
> To deal about and shuffle as I would,
> Let Selim never see the daylight spring
> Unless I shuffle out myself a king.
>
> (1539–44)

Human willpower can subjugate the impersonal force of chance just as shuffling, usually a randomizing act, here ensures that Selimus will get the card, or the royal status, he wants; and with no supreme being, there is no absolute morality to call it cheating. In turn, those who fail to take the initiative and accept their lowly station in life are not principled but contemptibly pusillanimous: as Richard says, 'Conscience is but a word that cowards use' (5. 6. 39). These characters free themselves by, as it were, emptying out the universe of its obstructions and inhibitions, and in so doing make themselves the most charismatic figures in their respective plays: it is always more fun to bustle than to jostle, and more theatrically exciting to watch, too.

The problem is that, in the end, jostle we must. In *Hamlet*, the rebels who seek to elect Laertes King of Denmark are said to be acting as if 'the world were now but to begin' (4.5.101); but in fact the world is far from new and far from flexible. Tamburlaine may have been exciting as the maker of his own identity and future, but the equivocal nature of his status as a cult figure is clear in an incident that took place in 1593, six years after his first appearance. That spring, a xenophobic poem threatening a massacre of the resident Fleming population was found, to official consternation, posted on the wall of the Dutch church in London; its author had signed himself 'Tamburlaine'. The association of Marlowe's hero with the seizure and exercise of power made his name a liberating mouthpiece for secret antipathies that were frowned upon by society's masters, and which could not be expressed in one's own person without the risk of state reprisals. But that pseudonymous circumspection is also to the point: if the poet identified himself with Tamburlaine, he is nevertheless least like him in assuming his name, because in doing so he pulls back from committing himself. The appeal of the character ultimately had little application to the constraining complexities of reality: he may easily be able to dominate the play's open landscape of atlas-derived place-names, but closer to home the will to power is held in check by the desire to continue living a safe, quiet life.

We can see this in another recurrent feature of 1590s history plays concerned with social mobility: their treatment of popular rebellions like the Jack Cade revolt in *Henry VI, Part 2*. At one level they draw overtly on the fantasy appeal of *Tamburlaine* in the way insurgents seek to appropriate the opulence and status of high rank, imaged in a familiar lush style: in *Edward IV, Part 1* (anonymous, but sometimes attributed to Heywood, 1599), the aristocratic traitor Falconbridge promises his plebeian followers,

> We will be masters of the Mint ourselves,
> And set our own stamp on the golden coin.
> We'll shoe our neighing coursers with no worse
> Than the purest silver that is sold in Cheap [Cheapside].
> At Leadenhall we'll sell pearls by the peek
> As now the mealmen use to sell their meal.
> In Westminster we'll keep a solemn court,
> And build it bigger to receive our men.
>
> (A5)

Yet if this is attractive, there is another side to rebellion. Elizabethan stage mobs are typically portrayed as capable of atrocities such as killing people for their literacy, as in *Henry VI, Part 2*, or even, in *Julius Caesar* (1599), for being a bad poet. Tamburlaine's majestic ambition was to 'ride in triumph through Persepolis' (2. 5. 50); if there is some thing slightly mock-heroic about Falconbridge's corresponding wish to 'ride in triumph thorough Cheap to Paul's' (C4²), there is something terrifying about it too.

Tamburlaine's real-life application was limited in metaphysical as well as in social and political terms: the culture's dominant assumptions about the universe included the notion of an all-powerful and just God, so the play's determinedly materialist version of history could be considered a somewhat partial representation of reality. Such an objection would, of course, best be satisfed by the received theory of tragedy which Marlowe had overturned—that is, by the kind of play in which the hubristic hero misplaces his faith in material things and is finally laid low by the implacable force of destiny, or Fortune, or the gods. It is understandable that some later writers should have reopened this as an available mode of interpretation, particularly when materialism had escalated into the even more provocative creed of atheism. Richard III, for example, is defeated at Bosworth by an enemy who prays before the battle and afterwards attributes the victory to providence. Today we tend to feel embarrassed by this kind of overt Christianity in Shakespeare's tragedies, which can look like an unworthily naïve retreat into conventional pieties, whereas in its own time it was probably just the concluding imposition of a relatively uncontentious world-view; yet our modern unease is not entirely anachronistic. The play may resemble the old tragedy in trumping Richard's libertarian atheism with a higher dimension of existence; the difference is that in this ending the play gainsays one of its own most fundamental pleasures, the amoral exuberance of its central character. It may reflect the inescapability of the real world, like the Dutch Church writer's pragmatic decision not to put his own name to his poison-pen poem, but, as in *Doctor Faustus*, it is not a conclusion to which we can wholeheartedly assent.

TRAGEDY AND HUMANISM

Tragedies always end in disappointment: that is what makes them tragic. The *Tamburlaine* plays were appealing, and refreshing, because they focused the sixteenth century's new philosophical sense of the boundless potential of humanity: Marlowe's hero creates himself and his destiny in the face of all social and political opposition. Tragedy proper attends to the obverse, the hero's failure to realize his full human potential, either because of the kind of world he lives in or the kind of self he makes through his own actions. As such, it too rests on the humanistic view of man which found its most eloquent spokesman in Hamlet: 'What a piece of work is a man! How noble in reason, how infinite in faculty, in form and moving how express and admirable, in action how like an angel, in apprehension how like a god—the beauty of the world, the paragon of animals!' (2. 2. 305–9) Alone among Shakespeare's tragic heroes, the Prince of Denmark has himself a developed sense of the tragic, which here activates the same disappointment, even before he continues, 'to me what is this quintessence of dust?' (309–10). We can see his mind's eye turning downward when he says that man, who bears comparison with angels and with gods, is also the paragon of animals, for that is humanism's dangerous trapdoor. The period's orthodoxy, inherited from medieval Christianity, gave mankind a comfortingly fixed place in the cosmic hierarchy between angels and beasts, but the humanist thinkers, whose protean creation myth Hamlet echoes, offered the more glorious and more frightening prospect of self-definition: man could rise to the perfection of divinity, but only with the corollary that he might alternatively degenerate to the ranks of the beasts; to use Hamlet's own terms, he could be Hyperion or a satyr. It is the same vertical scale that runs between *Tamburlaine* and tragedy, and the meaning of either depends on the contrasting possibility of the other: whereas, in the older conception of the genre, the mere fact of going down to destruction was tragic in itself, in *Doctor Faustus* damnation is tragic because there is also salvation. The essence of the experience is our sense of shortfall, of the disparity between the central character's potential and his achievement.

This is one reason why the tragedies of the period often focus on heroic characters. Many are war heroes like Tamburlaine: Titus Andronicus, Macbeth, and Coriolanus all return home early in their respective plays having taken a decisive part in winning a military victory, and Othello too has a formidable battlefield reputation. Others have a comparable superiority of imaginative or intellectual capacity, like Hamlet or, arguably, Brutus. Before Kyd and Marlowe, the greatness of office alone was enough to define a tragic hero, because all he had to do was fall from that high estate; but in the new tragedy, the heroes have a greatness of inherent character which defines their human potential and so marks out the extent of the tragic loss and waste which their fall entails. 'O thou Othello, that was once so good' (5. 2. 297): the sense of the superlative and the past tense in which it is mentioned are both to the point.

The tragedies which are usually felt to be easiest to analyse in this respect are the ones which have an early focus on a single, momentous act of will, like Lear's giving away his kingdom, or Faustus' signing away his soul, which creates the circumstances that lead on to destruction. This is a development of Aristotle's analysis of tragedy as proceeding from an act of significant error which he called *hamartia*. In the old tragedy, this might be a hubristic act which calls down the punishment of the gods; Tamburlaine's burning the Koran alludes to this concept in order to undermine it. In the new, however, it is a deed which fundamentally reduces a character's future options, delivering a previously free agent into the bondage of circumstance: there is an emphasis first on the process of choosing—to kill, to conspire, to conjure, to be or not to be—which is dramatized in the hero's soliloquies, and then on the consequences of that choice. Tragedies of crime are especially clear-cut in this respect, because the *hamartia*, usually murder, is both a moral rubicon and an event which overtly requires further action to deceive or frustrate the public mechanisms of justice. Thomas Middleton puts it well in *The Changeling* (1622) when Beatrice–Joanna, who has procured the death of her fiancé, is told that she has become 'the deed's creature' (3. 4. 136): it has remade her, and sin must now pluck on sin if she is not to be exposed as a murderess. Similarly, Macbeth is deluding himself when he says, after the assassination of Banquo, 'I am in blood / Stepped in so far that, should I wade no more, / Returning were as tedious as go o'er.' (3. 4. 135–7) He is not free to turn back, because his murders cannot be undone: it is symbolically apt that his wife, in her sleepwalking state, should believe herself unable to wash the blood off her hands.

However, there are many other tragedies in which the hero's free will is severely curtailed from the first. Beaumont and Fletcher's *The Maid's Tragedy* (1611) also begins with an act of choice which cannot be reversed, though not one that appears obviously tragic in its implications: the young courtier Amintor gets married. As the action develops, however, it becomes clear that the freedom of that choice was nugatory, because it was taken in ignorance: what Amintor didn't know was that his bride is also the King's mistress and is under orders not to consummate the marriage. In this kind of tragedy there is a sense not so much of the greatness as the pathetic littleness of the characters, and their suffering is a consequence not of choice but of compulsion. Occasionally, as in *The Spanish Tragedy*, it arises from the implacable and inscrutable operations of a metaphysical dimension of reality which is indifferent to individual human pain. In *Romeo and Juliet*, for example, the lovers' bad luck is so systematic, ranging from the accident of their birth as members of rival families to the miscarriage of Friar Laurence's letter to Romeo, that it is hard not to agree with the Friar in seeing the purposeful opposition of fate: 'A greater power than we can contradict / Hath thwarted our intents' (5. 3. 153–4). More often, however, the malevolent greater power is that of the state and its grandees, who use and destroy people whenever doing so is expedient to cement their authority, as the King dupes Amintor into being a respectable front for his lechery, and as the agents of the Roman state cause oppositional voices to 'disappear' in Ben Jonson's *Sejanus' Fall* (1603).

Both types of tragedy evoke regret, but of different kinds: one is regret for the annihilation of a human being, the other for the bleak and circumscribing condition of humanity. One owes much to Marlowe and the other to Kyd, but they both rest on the disappointed hope for something better which *Tamburlaine* had fostered. When King Lear meets the naked Edgar in the guise of Tom o' Bedlam, he asks the fundamental question which all tragic events pose: 'Is man no more than this?' (3. 4. 96–7). His answer is a nihilistic negative: no dignity, no expectations, no hope. Ours will be more equivocal: whatever calamity strikes, whatever tyranny galls, however petty or wretched the hero finally becomes, man can be more. That is what tragedy means.

Notes

1. Gosson, *Plays Confuted* and *The School of Abuse*, 181, 96–7.

2. Quoted by Thomas Lodge, *Wits Miserie, and the Worlds Madnesse* (London: Cuthbert Burby, 1596), 114.

EUGENE M. WAITH

Marlowe and the Jades
of Asia

Marlowe's power as a writer has never been doubted, and that power has commonly been associated with the portrayal of the passions. Shortly after his death, he was described by Peele as "Fitte to write passions for the soules below,/If any wretched soules in passion speake."[1] Drayton spoke of him as a prototypical poet, inspired by a prototypical *furor poeticus*:

> Neat Marlowe, bathed in the *Thespian* springs,
> Had in him those brave translunary things
> That the first Poets had, his raptures were
> All ayre, and fire, which made his verses cleere,
> For that fine madness still he did retaine,
> Which rightly should possesse a Poet's braine.[2]

Toward the end of the last century A. W. Ward wrote in much the same vein of Marlowe's power to move pity and terror:

> But during his brief poetic career he had not learnt the art of mingling, except very incidentally, the operation of other human motives of action with those upon which his ardent spirit more especially dwelt; and of the divine gift of humour, which lies so close to that of pathos, he at the most exhibits occasional signs. The element in which as a poet he lived was passion ... [3]

As Shakespeare warbled his native woodnotes wild, Marlowe, according to these critics, rent the air with an unending sequence of *cris de coeur*.

Ward seems to suggest what others have also thought, that Marlowe fails to deal adequately with complementary aspects of whatever experience he is portraying. This amounts to a complaint that Marlowe is restricted in vision and lacking in balance. I hope to adduce some evidence that this criticism is unfair and that, on the contrary, one remarkable feature of Marlowe's work is the multiplicity of his vision and his insistence on balancing one view against another. This is not to deny Marlowe's effectiveness in the portrayal of passion but to claim that in a variety of ways he constantly controls his portrayal.

Before going any further we must ask ourselves whose passions are to be subject of discussion. Peele, speaking of Marlowe's fitness "to write passions for the soules below," clearly refers to dramatic characters, while Drayton, also thinking of the plays, refers to the poet's own feelings—his "raptures." Ward implies, I think, that the raptures produced the passions, and he is also concerned with the emotions aroused in the audience. The emotions of author, character, and audience must all enter into the discussion. Though we cannot assume that the author feels exactly as one of his characters does, it is reasonable to suppose that he will seek to elicit a response corresponding to his own feelings *about* the characters and situations he is presenting—to make the audience share the emotions of the characters only to the extent that he does. When I speak of control, I have in mind the means by which the author may not only indicate the nature and intensity of the feelings of his characters but also determine the way in which the audience is to react. By so doing he reveals his own attitude toward the story he is dramatizing—an attitude which may be assumed temporarily and experimentally or may be rooted in his normal outlook on life. Because this attitude is an important part of his meaning, the control I refer to is an aspect of his technique not to be overlooked.

A scene in part 2 of *Tamburlaine*, to which Shakespeare paid the tribute of a parody, will serve both for an example and a symbol. A stage direction announces: "Tamburlaine, drawn in his chariot by Trebizon and Soria, with bits in their mouths, reins in his left hand, and in his right hand a whip with which he scourgeth them...." From the chariot Tamburlaine shouts his famous lines:

Holla, ye pampered jades of Asia!
What, can ye draw but twenty miles a day,
And have so proud a chariot at your heels,
And such a coachman as great Tamburlaine...?
The horse that guide the golden eye of heaven
And blow the morning from their nosterils,
Making their fiery gait above the clouds,
Are not so honored in their governor
As you, ye slaves, in mighty Tamburlaine.

The headstrong jades of Thrace Alcides tamed,
That King Aegeus fed with human flesh
And made so wanton that they knew their strengths,
Were not subdued with valor more divine
Than you by this unconquered arm of mine.[4]

It is a theatrical image of unforgettable brilliance, presenting eye and ear with this conqueror of conquerors who calls himself "the scourge of God." Let me sketch in the remainder of this brief scene. Tamburlaine is accompanied by his sons, his three faithful followers, and two more captive kings, who will draw the chariot tomorrow. These protest their treatment and are cruelly mocked and punished. The concubines of the captive kings are brought out and distributed among Tamburlaine's soldiers for their recreation. Stage direction: "They run away with the ladies." The scene ends with a long speech in which Tamburlaine outlines further conquests and imagines his triumphal return to Samarcand, describing the plumes he will wear in lines which Spenser found appropriate to use for the plumes of Prince Arthur in *The Faerie Queene*. Rising to an ecstatic pitch, Tamburlaine compares himself in his chariot first to Apollo and then to Jove:

So will I ride through Samarcanda streets,
Until my soul, dissevered from this flesh,
Shall mount the milk-white way, and meet Him there.
To Babylon, my lords, to Babylon!

                                        (II. 130–33)

No scene in all ten acts of this play depicts more clearly Tamburlaine's lust for power. Is this a passion which Marlowe shares or commends? Does he expect the audience to thrill with Tamburlaine at the prospect of more bloody victories, more cruel jokes? The questions are unexpectedly difficult to answer with assurance. The connotations of the triumphal chariot itself are various—glory, cruelty, pride. Many years before, the young gentlemen of Gray's Inn had been entertained with a classical tragedy of *Jocasta*, in which there occurred a dumb show of a king sitting in a chariot, "drawne in by foure Kinges ... Representing unto us Ambition...."[5] Running counter to any such moral interpretation of Tamburlaine's chariot, the rhetoric points to the chariot of the sun, bringing light or even enlightenment, and to the taming of wild mares by Hercules as one of his labors. There is cruelty in that story too, for King Aegeus is thrown to the wild mares to be devoured, but Marlowe reminds us that this wicked king had made them "wanton" by feeding them on human flesh. The violence of Hercules is both appropriate punishment and homeopathic cure, for immediately after feasting on King Aegeus, the mares become tame; a natural order has been restored. The allusion to these mares of the Thracian king has a special interest, since it probably points to the source of Tamburlaine's first words in this scene. It has been pointed out that Golding, in his translation of Ovid's story of the taming of the wild mares, called them "pampered jades of Thrace."[6] This labor of Hercules must be very close to the center of the meaning of Tamburlaine and his royal team.

There is nothing heroic, however, about the brutality of Tamburlaine's henchmen to the other captive kings, nor about handing out their concubines to the soliders like so many pieces of candy. These episodes color the whole enterprise with a savage humor which rapidly degenerates toward farce as the soldiers presumably chase the concubines around the stage and then run off with them—a burlesque rape of the Sabine women. One recalls the statement of the printer of *Tamburlaine* that he has omitted some "fond and frivolous gestures" which in his opinion detracted from the play but made a great hit in the theater. Were there some of these high jinks here? And if so, did Marlowe devise them, or did the eager actors of bit parts? All we can say for sure is that the text we have certainly invites comic treatment, and thus, momentarily at least, undercuts Herculean nobility. Then, as you will recall, the theme of Tamburlaine's immortal longings is sounded fortissimo, as his imagination soars from a roster of yet unconquered kingdoms to his entry into the heavens.

In this scene both Tamburlaine and his enemies give vent to strong passions, but I hope you will agree that in presenting them Marlowe has contrived to make the response to them complex. Excitement and awe mingle with revulsion and possibly even contempt. Thus the dramatist, like his hero, seems to whip forward with one hand while he reins in with the other, always determining the speed and guiding the direction of his chariot.

Certain of his devices for exerting artistic control have already become apparent. His use of allusion, his strange juxtapositions, and his unexpected strokes of humor will bear further examination, but there are also other devices to be examined; one is the use of a dramatic introduction. Marlowe's earliest play, *Dido, Queen of Carthage*, may have been written while he was still at Cambridge University, and its title page proclaims the collaboration of his fellow Cantabrigian, Thomas Nashe, though there are no clear evidences of Nashe's work in the play as it stands. I shall refer to it as Marlowe's play. The theme, of course, is the familiar love tragedy of Dido and Aeneas in Virgil's epic. There can be no secret for any literate member of the audience about the nature of the story he is about to see; it must be heroic in so far as it concerns the high destiny of Aeneas and pathetic in its portrayal of his desertion of Dido, who is to be the principal character. Knowing this much, one is startled by the un–Virgilian opening scene in which Jupiter is discovered "dandling Ganymede upon his knee," pulling feathers out of Mercury's wing to give his young favorite, offering these and other presents in return for love, and defying Juno to spoil his fun. The tone of the scene is flippant, worldly, and satirical. This is the way Jupiter disports himself when he is supposed to be ruling heaven and earth. When Venus enters, she loses no time in rebuking her father for his lascivious neglect of duty while her son Aeneas is being tossed about by a storm arranged by Juno. Goaded into responsibility, Jupiter goes about his business, though taking Ganymede along.

Virgil's story is now launched, but after this opening we no longer know what to expect. It might seem likely that all the rest would be in the vein of burlesque, though in fact nothing could be farther from the truth. When we have reached the funeral pyre, the bitter prophecy of the Punic Wars, and the triple suicide with which the play ends, we may look back to ask why the play starts as it does.

Marlowe accmplishes several things with his introduction. Its novelty has in itself some virtue—the suggestion of a fresh look at an old story. Its comic realism may also suggest that the author knows how the most respected gods and men behave, and can be trusted not to falsify his play with idealized characters. However, the chief effect of the introduction is to put the main story in perspective, not merely by showing, as Virgil does, how dependent human affairs are upon the whims of the gods, but also by adopting temporarily the viewpoint of gods, concerned but aloof. After Jupiter's departure, we move with Venus from Mount Olympus to near Carthage, where she disguises herself and hides to observe Aeneas and Achates. With her asides she maintains direct contact with the audience while the hero converses with his friend and looks for some trace of human habitation. We seem to see them through her eyes, and only when she leaves do we get what might be called a close–up of Aeneas. The effect of perspective is strengthened by a series of parallels which extend from the introduction into the main story in a disconcerting way. As Jupiter promises treats and gifts to his "little love," so Venus lures Ascanius, when she is abducting him, with similar offers, and so Dido takes Cupid in her lap, thinking he is Ascanius, and promises him to love Aeneas for his sake. Later on, it is Aeneas himself to whom she offers every luxury in return for his love. It is daring to present the great hero as the last in this sequence of love–objects, preceded by three spoiled boys. The emphasis is thereby thrown on the power of infatuation rather than on the greatness of the hero, and since this is Dido's story, the adjustment is appropriate. Her consuming passion is what counts. To the extent that Aeneas is analogous to Ganymede, Dido, of course, is analogous to Jupiter, and if her infatuation makes her oblivious of everything else, she is hardly more irresponsible than he is. What is merely pastime for Jupiter, however, is fatal to her, and thus the comparison of comic and tragic infatuation may lead to a somber reflection on human, as opposed to divine, existence. What Pope might have called the "machinery" of the play reveals and requires a complex attitude to Dido's passion.

Closely related to the device of an introduction is the presenter, who appears in three plays. In *Tamburlaine* he is called the Prologue, in *The Jew of Malta* he is Machiavel, and in *Doctor Faustus* Chorus. In each case he works in a

different way. The Prologue of *Tamburlaine, Part 1* is the envoy of the author
and the players who commends the play to our attention with the equivalent of
a brief "commercial": this is to be a serious play in elevated language, a better
buy than the standard fare. But he commits himself to no judgment upon the
hero:

> View but his picture in this tragic glass,
> And then applaud his fortunes as you please.
>
> (Prologue, II. 7–8)

In *Part 2* there is a little more publicity when he tells us that the great success of
Part I encouraged the author to write a sequel, in which "death cuts off the
progress of his pomp/ And murderous Fates throws all his triumphs down"
(Prologue, II. 4–5). Again the attitude toward the hero seems neutral except for
the suggestion that his fall may be an aweinspiring spectacle.

In contrast to this Prologue, the Machiavel of *The Jew of Malta*, expounds
his cynical views with engaging frankness, and having thus taken us into his
confidence, makes his sympathy for the hero apparent. To be sure, we are told to
"grace him as he deserves," but also urged: "And let him not be entertained the
worse/Because he favors me" (Prologue, II. 33–35). The Chorus of *Doctor Faustus*
again represents the players ("we must now perform/The form of Faustus'
fortunes"), but also makes an unequivocal judgment upon the hero, "swoll'n with
cunning of a self-conceit," and "falling to a devilish exercise" (Prologue, II. 7–8,
20, 23). At his appearance during the course of the play, the Chorus confines
himself to narrative, but at the end he draws the moral:

> Regard his hellish fall,
> Whose fiendful fortune may exhort the wise
> Only to wonder at unlawful things,
> Whose deepness doth entice such forward wits
> To practise more than heavenly power permits.
>
> (Epilogue, II. 4–8)

The attitudes of these presenters are closely allied to Marlowe's
manipulation of contexts. The failure of the Prologue to pass judgment on
Tamburlaine coincides with the absence of clear moral criteria within the play.
The hero gives allegiance to neither Christ nor Mahomet, and normally prays to
Jove. However, the Christian and pagan rulers appear to have no more
enlightened moral standards than the cruel and ambitious Tamburlaine. Since no
ethic is clearly established as a basis for judging the hero's conduct, the audience
is singularly free to "applaud his fortunes as they please," following the
admonition of the Prologue. Such a freedom is essential if the response to
Tamburlaine in his chariot, for example, is to be the complex one I have

described. In the context of a firmly established Christian ethic disapproval would heavily overbalance admiration.

In *Doctor Faustus* the situation is almost reversed. Here is a man whose desires are much more sympathetic to the average man than those of Tamburlaine. He longs for knowledge, and though he also seeks power, he would not harness his enemies to his chariot, massacre virgins, or kill his own child. Yet disapproval of Faustus's ambitions is an essential part of the meaning of the story. The Christian context must be preserved; the audience must not be free to applaud his fortunes as they please, but must be constantly reminded of the nature of his error. To this end the Chorus makes his plain statements at the beginning and the conclusion, and a Good and Bad Angel keep black and white clearly distinct in the morality play tradition. Against a background of conventional moral judgment Marlowe develops all that is appealing in his hero in the poetry which made the play famous. The effectiveness of the tragedy is due in part to this tension.

In *The Jew of Malta* Marlowe again makes use of stock attitudes but in an ironic fashion. The Machiavel, by proclaiming a highly unpopular point of view, damns in advance the hero to whom he is sympathetic. The avaricious Jew should in any case be anathema to a right-minded audience of the time, but especially so if he is also Machiavellian. It would seem that we know from the start how we must respond to Barabas. However, in the first scenes of the play, the representatives of Christian orthodoxy are so presented that the Machiavel's cynical view of the world seems almost justified. Is Barabas, like Tamburlaine, preferable to his enemies? The ironies of the presenter combine with ironies in the play to form a tissue of contradictory attitudes. At times they seem even to cancel each other out, rather than to support the complex balance seen in *Tamburlaine*. The obliqueness of presentation, brilliant as it is, comes near to defeating its own ends.

Although Marlowe's devices for qualifying or shifting opinion, for distancing characters or encouraging us to take them to our bosoms, are not uniformly successful, their virtuosity can always be admired, and they can be seen to great advantage even in a play in which they do not work perfectly. *The Famous Tragedy of the Rich Jew of Malta* is a case in point. It is a little disappointing in its totality, and yet it achieves some extraordinary effects. The complexities of Marlowe's presentation of Barabas are not limited to the use of the Machiavel as prologue and the exposure of Christian hypocrisy. They include the treatment of the company Barabas keeps—his friends and his daughter. He is seen near the opening of the play with three other Jews, who readily capitulate to Christian demands for half their money. Barabas refuses until too late and is punished. When he rages against the Christians, his friends behave like Job's comforters, tamely counselling patience. In contrast to them Barabas, miser that he is, can be seen as a man of spirit. As he says, they

Think me to be a senseless lump of clay
That will with every water wash to dirt.
No, Barabas is born to better chance
And framed of finer mold than common men
That measure nought but by the present time.

But then we may also contrast him with his daughter. Abigail is treated as badly as the innocent heroine of any melodrama, and her father is the chief offender. Much as he claims to love her, she is no more than a means to his ends, as we see in often quoted lines which inspired an even better known passage in *The Merchant of Venice*. When Abigail rescues Barabas's money bags for him, he cries, "O my girl,/My gold, my fortune, my felicity ... " and then: "O girl! O gold! O beauty! O my bliss!" as he "hugs his bags" (2.1.47–48, 54). It is a marvellously humorous moment in which his confusion of values stigmatizes him beyond doubt. When Abigail, in love, is compelled to be the means of luring her Christian lover to his death, the pathos of her plight is more marked and the cruelty of her father's behavior more repellent. If a certain grandeur in his character stands out in the company of his friends, it is meanness that we notice in his dealings with Abigail.

Her part in the story comes to an abrupt end when she decides to become a Christian and Barabas poisons her along with a conventful of nuns. Marlowe's attitude to this event is an uneasy blend of opposites. The girl is given an affecting little soliloquy just before her entry into the convent. Then at the moment of death she confesses to a friar, and pleads that her father's crimes be kept secret. In both instances pathos dominates, but the tone of the death scene suddenly shifts to something resembling *Ruthless Rhymes for Heartless Homes*:

ABIGAIL. And witness that I die a Christian.
FRIAR BERNARDINE. Ay, and a virgin, too—that grieves me most.
(3.6.39–40)

The comment of Barabas is more poetic: "How sweet the bells ring now the nuns are dead" (4.1.2). If incongruity is the soul of comedy, this must be one of the most intensely comic of situations, yet it is an uncomfortable kind of laughter that the scene produces. After such a buffeting by contrary winds one may wonder, "What next?" In this play Marlowe anticipates such devotees of the sudden change of mood as Bertolt Brecht.

The most interesting of all Marlowe's manipulations in *The Jew of Malta* is his regulation of the amount of individuality his hero is allowed to have at a given moment. Constant readjustments cause Barabas to appear now as a stock figure—melodramatic villain or comic butt—now as an aspiring and suffering man. Bernard Spivack and Douglas Cole have written well about Barabas as a morality play Vice, as a stage Jew, and as a Machiavel.[7] At the very outset the prologue leads us to expect a stereotype, and the initial stage image of the Jew, possibly in the traditional red Judas-wig, counting over his heaps of gold, can only confirm the expectation. Then the long first speech with its glittering references to "fiery opals, sapphires, amethysts," and "beauteous rubies" stamps the portrait of an individual upon the stereotype. To express the goal as the enclosure of "infinite riches in a little room" is to reveal an intensity of spirit which goes beyond routine avarice and what was thought to be Machiavellianism. The contrast between Barabas and his Jewish friends further stresses individuality. Next there is a scene with Abigail and a friar, in which Barabas feigns to be angry with her, while in asides he tells her how to fool the Christians and get some of his money back. Here he is obviously playing a part, but in doing so he is also becoming more of a Machiavel. As the man disappears beneath the disguise, the individual begins to disappear into the stereotype.

In the following scene he enters alone and once again reveals something of his inner feeling, in this case the anguish of his present situation:

> Thus, like the sad presaging raven ...
> Vexed and tormented runs poor Barabas.
>
> (2.1.1,5)

Then comes the scene with Abigail and the money bags, in which the stereotype takes over. Soon he is schooling himself to play the role of the villainous deceiver:

> We Jews can fawn like spaniels when we please,
> And when we grin, we bite; yet are our looks
> As innocent and harmless as a lamb's.
> I learned in Florence how to kiss my hand ....
>
> (2.3.20–23)

His speech to the slave Ithamore, when he tells how he kills sick people groaning under walls and goes about poisoning wells, seems almost a caricature of Machiavellianism, as if the stereotype were deliberately put on by Barabas to test the reactions of Ithamore. And shortly after this, he tells Abigail to behave "like a cunning Jew" in order to deceive the Christians. These suggestions that Barabas is aware of acting in accordance with the common stereotype of a Jew and a Machiavel add further complexity to the portrayal.

Ithamore, a basically simple character, is never anything but a Machiavellian villain, whose heartlessness is even more outrageous than that of Barabas, but so automatic that it is less shocking. Barabas refers to him as his "second self" (3.4.15) and, though not sincerely fond of him, makes the surprising, nearly fatal mistake of trusting him. Here and in the later trusting of Ferneze there appear to be chinks in the Machiavellian armor, but it is hard to say whether they have any meaning beyond their obvious contribution to the plot.

In the latter part of the play Barabas is almost as completely the stereotype as Ithamore. There is no longer any pathos in his complaints about being tormented as he plans his poisonings; for he and his enemies are clearly "weasels fighting in a hole." The ending, where Barabas drops into the cauldron prepared for the Turk, is farce of a savage kind, as Eliot recognized years ago. Only Barabas's indomitable vitality remains to draw us to him, and that is not enough to balk applause and a heartless laugh. Marlowe's shifting attitudes towards his protagonist are fascinating, but they seem at last to warp rather than add depth to the characterization.

The mixture of humor with pathos or horror, one of the conspicuous features of *The Jew of Malta*, poses, if possible, an even more difficult problem of interpretation in *Doctor Faustus*, where comic scenes of various sorts seem to come near destroying the effects created by the poetry. I shall not try to deal with the much discussed problem of the authorship of the comic scenes, but in my opinion Marlowe might have written most of them. The author of a special version of the play in which almost all comedy has been cut out poses the problem even more clearly than he may have supposed in saying:

> As a result of the removal of non-Marlovian dross from *Dr. Faustus* I realize I may have laid myself open to the charge of having left the play too short for performance in the theatre. Yet, as a practical producer, I cannot see that there is any real difficulty. Any producer, by the use of imagination, music, ballet and magical effects, could make the play into a full evening's entertainment.[8]

Indeed this version is far too short, and it is doubtful that "entertainment" of the sort envisaged would be any improvement over the comic scenes which have been excised. Whether or not Marlowe himself wrote these scenes, he must have intended to have something of the sort in the play. Most of the material, like that of the serious scenes, comes directly from the so-called *English Faust Book*.

There are two sorts of comedy to be considered. The first consists in burlesque of the main action, as in those scenes where clownish minor characters undertake some conjuring on their own. This kind of comedy belongs to a tradition going back at least to the *Second Shepherds' Play*. It is thoroughly congruent with other devices Marlowe uses for forcing a shift of point of view.

Another sort of comic effect appears in the scenes where Faustus is found using his powers for no more exalted purposes than playing tricks on the Pope, putting horns on the head of a doubting knight, or scaring a horse-courser. These are the scenes which are most likely to contain non-Marlovian additions; yet the disparity to which they point is an essential part of the story, for there is a basic frivolity in the learned doctor. Confusion of values is the source of his tragedy. The trouble with these scenes, artistically speaking, is that they prolong the mood of trivial fooling until the fate of Faustus's soul is almost forgotten.

The point which this second sort of comic scene should make is presented elsewhere more subtly and more satisfactorily by other means. In the early scenes, which everyone attributes to Marlowe, we can see how he balances the opposed characteristics of his hero. The poetry does full justice to the dynamics of aspiration, encouraging us to share Faustus's feelings as he says:

> O, what a world of profit and delight,
> Of power, of honor, of omnipotence,
> Is promised to the studious artisan!
>
> (1.1.54–56)

But when he adds, "How am I glutted with conceit of this!" his words equate aspiration with appetite as surely as the conventional comments of the chorus, who says, "glutted now with learning's golden gifts,/He surfeits upon cursèd necromancy." When he plans to have spirits bring him gold and fruits, read him strange philosophy, wall Germany with brass, and clothe students in silk, his want of discrimination shows that he is not only young in heart but also in brain—boyish if not infantile. In the scene where Faustus questions Mephistophilis about hell and accuses him of taking it much too seriously, it is the devil who has the orthodox and sensible scale of values and, in shocked tones, accuses Faustus of frivolity. Mephistophilis here plays the eiron to Faustus's alazon. The man who will not know what to do with his power when he gets it is plainly set forth, and the sympathy we have for him is qualified by awareness that he is making a fool of himself.

The final presentation of this fatal confusion of values is the scene at the end of the play where Faustus requests torture for the Old Man who has given him godly counsel and then addresses his magnificent lines to Helen of Troy. In context this speech functions precisely to show the choice of the lesser good dressed in all the beauty which sensitivity and imagination can contrive. Helen and the Old Man are emblematic as the representatives of Pleasure and Virtue who came to Hercules, but Faustus makes an un-Herculean choice, for "all is dross that is not Helena" (5.1.105). The lesson is crystal clear to the audience, and yet, thanks to Marlowe's poetry, so is the attraction of Helen. In all the best scenes of *Doctor Faustus* a delicately balanced view of the hero is maintained.

In *The Massacre at Paris* and *Edward II* Marlowe divides the interest among several characters instead of focussing so exclusively on one, as in *Tamburlaine*, *The Jew of Malta*, and *Doctor Faustus*. It is characteristic of him that he exploits this division of interest to achieve a multiplicity of points of view. The Duke of Guise, the Duke of Anjou (later Henry III), Catherine, the Queen Mother, and Henry of Navarre are all major characters in *The Massacre at Paris*. I shall deal with only the first two. In the present state of the text not much can be concluded, but it is at least apparent that an aspiring individual, one who lusts after political power like Tamburlaine, is here set in a context which guarantees disapprobation of his goal. The Duke of Guise is shown as the chief instigator of the massacre of Protestant leaders which took place on the feast of St. Bartholomew about twenty years before the writing of the play. He is introduced dispatching poisoned gloves to an enemy in the best Machiavellian tradition. However, immediately afterward, he reveals his ambitions in a speech worthy of Tamburlaine:

> Oft have I levelled, and at last have learned
> That peril is the chiefest way to happiness,
> And resolution honor's fairest aim.
> What glory is there in a common good
> That hangs for every peasant to achieve?
> That like I best that flies beyond my reach.
> Set me to scale the high pyramidès
> And thereon set the diadem of France;
> I'll either rend it with my nails to naught
> Or mount the top with my aspiring wings,
> Although my downfall be the deepest hell.
>
> (2.37–47)

Even the most Protestant and the most English man in the audience could hardly resist some slight quickening of the pulse. It is rhetoric of the sort that Edward Alleyn knew how to make thrilling. There is, alas, very little more of it in the play as we have it, but this sample shows what Marlowe was up to. It is as if he had chosen to elicit some measure of admiration in the most difficult circumstances possible.

We get another glimpse of his plan in the treatment of the Duke of Anjou. At first he is shown participating with Guise in the appalling massacre, though not sharing in the rhetorical splendor of mighty aspirations. He is eager enough for power but always takes the easiest path, and appears as something of a voluptuary, infatuated with his minions. At the end of the play, however, Marlowe exploits the very national and religious feelings which tell against the perpetrators of the massacre to swing opinion around to the dying Henry III. Murdered at the instigation of the Guise family, Henry turns against Rome and with his last breath sends greetings to the Queen of England: " ... tell her Henry dies her faithful friend." How Marlowe loved such turns! Because the play as it stands is crudely articulated, they are all the more apparent.

In *Edward II* the manipulation of feelings toward the main characters is accomplished with far greater subtlety. This dexterity, added to the structural sophistication and the highly effective portrayal of frustrated passion, makes the play one of Marlowe's most impressive. Its whole design is to give dramatic substance to the suffering of the King—to make the audience experience them with an immediacy which transcends moral judgment. In Holinshed's history, which Marlowe used, Edward's "troublesome reign" had a practical political moral:

> ... he wanted judgment and prudent discretion to make choise of sage and discreet councellors, receiving those into his favour, that abused the same to their private gaine and advantage, not respecting the advancement of the common-wealth ....[9]

I agree with such recent critics of the play as Harry Levin, Clifford Leech, and Douglas Cole, that the main emphasis of Marlowe's play does not fall here.[10] However, if Edward's personal tragedy is to be made persuasive, judgments of him as a ruler and as a man must be dealt with, and Marlowe does so by forcing revaluations of every important character—of those by whom and because of whom the King is judged, and of the King himself.

In the opening scenes the faults of the King are ruthlessly exposed. He is tactless, irresponsible, and self-centered, willing to disregard the feelings of the queen and the good of the state to indulge himself with his minion Gaveston. He appears to have no redeeming virtues. As the play progresses, however, it becomes possible to feel differently about King Edward as a result of Marlowe's treatment of other characters. Gaveston, for example, is revealed in the first speech as an opportunist, planning to exploit the King's homosexual infatuation for him. Edward's feelings, however ill-advised, seemed at least to be sincere. The more outrageously Gaveston behaves, the more Edward seems to be a victim. Then, when the barons, fiercely opposed to Gaveston, succeed in capturing him, his behavior changes surprisingly, and he gives some evidence of a genuine emotional commitment. His last moments are pitiful, and through him some of the pity is directed toward the King. The career of his successor, the younger Spencer, is almost identical in shape though not so fully portrayed. He too starts as an exploiter and ends as an admirer. When, toward the end of the play, he is captured with the King and Edward is led off to prison, Spencer is given the most eloquent praise of the King to be found anywhere.

The character of the Queen becomes another instrument for altering the opinion of the King. Pathetic at first, when Edward has turned from her to Gaveston, her loyalty to him only makes his behavior the more despicable. She even intercedes with the barons to have Gaveston recalled, hoping thus to win her husband's approval. But as he continues to neglect her she drifts into an affair with Mortimer and then into plots against the King. Similarly Mortimer, at first a sincere patriot whose concern for England makes Edward seem irresponsible, becomes increasingly interested in power for himself, and after seducing the Queen, aspires to the throne. By the time that these two have Edward in their power, and Mortimer is planning the King's murder, the sympathy we had for them at first has been transferred to their victim. Kent, the King's brother, is an excellent indication of the shifts in feeling which an audience might be expected to experience. At first he is loyal though disapproving; then he deserts to the barons; but after the defection of the Queen and Mortimer, he returns to the King's side and is beheaded for trying to rescue him from prison.

Thus the treatment of each of these characters contributes to the chief revaluation, that of the King, by damaging in various ways the case against him. In the last act Marlowe is free to concentrate on the horror of the King's confinement and murder. These episodes, which in themselves compel pity, are made the more moving by a marked rise in the pitch of Marlowe's rhetoric. Though the style is less flashy than that of *Tamburlaine*, there are many moving speeches in the last part of *Edward II*. One of the finest occurs in the scene where Edward is compelled to surrender his crown and is thereby brought to full recognition of the weakness which has ruined him:

> But what are kings when regiment is gone,
> But perfect shadows in a sunshine day?
> My nobles rule, I bear the name of king;
> I wear the crown, but am controlled by them,
> By Mortimer and my unconstant queen,
> Who spots my nuptial bed with infamy,
> Whilst I am lodged within this cave of care,
> Where sorrow at my elbow still attends,
> To company my heart with sad laments,
> That bleeds within me for this strange exchange.
>
> (5.1.26–34)

This is not a better king than the one who wanted only to frolic with his Gaveston at the opening, but Marlowe has made us painfully aware of his sufferings—of that inward bleeding caused by Edward's years of frustration. Our initial feelings have been eradicated.

Tamburlaine provided an approach to this topic by way of a symbol for Marlowe's guidance of his chariot. Another passage from the same play suggests a way of summarizing the evidence for Marlowe's control of his material. In a set piece in the last act of part 1, Tamburlaine reflects on beauty:

> What is beauty, saith my sufferings, then?
> If all the pens that ever poets held
> Had fed the feeling of their masters' thoughts,
> And every sweetness that inspired their hearts,
> Their minds, and muses on admirèd themes;
> If all the heavenly quintessence they still
> From their immortal flowers of poesy,
> Wherein, as in a mirror, we perceive
> The highest reaches of a human wit;

If these had made one poem's period,
And all combined in beauty's worthiness,
Yet should there hover in their restless heads
One thought, one grace, one wonder, at the least,
Which into words no virtue can digest.

(5.2.97–110)

Here is the aspiring poet who longs like his hero to conquer more and more territory, though he knows that there will always remain some unconquered region. No doubt the true meaning of the passage is very general: that no poetic endeavor can achieve absolute perfection; but it may be permissible to find a special application to Marlowe, suggested particularly by the word "restless." In the seven plays he wrote in his very brief career he appears as a vastly ambitious and gifted experimenter. No two of them use quite the same techniques. If something of his vision failed to be digested into words, if the conquered kings, those "jades of Asia," tired after going only twenty miles, Marlowe yet showed himself to be a remarkable coachman.

NOTES

1. *The Minor Works of George Peele*, ed. David H. Horne (New Haven: Yale University Press, 1952), p. 246.

2. "To Henry Reynolds Esq.," *The Works of Michael Drayton*, ed. J. W. Hebel (Oxford: Blackwell, 1932), 3: 228–29.

3. *A History of English Dramatic Literature* (London: Macmillan, 1875), p. 203.

4. *II Tamburlaine*, 4.4.1–4, 7–16; *The Complete Plays of Christopher Marlowe*, ed. Irving Ribner (New York: Odyssey Press, 1963). All references to Marlowe are to this edition.

5. *The Complete Works of George Gascoigne*, ed. J. W. Cunliffe (Cambridge: Cambridge University Press, 1907), 1: 246.

6. M.M. Wills, "Marlowe's Role in Borrowed Lines," *PMLA* 52 (1937): 902–3.

7. Bernard Spivack, *Shakespeare and the Allegory of Evil* (New York: Columbia University Press, 1958), pp. 346–53; Douglas Cole, *Suffering and Evil in the Plays of Christopher Marlowe* (Princeton: Princeton University Press, 1962), pp. 123–44.

8. *Doctor Faustus in a special version by Basil Ashmore* (London: Blandford Press, 1948), p. 99.

9. *Chronicles* (London, 1587), p. 342.

10. Harry Levin, *The Overreacher* (Cambridge: Harvard University Press, 1952), p. 88; Clifford Leech, "Marlowe's 'Edward II': Power and Suffering," *Critical Quarterly* 1 (1959): 181–96; Cole, pp. 161–87.

MARTHA TUCK ROZETT

Doctor Faustus

In *The Tragical History of the Life and Death of Doctor Faustus* Marlowe draws upon some of the oldest, most traditional elements from the morality play—The Good and Bad Angels, the Heavenly Man-Worldly Man dual-protagonist scheme unevenly embodied in the Old Man and Faustus, the spectacle of the Seven Deadly Sins, and the dragon, devils, and traditional gaping hell beneath the stage. Among these he placed a protagonist who seeks out damnation more explicitly than any morality play character had done, and who dies in a torment more terrible than anything the morality playwrights had dared to represent onstage. In the evolution of English drama, *Doctor Faustus* can be viewed as a final rejection of the original morality pattern, with its assurance that divine forgiveness remains always within reach. For a society that sought everywhere for signs of election, Faustus was the ultimate "other," deliberately embracing damnation in a blasphemous parody of Christ's sacrifice for man.

If *Doctor Faustus* were simply a didactic demonstration of the proud man's rebellion against God, it would lose much of its interest for scholars and audiences alike. What makes Marlowe's play so fascinating is its dramatic treatment of one of the most important issues of its day. At the core of the play is the same central paradox which defines Elizabethan Puritanism: predestined election to salvation or damnation determines the spiritual state of each soul at birth, yet repentance is everywhere and at all times possible and to be encouraged. Faustus is at once free to damn or redeem himself, yet he is constrained by a devil with whom he makes an irreversible pact. For the

From *The Doctrine of Election and the Emergence of Elizabethan Tragedy*. © 1984 by Princeton University Press.

Elizabethans, the haunting fear that they were living a life predetermined to end in damnation—a fear of becoming the evil selves of their most terrible imaginings—made Faustus' life a tragic reflection of what their own could be.[1] Repentance, before Calvin, had been the easy remedy for despair; by the 1580s and 1590s, it could be presented as the unattainable tragic ideal.[2] More than any other play of its age, *Doctor Faustus* confronts the essential question of man's freedom of choice, and the problematic relationship between free will and predetermined fate.

Marlowe also explores another related subject about which the Elizabethans were deeply ambivalent. Initially, much of Faustus' complexity as a character results from the audience's uncertainty about whether to enjoy or disapprove of his aspiration. A brilliant scholar, Faustus possesses the yearning for greatness that the Elizabethans admired. Spurred onward by a desire for knowledge, and the power that knowledge confers, he resembles some of the most admired aspiring minds of his age, men whose boldness and ambition could be signs either of damnation or election. He aims not downward at those things commonly associated with sin and wickedness, but upward at powers possessed by God and thus not at all wicked in themselves. Nor does he deny God's possession of them; like Tamburlaine, who styles himself the scourge of God, thereby implicitly acknowledging God's power and authority, Faustus aspires to godhead, thereby affirming God's omnipotence. Assuming God's uppermost position in the ordered hierarchy, both Tamburlaine and Faustus strive to acquire that position for themselves. In a sense, they are most blasphemous even as they are most orthodox, as Philologus was in *The Conflict of Conscience*. The fact that heroic striving was sometimes indistinguishable from blasphemous presumption made Faustus' dilemma a tragic one.

As in the case of the Tamburlaine plays, a fortunate discovery of a contemporary prose narrative gave Marlowe the basic outlines of his play. Faust, like Tamburlaine, was a legendary figure of more than human stature, around whom a body of material had begun to accumulate in the mid-sixteenth century, finally appearing in print in 1587 as the Spies *Faustbook*. The scholar, vagabond, and reputed magician named John Faust who lived and traveled in Germany in the early sixteenth century was, as the modern editors of the Faust material observe, "merely the lodestone about which gathered in time a mass of superstition which in turn is the deposit of centuries."[3] Accounts of earlier magicians, in particular the legends of Simon Magus and Theophilus, the first magus to enter into a compact with Satan, were widely known throughout the Middle Ages. These legends contributed specific elements to the Faust story, and, more important, created a set of conventional attitudes toward the Faust figure which Marlowe could use as he played upon his audience's expectations.

By the time it was formulated in the Spies *Faustbook*, the Faust legend had come to reflect the Lutheran condemnation of ungodly speculation, even as it continued to delight its readers with accounts of Faustus' exploits. The unidentified "P. F." translated the Spies Faustbook into English sometime before the end of 1592 (possibly before 1590), and it was this version of the legend that Marlowe used as his source.[4] *The History of the damnable life and deserued death of Doctor John Faustus*, as its title suggests, is markedly moralistic in bent, and the narrative voice comments freely and frequently on the doctrinal implications of Faustus' actions and the lessons learned therefrom. P. F. has no doubts about Faustus' state of election, as his observations at the end of the first chapter indicate:

> It is written, no man can serue two masters : and, thou shalt not tempt the Lord thy God : but *Faustus* threw all this in the winde, & made his soule of no estimation, regarding more his worldly pleasure than ye ioyes to come : therefore at ye day of iudgement there is no hope of his redemptio (p. 136).

Marlowe's counterpart to P. F.'s moralistic narrative voice is the chorus which frames the play with a prologue and an epilogue. Marlowe's prologue is deliberately evasive, characterizing the performance about to begin as "The form of Faustus' fortunes, good or bad" (Pro., 8).[5] Some fifteen lines later, however, the audience is given an image of Faustus as an Icarus figure, one whose "waxen wings did mount above his reach,/And melting, heavens conspired his overthrow" (21–22). The time sequence implied in these lines, as Max Bluestone has observed, is equivocal: did the heavens conspire, or bring about, Faustus' initial abjuration (the "mounting," or aspiration which preceded the "melting," and fall), or did the conspiracy occur only after and because of the failure of his aspirations?[6] Does the past tense of the verb "conspired" hint at predestined reprobation, and, if so, to what extent does Faustus cause his own overthrow? And, finally, does Faustus' overthrow or fall necessarily mean that, in P. F.'s words, there is no hope for his redemption at any point in the play? These are only some of the questions which the seemingly conventional prologue invites the audience to ask.

I. THE PURSUIT OF DAMNATION

In choosing Faustus as his protagonist, Marlowe gave his audience a character whose reprobation depended not merely on the subjective judgment of his condemners, but on a contract with the devil—an act performed onstage. This would necessarily create a relationship between audience and character which was quite different from the shifting sense of moral distance that the audience had felt for Tamburlaine. Even Philologus, the most explicitly damned morality play protagonist (in the original version), was not visibly and irrevocably damned, as Faustus seems to be after the completion of his contract with Mephostophilis. Indeed, Philologus' self-proclaimed reprobation was subject to all of the uncertainties and ambiguities characteristic of Puritan doctrine, as revealed, for instance, in this defense of Francis Spera by William Perkins:

> Yet they are much overseene that write of him as a damned creature. For first, who can tell whether he despaired finally or no? Secondly, in the very middest of his desperation, hee complaineth of the hardnesse of heart: and the feeling of corruption in the heart, is by some contrary grace; so that we may conveniently thinke, that he was not quite bereft of all goodnesse: though hee neither felt it then, nor shewed it to the beholders.[7]

The "who can tell" of Perkins' argument was an objection which could legitimately be lodged whenever a mortal presumed to pronounce upon the state of election of another mortal. Marlowe's audience knew this, and thus the theatrical effect of the contract signed in blood, with its implied parody of the communion ceremony, gave Faustus' transformation into the "other" a certainty and definition which never occurred in real life.

For the Elizabethan audience, Faustus' status as a reprobate depended not only on the scene in which his damnation is acted out literally in Act II; just as important are the preceding scenes in which he knowingly and deliberately seeks out damnation. Faustus embraces damnation not by blindly and impulsively committing a crime or succumbing to irresistible lusts, but, rather, as the result of a reasoned intellectual debate with himself. He begins by vowing to "live and die in Aristotle's works," but then impatiently rejects the art of logic because it affords "no greater miracle" than disputing well (I, i, 5, 9). The desire to effect miracles leads him to consider medicine, but he is dissatisfied with his ability to cure desperate maladies, and wants instead to be able to resurrect the dead. He then rejects the study of law, which merely "fits a mercenary drudge/ Who aims at nothing but external trash" (34–35). As he reviews these forms of knowledge he is urged onward by the desire to transcend human limitations, to be more than "but Faustus and a man" (23). And so he arrives at what the audience would have regarded as the admirable conclusion that "When all is done, divinity is best" (37). But of course this is not a conclusion, for, with hardly a pause, Faustus advances still further, toward a rejection of the Christian belief in salvation. He does so not out of ignorance, as a Turk or a Jew might do, but by entering into precisely the same activity in which Protestant preachers and laymen alike were zealously engaged—the reading of scripture and the piecing together of arguments from well-known tags and phrases.

Faustus rejects divinity on the strength of a syllogism based upon two frequently used verses from the Bible, each taken out of context:

> Jerome's Bible, Faustus, view it well:
> *Stipendium peccati mors est.* Ha! *Stipendium,* etc.

The reward of sin is death. That's hard.
Si peccasse negamus, fallimur
Et nulla est in nobis veritas.
If we say that we have no sin,
We deceive ourselves, and there's no truth in us.
Why then belike we must sin,
And so consequently die.
Ay, we must die an everlasting death.
What doctrine call you this? *Che, sera, sera*:
What will be, shall be! Divinity, adieu!
                              (I, i, 38–49)

The passages in their entirety read as follows in the Revised Standard Version:

> For the wages of sin is death; but the free gift of God is eternal life
>   in Christ Jesus our Lord.
>   (Romans 6:23)

> If we say that we have no sin, we deceive ourselves, and the truth is
>   not in us.
> If we confess our sins, he is faithful and just and will forgive our sins,
>   and cleanse us from all unrighteousness.
>   (I John 1:8, 9)

By omitting the corollary phrase of each text Faustus has entered into no daring and exotic apostasy such as Marlowe himself was accused of in the Baines note, but rather has stumbled in a familiar way by failing to consider the text as a whole.[8] As Kocher notes, the two parts of the passage from I John readily lent themselves to syllogistic treatment. In the "Dialogue Between the Christian Knight and Satan," by Thomas Becon, Satan accuses the Knight of not having kept the Ten Commandments and uses the words that Faustus quotes in an attempt to convince the Knight that he will be damned forever. The Knight rejoins by posing the gospel against the law, arguing that he can simultaneously acknowledge that he is a sinner "guilty of everlasting damnation," and believe in Christ, "by ... [which] faith all my sins are forgiven me. ..."[9] Whereas Becon's dialogue represents the dominant strain in Elizabethan Protestantism, Faustus, it has been suggested, takes the extreme Calvinist position; his "we" includes only the reprobate, and his fatalistic doctrine "What will be, shall be" excludes the Semi-Pelagian view so frequently invoked to temper the bleakness of the doctrine of election (i.e., that the believer, through his own efforts, can help bring about his salvation).[10]

As he proceeds to gloss his text, Faustus advances by means of questions and exhortations through stages of knowledge to an acceptance of God's word—

and beyond. But, instead of moving toward an understanding of the spirit behind the text, as a preacher would do, Faustus rejects the words of the Bible and seeks out their diabolical counterpart, the metaphysics of magicians and their "heavenly" necromantic books. These books, Faustus believes, will elevate him above emperors and kings, making him the ruler of a dominion that "Stretcheth as far as doth the mind of man," a dominion as unlimited as the ambitions of the Elizabethan aspiring mind. Faustus ends his speech with a conclusion based on another faulty syllogism: "A sound magician is a demi-god./ Here try thy brains to get a deity!" (I, i, 62–64.)

And so Faustus embarks on the "otherness" of damnation as a result of pursuing the "otherness" of Godhood; he descends to magic in hopes that it will get him a deity. Earlier in the speech Faustus had sought in physic the ability to "make men to live eternally,/ Or, being dead, raise them to live again" (I, i, 24–25), in a perhaps unconscious wishful identification with Christ (this curious identification reappears when Faustus completes his signing of the bond with Christ's words on the cross, "*Consummatum est*"). Though the audience would have recognized the presumption inherent in Faustus' desire for a deity, they would also have known that the other objects of his aspirations were, in themselves, neither wicked nor prohibited. The "world of profit and delight,/ Of power, of honor, of omnipotence" which he describes is not so very different from the promises which John Udall extends to the godly in *Two Sermons upon the Historie of Peters denying Christ* (1584):

> Solomon ... sheweth what the word of GOD shal bryng unto the lovers thereof: namely honour, ryches, long life and such like: which indeede figureth unto us al ioyes whatsoever, whyche the Godlye shall have in the lyfe to come.[11]

This figurative relationship between worldly accomplishments and the life to come was an important element in Protestantism, one which served to justify or legitimize the acquisition of wealth, among other things. That Faustus originally expresses such ambitions is not, therefore, a sign of damnation. It is even possible to see Faustus' discontent with his past achievements and his aspiration toward greater things as an analogue to the yearnings of the godly. What distinguishes Faustus from the godly, however, is the course of action on which he embarks to realize his ambition.[12]

The moment Faustus acts on his decision to reject divinity and pursue necromancy by sending for the the two magicians, his conscience, represented by the recurring dialogue between the good and bad angels, begins to resist. These two characters give voice to the concept of free will, the freedom to choose which Puritan theologians insisted upon despite its apparent inconsistency with the doctrine of election. As Perkins explained in a tract entitled "Of God's free grace and Man's free will": "Gods decree doth not abolish libertie, but only moderate

and order it; by inclining the will in milde and easie manner with fit and convenient objects, and that according to the condition of the will."[13] The Good and Bad Angels do not speak to Faustus in the manner of the virtues and vices of the moralities. Rather, they articulate the inner vacillations that Faustus experiences at crucial moments in the play, without his conscious awareness of their presence on stage.[14] In a sense, they are part of the ongoing dialogue or debate he has been engaged in from the beginning of the long opening monologue (in which he addresses himself by name seven times). Perhaps because Faustus is unable to imagine a merciful God who extends the possibility of salvation to all, his Good Angel's initial efforts to win him over contain no mention of God's mercy but only His "heavy wrath" (I, i, 73).[15] The Good Angel urges him to lay aside "that damned book" (i.e., damning book) and to read the Scriptures instead, as if to tell him that by reading on he would discover the fallacy of his syllogism. The Bad Angel offers promises rather than threats, and inclines Faustus' will in the direction of godhood: "Be thou on earth as Jove is in the sky,/ Lord and commander of these elements" (77–78).

The distinction that Marlowe makes between "Good" and "Bad" as embodied in the two angels is deceptively simple, and ironically at odds with the far subtler moral ambivalence that the audience feels toward the desire Faustus continues to describe after the angels exit. Of the list of extravagant commands he plans to give the spirits his magic will summon, the first is to "Resolve me of all ambiguities," a longing which many among his audience must have shared (81). He also wishes for gold and pearls (which recalls both the "external trash" of "mercenary drudge" he rejected earlier and the wealth Udall views as a prefiguring of heavenly joys), but plans to use his wealth to levy soldiers to drive out the Prince of Parma, a Spanish governor of the Low Countries in the 1580s and hated enemy of the Elizabethan audience. The magicians whom Faustus summons for his instruction also appeal to the audience's anti-Spanish sentiments: Valdes says, "shall they [the spirits] drag huge argosies" from Venice, "And from America the golden fleece/ That yearly stuffs old Philip's treasury,/ If learned Faustus will be resolute" (I, i, 131–34).

To this Faustus replies: "Valdes, as resolute am I in this/ As thou to live ..." (135–36). This phrase echoes ominously as the play continues: Faustus urges himself to be resolute again just before the signing of the deed in blood. Resolution was a quality he shared with the believers who remained firm in their conviction that they were among the elect. As William Burton told his listeners:

> ... in Gods service we must neither doubt of that which we do, nor waver in the performing of our uowes, neither must we do it fainedly, but with ful consent of heart and mind. Resolution is the thing indeed that we are here taught. Resolution in Gods matters is very requisite, as it is for a souldier in the field.[16]

But Faustus' resolution parodies that of the elect, just as Tamburlaine's assurance does: in each case Marlowe gives his protagonist qualities which his audience admired, but directs them to blasphemous ends. This resolution, rather than a predestination over which he has no control, is what prevents Faustus from repenting. Marlowe thus presents his audience with a paradox which in itself is a parody of the religious paradoxes of his age: had Faustus been weaker, he might have been saved. It is worth noting that P. F.'s Faustus lacks this resoluteness in the chapters that correspond to the early scenes of *Doctor Faustus*. He hesitates to commit his soul to Lucifer according to Mephostophilis' conditions, and, after the bargain is completed and he hears of the pain awaiting him in hell, he repeatedly becomes sorrowful and tries to repent. As M. M. Mahood points out, the *Faustbook* devils withhold Faustus from repentance by brute strength, whereas Marlowe's Faustus is always at liberty to repent.[17]

The resoluteness of Marlowe's Faustus is given even more emphasis by comparison with the remarkably human and hesitant Mephostophilis who appears as a result of his conjuring and blasphemy in Act I, scene iii. Using parts of three different discussions of hell in the *Faustbook*, Marlowe presents his audience with a tempter whose first act is an attempt to dissuade his prey from persisting in his pursuit of damnation. Marlowe ironically makes Mephostophilis more orthodox than Faustus in this scene: he speaks of the "Saviour Christ" and man's "glorious soul," while Faustus, in return, confounds "hell in Elysium" (I, iii, 48–49; 60). The questions which Faustus then proceeds to ask are a brilliantly transformed condensation of seven chapters in the *Faustbook*, which occur *after* the signing of the contract, rather than before.

Faustus begins by asking about Lucifer, whose fall from heaven because of his "aspiring pride and insolence" is being reenacted at this very moment by Faustus himself. Faustus then asks "And what are you that live with Lucifer?" The echoing effect of Mephostophilis' response summons up powerful, reverberating sensations of the eternal doom from which Mephostophilis is trying to avert the oblivious Faustus:

> Unhappy spirits that fell with Lucifer,
> Conspired against our God with Lucifer,
> And are for ever damned with Lucifer.
> (I, iii, 71–73)

Mephostophilis proceeds to give his famous description of hell as a state of mind rather than a place:

> Why this is hell, nor am I out of it.
> Think'st thou that I who saw the face of God
> And tasted the eternal joys of heaven
> Am not tormented with ten thousand hells

> In being deprived of everlasting bliss?
> O Faustus, leave these frivolous demands
> Which strike a terror to my fainting soul.[18]
>
> (I, iii, 76–82)

Marlowe has taken his cue from a didactic speech in his source, in which Mephostophilis tells Faustus that if he were a man, he would "humble my selfe vnto his Maiestie, indeuouring in all that I could to keepe his Commaundements, prayse him, glorifie him, that I might continue in his fauour, so were I sure to eniuy the eternall joy and felicity of his kingdome" (p. 158). The *Faustbook* description of hell is a compendium of physical description, vividly evoking the suffering of the damned, but without any sense that Mephostophilis has himself experienced suffering. Marlowe transforms these moralistic pronouncements into a fascinating depiction of damnation as "an ongoing process to the ultimate destiny," reflecting the Protestant's emphasis on the immediacy of damnation. As Douglas Cole observes, never before in English drama had a devil acted in this way.[19]

Marlowe's daring characterization of Mephostophilis emphasizes the diabolical nature of Faustus' pursuit of knowledge. Like Dent's reprobate in *A Pastime for Parents*, whose knowledge "doth puffe up," Faustus is "swoll'n with cunning of a self-conceit" (prologue, 20). He shares this preoccupation with self, as we have seen, with some of the most pious men of his age, yet the distortion implied by the word "swoll'n" alerts the audience to the degree of excess involved. The imagery of swelling is related to the motif of gluttony and surfeit and engorgement which, as C. L. Barber and others have shown, runs through the play.[20] But while food and drink appear in the play at a number of points, the appetite which Faustus most longs to satisfy is a craving for knowledge. As soon as the bargain with Mephostophilis is sealed, he begins asking questions about hell. The only true knowledge Mephostophilis offers him is based on his own experience of hell, and it is a definition, significantly, that can only describe hell as the absence of heaven.

> Hell hath no limits, nor is circumscribed
> In one self place, but where we are is hell,
> And where hell is, there must we ever be.
> And, to be short, when all the world dissolves
> And every creature shall be purified,
> All places shall be hell that is not heaven.
>
> (II, i, 119–24)

Faustus contemptuously rejects the warning implicit in this definition, and henceforth he receives only what Dent would call the knowledge of the reprobate, which is "generall and confused" rather than the "particular and certain" knowledge reserved for the elect. The knowledge of the reprobate is contained in the book Mephostophilis gives him, which the audience would recognize as a substitute for the Bible cast aside in Act I, scene i (the book is an important prop in this play). The shallowness of Faustus' newly acquired knowledge becomes evident as his efforts to "reason of divine astrology" are met with elementary and unsatisfying responses. Faustus' final question, "who made the world," cannot be answered at all, for the knowledge that God made the world is, again in Dent's terms, "spirituall and practiue, that is ioyned with obedience," and thus inaccessible to the reprobate.[21]

One of the most ironic uses Marlowe makes of the morality tradition is his transformation of Mephostophilis into the tempter in reverse. The devil with a fainting soul was an unprecedented concept in Elizabethan England. By presenting Mephostophilis in this way, Marlowe reminds his audience that all devils are ultimately instruments of God, just as scourges are. As George Gifford told his readers in a tract published in 1587,

> ... reprobat angels ... be instruments of Gods vengauce [sic], and executioners of his wrath, they doe not exercise power and authoritie which is absolute, and at their owne will and appointment, but so farre as God letteth foorth the chaine to giue them scope. Touching the reprobat, which despise the waies of God and are disobedient, we are taught, that God in righteous vengeance giueth them ouer into their hands ... therefore they come under the tirannie of wicked divels, which worke in them with power....

Among the greatest and "general mischiefes" of the Devil, Gifford observes, is his ability to "hold men from turning unto God by repentance." Lucifer and Beelzebub, Marlowe's more conventional devils, and the Bad Angel assume this role.

As Gifford's tract on devils makes clear, the fact that Faustus comes under the influence of the devil does not mean that he is reprobate. Gifford notes that

> ... these wicked fiends doe also set upon the faithful and elect people of God, for God useth them also as instruments for their triall, they tempt and trie them, they doe wrestle and fight against them, they buffet them, every way seeking to annoy and molest them both in bodie and soule.[22]

In keeping with the spirit of Elizabethan Protestantism, the play withholds definitive evidence that Faustus is not of the elect. Just as the preachers urged their listeners to believe that no sin was too great for God's forgiveness, so Marlowe uses the Good Angel and the Old Man as signals to the audience that even the selling of one's soul can conceivably be overcome by repentance.

Faustus thus remains both potentially elect and potentially damned until the final moments of the play, and, despite the fact that many members of the audience probably knew how the Faust story ended, they must have been caught up in the dramatic suspense. As they waited to see whether Faustus would repent before his twenty-four years ran out, they gave vent to some of their own anxieties about election.

II. REPENTANCE OR DESPAIR

Repentance and despair are the central theological issues in *Doctor Faustus*, and critics continue to debate about whether Faustus could have repented, and about the doctrinal implications of his inability to do so.[23] Faustus' opening soliloquy in Act II powerfully reveals how torn he is between the despair in God to which he is resolved and a lingering desire to repent:

> Now Faustus, must thou needs be damned,
> And canst thou not be saved.
> What boots it then to think on God or heaven?
> Away with such vain fancies, and despair;
> Despair in God, and trust in Beelzebub.
> Now go not backward; Faustus, be resolute.
> Why waver'st thou? O, something soundeth in mine ear:
> 'Abjure this magic; turn to God again.'
> Ay, and Faustus will turn to God again!
> To God? He loves thee not.
> The God thou serv'st is thine own appetite,
> Wherein is fixed the love of Beelzebub.
> To him I'll build an altar and a church,
> And offer lukewarm blood of new-born babes.
>
> (II, i, 1–14)

This soliloquy demonstrates the increasing skill at rendering the inner conflict of a morally and emotionally complex character that begins to appear in the tragedies of the 1580s and 1590s. In his dialogue between the "I" and the "thee," Faustus vacillates between his commitment to despair and its opposite, turning to God. The Elizabethan audience must have noticed the way Faustus aligns despair, trust in Beelzebub, and resolution against going "backward" toward God. This is the antithesis of repentance, which entails trust in God and a resolution to go forward. The speech rises to a peak of hope at its midpoint, with the repeated phrase "turn to God again," then falls downward, with Faustus' stark conclusion, "He loves thee not." His blasphemous love of Beelzebub, false church and altar, and pagan rite of bloodshed will replace the God, Church, and communion ritual of the orthodox Christian, or so at least he tells himself.

Although the soliloquy expresses sentiments that few Elizabethans would admit to, Faustus' desperate state of mind may well have been a common one in Elizabethan England, to judge from the many manuals in print designed to soothe troubled consciences. R. Linaker's *A Comfortable Treatise, for the reliefe of such as are afflicted in Conscience*, published in 1590, seems to speak directly to a soul in Faustus' spiritual condition. Using David and Paul as examples, Linaker argues that the more one is persecuted by temptations and punishments the more certainly he is chosen by God. If you doubt you are among God's chosen, you do so, he says, because your conscience prompts you to, a sign that God's spirit is bringing you to effectual repentance. Linaker might very well have seen in Faustus' speech evidence that he was saved, though he had succumbed to the "temptation of Satan ... [intended] to drive you to desperation." His remedy is as follows: "there is no cause why you shoulde believe him. First because hee is a lyar. Secondly because hee is your enemy, who meanes you no good at all." Linaker goes on to say that since Satan is a liar, you are to believe the opposite of what he tells you: if he says you are damned, be assured that you are saved.[24] He recommends that the sinner be aggressive with Satan and refuse to be browbeaten:

> And if, with his wily and uiolent temptations, hee [Satan] carrie you into anie sinne, let him be sure that he shal answere it, & not you: it shall be set on his score at the day of iudgement: because he was ye author of it & forced you against your wil as he did that holy man Job....[25]

How one makes sure that Satan answers for his temptations is not absolutely clear, however. As the audience undoubtedly knew, the cool reasonableness of Linaker's argument is seldom so easily accessible to the soul in torment.

Faustus' inability to shift the blame to Mephostophilis becomes clear in Act II, scene ii. The scene begins with Faustus repenting and cursing Mephostophilis, claiming that he has been deprived of the joys of heaven. To this Mephostophilis replies: "Twas thine owne seeking, Faustus; thank thyself" (II, ii, 4). Mephostophilis then quickly changes the subject, unlike his predecessor in the *Faustbook*, who, at the end of his account of what he would do if he were a man, reproaches Faustus at length:

> ... yea wickedly thou hast applyed that excellent gift of thine vnderstanding, and giuen thy soule to the Diuell: therefore giue none the blame but thine owne selfe-will, thy proude and aspiring minde, which hath brought thee into the wrath of God and vtter damnation.

To Faustus' rejoinder that "it were time enough for me if I amended," the

Faustbook Mephostophilis replies: "True ... if it were not for thy great sinnes, which are so odious and detestable in the sight of God, that it is too late for thee, for the wrath of God resteth vpon thee" (pp. 158–59). One wonders what Linaker would have advised Faustus to say to so eloquent and moralistic a devil. Marlowe deliberately makes his Mephostophilis much less forceful on this point, confident, perhaps, that his audience did not have to be told that Faustus' self-will and aspiring mind has brought him to his present condition. Nor does he wish to be so definite about what Faustus' present condition is; like Linaker, he lets the audience believe that Faustus may yet successfully shift the blame and the punishment—to Mephostophilis. Not until the very end of the play does Marlowe finally resolve the dramatic suspense which surrounds Faustus' state of election.

Rather than preach to Faustus as does his predecessor, Marlowe's Mephostophilis tries to divert him from thoughts of repentance, using the same kind of deceptive logic Faustus himself had used in Act I. Heaven was made for man, he tells Faustus; therefore man is more excellent than heaven. But his argument misfires, and Faustus concludes from it: "If heaven was made for man, 'twas made for me./ I will renounce this magic and repent" (II, ii, 10–11). At the mention of the possibility of repentance, the angels reappear. The Good Angel speaks first, urging Faustus to repent and promising that God will pity him. Faustus holds up against the first assault of the Bad Angel, who tells him, "Thou art a spirit; God cannot pity thee," by responding "Be I a devil, yet God may pity me;/ Yea, God will pity me if I repent." The Bad Angel rejoins ominously, "Ay, but Faustus never shall repent," sounding a note of predestined doom. Faustus abruptly shifts direction, and agrees: "My heart is hardened; I cannot repent./ Scarce can I name salvation, faith, or heaven" (18–19). Thus the dialogue ends with Faustus hardened of heart and resolved not to repent. The same kind of rhythm, in reverse, can be observed in the sermons and tracts: the despairing believer, led step by step by the preacher, is brought to an assurance of his election.

After another round of astronomical questions and answers, Faustus again begins to waver in his allegiance to the powers of hell. When Mephostophilis brushes aside his question with: "Thou art damned. Think thou of hell," Faustus responds, addressing his errant self: "Think, Faustus, upon God that made the world." He repeats his accusation against Mephostophilis: "'Tis thou hast damned distressed Faustus' soul./ Is't not too late?" The angels reenter, but, this time, the Bad Angel speaks first. "Too late," he echoes, to which the Good Angel responds, "Never too late, if Faustus will repent." Swept along by the Good Angel's assurance, Faustus reaches a conventional turning point in the process of redemption as he calls out, "O Christ, my Savior, my Savior,/ Help to save distressed Faustus' soul" (73–84).[26]

This heart-rending cry brings not comfort, but instead Lucifer and a slightly clownish Beelzebub, who with ease extract from Faustus his vow never to look on heaven or name God. They reward him with the extraordinarily crude and unconvincing display of the Seven Deadly Sins, whose talk of wenches' smocks and gammons of bacon, raw mutton, and fried stockfish seems hardly capable of delighting the soul of the Faustus, who earlier in the scene had recalled the sweet pleasure of Homer and Amphion's songs. Even if the spectacle could divert Faustus from thoughts of God, it could hardly convince the audience to do likewise; as they watched—and maybe enjoyed—the procession, their thoughts might have lingered upon the falsity of Lucifer's pronouncement that "Christ cannot save thy soul, for he is just./ There's none but I have interest in the same" (II, ii, 85–86). Christ, they knew, was the champion of that mercy which transcended and, if need be, overruled justice. Faustus' immediate acquiescence here is as doctrinally misguided as his original reading of Scripture; had he persisted a little longer, defying Lucifer instead of deferring to him, Christ would indeed have come to his aid—or so Marlowe's audience might have been tempted to think.

The interchange between Faustus and Lucifer that leads up to this turning point could easily have been a deliberate parody of the instructive dialogues that the preachers were fond of writing. In 1586, Marlowe's last year at Corpus Christi College, William Perkins, who was also in Cambridge, published "A treatise tending vnto a declaration, whether a man be in the estate of damnation, or in the estate of grace: and if he be in the first, how he may in time come ovt of it: if in the second, how hee may discerne it, and persevere in the same to the end." This treatise contains a series of dialogues between Satan and Christians of varying degrees of strength, or resolution. Here is the beginning of "A dialogue containing the conflicts between Sathan and a Christian":

Sathan.	Vile hell-hound, thou art my slave and my vassall, why then shakest thou off my yoake?
Christian.	By nature I was thy vassal, but Christ hath redeemed me.
Sathan.	Christ redeemeth no reprobates such as thou art.
Christian.	I am no reprobate.
Sathan.	Thou art a reprobate, for thou shalt be condemned.
Christian.	Lucifer, to pronounce damnation belongs to God alone: thou art no judge, it is sufficient for thee to be an accuser.
Sathan.	Though I cannot condemne thee, yet I know God will condemne thee.
Christian.	Yea but God will not condemne me.

Satan goes on to list the Christian's sins in lurid detail, but the Christian "dares to presume" on God's mercy, and insists that his afflictions are a sign of his salvation. The dialogue ends when the Christian asserts with finality: "I have true saving grace."[27]

Faustus is a mirror image of Perkins' Christian; he is the elect man of God in reverse. Where the Christian is strong, Faustus is weak; his irresoluteness when confronted by Lucifer and Beelzebub is the opposite of the Christian's persistence in his belief. Despair, then, is the absence of resolution; but it is also a terrible kind of arrogance, a refusal to accept as a gift the salvation one cannot earn. Without falling into arrogance, the believer must possess two kinds of confidence, a confidence in self and a greater, all-encompassing confidence in God, if he is to attain the greatly sought-after assurance of election.

The comic procession of the Seven Deadly Sins effectively dissipates the tension building in the audience as they are brought face to face with their own anxiety about election. This, and the scenes of comic conjuring that follow, are remarkably different in tone from the play's first two acts, and the considerable differences between the 1604 and 1616 texts make it difficult to arrive at conclusions about their dramatic and thematic purposes. The Elizabethan audience presumably enjoyed watching Faustus mock the pride of the Pope; indeed, for a strongly anti-Catholic audience, the humiliation of the Pope may even have seemed admirable, although the practical jokes at the banquet are hardly the awe-inspiring triumphs of a hero. Yet Marlowe does not let the audience forget that Faustus is potentially damned even in the midst of the fun. As the invisible Faustus is snatching dishes and cups from the hands of the Pope at the feast, the Pope crosses himself in protection against what he thinks is a troublesome ghost. Injured by the gesture, as devilish spirits are, Faustus strikes back at him. The Pope responds with lines that constitute a formula some variant of which can be found in countless Elizabethan or Jacobean tragedies:

> O I am slain. Help me, my lords.
> O come and help to bear my body hence.
> Damned be his soul for ever for this deed.
> (III, ii, 90–92)

To call one's enemy "damned" is a conventional insult in the Elizabethan theatre, but, here, the stock phrase reverberates with meaning, for the curse is literally fulfilled within the play. The friars proceed with the Catholic exorcism ritual, and, as Faustus mocks them, he again reminds the audience of his self-willed damnation: "Bell, book, and candle, candle, book, and bell,/ Forward and backward, to curse Faustus to hell" (95–96). The irony here is that the friars are superfluous, for Faustus has already cursed himself.

The comic exploits of the servants play a similarly ironic role, paralleling and hence debasing Faustus' great achievements. Robin's adventures with the stolen "conjuring book" remind the audience that the knowledge for which Faustus sold his soul offers little beyond trickery and is available to whoever possesses the book. These scenes, beginning in Act I with Wagner's mockery of Faustus' survey of the disciplines, and his promise to turn Robin into "a dog, or a cat or a mouse, or a rat, or anything," provide the audience with a set of familiar character types with whom to take refuge from Faustus' "otherness." Wagner and the clowns, after all, remain alive and unscathed at the end, despite their experiments with conjuring. They belong to the normal, everyday world, where the devil is only a character in a costume frolicking on the morality play stage.

In the midst of the final comic episode, the horse-courser scene, Faustus speaks his first soliloquy since Act II:

> What art thou, Faustus, but a man condemned to die?
> Thy fatal time draws to a final end.
> Despair doth drive distrust into my thoughts.
> Confound these passions with a quiet sleep.
> Tush? Christ did call the thief upon the cross;
> Then rest thee, Faustus, quiet in conceit.
>   (IV, v, 33–38)

There is a deliberate echo here of the line "Yet are thou still but Faustus, and a man" from the long monologue of Act I, scene i: Faustus' pact with Mephostophilis, he recognizes, makes him no less subject to death than before. He comforts himself with a trust in divine providence which his audience would have known to be presumptuous, for they had been taught that those who despair of forgiveness and those who gamble on God's mercy, expecting last-minute forgiveness, are equally damnable.[28] This reflective moment over, Faustus returns to his conjuring and mischief, which culminates in the appearance of Helen to the scholars. Their awed reaction to her "heavenly beauty" and gratitude for "this blessed sight" (V, i, 32, 35) are ironic reminders of the death which, as Wagner tells the audience in a prologue to the scene, rapidly approaches. Even more ironic are the first scholar's parting words of thanks: "Happy and blest be Faustus evermore" (36). The encounter with Helen, as Marlowe seems to suggest, makes Faustus momentarily happy, but damned forevermore.

At this point Marlowe introduces a new character, the Old Man, whose sudden and unprepared-for appearance is derived from the *Faustbook* incident in which Faustus dines with an old neighbor who tries to persuade him to repent. The Old Man is not of the same order of reality as the other human characters in the play; rather, he is an allegorical embodiment of divine love and mercy. He pleads with Faustus to turn away from magic, assuring him that his soul is still "amiable," or potentially elect, and that repentance is thus possible. Such is the Old Man's extra-human spiritual insight that he can see an angel hovering over Faustus' head, offering to pour a vial of grace into his soul (61 ff.). In a visual echo of the conflicting appeals of the Good and Bad Angels, the Old Man's presence onstage and his envisioned vial of grace are counterbalanced by Mephostophilis and the dagger, a symbol of despair, which he wordlessly offers

Faustus. Torn between the two, Faustus resumes the dialogue with himself in which he had been engaged in Acts I and II. Hell strives with grace for conquest of Faustus, and hell wins. Accused by Mephostophilis of disobedience to "my sovereign Lord" (as distinct from *the* sovereign Lord), Faustus quickly inverts true repentance and "repents" having offended Lucifer. Moreover, he seeks pardon for his "unjust presumption." This phrase is pointedly ironic, for Faustus has not presumed enough, and in the proper way, upon God's ability to forgive. What Faustus calls presumption has been in fact the absence of the godly believers' boldness and assurance in the face of all temptation. Similarly, the unlawful aspiration to godhood with which he embarked upon damnation is in fact the source of his unjust presumption.

In the Good Friday sermon of 1570, John Foxe assured his audience thus: "Be you willing to be reconciled, and you shall speede: come and you shall be received, holde out your hand to take what he will geue, and you shall have."[29] Like Foxe, the Old Man has presented the availability of salvation in the most generous of terms, but he has made it clear that salvation must be actively, not passively, sought out. For a moment, Faustus "feels" the comfort which the Old Man's words have attempted to convey, but, instead of holding out his hand, he succumbs to despair, the ultimate source of defeat to the human spirit. The preachers knew how easily the impulse to repent could turn into despair and warned most urgently against the pitfalls of "over-sharpe sorrow." As Perkins explained:

> When the spirit hath made a man see his sins, he seeth further the curse of the Law, and so he finds himselfe to be in bondage under Satan, hell, death, and damnation: at which most terrible sight his heart is smitten with feare and trembling, through the consideration of his hellish and damnable estate. ... All men must take heed, lest when they are touched for their sinnes, they besnare their owne consciences: for if the sorrow be somewhat over-sharpe, they shall see themselves even brought to the gates of hell, and to feele the pangs of death.[30]

Desperately intent on shunning the pangs of death, Faustus turns back to Mephostophilis and frantically offers to reconfirm his vow in blood, even though that vow, by its very nature, leads to certain death at the end of the twenty-four years. Marlowe has altered his source in a significant way here. In the *Faustbook*, the devil orders Faustus to "write another writing" (p. 215), whereas in the play Mephostophilis merely demands that Faustus "Revolt" (i.e., turn back—but the choice of words is ironic, reminding the audience as it does of the fallen angels who revolted against God).

Helen, who reappears at Faustus' request, represents Faustus' last effort to achieve superhuman stature—embracing her, he will be made immortal. Faustus seeks in Helen's embrace the satisfaction of appetite (Marlowe draws attention to this with the words "crave" and "glut"), then an escape from "Those thoughts that do dissuade me from my vow" (V, i, 90, 91). He deludes himself into thinking that heaven is in her lips, but just as he says this, the Old Man returns (in the 1604 text only), and undermines the soaring poetry of Faustus' declaration of love with these words:

> Accursed Faustus, miserable man,
> That from thy soul exclud'st the grace of heaven
> And fliest the throne of his tribunal seat!
> Satan begins to sift me with his pride.
> As in this furnace God shall try my faith,
> My faith, vile hell, shall triumph over thee.
> (122–27)

The Old Man's reappearance serves as an echo of the visual contrast of the preceding scene, in which the Old Man and Mephostophilis represented the alternatives of repentance and despair. Now the Old Man embodies salvation, and Helen, by contrast, can stand only for damnation. The Elizabethan audience certainly would have recognized that the final triumph of the scene, greatly overshadowing Faustus' delight in Helen, is the Old Man's, as he and the heavens laugh to scorn the proud Satan and ambitious fiends who torture him (the physical antithesis of Helen's embrace). As he flies unto God, the audience is perhaps reminded of the Icarus image as well as Faustus' flights in pursuit of knowledge and experience in Act III. To make the contrast explicit, Marlowe has the Old Man observe that Faustus has begun his doomed and inexorable descent to hell by flying *away* from "the throne of his [God's] tribunal seat."

The Old Man's exit is virtually an allegorical action; once he is gone, Faustus' damnation seems unavoidable. Yet, paradoxically, when Faustus takes his leave of the scholars, he is in many respects a more sympathetic character than he is at any other point in the play. Tragically, he understands with utter clarity the implications of his deed:

> And what wonders I have done, all Germany can witness—yea, all the world—for which Faustus hath lost both Germany and the world, yea heaven itself, heaven the seat of God, the throne of the blessed, the kingdom of joy, and must remain in hell for ever. (V, ii, 46–49)

The scholars urge him to call on God and he does, but ineffectually: "Ah, my God, I would weep, but the devil draws in my tears" (54–55). And so, knowing that his time has come, he dismisses the scholars, with a concern for their safety that makes him seem almost noble.

In the 1616 text, this scene is followed by the final appearance of Mephostophilis and the Good and Bad Angels. Here, for the last time, the play probes the ambiguities inherent in the theological concepts of election and free will. Mephostophilis once again instructs Faustus to despair, and Faustus turns on him with the accusation: "O thou bewitching fiend, 'twas thy temptation/ Hath robbed me of eternal happiness" (V, ii, 87–88). Surprisingly, Mephostophilis agrees, though earlier, as we have seen, he had told Faustus to blame himself. Now the traditional devil, gloating in the destruction he has wrought, Mephostophilis boasts:

'Twas I, that when thou wert i'the way to heaven,
Damned up thy passage. When thou took'st the book
To view the Scriptures, then I turned to the leaves
And led thine eye.
(90–93)

This speech has no counterpart in the *Faustbook*, unless one counts a very early speech of the *Faustbook* Mephostophilis in which he tells Faustus that when the devils saw him despise divinity and seek to know the secrets of hell "then did we enter into thee, giuing thee diuers foule and filthy cogitations, pricking thee forward in thine intent, and perswading thee that thou couldst neuer attaine to thy desire, vntill thou hast the help of some diuell" (p. 153). But Marlowe's Mephostophilis waits until his last speech to assume responsibility for Faustus' initial act of despising divinity. The renowned scholar thus is transformed into a puppet whose very act of reading is determined by the devil.

Critics have suggested that Mephostophilis' speech may not have been part of Marlowe's original design. W. W. Greg, for example, finds it hard to believe that Marlowe wrote this section, with "its piety and its frequent rimes," and concludes that the 1604 text, by omitting these speeches, "undoubtedly heightens the effect of the human tragedy." The 1616 text, on the other hand, keeps the action on "what can perhaps best be described as an allegorical plane" by including them. This plane is clearly inconsistent with the final tragic soliloquy. Greg suspects that the soliloquy in its present form was a second draft of an earlier, more conventional, speech, and that in the process of writing it Marlowe realized that the "morality" tone of the earlier section was inappropriate and that the dialogue with Mephostophilis and the Angels would have to be cut.[31] Certainly the tragic involvement Marlowe has cautiously reinforced in the farewell to the scholars is undermined by the reproaches of the two angels. Conventional pronouncements like "He that loves pleasure must for pleasure fall" (V, ii, 127) encourage the audience to see Faustus from a moral distance and judge him in simple and moralistic terms which do injustice to the complexity of his motives. The image of hell which the Bad Angel gleefully elaborates upon (accompanied, according to the stage direction, by a physical "hell" which "is discovered") is likewise extremely conventional in comparison to Mephostophilis' earlier arresting descriptions; this too suggests an earlier stage in the evolution of the play.

Finally the audience is left alone with Faustus, as they listen together to the clock strike eleven. The soliloquy that follows is the counterpart to the long speech with which the play began: once again, Faustus addresses himself, the "self" whom twenty-four years ago he instructed to "Try thy brains to gain a deity." Now comes the inevitable corollary: "thou must be damned perpetually" (V, ii, 132). The speech derives much of its power and urgency from the passage of time. Both Faustus and the audience await the next striking of the clock; both know that, despite all his power, Faustus cannot, after all, command the spheres of heaven to stand still, "That time may cease." Struggling like a trapped animal against the inexorable passage of time, Faustus is confined by a kind of moral gravity as well. He tries to leap up to God, but finds himself pulled down; he asks to be drawn up into clouds which might "vomit" him forth into heaven, only to find himself still on earth and on the stage. Desperately, he thinks of rushing headlong into the earth, of hiding from God's wrath beneath mountains and hills, of disguising and obliterating himself through Pythagorean transformation or dissolution into "little water drops"—all to no avail. Faustus experiences a sensation of physical entrapment which his soul cannot escape through metempsychosis as he descends to an eternal hell to which "No end is limited." This experience brings to completion the flights, the comic transformations, and the sense of unlimited possibilities that he had enjoyed throughout the play. The Elizabethan audience would presumably appreciate the moral symmetry here, yet Marlowe has drawn them into the experience of Faustus' desperation and fear so effectively that their involvement in his agony is at least as great as their detached judgment of him. As Faustus cries out to God, breaking up the rhythm of the blank verse with one outburst after another, he becomes more real than he has been at any other point in the play. Yet, paradoxically, he is now more fully and entirely the "other" than ever before. By dramatizing their own fear of hell and instinct for survival, Marlowe has brought his audience to an extraordinary degree of emotional involvement with a soul whose damnation is certain, an involvement from which, under any other circumstances, they would seek to detach themselves as much as possible.

Although Faustus' fate is resolved in this final speech, the play's theological ambiguities are not. Faustus cries out to Christ and God, and receives in return not the grace Foxe promised to those willing to be reconciled but a vision of God's "ireful brows" and heavy wrath. Is it because Faustus still fails to repent that he sees the outstretched arm as a bearer of punishment and not forgiveness? Is he wrong to assume that God "wilt not have mercy on my soul" (163)? In what way does his cry "My God, my God, look not so fierce on me" (184) constitute a plea for mercy devoid of the accompanying willingness to repent? An Elizabethan audience might have asked these questions, but they might also have finally realized that the offers of salvation extended by the Good Angel were illusory. As William Perkins observed, God does give the commandment "Repent and believe" to those who lack the requisite grace to do so. He explains that

> ... though in the intent of the Minister it have onely one end; namely, the salvation of all, yet in the intention & counsell of God, it hath diverse ends. In them which be ordained to eternall life, it is a precept of obedience: because God will enable them to doe that which he commandeth; in the rest it is a commandement of triall or conviction, that to unbeleevers their sinne might be discovered and all excuse cut off. Thus when the precept is given to beleeve, and not the grace of faith, God doth not delude, but re-prove and convince men of unbeleefe, and that in his justice.[32]

Perhaps this cutting off of all excuse was the Good Angel's intent when he encouraged Faustus to repent. Yet this is a judgment that an audience could only make in retrospect; when the words were originally spoken, it would have been an act of ungodly cynicism to doubt their sincerity.

Even if Faustus' damnation was predestined, he remains subject to the central paradox of Puritanism, which declares him morally and intellectually responsible for his own fall. Faustus acknowledges this in the final soliloquy, at least for a moment; after cursing his parents for engendering him, he corrects himself and says "No, Faustus, curse thyself." But in the next breath he adds "curse Lucifer/ That hath deprived thee of the joys of heaven" (178–79). Yet significantly, his last line contains still another reversal. With the final desperate offer to "burn my books" Faustus seems to recognize the causal link between his desire for knowledge and his damnation. His offer brings the play full circle to the very first words of the Good Angel: "O Faustus, lay that damned book aside." That "damned book" was laid aside only to be replaced by a still more damned one, which Faustus, at the end of Act II, scene ii, vowed to "keep as chary as my life" (171). Tragically, he failed to act upon his apparent disappointment with its contents when they fell short of the absolute and perfect knowledge he so desired. And just as tragically, he failed to realize that keeping the book meant relinquishing his life. That the final significance of this not be lost, Marlowe reminds his audience of Faustus' stature before the events of the play began. The final chorus, though it warns against his hellish fall, nevertheless pronounces Faustus to have been a learned man in whom "Apollo's laurel bough," the emblem of knowledge, once grew.

III. DOCTOR FAUSTUS AND THE DIDACTIC TRADITION

With its exhortation to the wise "Only to wonder at unlawful things" instead of practicing them, the chorus superimposes a traditional didactic ending on a play which has, in a sense, violated certain expectations its audience had brought to the theatre. As in *Tamburlaine*, Marlowe has taken a conventional literary form and inverted it: just as his audience might have expected Tamburlaine to undergo a well-deserved downfall, a sign of God's just retribution against the over-reacher, so that same audience could have awaited Faustus' final repentance as a sign of God's infinite mercy to the most hardened sinner. In writing *Doctor Faustus*, Marlowe assumed his audience's acquaintance with the logical counterpart of the *de casibus* formula, the fall and reformation of the flawed but eventually redeemed Christian. This was the dominant pattern of the morality play, as we have seen, despite the variations which were introduced during the final years in which the genre flourished. It was also a recurring structure in the published didactic literature of the Elizabethan age, much of it inherently dramatic in character, and very likely influenced indirectly by the religious drama.

One literary form which *Doctor Faustus* inverts is the saint's life, with its pattern of fall and repentance. As Susan Snyder has pointed out, the parody of a saint's life in *Doctor Faustus* is too consistent to be accidental. Faustus is "converted" to the devil after an orthodox early life, seals his pact with a diabolical sacrament, is "tempted" by the Good Angel and his own conscience and then "rescued" by his "mentor" Mephostophilis, performs "miracles," experiences a "heavenly" vision, and is received at death by his "master," Lucifer.[33] Marlowe and his audience were undoubtedly familiar with any number of saint's lives, including possibly some cast in characteristically Puritan terms. A good example is the account of the fourth-century Church father Eusebius, which Perkins presents in dialogue form in his treatise "whether a man be in the estate of damnation or in the estate of grace ..." (the source of the dialogue between Satan and the Christian quoted earlier). The story had long been popular among Protestant writers, evidently. Perkins' subtitle indicates that it was "gathered here and there out of the sweete and savourie writings of Master Tindall and Master Bradford."

The dialogue begins as Timotheus, the interlocutor, asks Eusebius to describe to him "how it pleased God to make you a true Christian, and a member of Christ Iesus, whom I see you serve continually with a fervent zeale?" Eusebius answers that:

> The fall of Adam did make me the heire of vengeance and wrath of God, & heire of eternall damnation, and did bring me into captivity and bondage under the divell: & my governour, and my prince, yea, and my God. And my will was locked and knit faster unto the will of the divel, than could a hundred thousand chaines bind a man unto a post. Unto the divells will did I consent withal my heart, with all my minde, with all my might, power, strength, will, and life: so that the law and will of the divell was written as well in my heart, as in my

members, and I ran headlong after the divell with full saile, & the whole swing of all the power I had; as a stone cast into the ayre commeth downe naturally of it selfe with all the violent swing of his owne waight. O with what a deadly and venemous heart did I hate mine enemies? With how great malice of mind inwardly did I slay and murther? With what violence and rage, yea with what fervent lust committed I adultery, fornication, and such like uncleannesse? With what pleasure and delectation like a glutton served I my belly? With what diligence deceived I? How busily sought I the things of the world? Whatsoever I did worke, imagine, or speake, was abominable in the sight of God, for I could referre nothing unto the honour of God: neither was his law or will written in my members, or in my heart, neither was there any more power in me to follow the will of God, then in a stone to ascend upward of it selfe.

Eusebius, like Faustus, has consented to the devil's will, although not explicitly out of aspiration to knowledge and god-like power. When the turn toward repentance first begins he resists it vigorously:

And besides that, I was asleepe in so deepe blindnes, that I could neither see nor feele in what miserie, thraldom, and wretchednesse I was in, till Moses came and awaked me and published the law. When I heard the law truely preached, how that I ought to love and honour God with all my strength and might from the low bottome of the heart ... then began my conscience to rage against the law and against God. No sea, be it never so great a tempest, was so unquiet, for it was not possible for me a naturall man to consent to the law that it should be good, or that God should bee righteous that made the law: in as much as it was contrary unto my nature, and damned me and all that I could doe, and never shewed mee where to fetch helpe, nor preached any mercie, but onely set mee at variance with God, and provoked and stirred me to raile on God, and to blaspheme him as a cruell tyrant.

The preaching of the law, Eusebius explains, was "the key that bound and damned my conscience," but "the preaching of the Gospel was another key that loosed me againe." First the law

... pulled me from all trust and confidence I had in my selfe, and in mine owne workes, merits, deservings, and ceremonies, and robbed me of all my righteousnesse, and made mee poore. It killed me in sending me downe to hell, and bringing me almost to utter desperation, and prepared the way of the Lord, as it is written of *Iohn*

Baptist. For it was not possible that Christ should come unto mee as long as I trusted in my selfe, or in any worldly thing, or had any righteousnesse of mine owne, or riches of holy wordes. Than afterward came the Gospel a more gentle plaister, which suppled and swaged the wounds of my conscience, and brought me health: it brought the Spirit of God, which loosed the bands of Satan, and coupled me to God and his will through a strong faith and fervent love. Which bands were too strong for the divell, the world, or any creature to loose.

After listening to his long account, Timotheus protests that "you doe too much condemne your selfe in respect of sinne." But Eusebius responds that "my nature is to sinne as it is the nature of a serpent to sting ... we are of nature evill, therefore doe we evill, and thinke evill, to eternall damnation by the law...."

Timotheus explains that his experience has been different: "As yet I never had such a feling of my sinnes as you have had, and although I would be loath to commit any sinne, yet the Law was never so terrible unto mee, condemning mee, pronouncing the sentence of death against mee...." To this Eusebius answers: "A true saying it is, that the right way to go unto heaven, is to saile by hell, and there is no man living that feeles the power & vertue of the blood of Christ, which first hath not felt the paines of hell."

And he continues "But the Lord which bringeth forth even to the borders of hell his best beloved when they forget themselves; knoweth also how well to bring them backe againe." In response to further questioning from Timotheus about his earlier life Eusebius describes how "the divell himselfe (as I now perceive) did often perswade my secure conscience that I was the child of God, and should be saved as well as the best man in the world: and I yeelded to his perswasion, and did verily thinke it." This confidence then gave way to despair, as "the divell changed both his coate and his note, and in fearefull manner cryed in my eares, that I was reprobate, his child: that none of Gods children were as I am, that this griefe of my soule was the beginning of hell. And the greater was my paine, because I durst not open my minde unto any for feare they should have mocked mee, and have made a jest of it."

Finally he went to a godly learned preacher, and after two or three days received promises of mercy, shown to him in "the booke of God." Now, says Eusebius: "I have had some assurance (in spite of the divell) that I doe appertaine to the kingdome of heaven, and am now a member of Iesus Christ, and shall so continue for ever." Timotheus then asks: "How know you that God hath forgiven your sinne?" Eusebius answers: "Because I am a sinner, and he is both able and willing to forgive me." Timotheus' questions persist, but Eusebius stoutly maintains: "I am certainly perswaded of the favour of God, even to the salvation of my soule."[34]

I quote from this at such length because I feel that the character of

Eusebius reveals much about the Elizabethan audience's response to Faustus. His account of his bondage to the devil has the same stubborn energy which Marlowe translates into a powerful drama, though Marlowe, following the legend he inherited from the *Faustbook*, makes it clear that Faustus' bondage to the devil is chosen, not inherited. Eusebius' subsequent disillusionment and bitter protest against the law of Moses corresponds to Faustus' rejection of Christianity after reading the two fragments from Jerome's Bible; this is perhaps Marlowe's most important addition to his source. The successive periods of confidence and despair which Eusebius experiences under the influence of the devil also have their counterparts in *Doctor Faustus*. Though Faustus never has the confidence of election that Eusebius had possessed, he is encouraged by Mephostophilis to feel a somewhat analogous sense of security at many points in the play. As in Eusebius' story, this encouragement ultimately changes to a bitter taunting. Faustus' despair is given far more emphasis than his security, and, significantly, it too derives in part from the kind of arrogance associated with unjustified confidence in election. Ironically, Faustus has a conviction of election in reverse: "The serpent that tempted Eve may be saved, but not Faustus" (V, ii, 42). It is this inverted assurance that prevents his final repentance, a repentance which some members of the audience might still have anticipated in the final moments of the play, accustomed as they were to accounts like Perkins' in which the protagonist is on the very brink of hell when the reversal takes place. Faustus' soliloquy frantically explores many forms of escape from the inevitable damnation that awaits him—but not repentance. And so, though like Eusebius he "lived as though there were neither heaven nor hell, neither God nor divell," Faustus dies a damned soul.

Notes

1. Cf. Robert G. Hunter in *Shakespeare and the Mystery of God's Judgments* (Athens, Georgia, 1976). Hunter believes that tragedy emerged from the fear that one is living a life predetermined by an apparently unjust God, a fear of hell. Whether this is a belief or just fear of a possibility, "it can be evoked as tragic terror and coped with through the familiar therapeutic process of tragedy" (p. 34). On our fear of becoming our evil selves as part of our response to *Doctor Faustus*, see Constance Brown Kuriyama in *Hammer and Anvil* (New Brunswick, New Jersey, 1980), p. 133.

2. Robert Potter, *The English Morality Play* (London, 1975), p. 129.

3. Philip Mason Palmer and Robert Pattison More, *The Sources of the Faust Tradition from Simon Magus to Lessing* (New York, 1936), p. 4.

4. Palmer and More believe that a reference to Pope Sixtus in the present tense in the English Faustbook indicates that the translation was made before his death in August, 1590 (*The Sources of the Faust Tradition*, p. 177). An early date for

the *Faustbook* would support the theory that *Doctor Faustus* was written right after *II Tamburlaine*, in 1588 or 1589. Paul H. Kocher is the major advocate for an early date for *Doctor Faustus*; his argument appears in "The English Faust Book and the Date of Marlowe's Faustus," *Modern Language Notes*, 55 (1940), 95–101. W. W. Greg is the major spokesman for the theory that *Doctor Faustus* was written in 1592; his argument appears in the introduction to his parallel text edition of the play, *Marlowe's Doctor Faustus: 1604–1616* (Oxford, 1950), and has been accepted by a majority of recent critics and scholars. However, Samuel Schoenbaum, in his revision of Alfred Harbage's *Annals of English Drama: 975–1700*, states that the argument for the early date has been "recently urged again" (p. 56), suggesting that Greg's word is by no means the last. Both the 1604 and the 1616 texts of *Doctor Faustus* borrow freely from the *Faustbook*: for example, the details of the conjuring scene, the magic circle, the thunder and lightning, the spectacular appearance of Mephostophilis in the form of a dragon and then his reappearance as a friar—all these come from the *Faustbook*. So do the visit to the papal palace and the snatching of the Pope's meat and drink (but not the escape of Bruno) and the appearance of Alexander and his paramour at the request of the Emperor. Marlowe also borrowed the tricking of the sleeping knight and his attempted revenge, the incident of the detachable leg, the deception of the Horse-courser, the pregnant Duchess of Vanholt's request for grapes, and the appearance of the beautiful Helen (who quite explicitly becomes Faustus' "bedfellow" in the *Faustbook* and bears him a child).

5. All quotations from *Doctor Faustus* are taken from *The Complete Plays of Christopher Marlowe*, ed. Irving Ribner (New York, 1963). For occasional distinctions between the 1604 text ("A text") and the 1616 text ("B text") I have used W. W. Greg's parallel text edition. I have tried to keep my critical interpretation of the play free from textual arguments and based on passages shared by the two texts, following the advice of Constance Brown Kuriyama in "Dr. Greg and *Doctor Faustus*: The Supposed Originality of the 1616 Text," *ELR*, 5 (1975), 171–97. Kuriyama believes that it is likely that both texts are "bad" in very different ways, but is inclined to agree with Fredson Bowers that the 1616 text is closer to Marlowe's original. Bowers' arguments appear in "Marlowe's *Doctor Faustus*: The 1616 Additions," *Studies in Bibliography*, 26 (1973), 1–18.

6. Max Bluestone, "*Libido Speculandi*: Doctrine and Dramaturgy in Contemporary Interpretations of Marlowe's *Doctor Faustus*," *Reinterpretations of Elizabethan Drama: Selected Papers from the English Institute*, ed. Norman Rabkin (New York, 1969), p. 35.

7. William Perkins, *A Golden Chaine* (London, 1635), p. 378.

8. Faustus' failure to complete the text in his syllogism was first noted by Helen Gardner in "Milton's 'Satan' and the Theme of Damnation in Elizabethan Tragedy," *Essays and Studies*, I (1948), reprinted in *Elizabethan Drama: Modern Essays in Criticism*, ed. Ralph J. Kaufmann (New York, 1961).

9. Paul H. Kocher, *Christopher Marlowe: A Study of his Thought, Learning and Character* (Chapel Hill, 1946), pp. 106–107.

10. Hunter, *Shakespeare and the Mystery*, p. 48.

11. John Udall, *Two Sermons upon the Historie of Peters denying Christ* (London, 1584), STC #24503, sig. B6r.

12. As Richard Waswo observes in "Damnation, Protestant Style: Macbeth, Faustus and Christian Tragedy," *Journal of Medieval and Renaissance Studies*, 4 (1974), a central tragic irony in *Doctor Faustus* is Faustus' loss of his finest quality, his ability to aspire (p. 81).

13. Perkins, *A Golden Chaine*, p. 740.

14. Joel Altman likewise sees a departure from morality play technique in Marlowe's use of the two angels: "In the early moralities, spiritual beings such as angels and devils had an objective reality quite external to the psyche of the protagonist, just as the personified vices and virtues were understood to exist within him. There was no tension between a personal, subjective consciousness and these forces. ..." Marlowe, however, uses these forces ironically, since his protagonist is attempting at this moment to assert his psychic autonomy. *The Tudor Play of Mind* (Berkeley, 1978), p. 381.

15. There has been considerable critical disagreement about the Good Angel's posture in this speech. Kocher, for example, uses it to support his theory that Marlowe's anti-Christian bias led him to present God as a wrathful Jehovah rather than a loving father (*Christopher Marlowe*, p. 118). Robert Ornstein takes a similar position in "Marlowe and God: The Tragic Theory of *Doctor Faustus*," *PMLA* LXXXIII (1968); he feels that for Marlowe the Godlike and the Christlike remain antithetical (p. 1385). I prefer the approach taken by Pauline Honderich in "John Calvin and Doctor Faustus," *Modern Language Review*, 68, 1 (Jan. 1973). She observes that "Marlowe calls up and sets against each other the images both of the benevolent God of the Catholic [or moderate Anglican] dispensation and of the harsh and revengeful God of Calvinist doctrine." There is an ongoing dramatic tension in the pitting of the two theological schemes against one another because we don't really know which one will win until the play ends (p. 12). This interpretation makes the play into a powerful and dialectical reflection of the range of possibilities open to the Elizabethans.

16. William Burton, *Davids Evidence or the Assurance of Gods Love* (London, 1592), STC 4170, p. 157.

17. M. M. Mahood, *Poetry and Humanism* (London, 1950), p. 70.

18. Interestingly, Marlowe borrows a phrase from the *Faustbook*, but transforms it utterly. In response to Faustus' demand to know the secrets of hell the Faustbook Mephostophilis boldly declares: "I will tell thee things to the

terror of thy soule ..." (p. 154). In *Doctor Faustus*, this becomes instead the terror of Mephostophilis' fainting soul.

19. The phrase "an ongoing process to the ultimate destiny" is Richard Waswo's; as Waswo points out, this attitude toward damnation was a clear departure from the medieval concept of damnation, which emphasized punishment after death ("Damnation, Protestant Style," p. 71); Douglas Cole, *Suffering and Evil in the Plays of Christopher Marlowe* (Princeton, 1962), p. 205.

20. C. L. Barber, " 'The form of Faustus' fortunes good or bad,' " *Tulane Drama Review*, VIII, 4 (Summer, 1964), pp. 106 ff.

21. Arthur Dent, *A pastime for Parents: or A recreation, to passe away the time; contayning the most principall grounds of Christian Religion* (London, 1606), STC #6622, sig. C6v. The emphasis on the book is more pronounced in the A text; Faustus requests the book of astronomical knowledge from Mephostophilis, but when he receives it, and Mephostophilis turns the pages, he says to himself, "O thou art deceived."

22 .George Gifford, *A Discourse of the subtill Practises of Deuilles by witches and Sorcerers. By which men are and haue bin greatly deluded.* (London, 1587), STC #11852, sig. D2r, H2v, D2r.

23. Kocher uses contemporary sources to show that Faustus could have repented and that he becomes one of those willful men who resist grace, a view also reflected in the *Faustbook*. This means that the audience is meant to view Faustus, not from the Calvinist perspective, according to which God hardens men's hearts, but from a more moderate Protestant perspective, according to which the initiative must come from man, who will not be damned unless he actively resists the grace God offers him (*Christopher Marlowe*, p. 110). Similarly, Lily B. Campbell sees Faustus as "one whose fate was not determined by his initial sin but rather as one who until the fatal eleventh hour might have been redeemed." See "*Doctor Faustus: A Case of Conscience*," *PMLA*, LXVII (1952), p. 239. Marlowe's insistence on ambiguity in respect to whether Faustus can or does repent is stressed by Susan Snyder in "Marlowe's *Doctor Faustus* as an Inverted Saint's Life" *Studies in Philology*, 63 (1966). Snyder notes that the play exhibits two patterns simultaneously, that fallen man cannot initiate repentance, and that repentance is a constant possibility (p. 565). This approach is also discussed by Max Bluestone, who regards Faustus as "neither repentant nor reprobate" ("*Libido Speculandi*," p. 79).

24. R. Linaker, *A Comfortable Treatise, for the reliefe of such as are afflicted in Conscience* (London, 1607; first edition, 1590), STC #15640, pp. 9, 22, 23.

25. Linaker, *A Comfortable Treatise*, p. 81.

26. Robert G. Hunter sees this moment as the *peripeteia* in *Doctor Faustus*; at this point, the play could become either "a comedy of forgiveness or a tragedy of God's judgment." Hunter notes that to the Calvinists in the audience, Faustus

has been damned all along, while to the non-Calvinists, his contrition is not sufficient (*Shakespeare and the Mystery*, pp. 55–56).

27. Perkins, *A Golden Chaine*, pp. 405 ff.

28. Cf. the official Elizabethan homily "How daungerous a thing it is to fall from God," cited in Cole, *Suffering and Evil*, p. 218.

29. John Foxe, *A Sermon of Christ Crucified* (London, 1570), STC #11242, p. 10.

30. Perkins, *A Golden Chaine*, p. 364.

31. W. W. Greg, *Marlowe's Doctor Faustus: 1604–1616*, pp. 126–32.

32. Perkins, *A Golden Chaine*, p. 724 (misnumbered 745).

33. Snyder, "Marlowe's *Doctor Faustus*," p. 566

34. Perkins, *A Golden Chaine*, pp. 381 ff.

PATRICK CHENEY

'Italian masques by night': Machiavellian Policy and Ovidian Play in *Edward II*

From the perspective of the present study, the dramatic poles of *Edward II* become two similar theatrical representations. In the opening scene, Gaveston plans to stage 'Italian masques by night' in order to 'best please his majesty' (I.i. 54, 70); and, in the penultimate scene, Mortimer commissions the henchman Lightborn to stage an 'Italian' rape by night in order to best kill his majesty (V.v).[1] Both the opening and the closing 'Italian masque' are at once Machiavellian and Ovidian, the synthesis of policy and play, as both Gaveston and Mortimer are adept in the 'arts' of both *Italian plotters*. If Gaveston plans like a Machiavel to stage the Ovidian 'comed[y]' (I.i.55) of 'Actaeon peeping through the grove' (66) in order to seduce his sovereign, Mortimer schemes like a Machiavel when relying on Lightborn in order to stage an Ovidian 'tragedy' (V.v.73) of bestiality and rape so horrible in its historical reality that not even Seneca could think of it: 'was it not bravely done' (115), Lightborn asks his accomplices, Gurney and Matrevis, before they kill him. We may wish to brood over the significance of this bifold, 'Italian[ate]' structure because it provides a clue as to how we are to situate Marlowe's Machiavellian 'play of policy' within his Ovidian career.[2]

For one thing, the bifold, Italianate structure permits us to account for what may seem most curious in a play nominally about an English sovereign: Marlowe allots space to a second 'tragic' hero, as the title page to the 1594 edition advertises: 'The troublesome raigne and lamentable death of Edward the second, King of England: with the tragicall fall of proud Mortimer.' Rather than

---

From *Marlowe's Counterfeit Profession*. © 1997 by the University of Toronto Press, Inc.

simply alerting us to a dual tragedy about the named principals, this printer's cue also reveals a dual representation of 'tragedy' in the rival 'arts' of Edward's primary favourite, Gaveston, and his primary competitor, Mortimer, as they vie for (Machiavellian and Ovidian) power over the king. Conceived in these terms, *Edward II* stages a narrative in which a Machiavellian schemer, Mortimer, uses an Ovidian plot to suppress and eliminate an Ovidian and Machiavellian schemer, Gaveston, as well as his 'successors, Spencer and Baldock' (Cartelli 131). This narrative consumes nearly the whole of the play—up until its last scene, when the Machiavellian Mortimer himself suffers a 'tragicall fall.'[3]

None the less, we need to come to terms with Marlowe's complete design. Although he emphasizes Mortimer's suppression of Gaveston, he briefly concludes with young Prince Edward's suppression of Mortimer. In this design, we can discover a model for Marlowe's poetics, including its fate, within Elizabethan culture. *Edward II* is a tragedy about 'the play of policy,' but it joins other late works—*The Jew of Malta*, *The Massacre at Paris*, *Doctor Faustus*, *Lucan's First Book*, and *Hero and Leander*—in emphasizing the individual's loss of *libertas*, his suppression by orthodox powers.[4]

In *Edward II*, Marlowe writes a 'tragedy' but conceals a strategy for overcoming his problem as a writer: with such heterodox views, how can he acquire authority as England's new counter-national artist? Gaveston's Ovidian art relying on Machiavellian policy, we shall see, inscribes a metatheatrical representation of Marlovian unorthodox theatre linking sex and politics; and Mortimer's Machiavellian policy relying on Ovidian play inscribes a metatheatrical representation of an orthodox art linking politics and sex that would seem to pertain to a rival or rival faction. In 1591 or 1592, who would these competitors be? Two rivals long known to Marlowe scholars suggest themselves: Spenser and Shakespeare. In the rivalry between Gaveston and Mortimer for possession of Edward, then, Marlowe may be implicating his own rivalry with his two colleagues for the ear and eye of Queen Elizabeth.

As the only play in the Marlowe canon putting an English king on the stage, Edward II writes nationhood more directly than *Dido*, the two *Tamburlaine* plays, or *The Jew of Malta*—plays that stage an African queen, an Eastern monarch, and a Maltese governor. 'Know,' agonizes Edward to Lightborn, 'I am a king' (V.v.88). As we saw in the introduction, Richard Helgerson argues that Shakespeare's history plays differ from those of Henslowe's playwrights: whereas 'Shakespeare's history plays are concerned above all with the consolidation and maintenance of royal power,' Henslowe's playwrights were preoccupied with 'the innocent suffering of common people' (*Forms of Nationhood* 234–5). By contrast, Spenser abandons a nationhood of 'absolute royal power' for a nationhood organized around 'aristocratic autonomy' (Helgerson 55). *Edward II* broods precisely over this tripartite structure. Our earlier glance at Gaveston's opening speech, however, revealed that Marlowe is not writing simply a nationhood of royal power, of the people's power, or of aristocratic power. Rather, he is writing a nationhood of *libertas*—in particular, free scholarship. We can trace this form of nationhood by focusing on Marlowe's metadramatic rivalry with his colleagues within the pattern of his Ovidian career.

Marlowe's strategy for managing poetic rivalry in the context of nationhood proceeds in three parts. First, he opens the play by using Gaveston to introduce the allure of his own Ovidian art. Second, he uses Mortimer to dramatize the suppression of this art by a rival faction. And third, he concludes by using Edward III to bring about the 'tragicall fall' of that faction.[5] In *Edward II*, Marlowe registers the reception his art was receiving among (more) orthodox circles, including those of Spenser and Shakespeare; and he accurately predicts his art's cultural fate, as that metonymic event, the 1599 burning of *Ovid's Elegies* by episcopal order, records. Evidently, Marlowe's *professional* purpose in *Edward II* is to counter his rival colleagues' censoring of his works. Complexly, he uses Mortimer's grim elimination of the weaker Gaveston to simulate the triumph of Marlovian art over Spenserian and Shakespearean art. That Marlowe should choose as his principal source for this project the orthodox text of Holinshed's *Chronicles* is at once a testament to his genius and a register of the secrecy required to carry out a program securing his authority as England's counter-national poet.

This thesis reconfigures the massive scholarship on Marlowe's 'debt' to Shakespeare, as well as throw into relief the less-well-documented debt to Spenser.[6] The sudden appearance of Shakespeare in Marlowe's representation of artistic rivalry marks a watershed event in his career; *Edward II* signals a changing of the Marlovian rival guard. As James Shapiro observes, 'in *Edward II* one can almost sense Marlowe playing at Shakespearean drama' (*Rival Playwrights* 91). This constitutes a change from the Tamburlaine plays, where Stephen Greenblatt and others sense Marlowe playing with Spenserian poesy. Scholars have long noted that a famous line spoken by Hamlet derives peculiarly from Mortimer—'and as a traveller / Goes to discover countries yet unknown' (V.vi.65–6). Is it possible that in Hamlet's metaphysical discourse on '[t]he undiscover'd country, from whose bourn / No traveller returns' (*Hamlet* III.i.78–9) Shakespeare is revealing that he found himself in Marlowe's anti-Gaveston faction? And is it possible that he found in Mortimer more than a critique of himself—that is, a sympathetic homage as well? If so, we can witness a feature of Marlovian rivalry that we have not yet seen: the 'rash' playwright's attempt to pay homage to a rival he is trying to eclipse.

In *Edward II*, then, written near the close of Marlowe's (counter-Spenserian) career, we may be intrigued to discover a partially sympathetic character named 'Spencer,' and it now becomes a special challenge to discover Marlowe evoking his first great rival. 'Spencer, sweet Spencer, I adopt thee here,' cries Edward (III.ii.144). What is of particular note is the change of Marlowe's representational attitude towards Spenser. Critics typically emphasize the 'maturity' of the play, and to the usual evidence we can add the mature handling of poetic rivalry. In this play, we can detect some changes from *Tamburlaine*. First, Marlowe no longer feels the need to 'plagiarize' Spenser in order to deconstruct him; he can proceed with more subtlety, relying on what Derrida calls 'trace[s]' (26).[7] Second, as with the more famous case of Shakespeare, here Marlowe has enough confidence to pay homage to Spenser, even as he tries to eclipse him. Finally, most complex of all, Marlowe now *unfolds* his traces of Spenser into both halves of the competition for the sovereign's will—*both* Mortimer and Mortimer's victims, Spencer and Gaveston.

Along with poetic rivalry, Marlowe matures in his reading of Spenserian nationhood. From *Dido* to *The Jew*, Marlowe sees Spenser writing a nationhood of royal power; in *Edward II*, he appears to recognize Spenser's 'ambivalence concerning absolute royal power' (Helgerson, *Forms of Nationhood* 55). If Spenser does end by championing 'aristocratic independence' (57), Marlowe may have come to discern an analogue, perhaps a conjunction, between his own Lucanic- and Ovidian-based nationhood of *libertas* and Spenser's nationhood of aristocratic power.[8]

WANTON POETS': GAVESTON'S MARLOVIAN THEATRICS

In the first part of his strategy, Marlowe introduces Gaveston as a successful Ovidian artist relying on Machiavellian policy.[9] The opening scene, showing Gaveston alone, then in dialogue with '*three* Poor Men' (s.d.), then alone again, functions as the play's prologue, with Gaveston '[d]ramatically positioned in the role of the play's Presenter' (Cartelli 123–4). Initially, Gaveston appears '*reading on a letter that was brought him from the King*' (s.d.); this is the first instance of what Marjorie Garber calls 'the material embodiment of the concept of countertext as counterplot' ('"Here's Nothing Writ"' 301), and it occasions the opening part of Gaveston's soliloquy:

> 'My father is deceas'd, come Gaveston,
> And share the kingdom with thy dearest friend.'
> Ah, words that make me surfeit with delight!
> What greater bliss can hap to Gaveston
> Than live and be the favourite of a king?
> Sweet prince I come; these, these thy amorous lines
> Might have enforc'd me to have swum from France,
> And like Leander, gasp'd upon the sand,
> So thou wouldst smile and take me in thy arms.
> The sight of London to my exil'd eyes
> Is as Elysium to a new-come soul.
>
> (*Edward II* I.i.1–11)

Marlowe's metadiscourse is evident in Gaveston's 'reading on a letter,' in his repetition of Edward's 'words,' and in his own phrase for his sovereign's language: 'amorous lines.' As the mention of Leander indicates, however, Marlowe contextualizes his metadiscourse in terms of his own 'Ovidian' career. Although we cannot tell whether 'Leander' refers to a *Hero and Leander* he has already written or advertises its advent, we inescapably find a self-reference.[10]

As if to emphasize the Ovidian career context of his historical tragedy, Marlowe presents his figure out of English chronicle voicing a well-known historical event (the 'decease' of Edward's 'father' and the recall of Edward's 'dearest friend') *as a revoicing of a famous Marlovian line*. Critics have long observed that Edward's quoted lines repeat with a difference the famous lines from 'The Passionate Shepherd to His Love' (Forsythe 699–700)—a repetition (or anticipation) that we have seen in *Dido*, the *Tamburlaine* plays, and *The Jew of Malta*: 'Come, Gaveston, / And share the kingdom with thy dearest friend.' Marlowe's self-imitation functions as a meta-imitation, and it inaugurates the Ovidian tragic mode, the 'amorous line,' which constitutes the political problem both in and of the play: what happens when an English sovereign *reads Marlowe*? He ceases to speak in his own regal or political voice (recorded in Holinshed); he breaks into Marlovian discourse. From the outset, the playwright contextualizes 'English history' in terms of Marlovian tragedy. The 'Edward' whom Gaveston enunciates is neither the 'historical' king who ruled between 1307 and 1327 (alas, he lies cold as stone in his grave), nor even Holinshed's 'Edward, the second of that name, the son of Edward the first' (rpt. in Thomas and Tydeman 351); rather, he is Marlowe's 'King, upon whose bosom [Gaveston wants to] ... die' (I.i.14). More technically, this sovereign is Gaveston's 'pliant King,' who '[m]ay [be] draw[n] ... which way ... [Gaveston] please[s]' (52), since Gaveston, not Edward himself, speaks Edward's words—'words that make [Gaveston] ... surfeit with delight!' By opening the play with a character in a dramatic fiction (Gaveston) voicing the words of a sovereign (Edward), who himself imitates an English chronicle writer (Holinshed), but who in fact imitates the play's own author, Marlowe alerts his audience to the most elemental passion of his play: not early fourteenth-century English politics or sodomy, but the complex literary system of communication that can best represent the problematic conjunction of politics and sodomy in late sixteenth-century England.

When Gaveston speaks in his own words, he does not extricate himself from this system, but clarifies what Garber calls, echoing Harry Levin, 'the play's overreaching author, Christopher Marlowe' (320). Quoting 'Marlowe' even more precisely than Edward does, Gaveston reproduces the key active words that echo through 'The Passionate Shepherd,' *Dido*, the *Tamburlaine* plays, and *The Jew*; these words succinctly represent the Marlovian conversion of an Ovidian ethics (*come, live*) into an Ovidian ontology (*be*): '*live* and *be* the favourite of a king? / Sweet prince I *come*.' Syntactically, Marlowe bookends the linguistic sign of ontology with twin signs from an Ovidian ethics: *live ... be ... come*. Ontology loses its virginal *telos*, imprisoned as a hapless mediator for sexual desire. Not simply do Gaveston's words echo Edward's; his system of literary imitation reproduces Marlowe's.

If we miss this system in the first six lines, Marlowe ensures that we become alert to it in lines 7 and 8, when he refers to 'Leander.' Here we are to see not simply an analogy between Leander's love of Hero and Gaveston's love of Edward, but Marlowe's attempt to rechannel the cultural flow of sanctified desire from heterosexualism to homoeroticism. We are also to see Marlowe's attempt to reinscribe the Machiavellian policy of Gaveston's designs in Ovidian terms. Given Marlowe's initial surge of metadiscourse, we can identify Gaveston's bridging word in his Leander simile, 'like'—the formal figural trope of similitude—as itself a fine metonym for the process of literary imitation. Marlowe repeats this strategy in the remaining lines and reveals its rhetorical direction: Gaveston's heroic, and even theologically charged return to 'London' stages the return of 'the play's overreaching author.'[11]

Within this metatheatrical system, Gaveston inscribes data from another Marlowe play: *Doctor Faustus*. Again, we cannot tell whether Marlowe is referring to a play he has written or is advertising a play he plans to write, but once more we inescapably detect a self-reference. Gaveston's 'surfeit with delight' resembles Faustus's 'surfeit ... upon cursed necromancy' (Pr.25; see V.ii.37). Similarly, Gaveston's 'greater bliss' resembles Faustus's 'chiefest bliss' (Pr.27). Finally, Gaveston's comparison of London to 'Elysium' resembles Faustus's 'confound[ing] hell in Elysium' (I.iii.61).[12]

In the first half of Gaveston's opening soliloquy, then, Marlowe uses self-quotation and self-reference to *trans-scribe* what Levin calls 'the pastoral fields of Ovidian lyricism' (32) within the Holinshedian genre pertaining to English historical tragedy. What both Edward's 'amorous lines' and Gaveston's subsequent lines voice is the linguistic current that in this play must be evaporated: not simply the playwright's usurpation of generic decorum—his intrusion of the Ovidian within the Holinshedian—but the absorption of the Holinshedian by the Ovidian: the refacing of English history by Ovidian *amor*. In Marlowe's hands, Holinshed's 'lines' indeed become 'amorous': they are Ovidianized.

The last half of Gaveston's opening speech, quoted in the introduction, does not refer to or quote from the author's works, but it does strike the tenor of another prologue, spoken by the 'presenter' of *The Jew of Malta*: 'Not that I love the city or the men, ... / As for the multitude, that are but sparks / Rak'd up in embers of their poverty' (12–21). Like Machevill, Gaveston voices insolence and contempt, relies on rhetorical question and exclamation, demystifies religious orthodoxy, and even tropes the 'soul's' international migration: '*Tanti*! I'll fan first on the wind, / That glanceth at my lips and flieth away' (22–3). Whereas the first half of Gaveston's speech proceeds in the Ovidian mode, the second half proceeds in the Machiavellian. If Gaveston first uses the Ovidian to voice his intimate relation with a single individual, he next uses the Machiavellian mode to detach himself from the nation.[13]

While Gaveston's discourse identifies him as a Machiavel, we can detect a change from *The Jew of Malta*. Machiavellian policy now serves Ovidian ends. London appears to Gaveston as Elysium not because it is a place worth loving intrinsically (for 'the city or the men'), but because it 'harbours him I hold so dear.' Ovidian intimacy, not Machiavellian power over the nation, becomes the *telos* of Gaveston's appetitive imagination.

The opening soliloquy, with its elaborate system of authorial self-presentation, intensifies a revolutionary strategy that we have witnessed in embryo form in earlier plays: Marlowe dramatizes his own authorship of a medium traditionally held to be void of 'the recital of the poet himself' (Plato, *Republic* III.394b). We should not be surprised, then, when Gaveston lapses into the allure of a Machiavellian plot for a new Ovidian theatre:

> I must have wanton poets, pleasant wits.
> Musicians, that with touching of a string
> May draw the pliant King which way I please;
> Music and poetry is his delight:
> Therefore I'll have Italian masques by night,
> Sometime a lovely boy in Dian's shape,
>
> ...
>
> Shall bathe him in a spring; and there hard by,
> One like Actaeon peeping through the grove,
> Shall by the angry goddess be transform'd,
> By yelping hounds pull'd down, and seem to die.
> Such things as these best please his majesty.
>
> (*Edward II* I.1.50–70)

Gaveston here projects his production of a 'masque' about the Ovidian story of Diana and Actaeon as a Machiavellian strategy for wooing his sovereign.[14]

If in Gaveston's first soliloquy Marlowe uses self-reference and self-quotation to identify Gaveston as a Marlovian Ovidian poet, in this one he offers a kind of 'dumb-show' of the Marlovian Ovidian art itself (cf. Sunesen). Among the rhetorical elements of this show, a few deserve attention. The first pertains to audience and purpose. Marlowe views his art as a form of political rhetoric, designed to persuade the power structure, especially the sovereign. Within the 'play,' that sovereign is English, yet few critics have contextualized Marlowe's politics in terms of his English sovereign.[15] Yet recent political critics do see Marlowe generally 'foreground[ing] ... the idea of patronage' and 'question[ing] ... the concept of the mis-advised monarch' (Shepherd 118, 122); or they see him boldly 'represent[ing] ... the execution as well as the deposition of a monarch,' localizing Mortimer through 'topical, or Elizabethan, associations' as 'contemporary preachers' who 'attacked theatrical excess' and who criticized 'Ralegh, Essex, Hatton and the others who devoted themselves to gaining and retaining, Her Majesty's pleasure' (Sales 113, 123–4, 126). We may endorse these comments but refocus them on Marlowe's subversion of monarchical power and his topical representations of Puritan attacks on the theatre and outbursts against the Queen's favourites. In *Edward II*, Marlowe challenges a writer like Spenser who was using his art to promote himself as a servant of a wise and just queen.[16]

To discover how Marlowe uses Gaveston's 'Italian masques by night' to function as a model of his Ovidian art designed to affect Elizabeth, we can profitably turn to an arresting element in Gaveston's soliloquy: the myth of Actaeon.[17] As Leonard Barkan observes, 'the story of Actaeon is one of the paradigmatic episodes in the *Metamorphoses*.'[18]

In the famous autobiographical poem, Book II of the *Tristia*, Ovid pauses to brood over the event he does not name because it compelled Augustus to banish him: 'Why did I see anything? Why did I make my eyes guilty? Why was I so thoughtless as to harbour the knowledge of a fault? Unwitting was Actaeon when he beheld Diana unclothed; none the less he became the prey of his own hounds' (103–8). Instead of answering the questions, Ovid lapses into myth. When we desire historical event, Ovid gives us timeless mythology. And yet our foiled expectation helps us to establish our own equation: we are to see Ovid as an Actaeon who '[u]nwitting[ly]' spied a divine figure in a way that compromised that deity's privacy, and therefore his own identity as a (human) poet.

We do not know the chronological relation between Ovid's penning of the Actaeon story in the *Metamorphoses* and the Actaeon-like espial that secured his banishment; hence, we lack access to Ovid's intent in placing the story within his counter-Virgilian epic.[19] Luckily, we need not solve the question for Ovid; we need only observe what Marlowe could have *seen*. By reading the *Tristia* into the *Metamorphoses* (as modern critics themselves do), Marlowe could see a representation of Ovid's own fate in the Augustan literary system: his playful use of an amorous art that becomes subjected to political tyranny—'the mercilessness of absolute power' (Otis 145). For Marlowe, as indeed for his own contemporaries, the Actaeon myth becomes the paradigmatic myth of Ovid's literary career.[20]

What is remarkable is not that Marlowe would appropriate the Actaeon myth to identify himself as an Ovidian poet par excellence (any astute writer could do that), but that his use of the myth in the prologue-like opening to *Edward II* should communicate so hauntingly our sense of his art near the end of his life. First, we often understand his art as an Ovidian 'comed[y]' of play redefined through the homoerotic vehicle of the Elizabethan theatre, in which 'a lovely boy in Dian's shape' works to 'hide those parts which men delight to see'; hence, under Gaveston's direction, the terribly unjust and haunting tale that Ovid tells in the *Metamorphoses* becomes the source for witty verbal play: the phrase 'By yelping hounds pull'd down, and seem to die' linguistically converts a tragedy ending in mutilation into a comic myth arriving at orgasm, as the well-noted Elizabethan pun on 'die' reveals (Deats, 'Fearful Symmetry' 246). Second, we see that Marlowe is predicting the necessarily *tragic* conclusion of such a project, as Gaveston dramatizes. By letting the second and the first conclusions collide, we can arrive at a third—a construct for Marlowe's paradigmatic representation of his art: paradoxically, he uses 'Sweet speeches, comedies, and pleasing shows' to 'peep ... through the grove.' Fusing the comic to the tragic, he uses erotic play to peer into the privacy of the Queen's political policy, making 'the goddess' *angry*. Ovidian play both masques and masks Machiavellian policy in order to fulfil Ovidian fate, not to conceal it.[21]

That Marlowe presents Gaveston as an Ovidian dramatist using an erotic art to move the sovereign may be confirmed by one subsequent 'career' image familiar from *Ovid's Elegies*, *Dido*, and the *Tamburlaine* plays: that of the chariot *cursus*. Gaveston tells Edward, 'It shall suffice me to enjoy your love, / Which whiles I have, I think myself as great / As Caesar riding in the Roman street / With captive kings at his triumphant car' (I.i.170–3). This is a bold thought, but a daring declaration, especially to a sovereign, and it situates Marlowe among contemporaries like Spenser, who were using their art to equalize themselves with their sovereign through self-presentation: the 'sovereigne of song' (*November* 25). The Ovidian origins of Marlowe's image emerge in scene iv of Act I, when Mortimer Senior quotes Ovid to refer to Gaveston's fate, '*Quam male conveniunt!*' (13: 'How ill they suit' [*Met* II.846–7]), with Warwick adding, 'Ignoble vassal, that like Phaeton / Aspir'st unto the guidance of the sun' (16–17). While Gaveston's linking of 'love' and 'car' has Ovidian origins, the image of the 'triumphant' Caesar also recalls Lucan—and so may subtly prepare for, and even trope, a Marlovian *meta* from tragedy to epic.[22]

'I SEE MY TRAGEDY WRITTEN IN THY BROWS': MORTIMER'S COUNTER-MARLOVIAN THEATRICS

In the second part of his dramatic strategy, Marlowe reconfigures Holinshed's depiction of Mortimer's 'tragic fall' via Machiavelli and Ovid in order to depict the counter-force to Gaveston's Ovidian comedy. In fact, the most significant change Marlowe makes to Holinshed lies in depicting Mortimer as Gaveston's enemy. To do so, Marlowe takes Holinshed's interspersed comments on Edward's revelry and makes them the topic of Mortimer's complaint against the king.[23] What is most notable is that Marlowe transfers Holinshed's 'antitheatricality' entirely to Mortimer in order to dramatize the motive for an antagonism that is itself the product of Marlowe's fancy.[24]

We can scrutinize Mortimer's indictment against Gaveston's and Edward's theatricality in terms of Marlowe's rivalry with 'the truly political animal among English sixteenth-century poets' (Crewe, *Hidden Designs* 89): Spenser.[25] The most significant borrowing for understanding Spenser's presence in the play lies in the phrase 'deads the royal vine.' Marlowe's phrase comes from the written

'message' spoken by the Herald, who has 'com'st from Mortimer and his
complices' (153), and it is addressed to Edward:

> That from your princely person you remove
> This Spencer, as a putrefying branch
> That deads the royal vine, whose golden leaves
> Empale your princely head, your diadem,
> Whose brightness such pernicious upstarts dim.
>
> (*Edward II* III.ii.161–5)

The lyricism or golden imagery here—'branch ... vine ... golden leaves ... diadem
... brightness'—has the general tenor of Spenserian discourse, but Charlton and
Waller were evidently the first to alert us to an actual borrowing from Spenser.

In *The Teares of the Muses*, published in the 1591 *Complaints* volume, and
thus available to Marlowe, Thalia, the Muse of Comedy, laments the defacing of
English comedy by those who turn the genre to 'a laughing game' (204). She
then pauses to lament the death of one individual who excelled in comedy: 'Our
pleasant Willy, ah is dead of late: / With whom all joy and jolly meriment / Is also
deaded, and in dolour drent' (208–10). We do not know the identity of 'pleasant
Willy.'[26] What is initially striking, however, is the possibility that Marlowe is
imitating a line topical in its significance: Spenser is praising a writer of comedies
whom he considers to be in his own literary circle.

The 'pleasant Willy' lines are part of a larger passage in which Spenser uses
Thalia to decry a group of poetasters ruining English comedy; the lines
immediately following read:

> In stead thereof scoffing Scurrilitie,
> And scornfull Follie with Contempt is crept,
> Rolling in rymes of shamles ribaudrie
> Without regard, or due Decorum kept,
> Each idle wit at will presumes to make,
> And doth the Learneds taske upon him take.
>
> (*The Teares of the Muses* 211–16)

As in the case of 'pleasant Willy,' we do not know here who Spenser has in mind.
William Renwick can avoid the obvious inference, that Lyly and the University
Wits are under attack, only by claiming that the passage was 'written about
1578–80' (209)—a conclusion rejected by recent scholars.[27] Indeed, the
penultimate and final lines look to be a troping of the University Wits, with their
'Learned' art of making organized around pride in the self, wit, and ultimately
will, as described by G.K. Hunter in his fine book on Lyly. The phrase 'scoffing
Scurrilitie' may suggest Nashe in his debate with Spenser's friend Gabriel
Harvey, which was raging in the bookstalls at precisely this time (see Moore), but

the phrase also echoes contemporary descriptions of Marlowe, as in the most famous, by Robert Greene in his 1588 *Perimedes the Blacksmith*: 'such mad and *scoffing* poets, that have propheticall spirits as bold as Merlins race' (rpt. in MacLure, ed., *Marlowe* 30; emphasis added). Spenser's diagnosis that such writers are controlled by 'Contempt' anticipates Greenblatt's observation: 'For Marlowe ... the dominate mode of perceiving the world ... is *contempt*' ('Marlowe, Marx' 46; emphasis in original).

But it is in the next stanza that we may find an even more precise representation of Marlowe, when Spenser contrasts the 'pen' of 'that same gentle Spirit' (usually identified as Spenser's own [Oram et al. 277] with 'the boldnes of such base-borne men, / Which *dare their follies forth so rashlie throwe*' (217–20; emphasis added). Spenser's phrasing recalls Greene's other construction for Marlowe, 'daring God out of heaven with that Atheist Tamburlan' (rpt. MacLure, ed., *Marlowe* 29), and thus Marlowe's own construction for Tamburlaine: 'His looks do menace heaven and dare the gods' (1 *Tamb* 1.ii.157). Spenser concludes by criticizing such a poet or poets for 'mockerie to sell' (222)—likely a gibe at Marlowe and the University Wits, who turned their university learning to profit by writing plays and pamphlets to suit vulgar taste.[28]

Given that Marlowe's 'vine' is 'royal,' he may also be responding to *Colin Clouts Come Home Againe* (written 1591; published 1595). Speaking of 'Cynthia' (Queen Elizabeth), Spenser writes: 'And eke to make the dead againe alive. / Her deeds were like great clusters of ripe grapes, / Which load the braunches of the fruitful vine' (599–601). Whereas Spenser tropes Elizabeth's 'deeds' as grapes loading the 'brauches of the fruitful vine,' Marlowe tropes 'Spencer's' deeds as a 'putrefying braunch' deading the 'royal vine.'[29] The vine at stake for Marlowe is certainly the traditional royal one, but as Charles Forker notes, 'the leaves that adorned the crown of *Edward II* ... were strawberry leaves, not vine leaves' (229). Marlowe's adjustment of the historical 'leaves' prompts us to speculate on the reason for the change.

Marlowe says that the vine Edward wears '[e]mpale[s]' his 'princely head'—'encircle[s] ... as with a garland' (Forker 229). The image of a garland made of vine suggests Bacchus, the god of wine and tragedy, as Spenser writes in the *October* eclogue of *The Shepheardes Calender*: 'O if my temples were distain'd with wine, / And girt in girlonds of wild Yvie twine, / How I could reare the Muse on stately stage, / And teache her tread aloft in bus-kin fine' (110–13). Possibly, Marlowe's change of Edward's strawberry garland to a vine garland contributes to the well-documented metadrama of the play: Edward's empalement by his own ivy garland metonymically renders the genre of 'historical tragedy' itself. Given that the image appears to respond to Spenser within a political or 'Elizabethan' context, we may wonder what it is that Spenser is empaling here.

The larger dramatic passage in which the Spenser borrowing occurs helps us formulate a response. The earl of Arundel is informing Edward and Spencer about significant courtly news—'for Gaveston is dead' (90)—and he uses a phrase that should alert us to the metadrama: 'Pembroke's men' (116). The Earl of Warwick, he reports, 'seiz'd' Gaveston in an 'ambush' of 'Pembroke's men,' to whom Gaveston had been 'deliver'd' (115–18). In the previous scene, Marlowe has actually staged this ambush, beginning with the stage direction to III.i: *Enter Gaveston mourning, [James,] and the Earl of Pembroke's Men.*' Warwick and '*his Company*' (s.d.) step forward to accost the procession, with the earl directing the action: 'My lord of Pembroke's men, / Strive you no longer; I will have that Gaveston' (6–7). This is splendid metadrama. For the acting 'Company' performing the ambush is named 'Pembroke's Men,' identified on the title page of the 1594 edition: 'Edward the second ... As it was sundrie times publiquely acted in the honourable citie of London, by the right honourable the Earle of Pembrooke his servants,' popularly called 'Pembroke's Men.' If we miss the identification between 'Pembroke's men' within the play and Pembroke's Men acting it, Marlowe ensures that we see it when he has the theatrically inclined Edward remark: 'In solemn triumphs and in public shows / Pembroke shall bear the sword before the King' (I.iv.349–50). Marlowe's strategy of relying on a historical family name out of the chronicles of *Edward II* to refer to the current Pembroke family and even his own theatrical patron, the Earl of Pembroke, also bears on the topic of Marlowe's staging of the 'Spencer' family and their relation to Edmund Spenser.[30]

Arundel's announcement of the death of Gaveston leads Edward to call immediately for 'Remembrance of revenge immortally' (140) against Warwick and Mortimer and to adopt Spencer as his new favourite: 'And in this place of honour and of trust, / Spenser, sweet Spenser, I adopt thee here' (143–4). That last line places 'Spencer' in the path of *succession*, and thus of literary imitation itself. Marlowe reiterates the phrase 'sweet Spenser' three more times in the play (IV.vi.72, 95, 110; cf. 'gentle Spencer' at III.ii.24). The phrase recalls an epithet for Edmund Spenser assigned by his own contemporaries, including Marlowe's friend and fellow street-fighter Thomas Watson, who in the 1590 'Eclogue Upon the death of ... Walsingham' had curiously used the phrase to describe Spenser as a tragedian: '*dulcis Spencere cothurno*'—sweet in the Spenser buskin—which Watson himself translated as 'sweet Spencer' (Cummings 70–1).[31]

Marlowe assigns the construction to the anti-Gaveston faction of Mortimer; thus, complexly, within a single scene we appear to find two conflicting responses to Spenser: the first calls him 'sweet' and 'adopt[s]' him 'here'; the second parodies his sweetness and disinherits him.[32]

For the most part, Marlowe's Spenserianisms come from Mortimer's enemies, especially Gaveston, Edward, and Spencer the Younger. As we have seen in the 'putrefying branch' passage, however, it is Mortimer himself who is responsible for such counter-Spenc/serian discourse. And it is Mortimer who most recurrently voices the play's metadrama—both for and against theatre.[33] Consider Mortimer's often-quoted condemnation of Gaveston at the end of Act

I, uttered to his uncle, Mortimer Senior (iv.401–18): 'Midas-like he jets it in the court ... / As if that Proteus, god of shapes, appear'd' (7, 10). What makes Mortimer impatient are three traits of Gaveston's character: he is 'basely born' (402); he is extravagantly theatrical in both action and dress ('proud fantastic liveries make such show' [409]); and he scorns the theatricality of others ('flout our train, and jest at our attire' [417]).[34]

Proteus is not merely the 'god of shapes'; he is also a figure for the actor, as revealed in 'The Prologue to the Stage at the Cock-Pit' prefacing the 1633 edition of *The Jew of Malta*, which describes Edward Alleyn, 'the best of actors': 'being a man / Whom we may rank with ... / Proteus for shapes' (4–10).[35] Marlowe links the Protean Gaveston with acting not merely by using ornate dress to trope theatrical costume (the 'fantastic liver[y]' of Gaveston is literally the actor's costume), but also by using both the word 'show' as a transition from the description of Gaveston's dress to the Proteus simile and the word 'appear'd' to end the simile itself.

Mortimer's speech thus crafts a fine piece of metadrama; it appears to represent Marlowe's rivals' indictment of Marlowe. The competitive indictment emphasizes Marlowe's Ovidian theatre, with its rich classical mythography out of the *Metamorphoses*, its foxy Machiavellianism, its biting 'contempt,' and its homoeroticism.

As Mortimer reappears, however, he increasingly resembles the theatrical agents he is rivalling. In Act II, scene ii, for instance, he becomes a Spenserian allegorist, arriving before his sovereign with an emblematic 'device' engraved on his shield (II), as he describes it to Edward: 'A lofty cedar tree fair flourishing, / On whose top branches kingly eagles perch, / And by the bark a canker creeps me up' (16–18).[36] Alert hermeneut that he is, Edward quickly construes the allegory: 'I am that cedar; shake me not too much. / And you the eagles; soar ye ne'er so high, / I have the jesses that will pull you down, / And *Aeque tandem* shall that canker cry / Unto the proudest peer of Britainy' (38–42).

To construct Mortimer's allegory of the kingly cedar tree, the protective eagle/barons, and the canker/Gaveston, Marlowe may have collated two sonnet allegories in Spenser's 1591 *Complaints* volume. Sonnet 7 of *Visions of the Worlds Vanitie* tells how '[h]igh on a hill a goodly Cedar grewe,' until '[s]hortly within her inmost pith there bred / A litle wicked worme' (1–7). Like Mortimer's allegory, Spenser's depicts the canker worm destroying the cedar tree. To find the birds and the cedar, we may turn to a related set of allegorical sonnets, *The Visions of Bellay*: 'Upon an hill a bright flame I did see, ... / Which like incense of precious Cedar tree, ... / A Bird all white, well feathered on each wing' (II: 1–6). Although the bird emerging from the flames is not the eagle, and the 'Cedar tree' appears inside a simile, Marlowe's imagination may have ranged over this recent publication and aligned it with the cedar/canker sonnet in the previous set of poems. While in both allegories Spenser places himself in the apocalyptic tradition, Mortimer politicizes the imagery in terms of English kingship. What is noteworthy is his sudden reliance on the Spenserian allegorical mode as a Machiavellian strategy for contesting his sovereign's (Ovidian) authority.

Hence, later in the scene Mortimer ridicules Edward by lapsing into theatrical discourse: 'thy soldiers marched like players, / With garish robes, not armour; and thyself, / Bedaub'd with gold, rode laughing at the rest' (182–5). Within the drama of the play, Mortimer is accusing Edward of foolishly showing up for a war by tricking out his soldiers like 'players' in their 'garish robes.' Within the play of the drama, however, Marlowe is inscribing the theatricality of his own dramatic action, through Edward, who is 'like' an actor, and through Mortimer, who voices the theatrical simile.[37]

Not surprisingly, the critic of Edward's theatricality turns to theatricality himself. In Act IV, scene i, Mortimer enters '*disguised*' (s.d.)—doubly dressed in an actor's costume. And in Act V, scene ii, he identifies his plan to assassinate the king as 'plots and stratagems' (78). To enact the 'plot,' he devises a two-pronged Machiavellian ploy. First, he will write a death warrant with equivocation: 'And therefore will I do it cunningly. / This letter, written by a friend of ours, / Contains his death yet bids them save his life: "*Edwardum occidere nolite timere bonum est*"' (V.iv.5–7). As he put it earlier to his mistress, Queen Isabella, 'a king's name shall be underwrit' (ii.14). Second, he will direct his principal actor, Lightborn, in the supreme Ovidian act of Machiavellian play.

Critics have long focused on Lightborn, in part because he is Marlowe's splendid creation, but recently they have emphasized Marlowe's use of Lightborn to lapse into 'allegory.'[38] As Lightborn himself reports to Mortimer in an autobiography reminiscent of those by Barabas and Ithamore in *The Jew of Malta*, he seeks to enact an allegory of Machiavellian policy: 'I learn'd in Naples how to poison flowers; / To strangle with a lawn thrust through the throat; / ... / But yet I have a braver way than these' (iv.31–7). As he hints in that last claim, he is a Machiavellian plotter in the homoerotic domain.

Yet it is his acting director who links Machiavelli with Ovid most directly. As soon as Lightborn exits, Mortimer lapses into the discourse of the Machiavel by actually quoting Ovid:

> The Prince I rule, the Queen do I command,
> ...
> I seal, I cancel, I do what I will;
> Fear'd am I more than lov'd: let me be fear'd,
> And when I frown, make all the court look pale.
> ...
> Mine enemies will I plague, my friends advance,
> And what I list command, who dare control?
> *Maior sum quam cui possit fortuna nocere.*
>
> (*Edward II* V.iv.48–69)

The Ovid quotation comes from the story of Niobe, the wife of Amphion, in Book VI of the *Metamorphoses*: 'I am too great for Fortune to harm' (195)—just before Fortune strikes her down, killing her husband (Amphion commits suicide) and their seven sons. Evidently, Marlowe finds the Machiavel in Ovid, and it does not bode well for his own Ovidian Machiavel, who is using his secret affair with a queen to bring about the downfall of a king. 'Fair Isabel,' he caresses her earlier, 'now have we our desire ... / Be rul'd by me, and we will rule the realm' (ii.1–5).

Thus both the penultimate and the final scenes of the play 'underwrite' an Ovidian 'tragedy' in the Machiavellian mode. In Act V, scene v, the murder scene itself, Lightborn begins and ends with self-reflexive delight in the deception he is enacting, rehearsing the principle of theatricality articulated by Stephen Greenblatt with respect to Barabas: 'he seems to be pursuing deception virtually for its own sake' ('Marlowe, Marx' 52). Lightborn begins with a cheerful soliloquy: 'So now must I about this gear; ne'er was there any / So finely handl'd as this king shall be' (38–9). And afterwards, he exclaims to the two men about to kill him, 'Tell me sirs, was it not bravely done?' (115)—the word 'bravely' functioning as a theatrical term (Cole, *Christopher Marlowe* 118). As with Barabas, critics have identified Lightborn as a figure for the Marlovian dramatist himself, constructing savage plots.[39] We may add that Lightborn is constructing savage plots against both his sovereign and the sovereign of song. Thus the king himself sees that he is being underwritten by Lightborn's Marlovian 'tragedy': 'I see my tragedy written in thy brows' (73). It is worse than this, for Marlowe relies on Holinshed to out-Seneca Seneca: *the tragedy is written in his bowels*:[40]

> they came suddenly one night into the chamber where he lay in bed fast asleep, and with heavy featherbeds or a table (as some *write*) being cast upon him, they kept him down and withal put into his fundament an *horn*, and through the same they thrust up into his body an hot spit, or (as other have) through *the pipe of a trumpet*, a plumber's instrument of iron made very hot, the which passing up into his entrails, and being rolled to and fro, burnt the same, but so as no *appearance* of any wound or hurt outwardly might be once *perceived*. (Holinshed, *Chronicles*, rpt. in Thomas and Tydeman 369; emphasis added)

'NOW ... BEGINS OUR TRAGEDY': EDWARD III'S COUNTER-MARLOVIAN THEATRICS

In the play's final scene, Marlowe inscribes the final part of his strategy. He dramatizes the suppression of Mortimer by orthodox forces, represented in the new king, the young Edward III. Here Marlowe pauses to juxtapose Edward's 'tragedy' with Mortimer's, as the Queen speaks it: 'Now, Mortimer, begins our tragedy' (V.vi.23). The director of this final drama is himself self-consciously theatrical, as the young king reveals when the Lord enters '*with the head of Mortimer*' (s.d.): 'Go fetch my father's hearse, where it shall lie, / And bring my funeral robes' (V.vi.94–5). Young Edward's directive recalls Dido's directive to Aeneas at the beginning of Marlowe's dramatic career: 'Warlike Aeneas, and in these base robes! / Go fetch the garment which Sichaeus ware' (*Dido* II.i.79–80). In the later play, we may discover a metadiscursive pun on 'hearse'—as Spenser had employed it famously in his Melpomene-inspired funeral Song of Dido in the *November* eclogue: 'O heavie herse, ... O carefull verse' (60, 62). Thus we may relish the theatricality dramatized when the boy calls for his actor's 'robes.' The final utterance of the play, spoken once the new king has his hearse and wears his robes, also resounds with the Senecan ghost of Marlowe's Ovidian and Machiavellian theatre:

> Sweet father here, unto thy murder'd ghost,
> I offer up this wicked traitor's head;
> And let these tears distilling from mine eyes
> Be witness of my grief and innocency.
>
> (*Edward II* V.vi.99–102)

Wilbur Sanders notes 'the unfinished air of the concluding lines' (128), and no modern critic has rested comfortably with them. What Frank Kermode says of Shakespeare's achievement in *Romeo and Juliet* (Introduction, *Riverside Shakespeare* 1057), we may counterfeit for Marlowe's profession in *Edward II*: that the play has a strong *professional* interest is clear; but Marlowe has now passed the stage when one could say, without too much injury to the work, precisely what that interest may have been.

NOTES

1. Cf. Deats, 'Fearful Symmetry': 'the play opens and closes with two similar rituals, the funeral of an older Edward and the assumption of royal power by an heir of the same name' (241). My approach differs from this and other structural approaches (Fricker; Waith, 'Shadow of Action'; McCloskey; Thurn, 'Sovereignty, Disorder'; see Forker's review [66–82]). Kocher, *Christopher Marlowe*, notes Marlowe's 'poetic realizations of the schemes of Mortimer and Gaveston' (205; see 291; Cutts, *Left Hand of God* 200–1; Brandt, *Christopher Marlowe* 156–9; and Deats, 'Fearful Symmetry' 255), but no one has isolated this rivalry in terms of Marlowe's Ovidian career.

2. Things have not changed much since Bakeless: 'All critics are generally

agreed that this is the maturest of Marlowe's plays and ... the latest' (2:4). On dating, which most assign to 1591–2, see Merchant xi–xii; Forker 14–17; and Rowland xiv–xv. Critics usually identify *Edward II* as a 'Machiavellian play of policy,' and they find a number of Machiavellian plotters, especially Gaveston and Mortimer (Cartelli 121–3, 128–33), but also Queen Isabella (Summers, *Christopher Marlowe* 172–4). Less often, critics mention Ovid (F.P. Wilson 133; Zucker 170–3; and Deats, 'Myth and Metamorphosis' 309, 311, 314, 316); but we need to take Marlowe's cues more seriously: Gaveston's Ovidianism; the recurrent references to myths from the *Metamorphoses* (I.iv. 16,172–3, 178–80, 407, II.ii.53–4, III.iii.82–3, etc.); and two lines quoted from Ovid's epic (I.iv.13 from *Met* II.846–7; and V.iv.69 from Met VI.195). As J. Bate remarks, '*Edward II* sometimes seems to require an extremely detailed recall of Ovid's Latin'(44). Of course, Marlowe mediates his synthesis of Machiavelli and Ovid with Seneca, as his quotation from *Thyestes* hints (IV.vi.53–4 from *Thy* 613–14; see H. Levin 99, 101).

3. Marlowe invents the rivalry between Gaveston and Mortimer. In Holinshed, Mortimer does not appear until after Gaveston is dead, when the Earl of Lancaster is 'the chief occasioner of his death' (rpt. in Thomas and Tydeman 360). See Fricker: 'for the first time in Marlowe's plays the hero [Edward] is confronted with an enemy of equal stature, namely Mortimer' (206). Critics debate the question of genre; Ribner's phrase, 'Historical Tragedy,' fuses the elements usually identified. See Clemen, '*Edward II*' 138; Bevington and Shapiro 263; and Forker's review (85, 86–91).

4. Cf. McCloskey on *Edward II* as 'the odd play out' (35). I do agree that 'Edward's story illustrates ... how circumstances in the world constrain human action and conspire to destroy human agents' (36). McCloskey identifies the loss of 'freedom' as 'the pattern of experience central to his play's meaning' (43), although she does not contextualize that 'story.'

5. See McCloskey, who examines the play's 'divided structure' (37), with 'the play break[ing] ... radically at Gaveston's death' (37, n. 3). On Edward III in the play, see Tyler 61–2.

6. On Marlowe's debt to Shakespeare in *Edward II*, see Forker's review (17–41). Although a few critics supply clues for Marlowe's debt to Spenser, no one has examined the topic.

7. For this thought, I am indebted to Chad G. Hayton, in an unpublished essay, 'Spenser, Marlowe, and the Dangerous Supplement': 'It should not come as a surprise that the traces of Spenser's influence on Marlowe become less visible as he matures as a poet. It would be a mistake, however, to assume that because Spenser's influence is less obvious it is less profound. Rather, we should take more pains to uncover the evidence of Spenser's influence'(3).

8. Lucan's obsession with *libertas* traces to his nostalgic desire to return

Rome to the days of the Republic, where the correlate of the Elizabethan aristocracy, the Roman nobility, reigned sovereign.

9. See Forker: '*Edward II* becomes more than usually significant as a piece of evidence in the ongoing study of Marlowe's perennially discussed but puzzlingly obscure psyche' (86). Greenblatt discusses 'Marlowe's implication in the lives of his protagonists' (*Renaissance Self-Fashioning* 221). In addition to Gaveston (Cartelli 127, 131), critics find Marlowe in Edward (Poirier 185), Baldock (H. Levin 104), the French spy Levune (Archer 80), and Lightborn (Cartelli 133–3).

10. Martindale observes: '*Meaning ... is always realized at the point of reception*; if so, we cannot assume that an "intention" is effectively communicated within any text' (*Redeeming the Text* 3). I am to contextualize Garber's deconstructive model, in which 'the act of writing or signing conveys ... a struggle for mastery of stage and text between the playwright and his inscribed characters' (301). Like Garber, I isolate 'the trope of writing and unwriting' (318), but I veer from her conclusion: that Mortimer is 'ultimately cancelled or slain by [his] own hands: ... by writing against the hand of the playwright' (320). Marlowe's use of written documents may derive from Holinshed, but the playwright alters the chronicler in representing the most important document—the letter containing the Bishop of Hereford's 'sophistical form of words' issuing Edward's murder, which Marlowe assigns to Mortimer: '*Edwardum occidere nolite timere bonum est*' (rpt. in Thomas and Tydeman 368–9; *Ed II* V.iv.11)

11. On Gaveston as intersecting Marlovian 'desire' and 'theatricality,' see Belsey, 'Desire's Excess' 88–9. Bullen long ago noted Marlowe's 'admirably drawn' portrait of Gaveston (rpt. in MacLure, ed., *Marlowe* 139); and Bullen's anonymous reviewer added, '"Edward the Second" might have been called "The Tragedie of Piers Gaveston"' (rpt. in MacLure 145).

12. Two of these conjunctions come from the prologue to *Faustus*, confirming the idea that the Gaveston scene functions as a prologue. Moreover, the *Faustus* prologue also includes an itinerary of works, including *Edward II* (see chapter 9). I respond to Cutts: 'Edward's missive to him [Gaveston] may sound like "Come live with mee ...," but it is not a Jupiter calling for a Ganymede to dangle on his knee. Gaveston likens himself to a Leander swimming across the English Channel of a Hellespont ..., but unlike Marlowe's own Leander, Gaveston *gasps* upon the sand ... Gaveston confounds London in Elysium, however, every bit as much as Faustus confounds Hell in Elysium' (*Left Hand of God* 203).

13. As Emily C. Bartels observes, the effect is to tie the discourse even more to issues of the state (personal communication, April 1996).

14. On this soliloquy, see Cartelli 123–7; and Bartels 167–70. I disagree with Tyler: 'Gaveston ... has elaborate plans for frivolous entertainments to keep "the plaint king" under his influence' (57).

15. For pertinent comments not pertaining to Elizabeth, see Ribner, 'Historical Tragedy' 146–7; Viswanathan 82–3, 89 (n. 6), 92; and Summers, *Christopher Marlowe* 155. Tyler best represents the tendency: 'The structure of *Edward II* ... is a double demonstration of how sexual motives enter the political scene, subvert its proper order, and engender a reaction designed to reassert that order' (64; see also 64–5).

16. See Ashby in his note on Warton's observations: 'It seems somewhat remarkable that Marlow, in describing the pleasures which Gaveston contrived to debauch the infatuated Edward, should exactly employ those which were exhibited before the sage Elizabeth' (rpt. in MacLure, ed., *Marlowe* 65). For a rare comment on the 'parallel between Edward and Elizabeth,' see Archer 77. See also Zunder 53.

17. Many critics comment on the Ovidian origin of this myth in the *Metamorphoses* without recognizing its localizing significance for both Ovid and Marlowe (Weil 161–2, 164; Zucker 170–1; and J. Bate 38–9, who none the less refers to 'the Renaissance reading of the myth as an emblem of the fate of those who peer into the sacred cabinets of princes' [39]).

18. Barkan, *Gods Made Flesh* 46. Barkan explains: 'transformation always succeeds in capturing the human essence of the subject and at the same time in filling us with uncomprehending wonder at the immanence and intimacy of otherwordly powers' (46). For other commentary on the Actaeon myth in the Renaissance, see esp. Vickers; Couliani 72–80; and Enterline.

19. Otis is cautious: 'There is no overt criticism of Augustus and his court (even Actaeon's *error* has probably nothing to do with the error that led to Ovid's banishment), but there is certainly an implicit criticism of Augustan ideology and practice' (145). Otis observes that the 'mention of Actaeon in *Tristia* II, 105 as an analogue of Ovid's own crime (*imprudenti cognita cupa*, 104) is of course suggestive'; he cites M. Pohlenz on the suggestion that Ovid gave to lines 142–3 of the story a 'personal nuance'; then he backs off: 'But the chronology is uncertain: Ovid could have thought of Actaeon as he did without a personal reason' (145, n. 1). In *Redeeming the Text*, Martindale takes Ovid's use of the myth in the narration of his *Carmen et error* seriously (60–2).

20. So Renaissance translators of Ovid thought. Although Ovid in the Exile Poetry relies on several myths to represent his predicament, the translators latched onto the first one Ovid uses: that of Actaeon. See Gower's translation of the *Fasti* (sig. A3^r); Sandys in his 'Life of Ovid' prefacing his translation of the *Metamorphoses* (sig. b1^v); and Catlin's 'To the Courteous Reader' prefacing his translation of the *Tristia* (sig. A3^r).

21. The record includes the comedic version of this construction: the 1587 letter from the Privy Council rescuing Marlowe's MA degree, on the grounds that 'it was not Her Majesty's pleasure that anyone employed, as he had been, in

matters touching the benefit of his country, should be defamed by those that are ignorant in th'affairs he went about' (qtd. in Nicholl 92). Riggs reminds us that the record also includes the tragic version: in a letter of August 1593, Sir Thomas Drury wrote to Anthony Bacon that 'the notablest and vildest articles of atheism [written by Marlowe] ... were delivered to Her Highness, and command given by herself to prosecute it to the full' (rpt. in Nicholl 304; Riggs, 'Marlowe Learns to Write,' MLA Convention, 1995). Nicholl's conclusion to *The Reckoning* resonates with the Actaeon myth: 'the cause of Marlowe's death was a perception—perhaps a momentary perception of political necessity. He died in the hands of political agents: a victim, though not an innocent victim, of the court intrigues that flourished in this "queasy time" of change and succession' (329).

22. In their editions, W.D. Briggs (114), Charlton and Waller (78), and Forker (152) all cite Peele's Edward I, while Rowland cites *The Massacre at Paris* and *Tamburlaine* (94). Yet Marlowe's linking of Phaethon with Caesar constitutes a virtual signature for the translator of Ovid and Lucan.

23. See Sanders 123. Thrice Holinshed describes Edward's behaviour in theatrical terms: Edward 'counterfeited a kind of gravity ... ; forthwith he began to play divers wanton and light parts'; 'the king might spend both days and nights in jesting, playing, banqueting'; and his revenging army is 'more seemly for a triumph' (rpt. in Thomas and Tydeman 351, 352, 356).

24. On Mortimer's theatricality, see Leech, *Christopher Marlowe* 127; and Cartelli 133–4.

25. In his detailed list of Marlowe's borrowings from his colleagues, Bakeless excludes Spenser (2: 27–40). None the less, criticism has turned up several borrowings (citations from the play differ from editor to editor; I cite Gill, ed., *Plays*, but give page numbers for other editions). Schoeneich identifies seven borrowings (99–101), although only the first four look like probable echoes, and only the second of real significance: (1) *FQ* I.vi.2 for Edward's 'wander to ... Inde' at I.iv.50; (2) *Mother Hubberds Tale* 487–99 for Spencer's courtly advice to Baldock at II.i.31–43; (3) *FQ* II.ii.10 for Edward's 'earth ... mother' at III.ii.128; (4) *FQ* III.ix.35 for Isabella's 'channel overflow with blood' at IV.iv.12; (5) FQ II.ix.48 for Edward's 'famous nursery of arts' at IV.vi.17–19; (6) *FQ* III.ii.15 for Edward's 'gentle words might comfort me' at V.i.5–6; and (7) *FQ* II.i.13 for Isabella's 'wrings his hands' at V.vi.18. Steane glosses two passages with 'the Spenser of *The Shepheardes Calender*' (208): II.iv.25–6 and II.ii.61–2. Both Godshalk (62) and Zucker (169) find Acrasia, the Bower of Bliss, and Spenser's idea of bestial transformation in Gaveston's dream of staging the Actaeon myth for Edward. And G. Roberts compares Spenser's use of Circe/Duessa at *FQ* I.viii.14 with Marlowe's use of Circe/Isabella at I.iv.170–4 (433–4). Among editors, W.D. Briggs accepts the first four of Schoeneich's seven borrowings (122–3, 134–5, 158–9, 171), cites Schoeneich 77 on the Spenserian origin of 'Renowmed' at II.v.41 (151), mentions one incidental comparison (144), and introduces one

substantial borrowing: FQ I.v.28 for 'iron car' at IV.iii.42–3 (171). Charlton and Waller accept the borrowings of 'Inde' (89), 'Renowmed' (134), and 'iron car' (160–1), add one incidental comparison with *Mother Hubberds Tale* (136), a potential borrowing of FQ III.i.39 for 'Whilom' at IV.vi.13, and another of *March* 76 and *FQ* I.i.3 for 'earns' at IV.vi.70 (173), but then introduce one borrowing of great significance: *Teares of the Muses* 210 for 'deads the royal vine' at III.ii.163 (146). Forker mentions Spenser twice, citing Charlton and Waller on *Teares* 209–10 for 'deads' at III.ii.163; and Briggs on FQ I.v.28 for 'iron car' at IV.iii.42–3. Finally, Rowland adds three Spenser origins: FQ IV.x.27 and III.xii.7 for 'Hylas' at I.i.43 (94); *Virgils Gnat* 339–44 on 'Tisiphon' at V.i.45 (119); and *FQ* I.x.57 on 'youngling' at V.ii.109 (122). All told, Marlowe critics have turned up around twenty potential borrowings from Spenser, with several significant indeed. These figures are not definitive; Chad G. Hayton discovers two more significant ones: *FQ* I.x.63:1–5 for IV.vi.17–23; and *FQ* I.xi.55: 8–9 for IV.vi.19–22. These figures indicate that at the end of his dramatic career, as at the beginning, Marlowe is contending with his first great precursor.

26. Speculation includes, in the 1928 words of Renwick, 'the names of Shakespeare, T. Wilson, Alabaster, and Sidney,' as well as 'Richard Tarlton,' though Renwick rules out all of these, because none is 'a writer of comedies'; he introduces the possibility of George Gascoigne, who first translated Ariosto's comedy *Suppositi* (210). More recently, Oram sees Willy as Sidney (Oram et al. 277), while Maclean sees a more 'plausible' allusion to Lyly (182).

27. Oram thinks a later date likely—in the early '1590s' (Oram et al. 263, 277n), and Maclean cites 'Thalia's lament and that of Euterpe' as evidence of 'at least' some late revision (182–3).

28. Rowland glosses Marlowe's 'deads' also by referring to 'Marivell's "lively spirits deaded quite" (*Faerie Queene* IV.iii.20)' (111). He means Marinell, and the line comes from canto xii. He could also have cited VI.vii.25. The peculiar usage appears to have been a favourite of Spenser's.

29. On the textual problem of Spenser's 'braunches,' see Smith and de Sélincourt 1: 520.

30. Thomson sees this principle working in 'Shakespeare's English history plays': 'Among the courtiers who watched these in performance would have been many descendants of the Knights and Earls who made up the *dramatis personae*' (28).

31. Spenser's contemporaries used several epithets to describe him and his poetry, but 'sweet' is especially recurrent. Citations with dates in the following catalogue come from Cummings's Critical Heritage volume: 'sweete Faery Queene' (Gabriel Harvey [1592] 53); 'sweete Poet' (Harvey [1593] 55); 'saith most sweetely' (William Webbe [1586] 56); 'sweete brest' (H.B. [1590] 64); 'sweet hunnie vaine' (Watson [1590] 70); 'saith most sweetly' (Francis Meres

[1598] 96); 'Sweete Spenser' (John Weever [1600] 101); 'A sweeter swan ... sweetly of his Fairey Queene he song' (anon., *The Returne from Parnassus* [1606] 116, 117); 'sweet singer' (Richard Niccols [1610] 124); and 'sweet Spencer' (William Browne [1616] 134). Among the list, Robert Salter's note 'Mr. Edmund Spenser' (1626) is historically perhaps the most important, since he transfers the epithet from Spenser's poetry to his person: 'The great contentment I sometimes enjoyed by his Sweete society, suffereth not this to passe me, without Respective mention of so trew a friend' (Cummings 146, n.). In his edition of *Edward II*, Merchant reminds us that the 1594 edition spells the name 'Spencer' as 'Spenser': 'There are some curious features in the speech-prefixes of the texts on which the present edition is based ... SPENCER is spelt Spenser' (5).

32. As noted, Schoeneich and others find Marlowe borrowing from Spenser just a few lines before the 'deads' passage, when Edward speaks of 'earth, the common mother of us all' (128); cf. FQ II.i.10: 'earth, great mother of us all.' Thus, within thirty-seven lines—between the 'earth' and 'deads' passages (128–65)—we can detect four borrowings or allusions to Spenser, to which I shall add two more, bringing the total to six, supplying overwhelming evidence that Marlowe is concerned with Spenser in the 'Spencer' scene. As we shall see in chapter 9, critics find Marlowe imitating the third Spenser passage in *Doctor Faustus*. Further evidence emerges in Schoeneich's discovery that Spencer's advice to Baldock to 'cast the scholar off, / And learn to court it like a gentleman' (II.i.31–2) borrows from *Mother Hubberds Tale*, when the Priest teaches the Fox deception (488–99). Marlowe's lines 'making low legs to a nobleman, / Or looking downward, with your eyelids close' (38–9) resemble Spenser's lines 'look[ing] ... lowly on the ground, / And unto everie one doo curtesie meeke' (498–9). See also Bredbeck: Marlowe's Spencer 'works through the channels of orthodox monarchical power' (73). In this light, Spencer looks to be a photograph of the Spenser who privileges a nationhood of royal power. To complicate things further. I observe that Marlowe's portrait of the theatrical Gaveston appears to be indebted to Spenser's description of the first two masquers in Busirane's Masque of Cupid in *FQ* III.xii.7–8: 'Fancy, like a lovely boy' and 'amorous Desyre, / Who seemd of riper years, then th'other Swaine.' As we have seen, Rowland cites the Hylas reference here for Marlowe's Hylas, and it is not hard to understand Marlowe's attraction to this homoerotic passage. Elsewhere, Sir John of Hainhalt's comment on the game of bidding base, 'We will find comfort, money, men and friends / Ere long, to bid the English King a base' (IV.ii.66–7), may have an origin in the *October* eclogue, when Piers refers to Cuddie's poetic art: 'In rymes, in ridles, and in bydding base' (5). Spenser and Marlowe are referring to the game of Prisoner's base, 'in which a player was safe only so long as he remained at his base' (Merchant 71; on Spenser, see Oram et al. 171). Finally, it seems striking that Marlowe should twice refer anachronistically to the St George legend: 'St. George for England' (III.iii.33, 35). Forker explains the 'anachronism': 'St. George was not adopted as the

patron saint of England until the reign of Edward III' (233); as Merchant puts it, 'This is Marlowe's addition' (65).

33. On Mortimer as a figure for the poet, see esp. McElroy 216, 218, 219.

34. Cf. Tyler: Mortimer's 'principal objection is that Gaveston is low-born (a point stressed by Marlowe but not by his sources)' (57). Voss suggests that 'Gaveston, and later Spencer, come to represent a challenge to the traditional hierarchy of birth which is the basis of the peers' social position and the backbone of the entire English state' (520), but he does not recall that Edmund Spenser repeatedly supports this hierarchy in *The Faerie Queene*.

35. See Sales on Proteus and acting (125–6). On Mortimer's speech, see Summers, *Christopher Marlowe* 166–7. Spenser had linked Proteus with the theater through his portrait of the enchanter Archimago (*FQ* I.ii.10).

36. Poirier links this allegory with vogues in Elizabethan literature but specifically to the one created by Lyly: 'when he [Mortimer] describes the *imprese* chosen by the noblemen, he refers to the custom of his own time and conforms to the vogue of euphuism' (187).

37. In this part of the scene, Mortimer repeatedly accuses Edward of subjecting himself to literariness; see II. 156–9, 176–7, and 187–94.

38. Thurn sees 'a perverse allegory of homosexual rape' ('Sovereignty, Disorder' 136); Bartels notes that Lightborn 'smacks of allegory' (158); and Forker links Lightborn with the 'emblematic figure' of 'good and evil' (88). H. Levin originally suggested that 'Lightborn's name reveals ... "Lucifer"' (101).

39. See Cartelli 133–4. Kocher, *Christopher Marlowe*, remarks: 'the humor of the play ... is summed up and made incarnate in Lightborn' (291).

40. See Bredbeck: the spit 'can be seen as an attempt to "write" onto him the homoeroticism constantly ascribed to him' (76).

M.C. BRADBROOK

Artificial Comedy and Popular Comedy: Shakespeare's Inheritance

1. ARTIFICIAL COMEDY: LYLY

It is not merely because his work, alone among that of early dramatists, survives in fair quantity and in good texts, that Lyly ranks beyond the other comic authors of his day. The plays are still actable, though not often acted.[1] In his own time their significance as a foundation for other men to build upon established them with the poems of Sidney and Spenser. Lyly set a standard, and shaped a model; and his limitations were part of his achievement.

Vigour was the chief virtue of early Elizabethan comedy; what was needed was a strong infusion of order and of grace. This was Lyly's gift, and it came to him in part from the Court Revels.

> Instead of ending an ordinary play with a masque-like denouement, Lyly sheds his compliment over the whole plot. Instead of framing a realistic story in a masque-like induction, Lyly makes his whole action approximate to the symbolic movement of the masque....[2]

Since Lyly's plays partook of the peculiar intimacy of the Revels, he could afford coolness and the reserve of his elaborate style. In revels and masques, actors and audience were literally joint performers for both took part in the final dances, and the chief spectators were often reflected in the slight story which served to support the spectacle and musical shows. Masque was the Elizabethan

From *The Growth and Structure of Elizabethan Comedy*. © 1955 by Chatto & Windus.

form of cabaret; the plays of Lyly, deputy master of the Children of St. Paul's, might be described as a cross between a floor show and a prize-day recitation.

The plays, however, as Professor Harbage has observed,[3] are *not* masques, but were intended to give the feeling of court entertainment to a wider public— though they were written with a special eye to complimenting Elizabeth. If some of the older theories on their 'inner meaning' now appear far-fetched, there is no doubt that at least *Sapho and Phao*, *Endimion*, and *Midas* had such significance. Like *Euphues*, the work on which their author's reputation was chiefly based, the plays also provided a model of elegant speech, and a mirror of manners. The appeal is to a critical and selected few. Negations and prohibitions are important; there is no fighting, no excitement, and no true love, but only wooing games. There is likewise no broad jesting; Lyly, alone among Elizabethan playwrights, observed decorum in the modern as well as the older sense.

The organization of Lyly's comedy depends on the symmetrical grouping of parts; the fable often seems a chess-play with animated chessmen. His role dictates the way in which any one character can move; none can modify, but metamorphosis, like the taking of a piece, transforms the pattern.[4] Women are turned into trees, birds, stones, monsters—ruled by the planets—constrained by the charms of a sorceress, or controlled by an old wise-woman. It is a world in which the rules of movement are fixed, but the powers governing them work arbitrarily. So, in real life, a courtier's role was fixed; his fate depended on luck and the uncertain temper of the great. The debate between Concord and Discord in *The Woman in the Moon* might apply to any of the plays; it is resolved by the goddess Nature, in a truly Lucretian fashion.

> Your work must prove but one;
> And in yourselves, though you be different,
> Yet in my service must you well agree.
> For Nature works her will from contraries.
>
> 1, 1, 26–9

Breaking the pattern by metamorphosis, love potions or other charms, does not make a progressive action: it works like the shift of focus in a perspective puzzle with cubes or pyramids: any visual reading may be reversed. It is no matter which of the two girls in *Gallathea* is ultimately to be transformed into a man, and so the audience is not informed.

Interest is intellectual, not sympathetic; the plays are full of gossip, laced with spectacle; declamation pipes, but passion disappears. Lyly is a lover of phrases, or at most of postures; his efforts to be philosophical end in diatribe, encomium, or backchat.

The form which he evolved is verbal; it is exquisitely phrased for youthful speakers, but not fully dramatic. Like Pygmalion's image, it wants the breath of life. But variety and control in language, and order in construction, were essentials which the drama had hitherto lacked, and these Lyly supplied. Learning joins with old wives' tales; jargon and proverbs with a clear central norm of speech. The earlier plays such as *Sapho and Phao* and *Endimion*, interlace two or three stories very loosely: the characters are hardly connected, and the plays fall into a succession of long tirades. *Midas* and *Campaspe* are Ovidian Romances in dramatic form; but the chatter of witty page-boys, riddles, jests, and songs break up their monotony of style. In *Love's Metamorphosis* and *Gallathea*, which are even more Ovidian, the extraordinary predicaments of the disguised and transformed lovers produce logical dilemmas: the fable now predominates. Even the clowns of *Gallathea* and the familiar setting on the banks of Humber do not destroy the play's artifice; the pace quickens, moving towards fantasy and farce. In the last plays, *Mother Bombie* and *The Woman in the Moon*, lovers, clowns, and pages are strongly contrasted in speech; the writing is richer and more varied than before. There is much more boisterous jesting: Pandora, compared with Midas, is made ridiculous by her transformation. Elegant courtly love is thrust into the background.

Lyly indeed always treats love as a disease which transforms, captivates, and makes its victims absurd. Though inescapable, it is really preposterous. Even when they are taken as models of elegant speech and correct sentiment, the lovers attract no sympathy. *Endimion* and *The Woman in the Moon* are the only plays to satirize women; yet Lyly always supplies the poison and antidote, Amor and Remedium Amoris, together. In his prologues he displays a diffident irony about his own intentions and, perhaps not altogether truthfully, disclaims all purpose of bestowing a shape upon the fancies of his audience.

> Our exercises must be as your judgement is, resembling water,
> which is always of the same colour into what it runneth.

In effect, the artifice and symmetry permit a wide liberty of interpretation. Oxford or Leicester will fit the role of *Endimion* equally well, and both have been discerned. Devotion itself in these plays, 'all breathing human passion far above', may become a symbol for the pursuit of fame or knowledge. As Petrarchan sonnet-form could be applied to education, religion or politics, so that allegory enabled the Elizabethan poet to use it as a formula for the discussion of any important intellectual issue,[5] so by the stiffness of his rhetoric and the rigidity of his fable Lyly cast a matrix, in which the audience could shape what forms they pleased. The symmetry of the sonnet form resembles the symmetry of Lyly's plays; today the effect is not one of flexibility and variety, but rather of consistency and even monotony.

Like the sonnets too, Lyly's drama relies on a façade of complete social assurance. The ultimate aim is self-mockery, achieved through invoking social standards, so inadequate as to be judged in the definition, against feelings so absurd as to be fittingly condemned even by such standards as these. The Sybil's definition of love from *Sapho and Phao* supplies an example.

> Love, fair child, is to be governed by art, as thy boat by an oar: for fancy, though it cometh by hazard, is ruled by wisdom. If my precepts may persuade (and I pray thee let them persuade) I would wish thee first to be diligent: for that women desire nothing more than to have their servants officious. Be always in sight but never slothful. Flatter, I mean lie: little things catch light minds, and fancy is a worm, that feedeth first upon fennel. Imagine with thyself all to be won, otherwise my advice were as unnecessary as thy labour....Be prodigal in praises and promises, beauty must have a trumpet and pride a gift. Peacocks never spread their feathers but when they are flattered, and Gods are seldom pleased if they be not bribed.

This *obbligato* continues for another fifty lines. In its irony and not quite trustworthy assumption of worldliness it may be compared with the attitude of Congreve's Angelica or Wilde's Mrs Allonby.

> She that marries a fool, Sir Sampson, forfeits the reputation of her honesty or understanding: and she that marries a very witty man is a slave to the severity and insolent conduct of her husband. I should like a man of wit for a lover, because I would have such a one in my power; but I would no more be his wife, than his enemy. For his malice is not a more terrible consequence of his aversion, than his jealousy is of his love.
>
> *Love for Love*, 5, 2

> The Ideal Man! O, the Ideal Man should talk to us as if we were goddesses and treat us as if we were children. He should refuse all our serious requests and gratify every one of our whims. He should encourage us to have caprices, and forbid us to have missions. He should always say much more than he means, and always mean much more than he says.
>
> *A Woman of No Importance*, Act II

The artifice of Congreve and Wilde, like that of Lyly, consists in presenting the spectator with what appears to be an authentic glimpse of an impossibly elegant world, which in its simplified outline and heightened speech makes no attempt at naturalism. This Contention between Manners and Passion is a sham fight, for Passion is present only as postulate; the informing mood is sceptical and evasive.[6]

There are later Elizabethan plays which have something of the wit and sparkle of Lyly, such as *Humour out of Breath*: there are others which have only a comparable symmetry, such as *The Wit of a Woman*:[7] but there are none which combine so gracefully an artificial form and a clear governing intention. Lyly, however, scarcely achieves full drama: the plays remain dramatic recitative. Each type of character has its appropriate speech, which is shared with the others of the group. The pages' retorts could be interchanged, as the lovers change their identity or even their sex, or as the gods turn mortal and reassume godhead. Constancy in change, unity in contrast, is the governing structural principle: yet in the final plays there is an approach towards popular form. In *Mother Bombie*, the setting is Rochester, and there is good store of homely proverbs: the play is cut to the English Plautine pattern of *Gammer Gurton's Needle* rather than the Italian Plautine of *The Comedy of Errors*. All the characters are countrified, and the theme is Crabbed Age and Youth.

> SPERANTUS: It is you that go about to match your girl with my boy, she being more fit for seams than for marriage, and he for a rod than a wife.
> PRISIUS: Her birth requires a better bridegroom than such a groom.
> SPERANTUS: And his bringing up another gate marriage than such a minion.
> PRISIUS: Marry gup! I am sure he hath no better bread than is made of wheat, nor worn finer cloth than is made of wool, nor learned better manners than are taught in schools.
> SPERANTUS: Nor your minx had no better grandfather than a tailor, who as I have heard was poor and proud: nor a better father than yourself, unless your wife borrowed a better to make her daughter a gentlewoman.[8]
>
> 1, 3, 7 – 20

The play is not interrupted with shows, such as those of Love's Metamorphosis—Ceres' tree and the delightful Siren who is directed to 'sing with a glass in her hand and a comb'. Lyly's rhetorical artifice now concealed a powerful unifying imagination, which welded together Ovidian, Italian and English tradition. He became the dramatist's dramatist, providing a model both for the youthful Shakespeare and the youthful Jonson.[9]

Both reacted against him, but it was the kind of reaction that presupposes a debt. Long before his death Lyly's achievement was already outmoded and his best work served for a target to the younger wits: but to him in particular the words of a modern writer would apply: 'Someone said "The dead writers are remote from us because we know so much more than they did." Precisely, and they are that which we know.'[10]

2. Popular Comedy: Peele, Greene, Nashe

Lyly at last approached popular drama: the 'merriness' of 'old *Mother Bombie*' became almost proverbial. Meanwhile, the men's companies were putting on plays which embodied much more directly the old traditions of the romances, whether saints' lives or tales of wandering knights.[11] Peele and Greene are the two authors most definitely associated with the attempt to raise popular comedy towards a simple form of art; the one a Londoner, son of the clerk to Christ's Hospital, the other the son of a Norwich saddler, both had reached the Universities, and therefore wrote themselves gentlemen. In their comedies, a variety of experiments proclaimed that comic form was as yet but inchoate. Yet comedy, though fluid, was not amorphous. The work of these men was in a common style which makes it impossible with any confidence to assign an exact contribution to each, and the popular comedy of the eighties is best considered as a whole. The shadowy contribution of Nashe, and the yet more shadowy one of Lodge[12] still leave several plays unfathered. A number were ascribed to Shakespeare, including the most popular of all, *Mucedorus*. These were comedies belonging at the time of publication to Shakespeare's own company; they reflect, however faintly, the popular view of Shakespeare's work; and they place him, where he was placed by Webster, in the line that leads from Peele and Greene to Dekker and Heywood.

In the most shapeless and primitive of such popular plays, Greene's *Orlando Furioso*, some foreshadowings of Shakespeare may be found. Less a gallimaufry than a farrago, this play has often been dismissed as hopelessly corrupt: yet within the popular kind it has a unity of its own—the unity of an old wives' tale. Orlando is a 'wandering knight' [2, 1, 638], one of the Twelve Peers of Charlemagne, and these worthies appear in the final scene, when the disguised Orlando fights with three of them before he is recognized as the man they seek. In the opening scene a parade of monarchs from the four corners of the earth appears to woo Angelica, with pompous Marlovian terms that in each case conclude with the same modest vaunt:

> But leaving these such glories as they be,
> I love (my Lord): let that suffice for me.

Orlando is chosen by Angelica, as his varied conclusion hints he will be.

> But leaving these such glories as they be,
> I love, my lord:
> Angelica herself shall speak for me.

His madness is induced by the wicked Sacrapant's hanging elegies and love poems upon the trees of the grove, which suggest that his lady is unfaithful: it is not as close to *As You Like It* as the opening scene is to the stately wooing of the Lady of Belmont. When her rejected suitors make war upon Angelica's father, and Orlando in the disguise of a poor soldier appears to win the day and to effect Angelica's rescue, as she is about to be executed at the demand of the peers of France, there seems to be a yet more distant glimpse of Posthumous and the sons of Cymbeline. The madness of Orlando, which leads to a good deal of low comedy, is finally dissolved by an unexplained Good Fairy who, appearing in the disguise of a poor old woman, charms him asleep with her wand and proceeds to recite her spell in Greene's best Latin. Orlando himself breaks into Italian, but only in the height of his madness. He beats the clowns, leads an army equipped with spits and dripping-pans to victory, and as a climax enters dressed like a poet, prepared to storm both heaven and hell, comparing himself to Hercules and Orpheus.

This attempt to unite old fairy tales with an Italian plot, scraps of Latin and Italian learning, Spenser, and the fashionable Ariosto, is held together by stage devices, such as the procession of kings—Orlando's rivals—at the beginning, and the combats of the Twelve Peers—his companions—at the end. It has been made without any ambition to impose a general design. The natural harmony lies in the *kind*, which is the fairy-tale;[13] in Lyly, this had been the minor ingredient and the Italianate form had predominated. Here the naïve attempt to put in something for everybody is justified only by the literal treatment of Lyly's theme—Love's Madness. This binds the play together and distinguishes it from such utterly shapeless monstrosities as *The Cobbler's Prophecy*. But it is still very close to the old romance.

The magician Sacrapant from *Orlando* mingles with *The Golden Ass* and legends of the English countryside in Peele's *Old Wives' Tale*, but here, as the title suggests, there is a greater degree of critical consciousness. The play has indeed been sometimes taken as a parody upon the kind of *Orlando Furioso*: but more modern critics have recognized its genuine 'dream quality', its 'fairy-like atmosphere of enchantments and transformation'.[14] In his earlier court play, *The Arraignement of Paris*, Peele had experimented in the adaptation of masque to drama: here he presented a series of riddles, shows, and songs, beautifully and subtly set in the humble frame of a cottage kitchen. Three benighted revellers are sheltered by Madge, the Old Wife whose tale forms the main play.

> ANTIC: Methinks, gammer, a merry winter's tale would drive away the time trimly; come, I am sure you are not without a score.
>
> FANTASTIC: I'faith, gammer, a tale of an hour long were as good as a night's sleep.
>
> FROLIC: Look you, gammer, of the giant and the king's daughter and I know not what: I have seen the day, when I was a little one, you might have drawn me a mile after you with such a discourse.

This is, of course, the Induction of medieval narrative adapted to dramatic form: it is the Dreamer of Chaucer's *Book of The Duchess* and *Parliament of Fowls* triplicated, with an old wife instead of a book to provide the Tale. The tone of the play is suggested by the names of the three revellers. The enchanted Well of Life, with its two golden heads rising from the water, the White Bear of England's Wood, and the dead man who rewards his benefactor, like Hans Andersen's Travelling Companion, are pure fairy-tale: the satire of Huanebango is directly topical: and, rarest of virtues in that age, the whole thing is brief and close-packed. Such delicate balance of diverse elements could be maintained only by a poet with some dramatic practice. Peele wrote for a wide audience: if his sympathies were with the city, for which he devised gorgeous pageants and shows, he could also celebrate the stately ceremonies of the Order of the Garter at Windsor Castle in a dream vision which is entirely in the Chaucerian mode. At the same time his name became attached to an old collection of Merry Jests, the kind which might have been used by countrified Master Silence in his wooing of sweet Ann Page at the humbler end of Windsor Town.[15]

James IV, Friar Bacon and Friar Bungay, and *George-a-Greene* are experiments in Comical History, of which *James IV* is much the most pretentious and least successful. The induction includes fairies and mortals, stoics and frolics; in the main play a patient wife, of the kind familiar in ballads and romances (Griselda or Constance), is subjected to severe trials before she recaptures the affections of the Scottish King. The figure of Dorothea, much praised as the first sympathetic heroine of English tragi-comedy, is a traditional one; the Machievel Ateukin, and the Merchant, Divine, and Lawyer who supply the graver notes, belong to quite a different tradition, and the two are not reconciled.

Friar Bacon and Friar Bungay was popular enough to evoke a second part, the fragmentary *John of Bordeaux*. It is a play of revelry among the country folk of Suffolk, with a good deal of local colour about Bungay, Fressingfield, and Beccles. Prince Edward hands over his part to the Fool, while he goes wooing a country maid. The keyword of the play is 'frolic': it occurs again and again. The king and courtiers make merry in an atmosphere of curds and cream, deer-hunting, and practical jokes; though Robin Hood does not appear, his spirit rules. The rival magicians conjure largely by way of entertainment: the play is full of shows. Friar Bacon's magic glass brings about the death of two Oxford scholars, whereupon he abjures magic, only to resume it in order that the Devil may carry off the Crown to hell, and the play concludes with a resounding prophecy of the birth of Queen Elizabeth.

Against this vivid and very notable medley may be set the ballad-story of *Fair Em, the Miller's daughter of Manchester*, the wretched *John a Kent and John a Cumber* of the ballad-maker Antony Munday, and the even more wretched anonymous *Wisdom of Doctor Dodypoll*, as proofs that plays of conjuring and magic are not as simple of composition as they seem. *Friar Bacon* has the charm of a mixed cottage nosegay; but in *John a Kent and John a Cumber* the bewildering succession of disguises, false spectres, and actions at cross-purpose which sustain the efforts of two Welsh princes to win their brides are so breathlessly crowded upon each other, that the effect is less like a poet's dream than a drunkard's double vision.

The patriotic note is most firmly struck in *George-a-Greene the Pinner of Wakefield*, where all the characters from the centenarian Musgrove to the infant Ned-a-Barley are aflame with heroism: George-a-Greene himself conquers the rebels single-handed, fights a bout with Robin Hood, and lives to feast the king, who in turn honours the Shoemakers of Bradford. In this play the characters have a solidity perfectly in keeping with the lively but well-planned action. There are a number of minor episodes, where the strength, fidelity, and true love of George are shown in turn. Bettris, his love, defines her role ballad-wise in the third speech she makes:

> I care not for Earl nor yet for Knight,
> Nor Baron that is so bold,
> For George-a-Greene, the merry pinner,
> He hath my heart in hold.

At the end of the play, George refuses a knighthood from the king, preferring to live a yeoman as he was born. Sturdy preference for kind hearts rather than coronets is typical of Comical History as a whole, and is always endorsed by the king, who himself relaxes among his subjects, in the style that Shakespeare revives for Henry V on the field of Agincourt.

The fashion of the Comical History was now almost completed. A king or prince revelling and giving his friendship to a particular craft, or a particular town: a strong love interest and a popular hero, magic and horseplay, songs and shows. *The Shoemakers' Holiday* descends from *George-a-Greene*, as *The Merry Devil of Edmonton* does from *Friar Bacon and Friar Bungay*.

A simple definition of comedy is given in the Induction to the popular success *Mucedorus*, where the figure of Comedy is opposed by Envy, who promises in the play martial exploits, severed legs and arms, and the cries of many thousands slain. It sounds indeed as if Envy had originally been Tragedy. Comedy replies:

> Vaunt, bloody cur, nursed up with tiger's sap....
> Comedy is mild, gentle, willing for to please,
> And seeks to gain the love of all estates:
> Delighting in mirth, mixed all with lovely tales,
> And bringeth things with treble joy to pass.
> Thou...
> ... delights in nothing but in spoyle and death.

At the end, this Demon King owns himself defeated by the Fairy Queen, and indeed the play contains nothing more daunting than a bear, which the hero slays as easily as Shakespeare's Orlando slays his lion. Prince Mucedorus is disguised as a shepherd for this feat; in his later disguise of a hermit he slays a cannibal by a cunning device to win his faithful princess Amadine. The clown falls over bottles of hay, runs away with a pot of ale, and keeps up a set of merriments, as well as making all the mistakes possible to the servant of the only villainous character in the piece. This pretty little romance, played before King James by Shakespeare's company, was printed more frequently than any other play of the time. It received additions, apparently at the time of the Poets' War, when Envy was given a poetic ally, a figure shaped in the likeness of Envy-Macilente from *Every Man Out of his Humour*—that is, Ben Jonson, the only begetter of the new satiric comedy.[16] *Mucedorus*, boldly attributed in the third Quarto of 1610 to William Shakespeare, relies simply on the ancient formula of true-love, disguise, wanderings in search of adventure, and 'such conceits as clownage keeps in pay'.

Transplanted into the hall of a great house, and exposed to the criticism of a learned audience, popular comedy dissolved into pageant. Nashe's *Summer's Last Will and Testament*, coming at the very end of this early season of comedy, is more like Spenser's procession of the months than it is like a full-fledged play. Spring with his morris dancers and songs –

Spring, the sweet spring, is the years pleasant king ...

—may play the prodigal, but such figures as Solstice, Orion the Hunter, Bacchus, and Harvest, though they appear in sequence, have none of the dramatic vitality which rules the disorder of *The Old Wives' Tale*. At far too great length, all the seasons are condemned; Summer makes his will to the sound of the dirge

Beauty is but a flower
Which wrinkles will devour,
Brightness falls from the air,
Queens have died young and fair,
Dust hath closed Helen's eye,
I am sick, I must die,
Lord have mercy upon us,

and goes out to the sound of a litany.

From winter, plague, and pestilence, good Lord deliver us.

Only in the figure of Will Summers, King Henry VIII's jester, who provides the Induction and acts as critic, can true dramatic energy be found. Will emphasizes the artificiality of the whole masque: he addresses the actors and tells them how to behave, jeers at their speeches and their roles, mocks the author, and appeals even to the prompter. The voice is that of Nashe himself; it is recognizable even as he comes in, pulling on his fool's coat 'but now brought me out of the laundry'. Here can be seen the first germ of the new critical comedy that appeared only after the great interregnum, of which this play, performed in October 1592 in the seclusion of Croydon, the Archbishop of Canterbury's country house, is a sharp memento. For, at the end of summer, in September 1592, the old order of comedy had come to an end. The Council declared a state of emergency. The plague had struck London: and all theatres were closed. For two long years the players tramped the countryside, acting among the simpler audiences such versions of the London repertories as they could collect. Companies broke, plays were allowed into print; and more important, playwrights disappeared. Marlowe was killed: Greene died theatrically cursing the players: Peele had sunk into illness and was to end by piteously appealing for charity to the deaf ears of Lord Burleigh: Lyly, in his poor lodging within the precincts of St Bartholomew's Hospital, was surrounded by brawling washerwomen and plague-struck inmates: Nashe took refuge first with the Archbishop of Canterbury at Croydon, then in the Isle of Wight with the Hunsdons: and Lodge, who in a later visitation of the plague, as practising physician, was driven to protest against the quacks who battened upon misery, went for a second voyage sailing the coasts of South America with Thomas Cavendish. None of these returned to the writing of plays.

3. THE SHAKESPEAREAN SYNTHESIS

The years 1592–4 mark a crucial turning-point in the history of the Elizabethan theatre. The one playwright who returned to London when at last the Council relaxed their ban was Shakespeare. At the first tentative opening performances of his company in June 1594, four plays were given: *Esther and Ashuarus, Hamlet, Titus Andronicus*, and *The Taming of a Shrew*. These plays were staged far out on the Surrey side, at Newington Butts, a mile beyond Southwark, and after ten days the company departed for their summer tour of the provinces. But hardly had the company returned than theatre building began, and by now not only Henslowe, but also such respectable citizens as Francis Langley, goldsmith by trade and member of the Drapers' livery, began to invest in a splendid new building. It was named the Swan, and stood in Southwark, for in his capacity as citizen and Draper of London it behoved Francis Langley to oppose playacting. Meanwhile, under the eyes of disapproving citizens, something very like two new livery companies emerged. The Chamberlain's Men at the Theatre and the Globe, the Admiral's Men at the Rose and the Fortune, were ahead of all competitors in talent, wealth, and popularity. The one company was led by Burbage, the other by Alleyn: both catered for mixed audiences of courtiers, citizens, and foreign visitors. The Earl of Worcester's Men came in a very poor third.

The two leading companies offered very different conditions to playwrights. It is from the date of his association with the Chamberlain's Men that Shakespeare emerges clearly into greatness. He was their chief writer, a full shareholder; this gave him stability and security; his great series of comedies and histories followed.

Those playwrights who wrote for the Admiral's Men were not in so happy a case. Henslowe, the financier, Alleyn's father-in-law, drove them hard, and they had no voice in the production. About half a dozen authors collaborated, cut down, rewrote, and expanded old plays. Speed was essential. Shakespeare produced two plays a year: Dekker and Heywood each produced about one a month. Their company billed one new play almost every week. The Admiral's kept to the older, simpler style of plot based on legend, folkstory, chronicle, and broadsheet. Later they became Prince Henry's Men, and after his death they soon broke. The kind of tradition they represented had had its day by 1612. The King's Men, as the Chamberlain's had now become, developed new interests at their private theatre, the New Blackfriars; but with Shakespeare's retirement they too had reached the end of an era. The period 1594–1616, the most important phase in English dramatic history, is one in which the old and the new, the traditional and the critical forms of drama grew into each other and through each other. This covers the span of Shakespeare's working life; it is also a period of unparalleled general fertility.

Before the interregnum, Shakespeare appears to have been the Johannes Factotum that Greene so angrily berated. His Lancastrian historics were popular enough; but some of his plays were even more artificial than Lyly's. If Egeon of *The Comedy of Errors* is to us a little too tragic for the Plautine tradition, he is no more so than the heroes of the learned Richard Edwards' *Damon and Pithias*, a play which Shakespeare evidently knew.[17] The elegance of the youthful Shakespeare's work is that of one who aspired to learning, and who inclined towards the great for patronage. After two years of trudging the roads, Shakespeare returned to sink his own interests in those of his company, and to become the poet of *A Midsummer Night's Dream* and *Romeo and Juliet*, plays of lyric beauty and low comedy wherein it is no longer possible to distinguish separate strands of the older kinds of play, for Shakespeare is here creating his own. These two plays are as original in form as his English history.[18] A tragedy which is based on the officially 'comical' and lowly subject of the loves of two private persons, and a May Game which is also artificial, are hybrids. Whether Shakespeare preferred acting to playwriting, as Saladin Schmitt has suggested, or whether he kept his roots in the little Warwickshire town where his family dwelt,[19] he remained a popular writer. If *Mucedorus* were wrongfully ascribed to him, he was capable, even at the end of his career, of refashioning that symbol of barbarity, *Pericles*, to his own ends. His plastic mind, absorbing and transforming the whole comic tradition as it had evolved up to that time,

> cast the kingdoms old
> Into another mould.

In Shakespeare's mature comedy—it is worth remembering that in comedy Ben Jonson put him above the classics—he presents 'a harmonious society in which each person's individuality is fully developed and yet is in perfect tune with all the others'.[20] While keeping to the old principle that comedy portrays characters, he profoundly modified it by deepening and strengthening each separate character, developing the relations between different characters, until the characters *became* the plot.

NOTES

1. *Campaspe* has been beautifully produced at Redlands School, Bristol.

2. Enid Welsford, *The Court Masque* (1927), p. 281.

3. Alfred Harbage, *Shakespeare and the Rival Traditions* (New York, 1952), p. 81.

4. Cf. below, Chapter VI, p. 79. On the physical level, Lyly clearly made full use of the resources of his stage. See, for examples, Richard Southern, *The Open Stage*, p. 110.

5. In this way, the sonnet form replaced the medieval religious allegory, in which almost *any* subject social, personal, or theoretical could be incorporated. It could also, of course, decorously conceal a particular story which might be far from decorous. The interpretations of Lyly's *Endimion* includes possible stories of bloodshed and adultery; my own interpretation of *The Women in the Moon* would link it with the story of Sir Henry Lee and his beautiful but flighty mistress, Anne Vere.

6. These three authors represent the purest artificial comedy of the English stage; it will be noticed that each of their three speeches comes from a woman, and that in Congreve and Wilde, while the romantic values are permitted ostensibly to triumph, neither the sermons of the reformed Angelica nor of the equally angelic Woman of No Importance can be compared with the tartness and vitality with which love is mocked.

7. For *Humour out of Breath*, see below, p. 170: it is about ten years later than Lyly and from Whitefriars. *The Wit of a Woman* is an early Jacobean play: the company is unknown. Its symmetry is of a much simpler kind: a quartet of girls, a quartet of young lovers, and a quartet of amorous old fathers, on the Plautine model. 'It is plotted like a catch', as K. M. Lea observes.

8. Compare the immaturity of *Campaspe*:

> *Sylvius*: Dost thou believe that there are any gods, that thou art so dogged?
> *Diogenes*: I needs must believe there are gods: for I think thee an enemy to them.
> *Sylvius*: Why so?

> *Diogenes*: Because thou has taught one of thy sons to rule his legs
> and not to follow learning; the other to bend his body every way and
> his mind no way.
> *Perim*: Thou dost nothing but snarl and bite like a dog.
> *Diogenes*: It is the next way to drive away a thief.
>   5.1.18–29.

9. Cf. below, Chapter VI, p. 78, and above, Chapter IV, p. 47. Lyly is the only English comic writer mentioned by Ben Jonson in his tribute to Shakespeare prefixed to the First Folio—except Chaucer.

10. T.S. Eliot, "Tradition and the Individual Talent' (*Selected Prose*, ed. Hayward, p. 25).

11. For tales of wandering knights, cf. Chapter II, note 1. The list of lost plays of the seventies and early eighties in Alfred Harbage, *Shakespeare and the Rival Traditions*, pp. 61–62, contains many names which suggest such themes. See also the reading of Captain Cox (Chapter II, note 10).

12. Nashe, son of a clergyman, was at St. John's College, Cambridge, with the other East Anglian, Greene. Lodge was the son of a Lord Mayor of London, and eventually became a landed squire himself. Only one drama by Nashe survives, and none entirely by Lodge; both collaborated in one or two other plays, but their dramatic gifts were negligible.

12a. The plot is that of Italian tragicomedy; it is roughly the same as that of W. Taylor, *The Hog hath lost his Pearl*.

13. See the Life of Peele by R. Horne, *Works*, ed. C.T. Prouty, Yale, 1952, vol. I, p. 90.

14. Peele's city pageants with the nymphs, soldiers, etc. resemble nothing so much as an animated Albert Memorial. The Collection of Merry Jests of George Peele, most of which are old stories, may be compared with the more famous Hundred Merry Tales (cf Benedick's taunt, *Much Ado About Nothing*, 2.1.134), or the Book of Riddles (*Merry Wives of Windsor*, 1.1.229), both aids to conversation much favoured by dull wooers.

15. *Mucedorus* was first issued in 1598, but belongs to the earlier decade. The third Quarto contains the addition at the end of the final exchange of Comedy and Envy which forms part of the War of the Theatres, and seems to be directed against Jonson. Since it emanated from Shakespeare's company, and Shakespeare's name was first associated with the enlarged play, this could have been the purge which he is said to have administered to Jonson. See below, Chapter VII, p. 101.

16. The thrice three Muses mourning for the death of Learning late deceased in Beggary (*Midsummer Night's Dream*, 5.2.52–53) appear in this play mourning for the imminent death of Pithias. See Chapter IV, p. 50. Egeon's adventures with his two sons remind me faintly of the story of that lost play of 'Placy Dacy'

(St. Eustace) which Manly discusses (see note 11 above) and which was given at Braintree, where Udall was vicar in 1534. Egeon is, however, derived from that medieval storehouse, Gower's *Confessio Amantis*.

17. For the idea that Shakespeare invented the English History see F.P. Wilson, *Marlowe and the Early Shakespeare*, Oxford 1953, pp. 106–108.

18. Cf. Chapter IV, p. 53. For Schmidt see note 19 to Chapter IV. Shakespeare lived in lodgings throughout his London career, whereas all the other established actors led highly domestic lives. Indeed, without a household in which a boy could be received, it was impossible for an actor to take a 'prentice.

19. Janet Spens, *Elizabethan Drama*, 1922 p. 32. Miss Spens lays great stress on Shakespeare's debt to festival games and the popular tradition in general. See the chapter 'Munday and the Apocrypha'. Munday wrote for the rival company, the Admiral's.

PAUL J. VOSS

Marlowe, Shakespeare, Spenser, and the Fictive Navarre

Your oaths are pass'd; and now subscribe your names,
That his own hand may strike his honor down
That violates the smallest branch herein.
Love's Labor's Lost (1.1.19–21)

Henry IV's reconversion to Catholicism in July of 1593 stunned many in England and effectively ended the publication of the news quartos from France. The abrupt halt to the reports, once so visible and replete with the very latest international news, largely ended England's fascination with the dashing king. Within weeks, all remaining English soldiers returned home, severing direct military ties with Catholic France. Navarre's coronation some months later received only scant attention in the English press. A lone extant news quarto, *The Order of Ceremonies observed in the annointing and Coronation of the most Christian King of France & Navarre, Henry the IIII. of that name*, covered the elaborate events of 27 February 1594 (see figure 8). The document, a detached and, when compared to the laudatory news quartos, remarkably dispassionate account of the coronation ceremony, neither praises nor condemns the French king per se. The English copy, "faithfully translated out of the French copy printed at Roan," contains much less polemic than previous news pamphlets, and, not surprisingly, no direct mention of the king's recent conversion to Catholicism. By making no allusion to the controversial change of religion, the report sanitizes the entire affair, affirming only that God's will, "having miraculously guided and advanced the king to the lawfull succession of the monarchy," must be observed.[1]

From *Elizabethan News Pamphlets: Marlowe, Shakespeare, Spenser and the Birth of Journalism.* © 2001 by Duquesne University Press.

Navarre's apostasy, however, did not go unnoticed in England; nor was it quickly forgotten. Three of Elizabethan England's finest writers—Christopher Marlowe, William Shakespeare, and Edmund Spenser—each turned Navarre into a character, the *only* historical personage to appear as a character in the writing of all three. This provides a strong testament to a continuing interest in the erstwhile Huguenot. Given the widespread English interest in French affairs, coupled with the charisma and popularity of Navarre, this unique literary nexus comes as no surprise. The characterizations of Navarre become more surprising, however, when closely considered. In each case, the Navarre presented in the literature makes an oath, breaks an oath, and/or explains a broken oath. While oath breaking itself often occurs in Renaissance poetry and drama, the various Navarres found in Marlowe, Shakespeare, and Spenser demonstrate both the singularity of the French king, and the profound effect his promises and broken promises had on Elizabeth and her soldiers, printers and their readers, authors and their audiences. The fictionalized accounts of Navarre, covered by the thin shroud of allegory or the equally pellucid trappings of the theater, stand as a signal event in late-Tudor art, an intersection where history and literature become virtually indistinguishable.

MARLOWE'S NAVARRE

On 1 August 1589, a Jacobin friar named Jacques Clément assassinated King Henry III of France.[2] Accounts of the assassination reached England quickly.[3] Some time after the murder, Christopher Marlowe began writing *The Massacre at Paris*, in which he dramatizes the murder and depicts Henry III, despite a warning from his minion Epernon, receiving the assassin-friar without concern:

> Sweet Epernoun, our friars are holy men
> And will not offer violence to their King
> For all the wealth and treasure of the world.
> Friar, thou dost acknowledge me thy King?[4]

In answer, the friar stabs the king.[5] As Henry III dies, he names Henry of Navarre as his heir. The king curses his enemies and asks Navarre to avenge his death. His final words reflect the bitterness and anger caused by the extended civil wars of religion:

> Navarre, give me thy hand: I here do swear
> To ruinate that wicked Church of Rome
> That hatcheth up such bloody practices,
> And here protest eternal love to thee,
> And to the Queen of England specially,
> Whom God hath bless'd for hating papistry.

$$(25.65–70)$$

Julia Briggs notes a potential irony in the oath for "those in the know." In reality, Henry III did not praise Elizabeth, England, or Protestantism, and he did not plead for vengeance against Rome, but urged instead Navarre's conversion to Catholicism.[6] Despite the (rather significant) departure, Marlowe's play, written and performed in England at a time when thousands of English soldiers traveled across the channel to assist the beleaguered king, ushered in a brief but intense literary preoccupation with French current affairs and the captivating personality of Navarre.

Before dying, Marlowe's Henry III gives one final set of instructions, coupled with a hopeful prayer, to Navarre and his lords:

> Fight in the quarrel of this valiant prince,
> For he is your lawful King, and my next heir:
> Valois's line ends in my tragedy.
> Now let the house of Bourbon wear the crown,
> And may it never end in blood as mine hath done!
>
> (25.90–94)

The hopes of the fictional Henry III notwithstanding, the reign of Henry of Bourbon, King Henry IV of France, began with bloodshed and war. In printed poems, news quartos, ballads, and on the stage, Navarre was indeed the "valiant prince" to English audiences. In Marlowe's play, Henry III dies shortly after his pronouncement, allowing Navarre to stand alone as the hope for a new future in France and a symbol of stronger ties with England. Indeed, in the "unfortunate theater" of real-life France,[7] a France not recreated in Marlowe's play, a renewed cycle of bloodshed and death involved England much more intimately than previous conflicts. Wars between the competing factions were frequent and bloody for the next three years. Thousands of soldiers lost their lives in battle, families were torn apart, and great cities were destroyed. In England, these dramatic events, presented in Marlowe's play and performed at the Rose theater, also found expression in the compelling narratives of the Elizabethan news quartos.

About eight months after Henry of Navarre became the king of France, two friars attempted to assassinate the new monarch. Although this attack resembles that against Henry III in a number of ways, including the involvement of friars, the resolutions do not. A news quarto reports the thwarted attempt against Henry IV:

> And his grace, being setled in his lodging, espied in the chamber of presence three men walking in the habit of gentlemen, whome hee knew not, but his hart gave him that they were not his friends ... These men being uppon the sodaine thus examined not knowing what to answer, kept such a faultering in their wordes, that therby they were suspected of evill, and their countenance declared ... where

uppon they were straight convayed to prison, and there being
narrowly examined, they voluntarily confessed that two of them were
friers of the order of Saint Frances, and the third was a Priest, and
how they were part of the number of twenty and foure that had
conspired and sworne the Kinges death.[8]

The specific third-person account came with a double-page woodcut graphically
depicting Henry observing the execution of the clerics. The impressive woodcut
and the corresponding narrative express the same strong message: traitors to the
king will die. The quarto contains another, more subtle, message as well: Henry
IV (Protestant King of France) is not Henry III (the late Catholic King of
France). Henry IV, God's anointed and protector of the new religion, will prevail
against any and all rebels who challenge a sitting monarch.

This news quarto reports events of June 1590, some months before
Marlowe completed writing his play. Conspicuous similarities exist between
Marlowe's play and the news report from France—two kings, two friars, two
assassination attempts. Marlowe may or may have not read about the attempt on
Navarre's life in the quartos.[9] R. B. Wernham, in fact, places Marlowe in
Flushing shortly after this period, and one "Christofer Marly" may have acquired
his material for the play firsthand.[10] The example does illustrate, however, the
ease with which events in France could move from page to stage—news from one
day became the drama of the next.

Marlowe conspicuously used contemporary French history in his play.
Although few dramatists explored current events on stage, this decision makes
sense, given Marlowe's travels to France, his service in the espionage system of
Walsingham, the time of composition, and his preference for the outrageous.
Vivien Thomas and William Tydeman have noted that recent French history
suited Marlowe especially well:

> He must have been well acquainted with the political and religious
> turmoil in France in this period. He was, in short, well qualified to
> write a play dealing with events so contemporary that, within two
> months of his death, its ending was to be overtaken by the final irony
> of Henry of Navarre's conversion to Catholicism in order to claim
> the throne of France.[11]

The Massacre, the first and only extant French chronicle history play of
Elizabethan England, deviates from the conventions of English chronicle history
plays in significant ways.[12] Unlike other chronicle history plays, the "chronicle"
used by Marlowe was not finished: the refashioning of France literally remained
a work in progress. So while Hall and Holinshed present a largely unchanging
pre-Tudor history for dramatists to adapt and recreate, a history of people long
deceased and events long concluded, the fluid history of France remained a

moving, unpredictable subject for both playwright and audience, a perfect study for a mercurial and unpredictable playwright like Marlowe.

This poses an intriguing question. Why was Marlowe the only Elizabethan playwright to employ contemporary French history for dramatic purposes? Hundreds of news quartos, ballads, essays, and commissioned prayers, not to mention the thousands of English soldiers who traveled across the Channel, demonstrate a prevailing, near-obsessive, interest in the French civil wars of religion. Yet Marlowe alone incorporated, without camouflage or allegory of any type, the religious and political turmoil of France into tragedy. The conspicuous absence of any additional surviving plays covering such a compelling subject suggests that adapting contemporary political affairs into a play carried potential for conflict and was perhaps best avoided. Marlowe's daring and fearlessness, so clearly exhibited in *Dr. Faustus* and *Tamburlaine*, take on another dimension in *The Massacre*.

Unfortunately, the only surviving edition of *The Massacre* raises many more questions about Marlowe's dramatic art than it answers. The corrupt version of the play, likely a memorial reconstruction, compresses seventeen years of French history into about 1250 lines of verse.[13] Curiously, such a short play requires a large number of actors. According to Scott McMillin, the play calls for 20 different speaking parts in the first 500 lines alone; only seven extant plays from the period call for more.[14] The garbled state of the undated octavo hinders both poetical and rhetorical evaluations, but still allows for an analysis of a contemporary English understanding of French history.[15] As many scholars note, the play as printed divides into two sections. Scenes 1–12 depict the St. Bartholomew's Day Massacre of 1572 and scenes 13–24 present events from 1587, concluding with the murder of Henry III in August of 1589. Marlowe obviously wrote the play after August 1589 and prior to his own death on 30 May 1593.

Based upon extant records, *The Massacre* was an extremely popular play when first performed. The Lord Strange's Men initially performed the play at the Rose Theater in January 1593. McMillan believes that this company "courted controversy and sensation more willingly than any other company of the 1580s and 1590s." The Lord Strange's Men often staged "drastic plays—drastic in dramaturgy and in political boldness, for they seize on controversial subjects and vivify them with new techniques of stagecraft that could not help but draw crowds."[16] This strategy obviously worked well with the intended audience. According to H. S. Bennett, although an outbreak of the plague closed the theaters a few days after the initial performance, the play grossed 3 pounds, 4 shillings, the highest of the season and nearly three times the average taking.[17] Given the extraordinary interest in the French wars and the attractiveness of the charismatic Navarre, this popularity, and the Lord Strange's willingness to stage the play, can be expected. Indeed it is odd that such an important and high profile turn of events did not spawn more plays.[18]

Like the real war across the channel, the action quickly turns bloody in The Massacre. Marlowe uses a variety of means, including poisoning, strangling, shooting, and stabbing, to effect 18 murders on stage. The deaths include the infamous slaughter of French Huguenots (witnessed by Sir Philip Sidney), the assassination of Henry, Duke of Guise, and the assassination of King Henry III, all of which occur prior to the accession of Henry of Navarre. Most of these events were reported in varying detail in both French and English pamphlets, and Marlowe obviously followed the events with interest. Penny Roberts argues that "Marlowe's depiction of events in France remains surprisingly true to the historical record" while it "acts as both a lesson and a warning to monarchs of the consequences of their actions."[19] Paul H. Kocher also traces the influence the early pamphlet literature had on Marlowe's play. Kocher suggests that Marlowe, in constructing his plot, "kept quite close to the facts of French history as the Protestants understood them." Kocher estimates that 50 pamphlets were written prior to Marlowe's death in 1593, but he makes no distinction between the political essay and the news quarto, or between French and English pamphlets. However, Kocher implies that Marlowe read the English versions, which were universally pro-Protestant, rather than the French pamphlets, many written by supporters of the Catholic League.[20]

Julia Briggs questions Kocher's analysis and his reading of the play as a piece of blatant Protestant propaganda. Briggs believes the play treats the murder of the Duke of Guise, the most visible member of the Catholic League prior to his death, with greater sympathy than acknowledged by Kocher. Briggs rejects reading the play solely as a polemical harangue directed at Rome. She contrasts the various acts of bloodshed between the Catholic and Protestant factions: "The rabid attacks on Catholics, Rome, and the Pope with which the play ends rather resemble a compulsive reopening of unhealed wounds than a pious manifesto for the future."[21] Debora Shuger agrees, arguing that "the Protestants are either helpless victims of prelatical malice or, in Coligny's case, no less cruel than their Romanist adversaries. As in the passion narratives, both villains and heroes deconstruct into interchangeable victims and avengers."[22] Indeed, to an audience in 1594, whether Protestant or Catholic, the cruel murders of the Huguenots, the Duke of Guise, and Henry III must have seemed in vain, for France once again served a Catholic king. Despite considerable bloodshed, the promise of a new France was momentarily thwarted.

Clearly, contemporary French history taught, warned, and informed English readers and theatergoers; English thinkers urge others to learn from the French conflict.[23] One contemporary document expresses just this belief: "The afflictions of France, may be Englands looking glasses, and their neglect of peace, our continuall labour and studie how to preserve it."[24] In 1594, Robert Persons also cautioned that England might suffer from civil strife similar to France's after Elizabeth's death.[25] The pages of the quartos continually use the crisis in France as an example for the English nation to avoid. Taken together, the warnings and cautionary tales juxtapose France and England in revealing ways. Many quartos begin with a brief homily against rebellion and disobedience. Authors frequently cite the miseries of Paris as effects of disobedience: "I coulde doe no lesse but lay it open to the view of the whole worlde that all the Cities in Christendome may take example by the same, and feare hereafter to attempt the like inhumane, unnatural, and most ungodly actions."[26]

Marlowe's use of French history in *The Massacre*, while direct, causes some confusion. It is quite clear, however, that Marlowe emphasizes Navarre's vow. The play, in fact, begins and ends with an oath spoken by Navarre. The initial oath, Navarre's marriage vows with Margaret, sister of then French King Charles IX, provides historical context and perhaps a bit of irony given the notorious philandering of Navarre.[27] Charles begins the play by calling attention to the ceremony:

> Prince of Navarre, my honorable brother,
> Prince Condy, and my good Lord Admiral,
> I wish this union and religious league,
> Knit in these hands, thus join'd in nuptial rites,
> May not dissolve till death dissolve our lives.
>
> (1.1–5)

Navarre responds to this wish affirmatively, stressing that he too is bound:

> The many favors which Your Grace hath shown
> From time to time, but especially in this,
> Shall bind me ever to Your Highness' will,
> In what Queen-Mother or Your Grace commands.
>
> (1.9–12)

Whether Navarre's initial vow-making created for the audience an immediate association with historical events (in this case Navarre's known perfidy) is difficult to ascertain. Navarre's second vow certainly did.

The final words of the play, also a vow spoken by Navarre, express a more resolute, more current, and more "English" sympathy aimed directly at an English audience:

> Come, Lords, take up the body of the King,
> That we may see it honorably interr'd;
> And then I vow for to revenge his death
> As Rome and all those popish prelates there
> Shall curse the time that e'er Navarre was king
> And rul'd in France by Henry's fatal death!
>
> (24.106–11)

The strong declaration, coming as it did initially in a January 1593 performance, complements the valiant Navarre of the news quartos. The words "I vow for to revenge his death" would have carried great force, especially given the numerous battles (using thousands of English soldiers) being fought for just such a cause at that very moment. The speech and the positive, patriotic ending may help account for the large audience, for both the quartos and the play enjoyed a marked popularity.

Despite the overwhelmingly strong support for Navarre in 1592/93 and the commercial success of the play, some critics view the fictional Navarre as "ambiguous" and a "problematical figure."[28] Leech believes it difficult to accept Navarre's oath that ends the play with "full seriousness."[29] These comments may reflect an ahistorical bias not apparent to Marlowe or his audience at the time of the writing. Perhaps we see Navarre as "ambiguous" or "problematical" because we know the subsequent record of his actions. We do not take his vows seriously because we know that Navarre did not keep them himself. However, it cannot be assumed that Navarre's future conversion creates ambiguities in the character as Marlowe penned it. To state that "by the end of the play all the protagonists but Henry IV are dead" and "[o]nly then can a solution to the religious troubles be found in the final and decisive political expedient, the king's conversion," confuses history and drama.[30] The play does not and could not depict Navarre's final conversion; nor does it endorse the notion of a "final and decisive" action. Moreover, as the following discussion of Spenser makes clear, the conversion itself, seen by some of Navarre's contemporaries as nothing more than "temporizing," certainly did not end all questions about the mercurial king. The final scene of the play, whether spoken and acted initially in 1593 and 1594 or in revivals in 1598 and 1601, in no way provides closure to the events.

It is important to see Navarre as the framing figure, both literally and figuratively, for the entire play. While the play begins with Navarre's marriage, it ends with Navarre's vow of revenge. Ultimately, Navarre stands as the lone survivor in a play of death. Kirk sees Navarre's final speech as a new union "openly swearing vengeance" against the Catholic League. Kirk argues that "with Queen Elizabeth symbolically present in the silent English agent, his vengeance is authorized and sanctified." Kirk does not explain how the silent English agent, a messenger of little note, authorizes or sanctifies such a pledge, nor does he suggest why either the historical or the fictitious Navarre needed any authorization or sanctification for such a vow. He did need Elizabeth's troops and money to be sure, but his quarrel with Rome or the Catholic League needed little authorization: Navarre had to defend himself or convert. Kirk sees the role of the English agent as controlling the French chaos and disorder: "Through the English agent, the *Massacre* recontains French disorder and this alternative view of French history."[31] But only for so long. Navarre's forthcoming conversion throws everything, once again, into a state of flux. The play actually accrues new meaning as a result of Navarre's actions.

According to Thomas and Tydeman, the scene "may well be interpreted as a dispassionate ironic comment on the cruel fanaticism of both sides."[32] While plausible, the comment does not note the additional layers of irony associated with the conversion or link the suddenly broken vows of the play with other remarkably similar vows in English literature. Moreover, it neglects the protean nature of the play—a play able to change its very meaning. The play as written and initially performed differs sharply from the play performed some months later; the ending to *The Massacre* actually changed *without* changing. When Marlowe finished the play, certainly prior to his death on 30 May 1593, the historical Navarre valiantly struggled to uphold both the oath and the promise proclaimed over his dying predecessor as the play concludes: Life continued to follow Marlowe's script. The reports back in England, fulfilling the vow made at the play's end, depict a valiant prince trying to destroy the Catholic League, defeat Philip II, and seek revenge on Rome. But within months of Marlowe's death, Navarre's conversion actually rewrote the ending of the play for the now-silent dramatist, adding a bitterly ironic dimension.

The ending of the resurrected play, dramatizing the now-broken oath of Navarre, silently registers the fractured alliance between England and France. It would be some years before the oath-breaking ceased to cause controversy. Unlike Shakespeare's comic rendering of a broken vow by Navarre in *Love's Labor's Lost* or Spenser's frank yet sympathetic treatment of Navarre's apostasy in book 5 of *The Faerie Queene*, Marlowe's final understanding of the unfulfilled promise remains a mystery. Audience reaction to any given play is never fixed, never certain, never predictable. Reaction and understanding may evolve or transform with time. It should be noted, however, that very few plays actually change without changing to the extent of *The Massacre at Paris*. Seeing the play in early 1593 would be a much different experience, a much different play even, than seeing the "same" play some months later. Recent events guaranteed a different audience reaction, a reaction partly governed by the conversion itself.

In a richly Marlovian fashion, the very instability of the ending can only be determined at a future date by an audience not yet imagined by the author. Leech says of the play's ending that "the world of the play is brought into juxtaposition with the world of the audience."[33] Actually, the very juxtaposition itself underwent change. It bears repeating that the "world of the audience" in 1594, an audience in an ever-changing world, understood the nature of Navarre's vows differently from an earlier audience. Perceptions, allies, hopes, and religions changed with palpable intensity during the intermission. Only an audience living during the summer of 1593, an audience invested in the fortunes of Navarre's oath, an audience of soldiers and parents of soldiers, of aristocrats and government officials involved in the war, could fully respond to such a sincere vow or to such a broken oath. Repeat performances and large ticket sales suggest a greater than usual interest in the play well into 1594; news of Henry's conversion to Catholicism and the return of the English soldiers during the previous year would provide an immediate network of advertisements for the play. Revivals in 1598 and 1601 continued to draw interest and spark controversy, suggesting an ongoing interest in French politics.[34] Without knowing it, Marlowe became the "experimental dramatist" he so often seems, in a manner even Marlowe himself could not have anticipated.[35] When considering the ending to Marlowe's play, one can only wonder if members of the audience laughed or cried, smiled or frowned, rejoiced or despaired at Navarre's final vow.

SHAKESPEARE AND THE NEWS QUARTOS

Shakespeare's *Love's Labor's Lost* serves as an excellent contrast to Marlowe, both in presentation and commentary. Whereas Marlowe presents the action largely stripped of fantasy or allegory, Shakespeare generally ignores the historical Navarre, creating rather an ironic and hypocritical comic figure while still exploring the effects of oath making and oath breaking. Yet Shakespeare's dependence on the news quartos seems more direct than Marlowe's; while Marlowe focused on intrigue and the character of Navarre, Shakespeare seems to be commenting, obliquely at least, on the entire presentation of news from France. Locating the precise documents that influenced Shakespeare gives new energy to both source studies and literary topicalism.

Shakespeare set many of his plays in exotic locations. Few of his non-history plays were set in England; most were set in Italy or elsewhere on the continent. Two comedies have French settings, *Love's Labor's Lost* in the court of Navarre, and *All's Well That Ends Well* in Roussillon, Paris, and Marseilles. *Love's Labor's Lost*, written about the time the French wars raged, captures little of the bloodshed and misery found in real life. The disjunction between the horrific and the comic merits examination. R. W. David, editor of the original Arden edition of the play, notes that "[n]o written source is known from which the plot might have been borrowed; there is, however, some reason to think that such a source did exist but is now lost. For every other play Shakespeare is known to have used some documentary original."[36] The absence of any surviving source, while causing concern for some students of the play, creates the artificial impression that the play exists free from a specific historical context. But despite its fictive status, *Love's Labor's Lost*, which uses names of well-known, living persons, is thoroughly grounded in a unique historical epoch—an epoch largely defined by the news quartos from France.

Shakespeare, like Marlowe and Spenser, used contemporary, living figures sparingly in his writings. In fact, only one play in the Shakespearean canon, *Love's Labor's Lost*, contains the names of persons actually living during the writing and performing of the play. Although some critics dismiss this nominal correspondence as trivial, the names of the male protagonists in *Love's Labor's Lost*, like significant names in other plays (e.g. Malvolio, Dogberry, Mistress Overdone, and Horatio), are important.[37] Given the extensive cultural interest in the French wars, not to mention the hundreds of printed texts describing the convoluted political scene, the names were undoubtedly familiar to most Elizabethans: King of Navarre (Henry not Ferdinand); Berowne (Armand de Gontant, Marshall Biron); Longaville (Henry of Orleans, the Duke of Longueville); Dumain (Charles of Lorraine, the Duke of Mayenne); Marcade (the Duke of Mercoeur); Boyet (Boyset, leader of the Huguenot forces). Allusions to a Holofernes, often dismissed as merely a stock character, also appear in tracts about Navarre, Mayenne, and the French civil war.[38] Both Navarre and Mayenne received considerable exposure in the quartos. Biron, described as "that valiant soldier & honorable man at armes," and Longaville also appeared in numerous quartos and other sources.[39] Scholars have long recognized the contemporary origins of the names, but few fully plausible explanations have been put forth.

Historical studies based upon source materials were once quite common. While Geoffrey Bullough's work remains valuable, such studies now appear infrequently, and some scholars discredit the attempts.[40] Recently, however, source studies have once again appeared. Graham Bradshaw, for example, states that looking at departures from source material can lead to very productive questions, which may lead to equally productive answers: "Noticing such departures can alert us to things in the play we had not noticed, and common sense suggests that they can provide a guide to dramatic intentions ... not to what we must think, but to what we are being given to think about."[41] Bradshaw's prudent remarks illustrate what is already accepted. Shakespeare often borrowed plots, characters, even entire passages from sources like Plutarch, Holinshed, and Ovid. Recognizing such borrowings and significant departures, additions, and omissions, offers a door into the mind of the dramatist. Yet such doors may close as well as open understanding. Recognition and proper appreciating of a topical allusion stands as a double-edged sword.

David Bevington, and more recently Richard Levin, notes the dangerous excesses that plague many source studies and topical readings. Bevington chronicles the "inglorious" history and often misplaced efforts of such literary detective work.[42] Equating dramatic characters with historical personages, whose identities can be determined only by unraveling mysterious clues and subtle allusions, too often produces a tangled web of suspect value. The evidence collected by Frances Yates in *A Study of Love's Labour's Lost*, while impressive, serves as a reminder of the dangers of too exact a topical reading. Yates creates a labyrinth of allusions and allegories, finding exact historical analogues to *all* characters and events in the play. Yates begins with the assumption that "Shakespeare, as a topical dramatist, is always indirect and subtle, never obvious and crude."[43] As Bevington points out, this assumption, while demanding an equally indirect and subtle *modus operandi*, creates a host of problems. Moreover, such a method asserts, curiously, that the names actually given by Shakespeare to the characters, apparently too "obvious and crude," are less meaningful than names *not* actually present in the drama, names uncovered only through diligent study. The search for mysterious topicalities, still with mixed results, continues.[44]

Levin also cites common problems associated with "a more prominent branch of the old historicism known as topicalism, which tries to show that a literary work is designed to allude to actual people or events of the time that are not presented in it." Levin demonstrates a major flaw in the numerous attribution studies. Simple enumeration, merely finding all the positive similarities between, say, Polonius and Lord Burghley, can be of use only if the analysis also considers differences in characterization as well. According to Levin, "an approach that simply enumerates ... positive evidence is thus fatally flawed, no matter how many items it enumerates."[45] Without considering the "negative evidence," enumeration alone becomes a self-confirming rather than a self-correcting system. Further, a topical reading that merely finds passing similarities between the character and the individual, especially correspondences that may be attributed to large numbers of people (like fathers who impart advice to their sons), has severe limitations for literary analysis.[46]

In this sense, *Love's Labor's Lost* is not a topical play at all. The play freely provides the names of the characters, complete with the setting in France, to the audience. No secret puzzles need solving; no mysterious allusions need identification. In other words, a literary analysis that considers the currency of these names, the concerns of the playwright, the attitudes of the audience, and the prevailing cultural ethos is not a topical analysis per se. In another sense, however, *Love's Labor's Lost* stands as Shakespeare's most topical play. It is difficult, in fact, to image how the play, whether written and revised in 1589, 1592, or 1595, could avoid being topical. How could a dramatist, for example, set a current play in Washington, D.C., mention prominent world leaders and adversaries, and still remain untopical? Would it be possible to stay wholly off topic and ahistorical using such important and widely recognized names? How could an audience watching the play in the 1590s condition themselves to ignore completely the dominant culture, church sermons, printing press, and ongoing events in France?

If, as Stephen Greenblatt suggests, one aim of literary criticism is to "enable us to recover a sense of the stakes that once gave readers pleasure and pain,"[47] the topical, or recognition of important, even life and death matters circulating within a given culture, must be explored. What about the play gave the audience pleasure and pain? Any number of variables. Could the depiction of Navarre and the bittersweet history surrounding the French King, be free from all irony, all editorializing, all conflict? Modern theories and common sense tell us no. According to the old historicism, it remains the job of scholars and critics to reconstruct, as nearly as possible, the rhetorical, philological, and dramatic techniques of the author, which, in turn, allow for greater appreciation of any given piece of literature. According to the new historicism, it remains the job of scholars and critics to be sensitive to all aspects of the play, the conspicuous and the less so, while focusing upon the various cultural forces at work in literary production. For both old and new historicists, part of that work concerns the historical record as Shakespeare and his audience understood and experienced it.

While Louis Montrose perceptively asserts that "Shakespeare's comedies insist upon their fictive status,"[48] any historical or new historical analysis of *Love's Labor's Lost* needs also to consider Shakespeare's decision to use names of such visible (and *living*) persons as Navarre, Biron, Longaville, and Mayenne in the play. The fictive and the factual can coexist; bridges often span the historical and the literary. As discussed below, Spenser directly, if apologetically, addresses the controversy surrounding Navarre's broken oath and conversion. Not insignificantly, Shakespeare's play also directly addresses the role of oath making and oath breaking. Andrew Kirk does not recognize this important component when he suggests that *Love's Labor's Lost* "merely adopts names from contemporary French historical figures."[49] By "merely" adopting the names, Shakespeare also adopted, to some extent, the accumulated actions associated with the names. As no characterization exists in a vacuum, the actions of Navarre and company need to be considered in relation to other representations also in circulation. No single source mentions the characters more prominently than the news quartos.

Love's Labor's Lost, with its many contemporary allusions, has long puzzled critics. Perhaps such difficulty stems from a confused historical context. While the quartos may not explain every facet of this complex, even ambiguous play, consulting the quartos may answer some troubling questions and dismiss some unpersuasive speculations. One such speculation should be discounted immediately: Despite the frequency of inside jokes and erudite puns, the play was not written exclusively or intended primarily for a coterie audience or members at court. Although the title page to the 1598 quarto of the play proclaims that the play was "presented before her Highnes this last Christmas," the evidence strongly suggests a more popular audience. In fact, interests that apply to large groups of people, allusions that mention current events, and the existence of more "universal" themes like the battle of the sexes or courtship rituals, make *Love's Labor's Lost* one of Shakespeare's most "popular" plays. Considering both the sources and contexts, any audience watching the play in a public theater in the 1590s would know more about current French politics than about other source material used by Shakespeare, including fourteenth century English history, Plutarch, or Ovid. The names of Navarre, Dumain, Longaville, and Berowne would be more recognizable than Hippolyta, Troilus, Shylock, or Sir Topas. Moreover, this audience would recognize a departure from a current source more easily than from the chronicle histories of Hall and Holinshed. It is also likely that Shakespeare, an "upstart" playwright in the early 1590s, would capitalize upon the widespread interest in France to attract an audience. How the young Shakespeare, a relative outsider to the workings of London, could begin writing for the more select audience of the coterie theater is more difficult to explain, especially when no coterie theaters existed between 1591 and 1598.

Aware of the conspicuous use of well-known names, many scholars attempt to date and read the play in light of French politics.[50] While the news quartos alone cannot date the play, they do provide evidence helpful in correcting mistaken assumptions. H. B. Charlton, whose essay remains a most thorough attempt to date the play, places composition in the later part of 1592. However, Charlton's flawed presupposition that English interest in the French wars peaked with the largely unspectacular Essex expedition of 1591/92 unduly influences his conclusions. The expedition, while closely followed at the court, received little attention in the popular press: only one news quarto chronicled the largely unsuccessful mission. If the Essex voyage marks the apex of public interest in the French wars, printers and publishers of the news quartos and other written matter failed to capitalize on this interest. Prior to the expedition, Charlton argues, public interest in the wars would not, could not, and did not justify the writing of a play starring Navarre and company. To support his conclusions, Charlton relies on the works of Harvey and Nashe as indicative of the popular tastes of Elizabethan society. While both men were deeply steeped in the literary culture, selecting Harvey and Nashe as *the* barometer of public interest is misleading. Charlton believes that "casual references" by either Harvey or Nashe in print support a post-1591 composition date: "We do not believe that English interest in the war was at this time [from late 1589 to mid 1591] sufficiently compelling to suggest any topical reference ... Neither the English populace nor the English court felt themselves concerned vitally: throughout 1589 and 1590 their interest was lukewarm."[51] Charlton's subjective criterion aside, extant documentation suggests a high level of English interest in France during all 1589, 1590, and early 1591. If publication after publication counts as evidence, the printers and publishers selling scores of quartos, sermons, prayers, and ballads did not gauge public interest to be "lukewarm" during those years.

Many quartos were printed in the 18 months prior to Essex's departure; Elizabeth had already sent thousands of English troops to aid Navarre. The pamphlets themselves, even excusing the hyperbole surrounding the reports, already see the importance of the conflict in a larger context. One early pamphlet from 1590, months before Charlton sees any "compelling" interest, describes Navarre's improbable victory over Mayenne and the Catholic League at Ivry in bombastic terms:

> The battle is so famous and memorable, that it is well worthie to be set forth in writing, & that this writing be confirmed with good testimonies. For otherwise the truer that the things shall be, the less credit will be given thereto.[52]

The document establishes, as do a large number of other quartos, poems, ballads, and songs written prior to the Essex departure, strong public interest in Navarre and the French wars.[53] G. B. Harrison's *The Elizabethan Journals* claims to be a "record of those things most talked about during the years 1591–1603."[54] The *Journals* contain dozens and dozens of entries for France, Navarre, and the French civil wars of religion. In fact, few if any topics between 1591 and 1594 generated more discussion, rumor, speculation, conjecture, or surmise than French politics. Such extensive coverage undermines Charlton's statement that "we shall hardly expect—and in fact, do not find—casual references to the French wars before the end of 1591."[55]

Consideration of the news quartos challenges another of Charlton's main arguments. He states that because Henry's army broke before the larger force of Parma in the summer of 1592, Henry, for the first time, "arous[ed] English sympathy" (264). Certainly this was not the case. Henry received both English attention and sympathy, not to mention great amounts of money and soldiers, well before the summer of 1592. Therefore, Charlton's assessment that "we may say that the summer and autumn of 1592 marked the highest level of English public interest in the French wars" is questionable (264). Public interest can be measured in a number of ways, but extant records found in the news quartos should be considered a more substantial indicator of public opinion than scattered allusions found in Harvey and Nashe or undocumented discussions in taverns or inns.

The inclusion of Dumain and the brief appearance at the end of the play by Marcade (the hated Duke of Mercoeur in the reports) in the company of Navarre, Biron, and Longaville are curious. Mayenne despised Navarre and fought him for the duration of the war, including the early battles at Arques and Ivry. No extant records suggest a friendly meeting of the enemy soldiers before, during, or after the date of the play. Why did Shakespeare use Dumain as a character? One handbook contains an interesting but dismissive passage:

> The Due de Mayenne, well known in Shakespeare's London for his role in the French Wars of Religion, is usually thought to have provided the name Dumaine. Unlike the originals of Longaville and Berowne, he was not an aide to the historical King of Navarre; rather, he was a principal enemy of the insurgent monarch, but this inconsistency would probably not have bothered either the playwright or his audience.[56]

The entry, while correct in its broad outlines, does not explain why Shakespeare used the name of a known enemy, often depicted as evil in the news quartos, in a comedy of love. Many English soldiers died fighting against Mayenne. Merely asserting that such an "inconsistency" did not bother an original audience fails to engage the issue. How, for example, could this indifference be accurately determined? Perhaps the grouping intrigued, confused, or angered the audience. Perhaps Shakespeare was making a political statement of his own. Such musings could be important.

Hugh Richmond also considers the inclusion of Dumain in the play. Richmond believes "Dumain" was mistakenly used by Shakespeare for General D'Aumont, a trusted general in Henry's army:

> The other uncertain identification among the lovers is Dumain, who cannot be the duc de Mayenne, as is sometimes asserted, for he was universally known and hated in England as the leader of the Catholic Guise faction against whom Henri and his troops were fighting. However, in many dispatches to England, we do find three names frequently recur among the King's wars council: Biron, Longueville, and d'Aumont.[57]

The hypothesis, however, remains unconvincing. The "many dispatches to England" cited by Richmond are all culled from one source, Antony Colynet's *The True History of the Civill Warres of France* (1591). Colynet's book, not really a "dispatch" at all, should be considered a more unlikely source for information than the thousands of quartos in circulation. Moreover, Mayenne was, as Richmond notes, well-known and quite universally despised by Protestants in England and ridiculed by some Catholics in France.

Other scholars posit a different source of information. Charlton asserts the primacy of oral testimony: "In Shakespeare's day the most obvious source of French news for both him and his audience would be the talk of the returned soldiers."[58] The speculation that returning soldiers provided the most obvious, accessible, and accurate reports to the folks back in London remains dubious. The vast majority of the conscripts from the Essex expedition (where accurate records still exist) came from shires outside of London; few returning soldiers needed to set foot in the city.[59] Even if returning soldiers mispronounced the name of d'Aumont, or Shakespeare consulted the text of Colynet, the myriad reports depicting Mayenne by name make the speculation all the more improbable: with so many documents containing the name of both Mayenne and d'Aumont, what accounts for the confusion? The quartos were too prominent and the wars too significant for such an "error."

A likely source exists that places Mayenne in the company of Navarre, Biron, and Longueville. At least three news quartos contain the names of the four primary characters from *Love's Labor's Lost* in the same report.[60] No one, to my knowledge, mentions the specific quartos that directly link the key names together.[61] The names of the characters surviving in a single document should put to rest the speculation about d'Aumont. Shakespeare's use of Dumain, no accident or misconstruction, should be considered an integral and intentional part of the play. Moreover, two of the quartos containing the names were printed in early 1590 and chronicle the famous battle of Ivry, well before Charlton or others see any English interest. This could easily place the moments of English interest and the composition of the play (if composition and public interest are linked in a causal manner) much earlier, around the summer of 1590 and well before the Essex expedition. Based upon source considerations and historical conditions, an earlier date of original composition of the play (i.e., mid-1590) cannot be discounted.

Perhaps the accepted division of three good guys (Navarre, Berowne, and Longaville) and one bad guy (Dumain) needs reformulation. This grouping, often troubling to critics, elides a more nuanced and historically accurate understanding of the characters. Although fighting against the Catholic League, Longueville, a loyalist Catholic, also served under Henry III and grew increasingly weary of the noncommittal Navarre.[62] Biron and Henry differed on many issues, including payment of soldiers and military strategy. Mayenne stood as the most visible member of the Catholic League. Taken together, the characters delineate a wide spectrum of political and religious opinions. They represent the divisions "so many and so intricate" mentioned by Francis Bacon in his assessment of the French civil wars, from the staunch Catholic to the ardent Protestant, led, not surprisingly, by the most mutable and changeable of men, Henry of Navarre.[63]

Shakespeare's experimental drama, or perhaps "imaginative journalism," might actually be suggesting a way to end the wars—with poetry and not pikes, sonnets not swords.[64] The instruments of war in the battle of sexes—poetry and flattery—are less destructive than other forms of artillery. Though romantic war replaces religious war, the combatants in both arenas strive for victory. The targets of the barbs in the play, all the male parties involved with the wars, need to learn a lesson. The literary war between the sexes, like the civil war raging in France, does not end in the play. Berowne's famous lines—"Our wooing doth not end like an old play; / Jack hath not Jill: these ladies' courtesy / Might well have made our sport of comedy" (5.2.866–68)—emphasize the failed negotiations of the lovers. The one year period, a romantic detente, must be observed before any marriage takes place. Distinct from all other comedies written by Shakespeare, the play provides no happy ending, no feast of celebration, no consummation.[65] While this lack of resolution often puzzles critics, it does more than merely challenge generic definitions: it mirrors the ongoing battles in France quite accurately, although quite differently than Marlowe. While the play may not be exactly a "work in progress," the relationships between the characters, like the peace negotiations and ongoing battles, certainly were.

The names of the characters should be considered as they exist in the play and not explained away as if they were an accident. Moreover, the combination of enemies and the array of political positions they embrace should cause us to look more closely at the play. As in his departures from established literary sources, Shakespeare's departure from a familiar contemporary source should intrigue and tantalize, not confuse or frustrate. David Bevington hints at a plausible solution when he acknowledges that the characters in the play "were unquestionably names in the news during the early 1590s" and that to "allude frivolously to these matters after 1589 ... Shakespeare would have had to be contratopical."[66] Albert Tricomi expands the idea of contra-topical drama. While noting that the delight and charm of *Love's Labor's Lost* stands in stark contrast to war ravaged France, Tricomi believes that a precise topical analysis is an impossible quest. He suggests a contra-topical, topsy-turvy reading of a decidedly festive comedy: "a deliberate inversion of the topical wherein these persons are charmingly transmuted from the French civil war into the fairy tale world of Nérac."[67] Tricomi attempts to answer the puzzling question of names not by suggesting an error in Shakespeare, but by looking at other possibilities.

Part of that inversion could center on broken promises. As we have seen in *The Massacre*, Navarre's real-life promises made a lasting dramatic impression; *Love's Labor's Lost* demonstrates that broken promises do so as well. Oaths and oath breaking were the subject of much cultural debate and literary treatment in Elizabethan England, and a surprising amount of scholarship covers oath making and swearing (distinct from cursing) in Shakespeare. *Love's Labor's Lost* figures prominently in this scholarship. Frances Shirley sees the play as the "most obvious use of a plot that turns on an oath and its violation, when Shakespeare is again making a serious point, this time about oaths taken lightly without real thoughts of the consequences."[68] The play begins with a serious accord, an ostensibly solemn vow taken among four young men. Yet in the comedy, the unnatural vow is anything but serious and solemn. The first 160 lines of the play, the lines that set the stage for all the ensuing action, discuss the nature of oaths and oath breaking. We *expect* the young men to break the strict contract even as they swear the oath and proclaim its value.[69]

Mary Ellen Lamb's fine essay focuses upon the breaking of oaths, both the historical and the fictive, in the play. Lamb takes a common-sense approach to the topical aspects of the play, highlighting that which serves both topical relationships and the demands of the fiction. According to Lamb, the topical should not be invested with more meaning than a literary source—changes in the topical should be expected and accepted: "The locus of meaning lies in the play itself, not in the play's relationship to its topical source."[70] Yet the topical source (and the displacement from the source) not only colors the narrative but helps provide the very "locus of meaning" Lamb seeks. Although both literary and topical sources should be treated with care, the newly topical casts a larger shadow for a diverse audience aware of the current event than a specific literary source read by far fewer members of the audience.

Obviously, oaths play a central role in the comedy. Shakespeare employed the word "oath" in his plays hundreds of times, but in no single play more than the 21 times in *Love's Labor's Lost*. The word "forsworn," the past participle of forswear, the breaking of an oath, appears 54 times in Shakespeare, but in no single play does the word appear more frequently than the 17 times in *Love's Labor's Lost*.[71] The question of broken oaths and justification for broken oaths saturates the play from the initial gathering of the lords to the departure of the ladies.

This simple observation, that Shakespeare repeatedly calls our attention to oaths and the breaking of oaths, not only links the play with both Marlowe and Spenser, it also helps establish a date of revision. The broken oaths of Navarre suggest that Shakespeare either, quite amazingly, anticipates the king's abjuration, or that the revision of the play took place after July of 1593. The lack of printed matter about Henry after this date contrasts sharply with the hundreds of extant documents, including news reports, broadsides, ballads, dedications, and plays written prior to that time. Writing a new play about Navarre after this date makes little sense; revising an older play to reflect new realities seems more plausible. *Love's Labor's Lost*, with Navarre as King, predates his conversion. Subsequent revision, which the 1598 quarto alludes to ("newly corrected and augmented"), took place after the king's conversion and the reopening of the theaters in 1594.[72] A recognition of Navarre's oath breaking also underscores the importance of the names. Appreciating the dramatic importance of the oath, and the significance of the names, saves a historical analysis from a reductive topicalism. The characters' names were part of the a larger literary context, as was the discussion of oaths and, more specifically, Navarre's forsworn oath.

The play begins with words spoken by Navarre about oaths and immortality. Making a vow to live a certain austere life, reasons the King, will insure lasting fame and memory:

> Let fame, that all hunt after in their lives,
> Live register'd upon our brazen tombs,
> And then grace us in the disgrace of death;
> When, spite of cormorant devouring Time,
> Th' endeavor of this present breath may buy
> That honor which shall bate his scythe's keen edge,
> And make us heirs of all eternity.
>
> (1.1.1–7)

The misguided quest for fame relies upon an equally misguided pledge to remain in the academy for three years, fasting once a week, sleeping only three hours per night, and forgoing the company of women. Despite such rigors, Navarre reiterates the importance of personal vows to Berowne, Dumain, and Longaville:

> Your oaths are pass'd; and now subscribe your names,
> That his own hand may strike his honor down
> That violates the smallest branch herein.

If you are arm'd to do, as sworn to do,
Subscribe to your deep oaths, and keep it too.

(1.1.19–23)

Navarre calls attention not only to the oath, but to the binding nature of the oath and the indignity of breaking such a vow.

Shortly after the serious discussion about honor and oaths, Berowne reminds Navarre of the impending visit by the French King's daughter. After reconsidering the diplomatic importance of the visit (he makes no mention of the romantic dimension), Navarre makes an exception to the recently sworn vow: "We must of force dispense with this decree; / She must lie here on mere *necessity*" (1.1.146–47, emphasis added). The word "necessity," the exact word Spenser later has Burbon [Navarre] use to justify his broken oath, captures the attention of Berowne, the most vocal critic of the proposed conditions.

Berowne, acting as a semi-choric figure, objects to much of the unnatural oath. Berowne, like the audience, understands the harshness of the pact. The audience expects the vows to be broken, for, as William Slights suggests, "we know that this way of combating 'cormorant devouring Time' is doomed to failure by the very nature of courtly young gentlemen."[73] Berowne sets up this expectation by noting that the vow, however conceived, will make them all promise breakers by necessity:

Necessity will make us all forsworn
Three thousand times within this three years' space;
For every man with his affects is born,
Not by might mast'red, but by special grace.
If I break faith, this word shall speak for me:
I am forsworn on mere *necessity*.

(1.1.148–53, emphasis added)

Berowne rejoices in the word "necessity," for it stands as a loophole to the contract, allowing Berowne and company to justify any decision, any change in plans, any broken promise. Shakespeare's comic treatment of the "necessity" question, a much less sympathetic or serious treatment than found in Spenser, suggests that such justifications are mere ploys for the undisciplined, inconstant lords.

The emphasis upon necessity may have other meanings as well. While the lords have many differences, they share one similarity: they are all men. In this play, to be a man means inconstancy, confusion, defeat, and humiliation. The women who control the action of the play mock the lords as they attempt to court the ladies and gain favor. Throughout the drama, the women have the upper hand, easily containing the fawning, bombastic men. In *Love's Labor's Lost* especially, the male characters receive harsh treatment. Rosaline, for example, says:

That same Berowne I'll torture ere I go.
O! that I knew he were but in by the week.
How I would make him fawn, and beg, and seek,
And wait the season, and observe the times,
And spend his prodigal wits in bootless rimes,
And shape his service wholly to my hests
And make him proud to make me proud that jests!

(5.2.60–66)

While the courting remains harmless enough, each male makes a vow of eternal love to the wrong woman and once again must admit to romantic perjury. The sentence imposed by the women, a one year period of abstinence, ironically recalls the initial vow so casually forsworn. In this battle of the sexes, the women prevail, handing out the sentences at the end of the play. They leave the scene in full control of the action—past, present, and future. Inconstancy and broken oaths are not perceived as terms of endearment, nor are the oath makers and oath breakers redeemed.

While other male characters in the play, including Moth, Armado, and Nathaniel, also receive sharp criticism from the ladies and the audience, Navarre and the lords incur the most stinging rebuke. The foolish Navarre and his followers are easy targets for the ladies; the words of the men and their tokens of love seem insincere and rushed. The women have little trouble overcoming the various expressions of love (sonnets, bracelets, gloves) and remain steadfast in their denial of the proposed affections.

Shakespeare may have returned to mocking Navarre in a later play as well. David Womersley argues persuasively that Shakespeare lampooned Navarre in *Henry V*. Womersley notes that during the summer of 1599, Henry IV, suddenly mentioned as a probable contender for the English crown, once again attracted the attention of English writers. At this moment, the argument goes, Shakespeare felt free to make the French king into an object of satire: "When Shakespeare put an image of Bourbon on a literal stage, he twisted that dignified self-image into a *buffo* counterpart to the embodiment of true regality he fashioned in the character of Henry V."[74] Although Womersley does not acknowledge the Navarre of *Love's Labor's Lost*, Shakespeare had already put a courting, oath breaking *buffo* Henry IV on stage some years prior.

The oaths that link the living Henry of Navarre and the fictitious Navarre from *Love's Labor's Lost*, like the names of the characters themselves, serve both a historical and literary function. Shakespeare could not set his play in France, use real names of real people, and highlight oath breaking without making some statement about the recently concluded actions across the channel. The captivating events in France afforded Shakespeare an opportunity to capitalize on the most discussed issue of the time while modifying the events to suit his comedic purpose. Far removed from the direct and combative Marlowe or the "sage and serious" Spenser, Shakespeare combines bitter enemies and transforms religious perjury into more benign romantic perjury, all the while turning oath swearers into oath breakers and men in love into fools. Unique among Shakespeare's plays, *Love's Labor's Lost* examines contemporary events considered important by large numbers of people and, once again, surprises us with the outcome.

SPENSER'S BURBON

William Ponsonby published books 1–6 of Spenser's epic poem *The Faerie Queene* in 1596. The woodcut illustration of St. George slaying the dragon discussed in chapter three tacitly introduces Navarre's presence into the poem, for the identical illustration appeared in some news quartos praising the French king. Navarre appears more conspicuously as Burbon in book 5 of *The Faerie Queene*. The relatively short "Burbon episode" covers only 23 stanzas (43–65) in canto 11. In the passage, Spenser represents Navarre's conversion with surprising candor. The episode stands as a significant anomaly in the poem: only this once did Spenser clearly identify and allegorize a still-living political figure other than Elizabeth I. The historical allegory surrounding Burbon's story, while embellished, does not attempt to hide the recent religious turmoil in France or Navarre's controversial abjuration. In fact, as Alison Shell argues, allegory "was potentially more open than other literary convention to topical or polemic interpretation."[75] Like Marlowe, Spenser confronts both the causes and effects of apostasy, climaxing with Burbon's abandonment of the shield of true religion. The inclusion of such recent, ongoing events, runs counter to the epic tradition and the role of the "poets historical" cited by Spenser in the "Letter to Ralegh."[76]

The epic poets mentioned by Spenser—Homer, Virgil, Ariosto, and Tasso—all largely refrained from including current events in their narratives.[77] According to the Letter, Spenser chose Arthur as his hero because the king stood "furthest from the danger of envy and suspicion of present time."[78] In other words, Spenser needed to devise a hero free from the usual infighting often associated with court politics, a protagonist acceptable to all political factions of the day. If Alistair Fox correctly (albeit cynically) argues that the "whole of Spenser's literary career, in fact, can be constructed as a concerted effort to gain, not simply monetary reward, but preferment at Court," the decision to cast Arthur as his hero displays prudence as well.[79] Any treatment of topical issues risked making enemies within the various factions of the Elizabethan court. Lessons of lasting political or moral value are harder to discern in the current event, disputes much more likely, and feelings more easily hurt: For the epic poet, historical perspective increases understanding. Selecting a relatively popular and largely unoffensive hero displays poetic understanding and political sophistication.[80]

Spenser's decision to incorporate current political events into book 5 of the poem, in addition to running counter to an epic tradition, creates further challenges for the poet. Instead of presenting history in an informative and entertaining fashion (Sidney's emphatic "to teach and delight"), the poet of recent or current history becomes an editorial writer, a partisan in the antagonistic sense of the word. Navarre's conversion, a recent event still hotly disputed and keenly felt by many, caused dissension among Elizabeth's government and military leaders. Spenser's decision to incorporate the matter demonstrates, perhaps, a Marlowe-like daring, for no other Elizabethan poet addressed the issue in print.

For understandable reasons, few commentators on the poem treat the Burbon episode in any depth: it appears to be a most straightforward historical treatment of a seemingly obscure situation that captured English attention for a short period of time. Elizabeth Heale calls the names in the episode and the intended allegory "transparent." Anne Lake Prescott, while admitting that "the thin veil of allegory" is "too thin for the taste of many readers," explores the complexities of the episode in detail, arguing that Spenser "meta-allegorizes the move from myth to actuality."[81] A. C. Hamilton provides the following nuts and bolts gloss:

> The historical reference is to the English intervention in France to support Henry IV against the rebellion of his subjects who were supported by Philip of Spain. As leader of the Huguenots, Henry fought against the Catholic League; later he renounced his faith in order to rule Paris.[82]

Although Hamilton does not expand on the significance of the renunciation, many English readers considered Navarre's broken promise far more than a historical footnote. The episode, coupled with the Belge and Irena cantos, merges into obvious historical allegory, "for here historical events do indeed structure the allegory of the poem."[83]

The Burbon episode, by more directly treating the individual actions of Henry of Navarre, provides Spenser's own account of the conversion while underscoring both his interest in and knowledge of the events. While fictionalized, the allegorical treatment of Burbon thrusts Spenser into contemporary politics and foreign affairs. Despite his residence in Ireland, Spenser must have received a fairly accurate account of the events in France. This is not to suggest that Spenser read the news quartos (home delivery of printed news was, after all, still a few generations away), and Spenser's exact relationship with the news quartos is difficult to ascertain. The episode does reiterate the importance, the centrality, of Navarre's conversion in the mid-1590s to Spenser and his readers. Spenser's rendering of Burbon suggests that his response to Navarre was complex, consisting of both censure and optimism, dismay and understanding.

At first glance, Spenser's narrative presents a rather common understanding of Navarre's actions from an English point of view. Prior to Burbon's introduction, Artegall notices a knight in "daungerous distresse" followed by a "rude rout him chasing to and fro" (5.11.44.2–3). Grandtorto, the "rude rout" chasing both Burbon and Flourdelis, represents the combination of usurpation and rebellion, joined together with Italian and Spanish interference. The mob attempts to oppress and capture the pursued knight. Despite the overwhelming odds against the knight, he battles bravely ("like a Lion wood amongst them fares") against the mob. During the heat of battle, the knight relinquishes his shield. Spenser vividly describes the event:

> And now they doe so sharpely him assay,
> That they his shield in peeces battred have,
> And forced him to throw it quite away,
> Fro dangers dread his doubtfull life to save;
> Albe that it most safety to him gave,
> And much did magnifie his noble name.
> For from the day that he thus did it leave,
> Amongst all Knights he blotted was with blame,
> And counted but a recreant Knight, with endless shame.
>
>   (5.11.46)

The harsh words Spenser uses to describe the loss of the shield (blame, recreant, shame) register the pain of betrayal felt by many in England and France after Navarre's conversion. The shield, given to Burbon "by a good knight, the knight of the Redcrosse," which clearly links Burbon with St. George and the Order of the Garter, magnified "his noble name." Moreover, the fellow "Knights" heaping opprobrium on Burbon for his displaced shield may allude to the Knights of the Order of the Garter to which Henry of Navarre belonged at the time of his conversion. While James W. Broaddus equates the loss of the shield with Burbon's lost "moral authority," creating a "clear example of a nation that is out of control, a society in which degree is no longer maintained," the shield represents more than individual virtue.[84] Not only did the knight lose his faith and spiritual compass ("that it most safety to him gave"), he also lost the respect and honor of all other knights. While Spenser acknowledges the "forced" nature of the decision, the overall tenor strongly condemns Burbon's actions.

It is only after the terrible deed that we learn the knight's name. Spenser's Burbon (Navarre, of course, was the first Bourbon king) introduces himself with a sense of guilt and regret over the misplaced shield and the loss of Flourdelis (the royal arms of France):

> My name is *Burbon* hight,
> Well knowne, and far renowmed heretofore,
> Until late mischiefe did uppon me light,
> That all my former praise hath blemisht sore;
> And that faire Lady, which in that uprore
> Ye with those caytives saw, *Flourdelis* hight,
> Is mine owne love, though me she have forlore,
> Whether withheld from me by wrongfull might,
> Or with her owne good will, I cannot read aright.
>
>   (5.11.49)

Burbon openly acknowledges his fallen reputation, noting how some "late mischiefe" had "blemisht" his once glorious name. To this point, the account closely parallels the fall of Navarre's reputation in England. Michael O'Connell argues that "in the allegorization of Henri of Navarre's change of alliance, the reader can see the almost comic doggedness of the poet's fidelity in pursuing the actual."[85] The allegory, however, does not end with stanza 49; Spenser's narrative goes beyond a rendition of actual historical events.

Artegall (often seen as an allegory of Essex, a friend and comrade in arms of Navarre) condemns the embattled knight in no uncertain terms for his decision to drop the shield of true religion given him by the Redcrosse Knight:

> But why have ye (said *Artegall*) forborne
> Your owne good shield in daungerous dismay?
> That is the greatest shame and foulest scorne,
> Which unto any knight behappen may
> To loose the badge, that should his deeds display.
>
>   (5.11.52.1–5)[86]

Artegall's words ("greatest shame and foulest scorne") clearly denounce Burbon's actions. Burbon then provides his justification for dropping the shield:

> To whom Sir *Burbon*, blushing halfe for shame,
> That shall I unto you (quoth he) bewray;
> Least ye therefore mote happily me blame,
> And deeme it doen of will, that through *inforcement* came.
>
>   (5.11.52.6–9, emphasis added)

Ultimately, Burbon claims the decision was not an act of "will," but rather "inforcement." Like his historical counterpart Henry IV, Burbon had little choice in the matter. The poem continues with Burbon's explanation of why he abandoned the shield of true religion:

But for that many did that shield envie,
And cruell enemies increased more;
To stint all strife and troublous enmitie,
That bloudie scutchin being battered sore,
I layd aside, and have of late forbore:
Hoping thereby to have my love obtayned:
Yet can I not my love have nathemore;
For she by force is still fro me detayned,
And with corruptfull brybes is to untruth mis-trayned.

(5.11.54)

Despite the apparent sincerity of Burbon, and the difficulty of his situation, the narrator continues to use the language of condemnation. Artegall responds with a direct challenge:

Certes Sir knight
Hard is the case, the which ye doe complaine;
Yet not so hard (for nought so hard may light,
That it to such a streight mote you constraine)
As to abandon, that which doth containe
Your honours stile, that is your warlike shield.
All perill ought be lesse, and lesse all paine
The losse of fame in disaventrous field;
Dye rather, then doe ought, that mote dishonour yield.

(5.11.55)

Speaking as an experienced soldier and knight, Artegall faults Burbon for his actions, reminding him that a true knight should be willing to die rather than face potential dishonor. The strong language and the unequivocal chastisement Burbon receives from Artegall notwithstanding, Spenser does not fully side with the Knight of Justice. After the lecture, Spenser allows Burbon to speak once again in self-defense, something that the English press did not allow the historical Navarre.

Burbon's response holds the key for understanding the entire episode. The embattled warrior, while admitting his error, also admits to a higher plan: a desire to recapture both Flourdelis and his shield once again. In the stanza, Burbon replies to Artegall's bold assertion that a valiant knight should prefer death to shame and apostasy ("Dye rather, then doe ought, that mote dishonour yield"). In a striking moment, Spenser allows Navarre both a rationale for past events and the hope for future action as well:

Not so; (quoth he) for yet when time doth serve,
My former shield I may resume againe:

> To temporize is not from truth to swerve,
> Ne for advantage terme to entertaine,
> When as *necessitie* doth it constraine.
>
> (5.11.56.1–5, emphasis added)

"Necessitie," the very word spoken by Navarre and Berowne in *Love's Labor's Lost*, stands at the heart of the matter. Burbon's plan, according to Spenser, requires waiting and patience. At some undetermined moment in the future, "when time doth serve," Burbon hopes once again to pick up the shield of true religion, his Huguenot faith. Although Artegall calls such action "forgery," it was the best-case scenario English Protestants and French Huguenots could envision. The important point, "to temporize is not from truth to swerve," a simulacrum, perhaps, of the frequently discussed Jesuit doctrine of equivocation, allows Burbon an explanation, a defense for his actions while granting his wistful supporters a ray of hope.

The invocation of "necessitie" thematically joins with the idea of "inforcement" from stanza 52. Both terms suggest a strong unwillingness on Burbon's part. The proverbial words "necessity hath no law" were frequently used in conjunction with oath-breaking. Oath breaking as a result of necessity has a very long history in Roman law and Germanic practice. In the sixteenth century, many such discussions took place, especially around debates of Machiavellian and anti-Machiavellian practices. In the fifteenth chapter of *The Prince*, Machiavelli writes that "[h]ence a prince, in order to hold his position, must acquire the power to be not good, and understand when to use it and when not to use it, in accord with *necessity*."[87] Robert Bireley investigates how numerous thinkers of the sixteenth century, including anti-Machiavellian writers Giovanni Botero and Justus Lipsius, viewed the practices expressed in *The Prince*.[88] The Flemish humanist Lipsius, well known to Navarre and invited to become a professor at the Calvinist academy of Bearn, was the "initiator and main proponent of the Neostoic movement."[89] Lipsius' 1584 work, *De Constantia*, translated into English and published in 1594 as *Two Bookes of Constancie* (*STC* 15694.7), advocates the virtue of remaining true to one's convictions. Against this backdrop, Navarre's inconstancy looms even larger.

The concept of necessity factored prominently into Spenser's analysis of Navarre's conversion. From the perspective of "necessity," Catholics and Protestants viewed Navarre's conversion quite differently. For Catholics, Navarre's conversion, a sincere and freely willed activity, did not come under duress or "necessity" of any kind. For Catholics to follow the former Huguenot, no evidence of any guile would be tolerated: the king either accepted the primacy of the Roman faith or he did not. Many Catholic preachers in fact, especially the friars in Paris, protested Navarre's conversion over fears of sheer hypocrisy and dissimulation.[90] Protestants, on the other hand, tended to cite "necessity" as a primary mover in the conversion, with the implication that Navarre only observed the external trappings of conversion and his sentiments remained, like those of many English Protestants, with the Huguenots.[91] Protestant apologists who still defended Navarre resorted to this argument: outward conformity need not measure individual faith. Viewed from this perspective, Navarre's actions, while still deplorable to Artegall and others, would appear less deplorable to a Protestant audience.

Spenser provides an interesting account of the events in France. No longer the "poet historical," Spenser emerges as the "poet-publicist." According to Spenser's version, Burbon acted foolishly, cowardly, and erroneously, but he also acted under duress, under "necessitie." Once the situation improves and the wild rout of the Catholic League and Spain no longer threatens his life, Burbon can again pick up the shield of true religion and rectify past wrongs. Spenser's optimistic presentation, a literary form of revisionist history and political spin control, gave the French king a rare opportunity in England: Burbon was finally allowed to present his side of the story. Few other forums existed for the rehabilitation of Navarre's damaged reputation.[92] As noted above, the news quartos no longer found the dashing Frenchman so attractive; poems and ballads covering his victories also disappeared.

David Womersley notes that after the conversion, Henry became increasingly a symbol of change and mutability. Womersley argues that Navarre "had become an object of suspicion. His recent actions revealed him to be a monarch without principle or gratitude."[93] One text published shortly after the conversion, *The Mutable and Wavering estate of France, from the yeare of our Lord 1460, until the yeare 1595*, actually makes Henry into the image of mutability:

> This noble and famous Prince who had for the space of foure or five and twentie yeeres so valiantly and fortunately defended the Gospell, and that with the hazard and perill of his owne life, freely exposing his royal person, his treason, his friends, and all other means whatsoever for the maintenaunce thereof, beganne to waxe calme in the defence of his profession, and to encline to that false and superstitious Religion of Rome, to the high displeasure of almightie God, the great dishonour of his princely Majestie, and to the extreme greefe and astonishment of all Protestants.[94]

The rueful yet philosophical story of French history presented in the book, published in England one year after Spenser's 1596 *Faerie Queene*, provides an illuminating context for the Burbon episode. In the space of two pages, constancy transforms into mutability:

> Thus this noble and renowned Monarke, the hope (as it were) of al that favored Gods truth, whom God had beautified with so many excellent graces and notable vertues, as courage, wisedom, zeale, and

constancy i[n] so many apparent dangers ... and to the admiration and wonderment of all men continually protected him in despight of all those who sought his ruine and overthrow, is another argument of the *mutabilitie* and interchangeable estate of all things in the world.[95]

The history of France ends within a couple of paragraphs, but not before leaving the reader with the impression of the complete and utter mutability of the French nation.[96]

As the book suggests, the growing consensus in England, and among Protestants on the continent, was that Navarre, beset with the self-inflicted wounds of shame and dishonor, could not be trusted. Spenser's form of history attempts to rehabilitate Henry IV after his conversion. However, Richard Mallette correctly states that "Burbon, of course, is freed from his assailants, at least temporarily, but the episode lacks the aura of final victory or the conclusive emergence of the good."[97] Through Burbon, Spenser provides an obvious explanation for the lack of a "final victory": Burbon must once again recapture his lost shield before the final chapter can be written. Only then will the "emergence of the good" take place.

Spenser's treatment of the Burbon episode works on a number of different levels simultaneously. Spenser clearly condemns the French king, noting the dishonor and shame engendered by his actions. Yet the poet also offers a softer, more humane, more sympathetic form of history.[98] By giving the apostate king a chance to speak in self-defense, Spenser's historical fiction provides an avenue previously unavailable to Navarre. No dramatic form of rehabilitation materialized: Marlowe was dead; Shakespeare employed irony. In the 1596 *Faerie Queene*, rehabilitation stems from the hope that someday, after the civil strife and turmoil in France subside, the proposed heir to the mantle of St. George may once again reclaim his role as cleanser of the faith. The "Letter to Ralegh" anticipates this move. In the Letter, Spenser differentiates between the "poets historical" and the mere historiographer. The poet historical enjoys a freedom to move about, for the "Poet thrusteth into the middest, even where it most concerneth him, and there recoursing to things forepaste, and divining of things to come, maketh a pleasing Analysis of all."[99] However, Navarre's future return to his Protestant faith, the "divining of thinges to come" spoken of in the letter, never actually came to fruition. So while in real life St. George does not always slay the dragon, likewise, the epic poet, despite the best public relations effort, could not always make a pleasing analysis of all.

THE FICTIONAL NAVARRE

Marlowe, Shakespeare, and Spenser depicted a dynamic and fluid Navarre in various ways. This fascinating nexus grants the modern reader an opportunity to consider the subtle and not so subtle characterizations of an intriguing personality. Henry of Navarre captured the English imagination in the early 1590s. Historical documents, including the news quartos and political essays, reveal in great detail the "factual" information surrounding these turbulent years. The "first order" meaning of the documents provide significant historical information. The imaginative literature allows for a host of "second level" interpretations. But as the evidence suggests, these interpretations are not unbounded. The archival record both limits and deepens our understanding of the works. The news quartos play a vital role in understanding the captivating figure of Navarre. While the history books tell us what happened and why, the plays and poems tell us what might have happened. The fictive imaginations of Marlowe, Shakespeare, and Spenser, while different from Elizabethan historians, are no less valuable than the various proclamations and news pamphlets. It could be argued, in fact, that the imaginative literature expands our understanding of the period: the plays and poems provide thoughtful, reflective responses to an important, epoch-making decision. Instead of the calculating, pragmatic Navarre found in history books, we may select Marlowe's brave and daring prince, Shakespeare's inconstant and foolish lord, or Spenser's ashamed and humbled king. Or, better yet, we may imagine a combination of the three.

Notes

1. *The Order of Ceremonies observed* (*STC* 13138; 1594), A2v.

2. The term "Jacobin," often used to describe Jacques Clément, is another word for Dominican, one of the four primary orders of friars. "Jacobin" specifically referred to French Dominicans, a group of friars often accused of arrogance. One contemporary states:

> The dessention might in time come to bring great damage to all orders of begging friars, amonst them the Jacopins [sic] were the chiefe and most esteemed, and presumed themselves to be the best. (*STC* 17450.3, F4).

The fact that Clément was a Jacobin friar certainly did not enhance their reputation among Protestants, but greatly endeared the Jacobins to fellow Catholics.

3. Shortly after the event, many accounts of the assassination were printed in England. According to the *Stationers' Register*, Edward Aldee entered a ballad on 4 September entitled "A Ffrenche mans songe made upon the death of the Ffrenche kinge whoe was murdered in his owne courte by a traterous ffryer of Sainct Jacobs order on the first daie of August 1589." The ballad, apparently, no longer exists; some years later, Aldee printed Marlowe's *A Massacre at Paris*. A later document from 1591, with the long title of *A second replie against the defensory and Apology of Sixtus the fift late Pope of Rome, defending the execrable fact of the Jacobine Friar, upon the person of Henry the third, late king of France* (*STC* 24913), repeated the refrain: "A Monke hath slaine the king, not painted or

pictured upon a wall, but the King of Fraunce, in the middle of his armie" (C3v). Years later, anti-Catholic literature printed in England still recounted the event. See, for example, Christopher Muriell's *An Answer unto the Catholiques Supplication*, an extended argument to King James I against Catholic toleration (*STC* 18292.3; 1603), which asks the question: "Did not a cursed Friar of France murder with a poysoned Pen-knife the last diseased French King?" (B4).

4. All citations to Marlowe's play are taken from *The Massacre at Paris*, ed. H. J. Oliver (London: Methuen, 1968).

5. For a more complete treatment of friars on the Renaissance stage, see Paul J. Voss, "The Antifraternal Tradition in English Renaissance Drama," *Cithara* 33 (November 1993): 3–16.

6. Briggs, "Reconsideration," 271. A. J. Hoenselaars, in *Images of Englishmen and Foreigners in the Drama of Shakespeare and His Contemporaries* (Rutherford: Fairleigh Dickinson UP, 1992), argues that "*The Massacre at Paris* ... was intended more to convey a sense of panic than to serve as a platform for national self-glorification" (79).

7. I borrow the phrase "unfortunate theater of France" from the news quarto *Remonstrances to the Duke of Mayne* (*STC* 5012; 1593). The various and anonymous writers of the quartos often employed theatrical metaphors to describe the protracted wars in France.

8. *A Briefe Declaration of the yeelding up of Saint Denis to the French King the 29. of June, 1590* (*STC* 13128), B1 –B1 v.

9. According to Vivien Thomas and William Tydeman, eds., in *Christopher Marlowe: The Plays and Their Sources* (London: Routledge, 1994), "any discussion of the sources of the second half of the play must necessarily be tentative and conjectural. There is a great deal of pamphlet material and it is difficult to establish how much of it Marlowe knew" (253).

10. R. B. Wernham, "Christopher Marlowe at Flushing in 1592," *English Historical Review* 91 (1976): 344–45. For additional biographical information on Marlowe, see Constance Brown Kuriyama, "Marlowe's Nemesis: The Identity of Richard Baines," in *A Poet and Filthy Play-Maker: New Essays on Christopher Marlowe*, ed. Kenneth Friedenreich, Roma Gill, and Constance B. Kuriyama (New York: AMS, 1988), 343–60.

11. Thomas and Tydeman, *Plays and Sources*, 252.

12. In 1598, Michael Drayton wrote three now-lost plays on the topic. The tone and content of the plays can only be surmised. Henry IV returned to the English stage in George Chapman's *Byron's Tragedy* (1608).

13. The Malone Society reprint of *The Massacre at Paris*, ed. W. W. Greg (New York: AMS, 1985), runs just under 1600 lines. Clifford Leech, in *Christopher Marlowe: Poet for the Stage*, ed. Anne Lancashire (New York: AMS,

1986), calls the octavo "one of the worst of the 'bad' Elizabethan dramatic texts" (147). See also the important discussion found in Laurie E. Maguire, *Shakespearean Suspect Texts: The "Bad Quartos" and Their Contexts* (Cambridge: Cambridge UP, 1996), esp. 279–81.

14. Scott McMillin, *The Elizabethan Theater & The Book of Sir Thomas More* (Ithaca: Cornell UP, 1987), 57. McMillin notes that "only twelve texts out of a total of 146 call for twenty or more speaking roles" (55).

15. Kristen Poole, in "Garbled Martyrdom in Christopher Marlowe's *The Massacre at Paris*," *Comparative Drama* 32 (1998), argues that the garbled speech actually exists as "a narrative feature of the play" (6). The printing of the play (*STC* 17423) in an undated octavo is unusual as the vast majority of Elizabethan plays were printed in quarto.

16. McMillin, *The Elizabethan Theater*, 60.

17. H. S. Bennett, ed., *The Works and Life of Christopher Marlowe* (New York: Gordian, 1966), 169.

18. Leech, in *Poet for the Stage*, notes that "in a sense *The Massacre* was a god-given subject for the dramatists of Elizabeth's later years, and it is surprising that this is our only extant play on the subject" (157).

19. Penny Roberts, "Marlowe's *The Massacre at Paris*: A Historical Perspective," *Renaissance Studies* 9 (1995): 441.

20. Paul H. Kocher, "Contemporary Pamphlet Backgrounds for Marlowe's *The Massacre at Paris*," *Modern Language Quarterly* 8 (1947): 151. The real difficulty for Kocher is "the sketchiness of the literature dealing with the years 1573 to 1589" (165).

21. Briggs, "Reconsideration," 278.

22. Shuger, *Renaissance Bible*, 120.

23. For an analysis of the influence of French history and political events on the development of English political thought, see Parmelee, *Newes From Fraunce*.

24. *The Mutable and wavering estate of France*, dedication.

25. Robert Parsons, *Conference about the Next Succession to the Crown of Ingland* (*STC* 19398; 1594), 216v.

26. *STC* 19197, A2. As discussed in chapter one, many other quartos warn English readers, implicitly and explicitly, that the civil unrest in France could happen in England as well. See, for example, *STC* 6878; 10004; 11273.5; 11285; 11287.5; 11727; 13128; 13139; 13147.

27. For a discussion of Navarre's well-known adultery, see Mary Ellen Lamb, "The Nature of Topicality in *Love's Labor's Lost*," *Shakespeare Survey* 38 (1985): 49–59.

28. Andrew M. Kirk, "Marlowe and the Disordered Face of French History," *Studies in English Literature* 35 (1995): 205; Briggs, "Reconsideration," 272.

29. Leech, *Poet for the Stage*, 155.

30. Roberts, "Historical Perspective," 441.

31. Kirk, "French History," 208, 209.

32. Thomas and Tydeman, *Plays and Their Sources*, 260.

33. Leech, *Poet for the Stage*, 158.

34. E.K. Chambers, *Elizabethan Stage* (Oxford: Clarendon Press, 1974), I, 323.

35. Edward Rocklin, "Marlowe as Experimental Dramatist: The Role of the Audience in *The Jew of Malta*," in *A Poet and Filthy Play-Maker: New Essays on Christopher Marlowe*, ed. Kenneth Friedenreich, Roma Gill, and Constance B. Kuriyama (New York: AMS, 1988), 129–42.

36. R. W. David, ed., *Love's Labor's Lost* (London: Methuen, 1951), xxviii. All citations from *Love's Labor's Lost* are taken from this edition.

37. For a more complete account of the names in Shakespeare, see *The Shakespeare Name Dictionary*, ed. J. Madison Davis and A. Daniel Frankforter (New York: Garland, 1995).

38. See, for example, *Martin Mar-Sixtus* (*STC* 24913; 1591). This piece of propaganda rails against the murder of Henry III (August 1589) and condemns League tactics and motivation in the ensuing civil wars. The Biblical Holofernes is mentioned repeatedly in the polemic:

And well known likewise is the famous story of the holy woman Judith, who to set free her own besieged city and people, took in hand an enterprise (God doubtless directing her thereunto) about the killing of Holofernes, then general of the enemies forces. (B3).

While the Holofernes in *Martin Mar-Sixtus* and the one in *LLL* have nothing in common, the name appeared in conjunction with Navarre, Mayenne, and others. Some scholars believe the pedant Holofernes was modeled after a contemporary literary figure like John Florio or Gabriel Harvey. Others suggest a link to Dr. Tubal Holofernes, a tutor in Rabelais' *Gargantua*. See also Manfred Draudt, "Holofernes and Mantuanus: How Stupid is the Pedant of *Love's Labour's Lost*?", *Anglia: Zeitschrift Fur Englische Philologie* 109 (1991): 443–51. For an analysis of Holofernes and Elizabethan spelling controversies, see Jane Donawerth, "Holofernes, the English Spelling Controversy, and Renaissance Philosophy of Language," *Proceedings of the PMR Conference* 8 (1983): 79–88.

39. *A True Declaration of the Honorable Victorie obtained by the French King in the winning of Noyan* (*STC* 13142.5), A3v–A4. Biron and Longueville, as discussed later, appear together in *STC* 11277.5 and *STC* 13131. The characters also appear in *The Mutable and Wavering estate of France, from the yeare of our Lord 1460, until the yeare 1595* (*STC* 11279; 1597), a long history book about recent and not so recent events in France.

40. According to Graham Bradshaw, *Misrepresentations: Shakespeare and the Materialists* (Ithaca: Cornell, 1993), Stephen Greenblatt once referred to the study of sources as "the elephant's graveyard of Shakespeare criticism" (32).

41. Ibid., 32.

42. David Bevington, *Tudor Drama and Politics* (Cambridge: Harvard UP, 1968), 1. Richard Levin, "Negative Evidence," *Studies in Philology* 96 (Fall 1995): 383–410.

43. Frances A. Yates, *A Study of Love's Labour's Lost* (Cambridge: Cambridge UP, 1936), 20.

44. For the most recent example of a "literary detective story" featuring Shakespeare's sonnets, see David Honneyman, *Shakespeare's Sonnets and the Court of Navarre* (Devon: Merlin, 1996). Honneyman attempts to uncover the "real" identities of figures found in Shakespeare's sonnets. Honneyman's novel though unpersuasive thesis suggests that Shakespeare's sonnets are translations of French originals that tell the story of Navarre (the Fair Friend), Marguerite de Valois (the Dark Lady), Du Bartas (the Rival Poet) and d'Aubigné (the ur-Sonneteer).

45. Levin, "Negative Evidence," 387, 386.

46. In a different essay, Richard Levin, "Another Source for *The Alchemist* and Another Look at Source Studies," *English Literary Renaissance* 28 (Spring 1998), notes that source studies remain "scandalously undertheorized" (220). Levin posits a taxonomy of relationships between any given text or event and a play. The news quartos, in this world view, would be classified as Class Beta Sources—a source with a close connection to the play, but only used for part of the drama.

47. Stephen Greenblatt, "Culture," in *Critical Terms for Literary Study*, ed. Frank Lentricchia and Thomas McLaughlin (Chicago: Chicago UP, 1990), 226.

48. Louis A. Montrose, "'Sport by Sport O'erthrown': *Love's Labour's Lost* and the Politics of Play," *Texas Studies in Literature and Language* 18 (1976–77): 528–52.

49. Kirk, "Disordered Face," 196. *In The Mirror of Confusion: The Representation of French History in English Renaissance Drama* (New York: Garland, 1996), Kirk expands his focus to cover a number of plays from the period.

50. Alfred Harbage, in "*Love's Labor's Lost* and the Early Shakespeare," *Philological Quarterly* 41 (1962): 18–36, supposes "that Shakespeare wrote the play about 1588–89 when the selection of names was logical, and revised it about 1596–97 when the retention of the names was permissible." Scholars have dated the play anywhere from 1588–98.

51. H. B. Charlton, "The Date of *Love's Labor's Lost*," *Modern Language Review* xiii (1918): 262.

52. *The true discourse of the wonderful victorie obtained by Henrie the fourth, neere Yurie, the fourteenth day of March 1590* (STC 13145), Blv.

53. See, for example, a song of praise written by Saluste du Bartas and translated by Joshua Sylvester entitled *A Canticle of the victorie obteined by the French King, Henrie the fourth. At Yurie* (*STC* 21669). The document was entered to John Wolfe on 15 April and 19 May 1590. The poem was also reissued as part two of The Triumph of Faith (*STC* 21672; 1592). Also see A*n Excellent ditty made upon the great victory, which the French King obtayned against the Duke de Maine, the fourth of March* (*STC* 13135).

54. G. B. Harrison, The Elizabethan Journals (New York: MacMillan, 1939).

55. Charlton, "Date," 263.

56. Charles Boyce, *Shakespeare A to Z* (New York: Facts on File, 1990), 164–65.

57. Hugh M. Richmond, "Shakespeare's Navarre," Huntington Library Quarterly 42 (1979): 203.

58. Not quite knowing what to do with the character of Dumain, Charlton, "Date," states: "The English contingent in Brittany in 1592 fought in conjunction with and for some time under Marshall Daumont. It is not at all difficult to imagine a confusion in soldier's ears between De Mayenne and Daumont: at all events it is easier to imagine this than to find a reason for including De Mayenne in the King's fellowship" (260 n. 2). Charlton is, moreover, incorrect about the reception of news in sixteenth century England. Publication and distribution of the thousands of quartos certainly received a much wider audience than talk of returning soldiers, especially if, as Charlton claims, only 1000 of the original 4000 of Willoughby's army returned home alive.

59. Exact figures are difficult to establish. Guy, *Elizabeth I*, 42–44, notes that, geographically, conscription rates were evenly distributed throughout the country, while socially, the lowest stratum of the population contributed the highest percentage of soldiers. Howell A. Lloyd, in *The Rouen Campaign, 1590–1592* (Oxford: Clarendon, 1973), notes that for the Rouen campaign, "exactly one half of the English shires were involved. All those of the south coast, and all the south-western shires, were omitted" (88). The government did not want to weaken the areas most immediately exposed to a possible invasion.

60. See, for example, *A Journall, wherein is truely sette downe from day to day, what was doone, and worthy of noting in both armies* (*STC* 11277.5), entered 20 May 1592; *A Discourse and true recitall of everie particular of the victorie obtained by the French King, on Wednesday the fourth of March, being Ash Wednesday* (*STC* 13131), entered 6 April 1590; *A recitall of that which hath happened in the Kings Armie, since the taking of the suburbes of Paris* (*STC* 13139), entered 22 January 1590. All three quartos contain the names of the four principals from *Love's Labor's Lost* (Navarre, Berowne, Longaville, and Dumaine) as well as other soldiers and battle information.

61. H. R. Woudhuysen, ed., *Love's Labor's Lost* (Surrey: Arden Shakespeare, 1998), notes that a "substantial pamphlet literature" covering the French wars existed and that "Shakespeare may have read some of these writings," but "none of this suggests Shakespeare was writing an allegorical, a political or a topical play" (68).

62. Wolfe, *Conversion*, 131.

63. Francis Bacon, *Letters and Life*, 1.160–61.

64. Richmond, "Shakespeare's Navarre," 214.

65. Some critics may contend that both *Troilus and Cressida* and *Measure for Measure* also depart from this formula. I do not consider *Troilus and Cressida* a comedy per se and *Measure for Measure* clearly announces three marriages (Claudio/Juliet, Angelo/Mariana, and Lucio/ prostitute), even if the marriage between the Duke and Isabella remains conditional: "if you'll a willing ear incline" (5.1.533). Dozens of studies analyze Shakespeare's comedies and the unusual ending of *Love's Labor's Lost*. See, for example, the pattern discussed in Northrop Frye, *A Natural Perspective: The Development of Shakespearean Comedy and Romance* (San Diego: HBJ, 1965). For a somewhat unjust critique of Frye's analysis, see Jean Howard, "The Difficulties of Closure: An Approach to the Problematic in Shakespearean Comedy," in *Comedy from Shakespeare to Sheridan*, ed. A. R. Braunmuller and J. C. Bulman (Newark: U Delaware P, 1986), 113–28.

66. Bevington, *Tudor Drama*, 15.

67. Albert H. Tricomi, "The Witty Idealization of the French Court in *Love's Labor's Lost*," *Shakespeare Studies* 12 (1979): 29.

68. Frances A. Shirley, *Swearing and Perjury in Shakespeare's Plays* (London: Allen and Unwin, 1979), 36. Additional studies also focus on oath making and oath breaking in other plays. See, for example, Elena Glazov-Corrigan "The New Function of Language in Shakespeare's *Pericles*: Oath Versus 'Holy Word,'" *Shakespeare Survey* 43 (1991): 131– 40; William Slights, "'Swear by Thy Gracious Self': Self-Referential Oaths in Shakespeare," *English Studies in Canada* 2 (June 1987): 147–60. For a history of cursing, see Geoffrey Hughes, *Swearing: A Social History of Foul Language, Oaths and Profanity in English* (Oxford: Blackwell, 1991).

69. For an interesting philosophical look at the actions of Navarre and company, see John Alvis, "Derivative Loves are Labor Lost," *Renascence* 48 (Summer 1996): 247–59.

70. Lamb, "Topicality," 55.

71. John Bartlett, *A Complete Concordance to Shakespeare* (New York: St. Martin's, 1990). The fact that *Love's Labor's Lost* accounts for more than 30 percent of the total times Shakespeare used the word suggests the importance of oaths and oath breaking in the play. Clearly, the play asks the reader to consider oaths and oath breaking as a central concern.

72. Title page claims do not, of course, provide incontrovertible evidence of revival or revision. The wordings, usually placed on the title page by the publisher, could be manufactured to stimulate sales.

73. Slights, "Self-Referential Oaths," 148.

74. Womersley, "France," 457.

75. Alison Shell, *Catholicism, Controversy and the English Literary Imagination, 1558–1660* (Cambridge: Cambridge UP, 1999), 25.

76. Many critics dismiss the notion that Spenser's "Letter to Ralegh," published only with the 1590 edition of the poem, can be used with any certainty to establish the poet's intentions. For an extended treatment of the letter, see Wayne Erickson, "Spenser's Letter to Ralegh and the Literary Politics of *The Faerie Queene*'s 1590 Publication," *Spenser Studies* 10 (1989): 139–74. See also A. Leigh DeNeef, "Raleigh, Letter to," *The Spenser Encyclopedia*, ed. A. C. Hamilton et al. (Toronto: University of Toronto Press, 1990), 581–84.

77. This is not to argue, of course, that Spenser followed a blindly classical course in writing *The Faerie Queene*. For an account of the relatively minor influence of classical sources on English Renaissance literature, see Murray Roston, "Spenser and the Pagan Gods," *Renaissance Perspectives* (Princeton: Princeton UP, 1987), 143–93. Roston argues "that *The Faerie Queene* could certainly not be described as classical in poetic form, in content, or in timbre" (144).

78. Edmund Spenser, *The Faerie Queene*, ed. A. C. Hamilton (New York: Longman, 1977), 737. All citations from Spenser's letter and the poem are taken from this edition.

79. Alistair Fox, "The Complaint of Poetry for the Death of Liberality: The Decline of Literary Patronage in the 1590s," in *The Reign of Elizabeth I: Court and Culture in the Last Decade*, ed. John Guy (Cambride: Cambridge UP, 1995): 229–57, 235.

80. As de Neef, "Raleigh," points out, some critics "object that the intention to make Arthur the central, unifying hero does not agree with the secondary role he plays in the poem" (581).

81. Elizabeth Heale, *The Faerie Queene: A Reader's Guide* (Cambridge: Cambridge UP, 1987), 142. Anne Lake Prescott, "Foreign Policy in Fairyland: Henri IV and Spenser's Burbon," *Spenser Studies* 14 (2000), 189, 207. Prescott, in "Burbon," *The Spenser Encyclopedia* (Toronto: University of Toronto Press, 1990), calls the allegory "irritatingly thin" (121).

82. Spenser, *The Faerie Queene*; 609n.

83. Michael O'Connell, *Mirror and Veil: The Historical Dimension of Spenser's Faerie Queen* (Chapel Hill: University of North Carolina Press, 1977), 13. Richard Mallette, "Book Five of *The Faerie Queene*: An Elizabethan Apocalypse," *Spenser Studies* 11 (1990): 129–59, believes that the Burbon episode, together

with the Belge episode, "need to be understood as a kind of apocalyptic diptych" (147).

84. James W. Broaddus, *Spenser's Allegory of Love: Social Vision in Books III, IV, and V of the Faerie Queene* (Madison, NJ: Fairleigh Dickinson University Press, 1995), 150–51.

85. O'Connell, *Mirror and Veil*, 154.

86. Some critics see irony in Artegall's words since he himself was earlier guilty of surrendering his own badge of justice to Radigund. According to T. K. Dunseath, *Spenser's Allegory of Justice in Book Five of The Faerie Queene* (Princeton: Princeton UP, 1968), "these critics are mistaken and have missed Spenser's point. There is no irony here, conscious or unconscious, for if there is any one Knight of Maidenhead in *The Faerie Queene* who has earned the right to instruct anyone about the meaning of his shield, it is Artegall" (222).

87. Machiavelli, *Machiavelli: The Chief Works*, translated by A. H. Gilbert (Durham: Duke University Press, 1965), 1: 57–58, emphasis added.

88. Robert Bireley, *The Counter-Reformation Prince: Anti-Machiavellianism or Catholic Statecraft in Early Modern Europe* (Chapel Hill: University of North Carolina Press, 1990). See also Kristen Neuschel, Word of Honor: Interpreting Noble Culture in Sixteenth-Century France (Ithaca: Cornell UP, 1989).

89. Parmelee, *Newes from Fraunce*, 119.

90. Wolfe, *Conversion*, 131–33.

91. For a discussion of necessity in Navarre's conversion, see the memoirs of Maximilien de Bethune, Due de Sully, as cited in Wolfe, *Conversion*, 123–25. See also, Ron Love, "The Religion of Henry IV: Faith, Politics, and War, 1553–1593" (Ph.D. diss., University of Southern California, 1986).

92. This is not to suggest, of course, that Spenser knew Henry IV or that the king encouraged Spenser's efforts to present a more sympathetic picture of the conversion. Further, the optimism voiced by Spenser's Burbon was unfounded. Disillusioned French Calvinists began to meet regularly after 1593, even considering the possibility of finding another Protector. Henry's promised Catholic succession also became a reality within the next few years. His marriage to Marie de Medici in 1600 and the birth of the future Louis XIII in 1601 all but insured the retention of his recently assumed Catholic identity.

93. Womersley, "France," 450.

94. *The Mutable and Wavering estate of france, from the yeare of our Lord 1460, until the yeare 1595* (STC 11279; 1597), N3v. Womersley, "France," 450, also cites part of this text as an example of the English perception of Henry's mutability.

95. *Mutable Estate*, N3v. Emphasis added. The British Library copy of The Mutable and Wavering Estate contains some interesting marginalia. A brief notation on the title page, "K. Henry 4 turned papist after he had 24 y. defe[n]ded ye Gospels," perhaps written by W. Dowling in 1646, displays both the blatant anti-Catholicism of seventeenth century England and the enduring legacy of Navarre's conversion.

96. Henry IV was not, of course, the first Frenchman to be charged with inconstancy. In the 1550s, Thomas Wilson, *The Arte of Rhetorique*, ed. G. H. Mair (1560; reprint, Oxford: Clarendon Press, 1909), stated that Italians were known for their wit, the Spanish for nimbleness of body, and "the Frenchmen for pride and inconstancie" (179).

97. Mallette, "Elizabethan Apocalypse," 148.

98. Prescott, in "Spenser's Burbon," states that "in making Burbon a timeserver, Spenser either agreed with Henri's papist enemies that the king was a liar or retained a frail hope that he was biding his time" (206).

99. Spenser, *Faerie Queene*, 738.

ALVIN B. KERNAN

Shakespeare's and Jonson's View of Public Theatre Audiences

Although the facts are well known, it seems still not to be well understood that the English Renaissance dramatists, Shakespeare and Jonson included, were the first writers to work in the market-place situation which has since become the characteristic social and economic condition of the literary artist. The building in London in 1576 of the first of many English public theatres, the establishment of large resident playing companies with star actors, the regular performance of plays in the capital six days a week before large paying audiences, and the consequent need for a great number of plays which would attract an audience of various tastes, provided for the first time a true market-place for poetry. The social historian, Christopher Hill, describes the new conditions for plays produced in the theatre in the following way:

> The way in which capitalist relations came to pervade all sectors of society can be illustrated from an industry not often considered by economic historians—the entertainment industry. ... The financial genius of James Burbage brought playing from a small-scale private enterprise to a big business. ... The drama was the first of the arts to be put on sale to the general public. Larger theatres brought bigger profits if the dramatist could draw his public. This created exciting new possibilities for the writers, though capitalism had its drawbacks too.[1]

From *Jonson and Shakespeare*. © 1983 by Austrailian National University.

I don't believe that Hill quite realises how serious those 'drawbacks' must have seemed to a contemporary writer, who, without preparation, was forced for the first time to think of his writing as work, of his poetry as a product produced for sale to the actors who controlled the theatres, bought the plays outright from their authors, and changed them at will. Nor were the authors familiar with a system in which their art became a commodity to be sold in a public place where its saleability depended on its attractiveness to a diverse audience with widely varying tastes drawn from all levels of society. In these new circumstances, no question was more persistent or more worrisome to them, judging by the evidence of the plays, than the nature and response of the new theatrical audience. Poets writing for a patron or for a small circle of friends addressed a limited group with shared values and an educated interest in poetry, particularly its style and its elegant expression of idealised themes in a manner approved by the courtly world. But the new audience of the public theatre was very different. First of all, it was large. Alfred Harbage, in his remarkable and still authoritative book, *Shakespeare's Audience* (1941), estimates that the public theatres had an average capacity of between 2500 and 3000 people, that the average daily attendance in one year, 1595, in the Rose Theatre was about 1000, and that about 21,000 people, about 13 per cent of the London population, went to the theatres in a given performance week in 1605—the one year for which he is able to work out the figures. This is a mass audience, and if we take into account all the varied evidence, it seems to have been a truly democratic audience, a cross-section of the population. Most contemporary descriptions of the audience were written from a hostile Puritan point of view and portray the 'common haunters' of the theatre, as Henry Crosse put it in 1603, in *Virtue's Commonwealth*, as

> the leaudest persons in the land, apt for pilferie, perjurie, forgerie, or any rogories, the very scum, rascallitie, and baggage of the people, thieves, cut-purses, shifters, cousoners; briefly an unclean generation, and spaune of vipers: must not here be good rule, where is such a broode of Hell-bred creatures? for a Play is like a sincke in a Towne, whereunto all the filth doth runne: or a byle in the body, that draweth all the ill humours unto it.[2]

This tradition of Shakespeare's brutal audience, idle apprentices, whores, pickpockets, swaggering soldiers and ignorant rustics, has had a long life, but we now know that the audience also contained ambassadors, noblemen, foreign travellers, gentlemen and -women, students and representatives of all classes. Harbage, who believed that this public theatre audience was a true democratic and popular audience in the best sense, concluded that

> the audience as a whole understood and appreciated what it bought and approved. Its approval could not have been easy to win ...

Shakespeare's audience was literally popular, ascending through each gradation from potboy to prince. It was the one to which he had been conditioned early and for which he had never ceased to write. It thrived for a time, it passed quickly, and its like has never existed since. It must be given much of the credit for the greatness of Shakespeare's plays.[3]

Harbage's view about the make-up of the audience is, when all the evidence is considered, surely the most correct one; but it is not clear that the playwrights shared his enthusiasm for this first national audience, and I would like to look at the ways in which Jonson and Shakespeare reflected upon the people in the audience on whom they were dependent for their livings. About Jonson's relationship with his public-theatre audiences there is little question. On the whole, they seem not to have liked his plays, hissing several of them from the stage, and he in turn, as Jonas Barish points out, 'far from conceding anything to the preferences of his audiences ... defiantly administered a double dose of what they had already spat out, as though to coerce them into swallowing his medicine even if they found it unpalatable, on the presumption that he knew better than they what was good for them'.[4] Barish catches precisely the characteristic Jonsonian stance towards his audience, lecturing, thundering at them, keeping 'schole upo' the Stage',[5] ridiculing lower-class clowns like Onion in *The Case is Altered* and gossips like Tattle, Expectation and Censure in *The Staple of News*. He is equally scathing towards young men of fashion, the 'Brave *plush*, and *velvetmen*'[6] who are advised, ironically, 'when you come to Playes, be humorous, looke with a good startch't face, and ruffle your brow like a new boot; laugh at nothing but your owne jests, or else as the Noblemen laugh'.[7] And in *Bartholomew Fair*, the audience at Lantern Leatherhead's puppet show, Jonson's reductive summary image of the public theatre, contains not one intelligent spectator in a full range of very common humanity, from the whore and pickpocket to the idiotic young gentleman Cokes, the zealous Puritan Zeal-of-the-Land Busy, and the thundering magistrate Overdo.

Jonson's openly scornful attitude towards his audiences dictated the methods he used to instruct them in their deficiencies and teach them the true values of theatre. In prologues, inductions, addresses to the reader, intermeans, and in internal scenes, such as the puppet show in *Bartholomew Fair* or the scene in *The Case is Altered* (I. ii) where Onion the clown praises the plays of Antonio Balladino (Anthony Munday), Jonson portrays the audience as ignorant, vain, childishly delighted with spectacular stage effects, fascinated with a good story, proud of their own unlearned judgements, quick to censure, sheeplike in their acceptance of the views of critics, wedded to the stock characters—fool, devil, vice—of the old theatre, faithful to such ancient get-pennies as Andronicus and *The Spanish Tragedy*, eager to sniff out scandal by identifying the characters as representatives of famous people, and in general indifferent to the values offered by a serious playwright like Jonson. In the place of such sensational fare he tried to force upon them the neo-classical standards which he believed, not altogether rightly, his own plays to represent: 'deeds and language such as men do use', carefully wrought and well-structured plays obeying the laws of classical drama, new and up-to-date materials, a revelation of folly designed through laughter to bring about moral improvement.

But of course it never worked, and the best relationship Jonson could imagine between himself and his audience was that of a legal contract, offered in the Induction to *Bartholomew Fair*, in which the author promises to present 'a new sufficient Play ... merry, and as full of noise as sport; made to delight all and offend none' (Induction, 81–3). In return he merely asks the audience to exercise its own true judgement, not to expect the play to repeat all the stale spectacular conventions of the stage, to indulge in no more censure than the price of their seat entitled them to, and to find no hidden references to actual people in the characters. Even this modest contract did not work, and at the end of his life, indignant at the 'malicious spectators' and 'the vulgar censure of his Play', *The New Inn*, he wrote the 'Ode to Himself' in the opening lines of which he declared the absolute antagonism between himself and his audience:

> Come leave the lothed stage,
> And the more lothsome age:
> Where pride, and impudence (in faction knit)
>> Usurp the chair of wit! Indicting, and arraigning every day
>> Something they call a Play.
> Let their fastidious, vaine
> Commision of the braine
> Run on, and rage, sweat, censure and condemn:
> They were not made for thee, lesse, thou for them.

With Shakespeare it seems to have been very different. He prospered in the public theatre, and the audiences made him rich and famous. But he may not, finally, have been much more easy with his audience than was Jonson. He did not harangue and instruct his audience directly like Ben Jonson, but he did often put an audience on stage in ways which suggest, very obliquely, his conception of the relationship of playwright, play, actors and audience. On five occasions, Shakespeare puts full-scale plays-within-the-play on stage, complete with audiences, and examines in some detail the response of the audiences to the performances and their effect upon them.

The first stage audience is Christopher Sly, the tinker in *The Taming of the Shrew*, who is picked out of the mud, where 'like a swine he lies', dead drunk, and carried, for the sake of amusement, to the house of a great lord. Here a little pretence is arranged for him in which he is richly clothed, waited on by servants, fed and wined, and presented with a fair wife in order to make him believe that he is in truth a nobleman who has been mad for a number of years and only dreamed that he was a drunkard breaking up the local alehouse. Sly has never seen a play before, thinking that a 'comontie', as he calls it, is like a 'Christmas gambold or a tumbling trick', but now he not only participates in one, but serves as the audience to another, *The Taming of the Shrew*, which is performed before him by a group of travelling players. In the internal *Shrew* play, Petruchio works on Kate in the same theatrical way that the Lord has worked on Sly, pretending that she is the opposite of what she in fact is, sweet of voice rather than railing, inviting rather than frowning, amorous rather than shrewish. The result on both these most unpromising audiences is nothing short of miraculous, at least in the simplest understanding of the play, for Kate the shrew is transformed by theatre into a loving wife, while Sly the drunken tinker at least believes he is become a lord:

> Am I a lord, and have I such a lady?
> Or do I dream? Or have I dream'd till now?
> I do not sleep: I see, I hear, I speak;
> I smell sweet savors, and I feel soft things.
> Upon my life, I am a lord indeed
> And not a tinker, nor Christopher Sly.[8]

There is surely some *naiveté* here, some warning about the danger of being so completely caught up in the illusion of theatre as to take it for reality, which is underscored in the old play, *The Taming of A Shrew*, where Sly finds himself in the end back in the mud again and sets off to tame his shrew in the way that Petruchio handled Kate. But in Shakespeare's play, though Sly concludes his speech about being a lord indeed with a request for 'a pot o' th' smallest ale', he is left inside his transformation, and we are left to consider the possibility even the crudest and most ignorant parts of humanity may be improved by a play which shows what man potentially can be.

Shakespeare's next stage audience, the young gentlemen of the court of the King of Navarre, and the Princess of France and her ladies in *Love's Labour's Lost*, are of much higher social station than Christopher Sly, but are a much less satisfactory audience. The internal play to which they are audience is 'The Pageant of the Nine Worthies', that 'delightful ostentation, or show, or pageant, or antic, or firework' presented in the posterior of the afternoon by several local rustics and pedants at the request of the King of Navarre to entertain the Princess. The Pageant is hideously miscast—no more unworthy Worthies could be imagined—and performed with epic ineptitude; but what might only be an embarrassing amateur theatrical made tolerable by the goodwill of the actors and their desire to show off and please their social betters is transformed into a complete rout by the bad manners of the young noblemen in the audience. Perceiving the ludicrous pretensions of the clown, the schoolmaster, and the curate to be Pompey, Alexander and Hector, the young lords hoot at the actors, interrupt their lines, argue with them, cause them to forget their parts, drive them from the stage in confusion, and bring the performance to an end by encouraging a fight between two of the actors. The mild remonstrance of one of the actors, Holofernes the schoolmaster, 'This is not generous, not gentle, not humble', goes unheeded by the stage audience, but it does remind the other audience in the theatre of the responsibility that an audience always has in making even the most wretched play work as well as it can by good manners, forbearance and a tolerance born of sympathy for those who are trying to serve and entertain them. In Love's Labour's Lost this sympathy is required not only because it manifests the good manners required of any audience with a pretence to civility, but because in 'The Pageant of the Nine Worthies' the stage audience is watching an image of its own ineptitude. The young nobles throughout the play have also been 'a little o'erparted' in trying to play a series of heroic parts, philosophers searching for eternal fame through study, lovers and Muscovites, parts which they have played about as foolishly as the rustics play their pageant. Some humility about our own deficiencies as players of our own self-chosen heroic roles in life, Shakespeare seems to be saying, ought to form a sympathetic bond between audiences and players, no matter how bad. We are all players, and not such very good ones either, and the theatre is the place where we come face to face with our own the—atrical selves. The experience if rightly understood should make not for a feeling of distanced superiority but of identification and sympathy.

This theatrical perspective is openly staged in *A Midsummer Night's Dream*, where Theseus and Hippolyta and the young lovers sit on their wedding night watching Bottom and his company of artisans turned actors make a 'tedious brief scene' and 'very tragical mirth' of a play of Pyramus and Thisbe. The play is as bad as can be imagined, 'not one word apt, one player fitted', but Theseus knows the necessity of the truly noble-minded audience giving the players

> thanks for nothing.
> Our sport shall be to take what they mistake;
> And what poor duty cannot do, noble respect
> Takes it in might, not merit.
>
> (V. i. 89–92)

'Noble respect' also knows that the imagination of the audience must make up for the deficiencies of the players; 'The best in this kind are but shadows; and the worst are no worse, if imagination amend them.' But noble respect, courtesy and imagination of this audience cannot quite, to use Theseus's word, 'apprehend' 'Pyramus and Thisby' as Bottom and his company play it, and so despite the best intents the noble audience chatters away loudly during the performance, making cruelly witty remarks about the players, and calling attention to themselves and their own superiority. Their bad theatrical manners do not help the play—but then what could harm it?—and their self-centred in attention surely does not deprive them of any meaning of the play, for what meaning could it possibly have? So at least it seems on the stage; but from the auditorium, where another audience sits, the scene looks remarkably different. We see not a group of real people laughing at a group of wretched actors in a ridiculous play, but a group of actors somewhat deficient in the imagination needed to apprehend the fantastic world of love and fairies and magic they have moved through, watching, without any self-consciousness whatsoever, another group of actors without any imagination whatsoever completely missing the point of the mysterious story of love and tragic death they are trying to present. Since both the stage players and the stage audience are imaginatively deficient, taking their own sense of reality as absolute, the audience in the theatre is inevitably reminded that they too may be somewhat too secure in turn in their own sense of reality, and that full apprehension of Shakespeare's play, *A Midsummer Night's Dream*, and its fantastic events requires of us both good-mannered tolerance of its performance and some suspension of our own disbelief, some imaginative willingness to consider the play as an alternative image of the world, no more fantastic, no more make-believe, than the image of ourselves and our existence we call reality.

One of the major defences of the English theatre during this period was that it had a positive moral effect upon its audience, and in *Hamlet* Shakespeare tests this contention directly by showing the reactions of an audience to a play presented in the King's palace, the very moral centre of the kingdom, before the King and Queen and the royal court, and depicting a crime directly affecting the welfare of the state. The audience's reactions to 'The Mousetrap or The Murder of Gonzago' are so baffling and unexpected that critics and producers have consistently invented additional actions and motivations for the characters in the stage audience. But if we take the text literally, it is clear that we have here a variety of inadequate and unsatisfactory audience reactions to a play which presents a close parallel to the murder of the old king of Denmark by the present ruler. The Queen, Gertrude, like the rest of the court, who are later identified by Hamlet as 'mutes or audience' to his death, gives no sign that she understands the relevance of the play to her own conduct or to events in Denmark. It may be, and is probable, as the evidence of the rest of the play suggests, that she knows nothing of the murder of her first husband, and that she is therefore unmoved by either the dumb-show or the action of the play depicting that murder. She is sensitive, however, to her 'o'erhasty marriage', but when the Player Queen vows eternal faith to her first husband in terms unmistakably bearing on Gertrude's situation, she either misses the reference to herself altogether or passes it off with an easy remark—'the lady doth protest too much, methinks'—which suggests that the play has not bitten very deeply into her moral consciousness, as very little does.

Claudius does, of course, know what is going on, probably from the beginning of the dumb-show which opens the play and certainly by the time that the murder is acted out on stage, and he rises in passion to call for lights. In the best manner of the moral theory of drama, the staging of his crime forces him to look inward to his heart, and he retires to the chapel to examine his conscience and pray for his soul. But there he concludes that he cares so much for the kingdom and the queen he has stolen that he cannot give them up, and so he plots another murder to protect himself and secure his worldly gains.

Even Hamlet, who has such elevated theories about playing and such scorn for the wrong kind of audience, 'who for the most part are capable of nothing but inexplicable dumb shows and noise', turns out to be a most unsatisfactory audience. Like the young nobles who, to the often-voiced distress of the playwrights, frequently sat upon the public stage during performances to show off their fine wit and dress, he intrudes upon the play, baits the actors, criticises their style, and comments in an audible voice on the action. Nor does the play have the desired moral effect upon him, any more than on Claudius, for while it confirms Claudius's guilt, it does not cause Hamlet to sweep to his revenge. After a period of fury, during which he stabs Polonius by mistake, he allows himself to be led tamely off to England. It can even be argued that Hamlet really misses the more general or philosophical meaning of 'The Murder of Gonzago', for the major portion of that play is taken up not by scenes relating directly to historical events in Denmark but with a long old-fashioned exchange between the Player King and Player Queen about the failure of human purpose in time and, in general, the lack of human control over fate. Hamlet eventually comes to the point of view offered by the Player King, accepting the divinity that shapes our ends and the providence in the fall of a sparrow, but though this sombre view of fate and will is the centre of the play the actors perform in Elsinore, it is not what Hamlet hears or understands at the moment of performance. His own self-absorption and preconceptions make him a poor audience and cause him to miss what the play might have told him.

Theatrical conditions are for once almost ideal in *The Tempest* where the playwright is a magician, his actors a band of spirits doing his immediate bidding, and his audience so 'charmed' that they accept the illusions he stages for them as full reality. Through his art and his spirit-actors, Ariel and his 'meaner fellows', Prospero is able to stage shipwrecks, emblematic banquets, a masque in which the gods are revealed and speak to men, and a tableau in which Ferdinand and Miranda play at chess. Through all these, and Prospero's many other theatrical contrivances such as Ariel's songs or the animal chase of Caliban and his companions through the woods, the various 'audiences' are perfectly protected from any real danger: 'Not a hair perish'd / On their sustaining garments not a blemish, / But fresher than before ... ' (I. ii. 217–19). But so complete is the theatrical illusion of reality on the magical island that the 'charmed' audiences are 'spell-stopped' and so completely absorbed in the spectacles they see that they are frequently drawn into the action. As a result, the play-wright is able to work his will on them and they experience fully and are morally transformed by the terror of shipwreck, the isolation of separation and exile, the wonder of the appearance of the gods of plenty. Ferdinand is brought to an understanding of the necessity for restraint and order. Alonso is brought to sorrow and repentance, and the playwright Prospero is brought by his own productions to forgive past injustices.

But even on this magical island, a geographic realisation of Hamlet's 'sterile promontory', where Shakespeare constructs his absolute 'idea of a theatre', the audience, like the playwright, theatre and actors, is finally not perfect. In their determined realism Sebastian and Antonio remind us of other Shakespearian stage audiences like Theseus and his court, or the King of Navarre and his companions, who through their unwillingness to suspend disbelief are unable to enter into the spirit of the play and are therefore unmoved by it. On the other hand, Caliban, Stephano and Trinculo, the groundlings in every sense of Prospero's theatre, are incapable of suspending belief, like Sly or Bottom and his fellows; and while they take the various performances Prospero arranges for them—for example, the dressing up in the stage costumes Ariel puts in their way—entirely literally, being 'red-hot with drinking', they too are not transformed, though Stephano does, rather oddly to my mind, phrase one of the major lessons of the island, albeit in a somewhat imperfect way, 'Every man shift for all the rest, and let no man take care for himself; for all is but fortune' (V. i. 256–8). The depressing effect of Caliban's literal-mindedness on theatre is made clear when his approach with his fellows Trinculo and Stephano causes the Masque of Juno and Ceres to '*heavily vanish*', with '*a strange, hollow, and confused noise*'.

Shakespeare knew very well what Ulysses tries to teach Achilles in *Troilus and Cressida*, in terms specifically suggesting the theatre (III. iii. 115–23):

> no man is the lord of anything,
> Though in and of him there be much consisting,
> Till he communicate his parts to others;
> Nor doth he of himself know them for aught
> Till he behold them formed in th' applause
> Where th' are extended; who, like an arch, reverb'rate
> The voice again; or, like a gate of steel
> Fronting the sun, receives and renders back
> His figure and his heat.

This is what the playwright in the public theatre, as well as Achilles the soldier hero, had to learn, and in his various presentations of stage audiences Shakespeare was obviously trying to instruct his actual audiences in the part they finally had to play in making the theatre 'like an arch, reverb'rate / The [play's] voice again'. By looking at images of themselves on the stage, he seems to have thought, an audience could become self-conscious about its own role in making theatre work and learn the importance of simple good theatrical manners: not talking while the performance is in progress, not sitting upon the stage and making sneering critical remarks on the actors, not breaching the circle of theatrical illusion, and, more positively, piecing out the crudities of spectacle or performance with imagination and supporting it with sympathetic understanding of the actors' desire to please. But Shakespeare went far beyond these mild, and usually humorous, remonstrances, for his stage audiences, taken in total, are designed to make a real audience at least consider, usually by means of negative example, the proper way to approach and conceive of a play. To take it too literally, to take it for reality, like Sly, Bottom, Caliban and even to some extent Hamlet, is to miss the real point and to interfere, as these audiences always do, with the effectiveness of the performance. To be too sceptical, however, like the King of Navarree, Theseus, or Sebastian and Antonio, and not to allow the play even the status of temporary illusion, is equally destructive. Too much disbelief breaks off Shakespeare's internal plays as frequently as too much belief.

To be fully effective and work the transformations of which it is ideally capable, Shakespeare seems to be saying, theatre must be felt by the audience to be a fragile illusion, at once real and unreal, requiring for its success not only the art of the playwright and the skill of the actors but a complex attitude on the part of the audience in which they accept and are moved by the play as if it were real, while at the same time knowing that it is not literally true. This theatrical epistemology, and the theatrical manners which are required by it, are supported and enforced by what we might call a theatrical metaphysic, which Shakespeare's internal plays again and again put before the stage audiences and the real audiences for their consideration. To put it most simply, all Shakespeare's stage audiences are themselves necessarily actors in fact, finally no more real in their assumed identities and actions than are the players and plays they scoff at and interfere with in various ways. And while the actors who make up the stage audiences are usually better actors than the players in the internal plays, they are totally unaware of their own status as actors, totally sure of their own reality, and completely insensitive to the fact that they have their existence only in plays which, while they maintain illusion more effectively, are no more real than the oftentimes silly and ineffective plays-within-the-play which they are watching. This perspective is maintained most subtly and extensively in Hamlet where all the world, not just 'The Murder of Gonzago', is 'a stage / And all the men and women merely players; / They have their exits and their entrances; / And one man in his time plays many parts'. But it appears most obviously in *A Midsummer Night's Dream* where Theseus, Hippolyta and the young lovers sit laughing at Bottom and his company performing the wretched 'Pyramus and Thisby', totally unaware that they are themselves merely players in the Lord Chamberlain's Company who exist in a play about Athenian dukes and Amazon queens, lovers and fairies, of which many in the real audience might well say, as Hippolyta does of 'Pyramus', 'This is the silliest stuff that ever I heard.'

Since these stage audiences are images of the actual audience, Shakespeare has contrived matters in a much more indirect way than Jonson to make his audiences consider whether their scepticism about Shakespeare's plays may not finally be as unwarranted as that of the stage audiences about the internal plays. Perhaps we too, we are forced to see, are only players unselfconsciously playing the roles of Smith and Jones in a larger play we arrogantly title *Reality*. Once an audience's certainty about itself and its world is unsettled in this way, and it is forced to consider itself as a group of actors, then it is in the proper theatrical frame of mind, poised between belief and disbelief, to accept the fiction of the play as both real and unreal. Real because it is worthy consideration as an alternative and possible image of the world, unreal because all images of the world, including the audience's, are no more than fictions, the 'baseless fabric of [a] vision'. If the revels end and the actors melt into air, so do

> The cloud-capp'd towers, the gorgeous palaces,
> The solemn temples, the great globe itself,
> Yea, all which it inherit, ... dissolve And,
> like this insubstantial pageant faded,
> Leave not a rack behind.
>   (*The Tempest*, IV. i. 152–6)

It is an interesting fact that Shakespeare, reflecting upon and trying to shape the response of the first large public audiences that poets had to work with and for, should have chosen to make his points by negative images. That is, he never shows us an entirely ideal audience, though Theseus expresses something like an ideal response, which he does not live up to, in his comment on the actors: 'The best in this kind are but shadows; and the worst are no worse, if imagination amend them.'

Most often the stage audiences are ill-mannered, imperceptive, and unchanged by what they see. They frequently reveal the effect of these attitudes on theatre by interrupting and halting the internal play before its conclusion. It may be that Shakespeare found that he could make his points about audience response and responsibility by showing what an audience should not be. This would, of course, make an audience more self-conscious than would the presentation of an ideal audience, with which we would easily and instantaneously identify, and consequently not become self-conscious about the role the audience has to play if theatre is to succeed. But it is also necessary, I believe, to take seriously the fact that the playwright who pleased his audience so well that he became rich and famous by doing so, expresses in his plays only suspicion and doubts of an audience ranging all the way from groundlings, like Sly or Caliban, who are 'for a jig or a tale of bawdry' and are 'capable of nothing but inexplicable dumb shows and noise'; through those like Gertrude and the courtiers in Elsinore who are merely 'mutes or audience to this act'; to great nobles like Theseus and a Prince of Denmark, who sits upon the stage making cynical remarks, dallying with his mistress, and putting the players out, 'leave thy damnable faces and begin. Come; the croaking raven doth bellow for revenge.'

While it seems inescapable that there is some distrust of audiences in all this, it is not certain that Shakespeare disliked and scorned his audiences, though we should note that such an attitude corresponds to the general sense of uneasiness about the public theatre audiences expressed by the other playwrights of the time, such as Jonson and Beaumont, but also, more indirectly, Kyd and Marlowe. But we can come somewhat closer to glimpsing, while probably still not pinning down, Shakespeare's own feelings about his audience and theatre by looking for a moment, in closing, at the standard configuration of his internal plays. In every case the play-within-the-play involves an upper-class aristocratic audience viewing with varying degrees of scorn and condescension a play, usually old-fashioned in style and awkward, or at least not totally satisfactory, in performance, put on by lower-class players, either amateur or professional. This structure appears most clearly in *Love's Labour's Lost*, *A Midsummer Night's Dream* and *Hamlet*; and in the latter two plays the philosophy or aesthetic underlying the upper-class scorn of the common players is made explicit: in Theseus's attack on imagination—'the lunatic, the lover, and the poet'—and in *Hamlet's* speech to the players. The configuration is less apparent in *The Taming of the Shrew* and *The Tempest*, but still in both cases there is an aristocratic presence, the lord who picks the drunken Sly out of the mud and arranges both internal plays simply for his own amusement, and the duke turned playwright, Prospero, who even while he practises his art scorns it as a 'vanity' and an 'insubstantial pageant', refers to the players, Ariel and his 'quality', as a 'rabble' of 'meaner fellows', and in the end abjures his 'rough magic', breaks his staff, drowns his book, and leaves his island stage to return to the more serious business of his dukedom in Milan.

The same pattern appears even in the briefer and less formally bracketed internal plays in Shakespeare. The Prince of Wales stands mockingly by while Falstaff, 'as like one of these harlotry players' as ever Mistress Quickly saw, plays the part of the King in an old-fashioned style, 'in King Cambyses' vein'. And Hal, of course, finds Falstaff's performance inadequate—'Dost thou speak like a king?'—and goes on to play the part superbly. Nothing seems more debasing to the Queen of Egypt than that her life and loves should be shown on the public stage:

> the quick comedians
> Extemporally will stage us, and present
> Our Alexandrian revels; Antony
> Shall be brought drunken forth, and I shall see
> Some squeaking Cleopatra boy my greatness
> I' th' posture of a whore.
>
> (V. ii. 215–20)

Even in Shakespeare's *Sonnets*, which constitute an apology for theatre, the lower-class poet, 'made lame by Fortune's dearest spite', who ultimately must make his living writing for the theatre, since patronage has failed him, labours under the shadow of the noble young man he tries to praise, and the aristocratic way of life and the courtly poetry it fostered.

If we want the historical equivalent of all this we need only turn to Sidney's *Apology* where from his aristocratic neo-classical perspective he describes a performance in the public theatre and scorns it for its mingling of kings and clowns, its greasy jokes and its lack of unity. But we should not conclude that the aristocracy and gentry were in Shakespeare's view the antagonists of the public theatre, for we know in fact that the court and the aristocracy on the whole favoured the theatre and protected it from middleclass Puritan and City attacks. Nor should we conclude that Shakespeare was only interested in performances before the court and aristocracy, even though he never openly shows us a public theatre, as Beaumont and Fletcher do in *The Knight of the Burning Pestle*, or Jonson does in *Bartholomew Fair*. Rather, and here I will conclude, I think that in Shakespeare's paradigm of the theatrical situation, the aristocratic audience or presence, represents an aristocratic artistic attitude towards the public drama, as is clear in Sidney, with which Shakespeare partly identified and which at the same time he opposed and criticised. The players and the play, on the other hand, have an equal ambivalence for him: lower-class, frequently awkward and 'o' erparted', old-fashioned in style and subject matter, ludicrously inadequate in the inability to create the necessary illusion of great battles, gorgeous places and solemn temples, they none the less in all their crudity are at least potentially capable of revealing profound truths, transforming human nature, making visible the farther ranges of reality, and telling us finally of the true nature of our existence as actors and our lives as plays. All this, if we will only see and listen in the right way.[9]

NOTES

1. Christopher Hill, *Reformation to Industrial Revolution: A Social and Economic History of Britain, 1530–1780* (Harmondsworth, 1969) p. 89.

2. Quoted in Alfred Harbage, *Shakespeare's Audience* (New York, 1941) p. 4.

3. Ibid., p. 159.

4. Jonas Barish, 'Jonson and the Loathed Stage', in *A Celebration of Ben Jonson*, ed. W. Blissett, Julian Patrick and R. W. Van Fossen (Toronto, 1973) pp. 31–2.

5. *The Staple of News*, Intermean after Act I, line 50.

6. 'Ode to Himself', line 32, appended to *The New Inn*.

7. *Every Man Out of His Humour*, I. ii. 57–60.

8. Induction, ii, 66–71.

9. Portions of this paper were first delivered as the 1979 annual Tupper Lecture at George Washington University, and permission to print these sections is gratefully acknowledged.

RICHARD DUTTON

Licensed Fools:
the 1598 Watershed

The policy of the Elizabethan government (which, for practical purposes, means the Privy Council) towards the business of playing is not always easily defined. It often has to be inferred from actions they either did or did not take, while anything they put into writing *may* need to be seen as a negotiating posture (in relation, say, to the City of London authorities) rather than as a settled will. In fact, it is probably a mistake to assume that they were consistent in their approach to these matters, which almost certainly never figured very highly among their most pressing concerns, or that they were all of one mind about them. Certain Councillors appear to have taken more of an interest at certain junctures, and perhaps nudged policy in a particular direction for a time. But the effects may only have been temporary.

I mention this as a prelude to a reconsideration of the Privy Council's actions in 1597–98, when they appear to have intervened in the theatre business more decisively than at any other time: first ordering the destruction of all the playhouses and latterly restricting London playing to two 'allowed' companies. In fact, rather bewilderingly, nothing came of the first order at all, while the terms of the latter unravelled somewhat in subsequent years. Nevertheless I want to argue that this *was* a decisive watershed, not in every particular but in laying down a framework of policy for handling the actors which would essentially remain in place down to the closing of the theatres in 1642. In these terms it was more significant, for example, than the taking of the major acting companies into royal patronage in 1603–4. And, as I shall argue, the actors and dramatists

From *Licensing, Censorship, and Authorship in Early Modern England.* © 2000 by Richard Dutton.

recognised this significance in the ways that they alluded to it in the plays of the period. Scott McMillin and Sally-Beth MacLean have established with detail and conviction what previous scholars had only inferred: that the Queen's Men, put together in 1583 by Edmund Tilney, Master of the Revels, were a product of deliberate court policy, instigated primarily by the Earl of Leicester and Sir Francis Walsingham (McMillin and MacLean). They were created as the largest and most prestigious company of the era to fulfil at least two functions: as a touring company (often dividing into two separate troupes) they were meant to show a repertoire of intensely loyalist and Protestant-orientated plays as widely as possible. And in the festive season, settled at least for a time in London, they were to supply the court with high-quality entertainment, their precedence putting an end to the rivalry between the patrons of other troupes for the prestige of performing there. In this latter capacity they dominated court entertainment between their inception and 1588.

In all of this 'the central government seemed ready to take charge of this burgeoning actors' industry and send it along calculated directions' (McMillin and MacLean, p. 17). This is what concerns me here, since the creation of the Queen's Men must be seen as the first step along the road towards the regulation of London-based playing which took something like final shape between 1598 and 1600. Yet in the 1580s the Privy Council had not yet settled on a definitive game-plan, since after 1588 the primacy of the Queen's Men was allowed to diminish; they 'began to share the court calendar with other companies in the seasons of 1588–9 and 1589–90, and ... lost the court advantage drastically in 1591–2' (McMillin and MacLean, p. 55). The reasons for this are not entirely clear: the company continued to tour until the end of the reign, and if its quality had been diminished it remained open to Tilney to reinforce it from other companies. But he did not do so, and we must suspect that this was not unconnected with the deaths of those Lords of the Council who had backed the company in the first place, Leicester in 1588 and Walsingham in 1590.

The other members of the Privy Council made no apparent effort to pursue alternative 'calculated directions' for the theatrical profession at this time. Strange's Men and Pembroke's Men enjoyed court precedence in the early 1590s; though their patrons were both influential men, neither was a Councillor, and it is not easy to discern anything resembling policy behind the prominence their companies achieved. It was only with the major reorganisation of the companies precipitated by the plague of 1593–94 (but perhaps not left to unfold randomly) that a new and more settled sense of policy emerged. When the theatres re-opened the Admiral's and Chamberlain's Men had been shaped as predominant companies, in ways that commercial practice alone would not explain. As Andrew Gurr puts it, 'In effect, from May 1594 onwards the Admiral's and Lord Chamberlain's companies knew themselves to be based in London as part of the government's policy, with accompanying privileges' (Gurr, 1996, p. 67). They were the only ones to act at court between December 1594 and February 1600.

Unlike the Queen's Men, however, there is no evidence that their repertoires were deliberately propagandist in nature; nor was provincial touring a primary element of their agenda.

As Gurr suggests, these arrangements arose from the concerted policy of the patrons of the two companies concerned, Lord Admiral Howard and Lord Chamberlain Hunsdon. Both were Privy Councillors, both were first cousins of the Queen, and Howard was, moreover, Hunsdon's son-in-law. Between them they seem to have dictated what was effectively Privy Council thinking on court and London theatre at this juncture, negotiating on behalf of their favoured companies with the city authorities who would have preferred to eradicate activities which they themselves could not control. But this fell far short of blanket support for the acting profession. By 1596 companies were denied the regular use of inn-yard theatres within the City of London's jurisdiction (which may have pleased the city authorities but certainly limited the number of acting venues).[1] And that year the Privy Council prevented the Burbages from using the Blackfriars as a theatre, following a petition from local residents—who included Hunsdon's own son. The Howard/Hunsdon exclusivity was disrupted, moreover, when Hunsdon died in 1596, to be replaced as Lord Chamberlain by Lord Cobham, a circumstance which may well have left its traces in the Falstaff/Oldcastle revisions in the *Henry IV* plays, since Oldcastle was an ancestor of the Cobhams (G. Taylor, 1985, 1987). The situation reverted to something like its earlier symmetry early in 1597 when Cobham in turn died, to be replaced as Lord Chamberlain by the second Lord Hunsdon.

Yet later that year the theatrical profession faced apparently the gravest of all the crises that beset it during Elizabeth's reign. Perhaps stung by the *Isle of Dogs* affair (the sequence of cause and effect is debatable), and urged on yet again by the City of London authorities who demanded 'the present staie & fynall suppressinge of the saide Stage playes, as well at the Theatre, Curten, and banckside, as in all other places in and abowt the Citie' (28 July), the Privy Council that very day temporarily suspended playing for the summer (which was not unusual, given the threat of plague) but ordered 'that also those play houses that are erected and built only for such purposes shalbe plucked downe ... and so to deface the same as they maie not be ymploied agayne to suche use' (Dutton, 1991, pp. 107–8).

Even Howard and Hunsdon signed the orders; and it is far from clear why they were not carried out.[2] Yet the eventual outcome of all this may suggest that it was never the Privy Council's intention to eradicate playing altogether, but rather to impose a more formal framework on the Howard/Hunsdon arrangements. The Chamberlain's Men, after all, had already lost the use of the Theatre in their dispute with the lease-holder, Giles Allen, and may yet have hoped for permission to use the Burbages' Blackfriars theatre. The Rose, where the Admiral's Men performed, was already sinking into the marsh on which it had been built. If all other public theatres were destroyed, *but the duopoly were given authority to start again in new premises*, the purposes of the Privy Council and those they patronised would have been ideally met. Indisputably, as William Ingram (1971–72) has argued, those who lost most in this crisis were Francis Langley, the owner of the new Swan Theatre, and Pembroke's Men who put on *The Isle of Dogs* there: parties outside the charmed circle, and competitors to it (three of the sharers in the Admiral's Men, indeed, had defected to Pembroke's). Langley, moreover, had incurred the wrath of another Privy Councillor, Sir Robert Cecil, in an entirely different matter. So the Privy Council order to destroy the theatres may effectively have been a smoke-screen for putting the Swan, in particular, out of business without publicly singling it out. Certainly, it was rarely used for playing after this. As for Pembroke's Men, just how 'lewd' *The Isle of Dogs* actually was we have no way of knowing, but the demonstrable effect of the Privy Council's investigation into it (largely conducted by the notorious torturer Richard Topcliffe) was that the company disintegrated before they had any chance of establishing themselves in London.

The following year a series of measures were instituted which perhaps made explicit what the Privy Council intended all along. Firstly (9 February) Parliament passed a new *Acte for punyshment of Rogues Vagabondes and Sturdy Beggars*, prescribing ever more vicious punishments for masterless men—explicitly including unlicensed players. Ten days later the Privy Council issued directives to the Middlesex and Surrey Justices, and to the Master of the Revels, for the first time publicly restricting the number of allowed acting troupes in the London area to two. The letter to Tilney specifies:

> Whereas licence hath bin graunted unto two companies of stage players retayned unto us, the Lord Admyral and Lord Chamberlain, to use and practise stage playes, whereby they might be the better enhabled and prepared to shew such plaies before her Majestie as they shalbe required at tymes meete and accustomed, to which ende they have bin cheeflie licensed and tolerated as aforesaid ... We thefore thought good to require you uppon receipt hereof to take order that ... none [may be] suffered hereafter to plaie but those two formerlie named belonging to us, the Lord Admyral and Lord Chamberlaine, unless you shall receave other direction from us.
>
> (Dutton, 1991, pp. 110–11)

It also requires Tilney to suppress an unnamed third troupe, who are neither 'bound to' him nor can be said to be rehearsing plays for performance at court.

What is not clear from the letter is whether the Privy Council were referring to an essentially new situation when they assert that 'licence hath bin granted', or whether they meant arrangements as they had in effect largely pertained since 1594, which they were in effect re-instating. Strictly speaking these precise arrangements could *not* have been in place all this time, since when

tween the privileged London companies and those in the Privy Council who
oked out for their interests.

An order of 22 June 1600 attempted to tighten the already very strict 1598
nditions: it reiterated the exclusive licences of the Admiral's and Chamberlain's
en, but restricted their playing to their 'now usual houses', respectively the
rtune and the Globe. There was a further ban on playing 'in any Common Inn
publique assemblie in or neare about the Cittie' and moreover 'forasmuche
hese stage plaies, by the multitude of houses and Companie of players, have
too frequent ... It is likewise ordered that the two severall Companies of
ers assigned unto the two howses allowed maie play each of them in their
rall howse twice a weeke and no oftener' (Dutton, 1991, p. 111).

Nothing, it would seem, could be clearer or more categorical. But in
tice things were nowhere near as clear-cut as this, as the Lords of the
ncil acknowledged when they concluded the order with the admonition to
Lord Mayor and the Justices of Middlesex and Surrey, to whom it was
essed: 'these orders wilbe of litle force and effecte unless they be dulie putt
ecution by those to whom yt appertaineth to see them executed'. Indeed,
dy by this date the duopoly of the Admiral's and Chamberlain's Men had
breached by the resuscitation of the boy companies, Paul's Boys and the
lren of the Chapel—both of whom would perform at court in the following
s season. Even more critically, another adult troupe, the Earl of Derby's
had already performed at court in the winter of 1599–1600, and had taken
sidence in the Boar's Head playhouse, in every respect flouting the Privy
cil's orders. Or, more precisely, flouting them in every respect bar one—
vere paying the Master of the Revels 15s. per playing week at the Boar's
and so apparently submitting to his authority, even though that was not
sed to extend beyond the two 'allowed' companies (Berry, 1986, p. 130).

Despite numerous reiterations by the Privy Council of the two-company
tion, Derby's Men remained at the Boar's Head unmolested, and
ned again at court in the winter season of 1600–1. In the autumn of 1601,
er, they were replaced at the Boar's Head by a new company, an
mation of troupes patronised by the Earls of Oxford and Worcester,
ould be known by the latter's name. They would perform at court in the
season, and finally join the Admiral's and Chamberlain's Men as a third
y 'allowed' adult company. Herbert Berry is not alone in seeing all this as
ld, not least in that the Privy Council emerges from it as wildly
tent—in 1597 apparently on the verge of eradicating the playhouses
er (and certainly stopping playing at The Swan for several years), but
er complaining rather lamely that their directives were not being
l, yet doing nothing about it: 'The Privy Council in Elizabeth's time
ntually have thought of theatrical enterprises as falling into one of three
es: 1) those that the central government for one reason or another would
y at all; 2) those that it would allow and take fees from but not protect

old Hunsdon died the company turned to his son as a patron ra
Cobham, and there was a period when the younger Hunsdon w
Councillor nor Lord Chamberlain. But they may simply be
details. Strikingly, the letter carries the authority of the whol
it relates specifically to actors patronised by only two of its
Lord Admyral and Lord Chamberlaine'. This needs to be set
Vagrancy Act; this reconfirmed the provision of the 1572 ac
companies to those 'belonging to any Baron of this Rea
honorable Personage of greater degree', but removing
companies might be licensed locally for performance by Jus

That is, taking the two measures together, the right
patronise acting companies were not infringed, but th
companies to perform in and around London (as Pembro
Hunsdon's Men had done, probably quite legitimately, in 15
to those patronised by members of the Privy Council itse
explicitly associated with the fiction that these companies w
the possibility of being invited to perform at court, and th
the Revels their logical regulator. The idea that public ac
to be rehearsal for court performance was an old fig-leaf
the Privy Council to protect the actors from the City au
them, for example, in April 1582, and was explicitly c
Mayor in 1592 when he sought Archbishop Whitgift's a
the actors, enquiring 'if by any means it may be devised
served with these recreations as hath ben accoustomed
may easily bee don by the privat exercise of hir M
convenient place)' (Dutton, 1991, pp. 49, 78–9).

What is new in 1598 is the very explicit limiting
perform on these grounds to two, that these two are
Councillors who are senior members of the royal ho
explicitly under the authority of the Master of the R
Tilney's public role for the first time. Although his S
had given him plenipotentiary powers over the thea
that in practice his dealings had only been with
unspecified) who stood a serious chance of performi
the Privy Council proposed that he join with a
someone appointed by the Lord Mayor of Londo
censor plays, which indicates that he was not in f
London region at that time. Indeed, he is not men
Isle of Dogs affair, presumably because he had not
have fallen to the Surrey magistrates. Uncompron
henceforth explicitly the controller of all permitte
cousin of Hunsdon and a rather closer one of H
originally secured the Revels Office for him), Ti

from local authorities; and 3) those that it would allow, take the same fees from, and protect from local authorities' (p. 130). The Swan after 1597 would fall into category 1, the Boar's Head from 1599 to 1602 into category 2, the Globe and Fortune from 1600, and the Boar's Head from 1602, into category 3.

The issue may be more intelligible, however, if we stop looking at the Privy Council as the driving force in all this. Clearly they were an interested party, and their authority could be all but definitive when they chose to exert it (as they did with The Swan). But the habit of reviewing events from a government-centred perspective, as if a modern Prime Minister or President was deliberately dictating policy—an approach so much encouraged by E.K. Chambers' beguilingly helpful assemblage of all 'Documents of Control' into a single, quasi-narrative appendix—may actually be very misleading (Freedman). I want to think laterally here, of the situation as it related to the regulation and censorship of printed books. From 1586 this was in the hands of the Church Court of High Commission, under the control of the Archbishop of Canterbury and the Bishop of London, though most of the day-to-day licensing was handled by their chaplains and other lesser clergy.

From a distance the Star Chamber decree setting this up looks like the imposition of an arbitrary and repressive government. The reality, however, was rather different. It was actually the Stationers' Company, rather than the government, who agitated for this development. Edward Arber, the Victorian editor of the Stationers' Register, observes that the 'Star Chamber decree of the 23 June 1586 ... was undoubtedly promoted, not by the Government, but by the principal Stationers chiefly as a protection for their own literary property as an article of commerce' (Arber, 3, p. 17: see below, Chapter 8 'Buggeswords'). The striking thing is that the Stationers' Company *already* had a monopoly of the English printing industry, under the terms of its 1557 charter. But it was a monopoly they found very difficult to enforce. John Wolfe in particular found ways of conducting business despite not being a Stationer. The 1586 arrangements changed the ground-rules (and Wolfe promptly became an extremely loyal and leading member of the company) since the licensing of books and the business of selling them henceforth went hand in hand.

That is, the legal framework was driven by a business imperative, securing an *enforceable* monopoly (or, strictly, a cartel since members traded independently) for the Stationers' Company: royal and church authority blended seamlessly with self-policing commercial privilege in a perfectly reciprocal pattern of patronage. The Privy Council directive of 19 February 1598 reads like a parallel case, and in my view was—to paraphrase Arber—if not undoubtedly, very probably 'promoted, not by the Government, but by the principal *actors and theatre owners* chiefly as a protection for their own *theatrical* property as an article of commerce'. There are no records to confirm this, but it makes the best sense of the evidence we have. Rather like the Stationers before 1586, the Admiral's and Chamberlain's Men after 1594 had established a *de facto* monopoly of regular

London and court playing, collaborating harmoniously (as far as we can tell) with Tilney. Lord Cobham's brief tenure as Lord Chamberlain may well have rocked the boat, while the *Isle of Dogs* business erupted outside the charmed circle, with destabilising effects on the whole industry which had to be taken seriously, given the (by now) entrenched opposition of the city authorities.

The Admiral's and Chamberlain's Men naturally sought to preserve their livelihood—and an arrangement whereby they publicly submitted to Tilney's authority and licensing in return for quasi-monopoly trading conditions must have suited them very nicely. As with the Stationers, the legal framework and commercial self-interest reinforced each other perfectly. There were, of course, differences between the 1586 and 1598 situations, but some were more apparent than real. The 1598 provisions do read as though Howard and Hunsdon were taking personal advantage of their positions to protect the interests of their companies (which perhaps they were); but this is not really so different from Archbishop Whitgift convincing the Court of Star Chamber—in reality only the Privy Council in another capacity, and he belonged to both—to set up a system of licensing which secured a comfortable income for a dozen of his clergy, at the same time as it tied the Stationers into bonds of mutual self-interest with himself and the government as a whole.

One real difference was that the Stationers determined their own membership. Although it was subject to many constraints, the acting profession had no such self-limiting mechanism. And the immediate response by those excluded under the 1598 restrictions was a determination to break into the privileged inner circle. The first to succeed were the boy companies. The Children of the Chapel had ceased commercial activities by the mid-1580s, while Paul's Boys stopped performing around 1590–1, possibly in the wake of the Martin Marprelate affair. But it has never been established what official action—if any—put them out of business or permitted them to restart. In the absence of evidence to the contrary it is sensible to conclude that there never was any intervention by the authorities—that they ceased performing because demand for them tapered off (possibly as a result of increased competition from London-based adult companies in the mid-1580s), and that they started up again when the demand returned, very probably because the Privy Council's action reduced the supply of drama on offer.

Their special patents as choir schools remained in force throughout, and from 1599–1600 they effectively joined the cartel of the Admiral's and Chamberlain's Men, under Tilney's authority, though official pronouncements from the Privy Council and elsewhere at this time continue to treat them as a special category, not as common players. (This was to change early in James's reign). Clearly, the Privy Council *could* have suppressed these activities if they had been determined to. The fact that they did not strongly suggests that the measures of 1598 were less a matter of clinical public policy than of collusion (reciprocal endorsement) between the agents of government and those in the profession with the resources and the patronage to negotiate privileged trading conditions. When others emerged with as persuasive a claim, the logic was to include them within the cartel rather than attempt to suppress them.

The Admiral's and Chamberlain's Men were perhaps less distressed than they might otherwise have been at *this* infringement of their privileges, because the boys offered something distinctively different: smaller and much more expensive theatres, a niche market perhaps only marginally in competition with their own. (There was even to be collaboration between the Chamberlain's Men and Paul's Boys over *Satiromastix*). But the 1598 arrangement also in practice left the door open to adult companies with the right qualifications: they established certain principles, but not the definitive numbers. Actors with a noble patron could still ply their trade in the provinces: and those with sufficient resources and patronage might bid to join the inner sanctum. This is what Derby's, and subsequently Worcester's Men, did. The privileges enjoyed by Derby's Men seem to have followed an intervention by their patron, or more precisely their patron's wife, who was Robert Cecil's niece:

> Good uncle[,] being importuned by my Lo: to intreat your favor that his man browne with his company may not be bared from their accoustomed plaing in maintenance wher of the[y] have consumde the better part of ther substance, if so vaine a matter shall not seame troublesum to you I could desier that your furderance might be a meane to uphold them for that my Lo: taking delite in them it will kepe him from moer prodigall courses and make your credit prevaile withe him in a greater matter for my good[.] So commending my best love to you I take my leave[.]
> Your most loving nece E. Derbye.
>
> (Berry, p. 34)

Unfortunately we cannot date this letter. But it is too much of a coincidence, given Cecil's pre-eminent position as secretary of state, that it should not to be associated with the particular favour shown to Derby's Men in the period 1599–1600.

It is indisputably the case that the admission of Worcester's Men to be another of the 'allowed' companies followed the intercession of the Earl of Oxford, still acting in effect as patron of at least part of the company. On 31 March 1602 the Privy Council wrote to the Lord Mayor, directing him to allow the new company to perform at the Boar's Head 'upon noteice of her Majesties pleasure at the suit of the Earl of Oxford'. The fact is that personal intervention, either with the Queen herself, or with an individual as powerful as Cecil, was quite capable of overturning the declared policy of the Privy Council—at least, that is, if the person making the intervention had the prestige of being a sixth (Derby) or seventeenth (Oxford) earl. Conversely, existing members of the

London cartel were equally free to use their own influence to try to protect their privileges. This must surely lie behind the directive of June 1600, which confirms the Admiral's and Chamberlain's Men as the only 'allowed' companies, but confines them to their 'usual houses'. Again, this looks like another arbitrary restrictive whim of government, anxious to assert its control. But in reality it raises the stakes in the patronage competition, and favours those who already have an advantage. Exclusive use of a purpose-built and authorised theatre becomes a minimum condition for joining the élite of the 'allowed' companies.

The strongest argument for this reading of events is its timing: the directive seems to have been issued as soon as The Fortune was complete. Indeed, it is the earliest evidence we have that The Fortune was ready for use.[3] Thus the Admiral's Men had caught up with the Chamberlain's Men, whose Globe had been completed about a year before. The Theatre had been dismantled to create The Globe, The Rose was deteriorating and its lease running out, use of The Swan was proscribed, and one of the conditions of the 1600 directive was that The Curtain should cease to be used for playing. The boy companies had their own theatres—Paul's Boys in the Chapter Precinct of St Paul's, while the Children of the Chapel gained the use of the Burbage's Blackfriars theatre, a measure of their difference from the adult companies. The whole situation clearly suited those *in possession*, and the directive merely reinforced the prerogatives of the status quo.

But in this it was not totally successful. In the late summer of 1599, just as The Globe was coming into use, the Boar's Head was refurbished for the use of Derby's Men, who had hitherto been touring in the provinces (Berry, p. 34–5). This was literally just outside the City precincts, and for that reason not subject to the proscriptions that had brought the regular use of inn-yard theatres to an end within London by 1596. But the patronage which gained Derby's Men an entrée at court that winter presumably kept the theatre safe in June 1600. Derby himself remains a relatively shadowy figure, though he must have had considerable influence at court. This was the period in which his involvement with the theatres was at its most intense. It was in June 1599 that George Fenner intriguingly recorded: 'Therle of Darby is busyed only in penning comedies for the common Players', and Derby also (significantly) financed the re-opening of Paul's Boys. His alliance by marriage with Cecil must have given an edge to his august title.

Yet somehow this did not translate into securing his actors a permanent place among the 'allowed' companies—merely a temporary sojourn. The sticking point may well have been that Derby, for all his influence and enthusiasm, was not a Councillor—the final hurdle built into conditions of membership in 1598. The Council itself, steered by Cecil, may tacitly have deferred to his status but denied his company formal recognition. This possibility is reinforced by what happened to those who succeeded Derby's Men at the Boar's Head and at court, but unlike them did break into the charmed circle of 'allowed' companies.

Oxford/Worcester's Men set up at the Boar's Head in late summer or early autumn 1601, appearing at court in January 1602. It was Worcester's name by which they were usually known—though as late as March 1602 Oxford was still sufficiently involved with them to intercede on their behalf, possibly with the Queen herself, though more likely the Privy Council acting in her name, and Worcester was present at the relevant meeting, signing the relevant documents (Berry, pp. 51, 57).

Oxford was not a Councillor, but Worcester was: he rose spectacularly as Essex fell, acquiring Essex's former post as Master of the Horse in April 1601 and being sworn into the Council that June—just before the new company came into being. However good their relations with their patron had been (and perhaps continued to be) those of Oxford's Men who joined the new company must have known that Worcester's patronage potentially carried with it something his never could. Being Master of the Horse he was equal in status in the royal household to the Lord Admiral and Lord Chamberlain. To this extent, the admission of a third adult company to the ranks of those patronised and authorised by the royal household and Privy Council was not a change of policy, merely a widening of the circle. It finally set the seal on a competitive process of reciprocal licensing and patronage that had been turning over at least since Tilney formed the Queen's Men, but reached something like definitive form in the years 1598–1602. The taking of all of the 'allowed' companies (except for Paul's Boys) into direct royal patronage may have removed a residual element of competition between the aristocrats whose liveries they had formerly worn, but in most other respects it did virtually nothing to alter the relationship between the acting community and the centres of power in the country, as they had been defined over these years.[4]

Much of this, of course, is guesswork, trying to make the best sense of events and documents whose full context we know very imperfectly. What I want to suggest now, however, is that the theatrical community itself recognised the events of 1598–1600 (or 1602) as a watershed, something that changed their status, and their relationships with both the court and the City, in a major way. Their plays from this period keep alluding to it. There is room for debate as to what these allusions finally tell us, but their existence is hardly to be doubted.

I start with *The Shoemaker's Holiday*, for which Henslowe paid Thomas Dekker on 15 July 1599, and these observations by R.L. Smallwood and Stanley Wells in their Revels Plays edition:

> In the spring of 1599, a few weeks before Dekker finished *The Shoemaker's Holiday*, Sir John Spencer, who had been Lord Mayor of London in 1594, had been temporarily committed to the Fleet for mistreating his only daughter Elizabeth, whose contract of marriage

to the Second Lord Compton, a young courtier close to the Queen, he bitterly opposed. Spenser continued to do all in his power to hinder the match after his release. He had been an unpopular Lord Mayor—there are records of his violent clashes with the London apprentices—and a firm opponent of the theatres, and the affair was the subject of gossip. It is not unlikely, as Novarr suggests, that the opening scene of *The Shoemaker's Holiday*, with a Lord Mayor doing his best to prevent his daughter's marriage to a courtier, would have struck a familiar chord with its first audiences, and that there would have been little doubt about the direction of their sympathies.

(Dekker, 1979, p. 25; see also Novarr; Stone)

In the context I have been outlining, I suggest such identifications are much stronger than 'not unlikely'. Dekker is crowing here over the 'misfortunes' of a known opponent of the theatres—one of those former Lord Mayors who must have been exasperated beyond measure by the 1598 developments, which effectively put the 'allowed' companies beyond their grasp once and for all. We can even imagine Tilney taking pleasure in the discomfiture of one of those who (in the 1592 negotiations with Whitgift) had sought to sever his links with the public theatres altogether: Dekker's ridicule remains just sufficiently anonymised that Spencer would have to make a fool of himself even to object to it.

But there is more here than simply a 'hit' at a known individual. *The Shoemaker's Holiday* is perhaps the classic example of the citizen comedy genre, which is commonly thought to have started in 1598 with William Haughton's *Englishmen for My Money* (like Dekker's, an Admiral's Men's play). As Alexander Leggatt argues, 'citizen comedy may be about citizens, but it does not necessarily uphold their values, nor was it necessarily written for them as an audience' (Leggatt, p. 4). In the hands of the boy companies the genre became openly satirical, ridiculing citizens' pretensions. But in these early examples, in the hands of Haughton and Dekker, the tone is affectionate, celebrating the city, its history, traditions, locales and heroes, like Dick Whittington and Dekker's own Simon Eyre. The romanticised view of the past may cover veiled criticism of the present—as Eyre's private munificence stands in marked contrast to the stark poor law and vagrancy legislation of the previous year. But the main thrust of such drama is to identify the theatres which stage it with the citizenry it celebrates: sharing together in the royal blessing which Dekker introduces into his play, a detail missing from Deloney and the other sources on which he draws.

There had always been a side of Elizabethan theatre that put it on the fringes of respectability, its playhouses located beyond the city limits to rub shoulders with brothels and prisons, its actors classed in legislation as no better than vagrants and masterless men—the side most clearly delineated by Steven Mullaney in *The Place of the Stage*.[5] But Mullaney underplays the extent that there was always a confederacy between the court and the leading acting companies which counter-balanced this marginalisation. In 1598 the balance tipped conclusively in favour of those lucky enough to be the 'allowed' companies, and that is what Dekker here celebrates. The theatres are no longer the city's shame, whatever its own authorities might think: they are its monuments, its places of wonder (as they clearly were to the foreign visitors who repeatedly voiced their admiration), sites on a par with John Stow's *Chronicles* which, in plays like this, relived its history and traditions.

And the actors are no longer little better than vagabonds: they are citizens, too. This is particularly stressed in the aptness of the subject-matter of *The Shoemaker's Holiday*, because cobbling is (as the play's subtitle and the Epistle to the 1600 quarto remind us) 'the Gentle Craft', a title with several mythic derivations, most of them stressing the grace of former monarchs to practitioners of the trade, who rose in status from the association, manual labourers aspiring (almost) to gentry. This neatly parallels what has happened to the actors of the 'allowed' companies ('the quality', as they were known), as Dekker is at pains to stress in the Epistle: '*To all good fellows, professors of the Gentle Craft, of what degree soever*. Kind gentlemen and honest boon companions, I present you here with a merry conceited comedy called *The Shoemaker's Holiday*, acted by my Lord Admiral's Players this present Christmas before the Queen's most excellent Majesty; for the mirth and pleasant matter by her Highness graciously accepted, being indeed no way offensive' (Dekker, 1979, p. 77). So Dekker effortlessly weaves together the citizens of London ('of what degree soever', though the emphasis is on gentlemen) and the Lord Admiral's Players, equally respectable subjects of her Majesty, equally engaged in their different 'gentle crafts', which are—an obeisance to Tilney's role—'no way offensive', as the Queen's patronage graciously confirms. Tilney and the Admiral's Men chose shrewdly when they selected this play for court performance, since it epitomises the relationship between the court, the actors and the City of London which the 1598 provisions dictate.

The other play they took to court that winter season, *Old Fortunatus*, again by Dekker, seems rather to look forward to the additional provisions of June 1600. In both title and theme it is a play about Fortune, who as a goddess repeatedly intercedes in the action. Given the circumstances of the play's composition, and their closeness to the building of The *Fortune*, it is impossible to escape the conclusion that the play would be seen in multiple senses as a celebration of the Admiral's Men's own good 'fortune'. At least one play of *Fortunatus* existed as early as 1596 and was in the Admiral's Men's repertoire. In November 1599 Henslowe made three separate payments to Dekker in connection with a 'whole history of Fortunatus', which seems to represent either a second part to the original play, or an amalgamation of two existing plays into a single new one; in either event Dekker received a total payment of £6, equivalent to the usual fee for a new play. But that is not the whole story, as Cyrus Hoy records:

The day after Dekker had received final payment for the play, we find Henslowe (under the date of what he terms 31 November) advancing the dramatist the sum of £1 'for the altrenge of the boocke of the wholl history of fortewnatus'. The reason for this is contained in Henslowe's entry of 12 December, where a further sum of £2 has been paid to Dekker 'for the eande of fortewnatus for the corte'. The play was being adapted for court performance, where it was duly played before the Queen on 27 December.

(Hoy, 1, p. 72)

This is unusual in the extreme. Firstly Henslowe pays Dekker a full fee for amending or adding to an old play, producing a text which we must assume the actors regarded as serviceable. But the very next day he engages him to rewrite the same material 'for the corte', paying yet another £3, a full half-fee. Nothing exactly parallels this in Henslowe's Diary, nor is there evidence elsewhere that it was usual to amend a text as extensively as is implied here for court performance.

Above all, it seems particularly odd that a text should be amended in this way before it could even be tried out on an audience. The usual assumption is that success in the theatre singled out a play for performance at court, possibly then amended under the guidance of the Master of the Revels. Here we have what amounts to the creation of a play especially—possibly even solely—for court performance (since Henslowe records no subsequent performances). Only Jonson's *Bartholomew Fair* and possibly Shakespeare's *The Merry Wives of Windsor* suggest themselves as comparable examples, so this was very unusual indeed—a uniqueness compounded by being published, in what is clearly an authorised edition, only weeks after that court performance (Stationers' Register, 20 February 1600).

I suggest that the only explanation for these unique circumstances must be prior knowledge, at least in court circles, that The *Fortune* was to be built. Roslyn Knutson argues that, since the contract for the new playhouse was not signed until 8 January, it can only have been 'a happy coincidence' that the Admiral's Men's purchased 'in November ... a play with the name of their playhouse in the title', though she recognises what good publicity it would be (Knutson, 1991, p. 82). But she ignores the payments made for revision in December and the special circumstances both of the court performance and of publication. This was more than publicity—it was the Admiral's Men basking in their new status, which was to be further confirmed in the building of the new theatre. It is in textual moments that Dekker certainly wrote for the court performance that this is most fully confirmed, as when the Goddess Fortune kneels before the Queen, acknowledging 'tis most meete/ That Fortune falle downe at thy conqu'ring feete' (5.2. 313–14) and the two old men who speak the Epilogue address Elizabeth as a 'deere Goddesse' whom they will entreat with 'praiers that we/May once a yeere so oft enjoy this sight' (Epilogue, 12–13: *Old Fortunatus* in

Dekker, 1953–61, I). The actors acknowledge that their 'Fortune' owes everything to the Queen, but hope to see their privileges confirmed in yearly court performances.

Chapman's *All Fools* is also obsessed with Fortune, though the date and provenance of the text that has survived makes it difficult precisely to locate in relation to these concerns. Henslowe paid Chapman for a play called *All Fools but the Fool* or *The World Runs of Wheels* between January 1598 and July 1599; the play that survives was published in 1605 as 'Presented at the Black Fryers, And lately before his Majesty'. E.K. Chambers argued that they were distinct plays: 'the change of company raises a doubt, and there is no fool in *All Fools*' (Chambers, 3, p. 252). But in a play where *all* the characters are fools, the absence of a distinctively scripted 'fool' is hardly conclusive (especially since, as I shall argue, 'fooling' and acting are sometimes suggestively synonymous at this time). Moreover, the text seems to retain distinct allusions to an outdoor theatre with a 'heaven' and 'hell' the Blackfriars did not have (Prologus, 3–4) and a date before the turn of the century is cited in the text: 'the seventeenth of November, fifteen hundred and so forth' (4.1.330: Chapman, 1968). Chapman presumably *did* revise the play for the Children of the Chapel, but this text seems to retain at least some earlier features. And it is here that its preoccupation with Fortune is so intriguing.

One of the principal characters is called Fortunio, while the Prologus twice links Fortune with the theatre: 'The fortune of a stage (like Fortune's self) / Amazeth greatest judgments ...', 'So Fortune governs in these stage events' (1–2, 33). Thereafter, the theme recurs repeatedly, most tellingly in the opening lines of both the final scenes: 'I see these politicians / (Out of blind Fortune's hands) are our most fools' (3.1.114–15); 'Fortune, the great commandress of the world, / Hath divers ways to advance her followers' (5.1.1–2); 'We will shift rooms / To see if Fortune will shift chances with us. Sit. ladies, sit. Fortunio, place thy wench ...' (5.2.1–3). It would, of course, be difficult to find a more common theme than Fortune in Elizabethan drama. But its very particular reiteration in this play seems pointed in a way that suggests an extra-textual referent, for which the new theatre is the prime candidate. Whenever precisely this text was penned, it seems to be part of an advertising campaign for the Admiral's Men new 'usual house', and so to stress the good fortune of those who are licensed to play at The Fortune.

There are numerous other plays in which Fortune (and, as we shall see, Globes) are foregrounded in such a way as to suggest extra-textual referents, which must surely be the theatres. Some seem more in the spirit of rivalry rather than advertising. We may, for example, suspect something of this in *Hamlet*'s badinage with Rosencrantz and Guildenstern, which leads eventually to the announcement of the players' arrival: Guildenstern claims that 'on Fortune's cap (Q2: 'lap') we are not the very button' but *Hamlet* twists their answers to put them 'In the secret parts of Fortune' (2.2. 218–19; 235). In the context of theatrical London c. 1600–1 (to which the text alludes repeatedly in other ways)[6], that is a coded way of acknowledging them as rivals, as the enemy. I shall return to this point.

For the Chamberlain's Men more generally I want firstly to turn to a play which was not new in 1598–1600 but a (presumed) revival from 1595–96. *A Midsummer Night's Dream* was first published in 1600 'As it hath been sundry times publickely acted, by the Right honourable, the Lord Chamberlaine his servants'. Roslyn Knutson proposes a close correlation between the publication of plays more than a year or so old, and their revival on stage, and cites this as a plausible example (1991, pp. 12–13, 81). Certainly, if the play was revived in late 1599/early 1600, Oberon's boast—'We the globe can compass soon/Swifter than the wand' ring moon' (4.1.94–5)—would have had a local and topical edge to it then, albeit not as resonant as the 'All the world's a stage' speech from *As You Like It* which Shakespeare must have penned with The Globe in mind. The possibility of a c. 1599 revival of *A Midsummer Night's Dream* is particularly intriguing from my perspective, since it is the only play I know where the Master of the Revels is himself brought on stage—Philostrate in the quarto text and Egeus in the folio, respectively Theseus's 'usual manager of mirth'. Strikingly, Philostrate figures much more prominently in the quarto text than (in this respect) does Egeus. In the quarto Philostrate is the one who outlines to Theseus the whole range of theatrical delights available on his wedding night and vainly attempts to prevent him having *Pyramus and Thisbe* performed. In the folio Egeus shares his lines with Lysander and the nature of his court post is sidelined by his plot centrality as Hermia's father. Editors of the play have (until recently) favoured the quarto version, but Barbara Hodgdon has argued to some effect that the folio is both dramatically and thematically more effective, providing a resolution of sorts to the Hermia/Egeus split which ignites the play's action (1986).

What we cannot know is when the differences between the two versions emerged. The publishing sequence prompts the assumption that the folio version is a post–1600 revision, but this is far from being a necessary conclusion. I simply want to point out that the quarto version is a peculiarly apt fable for the situation of the actors in 1599–1600—whether it was a simple revival or revised for the occasion. As my colleague, Richard Wilson (1993b), has argued it is a play about very English forms of censorship, in which the class-conscious deference of the 'mechanicals' compounds with their fear of giving offence to ensure a performance of utterly guileless 'entertainment'. And the services of a censor are unnecessary (despite suspicions elsewhere of 'satire, keen and critical') when Theseus is determined that 'never anything can be amiss,/When simpleness and duty tender it' (5.1.54, 82-3). By subscribing to this formula the Chamberlain's servants are indeed 'made men', secure in their 'sixpence a day' so long as they submit to Philostrate/ Tilney's authority. The common assumption that Shakespeare's play, like that of his 'mechanicals', was meant to celebrate an aristocratic wedding has long overshadowed the documented fact that it 'hath been sundry times publickely acted'—and so that it is a perfect allegory of relations between the acting companies and the court. The 1600 version, with its emphasis on Philostrate and his role, particularly mirrors Tilney's enhanced role as overseer of the 'allowed' companies from that time.

I want to argue, however, that the events of 1598–1600 left a much more substantial mark on the Chamberlain's Men than the in-jokes of this one play. They coincide with the single most significant change in their personnel during Shakespeare's career with them—the loss of Will Kempe and his replacement by Robert Armin. Despite the apparent residue of mutual ill-will in Kempe's gibes at 'my notable Shakerags' (in the 'humble request' to his *Nine Days' Wonder*) and *Hamlet*'s haughty strictures to 'those that play your clowns' it is far from clear why, or indeed when, Kempe actually left. He signed the lease for, and so became a shareholder in, The Globe in February 1599. David Wiles argues that he had left the company by the aulumn, partly because 'there is no obvious clown part in *Julius Caesar*, which was in performance by September' (p. 36). But what is the business of the Poet who tries to reconcile Brutus and Cassius, and is dismissed by the former with impatience at 'jigging fools' (4.3.137), if it is not an opportunity for one of Kempe's trade-mark jigs? Even the famous Nine Day's Morris to Norwich in February–March 1600 is not evidence that he had left the company, since it took place when the theatres were closed for Lent anyway; and though the published account of it (Stationers' Register 22 April that year) may register ill-will, it is not so abusive as to be categorical evidence that Kempe and Shakespeare were no longer working together.

The fact is that we do not know when Kempe actually left. We do know that he was with Worcester's Men by March 1602 (when Henslowe advanced him a loan) and so may well have been involved in the reformation of that company late in 1601. I have dwelled on this at some length because, to be honest, I wanted to find a causal connection between the developments of 1598–1600 and Kempe's leaving; but I have not done so. I toyed with a scenario in which Kempe's partly impromptu jigs no longer seemed safe in the repertoire of the 'allowed' companies, so his colleagues engineered his departure in order to make way for Armin as a player 'wise enough to play the fool', and discreet enough to do so comfortably within Tilney's rules. But the evidence is not there: all we know is that he left the Chamberlain's Men and joined Worcester's, but not before they too were an 'allowed' company. Such as it is, the evidence supports Wiles's conclusion that it was 'professional differences' (p. 36) that led Kempe to leave, rather than either personalities or the new framework of control. Jigs do seem to have continued to flourish in the theatres north of the city (with their citizen repertories) rather than in those south of the river.

So Armin's coming may not have been a planned replacement for Kempe. Indeed, they may have overlapped in the company. The witty cobbler who bandies words with the Tribunes at the opening of Julius Caesar has all the hallmarks of an Armin role, very different from the jigging Poet. What seems indisputable is that, quite early on in his association with the Chamberlain's Men, Armin became somehow associated with their new status as an 'allowed' company, and that this was semi-formalised in his 'licensed fool' roles. Wiles (p. 145) identifies seven of these between 1599 and 1605, mainly but not exclusively written by the company's resident playwright: Touchstone (*As You Like It*, c. 1599), Carlo Buffone (*Every Man Out of His Humour*, 1599), Feste (*Twelfth Night*, c. 1601), Thersites (*Troilus and Cressida*, c. 1601–2), Lavatch (*All's Well That Ends Well*, c. 1602–3), Passarello (*The Malcontent*, c. 1604) and the Fool (*King Lear*, c. 1605–6).

There were, of course, numerous other roles which shared some characteristics with these—Wiles identifies various 'orthodox clown parts' and 'latent clown parts' (pp. 150–1)—but the 'licensed fools' are particularly resonant precisely because their recurrent identity mirrors that of the acting profession as a whole. With the exception of Buffone, they are all servants of aristocrats and all uniquely licensed to speak their minds and not give offence (or be shielded from harm if they *do* give offence—the whip is invoked more than once, but never actually used). That is what the 1598 provisions established for the actors in the 'allowed' companies, with Tilney empowered to convey that licence. In all of these roles, therefore, Armin invokes a metadramatic dimension, a reminder of the precise rules—social and political, as well as aesthetic—under which the actors are allowed to 'hold a mirror up to nature'.

Even though the role and its conventions must have become a familiar one, Shakespeare in particular goes out of his way to write in the specific fact of 'licence'. So Olivia, defending Feste, reminds us all that 'There is no slander in an allowed fool, though he do nothing but rail' (1.5.89–91); Lafeu describes Lavatch as 'A shrewd knave and an unhappy', to which the Countess replies: 'So a is. My Lord that's gone made himself much sport out of him; by his authority he remains here, which he thinks a patent for his sauciness, and indeed he has no pace but runs where he will' (4.5.63–7); Achilles has to remind Patroclus about the fool he 'inveigled' from Ajax: 'He is a privileged man. Proceed, Thersites'; Goneril famously complains to Lear of 'your all-licensed fool' (folio; 1.4.183), who is threatened with the whip but never actually suffers it.

In each of these instances there are reasons within the action of the play itself why the issue should be raised. But its familiarity becomes so foregrounded as always to have extra-textual reference—which can often be linked to the wider status of the actors: their licensed cartel and their incessant rivalry within it. Lavatch's position in *All's Well*, for example, sets him up for a virtuoso broadside on Fortune, which can only be a slandering of the rival house ('Truly, Fortune's displeasure is but sluttish ...' 5.2.3–34).[7] Feste's position in *Twelfth Night* is particularly suggestive. He entertains the aristocrats in Illyria (usually by wittily ridiculing them to their faces), with a shrewd professionalism which insists above all on payment for his 'pains'. What is never fully explained is the streak of vindictive cruelty that runs through his treatment of Malvolio. Their mutual antagonism is established early on, but within the play Feste suffers no more at Malvolio's hands than do Toby, Andrew, Fabian and Maria. Yet when they tire of the trick played on him—indeed, begin to worry that it has gone too far—Feste persists in his 'exorcism', arguably taking the play beyond the confines of comedy. And his mockery persists to the very end, denying the play the all-inclusive resolution it so nearly achieves.

Malvolio the 'puritan' is, of course, the antithesis of the 'cakes and ale' world which is Feste's natural habitat, and it is easy enough to see this as a Lent/Carnival alternation in which for once—and for now—Carnival gets the upper hand. But this does not entirely square with what I have called Feste's professionalism: he is not responsible for the topsy-turveydom in Illyria, which derives from the self-indulgent aristocrats he serves. It is, rather, the condition of his trade: a world not dominated by self-love, misplaced grief and scrounging would have no time or appetite for the 'entertainment' he provides. A world in which Malvolio ruled would deny Feste an *economic* or *legal* existence, removing the licence of the 'allowed' fool because it would serve the interests of nobody who mattered. In these senses, like *The Shoemaker's Holiday*, *Twelfth Night* contains its riposte to those who would have closed down the theatres altogether. Feste's position as the 'licensed' fool exactly mirrors that of the 'allowed' actors who have survived that threat. The closing lines of his closing song acknowledge this, as he openly becomes their spokesman: 'our play is done,/And we'll strive to please you every day' (5.1.403–4).

Strikingly, though not untypically, it is neither Shakespeare nor the Chamberlain's Men who most fully articulate the special status of the licensed fool: it is Marston in *Antonio's Revenge* (1600). The hero, Antonio, disguises himself as a fool:

> *Antonio*   No, this coxcomb is a crown
>   Which I affect, even with unbounded zeal.
> *Alberto*   'Twill thwart your plot, disgrace your high resolve.
> *Antonio*   By wisdom's heart, there is no essence mortal
>   That I can envy, but a plump-cheeked fool.
>   O, he hath a patent of immunities,
>   Confirmed by custom, sealed by policy,
>   As large as spacious thought.
> *Alberto*   You cannot press among the courtiers
>   And have access to-
> *Antonio*   What! Not a fool? Why, friend, a golden ass,
>   A baubled fool are sole canonical ...
>
>   (4.1.9–19)

This was for Paul's Boys, but there is ample evidence that Marston has Armin and The Globe squarely in his sights. Balurdo, the play's 'true' fool, says 'Truth is the touchstone of all things' (1.3. 16–17, my emphasis), and there is endless playing (c.f. 'a golden ass') on Armin's formal standing as a goldsmith—an association which gave a particular edge to his 'touchstone' part. The pretensions of the new Globe (or 'world') are put derisively into perspective by Antonio's 'little toy of walnut shell and soap to make bubbles' (SD, head of 4.1.): 'Puff! hold, world! Puff! hold, bubble! Puff! hold, world!' (4.2.28–9).

This is all good-natured fun, and there is much more of it (see, for example, 4.2.30–53, where a 'fresh unsalted fool' is preferred to 'These vinegar-tart spirits'). But behind it Marston sees the key professional point: the licensed fool has 'a patent of immunities ... sealed by policy /As large as spacious thought'. The customary licence of an individual fool, like Will Summers at the court of Henry VIII, had become a matter of 'patent' and 'policy' for the 'allowed' actors who adopted its mantle under Tilney's authority. In practice, of course, this includes Paul's Boys, though Marston is hardly going to spoil a good joke by being so evenhanded. The privileges of the adult companies, at least for the time being, were a much more public issue. We probably see here some of the seeds of the so-called War of the Theatres, where the 'allowance' of the various parties *and their standing at court* is very much an issue.

In *Poetaster* Jonson was to accuse the adult actors, Histrio and Aesop (linked with 'your Globes' [3.4.201] and so with the Chamberlain's Men), of political connivance; they make accusations against both Ovid and Horace, for which Aesop is promised 'a monopoly of playing, confirm'd to thee and thy covey, under the Emperor's broad seal, for this service' (5.3.123–5). Part of Jonson's concern is undoubtedly that the cartel restricted his freedom as a writer to sell his plays on a free market. Conversely, Dekker in *Satiromastix* accuses Jonson of sour grapes, implying that his complaint against the cartel really boiled down to the fact that he did not control it himself, being anxious to 'beget ... the reversion of the Master of the King's Revels' (4.1.189–90: see Chapter 6 'Jonson: Epistle to *Volpone*').

The self-reflection of actors and playwrights on their privileged position did not end with the War of the Theatres, but rumbled on with modulations. Henry Chettle, the most prolific of the writers who figure in Henslowe's *Diary* and therefore an interesting test-case even though so little of his work has survived, produces a novel twist in *The Tragedy of Hoffman* (c. 1603), where the truly foolish prince, Jerome, talks to the fool-proper, Stilt, of writing a poem 'in praise of picktooths': 'I'll get a patent from the Duke, my father, for the *cum privilegio* for that poem *ad imprimendum solum*; besides, thou shalt have a privilege, that no man shall sell toothpicks without thy seal' (1.4.420–6). Chettle was a printer by trade and the cum privilegio was the royal licence for the exclusive printing rights to a work, a parallel from the print world to the 'sealed' status of the actors and their works.[8] And when Marston (if it was him) wrote the additions to *The Malcontent* for its performance by the King's Men, which included the creation of an entire fool-role for Armin, his emphases were rather different from those in *Antonio's Revenge*.

One of Passarello's chief refrains is on the velvet he now wears as a courtier, though he is no less a servant than ever he was; but he is very much in demand there—'the court cannot possibly be without me' (1.8.61–2)—as indeed are his fellows, since his lord 'keeps beside me fifteen jesters to instruct him in the art of fooling' (45–6). This is surely another direct equation of the licensed fool with the actors in general, here the whole company of the King's Men who with Armin have become indispensable appendages of the king's own household: velvet-clad servants, their licence so taken for granted it is scarcely necessary to mention it.[9] Of course, Goneril *does* mention it, quite venomously, in the last of Armin's true 'licensed fool' roles; it is painfully appropriate that he sings the very last snatch of Feste's 'When that I was and a little tiny boy' out on the heath as Lear's 'wit begins to turn', since we must understand that one consequence (a small, but not inconsiderable consequence) of the collapse of Lear's rule is the end of theatre itself. In a world where Edmund's Nature reigns, there is no place for licensed fools. The loyalty of Lear's Fool to his royal master is touching, but perhaps also inescapable. Just as Feste knows that Malvolio represents a threat to the entire privileged courtly world of licensed fooling, the Fool seems to know that without Lear he is (like Lear himself) nothing. Each depends on the other (in a prophetic vision down to 1642) for his essential validation.

Rather less fancifully, it may well be that the exasperation with Lear's 'all-licensed fool' echoes the widely-voiced complaints about the liberties taken by one acting company in particular, the Children of the Queen's Revels, who for a time became the only 'allowed' company not subject to Tilney's authority, when Queen Anne appointed her own licenser, Samuel Daniel.[10] Scandal after scandal beset the company: Daniel's own *Philotas* (1604), Chapman, Jonson and Marston's *Eastward Ho* (1605), Day's *Isle of Gulls* (1606), Chapman's *Byron* plays (1608), and others besides, even after we assume Daniel was removed from office. Roslyn Knutson's argument (1995) that the 'little eyases' passage in the folio *Hamlet* [2.2.337–62] is a late addition, aimed at this company at this time, rather than in 1600–1 as has traditionally been supposed, is entirely convincing. The Blackfriars boys, with their reckless satire, were in danger not only of 'the whip' themselves but of rocking the boat for the rest of the cartel as well. Shakespeare's earlier wry comedy about 'the private parts of Fortune' has progressed to something more serious: 'Will they not say afterwards ... their writers do them wrong, to make them exclaim against their own succession?' (2.2.347–51). Licence is never without limits, and Shakespeare obliquely voices concern about the future of the 'allowance' essentially contracted in 1598.

In fact the threat posed by the 'little eyases' faded after 1608, and the 'licensed fool' role seems to have passed into history, as the actors grew accustomed to its reality—the reality scornfully expressed by John Cocke, in his 'character' of 'A Common Player' (1615), that 'players may not be called rogues: *For they bee chiefe ornaments of his Majesties Revells*' (Chambers, 4, pp. 255–7). There continued to be stage fools, of course, including notable ones like the dramatist William Rowley, who (for example) wrote the role of Lollio for himself in his collaboration with Thomas Middleton, *The Changeling* (1622), while Middleton wrote the role of the Fat Bishop as a late addition for him in *A Game at Chess* (1624). In the former there is some ironic play on the fact that Lollio threatens the fools and madmen of the asylum he oversees with a whip, standing on its head the vulnerability of an Armin-style fool. But the greatest comic capital in both roles derives from Rowley's enormous size, rather than his licensed wit (Dutton, 1999, xxvi-xxvii). It is a measure of how assured the most privileged actors felt of their allotted place in the late Jacobean scheme of things (an assurance reflected in *A Game at Chess* and perhaps taken too much for granted with *The Spanish Viceroy*).[11] And it is a far cry from that moment in 1597 when the total eradication of the theatres seemed to be on the cards.

NOTES

1. There is evidence that inn-yard theatres within the City continued to be used after 1596. But no company was able to use one as a regular base, and that is the critical distinction here.

2. Glynne Wickham (1969) supposes that it was an elaborate bluff, that the privy Council were in effect challenging the City Council to buy out the owners of the theatres while playing was suspended (knowing that they would not be able to afford it). But this is undercut by the fact that the orders were issued to the relevant Surrey and Middlesex magistrates, not to the Lord Mayor. There is nothing in them to suggest that the magistrates were not supposed to carry out the destruction of the theatres forthwith.

3. This would mean it took just about six months to build, work having started on 17 January. This is comparable with The Globe, which in many respects it copied; that was reported to be newly built about five months after The Theatre was dismantled, though it was nine months (September 1599) before we can be sure it was ready for use, when Thomas Platter saw *Julius Caesar* there.

4. The major exception to this proposition is what happened to the Children of the Chapel, who became the Children of the Queen's Revels, were taken out of Tilney's control, and given their own licenser by Queen Anne, Samuel Daniel. See below.

5. See p. 192, Note 4.

6. As, for example, in Polonius's reminiscence of playing Julius Caesar (3.2. 103–4); *Hamlet*'s advice to the actors on acting (3.2.1–45) probably carried quite specific barbs for its original audience.

7. Thersites' 'privileged' position in *Troilus and Cressida* has few of these metadramatic resonances, which must fuel the common suspicion that it was not

(at least as we have it) written for the public theatre. His freedom to speak is only one among several that are carefully nuanced. Agamemnon tells Aeneas to 'Speak frankly as the wind' (1.3.253), while Ulysses begs his fellows 'Give pardon to my speech' (1.3.357), and Diomedes has to ask his enemies: 'Let me be privileged by my place and message / To be a speaker free' (4.4.130–1). The most resonant moment is perhaps where Cressida complains to Diomedes 'One cannot speak a word / But it straight starts you' and he replies 'I do not like this fooling' (5.2.103–4), but it is far from certain that theatrical 'fooling' is implied here, though Thersites is one of those watching this scene.

8. See Clegg, 1997a, pp. 8–11, on the status of *cum privilegio* licences.

9. There are parallels here with Autolycus in *The Winter's Tale*, not strictly a licensed fool but an analogous Armin role. He introduces himself as having 'serv'd Prince Florizel, and in my time wore three-pile' (4.3.13–14)—the rich velvet of a royal servant, though whether as a player or not is never specified.

10. On theatre in the court of Queen Anne, see Barroll, 1991b, and Lewalski.

11. On *The Spanish Viceroy*, see pp. 13, 49–50.

JAMES P. BEDNARZ

The Elizabethan Dramatists
as Literary Critics

Certainly it would be worth examining how the author became
individualized in a culture like ours, what status he has been given, at what
moment studies of authenticity and attribution began, in what kind of system
of valorization the author was involved, at what point we began to recount
the lives of authors rather than of heroes, and how this fundamental category
of "the-man-and-his-work criticism" began.
—*Michel Foucault*, "What is an Author?"

To judge of Poets is only the faculty of Poets;
and not of all Poets, but the best.
—*Ben Jonson*, Timber, or Discoveries

The legend of Shakespeare and Jonson's wit-combats is unarguably the most
famous case of poetic rivalry in the annals of English literature. This book
presents the theory that Jonson began in 1599 explicitly to define himself as
Shakespeare's opposite through his drama, and that Shakespeare, over the course
of the following two years, reacted in a series of metatheatrical plays answering
his challenge. The Poets' War—the most important theatrical controversy of the
late Elizabethan stage—commenced when Jonson, the younger playwright,
became "Jonson," the poet, by resisting Shakespeare's influence through the
invention of a new critical drama that he called "comical satire." The war
continued with added momentum when Shakespeare, in response, molded his

From *Shakespeare & the Poets' War*. © 2001 by Columbia University Press.

comedies to accommodate Jonson's satiric perspective while eschewing its self-confident didacticism. And the battle ended only after Shakespeare, having been stung by Jonson's attack on the Lord Chamberlain's Men in *Poetaster*, "purged" his rival in the guise of Ajax in *Troilus and Cressida*. It is consequently during the Poets' War that we find the first record of these writers' mutual commentary and criticism.

To our knowledge, Shakespeare and Jonson first crossed paths when they both wrote for the Chamberlain's Men between 1598 and 1599 and Jonson, using all the psychological ploys of a strong poet, defined himself through his drama in opposition to Shakespeare. Although Shakespeare is now often viewed merely as the butt of Jonson's process of self-creation, there is abundant evidence that he shaped his own literary representation in answering Jonson's criticism. This first occurred between 1600 and 1601 when, after an initial show of resistance, he increasingly appropriated Jonson's emphasis on satire in *As You Like It*, *Twelfth Night*, and *Troilus and Cressida*. Always ready to capitalize on literary fashions, he gradually reflected the hard edge of Jonson's new genre. But in doing so, he composed a kind of counter-trilogy to Jonson's three comical satires, *Every Man Out of His Humour*, *Cynthia's Revels*, and *Poetaster*, that combined plot parody and personal allusion to hoist the engineer on his own petard.

But any account of this first public dialogue between Shakespeare and Jonson is falsified by removing it from its historical context as part of the highly competitive culture of late Elizabethan commercial theater. At its most heated, the Poets' War converted three Bankside theaters—the Globe, Blackfriars, and Paul's—into military camps firing paper bullets at one another. Indeed, the Poets' War provides the fullest theatrical context currently available for understanding the interactive development of Shakespeare's work. Readers of Elizabethan drama have long noticed that in a series of interrelated plays written between 1599 and 1601—not only by Jonson and Shakespeare but also by John Marston and Thomas Dekker—there arose an intense and often acrimonious debate concerning the practice of dramatic representation. This controversy, to which Dekker referred in *Satiromastix* ("To the World," line 7) as the "Poetomachia" (or "Poets' War"), was a clash of opposing ideologies of drama initiated by Jonson in 1599 when he boldly attempted to reconstruct the premises upon which Renaissance popular theater was conceived. In self-proclaimed rebellion against established Elizabethan dramatic practice, Jonson, the *enfant terrible* of commercial theater, repeatedly claimed that he alone possessed a credible form of poetic authority, based on neoclassical standards that demolished his rivals' literary pretensions. Jonson's sense of election led him to mock competing plays and prominent rivals, especially Shakespeare, and to turn against his detractors in a struggle for poetic mastery from which, at the time, no decisive victor emerged. The first great dramatic criticism in England begins with this public dialogue—at once philosophical and personal—among Shakespeare, Jonson, Marston, and Dekker.

Recent studies have indicated that between 1599 and 1601 Jonson began a labor of poetic self-creation in his trilogy of comical satires. Here, in a more intense manner than he would ever attempt again, he fictionalized his own laureate status by creating a second self to assist in the management of his plays. These works, writes Richard Helgerson, "stand on the threshold of Jonson's career." He would never again write drama of this kind, "in which a character so clearly represented his own sense of himself."[1] Jonson subsequently receded into his work or hovered at its margins in prologues and prefaces. Once he abandoned comical satire, he was free from the absolutist mythology he had invented to sanction himself through this unique genre. Near the beginning of his career, however, in a supreme act of wish fulfillment, he projected himself into the roles of Asper, Criticus, and Horace in an effort to establish for himself and for his age a new paradigm of poetic authority. Jonson's autobiographical personae are interesting not only in themselves as symbolic acts of self-fashioning but also as the first examples in the history of English drama of a playwright self-consciously defending his status and explicitly defining the literary principles upon which his art is based.

There was never a consensus at the time, even among Renaissance humanists, on the status of the "author" or "poet" who wrote plays for the commercial theater. The word "poet," the early modern term for all creators of fiction, including drama, could suggest either a madman or a sage. "He is upbraidingly call'd a *Poet*," Jonson complains in *Discoveries*, "as if it were a most contemptible *Nick-name*" (8:572), even as he insists that his audience revise its meaning in response to his own unique performance. When feeling most at ease, Drummond notes, "he was wont to name himself the Poet" (1:150). Despite his best effort, however, the Poets' War staged the term's duality. The controversy can only be reconstructed, however, by examining the relation between Shakespeare's drama and a set of linked plays by Jonson, Marston, and Dekker that are almost off the map of contemporary criticism. My goal is to present the first comprehensive account of the Poets' War as a crisis of legitimation, a literary civil war during which Jonson's vanguard project clashed with the skepticism of Marston, Shakespeare, and Dekker, who literally laughed him off the stage. Disturbed by his satiric attacks, Jonson's rivals challenged the epistemological, literary, and ethical assumptions upon which he based his assertion of poetic authority. For in their most radical mood they were willing to object to what Thomas Greene calls Jonson's "centered self" and Jonathan Dollimore terms the philosophy of "humanist essentialism."[2] Yet by virtue of its insight into the insubstantial and transient condition of human consciousness, Shakespeare's modern sensibility paradoxically militated to confer a very different kind of authorship on him, making him both Jonson's most spectacular critic and his foremost beneficiary.

I

What initially attracted scholars in the nineteenth century, who first defined the Poets' War, was the fact that it consisted of a quarrel between rival playwrights embedded in a network of self-reflexive plays closely interlinked by patterns of literary allusion and personal satire. This research, best represented by Roscoe Addison Small's *The Stage-Quarrel Between Ben Jonson and the So-Called Poetasters*, demonstrated that the dramas that constituted this debate were not autonomous and self-contained. They were instead fused parts of a single historical moment of literary confrontation that pitted Jonson against Shakespeare, Marston, and Dekker, his principal rivals in the commercial theater. But while twentieth-century scholars usually gave pride of place to Small's short volume in their footnotes, they rarely examined either its merits or its mistakes.[3] Indeed, it is a scandal of contemporary criticism that on the four hundredth anniversary of the Poets' War, Small's brilliant but outdated treatise is still cited as the definitive work on this important controversy. This is particularly unfortunate since contemporary scholarship of Renaissance drama enjoys two advantages of belatedness—the accumulation of new evidence and a more sophisticated approach to topicality. In particular, the work of David Bevington, Oscar James Campbell, W. David Kay, Cyrus Hoy, E.A.J. Honigmann, and Richard Helgerson has made it possible to perceive with greater sophistication the controversy's theoretical, generic, allusive, and institutional dimensions.[4] It is, most importantly, through Bevington's study of "Satire and the State" in *Tudor Drama and Politics* that the Poetomachia has come to be viewed as a debate over substantive issues, in which

> the authors were committed to propositions far more essential than the fleeting notoriety of a name-calling contest. Nor do the purely commercial aspects of a theatrical rivalry explain away the basic dividing issue of the proper role of satire in a commonwealth shaken by religious and dynastic uncertainties.[5]

Bevington was able to demonstrate that the Poetomachia was primarily focused on the writer's responsibility to society. The task of modern criticism at its best has been both to account for the historical significance of the Poets' War and to limit its scope, turning it into a viable narrative. "Any criticism of any play bearing as a date of production one of the three years 1599 to 1601 which does not take account of this, for the time, stage-absorbing matter, must be imperfect and of small utility," Frederick Fleay, one of the first commentators, wrote at the end of the nineteenth century.[6] But the old historicists who rediscovered the Poets' War trivialized it by treating it more as a literary anecdote than as the most complex and thorough transaction of dramatic criticism in the English Renaissance. What is worse, their multiplication of unfounded biographical identifications brought their whole enterprise into disrepute. Fleay considered the Poets' War part of an ongoing "biographical chronicle of the English stage" in which literary allusions functioned primarily as vehicles for self-aggrandizement and invective. Yet even when they did interpret Renaissance drama, the old historicists were beset with crippling individual limitations. Despite rare flashes of perception, Fleay and Josiah Penniman displayed a proclivity for self-indulgent, allegorical lock picking, while Small, whose identifications were more accurate, made errors in assessing chronology.[7]

As a result of these interpretive problems, any new study of the Poets' War still risks being dismissed in one of two mutually contradictory ways: as a study of insignificant Renaissance gossip or as a naive literalization of fiction. Thus, one group of contemporary critics accepts the historical verifiability of the Poets' War but dismisses it as a "tiresome and obscure series of backbitings" that "wasted so much theatrical energy." And a second denies that the Poets' War was a Renaissance phenomenon at all, asserting that the very attempt to decipher its meaning is a symptom of pathology: a "Victorian heirloom, like a former source of innocent merriment which any amateur psychoanalyst can tell screens a neurosis or like great-grandfather's waste tract which never yielded its ore, serves chiefly as an ornate tribute to misapplied ingenuity."[8] Surely, both of these critiques cannot be correct: the Poets' War cannot be both a historically insignificant Renaissance phenomenon and a nineteenth-century critical fantasy. On the contrary, both are wrong—the Poets' War did in fact take place and merits close study as a major debate in the English Renaissance on the nature and function of drama. Only a synthesis of old and new histories can do justice to the quarrel's rich vein of personal satire while keeping in mind the issues of literary theory its topicality particularizes.

II

Alfred Harbage's mid-twentieth-century *Shakespeare and the Rival Traditions*, the next major reconceptualization of this controversy, defined it as a "War of the Theaters," a clash between rival repertory companies. Following his example, modern critics of Renaissance drama would continue to use the rubrics "Poetomachia" and "War of the Theaters" interchangeably. Yet only the first was coined at the time; the phrase "War of the Theaters" owes its existence primarily to nineteenth-century research.[9] Harbage, however, employed the latter to define the quarrel as an institutional competition, stoked by ideological interests in a struggle for economic and social power, between the public theaters and their private counterparts. According to his much disputed formulation, the revival of two private theater companies, the Children of Paul's at the end of 1599 and the Children of Queen Elizabeth's Chapel the following year, ignited a commercial "war" between them and the established adult acting companies. What was so appealing about Harbage's approach was that it seemed to provide the controversy with a sociological context—a model of commercial struggle between the adult actors, who performed in outdoor playhouses in the suburbs for audiences composed of heterogeneous classes, and the children of the private theaters in the city, who catered to an elite audience.[10] This premise, however, cannot sufficiently explain the Poets' War.

The turn of the seventeenth century was a period of intense theatrical competition, especially among three rival repertory companies: the Children of the Chapel at Blackfriars; the Children of Paul's, who performed on the grounds of the cathedral; and the Chamberlain's Men at the Globe. Yes, this rivalry was exacerbated by the Children's return; suddenly there were two more mouths to feed from the same general population of theatergoers. The Children of the Chapel and the Children of Paul's claimed to offer superior fare to a select audience and could therefore be seen as united in their challenge to the adult hegemony. The child acting companies drew their writers, however, from the public theater, recruiting Jonson, who had just composed his two Every Man plays for the Chamberlain's Men, and Marston, who had briefly toiled for Philip Henslowe and the Admiral's Men. And these writers felt as much competition with each other as they did with their peers in the public theater.

One can easily find major exceptions to Harbage's delineation of the rival repertories. Jonson's poetic manifesto *Every Man Out* was written for the public, not the private theater. The public theater sponsored his most explosive satire. He worked intermittently for both kinds of theater and satirized a portion of his audiences at the Globe *and* Blackfriars. He also criticized the dramatic offerings of the Chamberlain's Men and Paul's Boys and mocked their most successful poets, Shakespeare and Marston. Now while it is true that institutional rivalries existed between the adult and child companies, a variety of conflicts were experienced by the acting companies that performed in and around London at the end of the sixteenth century. Tension existed between the adult and child companies, between different child companies, and between rival adult companies. Robert Sharpe's stimulating but often unreliable study, *The Real War of the Theatres: Shakespeare's Fellows in Rivalry with the Admiral's Men, 1594–1603*, for example, emphasizes the ongoing commercial struggle between the two dominant public theaters. Furthermore, the Children of the Chapel and the Children of Paul's flung as many brains at each other as either tossed at the Chamberlain's Men. The major writers for these two private theaters between 1599 and 1601—Jonson and Marston—directed as much antagonism against each other as they vented against the adult companies. The public and private theaters, moreover, formed makeshift alliances against each other, as when the Children of Paul's and the Chamberlain's Men temporarily conspired against the Children of the Chapel in 1601. This, however, did not prevent Shakespeare, as I indicate in the first chapter, from pairing Jonson and Marston as slow Ajax and rank Thersites in his parody of the Poets' War in *Troilus and Cressida*. Between 1599 and 1601, Dekker worked for the Admiral's Men, the Chamberlain's Men, *and* the Children of Paul's. *Satiromastix* was produced by a private and a public company, and Dekker drew fire from Jonson for each of these affiliations. Harbage's institutional conflict is contradicted by yet another pattern of theatrical aggression. Jonson's comical satires at Blackfriars were critiqued by public and private theaters, by Shakespeare at the Globe, Marston at Paul's, and Dekker at both playhouses.

Associated with the Children of the Chapel between 1600 and 1601, Jonson heaped as much scorn on the Children of Paul's, their writers, and their managers as he hurled at members of the Chamberlain's Men. Both troupes were social, commercial, and literary rivals that, according to Jonson, merited criticism, and they responded by collaborating against him on *Satiromastix*. In 1599, Jonson attempted to create a visionary theater of social catharsis capable of fulfilling the highest expectations for drama enunciated by the leading humanist theoreticians of his day. The world that he represented to this end was peopled largely with humorist misfits who neglected the possibility of gaining their full humanity to pursue compulsively self-demeaning delusions. One would expect that Jonson's satiric drama would from the outset be plagued by official censorship. And indeed he was threatened from this quarter throughout his career, beginning with his earliest experiment in social criticism, the ill-fated *Isle of Dogs*. But what was equally devastating was the resistance his project encountered from his fellow playwrights, who, between 1599 and 1601, turned his satiric techniques against him.

Despite the personal tone of Jonson's quarrel with Shakespeare, Marston, and Dekker, the Poets' War was, on its most abstract level, a theoretical debate on the social function of drama and the standard of poetic authority that informed comical satire. This literary debate commands attention not only because it engaged the interest of Jonson, Shakespeare, Marston, and Dekker but also, more impressively, because they were willing to argue with incredible specificity about the basic issues of their art. In a passage in *Satiromastix* alluding to the conflict, Dekker comically explains that his colleagues have been attempting to dominate each other with such "*high words*" that they have appropriately written for players wearing "Chopins," their customary elevated shoes ("To the World," line 10). By 1599, the first permanent playhouses built in London were attracting a vast following, including an inner circle highly attuned to questions of theatrical politics. It was to this knowledgeable audience that the Poets' War was addressed, as the contenders ripped each other apart to bring these special spectators together.

III

Exciting new scholarship has been done on how Shakespeare and Jonson revised their work. This aspect of their activity is a vital part of this project, which suggests that Jonson added an interpolation to *Every Man Out* mocking Marston and Dekker and that Shakespeare inserted the "little eyases" allusion into *Hamlet* to deride Jonson at Blackfriars. More important in this regard, however, is the manner in which this self-revision was affected by both writers rethinking each other's dramatic forms. The techniques they evolved for mutual self-reflexivity required modes of interpretation that went beyond the formal limits of individual plays, as their discussion of self-construction helped create a sophisticated audience capable of attending to both the philosophical and personal issues involved in their debate. For this audience, individual dramas produced by competing theaters had to be played off each other for their competing meanings to arise. The Poets' War was consequently a series of literary transactions between writers of topically charged fictions who used their plays to master each other's language and drama. Often dismissed in our own time as a spectacle of self-advertisement calculated to generate publicity by furnishing its audience with the verbal equivalent of bear-baiting, its personal satire was nevertheless coordinated with a discussion of drama that was as entertaining and serious as theater itself. As Nestor remarks in *Troilus and Cressida*: "Though't be a sportful combat, / Yet in the trial much opinion dwells" (1.3.335–36). The Poets' War is, to borrow Gregory Bateson's distinction, a social game that tests the serio-ludic limits of theater, constructed "not upon the premise 'this is play' but rather around the question 'is this play?'"[11] The controversy was a source of amusement, but it would never have occurred if Jonson had not insisted on his unique status in a salient example of what Jacob Burckhardt identified as the Renaissance cult of the artist as hero.

In the aftermath of Fleay's wild enthusiasm for expanding the Poets' War to almost every drama written between 1599 and 1601, one of the most imposing problems that faces contemporary analysis is the need to establish a plausible chronology of the plays into which its metatheatrical strategies were written. The process of establishing the sequence is, however, fraught with all the difficulty that attends the dating of Renaissance plays, some of which were published long after they were first staged in altered forms that reflect subsequent revisions. A few insurmountable impediments of this kind will always exist, but we are currently in a better position than critics were a century ago to outline its historical dialectic. And if we work a series of refinements on the chronological models proposed by earlier scholars, the pattern becomes relatively clear.[12] We can currently retrieve enough of its development to conclude that the Poets' War had three phases, each of which was initiated by one of Jonson's comical satires followed by responses to it from Shakespeare, Marston, and Dekker. The conflict's duration can be fixed with reasonable precision as the period beginning with Jonson's bold claim to philosophical independence from the suffocating conventions of Elizabethan drama in *Every Man Out of His Humour* and concluding with his apology for *Poetaster* and Shakespeare's retort in the "little eyases" passage of *Hamlet*.

CHRONOLOGY OF THE POETS' WAR

	PHASE I		PHASE II		PHASE III
	Autumn 1599	1600	Autumn 1600	1601	Spring–Autumn 1601
	Globe opens / Paul's reopens		Blackfriars reopens		
JONSON	Every Man Out of His Humour ◆ ; Every Man Out (3.1.1–35; 3.4.6–40) ●		Cynthia's Revels ◆		Poetaster ◆ ; The Apology for Poetaster ◆
SHAKESPEARE		As You Like It ● ; Hamlet ●		Twelfth Night ●	Troilus and Cressida ● ; Hamlet (2.2.337–62) ●
MARSTON	Histriomastix ■	Antonio and Mellida ■ ; Jack Drum's Entertainment ■	Antonio's Revenge ■	What You Will ■	
DEKKER					Satiromastix ■ ●

● performed by the Lord Chamberlain's Men at the Globe
◆ performed by the Children of Paul's at the cathedral theater
■ performed by the Children of the Chapel at Blackfriars

Shaded areas indicate peripheral plays.
For dating, see the Chronological Appendix.

Between Jonson's aggressive manifesto and defensive apology, the Poets' War rioted across London's public and private stages in three waves of contention, each phase of which was triggered by a new comical satire. The center of my enterprise is structural morphology: the process through which the form of comedy and the status of the poet were suddenly foregrounded by Jonson in 1599. The three main sections of this book explore the strategic moves these three plays initiated as symbolic acts of literary criticism and the responses they elicited from Shakespeare, Marston, and Dekker, who measured Jonson's new drama against their own in the wake of his repudiation thereof. Answering Jonson play for play, plot for plot, they layered literary and personal allusions into their works, creating an interprofessional discourse fired by competition.

PHASE I

—*Every Man Out of His Humour* first performed by the Chamberlain's Men in autumn 1599.

—*Histriomastix, or The Player Whipped*, with imitations of *Every Man Out* and *The Case Is Altered*, performed by the Children of Paul's at the end of 1599.

—*Every Man Out*, with the addition of the Clove and Orange episodes, produced after Histriomastix in 1599.

—*As You Like It* acted by the Chamberlain's Men between January and 25 March 1600.

—Jack Drum's *Entertainment, or the Comedy of Pasquil and Katherine* first presented by the Children of Paul's, after *As You Like It*, between 25 March and 8 September 1600.

PHASE II

—*Cynthia's Revels*, or the *Fountain of Self-Love* premiered by the Children of the Chapel between 29 September and 31 December 1600.

—*Twelfth Night*, or *What You Will* produced by the Chamberlain's Men after 6 January but before 25 September 1601.

—*What You Will* originally presented by the Children of Paul's, after *Twelfth Night* but before 25 September 1601.

PHASE III

—*Poetaster*, or *The Arraignment* acted by the Children of the Chapel between late spring and 25 September 1601.

—*Satiromastix*, or *The Untrussing of the Humorous Poet* staged by the Chamberlain's Men and the Children of Paul's, after *Poetaster* but before 24 October 1601.

—*Troilus and Cressida* produced by the Chamberlain's Men, after the staging of *Poetaster* and *Satiromastix* but before 24 October 1601.

—The "Apological Dialogue" of *Poetaster* recited only once on the stage of the Blackfriars theater, after *Troilus and Cressida* but before 21 December 1601, effectively ending the Poets' War.

—*Hamlet* (first staged in 1600) acted with the addition of 2.2.337–62 (the "little eyases" passage referring to *Poetaster*, *Satiromastix*, and possibly *Troilus and Cressida*) by the Chamberlain's Men, near the end of 1601.

English drama and its criticism between Sidney's *Apology for Poetry* and Dryden's *Essay of Dramatic Poesy* underwent a complicated evolution. Drama criticism was at this time an emerging genre—a set of needs seeking realization that was steadily being formalized. It is generally agreed that no other critic between the time of Sidney's inauguration of English dramatic criticism and Dryden's validation of it contributed more to its development than Jonson. A strain of neoclassical criticism reverberates from Sidney through Jonson to Johnson and Dryden. Jonson's commentaries also had a profound impact on Shakespeare, Marston, and Dekker, who from 1599 to 1601 forged a culture of dramatic criticism *within* drama itself, building into their plays semi-autonomous strata of literary criticism that placed their works in relation to the theories and practice of their rivals. Under the competitive circumstances of the commercial theater that shaped their dissension, playwrights began the project of assessing their own quality.[13]

The question of how seriously we should take what *Hamlet* refers to as this "throwing about of brains" (2.2.358–59) can be answered in two different ways. It *was*, on one level, a publicity stunt calculated to draw attention to itself and an audience to the theater. In his "Apologetical Dialogue," Jonson charged that the only reason he had been attacked was for money. Predicting more personal satire in future plays, Dekker's Captain Tucca in *Satiromastix* promises the audience that, "if you set your hands and Seals to this," Jonson "will write against it, and you may have more sport," since his critics "will untruss him again, and again, and again" (Epilogue, lines 20–24), repeating the war's three phases. Marston's Lampatho Doria, his most complete caricature of Jonson in *What You Will*, fully appreciates the power of invective to attract spectators:

> This is the strain that chokes the theaters;
> That makes them crack with full-stuff'd audience.
> This is your humour only in request,
> Forsooth to rail; this brings your ears to bed;
> This people gape for; for this some do stare.
> This some would hear, to crack the Author's neck;
> This admiration and applause pursues.
>
> (2:266)

Jonson, however, foiled any plan to continue the War with his Apology for *Poetaster*, late in 1601. Nevertheless, its influence lingered, and several years later

George Chapman in his "Prologus" to *All Fools* complained that the recent restoration of Old Comedy had changed the nature of comedy itself:

> Who can show cause why th' ancient comic vein
> Of Eupolis and Cratinus (now revived
> Subject to personal application)
> Should be exploded by some bitter spleens?
> Yet merely comical and harmless jests
> (Though ne'er so witty) be esteemed but toys,
> If void of th' other satirism's sauce?[14]

Referentiality in comedy at the turn of the century, Chapman reveals, had made it difficult to write without engaging in an invective of "personal application." He could easily have answered his own rhetorical question: the change had occurred when the satiric spirit of Old Attic Comedy (represented here by Aristophanes' two greatest contemporaries) was revived by the Poets' War. Jonson's responsibility for creating this climate of invective ("your humour only in request") was, for his critics, the struggle's single most important issue. The Poets' War did not invent topicality. David Bevington has shown how personal allusion, a component of social satire, had effectively served as a political weapon in Renaissance drama. The stagequarrel merely refocused this satiric technique self-reflexively on the status of poets and players. It is widely known that Jonson criticized Shakespeare for the first time, along with Marston and Dekker, in *Every Man Out*, and that he would then go on to criticize the Chamberlain's Men, with escalating vehemence, in *Cynthia's Revels* and *Poetaster*, his final contributions to the Poets' War. Shakespeare, in reaction, criticized Jonson's new emphasis on satire through his parody of the melancholy Jaques, who would purge the world in *As You Like It*; his subversion of Jonsonian satire in the festivity of *Twelfth Night*; his purge of Jonson as Ajax in *Troilus and Cressida*; and his censure of the way the child actors had been used at Blackfriars in the "little eyases" passage of *Hamlet*. It was at this time that Shakespeare, along with Marston and Dekker, engaged in what Thomas Fuller, later in the seventeenth century, would refer to as a series of "wit-combats" with Jonson. The dialogue Fuller imagined as personal repartee can be traced back to this series of theatrical responses to *Every Man Out*, *Cynthia's Revels*, and *Poetaster* in *As You Like It*, *Twelfth Night*, *Troilus and Cressida*, and *Hamlet*. One primary objective of this study is to document the origin of the Shakespeare-Jonson legend in these seven plays. But the terms of Shakespeare's critical duel with Jonson between 1599 and 1601 become clear only when their criticism of each other is read against the simultaneous involvement of Marston and Dekker, who would find no place in the ensuing legend but were an important part of its making.

Jonson never considered Shakespeare to be one of the "band" of "*poetasters*" mentioned in the preface to *Satiromastix*: this barb is aimed only at

Marston and Dekker. And he never directly "represented" Shakespeare on the stage, as he had the others. Although critical, Jonson occasionally treated Shakespeare with a measure of deference never allowed to the "*poetasters*" and reserved only for a few contemporaries, including Chapman, Donne, and Bacon. He gives us, after all, our greatest elegy on his "beloved" Shakespeare in the First Folio as well as our most tender (yet not uncritical) personal recollection in *Discoveries* of this good-natured, witty man he "loved" (8:583). Yet it was in opposition to Shakespeare that he designed comical satire to displace romantic comedy. And it was Shakespeare who, in turn, criticized Jonson's new approach even as he submitted to its influence, moving from the romantic framework of *As You Like It* through the disturbing balance of romantic and satiric sentiment in *Twelfth Night* to the satiric nihilism of *Troilus and Cressida*. For as Shakespeare sought to contain Jonson's influence, he opened his work to his satire in order to contest its authority. Between 1600 and 1601, then, these comedies mark the poets' converging difference.

NOTES

Passages from Shakespeare's plays, unless otherwise specified, are quoted from *The Riverside Shakespeare*, ed. G. Blakemore Evans, 2nd ed. (Boston: Houghton Mifflin, 1997). I have lightly modernized spelling and some punctuation for all non-Shakespearean early modern texts. Quotations from Jonson's writings, including the "Conversations with Drummond," are derived from *Ben Jonson*, eds. C.H. Herford and Percy Simpson, II vols. (Oxford: Clarendon, 1925–1952). Quotations from Marston's dramas are from *The Plays of John Marston*, ed. H. Harvey Wood, 3 vols. (London: Oliver and Boyd, 1934–1939). Since this edition does not assign line numbers, references are by volume and page. His nondramatic poetry is quoted from *The Poems of John Marston*, ed. Arnold Davenport (Liverpool: Liverpool University Press, 1961). Passages from Dekker's plays are from *The Dramatic Works of Thomas Dekker*, ed. Fredson Bowers, 4 vols. (Cambridge: Cambridge University Press, 1953–1961). All citations from these works will hereafter be referenced in the text.

1. Richard Helgerson, *Self-Crowned Laureates: Spenser, Jonson, Milton and the Literary System* (Berkeley: University of California Press, 1983), 144.

2. Thomas M. Greene, "Ben Jonson and the Centered Self," Studies in English Literature 10 (1970): 325–48; and Jonathan Dollimore, *Radical Tragedy: Religion, Ideology, and Power in the Drama of Shakespeare and His Contemporaries* (Chicago: University of Chicago Press, 1984), 249.

3. What is most remarkable about Small's study, *The Stage-Quarrel Between Ben Jonson and the So-Called Poetasters* (1899; reprint, New York: AMS Press, 1966), is that, despite its mistakes and limitations, it explores the topicality of the

Poets' War with unprecedented success. In this regard, Small shaped a master narrative that has been accepted by twentieth-century theater historians from E. K. Chambers to Anne Barton with little reservation. The scope of his achievement, however, is diminished by his failure to conceptualize the issues of literary theory beneath the controversy's topical veneer. According to Small, the "stage-quarrel" between Jonson on the one hand and Marston, Dekker, and Shakespeare on the other was an escalating war of wits that began when Marston attempted to praise Jonson as a character called Chrisoganus in *Histriomastix* but enraged him instead, prompting Jonson to mock his vocabulary in *Every Man Out of His Humour*. This led to a series of plays in which these two playwrights traded caricatures: (*Jack Drum's Entertainment*, *Cynthia's Revels*, *What You Will*, and *Poetaster*), before Dekker and Shakespeare offered parodies of Jonson in *Satiromastix* and *Troilus and Cressida*. Based on Small's model, I have extrapolated the following sequence:

	JONSON	MARSTON	DEKKER
Histriomastix	Chrisoganus		
Every Man Out		Clove	Orange
Jack Drum's Entertainment	Brabant Senior		
Cynthia's Revels	Criticus	Hedon	Anaides
What You Will	Lampatho Doria	Quadratus	
Poetaster	Horace	Crispinus	Demetrius
Satiromastix	Horace	Crispinus	Demetrius
Troilus and Cressida	Ajax	Thersites	

4. The argument of this book has been particularly influenced by David Bevington's survey of the Poetomachia in *Tudor Drama and Politics: A Critical Approach to Topical Meaning* (Cambridge: Harvard University Press, 1968); Oscar James Campbell's *Comicall Satyre and Shakespeare's* Troilus and Cressida (San Marino: The Huntington Library, 1970); W. David Kay's *Ben Jonson, Horace, and the Poetomachia* (Ph. D. diss., Princeton University, 1968) and "The Shaping of Ben Jonson's Career: A Reexamination of Facts and Problems," *Modern Philology* 67 (1970): 224–37; Cyrus Hoy's The Dramatic Works of Thomas Dekker, 4 vols. (Cambridge: Cambridge University Press, 1980); E. A. J. Honigmann's *Shakespeare's Impact on His Contemporaries* (Totowa, N.J.: Barnes and Noble, 1982); and Helgerson's Self-Crowned Laureates.

5. Bevington, *Tudor Drama and Politics*, 279.

6. Frederick Fleay, *A Chronicle History of the London Stage: 1559–1642* (London: Reeves and Turner, 1890), 119.

7. See Josiah H. Penniman, *The War of the Theatres* (Boston: Ginn, 1897); and Small, *The Stage-Quarrel Between Ben Jonson and the So-Called Poetasters*.

8. Sydney Musgrove, *Shakespeare and Jonson* (Auckland: Pilgrim Press,

1957), 7; and John J. Enck, "The Peace of the Poetomachia," *PMLA* 77 (1962): 386. Gabriele Bernhard Jackson, *Vision and Judgment in Ben Jonson's Drama* (New Haven: Yale University Press, 1984), 29n, treats such analysis as irrelevant. "The question of the identification of Crispinus and Demetrius as Marston and Dekker and of Horace as Jonson along with all the subsidiary identifications which may or may not be valid," she writes, "are omitted as irrelevant to the subject under discussion." As a sop, she refers readers to Penniman and Small.

Enck's formalism is rooted in the early twentieth-century concentration on the so-called intrinsic qualities of literature instead of its "extraneous" context. This overreaction to the excess of nineteenth-century biographical speculation surfaces in the work of Oscar James Campbell, "The Dramatic Construction of *Poetaster*," *Huntington Library Bulletin* 9 (1936): 37–62; and Ernest William Talbert, "The Purpose and Technique of Jonson's *Poetaster*," *Studies in Philology* 42 (1945): 225–52. Any study of the Poet's War must consider: (1) the relation of literature to the personal and cultural conditions that produce it; (2) the intertextual patterns of imitation and parody that fuse separate works, causing their mutual dependence on each other for completion; and (3) the process of revision that yields variant texts irreducible to a single archetype.

9. Frederick Fleay in *A Chronicle History of the Life and Work of William Shakespeare* (London: John C. Nimmo, 1886) refers to this controversy as the "war of the theaters" (42) and as the "stage quarrel" (138); in *A Biographical Chronicle of the English Drama, 1559–1642*, 2 vols. (London: Reeves and Turner, 1891), 2:69, he uses a compromise formation and writes of the "three years' stage war between Jonson and Marston." By the time Penniman wrote *The War of the Theatres* (1897), this phrase had become common parlance. There is nothing inherently misleading about Small's reference to the "Poetomachia" as a "stage-quarrel"—once we recognize that this term is a conflation based on Jonson's confession to Drummond in 1619 that he had "quarrels with Marston" resulting from Marston's having "represented him in the stage."

10. Alfred Harbage in *Shakespeare and the Rival Traditions* (New York: Macmillan, 1952) tends to stereotype the audience of the private theaters as aristocratic degenerates, a gang of skeptical libertines. The adults' audience was, in this view, healthy, optimistic, and sincere, and the children's following was perverse, negative, and duplicitous. The popular theater was as well-adjusted as its democratic constituency and the private theater as twisted as the privileged class that patronized it. Current scholarship has revised this assessment by showing that members of the Inns of Court, who are often associated with the private theaters, demonstrated a wider range of tastes. Gray's Inn, for instance, sponsored Francis Bacon's masque for Queen Elizabeth and encouraged the philosophical tradition he advocated.

Harbage's social history of the theater has been challenged by Ann Jennalie Cook in *The Privileged Playgoers of Shakespeare's London, 1576–1642*

(Princeton: Princeton University Press, 1981). The question that Cook asks goes to the heart of his theory—who was attending theatrical performances in London on weekdays at two o'clock in the afternoon? Much of Shakespeare's audience must have come from a leisure class. Cook concludes that "the privileged represented the most consistent patrons of the drama, no matter where or when it was performed." The majority of gentlemen and would-be gentlemen thus "made it possible for them to dominate the audience of the huge public theatres as well as the small private playhouses" (273 and 272). But Martin Butler, *Theatre and Crisis, 1632–1642* (Cambridge: Cambridge University Press, 1984), in Appendix II, "Shakespeare's Unprivileged Playgoers 1576–1642," counters Cook's argument by pointing to the extensive evidence indicating that the public theaters had a mixed audience. The privileged were in attendance; but to assume that only this class (along with a small group of cutpurses and prostitutes) frequented the public theaters is wrong. It was against this mixed audience that the private theaters could offer, for a higher fee, to exclude some of the underclass. In doing so they created the aura of being elite. The higher tariff they imposed on their customers eliminated just enough of the "garlic-breathed stinkards" to be trumpeted for its snob appeal, even though the difference between the two audiences would have been more quantitative than qualitative in this respect. This de facto exclusion of the unprivileged was used as a premise to praise and bond (indeed to create) its "fashionable" audience.

The distinction between the outdoor and indoor theaters as "public" and "private" was based on a legal fiction used to allow the children to perform within London. Playhouses erected for the purpose of staging public performances were banished to the suburbs, and in 1599 the Chamberlain's Men exchanged one suburb for another, moving from the Theater and Curtain, in Shoreditch, half a mile outside the Bishopsgate entrance, northeast of the city, to the Globe in Southwark, centrally across the Thames. The theatrical entrepreneurs who backed the revived child acting companies at Paul's and Blackfriars circumvented the law by maintaining that their performances were actually "private" dress rehearsals for later presentations at court, although they charged a fee for admission that was at least double that of their competitors in the suburbs. This difference—a point of pride—could also be strategically enlisted, when necessary, to stigmatize the adult companies.

11. Gregory Bateson, *Steps to an Ecology of Mind* (New York: Ballantine, 1972), 182.

12. See the Chronological Appendix for the analysis behind my dating of the Poet's War plays.

13. Herbert Berry, *Shakespeare's Playhouses* (New York: AMS Press, 1987), 121, states that "we have no reviews of the thousands of productions that passed on the stages of Shakespeare's playhouses," and concludes that "this silence about how plays were played and received is one of the most important ways in which

our understanding of drama in Elizabethan, Jacobean, and Caroline times is sadly inferior to our understanding of drama in later times." But we have yet fully to examine the variety of Elizabethan criticism.

14. George Chapman, *All Fools*, ed. Frank Manley (Lincoln: University of Nebraska Press, 1968), lines 13–19.

15. Helgerson, *Self-Crowned Laureates*, 150; and Stephen Orgel, "What is a Text?" in *Staging the Renaissance: Reinterpretations of Elizabethan and Jacobean Drama*, eds. David Scott Kastan and Peter Stallybrass (New York: Routledge, 1991), 84, 87.

16. See Jeffrey Masten, "Playwrighting: Authorship and Collaboration," in *A New History of Early English Drama*, eds. John D. Cox and David Scott Kastan (New York: Columbia University Press, 1997), 357–82, and Leah S. Marcus, *Puzzling Shakespeare: Local Reading and Its Discontents* (Berkeley: University of California Press, 1988), 39, in which she writes of Shakespeare's theatrical career as occurring during a period "before the drama had been institutionalized as a branch of 'authored literature.' "

17. Harold Ogden White, *Plagiarism and Imitation During the English Renaissance: A Study in Critical Distinctions* (Cambridge: Harvard University Press, 1935), 201.

18. Joseph Loewenstein, "Plays Agonistic and Competitive: The Textual Approach to Elsinore," *Renaissance Drama* 19 (1988): 80.

19. Andrew Gurr, *Playgoing in Shakespeare's London* (Cambridge: Cambridge University Press, 1987), 113.

20. The estimate is proposed by Andrew Gurr, *The Shakespearean Stage 1574–1642*, 3rd ed. (Cambridge: Cambridge University Press, 1992), 213.

21. See Robert Weimann, *Shakespeare and the Popular Tradition in the Theater* (Baltimore: Johns Hopkins University Press, 1978); Annabel Patterson, *Shakespeare and the Popular Voice* (Oxford: Basil Blackwell, 1989); and Michael Bristol, *Carnival and Theater: Plebeian Culture and the Structure of Authority in Renaissance England* (London: Methuen, 1985).

22. Q1 *Hamlet* (sig. E3r), quoted from *Shakespeare's Plays in Quarto*, eds. Michael J. B. Allen and Kenneth Muir (Berkeley: University of California Press, 1981).

23. Steven Mullaney, *The Place of the Stage: License, Play, and Power in Renaissance England* (Chicago: University of Chicago Press, 1988), 52, 54.

24. Robert C. Evans, *Ben Jonson and the Poetics of Patronage* (Lewisburg, Penn.: Bucknell University Press, 1989), 9–10.

25. Franco Moretti, *Signs Taken for Wonders* (London: Verso, 1983; rev. 1988), 42.

26. Robert Weimann, *Authority and Representation in Early Modern Discourse* (Baltimore: Johns Hopkins University Press, 1996), 67, 1.

27. See Phyllis Rackin, *Stages of History: Shakespeare's English Chronicles* (Ithaca: Cornell University Press, 1990).

JAMES P. BEDNARZ

Jonson on Shakespeare:
Criticism as Self-Creation

"I will not do as PLAUTUS, ... beg a Plaudite, for go's sake; but if you (out of the bounty of your good liking) will bestow it; why you may (in time) make lean MACILENTE as fat as Sir JOHN FALSTAFF."

—Every Man Out of His Humour

In 1599 Ben Jonson invented comical satire—a new kind of drama that he conceived as an assault on existing theatrical conventions. In doing so, he not only precipitated a profound change in the structure of late Elizabethan drama but also instigated the Poets' War, a debate on the nature of poetic authority that arose in the subsequent attacks on and defenses of his bold dramatic experiment. In Jonson's First Folio, only three plays are designated (in early modern spelling) "comicall satyres": *Every Man Out of His Humour*, *Cynthia's Revels*, and *Poetaster*. Through this innovative trilogy he rejected the work of his competitors, especially Shakespeare, as inadequate for inducing the social catharsis that he then conceived as being the principal rationale for literary representation. Motivated by the humanist ideal of a theater of social transformation, Jonson originated a satiric form that embodied what G. K. Hunter has described as "an insistence on judgment, which is completely new in Elizabethan comedy."[1]

One major incentive Jonson had for inventing comical satire was that it provided him with an alternative mode of writing comedy in a late Elizabethan theatrical culture dominated by Shakespeare. It was at this early point in his career, writes Anne Barton, that the "young Jonson of the 1590's forged a comical

From *Shakespeare & the Poets' War*. © 2001 by Columbia University Press.

style for himself by dissenting from the Elizabethan popular tradition which achieved its finest realization in the comedies of Shakespeare."[2] The motto "*Non aliena meo pressi pede*" (I don't walk in other people's steps) that he emblazoned on the title page of *Every Man Out* epitomizes what Harold Bloom has eloquently termed "the creative mind's desperate insistence upon priority."[3] Still, Jonson never conceived of the poet as an autonomous creator. Instead, he held a dialectical view of representation that involved the simultaneous discovery and creation of meaning. He regarded imitation, the ability to "convert the substance or Riches of an other *Poet* to his own use," as a prerequisite for poetic achievement, and he urged writers "to make choice of one excellent man above the rest, and so to follow him, till he grow very He" (8:638). Yet he was aware of the danger of unreflective mimicry "wherein every man, forgetful of himself, is in travail with expression of another" and "we so insist in imitating others, as we cannot ... return to our selves" (8:597). A further complexity in Jonson's situation, however, is that in rejecting Shakespearean comic precedent in *Every Man Out* he purged *Every Man In* as well, or at least the part—its open-ended subjectivity—that most resembled Shakespeare.

I

Scholars once thought that Jonson had revolutionized Elizabethan theater by inventing the "comedy of humours" and that *Every Man in His Humour* was *the* pivotal play through which the younger dramatist established a new comic paradigm. And it was widely believed that its dark sequel, *Every Man Out of His Humour*, was an artistic dead end and theatrical failure. Yet, due to the pioneering work of W. David Kay, critics now generally agree that *Every Man Out*, not its predecessor, "marks a watershed in Jonson's work" and was recognized as such by his contemporaries. Prior to the composition of *Every Man Out*, Kay observes, Jonson had been "content to write superior plays of a popular nature, occasionally introducing new type characters to the stage but essentially following, not leading, the current dramatic fashion."[4] "*Every Man Out* represents a major change in psychic weather," concurs John Gordon Sweeney. Its innovation, he suggests, "is not just a new choice of subject or genre but a radical shift in Jonson's relation to his audience," toward "an amazing vision of theater as a real social force" that "transforms its spectators by calling on them to enact their own best selves."[5]

The most frequently cited explanation for this shift in Jonson's comedy in 1599 was formulated by Oscar James Campbell in the only comprehensive study of comical satire.[6] Campbell believes the Bishops' ban on the publication of verse satire in June of that year channeled its subversive energies into drama. Jonson's new form represented the return of the repressed; its distinguishing characteristic was its importation into drama of elements already present in formal verse satire, especially the controlling voice of the poet. But while parallels between these literary kinds do exist, Campbell reduces the genre of comical satire to the persona of the satirist, overestimates the influence of the ban on Jonson's work, and disregards the evolution of his dramaturgy from 1598 to 1599. Since Jonson was not involved in publishing verse at this time, he was unaffected by its censorship. Besides, the ban on satire seems to have been ineffective. When Jonson published *Every Man Out* in 1600, the fact that its title page designated it a comical *satire* did not prohibit it from being printed in at least two, if not three, editions that year, generating a minimum of 1,400 available copies. On the contrary, the quarto of *Every Man Out* met with less interference than its script had at the Globe, where Jonson was forced to change the ending by eliminating his depiction of Queen Elizabeth.[7]

In tracing the origin of comical satire to formal verse, Campbell neglects a more important factor: the process of generic revision that led Jonson from *The Case Is Altered* through *Every Man In* to *Every Man Out*. Anne Barton points out that these three early comedies involve a two-stage rebellion against Elizabethan comic conventions through which he increasingly estranged himself from the Plautine norm of *The Case Is Altered* that aligned his work with Shakespeare's. She endorses Kay's reformulation of Jonson's career when she explains that in *Every Man Out*, "he fought his way out of the brilliant but restricting manner of the early humour plays" with "the help of Aristophanes." Barton acknowledges that *Every Man In* was probably only "moderately successful" and that it did not bring "the kind of attention and acclaim that he received in the following year when ... he pushed his new method to a conscious, and very literary, extreme." But she also regards it as a transitional play that "mediates in certain important respects between *The Case Is Altered* and the three more rigorous and unbending comical satires which succeeded it."[8] *Every Man Out* established Jonson's reputation as an innovator, but it did so as the result of a revolution that began, however tentatively, with *Every Man In*.

Every Man In and *Every Man Out* are what Herford and Simpson call "humour comedies" to the extent that they postulate that character is determined by powerful psychological fixations to which Jonson, influenced by Galenic medical terminology, refers by analogy as "humours." Since "in every human body / The choler, melancholy, phlegm, and blood, / ... Receive the name Humours," Jonson explains in *Every Man Out*,

> thus far
> It may, by *Metaphor*, apply itself
> Unto the general disposition:
> As when some one peculiar quality
> Doth so possess a man, that it doth draw
> All his affects, his spirits, and his powers,
> In their confluctions, all to run one way.
> ("AFTER THE SECOND SOUNDING," LL. 98–108)

But applying the rubric "humour comedy" to both Every Man plays elides their major difference. The phrase *"every man in* his humour" suggests that consciousness is comprised of ineradicable compulsions. It furthermore implies a benign and self-deprecating acceptance of "humour" as a universal condition of subjectivity. Yet such a condition must always be psychologically imbalanced, limited by its partial perspective, and slightly absurd in its manifestations. It is bound to be appetitive and irrational. The phrase *"every man out of his humour,"* however, implies that "humour" induces a false consciousness that must be purged for a potentially ideal human condition to emerge. Since the term "humour comedy" flattens out this distinction, it is helpful to identify *Every Man In* as a humour comedy but distinguish it from the genre of comical satire created to supplant it. The linked titles of Jonson's Every Man plays suggest that the latter is a sequel, yet not a single character or plot strand from *Every Man In* is continued in *Every Man Out*. Like Jonson's original spectators, instead of finding *Every Man In, Part II*, we encounter a new fiction with new characters in a new genre that purged the theory of subjectivity implicit in his earlier poetics.

Humours seem ineradicable in *Every Man In* because they are produced by the four basic domestic relations that defined an Elizabethan middleclass household: descent (the father-son pairing of Lorenzo Senior and Junior); affinity (the husband and wife, Thorello and Biancha, echoed in Cob and Tib); consanguinity (the brothers Giuliano and Prospero); and service (the master-servant relation of the Lorenzos and Musco, Thorello and Pizo, and Doctor Clement and Formal). Each of these symbiotic social couplings engenders a characteristic set of interlocking psychological fixations. Lorenzo Senior is a humourist to the extent that his role as a father prompts him to worry excessively about his son's well-being, just as Lorenzo Junior's humour is shaped by a need to evade supervision. Thorello and his wife Biancha are spurred by the very condition of their union to suspect each other of being unfaithful. Prospero, the younger brother, is witty and carefree in the face of his disenfranchisement, while his older half-brother Giuliano has the peremptory temper of a privileged man. And just as Lorenzo Senior and Thorello seek to control their servants, Musco and Pizo assert their independence. The social bonds that conjoin these characters also divide them psychologically from one another.

This social *discordia concors* is presided over by the madcap magistrate Doctor Clement, who, at the play's conclusion, fosters festive tolerance by clearing up the misconceptions that have aggravated relations between the characters' stereotypical temperaments. A walking oxymoron, he amalgamates eccentricity and law, imagination and reason, symbolizing a benign acceptance of "humour" as the subjective container of perception. It is through Clement's intercession that Lorenzo Junior is pardoned for exhibiting the humour of youth, the overprotective father Lorenzo Senior is resigned to his son's pursuit of pleasure and forgives the impertinence of his servant Musco, the jealous husbands Thorello and Cob resolve to trust their wives, and the elder brother

Giuliano is encouraged to show less aggression toward Prospero, his younger sibling. Clement condones the humours of Lorenzo Junior and Musco—the rebellious son and servant—because he accepts the "wit" and "imagination" of high-spirited humour as expressions of a necessary *élan vital*. Elizabeth Woodbridge has observed that *Every Man In* lacks a coherent ethical perspective because the "line of division" that separates its characters is "drawn, not on a basis of honesty, but on a basis of wit." Such a play, she writes, "can scarcely be called moral, though no one would call it immoral either, unless it were a zealot. ... If it teaches anything it teaches that it is convenient to have a quick brain, a ready tongue, and an elastic conscience."[9] In other words, the high-spirited *Every Man In* tempers judgment with tolerance.

Jonson, however, sets limits on his generosity by his punitive treatment of Bobadilla, a cowardly soldier, and Matheo, a plagiarizing poet, who are punished for counterfeiting the gentleman's arts of arms and letters. Their crime is that (along with their naive imitator Stephano) they aspire to be members of the social class that Jonson celebrates at the center of his fiction through his sympathetic portrayal of Lorenzo Junior and Prospero. "Humour," Pizo explains, is "a monster bred in a man by self-love and affectation, and fed by folly" (3.1.157–58). Yet in *Every Man In* only these two charlatans are sentenced to be jailed and pilloried for pretending to be what they are not. Humour comedy, with its peculiar blend of saturnalian release and social conditioning, conforms to the norm of Elizabethan festive comedy. It liberates human desire from the restraint of unnecessary inhibition, even as it implies a necessary measure of self-constraint. It functions, moreover, as a vehicle for social reconciliation by balancing the divergent claims of its heterogeneous audience, predicating unity on the basis of tolerance and compromise. "The point of view, if not the subject matter, of *Every Man In His Humour* is almost Shakespearian," comments Robert Ornstein. "Here, near the start of his career, was a tolerant amused acceptance of humours that blunts the edge of corrective satire."[10] It is impossible to be out of one's humour in *Every Man In*, since "humour" is an inherent condition of subjectivity: social relations are dialectical, as are the perspectives they engender, so the best that characters can do is be accommodating. This sociability entitles most of them to a place at the promised wedding feast of festive comedy. But such a gathering must, to some extent, resemble a feast of fools.

Yet for all this movement toward social adjustment, what makes humour comedy problematic is its lack of psychological epiphanies. Although the humourists agree to be tempered, they never undergo a rigorous moral transformation. Though the characters partake in the shared experience of subjectivity, their idiosyncrasies isolate them from each other. This is why Gabriele Bernhard Jackson calls *Every Man In* a "comedy of non-interaction" in which "a group of personages in a state of chronic introspection is brought together by a central action which loosely unites them, or rather, brings them into proximity." This is different, she observes, from Shakespeare's "comedy of interaction," where minds transfigured together "grow to something of great constancy." In *Every Man In*, she concludes, there can be "no *together*, since each mind is transfigured separately," and "no mutual element can be deduced from the interweaving of confusions."[11] Brought together at last, the humourists of *Every Man In* still seem self-deluded and alone, and even to speak of their transfiguration, as Jackson does, is to overestimate the change in its denouement. What sets not only Shakespeare but also Chapman apart from Jonson at this time, Barton notes, is that "they freely embraced the idea that characters might change fundamentally, and for the better, as the result of one day's mirth."[12] But this distinction, I would caution, is only true for *Every Man In* and should remind us of the difficulty of making generalizations about Shakespeare's and Jonson's approaches to comedy. For Jonson based *Every Man Out* on the idea that consciousness could indeed be radically changed for the better by great theater. The kind of transformation he envisioned, however, was certainly not Shakespearean.

II

Arguing for the possibility of unassailable standards of judgment, Jonson's first comical satire pushes its characters and audience toward the perception of an empirical reality that purges the life-lies of appetitive humour. Humour comedy and comical satire are similar to the extent that the deep structure of both genres involves a series of converging plot lines in which mobile bands of characters display their obsessions. But they are antithetical insofar as *Every Man Out*—beginning with its startling opening scene—reevaluates *Every Man In*'s collective subjectivities.

Three trumpet blasts introduced plays in the Elizabethan public theater. These "soundings" formalized the playgoing experience and imparted an air of martial authority. They summoned spectators to attention, furnishing a formal transition between the world outside the theater and the events represented onstage. After the third sounding the Prologue spoke. All three comical satires, however, (and only these plays in the Jonson canon) are launched "after the *second* sounding," with scenes that invade the theater. When Asper, the presenter of *Every Man Out*, marches out on the stage of the new Globe—after the second sounding—he seems to voice real anger at a society in crisis as he outlines the need for Jonson's new genre:

> Who is so patient of this impious world,
> That he can check his spirit, or rein his tongue?
> Or who hath such a dead unfeeling sense,
> That heaven's horrid thunders cannot wake?
> To see the earth, cracked with the weight of sin,

> Hell gaping under us, and o'er our heads
> Black rav'nous ruin, with her sail-stretched wings,
> Ready to sink us down and cover us.
> Who can behold such prodigies as these,
> And have his lips seal'd up? not I: my language
> Was never ground into such oily colours,
> To flatter vice and daub iniquity:
> But (with an armed, and resolved hand)
> I'll strip the ragged follies of the time,
> Naked, as at their birth.
>   ("AFTER THE SECOND SOUNDING," LL. 4–18)

In the character sketches added to the First Quarto of 1600, Asper is one of only two characters (the other being "*the Author's friend*," Cordatus) immune from criticism. "*He is of an ingenious and free spirit,*" Jonson writes, "*eager and constant in reproof, without fear controlling the world's abuses. One, whom no servile hope of gain, or frosty apprehension of danger, can make to be a Parasite, either to time, place, or opinion*" (lines 1–6). And although Jonson's prefatory material describes him as the play's spokesman, Asper implies he is its author:

> Well I will scourge those apes;
> And to these courteous eyes oppose a mirror,
> As large as is the stage, whereon we act:
> Where they shall see the time's deformity
> Anatomiz'd in every nerve and sinew,
> With constant courage and contempt of fear.
>   ("AFTER THE SECOND SOUNDING," LL. 117–22)

After the induction, Asper returns as an "actor, and a Humourist" (line 214), taking on the role of his opposite, Macilente: a "*Scholar ... who (wanting that place in the world's account, which he thinks his merit capable of) falls into such an envious apoplexy, with which his judgement is so dazzled, and distasted, that he grows violently impatient of any opposite happiness in another*" (characters, lines 8–13). Asper acts this role until the play's climax, at which point he becomes himself again.

Saturated with metatheatrical allusions, comical satire announces the significance of its revisionism. In the play's superior moral community we invariably encounter two pivotal characters—the author's surrogate who invents "devices" to purge humourists and the monarch who sanctions him. Through this coupling of poet and sovereign—Asper and Queen Elizabeth in *Every Man Out*, Criticus and Cynthia in *Cynthia's Revels*, and Horace and Augustus Caesar in *Poetaster*—Jonson asserted that literary and political power were equal sources of moral authority. And since Asper, Criticus, and Horace are in various ways ideal self-projections, comical satire becomes the medium through which Jonson first postulates his own ideal status.

Despite Jonson's defense of his new genre's neoclassical poetics, its multiple plots are entirely unclassical. No matter how much he was influenced by ancient literary theory and practice, his rich plotting remained indebted to native dramatic traditions. *Every Man Out* takes shape from a different kind of old comedy: the estates satire of the morality tradition. Within its web of interconnected episodes, characters drawn from representative classes of English society are purged of their illusions in the third and fifth acts. The first of these purges occurs when Sordido, the grain hoarder saved from suicide by those he has starved, announces his conversion: "Out on my wretched humour, it is that / Makes me thus monstrous. ... / I am by wonder chang'd" (3.8.40–41, 55). The remainder are reserved for the fifth act, where a sequence of such climaxes ends the play.[13] To ensure that the audience recognizes their significance, Jonson's commentators, Mitis and Cordatus, analyze and predict them between scenes. In the chorus following Sordido's conversion, Mitis wonders "what engine" Jonson "will use to bring the rest out of their humours!" (3.8.95–96), and Cordatus advises him to expect "a general drought of humour among all our actors" (3.9.149). By the end of the fourth act, however, the impatient Mitis again queries how Jonson "should properly call it, *Every man out of his Humour*, when I saw all his actors so strongly pursue, and continue their humours?" Cordatus replies that Mitis will have to wait for the conclusion when, at the "height of their humours, they are laid flat" (4.8.163–68).

In Jonson's purge of festive comedy, the promise of the wedding feast that concludes *Every Man In* degenerates into a violent tavern scene in *Every Man Out*. Where *Every Man In* ends with the coupling of Lorenzo Junior and Hesperida, *Every Man Out* focuses on the disintegration of Delirio's marriage to Fallace. Unlike a festive comedy such as *A Midsummer Night's Dream*, which depicts the irrational attraction of unmarried lovers complicated by misalliances that end happily, *Every Man Out* traces the erosion of marriage through a husband's discovery of his wife's infidelity. Henceforth Jonson's treatment of sexual desire would be wholly subsumed by the "device" or "trick" of the exposure plot, which became the mark of his comedy in *Epicoene*, *Volpone*, and *The Alchemist*. By revising this pivotal motif, he challenged Shakespeare's concession to desire at the expense of judgment.

In Shakespearean comedy, marriage or its promise sanctions desire in a communal spectacle before the actors and the audience disband. His most radical closural variation before 1599 was to delay, not deny, the alliances of *Love's Labor's Lost* (which might have been realized in *Love's Labor's Won*). At the end of *Every Man Out*, however, romance is subjected to satire: Macilente leads the doting merchant Delirio to the debtor's prison where his pampered wife Fallace has come to seduce the dissolute courtier Fastidious Brisk. "Ay? is't thus," Delirio asks Macilente, who replies that he must either believe this ocular proof or cling to a delusion.

> MACILENTE Why, look you, sir, I told you, you might have suspected
> this long afore, had you pleas'd; and ha' sav'd this labour
> of admiration now, and passion, and such extremities as
> this frail lump of flesh is subject unto. Nay, why do you
> not dote now, signior? Methinks you should say it were
> some enchantment, *deceptio visus*, or so ha? If you could
> persuade yourself it were a dream now, 'twere excellent:
> faith, try what you can do, signior; it may be your
> imagination will be brought to it in time, there's nothing
> impossible.
>
> FALLACE Sweet husband:
>
> DELIRIO Out lascivious strumpet.
>
> (5.11.6–17)

Expressed in terms of a visual epistemology in which seeing is knowing, Delirio, the delirium of desire, recognizes his fallacy or Fallace. Against desire's tendency to falsify experience, Jonson brings to bear the pressure of a new empiricism. In Shakespeare's comedies, social conflict is routinely resolved by conceding error, subjectivity, and the contingency of perspective.[14] Macilente dares Delirio to assume the role of a Shakespearean lover by claiming that what he sees was caused by "some enchantment," "*deceptio visus*," "a dream," or "imagination," since "there's nothing impossible." Indeed, from *The Comedy of Errors* to *Twelfth Night*, Shakespeare's comedies are regularly resolved by granting the lie Delirio rejects. In *A Midsummer Night's Dream*, Delirio might have replied that he had "but slumb'red here / While these visions did appear. / And this weak and idle theme, / No more yielding but a dream" (5.1.425–28). He might have concurred with the similarly betrayed Hermia: "Methinks I see these things with parted eye, / When every thing seems double" (4.1.189–90). The jealous husband Ford, falsely suspecting his wife to be cuckolding him in *The Merry Wives of Windsor*, asks, "Is this a vision? Is this a dream? Do I sleep?" (3.5.139–40). The play answers yes in affirming his wife's unassailability, as from *the Comedy of Errors* to *As You Like It* Shakespeare predicates feminine constancy as an absolute against which to measure masculine betrayal.

Every Man Out ends with the masquelike epiphany of Queen Elizabeth, whose presence on stage cures Macilente: the envy (Macilente) that exposed desire (Delirio) is purged by judgment (Elizabeth). Asper becomes Macilente only to be transformed back into a pacified Asper when the queen's cathartic power "*strikes him to the earth dumb and astonished*," thus "*putting him clean* Out of his Humour" (3:602–603). As he explains, in Jonson's conclusion for performance before the Queen:

> ... in her graces,
> All my malicious powers have lost their stings.
> Envy has fled my soul, at sight of her, ...
> My stream of humour is run out of me. ...
> And I have now a spirit as sweet, and clear,
> As the most rarifi'd and subtle air.
>
> (LL. 2–15)

Gone is the crowded scene of social reconciliation that concludes festive comedy. Now only the poet-scholar-actor Asper and the impersonated queen share center stage as icons of moral authority. Comical satire is not a primarily negative or parodic genre, since it furnishes a counter-ideal for what it condemns. Delirio is disenchanted by Fallace, after which Macilente and, by implication, the audience are enchanted by Elizabeth. Comical satire recapitulates the happy ending of the comedy of humours. But *Every Man Out* shows a professional bias in narrowing the community that partakes in that moment to Asper and Elizabeth. The play that opens with defiance for the real ends with an ideal reverence.

Yet the original conclusion of *Every Man Out*—in which an actor impersonated Queen Elizabeth—proved to be so controversial that Jonson was forced to alter it, replacing the queen's appearance with an account of her effect. "It had another *Catastrophe* or Conclusion, at the first Playing," Jonson recalls in the First Quarto, which "many seem'd not to relish ... and therefore 'twas since alter'd" (3:602). Still, he defended his original choice as integral to his poetics, since he could not have discovered a more "*worthy* Figure, *than that of her Majesty's: which his* Election (*though boldly, yet respectively*) *us'd to a* Moral *and* Mysterious *end*" (3:602). As in the later masques that evolve from this experiment, the sovereign's "Figure" helps to stabilize the new genre. Why did it prove so inflammatory? Stephen Orgel plausibly explains that "when Ben Jonson mimed the queen openly, in *Every Man Out of His Humour*, the theater was considered to have overstepped its bounds, making the monarch subject to the whim of the playwright. Only Jonson would have presumed so far, using the power of royalty to establish the authority of his fiction." When actors are allowed to impersonate the monarch, David Kastan relates, representation tends to undermine rather than confirm political authority. What was dangerous about Jonson's representation of royalty in *Every Man Out* was that despite its encomiastic mood, it threatened, in Orgel's words, an "erasure of the distinction between sovereign and subject."[15] The form of political power collided with the power of literary form. When at the end of 1599 the play was produced at court, however, Elizabeth was content to have her actual presence create the necessary balance between poet and monarch, as Macilente addressed her directly in the play's third conclusion.

Modern readers of comical satire rarely focus on this important element of resolution. John Enck, for instance, writes that the "comic tempo" of *Every Man Out* features a single technique of "discontinuity" that "emphasizes ineffectuality through ardent schemes which, worthless from the start, come a cropper or dribble away." Through this technique, he concludes, Jonson established an "unprecedented" and "puzzling change" in theatrical representation that significantly "altered drama" at the turn of the century.[16] Yet comical satire is meant to leave its audience restored. Each play concludes with an idealized moment of concord: a pageant of the true poet and monarch. Whatever discontinuity may fragment society at large is transcended in this final moment of social rapport. Witnessing this spectacle of conversion, Jonson reasoned, would encourage spectators to undergo a cathartic purge of their own corresponding humours. The effect would be a purely moral comic equivalent of Aristotelian *anagnorisis*. The sight of Elizabeth, the antitype of Fallace, transforms Macilente back into Asper. Each of the three comical satires ends with a scene of social harmony that unites the Jonsonian poet and his responsive monarch.

Much late sixteenth-century satiric comedy, Walter Cohen observes, "structurally excludes a positive moral perspective from the action," since its "vigor derives from the disjunction between the social assumptions and resolution of the plot, on the one hand, and the implicit moral judgment by the author, on the other."[17] Comical satire breaks this pattern. L. C. Knights suggests that Jonson's plays "do not merely attack abuses in the light of an accepted norm, they bring in question the ability of the society depicted to formulate and make effective any kind of norm that a decent man would find acceptable." In his view, it was only in the poems and masques, prepared for an elite audience, that Jonson's "acceptance of shared codes in a given social order" encouraged him "to formulate and proselytize for an ideal."[18] But this is true only for Jonson's great Jacobean comedies. It was not the case in 1599.

III

A new sense of purpose led Jonson in *Every Man Out* to idealize both the nature of the theatrical medium he employed and his own role as a dramatist. Through comical satire he distinguished himself from his competitors by insisting that the putatively disgraced medium of commercial drama could serve as the basis for a specifically literary career. At the Globe, Jonson defined his new form of Aristophanic comical satire in opposition to Shakespeare's Plautine festive comedy and made this contrast an explicit theoretical concern of his drama. In one of the most suggestive exchanges between Mitis and Cordatus, the former worries that Jonson's new play might disappoint the Globe's audience, whose expectations of comedy are Shakespearean. In response to this criticism, Jonson's "friend" Cordatus defines the theoretical superiority of comical satire to the genre it was constructed to supplant.

MITIS   I travel with another objection, signior, which I fear will
             be enforc'd against the author, ere I can be deliver'd of
             it.

CORDATUS What's that, sir?

MITIS.   That the argument of his *Comoedie* might have been of
             some other nature, as of a duke to be in love with a
             countess, and that countess to be in love with the duke's
             son, and the son to love the lady's waiting maid: some
             such cross-wooing, with a clown to their servingman,
             better than to be thus near, and familiarly allied to the
             time.

CORDATUS You say well, but I would fain hear one of these
             autumn-judgements define once, *Quid sit Comoedia?* If
             he cannot, let him content himself with CICERO'S
             definition (till he have strength to propose to himself a
             better) who would have *Comoedie* to be *Imitatio vitae,
             Speculum consuetudinis, Imago veritatis*; a thing
             throughout pleasant, and ridiculous, and accommodated
             to the correction of manners: if the maker have fail'd in
             any particle of this, they may worthily tax him, but if
             not, why—be you (that are for them) silent, as I will be
             for him.

                                                 (3.6.191–211)

The influence of Jonson's dichotomy cannot be overestimated. For four centuries
critics have repeated its myth of a native, unlearned, romantic Shakespeare and a
classical, scholarly, satiric Jonson. There has been a tendency in criticism to
blame literary history for initiating, in Russ McDonald's words, "the process
which has dissociated Shakespeare and Jonson from each other, or, rather, joined
them, in a familiar and invariable relation," as "two distinct personae,"
employing antithetical philosophies and dramatic styles. It was through the
efforts of late seventeenth- and eighteenth-century critics, Jonas Barish has
maintained, that "the luckless Jonson was yoked to Shakespeare in an odious
tandem from which two centuries of subsequent comment would scarcely
extricate him."[19] Granted, literary history reified their differences, but Jonson
was *primarily* responsible for stereotyping their opposition in *Every Man Out.*
Barish and McDonald are right to insist that the rigid myth of Shakespeare and
Jonson as mighty opposites conceals significant similarities. But while it is helpful
and liberating to explore the common sources of Elizabethan comedy that they
shared, it is equally important to acknowledge their profound difference between
1599 and 1601. For their strategic intertextuality can best be understood within
specific historical horizons. There is hardly one "Shakespeare" or "Jonson," so
universal claims about their differences can only be misleading. Selecting the
Shakespeare of *As You Like It* instead of *Troilus and Cressida* for comparison with

the Jonson of either *The Alchemist* or *Bartholomew Fair* produces conflicting conclusions. Choosing either *Every Man In* or *Every Man Out* to represent Jonson's relation to Shakespeare similarly biases the results.

NOTES

1. G.K. Hunter, "English Folly and Italian Vice: The Moral Landscape of John Marston," in *Jacobean Theatre*, eds. John Russell Brown and Bernard Harris (New York: Capricorn, 1967), 85.

2. Anne Barton, *Ben Jonson, Dramatist* (Cambridge: Cambridge University Press, 1984), x. Percy Allen, *Shakespeare, Jonson and Wilkins as Borrowers* (London: Cecil Palmer, 1928), 45, had earlier noted that "Jonson's first attempts at drama probably found him, temporarily, under Shakespeare's influence among the Romantics. ... Romanticism, however, could not hold Jonson for long. Eager acquisition and absorption of classical learning, working upon an intensely satiric and rationalistic temperament—together, no doubt, with a tinge of native jealousy—drew him swiftly, and permanently, away from Shakespeare and his fellow romantics."

3. Harold Bloom, *The Anxiety of Influence, A Theory of Poetry* (New York: Oxford University Press, 1973), 13.

4. W. David Kay, "The Shaping of Ben Jonson's Career: A Reexamination of Facts and Problems," Modern Philology 68 (1970): 231. See also his discussion of *Every Man Out* in *Ben Jonson: A Literary Life* (New York: St. Martin's, 1995), 43–62.

5. John Gordon Sweeney III, *Jonson and the Psychology of the Public Theater: To Coin the Spirit, Spend the Soul* (Princeton: Princeton University Press, 1985), 18, 34. Sweeney writes that through comical satire Jonson "asks us to participate in significant theater, theater that promises self-knowledge and realizes the instructive potential of fiction" (9).

6. Oscar James Campbell, *Comicall Satyre and Shakespeare's* Troilus and Cressida (San Marino: The Huntington Library, 1970), 54–81.

7. See *Ben Jonson*, eds. C. H. Herford and Percy Simpson, 11 vols. (Oxford: Clarendon, 1925–1952), 3:410–11, for the difficulty of dating the third quarto, and 3:599–600, 602–3, and 9:185-86 for his alternative endings.

8. Barton, *Ben Jonson, Dramatist*, 44.

9. Elizabeth Woodbridge, *Studies in Jonson's Comedies* (1898; reprint, New York: Gordian Press, 1966), 29.

10. Robert Ornstein, "Shakespearian and Jonsonian Comedy," *Shakespeare Survey* 22 (1969): 43.

11. Quoted from the introduction to *Every Man in His Humor*, ed. Gabriele Bernhard Jackson (New Haven: Yale University Press, 1969), 2.

12. Barton, *Ben Jonson, Dramatist*, 47.

13. These concluding purges assume a mechanical regularity after Saviolina, a lady of the court, is tricked into accepting the country boor Sogliardo as a true gentleman and is consequently derided "out of her humour" (5.2.130). Shift, who had passed himself off as a fearless highwayman, is then forced by Puntarvolo to admit that he only pretended to be brave to "get my self a name, and be counted a tall man" (5.3.66–67). This confession, in turn, destroys Sogliardo's naive confidence in him. "Here," observes Macilente, "were a couple unexpectedly dishumour'd" (5.3.76). Macilente subsequently poisons Puntarvolo's dog, curing him of his excessive natural affection, and gleefully notes: "Puntarvolo and his dog are both out of humour" (5.3.77–78). Then, when Carlo Buffone mocks Puntarvolo, the distraught knight turns on him, seals his mouth with wax, and demands, "Now, are you out of your humour, sir?" (5.6.86). Fungoso, the parasitical man of mode who imitates the conspicuous self-display of Fastidious Brisk, is the next character to be purged, and after being threatened with arrest for debt, he bluntly renounces his obsession in familiar language: "Nay, I am out of those humours now" (5.9.45). Macilente then arranges for the doting husband Delirio to view his wife Fallace's infidelity with Brisk, a sight that opens his eyes to the absurdity of his fawning solicitude and exposes the passion of his wife and her lover. This crescendo of climaxes ends with a political epiphany, as Macilente, who has masterminded many of the play's satiric "devices," unexpectedly enters the presence of Queen Elizabeth and is himself purged of envy.

14. For a general explication of this phenomenon, see Ernest B. Gilman's *The Curious Perspective: Literary and Pictorial Wit in the Seventeenth Century* (New Haven: Yale University Press, 1978).

15. Stephen Orgel, "Making Greatness Familiar," in *Pageantry in the Shakespearean Theater*, ed. David M. Bergeron (Athens: University of Georgia Press, 1985), 23. David Scott Kastan, "Proud Majesty Made a Subject: Shakespeare and the Spectacle of Rule," *Shakespeare Quarterly* 37 (1986): 460.

16. John J. Enck, "The Peace of the Poetomachia," *PMLA* 77 (1962): 388.

17. Walter Cohen, *Drama of a Nation: Public Theater in Renaissance England and Spain* (Ithaca: Cornell University Press, 1985), 282.

18. L.C. Knights, "Ben Jonson: Public Attitudes and Social Poetry," in *A Celebration of Ben Jonson*, eds. William Blissett, Julian Patrick, and R. W. Van Fossen (Toronto: University of Toronto Press, 1973), 171.

19. Quoted from Russ McDonald, *Shakespeare & Jonson/Jonson & Shakespeare* (Lincoln: University of Nebraska Press, 1988), 1.

MATTHEW STEGGLE

The Other Side of the War: Marston and Dekker

Jonson's comical satires can be seen as polemical plays about literature in general and comic drama in particular. The representation of real people in them is a central, thematic part of their campaign that comic drama should be treated seriously. In this chapter, I look at the responses to Jonson, Marston's *What You Will* and Dekker's *Satiromastix*, and argue that each of these plays may be read in the same way. Each uses representation of real people as one of its means of conducting an argument about the status of professional drama, and to argue *against* Jonson's insistence that comedy is fundamentally a matter of text.

It was Jonson's attitude that produced his 1616 Folio, which—as the truism goes—set the precedent and laid the foundations for the academic study of English Literature; but it's an attitude that may appear a little simplistic next to *What You Will*'s celebration of the ludic and irrational, or the stance taken in *Satiromastix*, which sees performance as a continually negotiated compromise, and mocks the rootlessness of uncontextualised text. Perhaps unsurprisingly, neither of these plays has been especially well served by the academic disciplines whose origins they mock. Neither has attracted much secondary criticism, and uncertainties still surround the texts themselves. With *What You Will*, the uncertainties are the unavoidable starting-point.

WHAT YOU WILL AND FANTASY

What You Will is clearly a play with things to say about satire and comedy: two of its characters in particular, Quadratus and Lampatho Doria, discuss the subject

---

From *English Literary Studies*. © 1998 by Matthew Steggle.

explicitly and at some length. Specifically, mention is made of a current fashion for "railing" comedy, of a fashion for writing satires against named individuals, and (twice) of representing living people in stage comedies, so it is also fair to say that personal satire casts a long shadow over the play.[1] But any attempt to read *What You Will*'s poetics of satire and comedy must begin with making the case that there is or is not personation in the play. Most modern critics, led by Philip Finkelpearl, have developed readings of the play that reject the idea that personation is present or that Lampatho Doria has any particular reference to Ben Jonson. Instead, they read the play as a phase in Marston's artistic development, a work to be read only with reference to Marston's other plays and not for contemporary allusions. This is a shame, because *What You Will* champions inconsistency and playfulness, and is ill served by readings that seek to impose consistency on it. In particular Finkelpearl, in his efforts to accommodate a play starring an "Epicurean critic" within the oeuvre of a writer with a known partiality to Stoicism, is forced consistently to misjudge the tone, and to see the whole play as an aimless and depressing satire upon the Epicureanism it appears to celebrate: a manoeuvre of the sort that dogs Marston criticism, an invocation of what R. A. Levin has called "The philosopher's stone of parody."[2]

Although Finkelpearl's reading is almost thirty years old, it has underpinned all subsequent accounts of the play. In challenging it, and trying to reinstate the idea that this is a play built around satire of Jonson, I'm also challenging the basis of these later accounts. There are two main arguments for identifying Lampatho Doria as a specific caricature of Jonson: the portrayal of Lampatho as a character, and the links with *Cynthia's Revels*.

Jonson himself certainly represented Marston on the stage in *Poetaster* and, it is generally agreed, in *Cynthia's Revels* before that. In the Apologetical Dialogue to *Poetaster* the Author complains that his enemies' plays (that is, the plays of Marston and Dekker) have been attacking him personally—hence his response in this play. Years later, in conversation with William Drummond, Jonson explicitly stated that Marston had represented him on the stage.[3] In seeking whether there are any surviving plays in which to locate Marston's satire of Jonson, one must consider *What You Will* a leading contender. In particular, Lampatho Doria, one of the two feuding playwrights in *What You Will*, seems to have many points of contact with Jonson.

Arguing about topics like this was the favourite method of discussion in the nineteenth century, when it was all too easy to draw false parallels between characters and personalities on the basis of trivial resemblances, so care is needed. Indeed, several Victorian critics sought to find Jonson in Quadratus and Marston in Lampatho Doria, although after the work of R. A. Small it has become accepted that if Jonson is to be sought anywhere it is in Lampatho Doria.[4] Lampatho is an enemy of Quadratus, and satirises him, and threatens to write plays against him. Quadratus for his part criticises him for his railing, and insults him too. Furthermore, Lampatho's plays (as seen in Act V) are in rivalry with those of Quadratus. So Lampatho is to Quadratus as Jonson is to Marston, a rival satirical playwright.

Against this broad similarity, Finkelpearl puts a catalogue of biographical reasons why Lampatho Doria is not a caricature of Jonson. "Probably the most effective way to portray a public figure on the stage is to stress his best-known characteristics," but this is not done.[5] There are no references, argues Finkelpearl, to Jonson's bricklaying, or his background as an itinerant player, both of which would surely be gifts for any satirist, and which are used in Dekker's *Satiromastix*. This is true enough in itself, but his own examples show up the problem with using this as proof that Lampatho is *not* Jonson. He quotes, for instance Lampatho Doria's renunciation, near the end of the play, of his former self: "Lampoil, watch-candles, rug gowns and small juice, / Thin commons, four o'clock rising, I renounce you all" (1562–63).

It is true that in passages like this Lampatho Doria is pictured as a former university student: which Jonson, biographically speaking, was not. But Jonson's own self-fashioning as a scholar was so successful that the false idea that he had attended Cambridge was believed by Jonson's contemporaries and by editors as late as William Gifford.[6] And if we look at the presentation of Jonson or the Jonson-character in the three plays which no-one doubts to be involved in the War—namely *Cynthia's Revels*, *Poetaster* and *Satiromastix*—we find him presented in scholarly terms: indeed, terms which use precisely the objects named here. In *Cynthia's Revels* Crites is a "candle-waster"; "he smells all lamp-oyle"; and although not actually wearing rug, he is a "grogran-rascall"—wearing a similarly uncourtly fabric. In *Poetaster*'s Apologetical Dialogue the Author talks about the "pinching throes" of his writing endeavours lit by a "dumbe candle"; and the Horace of *Satiromastix*, "that Iudas yonder that walkes in Rug," that "staru'd rascall," writes by the light of a candle thematic enough to be specified in the scene-direction.[7] *Satiromastix* calls Jonson "self-creating Horace," and in *What You Will* it's the self-fashioned Jonson being satirised, while *Satiromastix* makes capital of the difference between the self-fashioned self and the sordid reality. This is the reason why *Satiromastix* digs up the stories of bricklaying and imprisonment, to create two contrasting versions of Jonson, while *What You Will* contents itself with the simpler and less inflammatory task of reducing Jonson to a single, unitary humour: the out-of-step ex-scholar.

Finkelpearl points out correctly that Lampatho does not obviously resemble Jonson. On the other hand, Jonson's "little fat HORACE," described as "pigmey" in *Satiromastix*, is no portrait of the tall and (at this stage of his career) raw-boned Jonson whom, in *Satiromastix* at least, the character is intended to represent.[8] So, perhaps surprisingly, physically accurate personal representation of the victim of one's satire was not put at a high premium in these plays. Finkelpearl also expresses concern that Lampatho Doria is not portrayed as "a professional man of letters."[9] But *What You Will* is very vague about how any of its characters make a living. They are all gallants, all—as Finkelpearl complains—on perpetual holiday. Insofar as Lampatho is a producer of court entertainments, he is portrayed as a professional man of letters, just as Crites is.

So Finkelpearl's point about personal appearance is irrelevant. It is not surprising that no allusion is made to Jonson's disreputable past. And the argument about Lampatho's career as a scholar tends to prove rather than deny the point. It therefore seems perverse to maintain Finkelpearl's doubts on grounds of biographical similarity, and one may conclude that Lampatho Doria does sufficiently resemble Ben Jonson.[10]

Secondly, *What You Will* has a relationship with the text of *Cynthia's Revels*. Indeed its reworking of some Jonson passages provides some of the best evidence for the date of *What You Will*. For instance, Jonson's Crites says:

> If good CHRESTUS,
> EUTHUS, or PHRONIMUS, had spoke the words,
> They would have moou'd me, and I should haue call'd
> My thoughts, and actions, to a strict accompt
> Upon the hearing: But when I remember,
> 'Tis HEDON, and ANAIDES ...

The trope reappears reversed in the mouth of Marston's Quadratus, and is combined with a second *Cynthia's Revels* tag:

> Should discreet Mastigophoros
> Or the dear spirit, acute Canaidus ...
> ·
>   ... once menace me,
> Or curb my humours with well-govern'd check,
> I should with most industrious regard
> Observe, abstain, and curb my skipping lightness;
> But when an arrogant odd impudent. ...[11]

Another instance of the connection between the two plays can be found a little later in the same scene, and again in lines spoken by Quadratus. Among the things satirised in *Cynthia's Revels* as symbols of frivolity are anchovies, caviar, fantasticness personified as the character Phantaste, and extravagance in clothing and headgear. Thus, the following speech by Quadratus, whose praise of fantasy may be considered an epigraph to all of *What You Will*, takes its opening verbal cues directly from *Cynthia's Revels*:

> A man can scarce put on a tuck'd-up cap,
> A button'd frizado suit, scarce eat good meat,
> Anchovies, caviare, but he's satir'd

And term'd fantastical by the muddy spawn
Of slimy newts; when, troth, fantasticness,
That which the natural sophisters term
Phantasia incomplexa, is a function
Even of the bright immortal part of man.
It is the common pass, the sacred door
Unto the privy chamber of the soul,
That barr'd, naught passeth past the baser court
Of outward sense; by it th'inamorate
Most lively thinks he sees the absent beauties
Of his lov'd mistress;
By it we shape a new creation
Of things as yet unborn, by it we feed
Our ravenous memory, our [invention] feast:
'Slid, he that's not fantastical's a beast.

(582-99)

Quadratus' praise of fantasy works by sliding together two different connotations of the word: "fantasticness," in the sense disliked by Jonson, and the fantasy as a faculty of the organic soul. In his general theory of the mind Quadratus is following Aristotle's *De anima*, elements of which were refracted through the three traditions of Arab scholarship, Neoplatonism, and Augustinian scholarship, and reassembled by Renaissance philosophers in a new form.[12] Although his argument is self-consciously fantastic itself, it is an accurate summary of the prevailing philosophical view, in which fantasy was an organ located in the anterior cerebral ventricle. It acted upon the data of the five external senses that common sense had processed, and converted them into "phantasmata"—images that were not mere copies of the outside world—which other organs of the brain, such as memory, could process. "Fantasticness," in that it is here given credit as the agency responsible for "a new creation," is made responsible for art: including the highly wrought and self-consciously showy piece in which this idea is contained, and including—as will be seen—even *What You Will* itself.

Theories of the organic soul provide something of a thematic key to *What You Will*. Elsewhere in the play, Lampatho describes how all his learning was in vain, with particular reference to his vain grapplings with the theories of the soul peddled by "Zabarell, / Aquinas, Scotus, and the musty saw / Of antick Donate."[13] In the main plot of the play, to which it must not be forgotten that Quadratus and Lampatho are merely accessories, the merchant Albano develops an uncertainty about his soul brought on by the fact that everyone thinks he is an impostor, merely an impersonation of Albano rather than the real thing:

The Samian faith is true, true, I was drown'd,
And now my soul is skipp'd into a perfumer, a gutter-master.

. . . .
                                        If Albano's name
Were liable to sense, that I could taste or touch
Or see, or feel it, it might 'tice belief;
But since 'tis voice and air, come to the musk-cat, boy:
Francisco, that's my name ...

                                        (1239–40, 1259–62)

The concept of the organic soul, and in particular of the interpretative power of
the fantasy—which is lacking in both Lampatho and Albano, unable to cope with
anything not directly discernible by mere "sense"—provides a unifying theme for
What You Will. Furthermore, the same imagery of the fantasy occurs in the
Induction, directly linked to statements about the nature of comic drama.

The Induction to *What You Will* sets up an opposition between two
characters, Doricus and Philomuse. Doricus is a devotee of fantasy, something
that becomes apparent quickly not merely through his direct mention of it but
through his associative, imaginative manner of speaking:

DORICUS: Marry sir, Signor Snuff, Monsieur Mew, and Cavaliero
          Blirt, are three of the most to be fear'd auditors that ever—
PHILOMUSE: Pish for shame, stint thy idle chat.
DORICUS: Nay, dream whatsoe'er your fantasy swims on,
          Philomuse ...

                                        (14–18)

Philomuse, on the other hand, is less tolerant of such unbuttoned frivolity. When
he mentions fantasy, it is in a derogatory context, as an example of one of the
things that an author should take no notice of in writing his work, along with
things like the reaction of the audience:

Shall he be crest-fall'n, if some looser brain
In flux of wit uncivilly befilth
His slight composures?
.....
Why gentle spirits, what loose-waving [vane],
What anything would thus be screw'd about
With each slight touch of odd phantasmatas?
No, let the feeble palsied lamer joints
Lean on opinion's crutches ...

                                        (28–30, 43–47)

The important thing about Philomuse's speech, shot through as it is with a vivid
imagery of sickness that weakens one's confidence in the speaker's self-

proclaimed healthiness and calmness, is that it is a *reductio ad absurdum* of an attitude of sturdy independence from the vagaries of the audience expressed, most notably, by Ben Jonson in *Cynthia's Revels*: "By—, 'tis good, and if you lik't, you may" (Epilogue 20). By contrast, what Doricus has to offer instead is a view of art, not as part of an author, but as a thing created by him:

> Music and poetry were first approv'd
> By common sense; and that which pleased most
> Held most allowed pass; no, rules of art
> Were shap'd to pleasure, not pleasure to your rules.
> Think you that if his scenes took stamp in mint
> Of three or four deem'd most judicious,
> It must inforce the world to current them
> That you must spit defiance on dislike?
> Now as I love the light, were I to pass
> Through public verdict, I should fear my form
> Lest aught I offer'd were unsquar'd or warp'd.
>
> (59–69)

The imagery is taken not from the body but from workmanship. Music, metal stamping and carpentry make their appearance in Doricus' alternative conception of art as an artefact: something external to the author. The author is deposed from a position of almost vatic authority to that of a mere artisan who must obey certain standards of workmanship. Where one might expect a Horatian stress on balancing the "utile" and the "dulce," Doricus concentrates instead purely upon the "dulce." In addition, he rejects literary precedent in favour of "common sense." Again, the vocabulary of the organic soul surfaces: common sense is what provides the raw material for the fantasy to work on.

Doricus' tirade has its effect. Chastened, Philomuse lapses into prose. Doricus asks him the genre of the play they are about to watch:

> DORICUS: Is't comedy, tragedy, pastoral, moral, nocturnal or history?
> PHILOMUSE: Faith perfectly neither, but even *what you will*, a slight toy, lightly composed, too swiftly finish'd, ill plotted, worse written, I fear me worst acted, and indeed *what you will*.
> DORICUS: Why I like this vein well now.   (87–91)

The spectators' active role in creating the play before them is stressed even in the title. Doricus throws onto the audience the responsibility of generically locating the play, if they think it worth their trouble. In its refusal to conform to any of the genres into which Elizabethan critics such as Sidney, Puttenham, Webbe and Meres had classified all drama, this piece refuses to play by the rules of these poetic systems. As can be seen in Envy's Induction in *Poetaster*, a large concern of Jonson is his fear of allowing the audience the sort of creatively interpretative role that they are allowed—indeed forced into—here, in making what they will of *What You Will*.

Likewise, one of the differences within the play between Quadratus (who is most definitely not "unsquared") and Lampatho relates to the works of art that they create. Lampatho is unable to judge the correct moment and the correct audience for his literary output. He tries to spring sonnets on the ladies at an inopportune moment, and offers a play for the Duke's entertainment which is so inappropriate in its moralising tone that it is never performed. Quadratus, on the other hand, fits his literary entertainments to the occasion, offering to "suit" the Duke's ears with "a subject worth thy soul: / The honour'd end of Cato Utican." The subject of this entertainment is souls, as it offers a discussion put into the mouth of Cato on "the soul's eternity." Not merely is it about souls, but it will affect the souls of its hearers: "O these are points would entice away one's soul / To break's indenture of base prentisage" (1962–63, 1971, 1982–83). This drama by Quadratus wears its learning lightly, as a functional aid to its ability to please its listeners. It earns its justification through the pleasure it gives, rather than depending on its moralising force (a force which is nevertheless clearly potential—after all, the subject, Cato, is famous for his virtue). The entertainment (which like Lampatho's is, through the exigencies of the plot, left forever undelivered) can be seen as a synecdoche for the rest of *What You Will*, and an example of the ideals of drama which it seeks to promote.

What You Will, in short, uses imagery of the organic soul to discriminate "good," fantastic drama such as that praised by Doricus and Quadratus, from the stiffer, stuffier model of composition favoured by Philomuse and Lampatho Doria. Furthermore, this latter model is to some extent parodic of the classics-based, text-privileging stance of Jonson's comical satires. It seems likely that personal satire of Jonson is an important part of Marston's technique here, although, admittedly, the ludic inconsistency of *What You Will* means that the attack on Jonson is not in the transparent mode adopted by *Satiromastix*. But then, *Satiromastix* does not just offer a different version of Ben Jonson: it also offers a third intellectual model of professional drama to set beside those of Jonson and Marston.

SATIROMASTIX: THE BAITING OF BEN JONSON

As with *What You Will*, so with *Satiromastix*. It's been neglected and misunderstood because it has been interpreted from a critical position with which it is not in accord. An example of this in miniature is provided by the question of its running-title—"The Untrussing of the Humorous Poet."

According to received wisdom, Jonson's *Poetaster* represents a coup over Dekker: Jonson rushed his play out before *Satiromastix* was ready, anticipating its characters and drawing its sting. Among the other details which it is assumed Jonson has scooped is the running-title of Dekker's play, since this phrase is used by Jonson's *poetaster*s of the play that they themselves are writing. But there are some self-evident problems with this scenario. Fifteen weeks, which is according to Envy, the amount of time taken to write *Poetaster*, is arguably a short time for the notoriously laborious Jonson, but it would imply that Dekker's play had lingered in composition for longer still: and Dekker was notoriously prolific.[14]

Furthermore, all the satire in *Satiromastix* as it stands is crucially dependent upon the characterisation of Jonson as Horace and on the role of Captain Tucca, both of which Dekker himself freely says (in the preface) are themselves dependent upon *Poetaster*. As for Rufus Laberius Crispinus and Demetrius Fannius, one cannot even argue that Jonson has pre-empted names envisaged by Dekker. These names are combinations of those of bad poets mentioned in the works of Horace, emphatically not the names of choice for sympathetic characters in any setting, let alone the early mediaeval.[15] It is a sign of what Julia Gasper calls the "condescending picture" painted of Dekker by critics that it has been assumed that Jonson outwitted him so completely by stealing his names and his subtitle, when clearly the reverse has happened.[16]

The reason, then, that Jonson in *Poetaster* appears so well able to predict what will appear in "The Untrussing" promised by Demetrius and Crispinus is not that he knows in advance what it will contain; on the contrary, it hasn't yet been written. Instead, it's because Dekker sets about writing a play that will fulfil all Jonson's predictions and take on Jonson on Jonson's own terms, complete with a version of the man himself.

Satiromastix, in its printed incarnation, opens with a dedicatory letter, and a flurry of Latin that is not at all characteristic of the play that is to follow. The preface explicitly distinguishes the classical "true *Venusian Horace*" from "Horace the second," author of "Euery Man in's Hvmour," "our new *Horace*."[17] Taking material that Jonson gives him, and altering the context to make the material ridiculous, Dekker does to Jonson's assumption of the character of Horace what he will go on to do to Jonson's own words. For instance, he describes the conflict in these terms:

> I care not much if I make description (before thy *Vniuersality*) of that terrible *Poetomachia*, lately commenc'd between *Horace the second*, and a band of leane-witted *Poetaster*s. They haue bin at high wordes, and so high, that the ground could not serue them, but (for want of *Chopins*) haue stalk't vpon Stages. (To the World 6–11)

The literal meaning is ostensibly favourable to Jonson, but it is undermined by irony. The grotesque classical coinage "Poetomachia," with its implication of deliberate pedantry, would not appeal to Jonson. Neither would Jonson be so immodest as to call himself "Horace the second," although Dekker is merely stating boldly the parallel *Poetaster* made implicitly between the two authors; Dekker's strategy here is merely to report Jonson's claim, but in a way that makes it appear self-evidently hubristic. By contrast, Dekker's tone is casual, self-mocking, and far removed from the "high words" of Jonson's side of the quarrel. The imagery of a physical struggle implicit in "Poetomachia" is carried on in the next paragraph: "All mount *Helicon* to *Bun-hill*, it would be found on the *Poetaster*s side *Se defendendo*" (To the World 20–21).

Again, Jonson would resist not merely the verdict here but the whole imagery of a fight. In the Apologetical Dialogue he refuses to state that *Poetaster* is part of a campaign: it's a once-only response to sundry impotent libels, a play of quite a different order to the material his opponents have been producing. Thus bringing in Mount Helicon here is a reminder of *Cynthia's Revels* (in which Helicon was prominent), and hence the fact that *Poetaster* was not so much of a one-off as Jonson disingenuously claimed. Dekker goes on:

> I wonder what language *Tucca* would haue spoke, if honest Capten *Hannam* had bin borne without a tongue? Ist not as lawfull then for mee to imitate *Horace*, as *Horace Hannam*? ... neyther was it much improper to set the same dog vpon *Horace*, whom *Horace* had set to worrie others.
>
> (To the World 32–35, 37–39)

Dekker's assertion has been most fully investigated by Tom Cain, who locates a "captayne Haname" on the fringes of theatrical life in the 1590s, pawning bed-linen to Henslowe. Cain further points out that there was a family named Hanham with strong links to the Middle Temple, which—if this Haname may be identified as one of them—would make him, like Charles Chester, or like Jonson himself, a figure on the margins of the Middle Temple society whose influence on comical satire appears to have been so important.[18] All this is even more involved, since a Tucca of very similar propensities to Jonson's had appeared in Guilpin's *Skialetheia* of 1598, as an auditor of some bawdy love poetry, leading to speculation that all three Tuccas, along with a handful of other characters in Marston's verse satires, are personations of the same person.[19] The problem with this is sheer lack of evidence: we have no biographical information on Hannam to prove or deny the resemblance, or to explain why he should be accorded any role (let alone a central role) in a conflict between playwrights. The Tucca of *Poetaster* is, as Herford and Simpson note, a *miles gloriosus* with strong affinities to Captain Shift and others of his genre: so Dekker's allegation must remain "not proven."

Again, the central importance of personal satire to these plays is highlighted, but of interest here is less the truth of this particular allegation, than the question of why Dekker makes it. It is phrased as an accusation of plagiarism against Jonson—that Jonson couldn't have made Tucca without taking Hannam's words. Dekker has taken over Jonson's material, but the Hannam allegation weakens Jonson's claims to have the authority to make accusations of plagiarism against Dekker.

Dekker does not differentiate between imitating a person's characteristic language, and taking words from a text that that person has written. In *Cynthia's Revels*, one finds the same lack of distinction between normal speech and authored text, notably in the gallants' discourse made up of jests stolen indiscriminately from dinner companions and from plays. To the twentieth-century mind, though, these are two quite different categories of theft. "Imitate" is a pun that not merely indicates that theft of Tucca's language and of Jonson's text is equally fair, but also links the theft in both cases with personation. Jonson "imitates" Hannam both in copying his "language" from him, and in making a forged representation of him. Likewise Dekker acknowledges his appropriation of characters from Jonson, and applies it to personation of him, as if appropriating material from him were a necessary part of personation.

And "honest Capten *Hannam*" is a figure outside the literary world in which the quarrel has functioned so far. This indeed is the way in which Dekker uses Tucca: whereas Demetrius and Crispinus (themselves professional writers) adopt reasonably conciliatory stances that acknowledge the literary importance of Horace's potential talent, Tucca still behaves with the uninhibited freedom of tongue and lack of literary scruple that Jonson gave him in *Poetaster*. Hence Tucca is described as "the same dog … whom Horace had set to worrie others." The question of whether Dekker's Tucca still constitutes a personation of Hannam is left conveniently unanswered. Dekker goes on to insist that he is not trying to escalate the quarrel any further:

> I protest (and sweare by the diuinest part of true Poesie) that (howsoeuer the limmes of my naked lines may bee and I know haue bin, tortur'd on the racke) they are free from conspiring the least disgrace to any man, but onely to our new *Horace*; neyther should this ghost of *Tucca*, haue walkt vp and downe Poules Church-yard, but that hee was raiz'd vp (in print) by newe *Exorcismes*. (To the World 42–47)

The phrase "The diuinest part of true Poesie" is just the kind of rhetoric over which Jonson was seeking to gain a monopoly by posing as the representative of true poetry: Dekker refuses to concede. Similarly, Dekker claims for the "naked lines" of his texts the same sort of victim-status as that Jonson likes to claim for his: Jonson's Envy had asked her minions to "Shew your rustie teeth / At euerie word, or accent" (Envy's Prologue 47–48). And even Envy herself resurfaces, complete with snakes, later in Dekker's preface: "*Enuy* feede thy Snakes so fat with poyson till they burst" (To the World 51–52).

Dekker says that his lines need not be tortured, as they have nothing to hide. But even here, as in the *Poetaster* Apologetical Dialogue, the limitation of personal application is a self-undermining statement. The work proclaims itself to contain no hidden satire, but then cannot name the person it admits to satirising openly. Likewise in *Poetaster* Jonson insisted "I vs'd no name" (Apologetical Dialogue 84). At no point during the entire War do the participants name their opponents by their real names: the strongest taboo of all on personal satire, the reluctance to name names as Aristophanes had done, remains strong. As will be seen, even this decorum was sometimes breached in later satirical drama.

Finally, Dekker's comment about "newe *Exorcismes*" should be noted. A striking fact about most of the plays in the War is the speed with which they went from performance to print. Presumably such topical plays dated badly, and would not be valuable in the repertoire very long. *Every Man Out* and *Jack Drum's Entertainment* were published in 1600; *Cynthia's Revels* in 1601. *Poetaster* appeared in print in 1602, as did *Satiromastix*.[20] Dekker's metaphor describes a second, ghostly War, as the series of plays came successively into print. But even the imagery of the "ghost" to describe this has a polemical intent. In describing the printings of these plays as "Exorcismes" of something that was only properly alive on the stage, Dekker differs from Jonson. From *Every Man Out* through to *The New Inn*, Jonson's quartos present themselves as a truer version of the play than that which had been acted, in terms of extra unacted material, and so on. Dekker does not subscribe to this model. In this effacement, the lines no longer even have limbs to torture: they have become incorporeal.

This second War in print overlapped with and influenced the War on stage; for it seems at least possible that the parts of Clove and Orange, the objects of offence in *Every Man Out*, were among the new and previously unperformed material which Jonson claimed to have added to the 1600 quarto.[21] Furthermore, it seems certain—from the accuracy of his quotations from it, discussed below— that Dekker had access to a printed version of *Cynthia's Revels* while composing *Satiromastix*. Another unique feature, then, about the War in the context of Renaissance English drama is not merely the interaction between rival plays, but the interaction between performance and print. In *Satiromastix*, this opposition manifests itself in an attack on textuality of all sorts.

Dekker's Horace is first encountered in his study, composing an ode, just as he was when introduced in *Poetaster*, although in that play composition was an apparently effortless process. It's an appropriate choice of opening, not just because odes were the forte of the historical Horace. After all, the ode, the "simple, and continued Song" mentioned in *Every Man Out* (Induction 250) etymologically speaking underlies comedy, tragedy—and parody. The ode in this scene of *Satiromastix* is in itself respectable enough, and a good pastiche of Jonson, but it dissolves into comedy when we see Horace in the process of composing it:

> To thee whose fore-head swels with Roses,
> Whose most haunted bower,

Gives life and sent to euery flower ...

. . . .

For I to thee and thine immortall name—
In—sacred raptures flowing, flowing, swimming, swimming:
In sacred raptures swimming,
Immortall name, game, dame, tame, lame, lame, lame,
Pux ha't, shame, proclaime, oh—

. . . .

Good, good, in flowing numbers fild with spright and flame.[22]

This scene is in fact a textbook example of Derridean deconstruction in the strict sense of the word—depriving a text of its monolithic power and unity by exposing the structures that construct it, and the rhyme-words that it chooses to repress, forget and reject.

A Derridean "logocentrism"—attribution of an almost divine stability to the relationship between signifier and signified—is perceived throughout as one of Horace's flaws. The ode, which at later recitations seems so spontaneous, is in fact a self-conscious act of writing. And it is typical of Dekker's strategy throughout the satirical subplot of *Satiromastix*: pieces of Jonsonian text, not just from *Poetaster*'s Horace, but also from Crites/Criticus of *Cynthia's Revels* and Asper in *Every Man Out*, are discredited by being uttered in farcical situations.

Satisfied with the finished version, Horace then recites the ode to his foolish sidekick and only ally, Asinius Bubo (for this version of Horace is deprived of the Augustan context and the extended circle of Maecenas so important in *Poetaster*), and they gossip and discuss the possibilities of Horace's social preferment. Other detailed echoes of Jonson in this scene have been recorded by Hoy, but the most important is this one:

> HORACE: Why should I care what euery Dor doth buz In
> credulous eares, it is a crowne to me, That the best
> judgements can report me wrong'd.
>
> ASINIUS: I am one of them that can report it.
>
> HORACE: I thinke but what they are, and am not moou'd. The
> one a light voluptuous Reueler, The other, a strange
> arrogating puffe, Both impudent, and arrogant enough.
>
> ASINIUS: S'lid do not *Criticus* Reuel in these lynes, ha Ningle ha?
>
> HORACE: Yes, they're mine owne.   (I.ii.149-158)

This exchange can be set beside the corresponding lines spoken by Criticus in the 1601 quarto form of *Cynthia's Revels*:

Why should I care what euery *Dor* doth buzze
In credulous eares? it is a Crowne to me,
That the best iudgements can report me wrong'd ...
. . . .
I thinke but what they are, and am not stir'd:
The one, a light voluptuous *Reueller*,
The other a strange arrogating *Puffe*,
Both impudent, and ignorant enough.[23]

The exactness of the similarities—apart from the confusion of "ignorant" with "arrogant," probably due to the word "arrogating" in the line above, and "moou'd" for "stir'd," "moou'd" appearing elsewhere in the speech from which these lines are taken—strongly suggests that this quarto was available to Dekker when writing *Satiromastix*, creating a unique interrelation of texts and performances.[24]

The significance of all these direct verbal borrowings from Jonson is revealed when Crispinus and Demetrius enter, in Crispinus' first major speech:

Horrace, Horrace,
To stand within the shot of galling tongues,
Proues not your gilt, for could we write on paper,
Made of these turning leaues of heauen, the cloudes,
Or speake with Angels tongues: yet wise men know,
That some would shake the head, tho Saints should sing,
Some snakes must hisse, because they're borne with stings.

(I.ii.204–10)

In these lines Dekker is rehearsing a version of the doctrine of "things indifferent" whose most famous reappearance in English literature will be in Milton's *Paradise Regained*.[25]

This idea insists that no object, or text, is so purely good that it is incapable of perversion or misapplication, not even the Scriptures. In *Paradise Regained* the Devil's persuasions are no less evil for being couched in biblical quotations, as words themselves do not carry an absolute value or power. The particular application of this idea to Scripture, reflected in Crispinus' imagery of angels and saints, is especially appropriate in view of *Poetaster*'s elevation of Virgil's text to almost scriptural status, as discussed above. Dekker's recognition that there will be no unanswerable answers—that not even the angels' song will get an unproblematic hearing—rejects the idea of natural language, viewing language instead as something negotiated by the parties involved.

In this scene, then, Dekker is undermining language's claims to be absolute, and hence undermining the Jonsonian idea that his play is an unambiguously virtuous text which must be protected at all costs from misinterpretation. Jonson fears the idea that the spectator is an active constructor of the drama they are watching—since at least part of the audience have "basiliske's eyes," and will try to "Peruert, and poyson all they heare, or see" (*Poetaster*, Envy's Induction 36, 39). Jonson wants a banished Envy and an inviolable text that the audience should passively accept, but the Envy in Dekker's Epistle is to die not by force but by her own poisonousness (Epistle 51–52). Dekker claims not to fear debate and dissent, seeing it as a process of moving towards truth. In fact, what Dekker proposes is a dialectical model of moral advice in general and satire in particular, in which "friends" can administer each other gilded "pills" for correction and improvement. This emphasis on reciprocity can be seen especially clearly—again in connection with the point about oaths—in Crispinus' next speech:

> Say you sweare
> Your loue and your aleageance to bright vertue
> Makes you descend so low, as to put on
> The Office of an Executioner,
> Onely to strike off the swolne head of sinne,
> Where ere you finde it standing; Say you sweare,
> And make damnation parcell of your oath,
> That when your lashing iestes make all men bleed;
> Yet you whip none. Court, Citty, country, friends,
> Foes, all must smart alike; yet Court, nor Citty,
> Nor foe, nor friend, dare winch at you; great pitty.
>
> (I.ii.227–37)

It is not merely that Dekker is denying Jonson a quasi-hieratic position as arbiter of morals: he is denying anyone that position. Dekker further rejects the Jonsonian (and Horatian) view that attacks on vice in general will not make the virtuous man "smart." Instead, he is constructing an audience of imperfect people, who do and always will fail to live up completely to perfect ideals, and whose attempts to do so are not helped by Jonson's caustic exposure of their shortcomings.

Furthermore, there is a repeated insistence on Horace/Jonson's overuse of swearing, reflected here in Crispinus' opening reference, and repeated a few lines later: "Say you sweare / And make damnation parcell of your oath." In the case of the character Horace, Crispinus has a point: even in this one scene so far, Horace has already made such oaths twice, both times, interestingly, in connection with his literary output. "Dam me ift be not the best [poem] that ever came from me," he says of the ode; and then a little later, "Dam me if I bring not [Tucca's] humor a'th stage" (I.ii.36, 132). Horace's "dam me" is the most powerful form of speech available, and the most dreadful oath one can make: it's an appalling thing to wish upon oneself, and besides, one can only be damned once. But, says Dekker, Horace/Jonson is using it and overusing it and not convincing his enemies at all. It is a point which the play comes back to again and again; Horace's swearing is mocked by the other characters in almost every scene in which he appears. Vain swearing is another example of the uselessness and powerlessness of mere language.[26]

Tucca's prose insults overlap thematically with the charges established by Crispinus and Demetrius in their blank verse. For example, Tucca warns: "That Iudas yonder that walkes in Rug, will dub you Knights ath Poste, if you serue vnder his band of oaths, the copper-fact rascal wil for a good supper out sweare twelue dozen of graund luryes" (I.ii.283–87). Again, the profligacy of Horace's oaths is under attack, linked this time not to debates about the textual status of scripture, but to an allegation of perjury; and this is typical of the way in which Dekker uses Tucca to provide a scurrilous biographical complement to the more theoretical and moral objections against Horace made by Crispinus and Demetrius. The end of this scene is a compromise. Tucca offers to be Horace's "Mæcenas" and to get Crispinus and Demetrius to provide scenes for the next of his "strong garlicke comedies" (I.ii.374, 334–35), thus insouciantly trampling on two of *Poetaster*'s main ideals, the virtuous patron and the idea of art as the product of a single, literary author. Subsequent scenes with Horace merely repeat this theme with variations, like *What You Will*'s satirical sub-plot and unlike the more linear structure of *Poetaster*. The stage action and the form of the chastisement may be different—the whipping with nettles, the stripping of Horace of his satyr's disguise—but the structure is the same. Therefore, these later scenes do not need discussion at length.

However, one later insult by Tucca is worth quoting in full, because it makes explicit the connection in the War between personal reputation and poetics:

> Thou call'st *Demetrius* Iorneyman Poet, but thou putst vp a Supplication to be a poore Iorneyman Player, and hadst beene still so, but that thou couldst not set a good face vpon't: thou hast forgot how thou amblest (in leather pilch) by a play-wagon, in the high way, and took'st mad Ieronimoes part to get seruice among the Mimickes: and when the Stagerites banisht thee into the He of Dogs, thou turn'dst Ban-dog (villanous Guy) and euer since bitest, therefore I aske if th'ast been at Parris-garden, because thou hast such a good mouth, thou baitst well; read, *lege*, saue thy selfe and read. (IV.i. 125–36)

To take the last insult first: Tucca refers to the benefit of clergy by which Jonson had saved himself from the gallows, a custom over which Jonson himself makes jokes, trying to privilege literacy as a tool for understanding drama (see *Cynthia's Revels* Induction 39–41). This is mainly gratuitous muck-raking, but the rest of the insult is more sophisticated.

On a straightforward level, there is clearly capital to be made out of the fact that Jonson, whose *Poetaster* includes so much satire against players as a class, should himself have been an actor. Furthermore, Dekker seeks to associate him not just with the permanent professional theatre in London, but with the even humbler world of the itinerant play-wagon: "the originall Dung-cart" of wit, as Jonson later called it. It was a world that was also mocked in *Histriomastix*, the play that seems to have ignited the War of the Theatres, and which *Satiromastix* seems to refer to in its title. *Histriomastix*, it is generally thought, portrayed Jonson as Chrisoganus, an impecunious writer who is at least a little above the mere travelling players for whom he is forced to write: but this passage collapses the distinction and pushes Horace/Jonson down to their level. Even the role allotted to Horace/Jonson, from Kyd's *Spanish Tragedy*, is a piquant one. "Mad Ieronimoes part" is the very role—irrational, threatening, out of control—that Jonson himself repudiates as undesirable in, for example, the *Bartholomew Fair* Induction. In fact, one effect of Tom Cain's proposed redating of *Poetaster* and consequentially of *Satiromastix* as well to the later autumn of 1601 would be to make the Ieronimo reference exquisitely apt and topical, for in September 1601, Jonson was being paid to write additions to *The Spanish Tragedy*—that is, he was actively involved in the very play which is here described as part of his old disreputable lifestyle.[27] What is more, "Mimicke," if we may judge from its appearances in Jonson's own language, is an especially pejorative word for an actor.[28]

Tucca's use of the word "Stagerite" is a startlingly erudite pun. It's a nonce-word, a *hapax legomenon* even in the *OED*. The pun is on "Stagirite," an inhabitant of Stagira, a title specifically of Aristotle, and even this word is so rare the *OED* does not record it until 1620.[29] The rest of the sentence describes of course the *Isle of Dogs* incident of 1597, so the pun in "Stagerites" insinuates that the *Isle of Dogs* was a gross violation of artistic standards as well as being imprudent: that Jonson has put himself outside the pale of the theories he espouses by his reckless satire, and is rejected both by the stage and by the theorists.

Finally, Jonson is said to have become a "Ban-dog." This insult contributes to a pattern of imagery of bears and dogs which has been present since the Epistle, where the talk was of setting dogs on Horace. Horace has since been described as "Hunkes," the nickname of the bear at Paris Garden, and Hoy suggests "Guy" and "Fulkes" in the extract above may well be the names of bears or dogs. The imagery of Horace as a *"Bearewhelp"* continues to the end of the play (I.ii.319: V.ii.185). The interesting thing about this is that bear-baiting was the main rival of the drama in the competition for a paying audience. Indeed, sometimes, as in the case of *Bartholomew Fair*, the bears and the actors boxed and coxed in the same theatre. Jonson's later plays are full of contemptuous references to "the bears within" (*Bartholomew Fair* Induction 52–53), who become emblematic of bad entertainment. But one does not need to look past 1601 to find examples of Jonson's dislike of the bear-pits. In *Poetaster* he likens the "multitude" who listen to his enemies to "the barking students of Beares-Colledge"—Paris Garden. He claims to be uninvolved, watching on "Pleas'd, and yet tortur'd, with their beastly feeding": and yet somehow the emotive verbs hint at a weakness in Jonson's armour on this point which Dekker, clearly, is seeking to exploit.[30]

Bear-baiting, then, becomes a metaphor for the War as Dekker and his side would like to see it. Casting Jonson as the bear is calculated to annoy Jonson immensely, and to discredit his pose of aloof supremacy from any sort of combat. So this paragraph of abuse by Tucca in fact represents a well-chosen and pregnant set of insults that attack his personal credentials, but in a way that is focussed on poetics. Tucca also speaks the Epilogue, which serves as an epitome of the difference between Dekker's approach and Jonson's, and might almost be said to be part of a manifesto for drama. Jonson's original Epilogue to *Poetaster* is lost, suppressed, he says in the quarto, by "authority"; but whatever it contained, on the basis of his other Epilogues it is unlikely to have been as colloquial as that delivered after *Satiromastix*. Captain Tucca speaks it in characteristic prose (as opposed to the verse more usual in Epilogues):

> Let's part friends. I recant, beare witnes all you Gentle-folkes (that walke i'th Galleries) I recant the opinions which I helde of Courtiers, Ladies, and Cittizens, when once (in an assembly of Friers) I railde vpon them: that Hereticall Libertine *Horace*, taught me so to mouth it. Besides, twas when stiffe *Tucca* was a boy: twas not *Tucca* that railde and roar'd then, but the Deuill and his Angels: But now, Kings-truce, the Capten summons a parlee, and deliuers himselfe and his prating companie into your hands, vpon what composition you wil. (Epilogue 5–13)

The allusion to the "Friers" is of course to the theatre of the Blackfriars, where *Poetaster* was played. Tucca is concerned with the theatre as a physical structure, with galleries and "two penny Tenants," and with rival theatres around the city: he is more concerned with the theatre than with the play, again a position antagonistic to Jonson.

Tucca is claiming that it was not the real Tucca who spoke in *Poetaster*; in fact, Tucca is alleging that Jonson personated him. The temptation is to take this allegation as evidence in favour of the Tucca/Hannam identification discussed above, but this is deeply problematic in view of the fact that Dekker would be trying to remedy the situation with a second personation. Also, the statement that Tucca was formerly a "boy," and has now grown—ostensibly a punning reference to the fact that *Poetaster*, unlike *Satiromastix*, was played by a boys' company—suggests that Tucca has developed as a character too: which would sit uneasily with the idea that he was a personation designed to reflect some external referent such as Captain Hannam. More plausibly, the allegation is cheekily retrospective, a final witty exploitation of the paradoxes of personation and plagiarism raised by Dekker in his preface.

As in *What You Will*, the success of the piece lies in the audience's hands: Dekker even falls into the same phrase, offering them "what composition you wil." The contrast again is with Jonson's parting shot in *Cynthia's Revels*: "By—, 'tis good, and if you lik't, you may" (Epilogue 20). Jonson's idea of an inviolable text whose virtues may not be appreciated by an audience is countered by an insistence that a play stands or falls by its audience's reaction.

Finally, this analysis of *Satiromastix*, personation, and the poetics of drama allows one to go back and reinterpret the main plot of the play, in particular the resolution, which has generally—and, I think, unjustly—been seen as a weak and hurried conversion of a tragic ending into a happy one. One notices, for example, that the scenes in which this conversion is effected are suffused with imagery of theatre. In short, King William intends to claim *droil de seigneur* upon the beautiful Celestine, bride of Wat Terrill, until she prevents him by taking poison. The King is appalled and contrite, whereupon it is revealed that the poison was only a sleeping drug and all ends happily. Imagery of drama appears in large quantities throughout this last Act, starting in the scene where Celestine and Sir Quintilian try to formulate a plan for the fatal evening:

> SIR QUINTILIAN: I, heer's a charme shall keep thee chaste, come, come,
> Olde Time hath left vs but an houre to play
> Our parts; begin the Sceane, who shall speake first?
> Oh, I, I play the King, and Kings speake first ...
> . . . .
> But to my part; suppose who enters now,
> A King ...
> . . . .
>   Then he speakes,
> Thus—thus—I know not how.
>
> CELESTINE: Nor I to answer him.
>
> SIR QUINTILIAN: No girle? knowst thou not how to answer him?
> Why then the field is lost, and he rides home,
> Like a great conquerour; not answer him?
> Out of thy part already? foylde the Sceane?
> Disranckt the lynes? disarm'd the action?
>   (V.i.55–58, 71–72, 76–82)

So the meeting with the King is being rehearsed as a dramatic event, but it is a dramatic event without a script. Sir Quintilian and Celestine are trying to work out a script—perhaps even predict a script—but it's not one that they already possess. (One could contrast, again, *Cynthia's Revels* where all the gallants already have scripts worked out.) It's precisely because the conclusion of their scene *isn't* a foregone conclusion that they need to rehearse it to work out how it will go.

When the event comes to be played out for real, it is set within the dramatic framework of a masque: Terrill's party are wearing masks, and enter "two and two with lights like maskers." The King, too, believes that his interview with Celestine will take a dramatic form, offering to help Celestine through "the Sceane of blushing," only to find that he is addressing her apparently dead corpse and "none plaies heere but death." Thereupon Terrill seizes the moment in a phrase that is almost Brechtian in its treatment of the dramatic illusion: "Now King I enter, now the Sceane is mine" (V.ii.36, 48, 52, 54, 61).

But Terrill, too, is deceived as to the sort of drama in which he is participating, mistaking it for a tragedy. The true nature of the drama in which they are participating is eventually revealed by Sir Quintilian, who declares: "I am an Actor in this misterie, / And beare the chiefest part," and reveals that the poison is not really fatal and that the generic resolution is really that of neither masque nor tragedy, but tragi-comedy. In terms of the imagery used to describe them, the death and resurrection of Celestine are dramatic events. Furthermore, it is important that the scene is a performance and not a script, since King William's self-recrimination and recognition of his guilt are, only caused by his erroneous belief that Celestine is dead—by the fact that he has been deceived by the dramatic illusion. Thus a play which will "wed a Comicall euent, / To presupposed tragicke Argument" is privileging the forgiving unpredictability of performance at the expense of text (V.ii.96–97, 113–14).

The same is true of the most glaring incongruity in the play. Everyone knows that, in the historical texts on which *Satiromastix* is based, Wat Terrill ends up murdering King William II. In unexpectedly converting the tragedy into a comedy, *Satiromastix* is rewriting English regnal history with an alarming freedom. (An obvious contrast is Jonson's *Sejanus*, weighed down with marginalia supplying textual warrant for its fiction.) Just as Dekker's Horace/Jonson is shown to have put too much trust in the power of texts, so *Satiromastix* ends by cocking a snook at the whole idea of a performed play being constrained by the prescriptions of historical texts.

In conclusion, this analysis shows that *What You Will* and *Satiromastix* pursue very different sets of poetics in their different reactions to the challenge of Jonsonian satire. Both, in different ways, attack Jonsonian logocentrism. *What You Will* actively celebrates the ludic, while in *Satiromastix* the relativity and limitation of fixed pieces of speech or text are treated more soberly. Whereas *What You Will* invokes ideas of fantasy and phantasmata to undermine the Jonsonian stress on self-sufficient decorum, *Satiromastix* uses imagery of drama and introduces a metadramatic instability. *What You Will* bypasses conventional poetics as far as possible; *Satiromastix* is prepared to mock them insofar as they underpin Jonsonian discourse, and use them offensively when they can help discredit Jonson. To Marston, Jonson is Lampatho Doria, an inept, pedantic gallant deaf to fantasy; to Dekker, he is Horace, an arrogant would-be laureate with a sordid past and a hardly less sordid present.

The resulting plays expose ideological tensions that lie at the heart of a struggle over what professional drama might be and might become. As playwrights define themselves more and more in oppositional terms, the War becomes an active force that pushes Marston into writing an Epicurean comedy, Dekker into broadening the intellectual and satirical limits of tragicomedy, and Jonson into writing *Sejanus*, the learned tragedy which he promised at the end of *Poetaster*.

NOTES

1. *What You Will* 520 (Lampatho threatens to write a satire against Quadratus); 1142 (Lampatho refers to the popularity of satirical comedies); 1555 (Quadratus says Lampatho might put him in a satirical comedy); 1915 (Quadratus wishes that Simplicius might be satirised in a comedy).

2. Finkelpearl, *John Marston* 162–77; Anthony Caputi, *John Marston, Satirist* (Ithaca: Cornell UP, 1961) 156–78, quotation from 169: Richard A. Levin, "The Proof of the Parody," *Essays in Criticism* 24 (1974): 312–16.

3. Jonson, *Conversations* 285–86; H&S I. 140.

4. Josiah H. Penniman, *The War of the Theatres* (Boston: Ginn, 1897) 137–43. The two characters certainly are similar in their social milieu and intellectual interests, leading to one description of Lampatho as a "teasing anamorphic double-portrait of the two rivals [Marston and Jonson]": *The Selected Plays of John Marston* ed. Macdonald P. Jackson and Michael Neill (Cambridge: Cambridge UP, 1986) Introduction xv.

5. Finkelpearl, *John Marston* 163.

6. John Taylor's elegy on Jonson, cited from H&S XI. 425; *The Works of Ben Jonson*, ed. William Gifford, Introduction 3.

7. *Cynthia's Revels*, III.ii.3,9,6; *Poetaster* Apologetical dialogue 213; *Satiromastix* I.ii.282, 309, I.ii.o (stage direction).

8. *Poetaster* IV.vii.24; *Satiromastix* I.ii.354.

9. Finkelpearl, John Marston 163.

10. Other similarities include Lampatho's "Jebusite" Catholicism; *What You Will* 514.

11. *Cynthia's Revels* III.iii.18–23 (cf. also III.iii.26–27); *What You Will* 567–74.

12. *The Cambridge History of Renaissance Philosophy*, ed. C.B. Schmitt and

Quentin Skinner (Cambridge: Cambridge UP, 1988) 464ff. provides an excellent guide to the reinterpretation of Aristotle's theories in the Renaissance.

13. *What You Will* 857–59. It is presumably through a profitable confusion with his namesake the heretic that Donatus here appears relegated to an incongruous "musty saw": an elegantly gratuitous dig at classical dramatic theory.

14. *Poetaster*, Envy's Prologue 14–17; Hoy, I.179.

15. H&S IX 535–36.

16. Gasper, *The Dragon and the Dove*, 1.

17. *Satiromastix*, To the World 54–55, 8, 27, 45. Even before the text proper starts, *Satiromastix* has appeared with a list of errata directed "Ad Lectorem," and a Latin quotation addressed "Ad Detractorem," both printed in Bowers' edition, I.306, 308.

18. Jonson, *Poetaster* ed. Cain, Introduction 48–49.

19. Cf. H&S IX.535: Hoy, I.188. Jonson's victim in *Every Man Out*, Charles Chester, had featured in *Skialetheia* under his own name, which also serves to suggest the closeness between verse satire and its dramatic equivalent: Everard Guilpin, *Skialetheia or a Shadowe of Truth, in Certaine Epigrams and Satyres*, ed. D. Allen Carroll (Chapel Hill: North Carolina UP, 1974), Satire II.47–51.

20. The two exceptions are *What You Will*, which was not in print till 1607, and *Histriomastix* (1610).

21. This point is argued by Hoy, I.183.

22. *Satiromastix* II.ii.1–3, 11–14, 20. As Evans (*Ben Jonson and the Poetics of Patronage* 147) points out, this piece is specifically parodic of Jonson's patronage poems.

23. This is the quarto text as it appears in the Bodleian copy, Malone 193 (1), for which H&S use the siglum B. Other quarto copies have readings that vary from this slightly, but not substantively; full details may be found in H&S's apparatus criticus at lines III.iii.8–10, 25–27.

24. Alternatively, one would need to contest that they were a memorial transcription from an earlier performance of the play. Cf. Hoy I.197, 309–10 for transcriptions from a performance of *Satiromastix*: the standard of recall is, significantly, much lower in these examples than it is for Dekker's reproduction of Jonson.

25. For a discussion of it there, and more generally of its other appearances in the thought of the period, see Stanley fish, "Things and Actions Indifferent: The Temptation of Plot in *Paradise Regained*," *Milton Studies* 17 (1983): 163–86.

26. See. e.g., I.ii.238–40, IV.i.157, IV.ii.182, IV.iii.178, V.ii.228, V.ii.323. And as Evans (*Jonson and the Contexts of his Time* 22–35) points out, another character too fond of oaths is King William himself.

27. Jonson, *Discoveries* 2677: *Bartholomew Fair*, Induction 106; Hoy I.195. Previously it had been assumed that Dekker was merely being prophetic.

28. See, for example, *Volpone* Dedication 57: "Where haue I beene particular? Where personall? except to a mimick, cheater, bawd or buffon, creatures (for their insolencies) fit to be tax'd." Or, *Cynthia's Revels* III.iv.20, where he brackets together "mimiques, jesters, pandars, parasites."

29. *OED* s.v. "Stagirite": there is, however, a prior use by John Marston, in *The Scourge of Villanie* IV.99. See *The Poems of John Marston*, ed. Arnold Davenport (Liverpool: Liverpool UP, 1961).

30. *Poetaster* Apologetical Dialogue 45, 48. Dekker, on the other hand, makes it clear in his preface that he welcomes audiences who enjoyed the first Tucca and now want to enjoy the second as well.

JONATHAN DOLLIMORE

The Revenger's Tragedy (c. 1606): Providence, Parody and Black Camp

Many critics have felt that if *The Revenger's Tragedy*[1] cannot be shown to be fundamentally orthodox then it cannot help but be hopelessly decadent. If, for example, it can be shown to affirm morality-play didacticism and its corresponding metaphysical categories (and hence idealist mimesis), an otherwise very disturbing play is rendered respectable. Moreover, the embarrassing accusation of a critic like Archer—that the play is 'the product either of sheer barbarism, or of some pitiable psychopathic perversion'—can be countered with the alternative view that it is a 'late morality' where 'the moral scheme is everything'.[2]

Numerous critics have tried to substantiate the morality interpretation by pointing to (i) the orthodox moral perspective which is, allegedly, implicit in characters' responses to heaven, hell, sin and damnation, and (ii) the extensive use of ironic peripeteias which allegedly destroy evil according to a principle of poetic justice. I want to challenge in turn each of these arguments.[3]

PROVIDENCE AND PARODY

In Vindice's rhetorical invocations to heaven there is a distinctive sense of mockery:

Why does not heaven turn black, or with a frown
Undo the world?—why does not earth start up,

From *Radical Tragedy*. © 1984, 1989 by the author.

And strike the sins that tread upon't?

(II. i. 254–6)

The implied parody of the providential viewpoint, the *caricature* of the vengeful god, becomes stronger as the play progresses:

> *Vindice*: O, thou almighty patience! 'Tis my wonder
> That such a fellow, impudent and wicked,
> Should not be cloven as he stood, or with
> A secret wind burst open.
> Is there no thunder left, or is't kept up
> In stock for heavier vengeance? [*Thunder sounds*] There it goes!

(IV. ii. 194–9)

Here the traditional invocation to heaven becomes a kind of public stage-prompt ('Is there no thunder left … ?') and God's wrath an undisguised excuse for ostentatious effect. In performance such lines beg for a facetious Vindice, half turned towards the audience and deliberately directing its attention to the crudity of the stage convention involved.[4] In effect, the conception of a heavenly, retributive justice is being reduced to a parody of stage effects. In the following pun on 'claps' heaven is brought down to the level of a passive audience applauding the melodrama: 'When thunder claps, heaven likes the tragedy' (V. iii. 47). Vindice becomes the agent of the parody and is invested with a theatrical sense resembling the dramatist's own: 'Mark, thunder! Dost know thy cue, thou big-voic'd cryer?/Duke's groans are thunder's *watchwords*' (V. iii. 42–3, my italics; cf. Vindice's earlier line: 'When the bad bleeds, then is the tragedy good'—III. v. 205).

It gives an intriguing flexibility to Vindice's role, with the actor momentarily stepping through the part and taking on—without abandoning the part—a playwright's identity. This identity shift is instrumental to the parody: at precisely the moments when, if the providential references are to convince, the dramatic illusion needs to be strongest, Vindice (as 'playwright') shatters it. He does so by prompting for thunder from the stage, by representing thunder as a participant in a melodrama waiting for its 'cue', and by re-casting the traditionally 'frowning' heaven as a spectator clapping the action. The convention linking 'heaven', 'thunder' and 'tragedy' is, together with its related stage effects, rendered facile; providentialism is obliquely but conclusively discredited.[5] The letter of providentialist orthodoxy and, perhaps, of censorship, are respected but in performance their spirit is subverted through a form of parody akin to 'the privy mark of irony' described in the Dedication to Beaumont's *The Knight of the Burning Pestle*.

Peter Lisca, in seeing the references to thunder and heaven as eliminating any doubt as to the play's 'sincere moral framework' (Lisca, p. 250), seems to miss an irony in tone and delivery which, in performance, would actually contradict the kind of moral conclusions he draws. Discussions of the extent to which a play is indebted to older dramatic forms are often marred in this way by an inadequate discrimination between the dramatic use of a convention and wholesale acceptance of the world view that goes (or *went*) with it. Obviously, the distinction becomes more than usually crucial when, as is the case here, the convention is being subjected to parody.

This play also exposes the hypocritical moral appeals which characters make to the providential order. An audience will, for example, simply *hear* the sermonising rhetoric of the Duchess' attack on illegitimacy:

> O what a grief 'tis, that a man should live
> But once i' th' world, and then to live a bastard,
> The curse o' the womb, the thief of nature,
> Begot against the seventh commandment,
> Half-dammn'd in the conception, by the justice
> Of that unbribed everlasting law.
>
> (I. ii. 159–64)

The hollowness of this rhetoric is, of course, compounded by the sheer hypocrisy of its delivery: the Duchess is seen speaking not from the pulpit, but in the act of seducing her stepson and inciting him to murder his own father.

Still in Act I there is a moral posturing more revealing even than that of the Duchess. Antonio, celebrating publicly his wife's 'virtue' (she has committed suicide after being raped) is seen to value it even more than her life. 'Chastity' and 'honour' emerge in fact as the ideological imposition and self-representation of the male ego in a male dominated world. What compels us to consider the episode thus is not the simple facts themselves but the fact of their caricature; thrown into exaggerated relief 'honour' and 'chastity' are turned inside out and held up for inspection. As with the interrogative representation of providence, parody here invites distrust, ironic distance and refusal. Thus, discovering his wife's dead body to 'certain lords' Antonio exclaims:

> be sad witnesses
> Of a fair, comely building newly fall'n ...
>
> *Piero*:   That virtuous lady!
> *Antonio*:   Precedent for wives!
>
> (I. iv. 1–7)

A language of artificial grandeur reeking of affected grief tells us that what is being celebrated is not her innate virtue but her dutiful suicide, her obedience to male-imposed terms of sexual honour:

> *Antonio*:   I joy
>   In this one happiness above the rest ...
>   That, being an old man, I'd a wife so chaste.
>
>   (I. iv. 74–7)

Chastity in this court involves a life-denying insularity dictated by male vanity, not disinterested virtue. Again, it involves a hypocrisy masked by an appeal to the providential order: 'Virginity is paradise, lock'd up./You cannot come by yourselves without fee,/And 'twas *decreed* that man should keep the key' (II. i. 157–9). Male relations of power and possession are sanctioned in terms of female virtue and providential design, while the death of Antonio's wife, though presented as the cause of ensuing conflict, is in fact the excuse for its continuation. In effect she is the instrument of a power struggle quite independent of her.

Peripeteias allegedly constitute the structural evidence for the providential interpretation of the play. Lisca for example has argued that its moral attitude 'proceeds from a Christian point of view (the Puritan)' and that the peripeteias indicate 'the intestinal division of evil itself, a division which while seeming to lead to multiplication ironically ends in cross cancellation' (pp. 242, 245). Often the assumption behind this approach is that peripeteia possessed an inherently providential meaning. This was not the case with Aristotle's definition of it and nor, at this time, with its use in the Italian *novelle* and the plays influenced by them.[6] In *The Revenger's Tragedy* the ironic reversal is manifestly bound up with Vindice's (and the theatre's) sense of artistry and 'jest' (V.i. 64) and what Nicholas Brooke characterises as a humour 'in marvellously bad taste' (*Horrid Laughter in Jacobean Tragedy*, p. 14). In particular the art of revenge is seen to aim at a vicious blend of the appropriate and the unexpected. Vindice's advice to Lussurioso on how to kill the Duchess and Spurio (whom they expect to find in bed together) is an extreme case in point: 'Take 'em finely, finely now ... Softly, my lord, and you may take 'em twisted ... O 'twill be glorious/To kill 'em doubled, when they're heap'd. Be soft,/My Lord' (II. ii. 169: II. iii. 4). Here both peripeteia and poetic justice are construed in terms of a villainous aesthetic delight. It is a mode of appropriation which makes for a kind of double subversion: the play not only refuses two principles of moralistic drama, it presses them ignominiously into the service *of* play. Likewise with its own formal closure: 'Just is the law above!' cries Antonio with orthodox solemnity in relation to the series of murders in the final scene; ''twas somewhat witty carried, though we say it' replies Vindice coyly, referring to one of the same. In that reply, as elsewhere, the play's mocking intelligence and acute sense of parody—the kind that 'hits/Past the apprehension of indifferent wits' (V. i. 134)—converge in a 'witty' subversion of Antonio's crude, providential rationalisation.

DESIRE AND DEATH

Inseparable from this play's subversion of some of the conventions of idealist mimesis is an alternative representation of the relations which bind sexuality, power and death. It centres on the frenetic activity of an introverted society encompassed by shadows and ultimately darkness—the 'heedless fury' and 'Wildfire at midnight' which Hippolito describes (II. ii. 172). The Court, 'this luxurious circle', is a closed world where energy feeds back on itself perpetuating the 'unnatural' act in unnatural surroundings: the location of the Duke's death is an 'unsunned lodge', 'Wherein 'tis night at noon'. Decay and impermanence stress the futility of each person's obsessive struggle for power. Yet there is no anticipation of otherworldly compensation, Junior's cynical rejection of the relevance of heaven to his impending death (III. iv. 70–4) being typical. The play's view of mortality is reminiscent of Schopenhauer; I quote briefly from his *Parerga and Paralipomena* simply to emphasise that it is not necessarily a view which entails a conception of man as inherently sinful or governed by divine law. The experience Schopenhauer describes is a contingent one with secular boundaries:

> The vanity of existence is revealed in the whole form existence assumes ... in the fleeting present as the sole form in which actuality exists, in the contingency and relativity of all things ... in continual desire without satisfaction; in the continual frustration of striving of which life consists ... Thus its form is essentially unceasing *motion* without any possibility of that repose which we continually strive after ... existence is typified by unrest. ... Yet what a difference there is between our beginning and our end! We begin in the madness of carnal desire and the transport of voluptuousness, we end in the dissolution of all our parts and the musty stench of corpses.[7]

One is reminded too of the more restrained, yet somehow almost as pessimistic, account of London by Tourneur (or whoever that 'C.T.' was)[8] at the opening of 'Laugh and Lie Downe: Or, the Worldes Folly':

> Now in this Towne were many sundrie sorts of people of all ages; as Old, and young, and middle age: men, women and children: which did eate, and drinke, and make a noyse, and die ... they were Creatures that serued the time, followed Shaddowes, fitted humours, hoped of Fortune, and found, what? I cannot tell you.[9]

In *The Revenger's Tragedy* this sense of court life as futile striving is intensified by the dramatist's insistence that here there is no alternative: activity occupying the immediate dramatic focus—'this present minute'—is made, through graphic 'off-stage' description, to appear as just a bolder representation of that which pervades the rest of life:

> My lord, after long search, wary inquiries,
> And politic siftings, I made choice of yon fellow,
> Whom I guess rare for many deep employments;
> This our age swims within him ...
> He is so near kin to this present minute.
>
> (I. iii. 21–6)

Moreover, characters move into the line of vision already 'charged' with a common motivating energy—sexual, aggressive or otherwise—which varies in intensity only depending on whether it is the dramatic foreground or background that they occupy. It is, consequently, a world whose sense ends with its activity—a world, that is, whose senselessness becomes instantly apparent when activity culminates in death. Vindice highlights this through a detached awareness which Tourneur exploits to full effect as part of a structural interplay between movement and stasis.

Movement illustrates repeatedly the forces that impel, but simultaneously constrain and destroy people; the most extreme is the sexual—the 'riot' of the blood (I. i. 11). 'I am past my depth in lust,/And I must swim or drown' says Lussurioso (I. iii. 88–9), testifying to the destructive yet compulsive force of desire. Social forces are powerfully realised as either grinding poverty or thwarted ambition—both of which render the individual vulnerable to court exploitation. Thus we see Hippolito being sent from court—

> To seek some strange-digested fellow forth,
> Of ill-contented nature, either disgrac'd
> In former times, or by new grooms displac'd—
>
> (I. i. 76–8)

while for Lussurioso 'slaves are but nails, to drive out one another'. For his second slave he demands one who,

> being of black condition, suitable
> To want and ill content, hope of preferment
> Will grind him to an edge.
>
> (IV. i. 69–71)

Both Machiavellian intrigue and lust are depicted as inherent aspects of the frenetic movement and become inextricably linked with it in imagination:

> *Vindice*:   my brain
>   Shall swell with strange invention; I will move it

> Till I expire with speaking, and drop down
> Without a word to save me; but I'll work—
Lussurioso: We thank thee, and will raise thee.

> (I. iii. 119–23)

The point is stressed throughout with the recurrence of that word 'swell' in imagery of tumescence: 'drunken adultery/I feel it swell me' (I. ii. 190–1); 'I would embrace thee for a near employment,/And thou shouldst swell in money' (I. iii. 76–7); 'Thy veins are swell'd with lust, this shall unfill 'em' (II. ii. 94); see also I. ii. 113 and IV. i. 63.

Movement involves an incessant drive for self-fulfilment through domination of others.[10] It is also represented as a process of inevitable disintegration; dissolution and death seem not in opposition to life's most frantic expression but inherent within it: 'O, she was able to ha' made a usurer's son/*Melt all his patrimony in a kiss*' (I. i. 26–7, my italics); 'I have seen patrimonies washed a-pieces, fruit fields turned into bastards, and, in a world of acres, not so much dust due to the heir 'twas left to, as would well gravel a petition' (I. ii. 50–3). The assertion of life energy does not stand in simple contrast to the process of disintegration but rather seems to feed—to become—the very process itself.[11]

Vindice's silk-worm image makes for the same kind of emphasis at a point immediately prior to the height of the dramatic action (the bizarre murder of the Duke with a skull, poisoned and disguised as a 'country lady'): 'Does the silk worm expend her yellow labours/For thee? for thee does she undo herself?'[12] (III. v. 72–3). Dissolution, the sense of helpless movement and lack of purpose are all concentrated in this image. The sense of uncontrollable movement towards dissolution also recalls Vindice's earlier lines where drunkenness releases barely conscious desire: 'Some father dreads not (gone to bed in wine)/To slide from the mother, and cling the daughter-in-law' (I. iii. 58–9). Here, in lines whose meaning is reinforced by the stress falling on 'slide' and 'cling', the involuntary action of a human being is reduced (casually yet startlingly) to the reflex action typical of an insentient being. In all these ways the futility and destructiveness of social life seem to have their source in some deeper condition of existence; at the very heart of life itself there moves a principle of self-stultification.

Contrary to this use of movement, the stasis with which it contrasts involves a form of detachment, the medium of insight and a limited foresight. Whereas to be caught up in the temporal process is to be blindly preoccupied with the present 'minute' (a recurring expression—see especially I. ii. 168; I. iii. 26; I. iv. 39; III. v. 75), the brief moments of inaction allow for a full realisation of just how self-stultifying is this world's expenditure of energy, of just how poor is the benefit of the 'bewitching minute'. It is reflected, initially, in the way Vindice's opening commentary is delivered from a point of detached awareness— a detachment represented spatially with him withdrawn into the shadowed region of the stage and directing attention at the procession. And at III. v. 50 ff., just before the (by now) anticipated climax, his own contemplative state directs attention to the lifelessness of the skull, a wholly static but tangible representation of death and a striking visual contrast to the frenetic activity of life in this court. Insight of this kind is limited to Vindice; by others it is actually evaded. Thus whereas Vindice realises that 'man's happiest when he forgets himself' (IV. iv. 84) but cannot in fact forget himself for very long, Ambitioso checks his realisation that 'there is nothing sure in mortality, but mortality' with a resolve to action: 'Come, throw off clouds now, brother, think of vengeance,/And deeper settled hate' (III. vi. 89–90; 92–3).

There is one view of the characters in this play which sees them as morality type abstractions—'simply monstrous embodiments of Lust, Pride and Greed' (Salingar, '*The Revenger's Tragedy* and the Morality Tradition', p. 404). But their sub-humanity indicates more: displaying considerable desire, some intelligence but little self-awareness, they fit this play's depiction of life lived obsessively and destructively within the dislocated social 'minute'. Moreover such awareness as does exist is turned inward, brought to bear on immediate desire, but always in a way that fails to discover a unified, autonomous self. Instead their soliloquies indicate the forces which in-form and dislocate them. The Duchess, for example, is first seen as a voice of 'natural' mercy pleading for her 'youngest, dearest son' (I. ii. 103). But in her first soliloquy, while presumably retaining this affection, she becomes the ruthless schemer intent on having her husband killed by his bastard son and herself having an illicit—in the terms of the play, 'incestuous' (I. ii. 175)—sexual relationship with the latter. Moments later, the bastard, Spurio, accedes to both proposals only to then repudiate the Duchess just as she repudiated her Duke: 'Stepmother, I consent to thy desires,/I love thy mischief well, but I hate thee' (I. ii. 193–4). Thus Spurio casts himself as the avenger, making the appropriate alliance, but in so doing makes a distinction in commitment that stalls all possibility of empathy. In the same soliloquy, brilliant, imaginative compression of mood and image suggests a dissolving of Spurio's present consciousness into the very circumstances of his conception: '... some stirring dish/Was my first father ... / ... drunken adultery/I feel it swell me' (ll. 181–2; 190–1). 'Impudent wine and lust' now infuse his veins such that 'Adultery is my nature' (l. 179), while alliteration and stressed single-syllable words give a rhythmic insistence blending into the 'withdrawing hour' to insinuate exactly the concealed activity in which he was 'stol'n softly':

In such a whisp'ring and withdrawing hour,
When base male-bawds kept sentinel at stair-head,
Was I stol'n softly

(I. ii. 187–9).

Imagery of sexuality becomes this play's most powerful signifier of a society deriving initial impetus from, yet finally stultified by, the contradictions within it. Thus the old Duke is sexually 'parch'd and juiceless'—one with 'scarce blood enough to live upon' (I. i. 9, 10)—yet his very impotence is paradoxically though not untypically the source of a sterile and destructive life force.

Given a world of dislocated energy as its dramatic subject, what kind of formal unity is such a play likely to possess? The answer is suggested in Vindice. Disguise, intelligence and the capacity to see the futility of others' endeavour, give him a kind of freedom. Yet it is at best partial and probably illusory, being, in effect, a knowledge of the fate of the society to which he is inescapably confined. It is as such that, at the play's close, he surrenders his life with comparative indifference, a surrender recalling his earlier expression of estrangement: 'My life's unnatural to me, e'en compelled/As if I lived now when I should be dead' (I. i. 120–1). Unemployed and with his family in poverty he articulates the tensions and contradictions of his world, becoming the focal point for those dimensions of the play which, though inextricably linked will not—indeed, cannot—be finally resolved into a single coherent 'vision'. Even when he is most apparently an agent—as for example in the famous fifth scene of Act III—he is really a victim and he knows it; hence his sharply alternating moods: detached, exhilarated, despairing, sadistic. Vindice as malcontented satirist is corrupted by the society he condemns because inescapably a part of that society; to put it another way, he condemns it because he is corrupted—inevitably corrupted by it. In this respect satirist figures like Vindice and Flamineo (*The White Devil*) share much in common with other malcontented rebels like, for example, Antonio (*Antonio's Revenge*), Bussy d' Ambois, and Edmund (*King Lear*): estrangement from society, whether because of poverty, dispossession, unemployment, injustice or thwarted ambition, provokes in them an aggressive reaction; heroic or criminal it adds up to the same thing: a desperate bid for reintegration. In its vindictiveness this bid becomes the contradictory attempt to destroy that which they are within and which they cannot survive without. The experience of estrangement reveals on the one hand the futility and worthlessness of the existing social order, on the other the estranged subject's dependence upon it; most extremely, to be reintegrated is to embrace destruction. Yet the alternative—estrangement itself pushed to an extreme—leads to poverty, mental collapse or suicide.

In *The Revenger's Tragedy* a vital irony and a deep pessimism exist in disjunction; if they are held together dramatically they are not in any sense aesthetically integrated, either in tone or character. And if there is an attitude yoking them by violence together it is not that of the unified sensibility once thought to characterise the period, but rather that of a subversive black camp. It is sophisticated and self-conscious, at once mannered and chameleon; it celebrates the artificial and the delinquent; it delights in a play full of innuendo, perversity and subversion; by mimicking and misappropriating their glibness it exposes the hypocrisy and deception of the pious; through parody it declares itself radically sceptical of ideological policing though not independent of the social reality which such scepticism simultaneously discloses. Vindice, living that reality in terms of social displacement and exploitation, lives also the extreme instability of his society and is led thereby to meditate on mutability and death. Even the meditation takes on a subversive edge because transferred from the study to that place to which Vindice's displacement has led him: the domain of sexuality and power, the 'accursed palace' where his brother finds him 'Still sighing o'er death's vizard' (I. i. 30, 50). Just as displacement compels action so the meditation is, as it were, enacted. Yet no one in the process is allowed the role of heroic despair; in relation to no one is human suffering made to vindicate human existence. To that extent *The Revenger's Tragedy* is beyond—or before—'tragedy'.

Notes

1. I am assuming nothing, nor contributing to the debate, about the authorship of this play.

2. Archer, *The Old Drama and the New*, p. 74; John Peter, *Complaint and Satire in Early English Literature*, p. 268. Instead of Archer's indignation, or Peter's rendering of the play respectable, another tradition of critics showed a deep fascination with 'Tourneur's' psychopathology. Thus J. Churton Collins writes that 'Sin and misery, lust and cynicism, fixed their fangs deep in his splendid genius, marring and defacing his art, poisoning and paralysing the artist' (*The Plays and Poems*, p. lvi), while T. S. Eliot, described the motive of the *Revenger's Tragedy* as 'truly the death motive, for it is the loathing and horror of life itself' (*Selected Essays*, p. 190).

3. These arguments are more fully outlined, and contested, in Jonathan Dollimore, 'Two Concepts of Mimesis: Renaissance Literary Theory and *The Revenger's Tragedy*,' pp. 38–43.

4. This is, perhaps, the 'pose of indignant morality' that Archer detected (*The Old Drama and the New*, p. 74) but misunderstood. But even Archer had misgivings: 'One cannot, indeed, quite repress a suspicion that Tourneur wrote with his tongue in his cheek' (p. 75). Indeed one cannot!

5. If, as seems probable, *The Revenger's Tragedy* was written after May 1606, such obliquity may, apart from anything else, have been an effective way of avoiding a tangle with the statute of that month to restrain 'Abuses of Players'. This act not only forbade the player to 'jestingly or profanely speak or use the holy name of God or of Jesus Christ, or of the Holy Ghost or of the Trinity', but also commanded that the same were not to be spoken of at all 'but with *feare and reverence*' (my italics). It is precisely this kind of 'feare and reverence' which is being parodied. The statute is reprinted in W.C. Hazlitt, *The English Drama and Stage*, p. 42.

6. See also J. M. R. Margeson, *The Origins of English Tragedy*, p. 136; G. Boklund has demonstrated how Webster uses repeated ironic reversals for an entirely different purpose—namely, to demonstrate that it is 'chance, independent of good and evil' which governs events in *The Duchess of Malfi* (The *Duchess of Malfi: Sources, Themes, Characters*, pp. 129–30). Webster's *The Devil's Law-Case* offers an overt parody of peripeteias and providentialist intervention not dissimilar to that found in *The Revenger's Tragedy* (see especially III. ii. 147–58).

7. From R. J. Hollingdale's selection, *Essays and Aphorisms*, pp. 51–4; for a complete edition of *Parerga and Paralipomena*, see E. F. J. Payne's two-volume translation.

8. See *The Works of Cyril Tourneur*, ed. A. Nicoll, pp. 16–18.

9. *Ibid.*, p. 275.

10. Compare Hobbes: 'I put for a general inclination of all mankind, a perpetual and restless desire of power after power, that ceaseth only in death' (*Leviathan*, chapter 11).

11. Compare Shakespeare's *Timon*: 'thou wouldst have plunged thyself/In general riot, *melted* down thy youth/In different beds of lust' (IV. iii. 256–8), and Spenser's Redcrosse, with 'The false Duessa', 'Pourd out in loosnesse on the grassy grownd,/Both carelesse of his health, and of his fame' (*The Faerie Queene*, 1. 7. 7).

12. Compare Montaigne: 'Men misacknowledge the naturall infirmitie of their minde. She doth but quest and firret, and vncessantly goeth turning, winding, building and entangling her selfe in hir own worke; as doe our silke-wormes, and therein stiffleth hir self' (*Essays*, III. 325). This image was a popular one, and the Montaigne passage was twice borrowed by Webster (see J. W. Dent, *John Webster's Borrowings*, p. 85).

JONATHAN DOLLIMORE

Bussy D'Ambois (c. 1604):
A Hero at Court

Bussy D'Ambois (c. 1604) occupies an interesting position in the radical drama of the period. Like the earlier plays it interrogates providence and decentres the tragic subject but now the emphasis is shifted; before, the emphasis had tended to fall on the first of these projects, now and henceforth the reverse tends to be the case.

SHADOWS AND SUBSTANCE

The very first line of *Bussy* repudiates stoic providence in a way even more direct than that found in the Antonio plays and *Troilus and Cressida*: 'Fortune, not Reason, rules the state of things'. Bussy is preoccupied with the instability of this 'state' (ie. the body politic): 'Reward goes backwards, Honour on his head;/Who is not poor, is monstrous' (I. i. 2–3). He repudiates politicians ('statists', 1. 10) who, with their 'Authority, wealth, and all the spawn of Fortune' are deluded into thinking they are everything whereas in fact—and in Time—they are nothing: 'Man is a torch borne in the wind; a dream/But of a shadow, summ'd with all his substance' (ll. 18–19). That word 'substance' had a fascinating range of meanings in this period not dissimilar from those it retains today. But it possessed an ambiguity more telling then than now: it could mean 'essential nature'—especially when, as here, it was contrasted with 'shadow' (cf. 'He takes false shadows for true substances', *Titus Andronicus*', III. ii. 80); alternatively, it could mean virtually the opposite—that is, not what man intrinsically is, but what he

---

From *Radical Tragedy*. © 1984, 1989 by the author.

acquires: 'Authority, wealth and all the spawn of Fortune' (1. 13). There is not here the Christian belief that the ways of the world tempt man from the ways of the spirit; on the contrary, man is seen to construct an identity from shadows because they are in some sense prior. What Montsurry says of princes—that 'form gives all their essence' (II. ii. 123)—is the view of man presented in this play: his essential nature goes missing as does the universe's teleological design; reluctantly yet determinedly Chapman concentrates on the social realities disclosed by their absence.

Given its political dimension, the play's opening stage direction—*Enter* Bussy D'Ambois, *poor*—is hardly less significant than its first line. Bussy's poverty runs quite contrary to the circumstances of his historical source. It is an innovation of Chapman's and serves as the pre-condition for Bussy's understanding of human identity and of the state. Exclusion and poverty give him—or rather force upon him—a true view of things yet one which is anything but disinterested; that is, they offer to Bussy a vantage point from which he experiences the relative worthlessness of the social order and, simultaneously, his dependence upon it. Monsieur politically exploits such dependence and his view of the exploited is simple: 'None loathes the world so much .../But gold and grace will make him surfeit of it' (I. i. 52–3). Tamyra later speaks of 'great statesmen' who 'for their general end/In politic justice make poor men offend' (III. i. 44–5); Monsieur is one such but with the important distinction that justice is not his objective. Bussy accepts Monsieur's offer of preferment but rationalises his choice: 'I am for honest actions, not for great'. He will, he tells himself, 'rise in Court with virtue' (I. i. 124 and 126). It is this rationalised—and compromised— position which characterises Bussy from here on.

Monsieur sends to Bussy, via Maffe, one thousand crowns. Maffe is the state servant who is eminently employable as an instrument of power because shrewd yet gullible: shrewd enough to play the game, gullible enough to internalise its rules. He has been instructed to give Bussy the money but has not been told why. Seeing the impoverished Bussy he asks: 'Is this man indu'd/With any merit worth a thousand crowns?' (I. i. 140–1). By 'merit' he means usefulness—specifically, the capacity to serve his master, Monsieur. Maffe thus invokes a criterion of human worth which is, as it were, second nature to those bound up in the struggle to maintain or achieve power. It is a criterion which Hobbes later makes the corner stone of his theory of the state: 'The *value*, or WORTH of a man, is as of all other things, his price; that is to say, so much as would be given for the use of his power: and therefore is not absolute; but a thing dependent on the need and judgement of another' (*Leviathan*, chapter 10). Maffe aspires to understand 'policy' (1. 202) but as he himself admits (ll. 199–200), he does not have the ears of great men, nor does he understand such men. His view of the court is both determined and ideologically distorted by his position within it—a position which, for example, leads him erroneously to assume a conventional range of potential roles for Bussy—the poet-pamphleteer, a soldier or joker. Bussy is angered by this and turns Maffe's criterion of merit back upon Maffe; referring to those parts of the latter's dress which signify his stewardship, he demands: 'What qualities have you sir (beside your chain/And velvet jacket)?' (I. i. 191–2). Thus Bussy taunts Maffe with being nothing apart from his position as state servant. Such is his own impending position, and such too is the recurring emphasis of this play: identity is shown to be constituted not essentially but socially.

Bussy arrives at court dressed in a new suit. His entry follows immediately after Henry and Montsurry have been criticising the vanity of dress. In the previous scene Bussy showed himself especially anxious not to have to appear at court 'in a threadbare suit' (I. i. 106). This anxiety is another aspect of the same awareness which prompted his interrogation of Maffe. In this society man's identity, like his worth, is, in the words of Hobbes, 'a thing dependent on the need and judgement of another'; more exactly, this identity exists in terms of the role ascribed to the individual by others or, alternatively, a role which he proposes for their ratification. It is precisely the courtiers' refusal to ratify Bussy's new role which leads to the quarrel in which five die. Bussy, manifestly insecure, is over-assertive. This prompts L'Anou to observe: 'See what a metamorphosis a brave suit can work' (I. ii. 118). But Barrisor's taunt is the more vicious for being even closer to the truth: 'This jealousy of yours sir, confesses some close defect in yourself, that we never dreamed of' (I. ii. 185–6). Unerringly he provokes in Bussy insecurity born of dependence. They vow to fight and so the first act concludes.

COURT POWER AND NATIVE NOBLESSE

Monsieur and the King eulogise Bussy, or rather they construct for him a conception of himself as innately noble, self-determining and uncompromised. To the extent that he 'lives' this identity he becomes not in fact autonomous but the more exploitable. Monsieur is especially accomplished in achieving this. His initial description of Bussy as incomparably heroic (I. ii. 140–6) is not a spontaneous recognition of him as such but the testing out of a predetermined role for him. Monsieur's hyperbole picks up on something more general: even as a life and death struggle is developing between Bussy and Guise, a self-consciously theatrical court is construing it as performance; for the king the quarrel is a kind of entertainment (1.147) while L'Anou (later to die in the fight) describes it as 'one of the best jigs that ever was acted' (I. ii. 152). By the close of this scene Bussy has taken on the part devised for him by Monsieur. Later, after Bussy has deserted him, Monsieur gives a very different assessment of his former protégé, one which speaks very much to the conditions in which he found him. Lacking a rational soul, he is, says Monsieur, not 'diffused quite through' with that which would make him all 'of a piece'. As such he is unpredictable and erratic; he is, in effect, the decentred, soulless subject who 'wouldst envy, betray,/Slander, blaspheme, change each hour a religion,/*Do anything* ...' (III. ii. 349–56, my italics).

Bussy, once raised by Monsieur (the king's brother) is taken up by the one person even more powerful: the king. To the latter Bussy becomes protector and play-thing ('my brave Eagle', IV. i. 108). The king's similarly hyperbolic praise of Bussy is especially revealing at the point where he indulges in role reversal; Bussy is, he says—

> Man in his native noblesse, from whose fall
> All our dissensions rise; that in himself
> (Without the outward patches of our frailty,
> Riches and honour) knows he comprehends
> Worth with the greatest: Kings had never borne
> Such boundless eminence over other men,
> Had all maintain'd the spirit and state of D'Ambois.
>
> (III. ii. 91–7)

Subscribing to the myth of transcendent virtue in another permits the ruler to mystify the true extent of his own material power. This comes across quite clearly in the scene where Bussy is pardoned by the king. He declines the pardon, insisting that he has committed no offence when events are considered in the light of his essentialist autonomy: 'Who to himself is law, no law doth need' (II. i. 203). The king replies: 'Enjoy what thou entreat'st, we give but ours', which might be glossed: enjoy your illusion of autonomy only in so far as it does not transgress my authority. Indeed, thus encouraged and controlled, Bussy's mythical autonomy will actually enhance that authority. One indication of the extent to which Bussy's *virtus* is shown to be not innate but the effect—and thus the vehicle—of court power is the way he takes on the hyperbolic terms in which Monsieur had set it up:

> What insensate stock
> Or rude inanimate vapour without fashion,
> Durst take into his Epimethean breast
> A box of such plagues as the danger yields,
> Incurr'd in this discovery?
>
> (IV.ii. 9–13)

Even more conclusive (and in the same scene) is the moment when the hyperbole, and indeed *virtus* itself, is shown to dissolve into the policy of which it was only ever the effect; plotting against Monsieur, Bussy declares: 'I'll soothe his plots: and strew my hate with smiles ... And policy shall be flank'd with policy' (ll. 155, 161).

The play does not merely show noblesse defeated by policy. Were this in fact the case it might be legitimately defined as humanistic tragedy in the sense already outlined in chapter 2: that is, a tragedy of defeated potential in which the defeat only confirms the potential. Rather, the play shows the putative noblesse to be the effect of policy and thus, by noblesse's own essentialist criteria, to suffer erasure.

Bussy dies in a scene which begins with one of the most direct repudiations of teleology, providence and natural law to be found anywhere in Jacobean tragedy:

> Nature hath no end
> In her great works, responsive to their worths,
> That she who makes so many eyes, and souls,
> To see and foresee, is stark blind herself:
>
> So nature lays
> A mass of stuff together, and by use,
> Or by the mere necessity of matter,
> Ends such a work, fills it, or leaves it empty
> Of strength, or virtue, error or clear truth.
>
> (V. iii. 1–4; 12–16)

Even the play's supernatural dimension works against providence. In fact Act IV, scene ii works as a burlesque of the supernatural similar to that which we have already seen in *The Revenger's Tragedy* (above, pp. 139–43; Chapman's is of course the earlier play). Behemoth and his spirits are shown to be incompetent (1. 60) and at cross purposes (ll. 73–5); finally they exit ('descend') in disarray advising that Bussy have recourse to 'policy' (1. 138). In fact they seem themselves to be instruments of policy: they are controlled by 'Fate' while 'Fate's ministers' are said to be 'The Guise and Monsieur' (V. ii. 61–2; cf. the association of 'Destiny' with 'Great statesmen' at III. i. 43–4). Thus the significance of the supernatural comes back, via a kind of closed circuit, to the secular.

Just as Monsieur rejects the notion that nature is encoded with a teleological design, so Bussy dies repudiating the existence of the soul (once again the disintegration of providentialism is accompanied by this decentring of the tragic subject):

> is my body then
> But penetrable flesh? And must my mind
> Follow my blood? Can my divine part add
> No aid to th' earthly in extremity?
> Then these divines are but for form, not fact.
>
> (V. iii. 125–9)

Echoing lines from his opening speech he adds:

> let my death
> Define life nothing but a Courtier's breath.
> Nothing is made of nought, of all things made;
> Their abstract being a dream but of a shade.

(V. iii. 131–4)

The sense of those last two lines is as follows: 'all things are created from and return to nothing. Therefore the idea of substantial essence is an illusion'.[1]

NOTE

1. For a diametrically opposed reading of *Bussy* and one firmly within the perspective of essentialist humanism, see Richard S. Ide's *Possessed With Greatness* (1980): 'Bussy does not renounce his heroic conception of self at death. Rather he transcends it by progressing to a higher, more admirable mode of heroism ... "outward Fortitude" is not rejected, but ... improved upon by an inner fortitude equally extraordinary, equally heroic, and in this situation morally superior' (p.99).

GAIL KERN PASTER

Parasites and Sub-parasites:
The City as Predator
in Jonson and Middleton

Our *Scene* is *London*, 'cause we would make knowne,
No countries mirth is better then our owne,
No clime breeds better matter, for your whore,
Bawd, squire, impostor, many persons more,
Whose manners, now call'd humors, feed the stage.
[*The Alchemist*, prologue 5–9]

In Jonson's wry joke about the excellent badness of London, the self-congratulation of masque and pageant reappears in a new, ironic light. London becomes an ideal commonwealth only for satirists feeding the stage. The abundance and prosperity attributed in the entertainments to exemplary government has here bred better matter for whores and rogues; the social behavior held up for civic emulation has now become the source of comic spleen. Jonson's mocking boast about London as exemplary comic subject represents the other side of the coin: instead of a society "joyfully contemplating its well-being," we have a society ironically contemplating its viciousness.[1] Ideal reciprocity has given way to obsessive striving for place.

Of the many playwrights who contributed to the rapid emergence of city comedy early in the seventeenth century, Jonson and Middleton, heavily involved with the city comedies and with court or civic entertainments, represent most clearly the polarized attitudes toward the city which is my continuing focus. Middleton's career as a pageant writer begins in earnest in 1613, the same year his finest city comedy, *A Chaste Maid in Cheapside*, appeared at the Swan.[2] At the

From *The Idea of the City in the Age of Shakespeare*. © 1985 by the University of Georgia Press.

same time that Jonson was undertaking commissions to portray the court as classical or Arthurian heroes, the usurer had become the type of contemporary villain because he symbolized "forces of aggression, ruthless materialism, aspiration and anarchy in Jacobean society."[3] Part of the discrepancy between the city as it appears in the playwrights' entertainments and the city as it appears in their plays may be attributed to the usual differences between a city as it ought to be and a city as it is. The problem with this inference is that it requires not only a simplistic dismissal of the idealization in the entertainments but a simplistic acceptance of the satire in the comedies as well. In fact, exaggeration in both directions links the genres, laus lining up quite specifically against *vituperatio* for antithetical literary treatment. Thus the festival celebration of the present moment is echoed negatively in the insistence of the comedies that times have never been worse. "Every part of the world shoots up daily into more subtlety," laments the courtesan's mother in Middleton's *A Mad World, My Masters* (1.1.140). She would prefer less competition. In *The Devil Is An Ass*, Satan mocks Pug for underestimating London vice: "We must therefore ayme / At extraordinary subtill ones, now" (1.1.115–16). If the entertainments require dressing up topography and people in heroic or allegorical trappings, the city comedies require the reverse—a symbolic dressing down, an apparent removal of artifice. In the Induction to *Michaelmas Term*, personifications of the four London law-terms enter dressed in "civil black"—the color belonging both to the gowns of city officials and to the devil. Serious moral intent and artful selection are quickly denied, however, in Michaelmas Term's offhand comment: "He that expects any great quarrels in law to be handled here will be fondly deceived; this only presents those familiar accidents which happen'd in town in the circumference of those six weeks where of Michaelmas Term is lord" (Induction, 69–73).[4]

A similar disclaimer against artifice is presented more elaborately in the induction to *Bartholomew Fair*. As part of his contract with the spectators, Jonson asks his audience to expect no better than a fair will afford; what is probable in a fair is absolutely essential in a play about a fair by an author "loth to make Nature afraid in his *Playes*" (129). Jonson also insists on the social realism of *The Alchemist* by setting the play "here, in the friers" (1.1.17), which is a reference to the place of the play and to the place of the playhouse as well.[5] Such insistence on creative self-limitation, on treating only what the "familiar accidents" of the city have provided, functions like the symbolic decoration of the entertainments. Both assert that the city, rather than the playwright, is ultimately responsible for its praise or blame.

This assertion is essential to urban portraiture in the city comedies precisely because that portrait is so negative. If the masques present a benign world where natural law has been brought under human control, the comedies offer a polar image of urban society in the sway of natural law as predatory appetite. In such a city, the idea of community means that each character defines place only in terms of his self-interest. The members of this community have ties not to each other, but only a direct tie of self-interest and survival to the city itself. The participation and unity so central to masque and pageant turn out here to be the main-springs of intrigue. Civic order in such a city is as fixed and as self-perpetuating as the order of masque and pageant. Instead of the benevolent circle of reciprocities, however, the satiric city regulates the lives of its citizens through a ruthless and competitive predatory cycle that gives every rogue his gull, dooms every guller to be gulled himself, values intellectual cunning over moral integrity, and rewards no one.[6] Patterns of predatory behavior underlie the action of all these comedies in varying degrees and turn the comic convention of "the biter bit" into a summary judgment of urban society. The predatory order comes to take on the universal validity of natural law.

Jonson and Middleton make the impersonal operations of the predatory cycle believable by creating an urban atmosphere in which aggressive individualism has become an accepted behavioral norm and reductive conceptions about human nature hold sway. Such an atmosphere becomes an implicit counterstatement to the pageants' praise of mercantile adventurism as the source of so much civic benefit. Community in the city comedies does have a common world-view, like the communities of masque and pageant. This community, however, because it is degenerate, simply accepts ruthless self-interest as governing human behavior. It assumes what in fact usually turns out to be true—that each man is like his neighbor in being his neighbor's enemy.

A good index to the moral temper of these comedies is their general depiction of women, because the idealization of women which we found to be so conventional in praises of cities is here turned around. London is a reverend mother in the entertainments; the mothers in city comedy may well be bawds. Female sensuality, a given in most city comedy, is particularly common in Middleton. The unmarried woman is often a courtesan, the virtuous virgin is almost an anomaly. But the most common female type is the wife whose leisure feeds sensuality and makes time for adultery. Examples abound, from Fallace in *Every Man Out*, to Mrs. Harebrain in *A Mad World, My Masters*. Female sensuality is most often expressed as cliché in city comedy, the inevitable complement to the endless cuckoldry jokes. Andrew Lethe, for instance, assumes that Thomasine Quomodo's objections to him as prospective son-in-law concern her designs to have him "as a private friend to her own pleasures" (*Michaelmas Term*, 1.1.201–11). But she is outraged at the suggestion because "'tis for his betters to have opportunity of me" (2.3.7–8). The gallants Rearage and Salewood make casual conversation comparing a "little venturing cousin" to a "virgin of five bastards wedded" (1.1.9,15). *A Chaste Maid in Cheapside* is supposed to sound oxymoronic, like Dekker's *Honest Whore*.[7] In *Bartholomew Fair*, Mrs. Littlewit accepts Knockem's argument that "it is the vapour of spirit in the wife, to cuckold, now adaies; as it is the vapour of fashion, in the husband, not to suspect" (4.5.50–51). The sensuality of city wives is such, according to Ramping Alice, the punk of Turnbull, that "the poore common whores can ha' no traffique, for the privy rich ones" (4.5.69–70). Touchwood Senior keeps a stable of gullible young men around to marry the wenches he has ruined, and Middleton often makes the trick of his plots the marriage of an unknowing man to a whore.

The significance of female sensuality for the city is that sexual stereotypes finally become expressive of pervasive cynicism. Middleton's citizens assume gallants to be lecherous—and are usually right. If merchants like Quomodo seem not to be particularly interested in sex, it is because they have traded sexual prowess for financial gain and value women at a lesser rate than "that which she often treads on, yet commands her: / Land, fair neat land" (*Michaelmas Term*, 1.1.100–101).[8]

The corollary to treating people like property is to treat property like people. In *A Trick to Catch the Old One*, Witgood apostrophizes to his newly recovered mortgage in the diction of a lover: "Thou soul of my estate I kiss thee, / I miss life's comfort when I miss thee" (4.2.87–88). Old Hoard waxes as rhapsodic about the lands he thinks his rich widow owns: "When I wake, I think of her lands—that revives me" (4.4.6–7). Perhaps it is this habit of humanizing property while dehumanizing people which makes credible the casualness G. J. Watson has noticed in *A Trick to Catch the Old One* with which characters accept vicious sharking as the way of the world.[9] After Lucre and Hoard quarrel over the right to cozen a young heir, Lucre appeals to the way of the world in his defense: "I got the purchase, true: was't not any man's case? Yes. Will a wise man stand as a bawd whilst another wipes his nose of the bargain? No, I answer no in that case" (1.3.11–14). Dick Follywit, the most sympathetic character in *A Mad World, My Masters*, lightheartedly describes the downfall of his own higher nature: "I was wont yet to pity the simple, and leave 'em some money; 'slid, now I gull 'em without conscience" (1.1.19–21).

This acceptance of human baseness as predictable and thus natural is reinforced by the evident physicality of human nature: the community becomes merely a collection of appetites. This low assessment of human nature is particularly apparent, perhaps, in *A Chaste Maid in Cheapside*. Middleton fixes the mental focus of all Cheapside well below the navel: his characters are preternaturally alert to obscene innuendo, which they find everywhere. Characterization in the play is almost exclusively a matter of sexual capacity and proclivity, which serves to lower our mental focus as well in what R. B. Parker has called the mood of a soiled saturnalia.[10] Jonson's depiction of the human animal tends to be less exclusively sexual than Middleton's, but it is not more exalted. Pig-woman Ursula, the life-force of *Bartholomew Fair*, "is all fire, and fat, ... I doe water the ground in knots, as I goe" (2.2.50–52). The urge to relieve themselves brings Mrs. Overdo and Win Littlewit to Ursula's booth, where Knockem persuades them to become "birds o'the game." Jonas Barish has noted the frustration of physical function in *Epicoene* epitomized by LaFoole's captivity with a full bladder in a locked closet.[11]

Even apart from scatology, Jonson customarily associates his characters with unattractive physical images that almost turn the urban landscape into an Elizabethan junkyard. In *Bartholomew Fair*, there is Joan Trash's gingerbread, "stale bread, rotten egges, musty ginger, and dead honey" (2.2.9–10), or Bartholomew Cokes's brain, "hung with cockelshels, pebbles, fine wheat-strawes, and here and there a chicken's feather" (1.5.95–97). All this is as nothing compared to *The Alchemist* with its whelps, black and melancholic worms, powdercorns, dunghills, moldy slippers, rats, stills, glasses, spiders, brooms, and dust.[12] Perhaps the urban landscape is less finely enumerated in *Volpone* not only because it is set in Venice, but also because humanity there has already turned animal. For both writers, however, the point of emphasizing physiological function and of creating such a dense material substratum is to belie any claim that urban man controls either himself or his environment. The city is not the home of the life of reason, as it was for the ancients; nor is it proof of man's spiritual aspirations and capacities, as it was for the Italian humanists. The unattractive solidity of the city and the animal-like behavior of its people fix human nature in the city firmly in the bottom half of the chain of being.

The predominance of predation in city comedy makes the nature of human association not only ruthless but interdependent and involuntary as well. The material resources of these cities are so limited that the rogue is completely dependent on rich conies or foolish benefactors; they are his food. And he must always conduct his affairs under the threat of ferocious competition. Middleton's Quomodo, who habitually rationalizes his activities as the normative response to class conflict, seems thoroughly imbued with the competitive spirit, praising the man who "never walks but thinks, / Ne rides but plots" (*Michaelmas Term*, 1.1.96–97). Competition makes class solidarity a mere illusion. Quomodo's man Shortyard has no compunction about cheating Quomodo's foolish son Sim, and the gallants Rearage and Cockstone wait cynically for the naive newcomer Easy to get the "city powd'ring" (1.1.56). In *Bartholomew Fair*, although Leatherhead calls Joan Trash sister, he quarrels fiercely over territory: "hinder not the prospect of my shop," he tells the gingerbread seller, "or I'll ha'it proclaim'd i'the *Fayre*, what stuffe they are made on" (2.2.4–6). The economic scramble not only divides members of a class, but also members of a family as well.[13] Theodorus Witgood in *A Trick to Catch the Old One* wants to recoup what his uncle has taken from him, just as Dauphine Eugenie wants to make sure of Morose's legacy. Dick Follywit explains what has turned him to cony-catching in general and to grandfather-catching in particular: "I shall have all when he has nothing; but now he has all, I shall have nothing" (*A Mad World, My Masters*, 1.1.41–42). Family ties are so attenuated by the competitive struggle that Middleton's young men sound just like Plautus's wishing for the deaths of their elders. Fitsgrave asks the young gallants of *Your Five Gallants*, "Are your fathers dead, gentlemen, you're so merry?" (4.8.288–89).[14] Follywit explains filial coldness as a natural response to paternal closefistedness: "they cannot abide to see us merry all the while they're above ground, and that makes so many laugh at their fathers' funerals" (1.1.45–47). And his attitude is confirmed by Lucre's denial of the nephew by whom he has profited: "If he riot, 'tis he must want it; if he surfeit, 'tis he must feel it; if he drab it, 'tis he must lie by't; what's this to me?" (*A Trick to Catch the Old One*, 1.3.30–32).

Ironically, the consequence of denying familial or communal bonds is to reassert them in the parodic form of inverted community. Involuntary fellowship becomes the order of the day, as when Pursenet complains that "a man cannot have a quean to himself! let him but turn his back, the best of her is chipt away like a court loaf" (*Your Five Gallants*, 3.2.97–98). However, he achieves self-command by realizing the impossibility of keeping anything to oneself in the city. Sharing finally represents a cyclical order by which all live:

> Does my boy pick and I steal to enrich myself, to keep her, to maintain him? why, this is right the sequence of the world. A lord maintains her, she maintains a knight, he maintains a whore, she maintains a captain. So in like manner the pocket keeps my boy, he keeps me, I keep her, she keeps him; it runs like quicksilver from one to another. [3.2.100–07]

The age-old hierarchies remain, but reciprocity here ironically opposes the bountiful order of masque and pageant. The emblem of cyclical order in the play is a chain of pearl which travels around the circle of gallants by gift and theft. The crucial recognition occurs when, tracing the ownership of the jewels, the gallants learn they are all parasites and thus form a community of interests. "'Sfoot," declares Goldstone, "I perceive we are all natural brothers" (4.7.213).

In most of the plays, this recognition of ironic fellowship is less conscious. But because such sharing is always involuntary, it seems to result inevitably from the discrepancy between the limited resources of the city and the limitless appetites of its citizens. Over and over action reinforces the fact of limit. In all *Bartholomew Fair*, there is apparently one chamber pot, while Ursula's fear that she and Knockem will be "undone for want of fowle" (4.5.14) persuades Knockem to turn to Mrs. Overdo and Win Littlewit. Jonson's alchemical rogues pretend to transform men and matter, but all they really do is broker money and goods. A similar illusion about the meaning of gold deceives *Volpone*, Mosca, and the suitors, for *Volpone* elevates gold into a symbol of aspiration beyond the fact of limit or, more importantly, need of community, surpassing "all sublunary joys in children, parents, friends" (1.1.17). *Volpone* declares himself outside the common exchange of gold for labor, since he lives by "no trade, no venter" (1.1.33). For their part, the suitors regard him as the city merchants regarded the fabled Indies—as an investment repaying tenfold the worth of ventured goods. But the predatory cycle of city comedy is at its barest in *Volpone*, where the sequence of visits probably represents the order in which birds descend on carrion.[15] Abundance in Venice is so illusory that even souls seem to be in short supply. Androgyno admits having shared his with Pythagoras, Crates the Cynic, and Euphorbus killed at Troy. In such a world, *Volpone* at best could only get what his clients give and ends up getting exactly what they do—nothing.

Reciprocity, it would appear, governs the predatory city no less than the ideal commonwealth of masque and pageant. The urban communities here live not off land, but off each other. As Edward Partridge comments about *Volpone*, "the final food is man."[16] This recognition propels Mosca's self-delighted soliloquy, when he understands that he epitomizes the rest of the world; what everyone else does by nature and without knowing, he knows and does best of all: "almost / All the wise world is little else, in nature, / But Parasites or Sub-parasites" (3.1.11–13). The sub-parasites in *A Trick to Catch the Old One* are Hoard's two friends Lamprey and Spitchcock, voracious eel-like fish. In *Michaelmas Term*, Dick Hellgill describes the town gallants as "gilded flies" upon the flesh of the Country Wench (1.2.48). Characters' amusement at the follies of their neighbors becomes the appetite of the intellect, predation sublimated.

The only resource of the city is its people, actors in the urban comedy. The purchase of any other resource is as illusory as Volpone's gold or the alchemical promise. Unfortunately, like other city dwellers, these comic citizens had regarded their mother city as truly bountiful, if only for them. Thus Michaelmas Term sees his law term as a version of the natural cycle, this "autumnian blessing" of a "silver harvest" (1.1.6,10). When he wonders if gulls come up "thick enough," he is told, "like hops and harlots, sir" (14–15). The outcome of all the city comedies, however, reinforces the fact of limit by closing the circle of reciprocity—the biter, no matter how clever or sympathetic he may be, is always bit. The ironic severity of urban limit makes Follywit's bride his grandfather's whore or Hoard's wife Witgood's whore; it explains why Lovewit will return to town to end the venture tripartite and why Overdo will find no enormities at the fair; or it makes Morose's hopes for a silent woman absurd. Comic convention operates as natural law, the ruthless circularity of the urban game.

This figure of the circle, although it may symbolize perfection as in masque or pageant, can also symbolize empty, meaningless movement.[17] The circularity of action in urban comedies, seen as a function of the predatory cycle, ironically produces the illusion of bewildering change without effecting any real change at all.[18] Characters come up to the city in the hope of self-transformation, a hope that also motivates such natives as Dapper and Drugger in *The Alchemist*. One of the first apparent changes the city works on the newcomer is to separate him from his roots, resulting in loss of identity for Lethe and the Country Wench in *Michaelmas Term*. Loss of identity in Lethe is loss of memory, since he cannot remember his acquaintance of the night before. Both he and the Country Wench are unrecognizable to their parents, and the Country Wench confesses, "I scare know myself" (3.1.30–31).[19] For such characters, new clothes are the most obvious symptom of illusory change. Clothes have the power to prevent parents from recognizing children, as in *Michaelmas Term*, or to swallow up land, as when Carlo tells Sordido to become a gentleman by turning "foure or five hundred acres of your best land into two or three trunks of apparel" (*Every Man Out*, 1.2.41–42). For the pander Dick Hellgill, clothes have more substantiality than people: "What base birth does not raiment make glorious? And what glorious births do not rags make infamous? Why should not a woman confess what she is now, since the finest are but deluding shadows, begot between tirewomen and tailors?" (*Michaelmas Term*, 3.1.1–5).

The dramatists want us to recognize that the change effected by costume is only outward, and thus illusory. So also, however, are the transformations effected or merely promised by the transfer of lands, goods, or gold, primarily because possession in such predatory cities is only temporary. Although the predatory cycle guarantees change as instability, it precludes change as gradual amelioration for the individual or society. Predation also precludes the historical process always associated with cities: there can be no change in the closed circle of the predatory system, merely recycling. Though each of the city intriguers thinks himself capable of effecting change for himself by standing at the end of the predatory chain to receive all the spoils, he proves to be a member of the commonwealth offering as nourishment to the next man what he had taken from the last. There are bitter moments when, at the height of success, the schemer may realize the circularity of urban activity and the purposelessness of his behavior. Quomodo, although imagining himself immune, anticipates that his son will be gulled: "our posterity commonly foil'd at the same weapon at which we play'd rarely" (4.1.84–85). Instead of releasing Quomodo from the predatory cycle, however, this recognition only affixes him more closely to it by prompting his catastrophic decision to counterfeit death. The decision allows Shortyard to gull Sim Quomodo and returns Quomodo's newly acquired lands to their rightful owner, Easy. For urban game-players, there is no way out or up. The city exacts a brutal justice in the self-perpetuating order of the predatory cycle. *Volpone*'s gold ends up bequeathed to the city's incurables, a condition bitterly descriptive of nearly the whole city. In such comedies, the city awards itself the only victories.

One reason that predation is so frightening an image for civic life in city comedy is that there is really no other place to go. "Alas, poor birds," laments Shortyard's boy about the incoming countryfolk, "that cannot keep the sweet country, where they fly at pleasure, but must needs come to the city to have their wings clip'd" (3.2.19–21). Masque and pageant make a similar assumption about their own centrality, as we have seen. In the comedies, however, the centrality of the city is less an attribution of supreme value than a recognition of the limited capacity and unlimited appetite of social man. Rome is central in Juvenal's satires, we recall, because he cannot finally escape its magnetic pull, caught as he is between hatred and fascination. Both Jonson and Middleton find an analogous inevitability in urban settings: no one escapes being drawn into the predatory chain of events.

Much of this suggested centrality in Jonson's comic city results from his skill at deploying the classical unity of place, particularly in the four great comedies from *Volpone* to *Bartholomew Fair*. Each setting in those plays has a magnetic attraction of its own, which functions as an intensification of the attraction which the city as a whole seems to have for country. It is a crucial part of the opening business of each play to demonstrate the attraction of the setting (as in *Volpone* and *The Alchemist*) or to orchestrate a movement into it (as in *Epicoene* and *Bartholomew Fair*).

Each setting, furthermore, becomes progressively more inclusive and seemingly more compelling than its predecessor. The bedchamber that draws predatory birds in *Volpone* is succeeded by Morose's house in *Epicoene*, invaded by a college of ladies and their followers. The alchemical rogues would like to draw into their house in the Friars whoever has not left the plague-ridden city.[20] But the Smithfield fairground does attract everyone, and Jonson strains the limits of coherent dramatic plotting to prove it.[21] More important, Jonson gives his settings a civic dimension, making them expressive not only of the characters but also of an idea of the city as well.

Volpone for instance is structured neatly around a contrast between private and public space. More precisely, the contrast between Volpone's house and the Venetian courtroom is mediated by the neutral, communal space of the piazza, where Volpone is free to erect his mountebank's platform. Each of these settings becomes a theater within the theater, containing scenes from different dramatic, or quasidramatic, genres—the deathbed scene, the seduction scene, the mountebank's spiel, the judgment scenes. For Volpone, other places are secondary to the prime space of his bedchamber, which is as essential to his security as London, *camera regis*, was to the king's. His claim to physical centrality is supported by the behavior of the suitors, who identify their deepest selfinterest with the outcome of events in the Magnifico's chamber. Private space stimulates private interest and the reverse; anyone who acts in Volpone's bedchamber has entered a competition that opposes his own interests to the community's. Jonson even suggests that Volpone's bedchamber is itself a kind of city. Alberti argued that a "city, according to the Opinion of Philosophers, be no more than a great House, and ... a House be a little City" (*De re aed.*, bk. 1, chap. 9, p.13). The members of Volpone's household—Nano, Androgyno, Castrone—represent a spectrum of deficiencies, a parody of urban variety. They also provide this city's version of civilization, offering parodies of history and culture in their little entertainment. And, as Alvin Kernan has pointed out, Volpone's initial act of worshipping his gold attempts to redefine Renaissance cosmology and religious belief.[22] Volpone's house, moreover, redefines the nature of human bonding. By persuading Corbaccio to disinherit his son and Corvino to prostitute his wife, Volpone attempts to destroy the two bonds in which a city has most at stake. He would reduce all bonds, social and familial, to the single, material bond implied in a legacy.

Volpone's claim of physical centrality is thus also a claim of supreme civic authority which goes essentially undisputed until act 5. Our awareness of Mosca's greater power in the role of hypocritical servant helps to prepare for Corvino's flogging of Volpone in the piazza and, more importantly, for Volpone's defeat in the courtroom. Until the final judgement scene, Volpone suffers only partial and temporary setbacks, yet he does so because he has ventured outside his secure chamber. Even Volpone's performance on the mountebank's stage, usually regarded as an expression of the genuine, dangerous individuality of the Renaissance actor, brings Volpone an unaccustomed vulnerability.[23] So does his involuntary introduction to the courtroom in act 4, as he says:

> I ne're was in dislike with my disguise
> Till this fled moment; here, 'twas good, in private,
> But in your publike, *Cave*, whil'st I breathe.
>
> [5.1.2–04]

In one sense, then, the courtroom of the Scrutineo demonstrates the triumph of public over private, the triumph of the city over the dangerously outsize house within it. Yet this earthly city is no ideal, for there is a large discrepancy between the operations of ideal justice and the accidental justice that reveals these rogues. Venice has institutions that are supposed to govern civic life. But the ideal operation of those institutions requires a moral integrity which is lacking in the corrupt and greedy Venetian justices and which is ineffectual in Celia and Bonario. The moral denouement here results from a falling-out among the rogues, which Jonson presents as inevitable: "Mischiefes feed / Like beasts, till they be fat, and then they bleed" (5.12.150–51). Only the self-limiting nature of the urban law of universal appetite saves Venice from the two rogues whose vitality, wit, and greed epitomize its worse and its best self. The Scrutino merely pronounces judgment on an intrigue that has already run its course.

In *Epicoene*, Morose's house provides a setting comparable to *Volpone's* bedchamber. Once Jonson has defined the relationships among the members of the other households in the play, the crucial action is to move the city to Morose since he will not go to it. Like nature, the city abhors a vacuum. It seeks to open up and fill urban space that Morose would keep completely private, filled only with the sound of his voice. Descriptions of Morose's house suggest that, like Volpone, he is trying to create a theater within the theater, a city within a city. He claims that he does not "neglect those things, that make for the dignitie of the commonwealth" (5.3.56–57), but his actions contradict all that commonwealth customarily means. He is a city planner in reverse; instead of valuing easy movement among parts of the city, "hee hath chosen a street to lie in, so narrow at both ends, that it will receive no coaches, nor carts, nor any of these common noises" (1.1.167–69). He is also a master of fortifications, rather like the cook in *Neptune's Triumph*, double-walling his rooms and caulking his windows. But for Jonson as for the Romans a city of one is a contradiction. Morose is even more solipsistic than Catiline or Tiberius, Jonson's other spectacular city destroyers. He is a spider, spinning from his innards the web of words that is his home. And like the spider, he becomes a version of the bad artist—the bad architect as well as the bad poet—thinking wrongly with a later, Miltonic version of the bad architect and poet that the mind can be its own place. The city begins for Morose as it began for presocial man when he discovers that he does not suffice for his own needs—the need being Morose's desire to disinherit Dauphine. Once Morose has committed himself to marriage, the building block of a community, he cannot prevent as much community as exists here from moving in to share his space, merging the city outside with the city inside. Jonson does not present community victory over this antisocial individual as an unambiguously happy event. The community takes too much pleasure in the torment of its major victim, dehumanizing him as he attempted to dehumanize them until he is forced to confess, "I am no man, ladies" (5.4.44).[24] Morose is not the only would-be domestic tyrant in the play. Mrs. Otter, who "would bee Princesse, and raigne in mine owne house" (3.1.33–34), finds her power restored finally with the submission of her husband. Perhaps justice lies in the fact that Morose, who does not really want a wife, does not in the end have one. But the familial bond he has sought to deny is finally the one he cannot avoid: Dauphine, the source of his torment, is also the source of his release. The success of this community's invasion of the city of one does demonstrate explicitly what other city plays leave implicit—that the city can neither be denied, silenced, nor evaded. It is the nature of the city and the houses and playhouses within it to be as inclusive as possible, even if the urban community is far from ideal.

Jonson changes ground in *Bartholomew Fair*, from a city inside a city to a city outside the walls. By using a familiar spatial symbol like the fair-grounds, Jonson can also draw upon the spatial symbolism of the medieval stage. Placed at stage-left, Ursula's barbeque pit would represent hell-mouth; the puppet booth, at stage-right, would signify the play's "heaven," where the final orderings take place. The stocks at down-center become a fitting emblem for the trials of this life.[25] Such a staging allows the fair to represent not just holiday but everyday as well. This suggestion is reinforced at the opening of act 2 when Adam Overdo presents the fair as a civic proving-ground while Leatherhead and Joan Trash set up their booths onstage behind him. His presence as authority-in-disguise, his ostentatious allusions to the classical past, and his refrain—"Well, in Justice name, and the Kings; and for the commonwealth" (2.1.1–2;48–49)—prepare us to regard action at the fair as a genuine test case of "the nature of our people, / Our city's institutions, and the terms / For common justice" (*Measure for Measure*, 1.1.9–11). That Overdo is himself undone by the fair affects the validity of the social test no more than the similar exposure of the duke in *Measure for*

Measure.[26] Jonson's aesthetic contract with his audience yields to a more complex presentation of the social contract which underlies the fair itself and the idea of the city which it expresses. For all their disparateness before and during the fair, the fairgoers do function as a minimal community simply because each has identified a reason to collect in the same space. The parallel with citizenship is clear. Whether opposed to the fair or not, the fairgoers share a status that for the occasion highlights and limits other differences among them. In its concentration, the fair is even more a city than the city itself, its notion of reciprocity simpler but no less fundamental since everyone at the fair expects to get or lose something in its course. That Jonson intends us to accept the fair world as a manic version of everyday rather than as an alternative to it is clearest in the experience of Overdo himself. His expectation of finding enormities ignores Jonson's warning against those who would expect servant monsters or "better ware then a Fayre will affoord" (115–16). Furthermore, like the city itself, the fair is only apparently chaotic. While it may intensify normal social and comic processes, Jonson has insisted at the beginning that it will not deviate from them. And if the fair breaks down preexisting relationships, it serves its own best interest in creating new ones—the two marriages in prospect at the end.[27]

But none of Jonson's plays, not even *Bartholomew Fair*, exceeds *The Alchemist* in a significant interpretation of the city through extreme adherence to unity of time and place. By setting the play in the Blackfriars neighborhood in 1610 and making the fictive time coterminous with performance, Jonson attempts to make the stage an extension of everyday reality.[28] The effect is not only to imply that the audience is capable of being gulled like Dapper or Drugger; it is also to make the audience into Blackfriars neighbors doing exactly what the trio is always worrying about—listening in. Edward Partridge has noticed the martial and political references that join the alchemical imagery that pervades the play, references that John Mebane has recently argued constitute Jonson's attack on the radical millenary and utopian movements of his day.[29] But the gulls, too, have civic pretensions. Epicure Mammon wants, among other things, to eradicate disease, age, poverty, and other social ills. Like the merchant princes of the pageants, he would disperse his fortune in pious works and public service. That solutions to such problems should come as pallid afterthoughts to elaborate sensual fantasies suggests a disproportion between self-interest and public service in the amassing of great speculative fortunes which the pageants overlook. The temporal ambitions of the Anabaptists are more explicit, although their willingness to use bribery satirizes the corrupt "civil *Magistrate*" (3.1.42) no less than the religious enthusiast.

Here, as in *Volpone*, Jonson uses the city within a city to imply inevitable defeat for all who dream of turning the age to gold. The gulls imagine the one prosaic city house in the play as the home of the Queen of Faery, Novo Orbe, the seat of necromancy, an alchemical laboratory, a school for quarreling, and a matchmaker's data bank. Yet even its fictive reality is an illusion. What Jonson makes especially absurd about his gulls' illusions is their expectation that actuality can ever be more than actuality, that a city can be other than the sum of everyday. Our recognition of this absurdity becomes inescapable when Jonson turns the focus of the play inside out with the arrival of Lovewit and the neighbors, preparing the audience for the moment when he will turn them out, too, into the actual world of the Blackfriars. Transformation will occur only in the least ambitious character of all; Dame Pliant becomes Mistress Lovewit. The commonwealth promises once again to renew itself, but the promise in so cynical a union is ironic.

Thus *The Alchemist* represents an intensification of the dramatic strategy which Jonson uses to good effect in the other three great comedies. His urban settings take on a suggestion not simply of probability, but of inevitability in an emphatic use of the metaphoric dimensions of the Elizabethan stage. Jonson demonstrates the symbolic centrality of his urban settings by offering no alternative. Most Jonsonian characters live physically constricted lives. Morose never leaves his house. Volpone, who seems to have spent three years entertaining suitors in his chamber, encounters disaster each time he leaves it. Face makes forays into plagueridden London, but we only see their results. Only Bartholomew Fairgoers represent an apparent exception, since they are not trapped in one place and the fair is temporary. Yet the fair, man-made like Jonson's other environments, cannot escape the implication that man—not nature—is responsible for what goes on within it.[30] Such a recognition explains the poverty of nature imagery in Jonson's plays, a lack directly attributable to the characters.[31] There is much more nature imagery in the masques. The satiric meaning these dramatic characters attribute to their settings is a function not of their importance but of their dramatic creator's skill and ethos. In all four of the comedies, for instance, there is an evident, highly charged tension between the narrow physical scope of the scene and the complexity of the action and atmosphere it contains. Jonson evokes the urban world by filling up his stage with diverse people, an often immense range of physical reference, and a tangle of linguistic accents. The contrast with the ordered materiality of the masque world is conspicuous. Part of the action of any masque is one of selection— excluding or transforming certain environments, extolling uniformity in the masquers. Unacceptable landscapes vanish, while characters from the city act their parts in the antimasque and either leave or step aside for the advent of their social superiors. The ideal community is thoroughly at one with a benevolent, pristine natural world that it understands and in some measure controls. The operating principle of the ideal commonwealth, like all the ideal cities of the Renaissance, is one of controlled inclusiveness. But inclusiveness in the comic communities represents diversity without distinction, the antithesis of hierarchy.[32] Jonson's comic societies include one fox, one fruitfly, one crow, one vulture, two parrots, and a hawk; or three rogues of differently disreputable backgrounds who assume different roles while gulling one tobacconist, one lawyer, one quarrelsome rustic, two Anabaptists, one knighted voluptary; or one near idiot, his tutor, one lunatic, one disguised justice, and so forth.[33] The degree and uniformity of the masque has yielded to disorderly heterogeneity, to the sensation of uncontrolled inclusiveness—a city planner's nightmare. Even so, these communities are communities because they are packed into the same dense urban space.[34] Morose cannot prevent the city from moving in on him any more than he can prevent his wife from talking. The fair takes its own course despite the attempts of Overdo, Busy, and Wasp to control it. And the biggest problem for the alchemical trio—where they are going to put everyone—is a miniature version of the basic urban dilemma. Furthermore, the density of verbal texture in these plays ties the Jonsonian characters even more firmly to their settings and gives their heterogeneity correspondences throughout the microcosm. Like the characters in the antimasque, these are characters tied to and expressed by the objects in their worlds.

Thus, if the sense of centrality which the masques and pageants create for the places they celebrate confirms a sense of spaciousness in order and decorum, the kind of centrality to which the comic city aspires produces an imitation of chaos. This is the negative side of the pageants' glorification of urban abundance. The city is so crowded, so complex, so full, and so dramatically sufficient to the action that its inhabitants are almost inevitably deluded into thinking that it and they are complete and essential.

Of course Jonson delights in the imaginative power of his comic cities and of the real city they imitate. But the juxtaposed visions of the communities in the comedies and the communities in the masques—a rough juxtaposition of real and ideal—suggest an imaginative division in Jonson comparable to the division we found in Juvenal.[35] He cannot reject the disorderly city that so fascinates him any more than Juvenal can leave Rome. And, although it is true that the approximate justice of Jonson's denouements may imply recognition of a more perfect city, that justice is far more rigorous in *Volpone* and *Epicoene* than it is in the two later comedies where the city is most disorderly. Order as a social phenomenon within the plays yields to order as an aesthetic phenomenon achieved by the playwright alone. He is the urban alchemist, transforming the materials of actuality into art. The regularity, uniformity, and unanimity so essential to the masque give way to a comic celebration of the urban particular, even if the place is as dirty as Smithfield and as stinking every whit.

Perhaps Jonson did see the image of an ideal city reflected in the splendor of the court on masquing nights. But the ideal city itself can only have existed for him as it did for the Platonic Socrates—in heaven. In order to celebrate ideal community on earth, he had to bring in the antimasque.

Instead of concentrating narrowly on a specific place and group of characters, Middleton focuses interest on a generalized scene or action, as titles like *A Mad World, My Masters* or *Michaelmas Term* or even *A Chaste Maid in Cheapside* suggest. Middleton is less interested in outsize personalities than in the pervasive qualities of a scene. The symbolic household in Jonson yields to a symbolic region, like Cheapside, or a symbolic season, like *Michaelmas Term*. Jonson uses the city as a place in which giant predators lure victims into their restricted spaces, analogues for the city. But, although Middleton does invest Quomodo's darkly lit shop with infernal implications, it is less important than Jonson's important interiors.[36] In general, Middleton allows a sense of the entire city to control mood and to provide the chief thematic unity of a play. Furthermore, instead of Jonsonian constriction Middleton presents the first effects of the city as a sense of liberating opportunity and unrestricted freedom of action that will prove to be a trap only at the end. His characters are far freer than Jonson's to move around, within, and beyond the confines of the city; they have the illusion of psychological free space. And, in at least two of the city plays—*Michaelmas Term* and *A Mad World, My Masters*—Middleton opens the action on street scenes and rapidly introduces characters from each of the several groups that make up the multiple plot.

These public scenes enable Middleton to make his characters part of a much larger, seemingly openended community that stretches out beyond the confines of the stage and defines the city as a treasure house of financial and social opportunity. Encounters on the street set various subplots in motion. In *A Trick to Catch the Old One*, Theodorus Witgood regards London as the only place to recoup his bankrupt fortunes. And, sure enough, the first person the theater of the city presents is his designated prey, Uncle Lucre the usurer, locked with his adversary Hoard in the very attitude of combat that will ensure Witgood's success. In *Michaelmas Term*, right after Quomodo describes the land he intends to possess in Essex, he spots the owner of the land, Master Easy, whom the city seems to have offered to his hand. "That's he, that's he!" (1.1.115), rings out from the merchant with the exultation of the hunter spotting long-sought-after game. Easy himself, who has had to wait until his father's death to come up to the city, is welcomed with the assurance that "here's gallants of all sizes, of all lasts" (1.1.44). He responds with a declaration of new-found independence from rustic confinement: "You have easily possess'd me, I am free;/Let those live hinds that know not liberty" (1.1.47–48). His attitude is quite specifically antipastoral, probably meant to remind us ironically of those, like Rosalind and Touchstone, who flee court or city for the sensation of liberty in Arden.[37]

Something more is going on here than comic economy of predictable coincidence. Middleton uses coincidence to suggest urban opportunity, the heady sense of possibility experienced most strongly by the newcomer but clearly available to a seasoned native like Quomodo. As we shall see, Shakespeare achieves much the same effect, with an even more manic intensity, in *The Comedy of Errors*, where the wandering twins walk the streets of Ephesus only to be presented with a ready-made dinner, wife, household, girlfriend, chain of gold, and set of acquaintances. And, rather like *The Comedy of Errors* again, this bustle of activity on Middleton's streets provides more community and generates more relationships than individual city dwellers may desire or comprehend. His introductory scenes demonstrate a large network of relationships tying his characters together, but the same expansiveness prevents those characters from fully appreciating it. For Middleton, the city creates community and makes it ironic or perverse at the same time. Dick Follywit and Frank Gullman, the courtesan, are part of the same community in *A Mad World, My Masters* not simply because both can walk out onto the same stage at different moments of the opening scene, but also because they share without knowing it a close relationship with the same man: Follywit's grandfather, old Sir Bounteous, is Gullman's lover. This relationship will be superseded by an even closer one when Follywit marries Gullman. Gullman herself is a common bond between Penitent Brothel and Master Harebrain, since by making her his wife's best friend Harebrain enables Gullman to function as Penitent Brothel's bawd.

The irony of unconscious relationships permeates the atmosphere and defines the nature of community in Middleton's other plays, too. In *Michaelmas Term*, Master Rearage withdraws from the stage to avoid being seen by Quomodo, who does not want him as his daughter's suitor. At almost the same time Quomodo singles out Easy, planning a relationship of which Easy is as yet unaware, but winding up with a relationship he did not plan: Easy, at least temporarily, marries Quomodo's wife. The street provides the upstart Andrew Lethe with an old mother he can refuse to acknowledge because she does not recognize his new appearance. His old mother will become his new servant. In *A Chaste Maid in Cheapside*, the Welsh woman whom Sir Walter Whorehound presents as his niece is actually his mistress, while Mistress Allwit's baby whom he acknowledges as his godchild is actually his bastard. Yellow-hammer, taking an order for a ring from Touchwood Junior, sees him only as a customer and not a future son-in-law.

For Middleton, this loose web of multiple relationships creates more ironic possibilities and a more effective sense of urban life than the intensifying technique of Jonson's crowded interiors and narrowly compressed actions. His characters, unlike Jonson's, have relationships and connections extending beyond the play. A recent editor of *A Trick to Catch the Old One* points out the number of nameless people we hear about, but never see: the widow hunters Witgood mentions in 3.1.253–58; the widows hunting Witgood whom Lucre imagines in 2.1.310–19; or the matches that Lucre boasts of having made in 2.1.333–35.[38] The effect of this extension is to imply that what Middleton dramatizes has been selected almost at random from an urban abundance of comic material—like the humors crowding the stage which Jonson mentions in the prologue to *The Alchemist*. The potential of the city for comic opportunity is most obvious in *A Chaste Maid*, perhaps because the multiple relationships among the characters make the cast appear larger than it is. Richard Levin has counted four separate main actions in the play affecting four households—the Yellowhammers, the Allwits, the Kixes, and the Touchwoods. The resulting subplots are comparable in complexity to those in *Bartholomew Fair*.³⁹ Here, however, Middleton makes the multiple plot expressive of a complex urban community that stands for a larger, more complex community implied in the Allwit christening or the young lovers' mock funeral.

Middleton's interest in establishing the representativeness of his characters is particularly important in *A Chaste Maid in Cheapside* because of the extremes of sexual license which it depicts. (This is a community that has so thoroughly lost normative social control of basic biological function that it makes Vienna in *Measure for Measure* look well run by comparison.) At the beginning of act 2, for example, Touchwood Senior comments ironically on a new Lenten severity as evidence for civic order, in a speech that takes away in the last three lines what it had granted before:

> There has been more religious wholesome laws
> In the half circle of a year erected
> For common good, than memory ever knew of,
> Setting apart corruption of promoters,
> And other poisonous officers that infect
> And with a venomous breath taint every goodness.
>
> [2.1.112–17]

The speech contains a deeper irony, prompted by our awareness of sexual profligacy and the other varieties of sexual irregularity in the play completely untouched by "religious wholesome laws." Touchwood himself will have good reason to be grateful for civic corruption since the prospect of obtaining a salable loin of mutton prompts the two Lenten promoters to keep the basket in which the Country Wench has deposited her baby—adulterously fathered by Touchwood himself. The praiser of civic order also tells us he hinders every haymaking by the pregnancies he causes, and by the end of the play he will have impregnated Lady Kix with an illegitimate heir to the fortune Sir Walter Whorehound expects to inherit. By insisting on the Kixes's own satisfaction in the matter and on Sir Walter's unworthiness as heir, Middleton prevents us from making simple moral judgments.⁴⁰ (What is clear is the ineffectuality of law to adjudicate Lenten behavior or legitimate succession in Cheapside.)

Allwit, too, exemplifies the disparity between public order and private misrule. His status as wittol has not made him immune to social concern: he too exclaims against promoters and appears shocked by Sir Walter's intention to stand as godfather to his own bastard. And, although his own behavior attests to a remarkable combination of shamelessness, laziness, and greed, he is as disgusted by the incontinent gluttony of the Puritan gossips as he is by their professions of humility and struggles for precedence at the christening. (Throughout the play, such formal social structures as those personified in the promoters or represented by the christening prove not only corrupt but also powerless either to express or to regulate actual behavior.)

A more effective method of social control seems to exist in the informal pressure of the community on the Yellowhammers when they try to prevent Moll from marrying Touchwood Junior. The activities of the promoters, and the reactions of other characters to them, have already hinted that few actions in Cheapside go unobserved. This is one negative aspect of the group solidarity celebrated in the civic pageants or the masques. But, if the nameless promoters represent official forms of surveillance, equally anonymous watermen and Cheapside neighbors condemn the Yellowhammers for their cruelty to Moll. Fear of the neighborhood motivates Yellowhammer's decision to stay away from Moll's funeral:

> All the whole street will hate us, and the world
> Point me out cruel: it is our best course, wife,
> After we have given order for the funeral,
> To absent ourselves till she be laid in ground.

> [5.2.92–95]

Sir Oliver declares he "would not have my cruelty so talk'd on/To any child of mine for a monopoly" (5.3.27–28). The funeral itself draws "such running,/Such rumours, and such throngs" (5.3.20–21) that the Yellowhammers' behavior seems prudent. And the community becomes partially responsible for the lovers' wedding when they arise from their coffins.

There is also a suggestion, however, that the emotional outpouring of the community here is prompted by the self-indulgence so evident at the Allwit christening. The Puritan gossips are sloppily demonstrative to the Allwit baby and to Tim Yellowhammer, while Lady Kix spends much of the play in tears. Emotional indulgence thus becomes part of the general lack of self-restraint throughout Cheapside. If social control first requires self-control, Cheapside seems virtually ungovernable. Allwit's question to the promoters—"What cares colon here for Lent?" (2.2.79)—could stand as motto for the play. The Kixes's offer to house the Touchwoods will not curb Touchwood's ungovernable potency; the play is not even sure that it should.[41] But Sir Oliver will provide Touchwood with a sexual outlet that may lessen the social damage he has heretofore created. And Sir Oliver will take Allwit's place as the contented cuckold of Cheapside. The best that the mind can do in Cheapside is exemplified in Tim Yellowhammer's syllogistic attempt to prove his newly married whore an honest woman.

This sense of social panorama in Middleton's comedy eventually creates a symbolic centrality for his cities no less powerful than it is for Jonson's. The magnetism of the city appears strongest, perhaps, in *Michaelmas Term* where the seasonal influx of visitors and returning natives demonstrates the city's "contentious fathom" (Inductio, 7). The city reaches out to grasp all that the country has to offer. The city harvests the crop the country plants:

> And what by sweat from the rough earth they draw
> Is to enrich this silver harvest, Law;
> And so through wealthy variance and fat brawl,
> The barn is made but steward to the hall.
> Come they up thick enough?
>
> [Inductio, 9–13]

Michaelmas Term makes much use of the familiar city-country contrast, in part to underscore the comic contrast between Easy's desire to leave his country estates and Quomodo's desire to possess them. But, although *Michaelmas Term* regards conscience as a garment to be discarded in London, Middleton himself blurs any distinction between country virtue and city vice in the characters who actually come up.[42] The Country Wench is only too eager for a taste of city life. Her transformation by fashionable clothes repeats that of Andrew Lethe, which predates the play. Their metamorphoses demonstrate that shape-shifting is not a device restricted only to the citizenry. And their marriage at the end of the play, which Lethe regards as an unjustifiable humiliation, actually unites two country characters of comparable social backgrounds.

Michaelmas Term is also the play in which Middleton most strongly emphasizes the city's sense of itself as a world apart, with its natural law and internal dynamic. Another symptom here of the predatory relation of the city to the countryside is the urban characters' appropriation of nature imagery to rationalize a hunter-victim relationship that they regard as universal. Gulls are lambs to be fleeced, bucks to be struck, and trouts to be caught. *Michaelmas Term* describes writs as "wild fowl" that return with "clients, like dried straws, between their bills" to use for nest building (Inductio, 57, 60). Characters' frequent use of such urban adages establishes the predominance of class consciousness among citizens and gentry. Even the characters in this play regard the warfare between the two classes—"our deadly enmity, which thus stands: / They're busy 'bout our wives, we 'bout their lands" (1.1.106–7)—as a social truth almost too tired to be worth repeating. Quomodo is as aware as we are of the utter conventionality of his social aspirations to own land, to educate his son and to marry his daughter to a gentleman. His confidence about gulling Easy stems less than Shortyard's skill than from the victim's predictability:

> Keep foot by foot with him, out-dare his expenses,
> Flatter, dice, and brothel to him;
> Give him a sweet taste of sensuality;

Train him to every wasteful sin, that he
May quickly need health, but especially money.

[1.1.120–24]

The fascination that the city holds for newcomer Easy is complemented by
the equal appeal that the country holds for Quomodo, the quintessential citizen.
The country is not, however, any more real an alternative to London in
Michaelmas Term than it is in Jonsonian comedy. Quomodo's descriptions of the
natural landscape have the tone as well as the essential unreality of vision:

> Oh, that sweet, neat, comely, proper, delicate parcel of land, like a
> fine gentlewoman i'th' waist, not so great as pretty, pretty; the trees
> in summer whistling, the silver waters by the banks harmoniously
> gliding. [2.3.82–86]

Quomodo laughs to think "how the very thought of green fields puts a man into
sweet inventions" (4.1.79–80), which in this case are apparently unfamiliar sexual
daydreams. But Quomodo never really imagines himself as anything other than
a citizen of London. The city provides the essential context for his most rapt
dreams of landowning, the mirror for his self-admiration. Thinking he will now
be "divulg'd a landed man / Throughout the Livery," (3.4.5–6), Quomodo turns
himself into the subject of an imaginary London conversation:

> —Whither is the worshipful Master Quomodo and his fair bedfellow
> rid forth?—To his land in Essex!—Whence comes those goodly load
> of logs?—From his land in Essex!—Where grows this pleasant fruit?
> says one citizen's wife in the Row.—At Master Quomodo's orchard in
> Essex. [3.4.13–17]

Even for a citizen like Quomodo, however, the city is no less a trap than it is for
the gulls he fleeces. His acquisitiveness so alienates his family that they rejoice in
his death. And Quomodo listens, ashamed, while his fellow liverymen disparage
both him and his fortune: "Merely enrich'd by shifts/And coz'nages" (4.4.16–17).
Because Quomodo cannot prevent Sim from losing his patrimony as the other
prodigal sons of the play lose theirs, Quomodo himself ends up behaving
prodigally. Like Easy he has foolishly set his hand to a deed that takes all his
property away and that cannot be remanded by the profession of ignorance: "I
did I knew not what" (5.3.72).

Having the "freedom of the city" in this play becomes an increasingly
ironic phrase. Formally it designates those who belong to one of the livery
companies in the city; informally, it connotes insider status, as when Dick
Hellgill tells the Country Wench, "Virginity is no city trade,/You're out o'th'
freedom, when you're a maid" (1.2.43–44). *Michaelmas Term* describes his hand

as free from restraint or scruple. Easy is repeatedly described as free and fresh, free-breasted, meaning free from suspicion, free to spend, and vulnerable. Easy is free in a different way after losing his lands to Quomodo. "Y'are a free man," Quomodo tells him, ironically, "you may deal in what you please and go whither you will" (4.1.49–50). Freedom here is just another word for nothing left to lose.[43] But the idea of freedom rebounds ironically on Quomodo since Easy is also free to marry Thomasine Quomodo, just as she imagines herself free to marry him. In the end the freedom of this city exists for no one. Quomodo ends up being his "own affliction" (5.3.164), free neither from himself nor from his awareness of having been cuckolded. But the play is especially grim in its denial of distinction between gulls and rogues and natives and newcomers in the successive stages of the "city powdering." The veteran gallants regard newcomers like Lethe and Easy with some condescension. But they too have been deceived by Shortyard's impersonation of Master Blastfield and are just about to turn on him when he assumes a new identity. The country parents who travel to the city in the course of the action have difficulty recognizing their off spring, but Quomodo also has been deceived by Lethe's transformation from Andrew Gruel to fashionable gallant. The Country Wench's father has not learned enough from a youthful experience as urban victim to detect his daughter under her new clothes. The most he manages is to realize that he serves no gentlewoman, but a bawd. What unites the country people is not a common commitment to simple virtue, but a common identity as past, present, or future victims of the city powdering. Lethe's mother and the Country Wench's father almost immediately lose their freedom since necessity turns them into servants. Middleton refuses, however, to idealize any of his countryfolk, sharply undercutting the country father's status as spokesman for rural virtue and giving Mother Gruel a sexual appetite for young courtiers comparable to—if more grotesque than—Thomasine Quomodo's.

The entrapping magnetism of the city thus becomes part of a patterned temporal sequence which—like the predatory cycle with which it is aligned— effectively negates the possibility of positive urban change. The city alone benefits from this pattern, since it serves to perpetuate the city's imaginative appeal. In this sequence, gentry like Easy come up to town and lose their money by gambling or whoring and their patrimony in a commodity swindle. Debt- and disease-ridden, they may remain in the city like Rearage and Salewood and think of the country only for rent collections. They may, like the country father, finally reject "this man-devouring city" entirely and return to rural poverty.

This Juvenalian rejection of the city counts for very little in the moral vision of the play. More significant is the circularity within which the merchant class is trapped. Turning their profits into the means to purchase gentlemanly status means becoming prey to sharpers like themselves. Recognition of this irony is so widespread in city comedy that Jonson rings a final change on it in *The Devil Is an Ass*, when Plutarchus begs his father not to make him a gentleman:

In a descent, or two, wee come to be
Just i' their state, fit to be coozend, like 'hem.
And I had rather ha' tarryed i' your trade.

[3.1.28–30]

But the importance of this pattern for the satiric thrust of city comedy is to suggest at least one way that the city ensures its survival as the ultimate predator. If every swindling citizen is either a potential gull or the producer of gulls, there will always be prey for the predatory city. It is the one commodity that transcends the fact of limit. For Middleton, the contentious fathom of the city is so powerful that it allures the countryman and traps the citizen. The city's power is a product of the greediness of the city's embrace, because the city is a version of the Renaissance overreacher, unwilling to let anyone or anything go.

NOTES

1. The phrase is Jonas Barish's in *Ben Jonson and the Language of Prose Comedy* (1960; reprint, New York: Norton, 1970), p. 244.

2. For this date, see Parker, ed., *A Chaste Maid in Cheapside*, p. xxviii–xxxv.

3. Gibbons, *Jacobean City Comedy: A Study of Satiric Plays by Jonson, Marston, and Middleton* (Cambridge: Harvard University Press, 1968), p. 30. The other standard treatment of city comedy is by Alexander Leggatt, *Citizen Comedy in the Age of Shakespeare* (Toronto: University of Toronto Press, 1973).

4. In seeing a significant thematic purpose to the induction, I disagree with Ruby Chatterji, "Unity and Disparity in *Michaelmas Term*," SEL 8 (1968): 352.

5. See F. H. Mares, *The Alchemist*, Revels Plays (London: Methuen, 1967), p. xlvii.

6. Gibbons, *Jacobean City Comedy*, pp. 153–55.

7. Parker, ed., *A Chaste Maid*, p. xlvii. For other discussions of women in Middleton, see Caroline Lockett Cherry, "The Most Unvaluedst Purchase: Women in the Plays of Thomas Middleton," Institut für Englische Sprache und Literatur (Salzburg: Universität Salzburg, 1973), pp. 62ff. See also Leggatt's chapter, "Chaste Maids and Whores" in *Citizen Comedy*, pp. 99–124.

8. On the sex-money equation, see Richard Levin, *The Multiple Plot in English Renaissance Drama* (Chicago: University of Chicago Press, 1971), pp. 168–74; also George E. Rowe, Jr., *Thomas Middleton and the New Comedy Tradition* (Lincoln: University of Nebraska Press, 1979), p. 64.

9. Watson, ed., *A Trick to Catch the Old One*, p. xxi. All quotations refer to this edition.

10. Parker, pp. xlvii–lvi.

11. Barish, *Ben Jonson and the Language of Prose Comedy*, p. 181.

12. See Alvin Kernan, *The Cankered Muse: Satire of the English Renaissance* (New Haven: Yale University Press, 1959), pp. 168–70; also, Alvin B. Kernan, ed., *Volpone*, Yale Ben Jonson Series (New Haven: Yale University Press, 1974), pp. 9–10.

13. Samuel Schoenbaum, "*A Chaste Maid in Cheapside* and Middleton's City Comedy," in *Studies in the English Renaissance Drama:In Memory of Karl Julius Holzknecht*, ed. Josephine W. Bennett, Oscar Cargill, and Vernon Hall, Jr. (New York: New York University Press, 1959), p. 292.

14. I have treated the connections between Middleton and Plautus at length in "The City in Plautus and Middleton," *Ren D*, n.s. 6 (1973): 29–44.

15. Edward B. Partridge, *The Broken Compass: A Study of the Major Comedies of Ben Jonson* (London: Chatto and Windus, 1958), p. 85.

16. Ibid., p. 107.

17. Alvin B. Kernan, *The Plot of Satire* (New Haven: Yale University Press, 1965), p. 153.

18. I disagree, implicitly, with Rowe here who finds more evidence of urban change in this play than I do; see his *Thomas Middleton and the New Comedy Tradition*, p. 64.

19. See Levin, *The Multiple Plot in English Renaissance Drama*, pp. xvi–xvii; also Rowe, *Thomas Middleton and the New Comedy Tradition*, p. 66, and Chatterji, "Unity and Disparity," pp. 360–61.

20. See Alan C. Dessen, *Jonson's Moral Comedy* (Evanston, Ill.: North-western University Press, 1971), pp. 108–9.

21. See Levin, *Multiple Plot in English Renaissance Drama*, pp. 207–11.

22. Kernan, ed., *Volpone*, pp. 1–2.

23. See George R. Kernodle, "The Open Stage: Elizabethan or Existentialist?" *Shak S* 12 (1959): 3; see also Kernan, ed., *Volpone*, textual note to 2.2.2.

24. Barish, *Ben Jonson and the Language of Prose Comedy*, p. 183.

25. On the staging of *Bartholomew Fair*, see Eugene M. Waith's edition of the play for the Yale Ben Jonson Series (New Haven: Yale University Press, 1963), p. 214; and R. B. Parker, "The Themes and Staging of *Bartholomew Fair*," *UTQ* 39 (1969–70): 294–96.

26. A parallel pointed out by Leo Salingar, "Crowd and Public in *Bartholomew Fair*," *Ren D*, n.s. 10 (1979): 158.

27. Levin, *The Multiple Plot in English Renaissance Drama*, pp. 207–11.

28. See Mares' edition of *The Alchemist*, p. xlv.

29. John Mebane, "Renaissance Magic and the Return of the Golden Age: Utopianism and Religious Enthusiasm in *The Alchemist*" *Ren D* 10 (1979): 117–39.

30. I have treated the theme of Jonson's confined settings at more length in "Ben Jonson's Comedy of Limitation," *SP* 72 (1975): 51–71. See also a more recent discussion by Patrick R. Williams, "Jonson's Satiric Choreography," *Ren D*, n.s. 9 (1978): 121–45.

31. See Barish, *Ben Jonson and the Language of Prose Comedy*, pp. 181–82.

32. Waith, ed., *Bartholomew Fair*, p. 11.

33. Gabriele Bernhard Jackson, ed., *Every Man in His Humor*, Yale Ben Jonson Series (New Haven: Yale University Press, 1969), p. 15.

34. In "Crowd and Public in *Bartholomew Fair*," Salingar remarks that the characters "affect one another chiefly by contiguity" and concludes that "they are not a community but a crowd." Yet crowdedness is a chief characteristic of urban life then as now; it may be truer to say that the characters in the play are a crowd in the process of discovering themselves to be a community.

35. On the relationship of Jonson's platonizing beliefs in universal truth to the question of setting, see Gabriele Bernhard Jackson's discussion of the "truthful setting," in *Vision and Judgment in Ben Jonson's Drama* (New Haven: Yale University Press, 1968), pp. 77–94.

36. This is Rowe's observation in *Thomas Middleton and the New Comedy Tradition*, p. 64. He also ties this observation to the influence of the morality play tradition noticed by Gibbons in Jacobean City Comedy, p. 129.

37. Rowe comments that the youths' journeys from country to city symbolize "their acceptance of chaos," *Thomas Middleton and the New Comedy Tradition*, p. 65.

38. Watson, ed., *A Trick*, p. xix.

39. Levin, *The Multiple Plot in English Renaissance Drama*, pp. 194–202.

40. On this subject, see R. B. Parker, "Middleton's Experiments with Comedy and Judgment," in *Jacobean Theatre*, ed. John Russell Brown and Bernard Harris, Stratford-upon-Avon Studies, no. 1 (London: Edward Arnold, 1960), pp. 179–99.

41. Parker comments on the ambiguities of the portrayal of fertility in the play; see ibid., pp. l–li. He thus undercuts Arthur F. Marotti's account of the festive qualities of the play in "Fertility and Comic Form in *A Chaste Maid in Cheapside*," *Comp D* 3 (1969): 67.

42. Rowe comments that the induction associates "the country with purity and goodness," in *Thomas Middleton and the New Comic Tradition*, p. 63; but the play as a whole treats the country as irrelevant to the action except as it functions as an illusory goal for Quomodo and provides a supply of gulls.

43. See Rowe's excellent discussion of the allied subjects of prodigality and freedom in ibid., pp. 63–67.

LEAH S. MARCUS

Pastimes and the Purging of Theater:
Bartholomew Fair (1614)

"And never rebel was to arts a friend," John Dryden observed in *Absalom and Achitophel*. That notion is, of course, untenable: one wonders what John Milton would have made of it. But it was a common perception in seventeenth-century England, at least in certain circles. Traditional pastimes and the theater were parallel cultural forms in that they held the same ambivalent status, outside the rules of ordinary life, yet integrally bound up with it. They tended to happen together, masques, plays, and traditional games all being particularly rife at holiday times and enjoyed in the same places—at court and, in the London area, in the no-man's-land of the liberties, outside the City's legal jurisdiction and under the protection of the crown. Queen Elizabeth I had been an avid, if frugal, supporter of the drama, and the "precise people" who had ventured to condemn plays and players during her reign had sometimes acknowledged warily that they were opposing a group "privileged by a Prince."[1] Under the Stuarts, however, defense of the drama came to be much more closely tied to defense of the monarchy. As in the case of the *Book of Sports*, James I deliberately forced the issue. He made the theater a royal monopoly—a branch of his prerogative—so that anyone attacking the drama was assailing an aspect of his power.

Enemies of the stage regularly charged that plays rested on lies and hypocrisy, reminding their readers that the Greek word *hypocrite* had meant both actor and pretender. But defenders of the drama were quick to return the charge. Those who muttered against plays and masques were "open Saints and secret varlets" who concealed their true natures for nefarious ends.[2] In *Love Restored*,

From *Staging the Renaissance*, eds. David Scott Kastan and Peter Stallybrass. © 1991 by Routledge, Chapman and Hall.

when Robin Good-fellow is accused of hypocrisy, he answers, "We are all masquers sometimes." The joke operates on a number of levels. Robin is in fact a member of the theatrical company The King's Men, playing the part of Robin Goodfellow, a spirit of country jollity, who, in turn, has attempted to pass himself off as a hypocritical Puritan feather-maker—disguise upon disguise upon disguise. But his challenger is also an actor and therefore also a "hypocrite," a player of roles. The need to act, mime, and take pleasure in such functions, Robin implies, is a natural human trait. It can either uplift or debase, depending on the degree to which it is acknowledged and therefore made open to regulation and refinement. This is a standard Jacobean argument for the drama, as for other traditional customs. By extension, it is an argument for the royal monopoly. By claiming the power to "license" and regulate it, James was ensuring that the human needs it met would be channeled to the betterment of the nation. Otherwise, the argument went, those needs were likely to be driven underground, twisted toward evil and seditious ends.

Bartholomew Fair is pervasively grounded in contemporary controversy over theatrical arts and traditional pastimes and trenchant in its commentary upon those Plutuses—Puritan or otherwise—who made it their "lawful" calling to challenge the authority of the king. The play has inspired fine commentary from a number of perceptive critics. But opinion has divided sharply over whether it is (to use one of its own recurrent puns) a foul play or a fair one—a dark indictment of human irrationality and moral decay or a celebration of the rejuvenating energies of folly and festival disorder.[3] A study of its "occasion" will demonstrate that Jonson fully intended to have it both ways. He immerses his audience in the seamy squalor of Smithfield and exposes the vice and blasphemy which can lurk behind noble ideals like law and religion and education. The shabby, tinsel world of Bartholomew Fair seems to slough off higher cultural forms as irreconcilable with its nature. But Jonson's fair is not all foulness, and those who would have it so must reckon with some awkward incongruities.

In the Prologue to the king, Jonson warns James not to expect too much from his fair but nevertheless promises "sport" and, for a "fairing," the gift traditionally offered by those returned from a fair, "true delight."[4] James would presumably have been amused by the fair's grotesques and, beyond that, would have found rare "sport" in the play's unmasking of what he habitually identified as two major species of rebel against his authority: the Puritan who uses religion as a cloak for personal aggrandizement and the judge who argues for the supremacy of law, meaning by that the supremacy of himself. But the true delight Jonson proposes is a wider pleasure than the sport of seeing one's enemies exposed. The play carries too many echoes from contemporary defense of public mirth, echoes even from the Anglican liturgy for the Feast of Saint Bartholomew, an official holiday of the Church, for its "fair" festival side to be discounted. Unlike some of his sons, Jonson was seldom one to romanticize popular sports— he does not allow his audience to lose contact with their raucous, gritty earthiness. There is considerable tension in the play between the "fair" and the "foul" levels of its argument. But in *Bartholomew Fair* the author's ambivalence, or at least some of it, is channeled into defense of the king. The "fairing" offered King James is the "true delight" of seeing one's cherished beliefs about the potential functioning of plays and pastimes reflected in the uncommon looking glass of a play about plays and pastimes.

In both the Induction to the Hope audience and the Prologue to King James, Jonson adamantly denies that *Bartholomew Fair* is meant to satirize individuals. In the Induction he wards off any "state-decipherer, or politic picklock of the scene" so "solemnly ridiculous as to search out" models for the personalities who wander his fair, and in the Prologue to James he again protests that he writes "without particular wrong, / Or just complaint of any private man / Who of himself or shall think well or can" (Fair, 23, 33). This formulation effectively shields *Bartholomew Fair* against accusations of slander. If any individual is so rash as to protest that he has been singled out for reflection in the unflattering mirror of the play, it will be because he cannot think well of himself. His protest will be motivated (according to the standard theory) by secret recognition of his own culpability and will therefore amount to a confession that he needs the play's tart correctives. And yet Jonson's pious caveats against politic picklocking have the effect of whetting our curiosity for precisely the activity he warns us against. Several modern critics, suspecting that the poet doth protest too much, have set out to identify historical figures as the butts of Jonson's satire and found striking parallels among his contemporaries. The Lord Mayor of London in the year 1614, like Adam Overdo, ferreted out dens of iniquity through spies and went "himself in disguise to divers of them"; he also seasoned his discourse with references to classical authors, much in Overdo's style. The famous Banbury Puritan William Whately, known as the "roaring boy of Banbury," habitually preached at fairs, as Zeal-of-the-Land Busy does, to gather a "fairing of souls" for God. *Bartholomew Fair* was a favorite time for Puritan invective against the drama because the crowds of fairgoers visiting London filled the playhouses to overflowing.[5]

Jonson almost certainly expected a similar picklocking on the part of his contemporary audience, but that does not mean that his warnings against it are entirely disingenuous. When the poet steers us away from attempts at specific identification he is not denying that parallels with contemporaries can be found, but advising us not to dwell on them at the expense of larger issues. Many Puritans preached at fairs; several Lord Mayors played detective. Overdo's bustling in search of "enormities" and his grave distress over the corrosive effects of puppetry and poetry also recapture the attitudes of a number of contemporary Justices of the Peace, whose court records are full of similar opinions and long lists of "notable outrages." There are even intriguing parallels between Overdo and Chief Justice Edward Coke, the king's principal opponent in issues of royal prerogative.[6] But we are not encouraged to stray in search of particulars. Jonson's characters are composites, representative of contemporary anti-court attitudes and argumentative styles; his play analyzes tendencies they have in common, especially their worship of law.

For a play about holiday license, *Bartholomew Fair* is curiously permeated with legalisms. Before it even gets underway, the Hope audience is invited to accept a formal contract granting them lawful right to criticize the work in proportion to the price of their tickets; they are authorized to sit in judgment on their "bench" like justices of the King's Bench (*Fair*, 31). The play itself teems with legal authorities: Busy, Overdo, Wasp, and Littlewit all see themselves as lawgivers in their respective realms of religion, secular government, education, and poetry. There is much talk in the play of licenses and warrants—proofs of legitimacy without which little can be accomplished. At the height of the fair's swirling madness, Trouble-all requires legal sanction even for the act of losing a cloak or downing a pint of ale. There is also much talk of license in the opposite sense of freedom from the authority of law—a liberty which the fair's hostile observers find licentious. Words like liberty, law, license, and *judgment* seem forever to be sliding out of meaning in the chaos of Smithfield, so that our sense of what is lawful is seriously impaired. Most of those making it their business to enforce some legal system end up in the stocks, like common transgressors of law; the legal documents juggled at the fair finally authorize actions contrary to what they first specified as lawful. One of the play's overriding themes is the *tu quoque*—let him who is without sin cast the first stone. Taken literally, this precept would undo all human capacity to penalize breaches of law.

Bartholomew Fair's emphasis on legalisms has struck a number of readers, but we have failed to recognize how Jonson's *tu quoque* applied to contemporary circumstances.[7] *Law*, *license*, and *liberty* were loaded words in 1614, as thick in the air about London as they are in the vapors of *Bartholomew Fair*. Jonson deliberately clouds the atmosphere of his play with legalistic obscurities in order to undercut what he saw as a contemporary tendency to worship legal authority. His target is not the law itself, but the abuse of law. Beneath its surface of folly and obfuscation, *Bartholomew Fair* is a lucid and elegant defense of royal prerogative, particularly the king's power to "license" plays and pastimes, against those contemporaries who grounded their opposition to such "licentious enormities" in the doctrine of the supremacy of law.

The play is aimed specifically at two parallel areas of contemporary dispute over law and license: the drama, under the authority of the king, and the pleasure fair of St. Bartholomew, under the authority of the London Corporation. In his Induction to the Hope audience, Jonson playfully establishes the identity of two things: his play, performed under license by the king's Master of Revels in the newly opened Hope Theater, Bankside, on the night of 31 October 1614 and the fair of St. Bartholomew, allowed by royal charter and proclaimed annually in Smithfield by the Lord Mayor of London from the twenty-fourth to the twenty-sixth of August. Jonson acknowledges that some of his more literal-minded viewers may, like the Hope stage keeper, object to the play's lack of such fine fixtures of the fair as the juggler and "well-educated ape"; nonetheless, Jonson assures us, his "ware" is precisely the same. He has even observed a "special decorum" as regards unity of place, the Hope Theater "being as dirty as Smithfield, and as stinking every whit" (*Fair*, 34). This "special decorum" serves an important rhetorical function. It forces us to see the similarities between the two and therefore points out the inconsistency of those contemporaries, particularly in London, who damned the "license" of the king's theater on all sorts of high moral grounds but managed to tolerate their own fair. The *tu quoque* of *Bartholomew Fair* is aimed especially at them.

For decades, as any student of theatrical history knows, the City fathers had opposed virtually all dramatic activity in and about London, as the king's old enemies, the Kirk, had in Edinburgh and for many of the same reasons. But the patents issued by James I to his own acting companies specifically exempted them from local restrictions. Although privy council records for the period have not survived, we know from numerous other sources that the years just before 1614 were a time of tug of war between the king and his privy council on one hand, and the Mayor and the City Corporation on the other. The king claimed power to license plays and players in and around London, and to override local ordinances against them; the City claimed the right to curb the royal monopoly within its liberties through enforcement of its own and parliamentary ordinances.[8] But what the City fathers condemned when it produced revenue for the king, they found considerably less objectionable when it produced revenue for themselves. Bartholomew Fair had two parts and it is important that we keep them straight. There was, first of all, the cloth fair, mostly business, which took place within the walls of St. Bartholomew Priory; its revenues went to Lord Rich, owner of the priory. Secondly, there was the pleasure fair outside the priory walls; Jonson's play deals almost exclusively with the pleasure fair, whose profits went to the London Corporation.[9] The area of the pleasure fair had not become part of the liberties of London until 1608. In that year, reportedly in return for funds to build a new Banqueting House, the king offered the city a new charter which specified that the "circuit, bounds, liberties, franchises, and jurisdictions" of London be extended to include the area around the priory, noteworthy for its annual fair, and Blackfriars and Whitefriars, noted for their theatrical connections.[10] Just as he was asserting royal control over the culturally marginal institution of the theater, he invited the City to try its hand at coping with the fair. However, while City fathers applied their new authority over Blackfriars and Whitefriars to curb the drama as much as they could, they showed less zeal in Smithfield. There was a notable "reform" in 1614: the muddy swamp of the fairgrounds was paved at City expense and made a "clean and spacious walk." The impetus for this improvement came from the king, who sent a letter to the Lord Mayor ordering it done. The Lord Mayor obeyed only after considerable protest.[11]

It is easy to see how these inconsistencies could be viewed by unsympathetic observers. So long as the City Corporation allowed in their fair the same liberties they condemned in the theaters, their high-sounding arguments about law and morality could appear purely self-serving. We need not, of course, agree with this prejudiced assessment. The king was acting as much in his interest as Londoners were in theirs. But the king's supporters would have drawn additional ammunition from the subsequent history of the fair. *Bartholomew Fair* was not suppressed during the Interregnum. When plays and traditional holiday pastimes had been banished from all of Britain by act of Parliament, similar frivolities were still allowed at the fair. Even its puppet theater, with its plays of "patient Grisel," "fair Rosamond," and Suzanna survived, as diaries and pamphlets from 1648, 1651, and 1655 record.[12]

Jonson's equation between fair and play therefore functions as an indictment of the king's London opposition, but an indictment tempered with mercy. He advises its grave citizens and judges not to carry on about the "enormities" of the royal monopoly of the drama until they have curbed the "enormities" of their own fair. In the process, they will come to recognize that they themselves participate in the imperfection for which they castigate others. At the end of the Induction, Jonson asks his viewers to judge the "ware" of his play by precisely the same standards that they would the wares of the fair; otherwise, the poet will "justly suspect that he that is so loth to look on a baby or an hobbyhorse here, would be glad to take up a commodity of them, at any laughter, or loss, in another place" (*Fair*, 34). That "other place" is Smithfield. Sober sorts who shrink from the vanities of the playhouse while allowing themselves to profit from the vanities of the fair are counseled to look to their motives.

If Jonson's case against the City of London is to gain conviction, however, he must demonstrate his proposition that the "ware" of the play and the "ware" of the fair are in fact the same. On the most obvious level, he accomplished this by making the two events coterminous. The fair is the play and the play, except for its opening scenes, is the fair. Any objection to the scurrility of one is at once an admission of the foulness of the other since the two are indistinguishable. Both are episodic in structure: the Induction enumerates the "sights" of the play as though they were a succession of spectacles at a fair, and the visitors to the fair watch its changing scene as they would the scenes of a play. Like a play, the fair has its "prologue" of a cutpurse and "five acts," its "orations" and its "tragical conclusions," and a player (Wasp) who is "Overparted" (*Fair*, 91, 96, 100). But Jonson is considerably wittier than that; the landscape of the fair symbolically recapitulates aspects of the Hope Theater, particularly those features its enemies found most reprehensible.

The poet sets us along the path of interpreting his work by pointing out a first element of correspondence between the two—their foulness—Smithfield and the Hope being equally "dirty" and "as stinking every whit" (*Fair*, 34). But the two locations have other physical features in common. The stage at the Hope was not the usual fixed platform, but a movable scaffold resembling the street stages used at fairs.[13] A major contribution to the Hope's stench was that it also served as a Bear Garden and the animals were stabled nearby. On alternate days its scaffold stage was removed and bearbaiting took the place of plays. After 1616 the theater was given over exclusively to bearbaiting, another monopoly of the king's and a frequent form of entertainment at court. City authorities opposed the sport as a danger to public order. In 1583 when a Paris Garden scaffold had collapsed during a Sabbath baiting, the Lord Mayor and other authorities had attributed the catastrophe to the wrathful hand of God, and the sport was not permitted in London.[14] But the City's own fair nevertheless boasts its own holiday bearbaiting: Ursula, the gargantuan brawling "enormity" at the heart of it, has a name signifying *little bear* and she is forever being baited by the other characters. Knockem calls her "my she-bear" and she disdains the "lion-chap" with which he snaps at her (lions did in fact bait bears—a variation on the sport introduced by King James himself). But her encounter with Knockem is a mere opening skirmish. When Quarlous and Winwife enter her booth, the baiting begins in earnest. They snap at the "she-bear," seeking to wear her down with wit, and she roars back with epithets which turn them into her dogs: "dog's-head" and mongrel "trendle-tail" (*Fair*, 80). She begins to tire, but after a brief mêlée and a scalding, she emerges the wounded but triumphant "Ursa major," as bears against dogs generally did.

Jackson Cope has pointed out that Jonson associates Ursula with the standard symbols of Ate, goddess of mischief and discord.[15] However Londoners may rail against royal bearbaiting as a source of riot and disorder, they harbor an equivalent manifestation of the Goddess Discordia in the center of their own fair. Just as the Hope Theater, in the Liberty of the Clink and safely out of their jurisdiction, was transformed into a bear ring every other night, so the "theater" of the fair becomes a ground for the baiting of Ursula. We know that puppet plays were sometimes performed after the baitings at Paris Garden, and the same custom was probably continued at its successor, the Hope. If, as some critics have suggested, Ursula's booth was either adjacent to or actually transformed into the puppet theater for act 5, then the imitative sequence is even closer. The scene of the fair becomes in turn a bear garden and then a puppet stage, as the Hope Theater did in 1614.[16]

Once Jonson's symbolic equivalence is established, it is easy to recognize how the particular types of foulness which surface in his fair parallel the vices City fathers berated in the theater. They condemned plays as the "occasyon of frayes and quarrelles" and argued that tolerance for the theater had brought the fall of Rome,[17] but their fair harbors equal disorder. In act 4, with its complicated and pervasive wrangling, any remaining semblance of social coherence breaks down into lawlessness. They complained that the theaters were a favorite resort of cutpurses and suppressed the jigs at the end of plays ostensibly for that reason in 1612, but at *Bartholomew Fair* cutpurses do a thriving business under the very noses of the authorities. They condemned plays as "very hurtfull in corruption of youth with incontinence and lewdness" and the "alleurynge of maides" into debauchery,[18] but their fair is equally rife with sexual laxity and in a more organized form. Even upstanding citizens like Win and Mrs. Overdo are easily enlisted among "my Lord Mayor's green women" (*Fair*, 146).

Plays, according to City authorities, were reprehensible even when they did not spawn worse forms of vice because such mere tinsel and trifles foolishly wasted "the time and thrift of many poore people." The fair is also crowded with cheap allurements and the promise that drums and rattles can transform a life. "What do you lack?", its vendors cry to all comers, and Bartholomew Cokes, a young person notably poor in judgment, heeds their cry, loading himself up with baubles more obviously superfluous than anything he would find at the theater. As Jonson may have known, Bartholomew Fair had been founded by a notable trifler, the court jester of King Henry I.[19] For Jonson's most unsympathetic contemporaries, plays were nothing less than madness: "What else is the whole action of Playes, but *well personated vanity*, artificiall folly, or a lesse Bedlam frenzie?"[20] Yet the madness of the stage yields nothing to the "frenzie" of the fair, which boasts its traditional resident maniac Arthur O'Bradley, which teems with fools natural and "artificiall," and where the very notion of sanity threatens to dissolve altogether.

Jonson's portrait of the fair also speaks to anti-theatrical arguments of an overtly Puritan stamp. Extremists among the Puritans likened playhouses to hell itself, calling them "devil chappels" and evoking lurid visions of the actions on stage as the machinations of demons, half-hidden in the stychian smoke of tobacco.[21] The same can be said of the fair. It is shrouded in noxious "vapors" and its center, Ursula's booth, is its bottomless inferno, belching forth fire and fumes. "Hell's a kind of cold cellar to't, a very fine vault" (*Fair*, 65), or if not Hell itself, then the hellish fires of paganism. Some of the most avid play-scourgers condemned drama on account of its heathen origins and its association with Roman fertility rituals and sacrifices, an argument which receives satiric short shrift in Jonson's own "*Execration upon* Vulcan" when he describes Puritan reaction to the burning of the Globe Theater in 1613:

> The Brethren, they streight nois'd it out for Newes,
> 'Twas verily some Relique of the Stewes:
> And this a Sparkle of that fire let loose
> That was rak'd up in the *Winchestrian* Goose
> Bred on the *Banck*, in time of Poperie,
> When *Venus* there maintain'd the Misterie.
>
> (*Jonson*, 8:209)

But as Jonson and other contemporary classicists knew, fairs, festivals, plays, (and even brothels), had been closely related cultural forms in classical times, found together as part of the same ceremonial structures. Jonson steeps his fair in paganism. It has its resident deities and heroes, an "Orpheus among the beasts," a "Ceres selling her daughter's picture in ginger-work," its Neptune and its Mercury, its "oracle of the pig's head," its overlay of fertility symbols and blessings for increase, its leafy pagan bowers (the fair booths), and its ritual sacrifices with fire "o' juniper and rosemary branches" (*Fair*, 76, 93). Eugene Waith suggests that the staging of the play may have been designed to emphasize the fair's connection with medieval and classical conventions: "The booths recall the mansions of the old mysteries, and more dimly, the houses of Plautus and Terence" (*Fair*, 217).

But Jonson's strongest argument for the hypocrisy of City authorities comes from the fact that all the dramatic arts they declaim against when supervised by the king, they permit in debased form as major attractions of the fair. The Smithfield area had lingering theatrical associations of its own. The royal office of the revels, which prepared masques and plays for court, had until 1607 been located near Smithfield, and Inigo Jones himself had been born in Saint Bartholomew Parish. Jonson certainly had this fact in mind, despite his disclaimers, when he created the character of Lanthorn Leatherhead, whose booth peddles the debased shards of masquing—puppets and tinsel baubles.[22] But the only masque contemplated at the fair is the forty-shilling wedding masque for Bartholomew Cokes—a travesty of the noble spectacles at court—to be scrapped together out of Leatherhead's fiddles and toys, Nightengale's doggerel, and Joan Trash's gingerbread. Smithfield was also associated with plays. The old interludes performed at Skinner's Well, some of them probably in connection with the Feast of St. Bartholomew, the patron saint of Skinners, had died out—perhaps as late as the 1580s[23]—but puppet plays, some of them with religious themes, were allowed at the fair. Near Smithfield there was also a theater, the notorious Red Bull, derided by contemporaries for catering to the lowest citizen tastes and noted from time to time for its attempts to stage opposition plays.[24] Appropriately, then, the reigning dramatic authority at the fair is John Littlewit, who stands upon the supremacy of law (his own) in the kingdom of wit. His wife is as well dressed as any of the wives of the players, and the local Justices of the Peace are on his side. While those "pretenders to wit," the "Three Cranes, Mitre, and Mermaid men," are dependent on "places" at court for their livelihood, he can "start up a justice of wit out of six-shillings beer, and give the law to all the poets and poet-suckers i' town" (*Fair*, 37).

But Littlewit's "dainty device" of a bawdy puppet play stands up rather poorly alongside the work of his rivals, the "Three Cranes, Mitre, and Mermaid men." His puppet play has all the external trappings of a regular stage play: "motions" and other visual effects, elaborate costumes, and an audience with the usual complement of dimwits who fail to understand the nature of dramatic illusion. In Littlewit's play, however, there is precious little but scurrility and illusion. Through the puppet play, Jonson cleverly exposes Smithfield theatrical tastes, which ran from empty spectacle to simplified rehash of the classics.[25] As Leatherhead explains, to play by the "printed book" would be "too learned and poetical for our audience" (*Fair*, 164). City moralists were tireless in condemning the "license" of the great theaters about London, yet allowed puppet plays at the fair—a drama deprived of noble essence and shabbily jumbled together like baubles from Leatherhead's stand.

Bartholomew Fair does have its would-be correctors: Humphrey Wasp, who buzzes against it out of some secret and incomprehensible wrath; Adam Overdo who tolerates the fair in theory but seeks to curb its enormities in the name of civic zeal; and Zeal-of-the-Land Busy, who declaims against plays, fairs, toys, and every sort of sport on grounds of Puritan principle. On the face of it, this acknowledgment of reforming efforts by contemporary magistrates and religious leaders would seem to blunt the force of Jonson's indictment. If the opponents of the king's public mirth were simultaneously working to redress kindred evils under their jurisdiction, then they were not easily accused of hypocrisy. But they all fail. At the end of the play, they have been disarmed and silenced while the fair continues unabated. And they all fail for the same basic reason: they are so blinded by their own unrecognized faults that they cannot discover what lies beyond. In the mirror of Jonson's play (which is simultaneously the fair) they unwittingly see themselves and their own secret vice. Each learns that the *tu quoque* applies to him.

NOTES

1. E.K. Chambers, *The Elizabethan Stage* (Oxford: Clarendon, 1923), 1:129–30; and William Rankins, *A Mirrour of Monsters: Wherein is plainely described the manifold vices ... caused by the infectious sight of Playes ...* (London, 1587), fol. 2. The Dryden quotation is from *Absalom and Achitophel*, line 873.

2. See the commendatory poems to Heywood's *Apology*, especially Richard Perkins's, fols. 22v–23r; William Prynne, *Histrio-Mastix* (London, 1633), 160; and Ian Donaldson, *The World Upside-Down: Comedy from Jonson to Fielding* (Oxford: Clarendon Press, 1970), 66–69.

3. I have tried to be exhaustive in my reading of *Bartholomew Fair* criticism and have gleaned some insight from nearly every piece I have read. I cannot hope to be exhaustive here; I mention only those works to which my own discussion is most greatly indebted. These include, among the "fair" critics, Jonas Barish, *Language of Prose Comedy* (Cambridge, Mass.: Harvard Univ. Press, 1960), 230–39; Joel H. Kaplan, "Dramatic and Moral Energy in Ben Jonson's *Bartholomew Fair*," *Renaissance Drama*, n.s. 3 (1970): 137–56; Richard Levin, "The Structure of *Bartholomew Fair*," *PMLA* 80 (1965): 172–79; Michael McCanles, "Festival in Jonsonian Comedy," *Renaissance Drama*, n.s. 8 (1977): 203–19; C. G. Thayer, *Ben Jonson: Studies in the Plays* (Norman, Oklahoma:

Univ. of Oklahoma Press, 1963), especially his discussion of Jonson's use of classical motifs; Eugene M. Waith's introduction to *Ben Jonson: Bartholomew Fair* (New Haven: Yale Univ. Press, 1963), 1–22; and above all, Ian Donaldson's stimulating discussion in *World Upside-Down*, 46–77 (note 2 above); and Susan Wells, "Jacobean City Comedy and the Ideology of the City," *ELH* 48 (1981): 37–60.

Among critics who emphasize the foulness of the fair, I am especially indebted to Jackson Cope, "*Bartholomew Fair* as Blasphemy," *Renaissance Drama* 8 (1965): 127–52; and Guy Hamel, "Order and Judgment in *Bartholomew Fair*," *University of Toronto Quarterly* 42–43 (Fall 1973): 48–67. In "Infantile Sexuality, Adult Critics, and *Bartholomew Fair*," *Literature and Psychology* 24 (1974): 124–32, Judith Kegan Gardiner sorts out various critical responses to the play in terms of its distinctive atmosphere of sexual regression. One of the best studies of the play's historical and economic context is Jonathan Haynes, "Festivity and the Dramatic Economy of Jonson's *Bartholomew Fair*," *English Literary History* 51 (1984): 645–68. L. C. Knights, whose studies of the contemporary context in *Drama and Society in the Age of Jonson* (London: Chatto & Windus, 1937) are otherwise most helpful, does not discuss *Bartholomew Fair* at all. In his essay "Ben Jonson, Dramatist" in Boris Ford, ed., *The New Pelican Guide to Literature 2: The Age of Shakespeare* (1955; reprinted, New York: Penguin, 1982), he claims that the play's "fun is divorced from any rich significance" (p. 416). My thanks also to Michael Shapiro, who generously allowed me to read his manuscript on the play.

4. Ben Jonson, *Bartholomew Fair*, 23.

5. For the activities of Lord Mayors, see Marchette Chute, *Ben Jonson of Westminster* (New York: Dutton, 1953), 215–16; E. A. Horsman, ed., *Bartholomew Fair* (Cambridge, Mass.: Harvard Univ. Press, 1960), xx–xxi; and David McPherson, "The Origins of Overdo: A Study in Jonsonian Invention," *Modern Language Quarterly* 37 (1976): 221–33. The 1613 Lord Mayor's Show had depicted just such activities as Overdo claims to engage in as laudable, so that Jonson's play can be seen on one level as an undoing of the previous year's pageant, just as *Love Restored* "undoes" the pageant for 1611. See David M. Bergeron, "Middleton's Moral Landscape: *A Chaste Maid in Cheapside* and *The Triumphs of Truth*," in *"Accompaninge the Players": Essays Celebrating Thomas Middleton, 1580–1980*, ed. Kenneth Friedenreich (New York: AMS Press, 1983), 133–46. For the Puritans see also the Dictionary of National Biography for Whatley; Henry Morley, *Memoirs of Bartholomew Fair*, 4th ed. (London: George Routledge & Sons, 1892), 140–41; the prefatory biography of William Whatley in his *Prototypes, or the Primarie Precedent ... Practically applied to our Information and Reformation* (London, 1640); and W[illiam] D[urham], *The Life and Death of that Judicious Divine, and Accomplish'd PREACHER, ROBERT HARRIS, DD.* (London, 1660), 25. John Stockwood's *A sermon Preached at Paules Crosse on*

Barthelmew day, being the 24, of August 1578 (London, 1578) is a splendid example of an attack on the theater made in connection with the fair.

6. Like Overdo, Coke was an "upstart" judge, had a loose and meddling wife, and was "silenced" by being removed from his post of Chief Justice of the Common Pleas to the post of Chief Justice of the King's Bench on 25 October 1613, a year before the premiere of Jonson's play. See Thayer, *Ben Jonson*, 144; and Catherine Drinker Bowen, *The Lion and the Throne: The Life and Times of Sir Edward Coke* (Boston: Little Brown, 1951), 125–26, 313–50.

7. See especially Donaldson, *World Upside-Down*, 50–59; and Wells, "Jacobean City," who has shown the play's engagement with issues relating to royal licensing. I am also indebted to Steven Mullaney's work on the ideology of theatrical marginality, in *The Place of the Stage: License, Play, and Power in Renaissance England* (Chicago: Univ. of Chicago Press, 1988).

8. In the absence of Privy Council records, elements of the conflict must be pieced together from other sources. For the general conflicts between the king and the City or town corporations during these years, see Chambers, *Elizabethan Stage*, I:337–38 and 4:249 (which describes a inflammatory 1608 sermon by William Crashaw that may have touched off a renewal of the old controversies in London); and Virginia Cocheron Gildersleeve, *Government Regulation of the Elizabethan Drama* (New York: Columbia University Press, 1908), 44–214. For an account of the controversy as carried out through pamphlet warfare, see Elbert N. S. Thompson, *The Controversy Between the Puritans and the Stage* (1903; rpt New York: Russell & Russell, 1966), 134–42; Richard H. Parkinson, ed., *An Apology for Actors (1612) by Thomas Heywood, A Refutation of the Apology for Actors (1615) by I. G.* (New York: Scholars' Facsimiles & Reprints, 1941); and for individual literary works which argue one side or the other, Robert Tailor, *The Hogge Hath Lost His Pearl* (printed in 1614), a play performed illegally by apprentices in 1613 and popularly taken to be about the controversy between the Lord Chamberlain and the Lord Mayor (a proof of the strength of the controversy in the public mind, since the work itself seems to carry only scattered references); *Hogge* is reprinted in Robert Dodsley, *A Select Collection of Old English Plays*, ed. W. Carew Hazlitt, vol. 11, 4th ed. (1875; reprint, New York: B. Blom, 1975), 423–99. See also the dedicatory poems to Heywood's Apology; the contemporary sermons and characters cited in Chambers, *Elizabethan Stage*, 4:254–59; and the skirmishes recorded in G. E. Bentley, *The Profession of Dramatist in Shakespeare's Time: 1590–1642* (Princeton: Princeton Univ. Press, 1971), 175–76. Coke himself had argued that local magistrates had the power to suppress the "abuse of *Stage Players*" at least in some cases. See *The Lord Coke His Speech and Charge* ... (London, 1607), sig. H2r.

9. Morley, *Memoirs*, 80–114.

10. Morley, *Memoirs*, 112; Chambers, *Elizabethan Stage*, 2:480. For an account of some of the limitations of the charter, see also Valerie Pearl, *London*

and the Outbreak of the Puritan Revolution: City Government and National Politics, 1625–43 (London: Oxford Univ. Press, 1961), 27–33.

11. Morley, *Memoirs*, 114; and for continuing pressure, *Analytical Index to ... the Remembrancia ... AD 1579–1664* (London: E. J. Francis, 1878), 471.

12. Morley, *Memoirs*, 172–81.

13. C. W. Hodges, *The Globe Restored: A Study of the Elizabethan Theatre*, 2d ed. (London: Oxford Univ. Press, 1968), 63.

14. Chambers, *Elizabethan Stage*, 2:453–54, 470–71; Gildersleeve, *Government Regulation*, 165.

15. Cope, "*Bartholomew Fair* as Blasphemy," 143–44.

16. See Hamel, "Order and Judgment," 63; William A. Armstrong, "Ben Jonson and Jacobean Stagecraft," in *Stratford-Upon-Avon Studies I, Jacobean Theatre* (London: Arnold, 1960), 54; the discussion of staging in Fair, 205–17; and Elliott Averett Dennison's excellent "Jonson's *Bartholomew Fair* and the Jacobean Stage," Ph.D. diss., Univ. of Michigan, 1970, 49.

17. Gildersleeve, *Government Regulation*, 156; and for later recapitulation of the same arguments, the anti-theatrical sources cited in note 8 above.

18. Quoted in Gildersleeve, *Government Regulation*, 164 and 156.

19. Gildersleeve, *Government Regulation*, 164; and Morley, *Memoirs*, 1–19.

20. Prynne, *Histrio-Mastix*, 174.

21. The most colorful example I have found is William Rankins's *Mirrour of Monsters* cited in note 1 above. Rankins later fell into the very vice he declaimed against and applied his fertile imagination to the writing of plays. See Elbert N. S. Thompson, *The Controversy between the Puritans and the Stage* (New York: Holt, 1903), 89.

22. Chambers, *Elizabethan Stage*, 1:102–3; and for the early life of Inigo Jones, Peter Cunningham, *Inigo Jones: A Life of the Architect* (London: Shakespeare Society, 1848), 1–4. Cunningham points out that Jones's father was a clothworker who lived in the clothworkers' area and is therefore certain to have had very close connections with the Smithfield cloth fair.

23. See Chambers, *Elizabethan Stage*, 2:119; Heywood, *Apology*, sig. G3r; and John Stow, *A Survey of London*, ed. C. L. Kingsford (Oxford: Clarendon Press, 1908), 1:16, 104. Morley (*Memoirs*, 65–67) speculates that religious plays may have survived in the Smithfield area even into Ben Jonson's adulthood.

24. On the reputation of the Red Bull, see G. E. Bentley, *The Jacobean and Caroline Stage* (Oxford: Clarendon, 1968), 6:238–47; on the staging of opposition plays, Margot Heinemann, *Puritanism and Theatre* (Cambridge: Cambridge Univ. Press, 1980), 231–32; and on the unlicensed theater, Chambers, *Elizabethan Stage*, 4:327. Thomas Dekker's *If This Be Not a Good Play, the Devil Is*

in It, a nearly contemporary opposition play, was, according to its 1612 title page, acted at the Red Bull. See also Martin Butler, *Theatre and Crisis 1632–1642* (Cambridge: Cambridge Univ. Press, 1984), 181–250.

25. Jonson may have had in mind works like Thomas Heywood's four plays in badly rhymed couplets on the golden, silver, bronze, and iron ages; they had been acted at the Red Bull and were published in London between 1611 and 1613.

STEPHEN ORGEL

The Royal Spectacle

Why did the Renaissance consider perspective settings and spectacular machinery particularly and exclusively appropriate to courts? The question is capable of several kinds of answers; we have already touched on two of them. Illusionistic theaters made of their audiences living emblems of the aristocratic hierarchy, and their costly scenic wonders constituted a prime instance of royal liberality, exemplifying the princely virtue of magnificence. But though both these answers point to significant qualities of the Renaissance spectacular stage, they do not really touch on the central issues: Why the intensity of interest in this mode of asserting the hierarchy? Why the enormous investment in this particular expression of magnificence? These are, at bottom, basic questions about the way in which the age saw itself.

Up to this point I have confined my discussion to drama; but, as we have seen, settings and machines were not used primarily for the production of plays. The new stage was developed largely for court masques, which were not, to the Renaissance, a kind of drama. It is important to begin by insisting on the difference between the two genres and by stressing the depth of the age's commitment to the masque as a form of expression. Masques were essential to the life of the Renaissance court; their allegories gave a higher meaning to the realities of politics and power, their fictions created heroic roles for the leaders of society. Critics from Puritan times onward have treated them as mere extravagances, self-indulgent ephemera. But in the culture of the Medici grand dukes, the courts of Navarre, Anjou, Valois, and Bourbon, the Venetian republic,

From *The Illusion of Power*. © 1975 by the author.

the Austrian archdukes, Henry VIII, extravagance in rulers was not a vice but a virtue, an expression of magnanimity, and the idealizations of art had power and meaning. This was the context in which James I, and above all Charles I, saw their own courts.

To the Renaissance, appearing in a masque was not merely playing a part. It was, in a profound sense, precisely the opposite. When Inigo Jones and Ben Jonson presented Queen Anne as Bel-Anna, Queen of the Ocean, or King James as Pan, the universal god, or Henry Prince of Wales as Oberon, Prince of Faery, a deep truth about the monarchy was realized and embodied in action, and the monarchs were realized in roles that expressed the strongest Renaissance beliefs about the nature of kingship, the obligations and perquisites of royalty. Masques were games and shows, triumphs and celebrations; they were for the court and about the court, and their seriousness was indistinguishable from their recreative quality. In England the form had roots in a strong native tradition of mummings and disguisings. It came into its own artistically with the accession of the first British Renaissance monarch, Henry VIII, who loved playing the central role in any enterprise, and retained the great composer William Cornysshe and the musicians of his Chapel Royal to provide his revels. For the next century and a half masques were staple elements of the Christmas and Shrovetide seasons, and formed an indispensable part of the courtly celebration of any extraordinary event, whether personal, social, or political—a royal marriage, the visit of a foreign dignitary, the conclusion of a treaty. In form they were infinitely variable, but certain characteristics were constant: the monarch was at the center, and they provided roles for members of the court within an idealized fiction. The climactic moment of the masque was nearly always the same: the fiction opened outward to include the whole court, as masquers descended from pageant car or stage and took partners from the audience. What the noble spectator watched he ultimately became.

The greatest problems in such a form are posed by protocol. Masquers are not actors; a lady or gentleman participating in a masque remains a lady or gentleman, and is not released from the obligation of observing all the complex rules of behavior at court. The king and queen dance in masques because dancing is the perquisite of every lady and gentleman. But playing a part, becoming an actor or actress, constitutes an impersonation, a lie, a denial of the true self. Hence "Woman-Actors," said William Prynne in 1633, with a large body of British opinion behind him, were "notorious whores."[1] For speaking roles, therefore, professionals had to be used, and this meant that the form, composite by nature, was in addition divided between players and masquers, actors and dancers. In the hands of Ben Jonson and Inigo Jones, this practical consideration became a metaphysical conceit, and the form as they developed it for James I and his queen, Anne of Denmark, rapidly separated into two sections. The first, called the antimasque, was performed by professionals, and presented a world of disorder or vice, everything that the ideal world of the second, the courtly main masque, was to overcome and supersede.

The masque presents the triumph of an aristocratic community; at its center is a belief in the hierarchy and a faith in the power of idealization. Philosophically, it is both Platonic and Machiavellian; Platonic because it presents images of the good to which the participants aspire and may ascend; Machiavellian because its idealizations are designed to justify the power they celebrate. As a genre, it is the opposite of satire; it educates by praising, by creating heroic roles for the leaders of society to fill. The democratic imagination sees only flattery in this sort of thing, but the charge is misguided, and blinds us to much that is crucial in all the arts of the Renaissance. The age believed in the *power* of art—to persuade, transform, preserve—and masques can no more be dismissed as flattery than portraits can. We do not consider portraits less "serious" than historical or religious or mythological paintings; nor do we assume that they have meaning only to their sitters; nor do we believe them to be beneath the dignity of a Titian or a Rubens.

It is probably the ephemeral quality of the form that really disturbs us most, conditioned by a strongly moral sense of artistic economy—all that money for only two performances! In fact, this was a standard Puritan objection to the masque, though with an important difference: the Puritan objection did not distinguish the masque from any other kind of art. Cromwell also closed the theaters, sold off the royal picture collection, and ordered statues defaced. We, however, do distinguish the arts; we assume that the ephemeral nature of the masque calls into question not only its potential as an investment, but even its seriousness. Behind this is another moral assumption, generally unacknowledged: that artists ought not to take such a form seriously; and that if they say they are doing so, they are dissembling their true motives. These claims are very common among modern scholars, but a little historical perspective will allow us to dispose of them. Renaissance festivals were the province of the greatest artists of the age; their number included Leonardo, Dürer, Mantegna, Holbein, Bronzino, Rubens, Buontalenti, Caron, Primaticcio, Callot, Monteverdi, Ferrabosco, Dowland, Campion, Lawes, Ronsard, Sidney, Jonson, and Milton. Masques and triumphs regularly had enormously elaborate and complex philosophical and symbolic programmes; the idea that these were somehow inappropriate to the form is both historically inaccurate and on the face of it illogical. No such charge appears until well into the seventeenth century, at which time it is rightly considered very new, and, as we shall see, both subversive and revolutionary. The question of seriousness, however, does bring us back to the main issues. A look at the exchequer records will show us that the court was indubitably serious about masques, and believed that there was some point in having the most distinguished artists devise them. In what ways, then, were masques serious?

Let us begin with the ways in which the age saw the monarchy. The Renaissance had many concepts of kingship, but central to all of them was the notion of the ruler as an exemplary figure. This was true whether he was conceived as God's regent on earth or as a Machiavellian politician, and throughout all the gradations in between. An Aristotelian might maintain that to be a good king it is necessary to have all the virtues, and a Machiavellian object that it is necessary only to seem to have them; but in either case it is the *image* of the monarch that is crucial, the appearance of virtue, whether it accords with an inner reality or not. The theatrical metaphor was a natural expression of such an attitude: "We princes, I tell you," said Queen Elizabeth, "are set on stages, in the sight and view of all the world duly observed."[2] James I made this a precept for his heir in his handbook of kingship, *Basilikon Doron*: "A King is as one set on a stage, whose smallest actions and gestures, all the people gazingly doe behold."[3] The monarch must not only impose good laws, he must exemplify them "with his vertuous life in his owne person, and the person of his court and company; by good example alluring his subjects to the love of virtue, and hatred of vice. ... Let your owne life be a law-booke and a mirrour to your people, that therein they may read the practise of their owne Lawes; and therein they may see, by your image, what life they should leade."[4]

Masques were the festal embodiments of this concept of monarchy. To Ben Jonson, far from being flattery, they were "the mirrors of man's life, whose ends, for the excellence of their exhibitors (as being the donatives of great princes to their people) ought always to carry a mixture of profit with them no less than delight."[5] Nor was the profit conceived in general or abstract terms. Court masques were always topical; under Charles I they argued the royal case in current political and legal disputes with an energy and ingenuity that suggests that the king must have been actively involved in their composition. Charles was not merely being entertained by his masques; the form was an extension of the royal mind, and—despite the universal British prejudice against actors—to take the stage was a royal prerogative. Perhaps the clearest illustration of how important the crown felt this prerogative to be may be found in the case of William Prynne, whose harsh words on women actors have already been cited.

Prynne was a barrister of Lincoln's Inn, an energetic and at times fanatical Puritan polemicist. In 1633 he published a gigantic attack on the theater entitled *Histrio-Mastix, or the Scourge of Players*. The book consists of a thousand pages of circular arguments and lunatic fulminations, but its authorities are the Bible and the church fathers, and it therefore carried weight with Puritan readers. The royal interest in drama is naturally, for Prynne, especially reprehensible. Watching plays is declared to be the "cause of untimely ends in Princes," and the histrionic Nero is adduced as an example. "Women-Actors, notorious whores" appears as an entry in the index; the king's attorney general took it to be an aspersion on the queen's participation in court theatricals. Prynne denied the allegation, but the evidence was considered ample, and he was arrested and charged, not with libel but with high treason. He was convicted by the Star Chamber and sentenced to life imprisonment, fined £5000, pilloried, expelled from Lincoln's Inn, deprived of his academic degree, and his ears were cut off by the public executioner.

Prynne was guilty not merely of an attack on the queen. There were many such that went unnoticed; against her Catholicism, her associates, her growing influence over the king. It was the attack on the queen as actress, on the royal theatricals, that was treasonable. The loss of Prynne's ears, freedom, and livelihood did not seem to the court too severe a penalty, nor did it seem to Prynne's Puritan supporters a punishment suffered in a trivial cause. Both sides rightly saw *The Scourge of Players* as a call to revolution, and Prynne became a popular hero.

Court masques and plays, then, were recognized to be significant expressions of royal power. The most important Renaissance commentary on the subject is itself a theatrical one, Prospero's masque in *The Tempest*. It is, of course, not a real masque, but a dramatic representation of one, and it is unique in that its creator is also the monarch at its center. This is Shakespeare's essay on the power and art of the royal imagination. By 1611, when *The Tempest* was produced at Whitehall before the king, the playwright's knowledge of the work of Jones and Jonson must have been intimate. With James's accession in 1603 Shakespeare's company had come directly under the king's patronage; he and the other directors were made Grooms of the Chamber, members of the royal household, and wore the royal livery. We know that after 1612 the King's Men were the regular professional players employed in the Christmas masques, and it is reasonable to assume that they had been at least occasionally so employed from the beginning of the reign. That all this conferred a new status on the company of actors is attested by the fact that around 1612 they also began calling themselves not merely the King's Men or the King's Servants, but Gentlemen, the King's Servants. Shakespeare's figure of Prospero, the royal illusionist, derives from a profound understanding of court theater and the quintessentially courtly theatrical form of the masque. Masques are the expression of the monarch's will, the mirrors of his mind.

Prospero produces his masque to celebrate the betrothal of his daughter Miranda to Ferdinand, heir to the throne of Naples; it is both a royal masque and a wedding masque. The lovers are shown a pastoral vision, presided over by Ceres and Juno. The goddess of agriculture directs the play back to civilized nature, away from Caliban's search for pig-nuts and the mysterious scammels, away from his dams for fish; and the goddess of power takes on her most benign aspect as patroness of marriage, pointing the way to a resolution of political conflicts, to the proper exercise of authority and the uniting of ancient enemies in nuptial harmony. All the destructive elements of love have been banished. Venus and Cupid, confounded by the chaste vows of Ferdinand and Miranda, are safely elsewhere. The agent of all this is Iris, the rainbow, the messenger of heaven and the pledge of God's providence after the universal flood.

The Tempest is temporally the most tightly and precisely organized of all Shakespeare's plays, the only one in which the action represented takes precisely as long as the performance of it. But the action of Prospero's masque has a different time scheme; it moves from "spongy April" through spring and high summer to the entry of "certain reapers," "sunburnt sicklemen, of August weary." After this Ceres promises Ferdinand and Miranda not the coming of winter, but

> Spring come to you at the farthest,
> In the very end of harvest.

The masque's world is able to banish even winter. As its love contains no lust, its natural cycle includes no death. Appropriately, it is at this point that the magician interrupts his creation to recall himself and the play to the other realities of the world of action. "I had forgot that foul conspiracy of the beast Caliban": it is precisely death, in the persons of Caliban, Stephano, and Trinculo, that threatens at this very moment. Prospero's awareness of time comprehends both masque and drama, both the seasonal cycle of endless fruition and the crisis of the dramatic moment. This awareness is both his art and his power, producing on the one hand his sense of his world as an insubstantial pageant, and on the other, his total command of the action moment by moment.

Prospero's vision of nature, then, is a vision in two senses. First, it is an imaginative projection for an audience—both the lovers and ourselves—of an ideal, a world of ordered and controlled nature from which all the dangerous potentialities have been banished. But it is also *Prospero's* vision, something unique to him, and a realization of the qualities of mind that have been controlling the play. The masque, with its apparitions and songs, and even more directly the tiny spectacular charades that Ariel performs for the shipwreck victims, are the royal magician's power conceived as art. In an obvious way that power is the power of imagination, but only if we take all the terms of the phrase literally. Imagination here is real power: to rule, to control and order the world, to change or subdue other men, to create; and the source of the power is imagination, the ability to make images, to project the workings of the mind outward in a physical, active form, to actualize ideas, to conceive actions.

The mind for Prospero, then, is an active and outgoing faculty (not, that is, a contemplative one), and the relation between his art and his power is made very clear by the play. His control over nature is exemplified in the masque, performed by spirits, extensions of his will, who act, in both senses, at his direction; Ariel, the spirit of air, is his servant; the destructive elemental forces are his to command. After the storm he has raised at the play's opening, he lays aside his wand, the symbol of his power, with the words "Lie there my art."[6] Miranda describes his power in the same terms:

> If by your art, my dearest father, you have
> Put the wild waters in this roar, allay them;

and she continues,

> Had I been any god of power, I would
> Have sunk the sea within the earth. ...[7]

Prospero is, of course, that god of power his daughter wishes to be: it is primarily his authority over elemental nature that is, for the age, godlike.

Modern critics are made exceedingly uncomfortable by the idea of Prospero as God. Can Shakespeare have meant to deify a figure so arbitrary, ill-tempered, vindictive? But Renaissance Christianity was not a comforting faith; we find Milton's God equally unsympathetic, and for similar reasons. Even the gentle George Herbert characterizes Christ in terms that are strikingly reminiscent of Miranda's view of her father: "Storms are the triumph of his art"; and a few lines later refers to him explicitly as "the God of Power."[8] We want our God all love, our Jesus meek and mild, but Herbert's God is, like Prospero, a god of storms and power too.

As with gods in the Renaissance, so with kings. Here is the legal philosopher John Selden on the right of monarchs to bar their territorial waters to foreign shipping:

> For, seeing it is in the power of an Owner, so to use and enjoy his Own ... , it cannot be amiss for any one to say, that the Seas, which might pass into the Dominion of any person, are by the Law of Dominion shut to all others who are not owners or that do not enjoy such a particular Right; in the same manner almost as that, whereby in that Winter-season they become unnavigable by the Law of Nature.[9]

Selden was not a fanatical supporter of Divine Right; on the contrary, he was a strong and litigious opponent of the autocracy of Charles I. Nevertheless he assumes that the appropriate analogy to the royal will in a commonwealth is the law of nature.

Again and again masques draw the same analogy. Pastoral, that traditionally contemplative mode, becomes an assertion of royal power; and the use of pastoral in masques is a remarkable index to the age's changing attitudes toward the monarchy. We may trace in this a significant development. In the early years of James I, when a pastoral scene appears as part of a sequence, contrasted with cities or palaces, it invariably comes at the beginning and embodies the wildness of nature or the untutored innocence that we pass beyond to clear visions of sophistication and order, usually represented by complex machines and Palladian architecture. But after about a decade, from 1616 onward, this sequence is reversed. When pastoral settings appear they come at the end, and embody the ultimate ideal that the masque asserts. For the earlier sequence we might take as the normative masque Jonson's *Oberon*, which opens with "a dark rock with trees beyond it and all wildness that could be presented," then moves to a rusticated castle, and concludes with a Palladian interior. For the later sequence, a good example is Jonson's *Vision of Delight*, which opens with a perspective of fair buildings, changes to mist and cloud, and concludes with the Bower of the Spring. There are of course any number of other instances, but the important point is that the sequences are invariable: in a Stuart court masque with this sort of structure, when a pastoral scene appears before 1616 it always comes at the beginning, after 1616 it always comes at the end.

Obviously two different notions of both nature and the function of pastoral are at work here. But the change is really more interesting for what it says about the masque and its patrons than for what it says about pastoral—it is no news that to the Renaissance, nature was either better or worse than civilization. There is more than mere contrast in Jones's and Jonson's transitions. In the early productions they conceive the masque as starting somewhere else, very far from the realities of Whitehall: a landscape, a great red cliff, an ugly hell. But the work concludes with the realities of the court: the queen on a throne surrounded by her ladies, or in a classical House of Fame; the Prince of Wales emerging from a Palladian *tempietto*. The architecture of these final visions extends the architecture of the colonnaded and galleried Banqueting House in which the performance itself is taking place, just as spectator merges with masquer in the great central dance.

But the later productions tend to start with the realities of Whitehall—in the cellars, in the court buttery hatch, or most often simply in the masquing hall itself, and the masque begins by claiming that what is taking place is not fiction but reality. Indeed, in the most extraordinary example, Jones, ignoring Jonson's text (which demands an indoor scene) opens *Time Vindicated* (1623) with a perspective setting of the façade of his own uncompleted Banqueting House. Even this, London's new Palladian masterpiece, is rejected in favor of a final pastoral vision of Diana and Hippolytus in a wood. The Caroline productions go even further, and tend to resolve all action through pastoral transformations. The apotheoses of nature become immensely complex and inclusive visual statements about the commonwealth, accommodating within their vistas even traditionally anti-pastoral elements—distant views of London, the fleet in full sail, the fortified castle at Windsor.

What is recorded in these productions is the growth of a political ideology. The masques of James I and Charles I express the developing movement toward autocracy—it is not accidental that Jones's pastoral visions become most elaborate during the 1630s, the decade of prerogative rule. Monarchs like Charles and his queen are doubtless attracted to the vision of themselves as pastoral deities because the metaphor expresses only the most benign aspects of absolute monarchy. If we can really see the king as the tamer of nature, the queen as the goddess of flowers, there will be no problems about Puritans or Ireland or

Ship Money. Thus the ruler gradually redefines himself through the illusionist's art, from a hero, the center of a court and a culture, to the god of power, the center of a universe. Annually he transforms winter to spring, renders the savage wilderness benign, makes earth fruitful, restores the golden age. We tend to see in such productions only elegant compliments offered to the monarch. In fact they are offered not to him but by him, and they are direct political assertions.

We might compare John Selden on the king's will as the law of nature with Jonson's justification of the appearance of spring in midwinter in *The Vision of Delight* (1617). The dialogue is between Fantasy and Wonder, embodiments of the creativity of the artist and the response of the spectator. Wonder asks,

> Whence is it that the air so sudden clears,
> And all things in a moment turn so mild?
> Whose breath or beams have got proud Earth with child
> Of all the treasure that great Nature's worth,
> And makes her every minute to bring forth?
> How comes it winter is so quite forced hence,
> And locked up underground? ...
> Whose power is this? What god?

Fantasy replies, gesturing toward King James,

> Behold a king
> Whose presence maketh this perpetual spring,
> The glories of which spring grow in that bower,
> And are the marks and beauties of his power.[10]

What is expressed through the unseasonable glories of nature and the scenic marvels of Vitruvian mechanics is royal power. The choir takes up the theme, turning it to a political affirmation, and initiating the court's revels:

> 'Tis he, 'tis he, and no power else
> That makes all this what Fant'sy tells;
> The founts, the flowers, the birds, the bees,
> The herds, the flocks, the grass, the trees
> Do all confess him; but most these
> Who call him lord of the four seas,
> King of the less and greater isles,
> And all these happy when he smiles.
> Advance, his favor calls you to advance,
> And do your this night's homage in a dance.[11]

The culmination of pastoral is, in the masque, the state and the court.

Or again, Jonson's *Mercury Vindicated from the Alchemists at Court*. The masque opens with alchemists practising below stairs; they have enslaved Mercury in their search for the Philosophers' Stone. They succeed, however, in producing only the deformed creatures who dance the antimasque. A seventeenth-century spectator would have seen more than contrast in the subsequent transition to the Bower of Nature: Mercury is the patron of alchemy precisely because he is the active principle in nature, and the concluding vision places him in his proper context. The metamorphosis is effected by the god himself invoking the present majesty, King James: "Vanish with thy insolence, thou and thy imposters, and all mention of you melt before the majesty of this light, whose Mercury I profess to be, and never more the philosophers'".[12] At this *the alchemists*' workshop vanished, and "the whole scene changed to a glorious bower wherein Nature was placed with Prometheus at her feet." Prometheus signified to the Renaissance human potentiality. As Mercury is freed, so Nature is restored by the royal power: "How young and fresh I feel tonight," she sings. The masque concludes, through its pastoral vision, with a living emblem of man's creativity.

Jonson's final masque, the pastoral *Chloridia*, with Queen Henrietta Maria at its center, and addressed to King Charles, abandons entirely the passive and contemplative aspects of the form, and becomes a hymn to the life of action. It manages to include among its various nymphs, floods, rivers, fountains, flowers, the very uncharacteristic figure of Fame, that arch-enemy of pastoral contentment, that last mental infirmity, that source of laborious days. She is accompanied by personifications of Poetry, traditional enough in pastoral, but also by History, and the city arts of Architecture and Sculpture, all uniting to sing the praises of the Caroline monarchy.

The vision of nature controlled by the human intellect is a central way of expressing the sovereign's place in the Renaissance universe. This is why the ceilings of palaces are so often, like the Whitehall Banqueting House, decorated with paintings depicting the apotheosis of the monarchy within a benign heaven. We put roofs on our houses because without them we are at the mercy of the weather. But having done so, the Renaissance ruler went on to create an alternative heaven, asserting his control over his environment and the divinity of his rule through the power of the art at his command. All this is a fantasy, no doubt; but it is a fantasy not only of monarchists and their artists. It is the chief end of Baconian science as well. "Of the sciences which regard nature," wrote Bacon in *The Great Instauration*, "it is the glory of God to conceal a thing, but it is the glory of the King to find a thing out."[13] The glory of the *king*, not of the scientist. The Renaissance empiricist was able to list among the promised benefits of the new learning the most fabulous wonders of masques: dominion over the seasons, the raising of storms at will, the acceleration of germination and harvest.[14] Every masque is a celebration of this concept of science, a ritual in which the society affirms its wisdom and asserts its control over its world and its destiny.

For modern readers, the scientific assumptions of the masque and the stage that was created for it require particular emphasis, because we are much more likely to view the form in terms of magic than of science. Thus a recent and very influential critic writes that the elaborate mechanics of the masque "were being used, partially at least, for magical ends, to form a vast moving and changing talisman which should call down divine powers to the assistance of the monarch."[15] Possibly; but no contemporary observer ever writes about the form in this way, and when the creators of masques explain what they are doing, it has nothing to do with magic. It has to do with wit and understanding, with the ability to control natural forces through intellect, with comprehending the laws of nature, and most of all, with our own virtue and self-knowledge. There are, to be sure, ways of describing virtue, knowledge, and science as magic, but that is not how the masques describe them. And when magic appears in the masques, it is regularly counteracted not by an alternative sorcery, black magic defeated by white magic, but by the clear voice of reason, constancy, heroism. Inigo Jones wrote that he had devised his splendid costume for Queen Henrietta Maria in *Tempe Restored* "so that corporeal beauty, consisting in symmetry, color, and certain unexpressible graces, shining in the queen's majesty, may draw us to the contemplation of the beauty of the soul, unto which it hath analogy."[16] Masques are not magical talismans, they are analogies, ideals made apprehensible, so that we may know ourselves and see what we may become.

This is not to say that such a patron as Charles I did not rely on these visions of permanence and transcendence in a way that we may call magical. There are always people who believe in magic. He also relied on judicial decisions, architectural façades, and depictions of himself in imperial trappings in precisely the same way, and, like all magical thinkers, without any ability to perceive such phenomena in relation to their real effects. But insofar as the texts give us evidence, Jones and his poets did not think of their creations in this way. What is provided for the court is not a mystic charm, but roles to play that relate the present to the heroic ideals of the past on the one hand, and to the immutable laws of nature on the other. They teach, they celebrate virtue, they persuade by example; they lead the court to its ideal self through wonder.

So the king is allegorized in ways that imply intellect, control, power: as Neptune, tamer of the elements, or Pan, the god of nature, or the life-giving sun, or, in a Jonsonian *tour de force*, as pure energy, a principle of physics, through whom the ultimate mysteries of infinite power and perpetual motion are finally solved:

Not that we think you weary be,
For he
That did this motion give,
And made it so long live,
Could likewise give it perpetuity.

Nor that we doubt you have not more,
And store
Of changes to delight;
For they are infinite,
As is the power that brought those forth before.[17]

Jonson's metaphor expresses not only the absolute authority increasingly asserted by the Stuart monarchy, but even more the age's wonder at the infinite possibilities of machinery scenic or otherwise. The metaphor will seem less far-fetched if we set beside it a passage by Marsilio Ficino, the great Florentine neo-Platonist, discussing mechanical models of the heavenly spheres:

> Since man has observed the order of the heavens, when they move, whither they proceed and with what measures, and what they produce, who could deny that man possesses as it were almost the same genius as the Author of the heavens? And who could deny that man could also make the heavens, could he only obtain the instruments and the heavenly material, since even now he makes them, though of a different material, but still with a very similar order?[18]

This is the context within which the court audience saw the masque, with its scenic illusions and spectacular machines: as models of the universe, as science, as assertions of power, as demonstrations of the essential divinity of the human mind. The marvels of stagecraft—the ability to overcome gravity, control the natural world, reveal the operation of the heavenly spheres—are the supreme expressions of Renaissance kingship.

NOTES

1. In *Histrio-Mastix, or the Scourage of Players*, 1633. See below, pp. 43–44.

2. J. E. Neale, *Elizabeth I and her Parliaments* (New York, 1958) 2:119.

3. C. H. McIlwain, ed., *Political Works of James I* (Cambridge, Mass., 1918), p. 43.

4. *Ibid.*, p. 30.

5. *Love's Triumph through Callipolis*, lines 3 ff.

6. 1.2.25.

7. 1.2.1–11.

8. "The Bag," lines 5, 9.

9. *Mare Clausum* (London, 1663), f2r.

10. Lines 164–192.

11. Lines 194–203.

12. Lines 166 ff.

13. R. F. Jones, ed., *Essays, etc.* (New York

14. *Magnalia Naturae*, in Bacon's *Works*, (London, 1887–1892) 3:167–168.

15. Frances Yates, *Theatre of the World* (Lo

16. Lines 361–364.

17. *News from the New World*, lines 342–35

18. From *Platonic Theology*, trans. Josephi *History of Ideas* 5 (April, 1944):235.

G.K. HUNTER

Tragicomedy

Philip Sidney thought of tragicomedy as a 'mongrel' form, supposing that both social decorum and classical tradition (not easily distinguished) demanded a mutual accommodation of form and content such as comedy and tragedy separately provide. Battista Guarini, in the practice of *Il pastor fido* (1590) and the theory of the *Compendio della poesia tragicomica* (1603), looked rather for the tension of potential imbalance that an integrated form offering near-death but no-death provides, and argued that this was a more appropriate mode for a Christian civilization. Fletcher's *The Faithful Shepherdess* (1608) brought this baroque ideal to the attention of the London audience of the boys' theatre. But even this élite group was not much taken with such continental novelties. They were looking, Fletcher tells us in his Preface, for 'a play of country hired shepherds ... sometimes laughing together, and sometimes killing one another' (as in Greenian pastoral romance). True pastoral tragicomedy, he declares, is not an alternation of kissing and killing, but is defined by the fact that 'it wants deaths, which is enough to make it no tragedy, yet brings some near it, which is enough to make it no comedy; which must be a representation of familiar people, with such kind of trouble as no life be questioned, so that a god is as lawful in this as in a tragedy, and mean people as in a comedy'.

It is no accident that these remarks relate to a play written for the boys' theatre. I have described their repertory as one of self-conscious innovation, in which static satire (which limits mobility of character) and dynamic comedy (that opens it up) struggled for union. In 1604 Marston defined the resultant form (as

---

From *English Drama 1586–1642: The Age of Shakespeare*. © 1997 by Oxford University Press.

it appeared in *The Malcontent*) as *Tragiecomedia* in the Stationers' Register and as *aspera Thalia* in the dedication. In practice, of course, 'wanting deaths but bringing some near it' was already characteristic of both public and private theatre; the plays of prodigals (see Chapter 8) fulfil this requirement almost in excess, requiring their protagonists to stand under the gallows before the charges can be dropped and the hero returned to happiness. But Fletcher adds a dimension incompatible with this when he speaks of 'such kind of trouble as no life be questioned', which seems to imply that the 'bringing some near' to death cannot be handled too realistically. We must, presumably, be assured that we are watching a world in which the threats are too stylized (as in pastoral) to cause any actual anxiety.

William Empson has pointed out with exemplary élan, in his Some Versions of Pastoral, that pastoral is basically concerned with imaginary solutions to class divisions. In the sixteenth century the only acceptable solution required that the division be preserved but that its political meaning become invisible. This is the mode of *The Faithful Shepherdess* (though not of Sidney's *Arcadia*) and we can see the Beaumont and Fletcher dramaturgy up to this point as a set of steps to turn the standard play forms towards that invisibility.

The Prologue to *The Woman Hater* (1606) illustrates the degree of self-consciousness involved, not only of fashion ('Gentlemen, Inductions are out of date, and a Prologue in verse is as stale as a black velvet cloak and a bay garland'[1]) but of the authors' own contribution to the change:

> I dare not call it a comedy or tragedy; 'tis perfectly neither .... Some things in it you may meet with which are out of the common road: a duke there is, and the scene lies in Italy, as those two things lightly we never miss. But you shall not find in it the ordinary and overworn trade of jesting at lords and courtiers and citizens, without taxation of any particular or new vice by them found out but at the persons of them. Such he that made this thinks vile; and for his own part vows that he did never think but that a lord born might be a wise man and a courtier an honest man. (Prologue, ll. 12–26)

One thing is clear in this Prologue: the satiric impulse that lies behind the dramaturgy of Marston and Jonson (with its sharp antinomies in style and structure) is being disowned (as is, one might add, the whole tradition that descends from the Morality play). The author, we are told, 'means not to purchase [his audience] at the dear cost of his ears' (as the authors of *Eastward Ho* had been in danger of doing).[2] The loosely articulated plot is carried by a smooth and fluent verse that engages our admiration but distances it. This is an Italian dukedom, as the Prologue says, but the court's corruption is presented as a source of laughter not anger, and the duke's political function is mentioned only to be denied. We begin with the 'humorous' duke getting up at four in the morning.

His courtiers guess that this is the beginning of a disguised duke play. Has he risen 'to cure some strange corruptions in the commonwealth' or 'to walk the public streets disguised / to see the street's disorders'? No. 'I break my sleeps thus soon to see a wench' (I. i. 11–29).

There is no evidence that *The Woman Hater*, in spite of its claim to novelty, raised much interest. The second Beaumont and Fletcher play, *Cupid's Revenge* (c. 1607–1612), seems, however, to have been one of the most prized properties of the Queen's Revels company,[3] as that body passed through its various transformations.[4] It was played at court in 1612, 1613 (twice), 1624, and 1637. This time the authors start from the tragic end of the spectrum, picking up a melodramatic confrontation with evil from Sidney's *Arcadia*.[5] A tense political situation is offered, but politics is evaded. An infatuated old king is destroying the integrity of the State, but the noble prince cannot deal with what is happening except in terms of personal relationships. Cynical commentary by the courtiers is presented but is not given any political significance; their attitudes point to natures disengaged from any active interchange with the system. The 'humours' that drive the characters confine them to set roles, but these are not held up to scorn; they are shown merely as representations of social fact.

Beaumont and Fletcher's enormously popular play for the boys, *The Scornful Lady* (1613–1616), begins as if it was going to be a Middletonian city comedy. The young heir loses the mortgage on his estates to a city usurer. And, as usual, the usurer's next target, a rich city widow, is more affected by the young heir's sexual potential than by the old man's money bags. But no intrigue emerges from this situation. The prodigal heir recovers his fortune without wit or reformation. Opposites are placed in relation to one another as psychological elements not as pressures in society and can be resolved without social consequence. The young man's erotic energy is separated from economic and political disruption; his desires can be fulfilled without bringing into play the contradictions of society. The usurer repents and gives away his money; the economic potential of the story is lost in the complexities of the struggle for personal 'maistrie' in the will-she-won't-she main plot.[6]

In these terms it does not appear that Fletcher's *The Faithful Shepherdess* is, as often thought, an extraordinary diversion from the main line of the Beaumont and Fletcher canon. One can recognize that, though it comes at the issue from a different direction, it centres on the same reduction of politics to erotics as has been noticed above. Chastity has become the controlling feature of social life in this never-never land of self-sufficient amours. Varieties of sexual arrangements are presented (as elsewhere in the *œuvre*) but all are subjected to a single standard, enforced in Clorin's reeducation establishment. The liberation of the female voice, even inside the practical arrangements of Jacobean social life, is one of the triumphs of this new depoliticized drama; but the failure of *The Faithful Shepherdess* in the playhouse seems to show us that Italian avant-gardism had pushed the point beyond what London was prepared to tolerate.

This same time saw a number of institutional changes, however, that altered the balance of audience and dramaturgy in the capital and affected the fortunes of tragicomedy. In Chapter 7 I have already spoken about the collapse of the boys' theatres in this period.[7] The King's Men reacquired the boys' space in the Blackfriars in 1608, but seem not to have occupied it until 1610, when the plague abated. Some of this time was no doubt spent considering the dramaturgy that could marry the innovations of the children to the ever-popular romantic adventures of the adult stage. And Shakespeare, as a shareholder, was no doubt part of this consideration. Did he respond by writing a new kind of comedy (now usually called 'romance')?[8] We cannot be sure whether Pericles was planned before the buyout of the Blackfriars, but the uncertainty should not prevent us from considering dramaturgical connections.

Perhaps even more important for the future of the company than Shakespeare's gear change was Beaumont and Fletcher's move from the boys to the men.[9] Though *The Faithful Shepherdess* had been a flop, the literary and social avant-garde rushed to its rescue, attaching their poetic testimonials to the quarto publication (probably in the same year). So there was some approval of Guarinian tragicomedy among the cognoscenti. The thirty-eight poems set before the 1647 Folio of the Beaumont and Fletcher *Comedies and Tragedies*,[10] written by all the most distinguished cavalier wits and poets of the time, tell us retrospectively that the King's Men had found a key to the taste of a newly self-conscious literary élite, so ensuring dominance in court and polite drama throughout the first half of the century.

Four interconnected aspects of the compromises in dramaturgy that the institutional change produced can be described here: Shakespearian Romance, collaboration and contrast between Shakespeare and Fletcher, a Fletcherian dramaturgy centred on tragicomedy, a more diffused taste for tragicomedy by Fletcher's contemporaries and imitators.[11] I treat these topics in that order.

SHAKESPEARE AND ROMANCE

The standard chronology tells us that some time around 1607 Shakespeare wrote Pericles, as the first in a series of four plays—Pericles (1606–1608), *Cymbeline* (c.1608–1611), *The Winter's Tale* (c.1610–1611), and *The Tempest* (1611)—that are not only closely related to one another in structure but are different from all the comedies he had written before. *Pericles* seems to mark a decisive turn in Shakespeare's dramaturgy,[12] and perhaps for this reason (as well as the obvious corruption of the extant text) it looks a less finished product than the plays which followed.[13] Indeed it is only in the twentieth century (following the establishment of a consensus chronology) that critics have taken to arguing its genre; but the popularity of the play in its own age tells us that contemporaries did not find generic indeterminacy a bar to popular esteem; it was reprinted five times between 1609 and 1635 (giving it second place in the Shakespeare quick reprint stakes—*I Henry IV* comes first). The source story, Which Shakespeare had already used for the Aegeon plot in *The Comedy of Errors*, is drawn from the Latin (perhaps originally Greek) romance of *Apollonius of Tyre*. Two English versions of this are used in the play: Gower's, from the *Confessio amantis* of the late fourteenth century, and Lawrence Twine's *The Pattern of Painful Adventures: Containing the History of Prince Apollonius* (1594; 1607). Even if Shakespeare's attention was stimulated by the 1607 publication of Twine, none the less it was Gower he chose as his presenter, and the choice indicates something about the response he was aiming at. Gower begins by telling us that this is 'a song that old was sung', one which

> Hath been sung at festivals
> On ember eves and holidays,
> And lords and ladies in their lives
> Have read it for restoratives.
>
> (Act I, Chorus, ll. 5–8)

The story is presented to an audience with 'wits more ripe' as a distanced and naïve piece of ancient fiction. They are invited to construe it from the vantage point that allows sophisticated persons to enjoy fairy stories and folk-tales, narratives of marvels and surprises, flat characters, sudden conversions, long-drawn-out alternations of good and bad fortune. Tragic emotions are presented in terms of description rather than experience, and suffered across the many contrasting locations that exemplify, and to some extent predetermine, the alternations of sorrow and joy (and of the generic modes that convey them). But Shakespeare's concern is not only to flatter the audience's sophistication; he uses the story to focus for naïve as well as sophisticated the pattern of an individual's struggle to maintain identity in an essentially unstable world—the same pattern as in the Henslowe historical romances. In these terms *Pericles* seems well designed to appeal to the mixed audience of the Globe and the Blackfriars.

Ben Jonson thought *Pericles* 'a mouldy tale',[14] and by neoclassical standards almost everything is wrong with it. But public approval clearly encouraged Shakespeare and company to build on its success. Sophisticated nostalgia for older modes may be seen as a key to open up a new dramaturgy at once artful and emotional, distanced and immediate, romantic and comic.[15]

In writing in this way, Shakespeare was not flaunting innovation. He was, in fact, returning to the mainline taste of the Elizabethan theatre. E. C. Pettet in his *Shakespeare and the Romance Tradition* notes that the new Shakespearian mode aimed 'deliberately at the far-fetched, the astounding and the incredible ... quite unhampered by any considerations of verisimilitude ... With realism jettisoned, extravagance becomes a virtue' (p. 163).[16] It would be hard to find a better description of such paradigms of the Henslowe repertory as *The Four Prentices of London* (1592–c.1600), *Look About You* (c.1598–1600), *The Blind Beggar of*

Alexandria (1596). The revised version of *Mucedorus*, played at court by the King's Men-in 1610, is sometimes cited as evidence of a resuscitated taste for romance, but a look at the overall repertory detects no need for resuscitation. The deservedly obscure play, *The Thracian Wonder*, attributed to Webster and Rowley in the first and only edition of 1661 and dated 1599—c.1600 in Harbage—Schoenbaum shows us how closely Shakespeare's romances can be anticipated (or reproduced—the dates are impossible to fix) in the popular repertory.[17] But there is no need to suppose direct contact. The plot of *The Thracian Wonder* comes from Greene's Menaphon (of 1589, 1599, 1605, 1616), while the plot of *The Winter's Tale* comes from Greene's *Pandosto* (reprinted twenty times before 1700). The continuity of these romantic confections across (and far beyond) the lifespan of Elizabethan drama points to their centrality in the taste of the time, whatever Jonson or Marston had to say about 'unpossible dry fictions' (see p. 262). The basic mechanisms of the mode (loss of status and identity, exile, incoherent travel punctuated by idyllic resting places, plots straggling across large tracts of time, marvellous coincidences, violent but inconclusive passions) not only persist inside the historical romances; they lurk behind the realism of the Prodigal Son plays and now they re-emerge in Shakespeare's repertory in their full Greenian form.

We see him now, at the end of his career, no longer controlling romance by what I have called 'unindulgent' structures (p. 390), but accepting romantic premises without seeking to balance them, either by the commentary of cynical clowns[18] or by the trickery of competent women. The central characters are now left open to change of fortune without any compensating idea that fortune can be *made*. In consequence, the double-plot structure, as a formal expression of balance, now carries less burden. When these late plays break in two, the contrasting halves are laid end to end and measure social distinction less than the chronological gap between destruction and reparation. Yet for all the arbitrariness of the plots, one may argue that they still display the mixed-mode kind of unity that Guarini had recommended; they are held together by a unified poetic that demands a response somewhere between sad acceptance of evil and a vision of love.

It is *The Winter's Tale* that confirms, beyond the other 'romances', the continuity[19] of these plays with the romantic taste of the 1590s. The political issues evident in *Pericles* and *Cymbeline* are attenuated here, and dominated by purely personal emotions. These bring into clearest view the primacy of an idea that in *Pericles* and *Cymbeline* only shares the limelight—the idea of power vested in the innocent girl whose self-sufficiency enables her to penetrate behind the political evil that controls the world. And so she can play a queen and reinvent the ideal world that the 'real' authority of the king her father could only destroy.[20] In *The Tempest* the pattern is seen largely in retrospect. The play begins at the point that *The Winter's Tale* reaches only in Act IV. The generating evil is now in 'the dark backward and abysm of time' and a continent apart. But once again the heritage of shared political corruption has to be relived in personal anguish before it can be converted into reparation, once again less by action than by a change in moral vision. Prospero is both victim and (as he intends) victimizer; and so the turning of evil into good, revenge into forgiveness, tragedy into comedy, has to be achieved inside the father's mind; the recuperative innocence of the daughter[21] is an adjunct but not a cause. The key exchange that points us to the transformation is handled in the more abstract and impersonal terms of Ariel's commentary on the sorrow and bewilderment of the imprisoned evildoers: 'if you now beheld them, your affections / Would become tender' and Prospero's response: 'Hast thou, which art but air, a touch, a feeling / Of their afflictions, and shall not myself, / One of their kind, that relish all as sharply / Passion as they, be kindlier moved than thou art? ... The rarer action is / In virtue than in vengeance' (v. i. 18–28). The distanced calm of *The Tempest* reveals it as more a commentary on Shakespeare's Romance dramaturgy than an enactment of it.

SHAKESPEARE AND FLETCHER

Shakespeare's romances can be linked not only to his own comedies but to the whole tradition of popular romance that spans the period. The tragicomedies of Beaumont and Fletcher, on the other hand, exemplify the new dramaturgical ideals that were to dominate the London theatre until 1642. Shakespeare uses the romantic evocation of wonder to suggest the capacity for redemption in human nature, set against larger patterns of selfishness and love, loss and recovery, manipulation and innocence; Beaumont and Fletcher use very similar patterns to suggest rather the indeterminacy of human experience in what Herbert Blau has called 'a repertoire of intense emotions achieved ... without any essential continuity or metaphysical ground.'[22] Yet the two modes share a great deal, and there is one play which ought to show what happens when shared authorship brings the two dramaturgies together.

The Two Noble Kinsmen (1613–1614) is described on its title-page as 'written by the memorable worthies of their time, Master John Fletcher and Master William Shakespeare, Gentlemen'. The plot's derivation from Chaucer's *The Knight's Tale* places it in the same region as the first half of *Pericles*, the region of chivalric love and honour, with the winning of noble ladies by deeds of prowess. But in *Pericles*, disillusioning experience leads the knightly hero into a humanized world we can respond to more directly. In *Two Noble Kinsmen* we are never allowed to be this close to the rituals of Palamon and Arcite, Theseus and Emilia. The bourgeois sub-plot in which a rustic lover has to take the name of Palamon in order to secure the attention of his beloved, remains too remote from the actions it parodies to provide any kind of bridge.[23] This regularly disappoints those who come to The *Two Noble Kinsmen* looking for Shakespeare's internalizing dramaturgy. But we should notice not only that ritual appears recurrently in Shakespeare's Romances (the oracle in *The Winter's Tale*, the 'banquet' in *The Tempest*), but that Fletcher also seems to have given up something of his characteristic quality—his typical complexity of plot and switches of focus. In its stately and muted mode of action perhaps we should see *Two Noble Kinsmen* as a work of two authors trying not to tread on one another's toes.

To get a purchase on the similarities and differences between Shakespearian romance and Fletcherian tragicomedy it is probably better to look at plays, written close in time, in which the separate authors are committed to their separate modes. The dates of *Philaster: or Love Lies a-Bleeding* (1608–1610) and *Cymbeline* (c.1608–1611) do not supply answers to the standard question, 'who learned what from whom'. Yet the two plays can surely be called contemporaries; we can see them responding (in similarity and difference) to the same pressures and fashions. And so we can understand both what was available and what was chosen.

Andrew Gurr, in the introduction to his edition of *Philaster*,[24] has suggested that the authors draw on their romance sources—Sidney's *Arcadia* (as in *Cupid's Revenge*) and Montemayor's Diana—less for the sake of the stories than for the conventions of character (or rather, ethos) that the stories exemplify,[25] particularly the conventions of idealized love set in confrontation with cynical lust, and of honourable self-sacrifice in the face of a corrupt world, found in both men and women. These are conventions, we should notice, that define individuals rather than societies; their relevance to action in the public sphere remains oblique.

Philaster begins with a description of a political situation: Sicily is ruled by a usurper, though the rightful heir (*Philaster*) still lives in freedom, protected by the knowledge that any harm done to him will result in a popular uprising. We hear of the king's plan to strengthen his hold on the country by marrying his daughter and heir to a Spanish prince. A situation in delicate balance between political possibilities is thus set up; but the play is not interested in advancing along political lines. It immediately moves its focus to the sex lives of the persons involved; and the central issues of the play will recurrently show us political ends as only reachable by sexual means. The Spanish prince hopes to be given immediate access to the bed of his betrothed, but, repulsed by the chaste princess as a gross boor, he quickly satisfies his needs elsewhere; the political plot can now be frustrated by a revelation of his unsuitability as a husband (or so we might think). The princess and the true heir are chaste and ideal lovers, but slander from the Spaniard's mistress—that the princess has sexual relations with *Philaster's* page Bellario (actually a girl in love with *Philaster*)—is easily believed in this cynical society, even by *Philaster* himself. The ideal characters are rendered politically impotent by the waves of grief and anger, condemnation and self-reproach, that sweep them from side to side. Aiming at generosity and nobility they are unable to turn their ideals into actions. The moral anarchy of a society unable to separate private from public can be ended only when political necessity breaks into the magic circle of personal distress. The king arrests the prince, and the populace rises in revolt. National stability can be restored only by the marriage of prince and princess—a stability now based on personal qualities of chaste and selfless virtue; innocent love and political correctness become joint enabling powers, so that misrepresentations can be cleared up and all can end happily.

An analysis of *Cymbeline* yields a very similar pattern: chaste love in Posthumus and Imogen, forbidden by the king, spotted by evil lust in Iachimo and Cloten, leads to female self-sacrifice, guilt and agony over loss of identity, all caught up in the political issues of a remote time which can achieve peace only when purity of motive is revealed as the ethical basis of the state. But ethics is not buried under cynicism in *Cymbeline* as in *Philaster*, so that redemption can be more easily believed. Shakespeare's good characters have a sustaining continuity in their sense of self and world which enables them to take responsibility for their reactions. We can easily understand the movement of their lives even while the changing world is forcing them to change position. Likewise with the evil characters: Iachimo, the Queen, Cloten show qualities which are individual rather than representative. And so we understand their changes of role as aspects of character rather than justifications for the theatrical *frisson* of surprise. The Queen, who is in part a fairy-tale witch like that in *Snow White*, and Cloten, the traditional uncouth witch's son (like the 'losel' in *The Faerie Queene*, III. vii), lead the nation in its patriotic defiance of Rome, and they are 'sorely missed' when the Romans attack; but we are invited less to gasp at the shift of focus than to register how a person who seems vicious in one context can be virtuous in another. Posthumus first exalts and then curses the sexuality of Imogen, and so finds himself, like *Philaster*, caught between opposed emotions. But these personal issues do not become mirrors of state policy; we see them cross-cut and counterchecked by other personal business. The heroine herself can show us, in typical Shakespearian fashion, a more direct way of drawing on resources of character to overcome misfortune.

A glance at the denouements of the two plays shows some of the ways in which these distinctions shape the meanings we attach to the action. The denouement of *Philaster* works as a series of increasingly desperate reversals as characters are required to deal with situations they cannot understand and actions they cannot justify. The fourth act in the woods has shown us *Philaster* dragged into meaninglessness, stabbing the Princess (although not wishing to), being wounded by an intervening 'country gentleman'—who seems incapable of understanding the protocol of courtly stabbing—crawling away into the forest (while not wishing to), finding his page Bellario asleep, wounding him to deceive the pursuers (and immediately regretting it), being hidden by Bellario, who would rather die than betray his master, allowing the pursuers to drag Bellario away, and then crawling out of the brush to demand that they recognize that he himself is the guilty party. The fifth act finds *Philaster*, the Princess, and Bellario all in prison. Each one wishes to die for the others. But the populace revolts, captures and tortures the Spaniard. *Philaster* must take charge, and can save the day and the Spaniard by marrying the Princess. But even at this point there is a last twist to the tale. The accusation of unchastity between the Princess and Bellario resurfaces. Bellario must be stripped and tortured. The melodrama of this occasion produces the surprising discovery that the page is a girl; and so the Princess *must* be innocent, and all is well—but only for the moment, we must feel, in a world so composed (like a Matisse painting) of brilliant juxtapositions on a flat surface.

The concentration in this process is on states of mind (rather in the mode of *nouvelle vague* films), not on the alternative lines of action available to a unified moral purpose.[26] In *Cymbeline*, however, the denouement is not expressed by an alternating current between emotional polarities, but must be discovered in the destiny the gods have laid up for the family and the state. The Act V changes of Posthumus from Roman to Briton and back to Roman again represent not only an emotional switchback but an effort—controlled by the need to achieve a single and well-understood end—to die in expiation for his sin against Imogen. The major change in him is achieved by the vision of Jupiter and his parents, where he learns that 'the strength of the Leonati' he thought he needed to face guilt is in fact a strength needed for life. This gives him (and us) an assurance that *Philaster* does not search for—that the apparent psychological instabilities are only the troubled surface of a stable universe. The extraordinary series of recognitions in the last scene is not only a theatrical *tour de force* but also an enactment of the interconnected strength of this world, as each revelation inevitably triggers the next one (as Iachimo's confession leads to Posthumus', Posthumus' to Imogen's, Imogen's to Pisanio's, Pisanio's to the tale of Cloten's mission, the tale of Cloten to Guiderius' confession, Guiderius' to Bellarius'), so that the whole tangled skein is reduced to a straight thread, as predicted in the tablet that Jupiter handed down. The stability of the British state is not underwritten by the forced conversion of the king's character as in *Philaster* ('Let princes learn / By this to rule the passions of their blood' (V. v. 216–17)), but by a conjoint acceptance of the supernatural order that stands above kings:

> Laud we the gods,
> And let our crooked smokes climb to their nostrils
> From our blest altars.
>
> (V. v. 476–8)

As the camera draws back for the final take, what is revealed in these late Shakespeare plays is that the whole scene corresponds to a pattern laid up on high, now miraculously reassembled out of all the jarring elements that have seemed to compose it. The dead are returned to life, not merely in the discovery of their lost social identities, but as recreated out of emptiness, from the despair and helplessness that has imprisoned them in their pasts, making them no longer able to imagine renewal. The catatonic *Pericles*, who has seen his wife's coffin and daughter's tomb, Imogen, who has seen her husband's dead body, the guilt obsessed Leontes, the revenge obsessed Prospero, are all rewarded for an underlying continuity of purpose they did not know they possessed. The excitement of a Beaumont and Fletcher tragicomedy, on the other hand, depends on final truths emerging with a shock of surprise. Only thus can the brilliance of its alternations be secured.

FLETCHERIAN TRAGICOMEDY

The poems in the 1647 folio hold up for particular admiration two aspects of Fletcher's dramaturgy: first, his portrayals of soldierly honour (Mardonius, Arbaces, Melantius) and of female pathos (Aspatia, Bellario, Lucina, Arcas)—the two polarities of his tragicomic mode—and, secondly, his 'wit', his artful poise, seen as a middle point between the smoothness of Shakespeare and the weightiness of Jonson, so that he can draw on the qualities of both. The description has remained extraordinarily constant through time, though the values encoded have been reversed. This is not surprising, for we must allow that the 1647 praise itself encodes a particular historical moment. The volume is clearly a royalist manifesto; the authors are being co-opted into a celebration of the (now-closed) theatre as a royalist institution: and, as that political and ethical connection raised their esteem in 1647, so in later centuries it has damaged it, Fletcherian tragicomedy coming to be seen as 'decadent', reflecting in its 'evasiveness' (between tragedy and comedy) courtly society's flight from responsible action, and so the conditions that led to the Civil War.[27]

These 'historical' judgements are neither focused enough to describe the actual characteristics of Fletcherian tragicomedy nor comprehensive enough to allow for the overlap between Fletcher's tragicomedy and his comedy (discussed above, pp. 409–15). Fletcher, like other prolific playwrights of the period (Middleton, Dekker, Heywood, Shakespeare), was a dramatist before he was an ideologue, and moved his ethical assumptions to suit his dramatic focus.[28] Moreover, the 'Fletcherian' combination of passionately individual and socially farcical manifests itself in a great variety of forms, many of which are tragicomic only in the traditional sense that they mix comic and tragic impulses, subject characters to life-threatening violence and then restore them to happiness. One may instance the disguised maiden's flight from patriarchy and her wanderings in forests full of outlaws in *The Pilgrim* (1621); printed 1647); the haphazard criminality of deracinated gentlemen and their disguised sisters in *The Night Walker or the Little Thief* (1611; printed 1640); the disguised maidens' pursuit of their philandering seducer in *Love's Pilgrimage* (?1616; printed 1647); the pseudo-historical labyrinth of usurpation in *Beggar's Bush* (c.1615–1622; printed 1647), with its lost heirs, disguise among gypsies, fortunes lost at sea; or the Spanish cloak-and-dagger imbroglio of *The Chances* (1613 X 1625); printed 1647), where random passers-by find themselves caught up with royal babies passed out of doorways, distressed beauties demanding protection, and duels in which the fighters cannot guess what is going on. In terms of the Guarinian ideal of a mixed genre sustained in coherent continuity by the balance of opposite points of view, these are very rough and ready approximations, where Guarini's interlacing of different levels of the plot is sacrificed to the standard excitements of a quick moving narrative. In Fletcher's handling of such plots, there is very little that would surprise Henslowe or Alleyn or that requires us to change our nomenclature from romance to tragicomedy.

There are, of course, clear distinctions to be made. Characters placed in worlds of indeterminate ethos are given little chance to impose themselves on the action.[29] The Fletcherian handling of these romantic stories concentrates less on heroic patience and active response than on emotional confusion, often of military men stranded in an unstable and corrupt society (as in *The Loyal Subject*). The hero has still, of course, to be a potential man of action, but he hardly ever needs to fight on stage; militarism has become a quality of character rather than performance, so that 'honour' appears as an ethical issue to be investigated rather than a duty to be fulfilled.[30] Constancy in love, rather than in war, is recurrently invoked as the true test of honour (as also, outside Fletcher, in Heywood's *The English Traveller* (c.1627), Ford's *Love's Sacrifice* (?1632), Shirley's *Love's Cruelty* (1631; printed 1640)). The usurer is still a characteristic blocking figure but is no longer a central source of dismay.[31] Intrigue is more tightly organized, but with a greater variety of interlocking mechanisms; double plots remain common (very often in the standard mode of romantic main plot, comic sub-plot),[32] but tend to be held together as contrasting aspects of a single world judged by a single social standard, so that they seldom offer antithetical visions of life. Thus there is no sense in which the parasite Bessus in *A King and No King* can break out into a different dimension, as does the parasite Parolles in *All's Well that Ends Well* with his 'simply the thing I am / Shall make me live' (IV. iii. 333–4). Bessus can offer only a debased version of the ethos ruling elsewhere in the play, and so with Syphax in *The Mad Lover* or Perez in *Rule a Wife*. Instead of socially contrasted plots, Fletcher generally prefers cognate actions where brothers or sisters or companions work out the same attitudes in different adventures.[33] Though the liaison des scènes is not yet a shibboleth, we can feel the stress on continuity getting closer as playwrights learn to avoid the unmediated transitions of the Elizabethan stage that carry us without preparation from one matter to another, related only by analogy—what Harbage calls 'plot ellipses'.[34]

The central suppositions of Fletcherian tragicomedy have been masterfully analysed in Eugene Waith's *The Pattern of Tragicomedy in Beaumont and Fletcher*. These, Waith finds, derive from the co-presence of two impulses inside a single situation, one involving distance, the other requiring immediacy, one pointing to romance and idealism, the other to satire and reductive realism: 'operating together they produce the theoretical, the factitious, the hypothetical'.[35]

If we set this formula against that which sustained the romances of the Henslowe dramatists, we can see the change as a shift in the relation of character to context. Heywood's *The Royal King and the Loyal Subject* (1602–1618; printed 1637) creates reality for its characters by making their beliefs reflections of the system they live in. The warrior monarch and his Earl Marshal display the esteem of great comrades-in-arms for one another's magnanimity, daring, outspokenness. But in peacetime they are faced by an equally clear assumption that they are now sovereign and subject. This is a clash of characteristics that exemplifies the basic structure of feudal society, where the political is always having to be renegotiated as a form of the personal.[36] So there is ample space for villainy to subvert the negotiation. But so many values are shared here that a return to a stable understanding appears, inevitably, as a confirmation of the agreed value system underlying the whole play.

One can see why this plot appealed to Fletcher. His *The Loyal Subject* (1618 (revised ?1633); printed 1647) offers a much more complex political diagram, in which the loyal subject can no longer cling to a standard morality and so appears much more an isolated 'humour', finding no consensus outside himself; his theatrical force becomes that of paradox. His loyal emotions have to focus on a duke who is without royal qualities. And they must do so without support from his natural constituency, those military purists (his son and his captains) who wish to destroy the political hierarchy (the only thing he can be loyal to) in the name of military ethics. The contradiction that Fletcher has set up between personal beliefs and a corrupt social scene stresses the theoretical status of both: no resolution can be imagined except by a *coup de théâtre*.

What is perhaps the most brilliant tragicomedy in the Beaumont and Fletcher canon, *A King and No King* (1611; printed 1619), tells a story of puzzling incompatibility between values that stands somewhere between The *Two Noble Kinsmen* and *The Loyal Subject*. It is a more accessible play than either, because Arbaces, the hero, manages to contain laughter and wonder inside a single believable character. This quality transforms the contradictions in which he is involved from the remote and the ritualized into a brilliantly tragicomic immediacy of theatrical presence. Arbaces begins as a sharply foregrounded comic figure, a successful general, like the loyal subject, enamoured of his own (genuine) virtues, and possessed of a gay determination to impose equal happiness and virtue on all men around him. When tragedy strikes him, in the form of an incestuous passion for his supposed sister, Panthea, his comic self-assurance, and his determination to take every problem by the shoulders and shake it into conformity create a simultaneously comic and tragic effect, characteristically Fletcherian in its use of personal, domestic, and potentially comic means to cope with political issues and tragic dilemmas. The use of incest to create the tragic potential has been objected to (most categorically by Thomas

Rymer[37]) but in fact the dramaturgy ensures that it is never more than a hypothetical topic upon which Fletcher can compose arias of passion and despair. We can appreciate these for their rhetorical power without being convinced that reality will justify their force.[38] Indeed, our distance allows us to suspect that the incest theme exists only as a further reflection of Arbaces' emotional excess; and it is one of the play's pleasures to discover that we are right.

The indeterminacy of a psychology that seems realistic in separate moments but wildly improbable in its alternations enables Fletcher to generate an exciting drama of surfaces (like a Fauve painting); a series of unprepared reversals of attitude keep us continually on the edges of our seats. *The Mad Lover* (1617; printed 1647) offers us again the paradox of a great and successful general, somewhat given to talking about his exploits, whose happiness in himself is destroyed by love. When Memnon meets the princess he is stunned into silence; he no longer knows who he is and can think only to impress her by a deed of suicidal courage, to give her as a gift the heart cut out of his body. The collision between grandeur and absurdity thus set up is never resolved (as it is in the case of Arbaces); clearly the effect that Fletcher is after, the sense of paradox and indeterminacy in experience, does not require it to be.

The often remarked rhetorical fluency of the Beaumont and Fletcher verse—its projection of strong emotions that define situations but stand apart from character—is an important part of the tragicomic effect. If we compare it to the distorted syntax of Shakespeare's last plays[39] we can see how far the psychological extremism of one stands from the other's careful orchestration of pathos and potential violence—in a scene of naturalistic dialogue like the following. Young Archas, the general's grandson, disguised as Alinda, is the Princess Olympia's beloved companion. But 'she' has also attracted the attentions of the corrupt duke, and it is supposed he has seduced her:

> ALINDA. Madam, the Duke has sent for the two ladies.
> OLYMPIA. I prithee go: I know thy thoughts are with him.
>   Go, go, Alinda, do not mock me more.
>   I have found thy heart, wench, do not wrong thy mistress,
>   Thy too much loving mistress: do not abuse her.
>
> . . . .
>
> ALINDA. Oh, who has wronged me? who has ruined me?
>   Poor wretched girl, what poison is flung on thee?
>   Excellent virtue, from whence flowes this anger?
> OLYMPIA. Go ask my brother, ask the faith thou gav'st me,
>   Ask all my favours to thee, ask my love,
>   Last, thy forgetfulness of good: then fly me.
>   For we must part, Alinda.

ALINDA.   You are weary of me.
 I must confess I was never worth your service,
 Your bounteous favours less; but that my duty,
 My ready will and all I had to serve ye—
 O heaven, thou know'st my honesty.
OLYMPIA.   No more.
 Take heed, Heaven has a justice. Take this ring with ye,
 This doting spell you gave me; too well, Alinda,
 Thou knew'st the virtue in't; too well I feel it:
 Nay keep that too, it may sometimes remember ye,
 When you are willing to forget who gave it,
 And to what virtuous end.
ALINDA.   Must I go from ye?
 Of all the sorrows sorrow has—must I part with ye?
 Part with my noble mistress?
OLYMPIA.   Or I with thee, wench.
ALINDA. And part stain'd with opinion? Farewell lady,
 Happy and blessed lady, goodness keep ye:
 Thus your poor servant full of grief turns from ye,
 For ever full of grief, for ever from ye.
 I have no being now, no friends, no country,

 . . . .

OLYMPIA.   How she wounds me!
 Either I am undone or she must go: take these with ye,
 Some toys may do ye service, and this money;
 And when ye want, I love ye not so poorly,
 Not yet, Alinda, that I would see ye perish.
 Prithee be good, and let me hear; look on me,
 I love those eyes yet dearly; I have kiss'd thee,
 And now I'll do't again: farewell Alinda,
 I am too full to speak more, and too wretched.   *Exit*
 ALINDA. You have my faith, and all the world my fortune.
                 Exit
       (*The Loyal Subject*, IV. i. 1–57)

It will be noted how effectively the rhetoric here conveys realistic emotions, but with a force of expression that has no basis in fact (for we know that Alinda has not been seduced). The emotions are thus cut off from any external consequence in action;[40] they are turned in on themselves as specimens of a poetic management which undermines the truth of the situation at the same time as it magnifies its emotional power,[41] and so substitutes connoisseurship for identification. Or take the more violently passionate dialogue (now usually attributed to Beaumont) between Philaster and his page, Bellario:

PHILASTER. She kisses thee?

BELLARIO.   Never, my Lord, by heaven.

PHILASTER. That's strange; I know she does.

BELLARIO.   No, by my life.

PHILASTER. Why then she does not love me. Come, she does.
      I bade her do it; I charged her by all charms
      Of love between us, by the hope of peace
      We should enjoy, to yield thee all delights
      Naked as to her bed. I took her oath
      Thou shouldst enjoy her. Tell me, gentle boy,
      Is she not parallelless? Is not her breath
      Sweet as Arabian winds when fruits are ripe?
      Are not her breasts two liquid ivory balls?
      Is she not all a lasting mine of joy?

. . . .

      Thou think'st I will be angry with thee. Come,
      Thou shalt know all my drift; I hate her more
      Than I love happiness, and placed thee there
      To pry with narrow eyes into her deeds.
      Hast thou discovered? Is she fall'n into lust,
      As I would wish her? Speak some comfort to me.

BELLARIO. My Lord, you did mistake the boy you sent.
      Had she the lust of sparrows or of goats,
      Had she a sin that way, hid from the world,
      Beyond the name of lust, I would not aid
      Her base desires; but what I came to know
      As servant to her I would not reveal
      To make my life last ages.

                                          (III. i. 193–224)

What we see here is Philaster and Bellario aiming at one another their
powerfully realized and fluent theatrical emotions. As the power struggle swings
to and fro, we see each contestant being made to take up the position that will
best undercut the other, pushing into extremity both the obsessive imagination
of total disloyalty and the assertion of total loyalty (Bellario bids *Philaster* to 'hew
me asunder, and whilst I can think, / I'll love those pieces you have cut away /
Better than those that grow' (III. i. 245-7). One line of assertion in the dialogue
is known to be true, the other false, and it may be assumed that the true will
triumph in the end; but this distinction matters little; it is the power of the
rhetorical strokes that marks our pleasure in the game. It is not a case of the art
pointing to the suffering but of the suffering pointing to the art.

We find the prefatory material for the 1647 Folio making the same point.
Shirley's Epistle speaks of 'passions raised to that excellent pitch and by such

insinuating degrees that you shall not choose but consent and go along with them ... and then stand admiring the subtle tracks of your engagement'. Just so![42]

OTHER TRAGICOMEDIES

Describing Fletcherian tragicomedy, I have spoken of the instability of the situations set up and of the hypothetical responses therefore imposed on the characters. The tragicomedies of Massinger, Middleton, and Webster, while not to be described simply as products of 'the school of Fletcher', show the extent to which these techniques continued to offer different writers opportunities each could exploit in his characteristic way, usually in terms of more slow-burning and so less brilliantly illuminated emotions than Fletcher uses.

It is not surprising that Philip Massinger, Fletcher's recurrent collaborator, should stay closest to Fletcher's model. *The Maid of Honour* (c.1621?1632) sets up the contradictory structure of tragicomedy by using (like Fletcher) a corrupt court as the context for noble aspirations. Bertoldo is a warrior purified in battle, presented in strong contrast to his cowardly and time-serving brother, the King. Camiola, the 'Maid of Honour', is a great lady, scornful of the courtlings who come to woo her, carrying recommendations from the king. The mutual esteem of these two figures of virtuous opposition cannot be resolved, given the world they live in, by tragic loss or comic fulfilment. When Bertoldo is captured in battle in his quixotic attack on Siena, the King refuses to ransom him. Camiola will sell her estate to right this wrong. But Bertoldo cannot secure his release without permission from the Duchess of Siena; and she will grant it only in return for a promise of marriage. Prospect of the power his brother has denied him makes Bertoldo accept the proposition. But Camiola's dignity persuades the Duchess that Bertoldo cannot be the man of integrity she took him for. Camiola sends for a priest, not to marry her, but to secure a monastic refuge from the twists and turns of the tragicomic world. Bertoldo must restore his honour in the Christian warfare of the Knights of Malta. The tragicomic form thus validates a middle space between acceptance of the status quo (comedy) and transcendence of its limits (tragedy), in which noble natures are too mired in the world to achieve more than half lives dedicated to selflessness.

Middleton's *More Dissemblers Besides Women* (?1615; printed 1657) tells a very similar story of a great lady's renunciation of the shifts and subterfuges that are needed to succeed in love. When we first meet the Duchess she is an icon of chastity, dedicated to the memory of her late husband. But, when she sees Andrugio, her heart melts, and she becomes an expert player in the game of deceptions and disguises she finds all around her. However, understanding the steps she would have to take to secure her desires, she prefers nobility to success and retreats from involvement.

Middleton and Rowley's *A Fair Quarrel: with the new additions of Mr Chough's and Trimtram's roaring, and the bawd's song* (c.1615–1617) handles a similar mismatch between the impulse to honour and a real world in which intention must twist before it can reach action; but the process is seen this time from a masculine point of view and in an uncourtly (English) setting. Captain Agar and the Colonel return from warfare and immediately find themselves embroiled in family quarrels about money. Tempers rise. The colonel calls Agar 'the son of a whore'; they must fight to clear their consciences. But what must Agar do when his mother tells him (to ensure his safety) that the charge is not a slander but a truth? Agar's honour tells him that he must not fight on this theme, and so he is disgraced. But when he is called a coward he is freed from the inhibition, and he gravely wounds the Colonel. Now it is the Colonel's turn to show exemplary honour; he must recompense Agar for the insult: he will bequeath his estate to his sister and his sister to Agar.[43] She objects, of course, but allows that this is the only way family honour can be cleared. Meanwhile, on the nonmilitary side of the story, love and money are secured by trickery and military decorum is parodied in a school of 'roaring boys'. The choice of honour appears in this context as a purely hypothetical virtue, not validated by anything outside itself, but still demanding the allegiance of good men.

Middleton's *The Witch* (c.1609–c.1616) handles the discontinuities of the tragicomic plot from an opposite direction. Here we do not meet characters of honour trying to live inside a world governed by alternative assumptions. Instead, we find a cast of characters intent on tragic violence, but required to pursue their aims not in a world of real action but in a hall of mirrors, so that no move ever leads in the direction intended. We begin with a grand tragic gesture in which the duke (as in Davenant's *Albovine*) requires the duchess to pledge him in a cup made from her father's skull. The duchess plans revenge. But everything thereafter goes awry. The duchess seduces Almachildes, so that she can require him to kill the duke. Faced by the alternative of execution for attempted rape, he does the deed (as it seems) and now he must be killed in his turn. But it was not the duchess he was in bed with, and neither duke nor assassin dies. In a second plot a jealous husband kills his wife and her supposed lover, and then himself falls into a vault and dies. But again no one dies in fact.[44] This is to push the Guarinian definition of tragicomedy, as wanting deaths but bringing some near it, to such a degree of absurdity that one wonders if Middleton is not simply playing games with the tragicomic convention of evil turned into good. The local witches (whose songs somehow got into the printed text of *Macbeth*) offer all the characters of possibility of short cuts that will lead intention directly into effect. But the offer exceeds the result; even the witches are hobbled by discontinuity: they too are simultaneously threatening and comic, as pleased with a marzipan toad as with 'the privy gristle of a man that hangs'. Their charms quickly lose their efficacy or are overtaken by natural causes. The complex world cannot be simplified by their interventions.

Webster's *The Devil's Law-Case; or when women go to law the devil is full of business* (1610–1619) is more like Webster's two great tragedies than it is like the other tragicomedies considered here. Yet one can see that it resembles them in its use of labyrinthine plotting to turn evil intentions into improbable agreement and so fulfil the central issue of its form (it is called *Tragecomedy* on the title-page). In Webster's tragedies society exists only to serve the lusts and ambitions of the princes in power; the individual who tries to break free is quickly eliminated. In *The Devil's Law-Case*, however, we meet a bourgeois society in which power (and so the capacity to resist and achieve success) is made available in many forms to many people. Romelio, the protagonist, resembles Flamineo and Bosola, the tool villains in the tragedies, in his relish for corruption, his opportunism and wry self-awareness; but as a wealthy merchant he is his own master, constantly able to redefine his aims as one check after another requires him to trim his course, always in motion, always enjoying himself, like Marlowe's Barabas whom he so closely resembles. But, unlike Barabas, Romelio is subject to a power above himself: not that of the duel-fighting aristocrats, who are quite démodé here, but the power of the law to disentangle point by point the lies, deceptions, and inventions that have snared everyone in the complex society of the play. And so the law becomes the instrument by which tragedy is turned into tragicomedy, as the murderous intentions that bring many 'near death' are turned into legal debates, where lost identities become evidence in court, pieced together to create a denouement. And so, having discovered their actual relationships, the pregnant nun, the two supposedly dead aristocrats (the Palamon and Arcite of the story), and the Romelio family can survive, not only to enjoy happiness with one another but to use the money that has been the cause of so much complex plotting to achieve the most virtuous things imaginable—build nunneries and equip galleys to fight the Turks.

Fletcherian tragicomedy is probably the last substantial generic innovation to take possession of the Elizabethan stage—'substantial' because, as noted above, it proved capable of absorbing many different kinds of emphasis. In its late development it looks symptomatic of the direction in which the whole process of Elizabethan drama was moving, from poetry to plot manipulation, from emotions described to emotions enacted, from passion to prudence, from imagination to reality, from a form designed primarily for a poetic response to one that thrives on theatrical discoveries. The first heirs of the tradition (the Restoration critics and comic dramatists) assumed that the movement could be called progress—progress towards their own aesthetic, of course. It had liberated the theatre, they supposed, from the predetermining judgements imposed by fixed genres and allowed it to hold up a genuinely reflecting mirror to the accidental quality of real life. From a modern literary standpoint, however, the development of Elizabethan drama is the story not of progress towards rational representation, but a process of decline, not to say betrayal[45]—a betrayal of poetic truth and of the shared moral meanings that genre strictly applied gives to the image of society.

The critic as historian, looking at these alternative judgements, must recognize that they raise a specific question about his enterprise. He can allow that both points of view are justified, for hypotheses to 'prove' each view exist; but the contradiction between them can be resolved only by constructing an infinite regress of further hypotheses. In this book I have sought to avoid the too-easy unification that comes from either sentimentalizing the past (by assuming that its values are our own) or from demonizing it (for its failure to be politically correct). I assume that the first impact of Elizabethan drama on readers and spectators in the present is likely to be one of recognition—a recognition of the present in the past; I hope to complement that by a recognition of the past in the present, as when we register the contradiction the detail of the past imposes on the limiting certainties and unnoticed presuppositions of the present. In this situation the critic must, like Desdemona, confess to a 'divided duty'—a duty to compose an intelligible picture, faced by a contradictory duty to evoke the shadows that speak to us in strange tongues from behind the particular structures that can be described. The multiplicity of these semi-intelligible voices cannot be reduced to any unison, let alone the unison of today, but the duty to record their challenge to neat coherence must be (and I hope has been) acknowledged.

NOTES

1. Cloak and garland provided the characteristic dress for Prologue actors.

2. Of course such assertions of innocence are standard features of plays that are clearly uninnocent. *The Woman Hater* does contain elements that could be part of a political satire, but they are organized in a way that defuses such potential.

3. See John H. Astington, 'The Popularity of *Cupid's Revenge*', SEL 19 (1979), 215–27.

4. See below, n. 7.

5. Technically speaking, Cupid's Revenge is a tragedy; but, as E. M. Waith remarks, 'if all the characters were saved from death and if the play ended in repentance and reconciliation, its total effect would be very little different' (*The Pattern of Tragicomedy in Beaumont and Fletcher* (New Haven, 1952), 14). Cf. Una Ellis-Fermor, *The Jacobean Drama* (London, 1936), 205: 'Something, then, in the mood ... has disabled us from distinguishing, in the world we are now moving in, the characters, emotions and events that will lead to tragedy from those that will lead through romantic stress to escape'.

6. On this see further pp. 412–13.

7. The transfer of the Queen's Revels boys to the Whitefriars playhouse in

1609 should probably be seen as part of their ghostly afterlife. By 1613 they had combined with the Lady Elizabeth's Men, the combined company alternating for a time between the private theatre and one or another of the public ones. The original boys' company was by then reaching adult status. In a lawsuit of 1635 the Burbages explain the takeover by the King's Men: 'the more to strengthen the service, the boys then wearing out, it was considered that house [the Blackfriars] would be as fit for ourselves' (Chambers, ii. 509 n. 7). It must be supposed that 'the boys then wearing out' means they were already adults and showed that the playhouse was appropriate for a truly adult company.

8. Edward Dowden, in his *Shakespeare* (1876), seems to be the first person to use the word 'romance' for this purpose. He says that these plays 'have a grave beauty, a sweet serenity which seems to render the name "comedies" inappropriate ... Let us then name this group ... "Romances" ' (p.56). It is worth noting that the word appears in Dowden as part of an effort to construct an artistic chronology. My sometime pupil Chris Cobb has pointed out a startlingly prescient definition of romance in Hazlitt's notes on *Cymbeline* in his *The Characters of Shakespeare's Plays* (1817) (ed. Howe, iv. 179). Hazlitt calls the play 'a dramatic romance' and says that the reading of it 'is like going a journey with some uncertain object at the end of it ... Though the events are scattered over such an extent of surface, and relate to such a variety of characters, yet the links which bind the different interests of the story together are never entirely broken ... The ease and conscious unconcern with which this is effected only makes the skill more wonderful.' But Hazlitt never uses the word 'romance' in his discussions of the other plays in the group. Lacking the support of chronology, he cannot see the characteristics he describes so well as generic markers for a whole set of plays.

9. John Danby (*Poets on Fortune's Hill* (London, 1952)) notes that Beaumont and Fletcher's plays 'could easily compete with the popular theatre in dramatic stir and skill; they had something to offer, too, to the aristocrat ... whose connoisseurship was reserved for 'wit' (p. 180).

10. To avoid recurrent excursions on theories of authorship I follow the 1647 Folio's concept of a coherent canon of Beaumont and Fletcher plays, even though modern scholarship has anatomized the corpus into elements attributed to Beaumont, Fletcher, Massinger, Field, and Daborne. I attribute the authorship of all fifty or so plays to 'Fletcher' (meaning 'the school of Fletcher'). He seems to be the most recurrently present of all the collaborators, and to have provided the model dramaturgy that others followed. The 1647 poems recurrently speak of the volume as 'Master John Fletcher's Plays' (25 poems are addressed to Fletcher, 4 to Beaumont, 5 to the two of them (4 address the stationer, the edition, etc.)). On the other hand, it is now generally believed that Beaumont wrote the major part of plays in which he collaborated.

11. Lois Potter ('True Tragicomedies', in Nancy K. Maguire (ed.),

Renaissance Tragicomedy (New York, 1987), 196–7) has noted that there is no consistent use of the word 'tragicomedy' in this period (the same is true of 'comedy', 'history', and 'tragedy'). But it can also be said that a majority of the Fletcher plays most esteemed in 1647 and now (for example, *Philaster*, *A King and no King*, *The Humorous Lieutenant*) appeal to a specific taste that is easy to call tragicomic, given their romantic excess, contradictory and violent emotions, happiness snatched at the last moment from despair, laughter (often contemptuous laughter) attached to corrupt characters.

12. The shift can look logical if one pursues Shakespeare chronology looking for continuities. The romantic comedies show us heroines who know what they want and have a fairly good idea how to get it. The 'middle comedies' (*Measure for Measure* and *All's Well*—perhaps *Twelfth Night* belongs here as well) have heroines either puzzled about what is to be desired (*Measure for Measure*) or who face great difficulty in knowing how to secure it (*All's Well*). Helena has to learn that she is not in a romantic comedy but must embrace self-abnegation ('Come night, end day! / For with the dark, poor thief, I'll steal away') before she can have what she wants. She thus provides a preview of the later heroines, Marina, Imogen, Perdita, Miranda, who, though royal children, are given little or no power to impose themselves on the world and have to wait with passive endurance until fortune finally provides what effort could not achieve: time 'gives them what he will, not what they crave' (*Pericles*, II. iii. 47).

13. If we allow that the plan of the play is of Shakespeare's devising—and many would not (it is not included in the First or Second Folios)—we must also allow that he could never have envisaged it as a tightly organized piece. Clearly the text we have does not represent Shakespeare's language with any accuracy and this no doubt adds to our sense of incoherence in the structure.

14. Jonson, 'Ode to Himself', published with *The New Inn*.

15. The record seems to show that the impressiveness of the theatrical past weighed heavily on Jacobean taste. In 1615 John Chamberlain remarked of court performances that 'our poets' brains and inventions are grown very dry insomuch that of five new plays there is not one pleases, and therefore they are driven to furbish over the old, which stands them in best stead and brings them most profit' (The *Letters of John Chamberlain*, ed. N. E. McClure (2 vols.; Philadelphia, 1939), i. 567).

16. (London, 1949), 163.

17. The play tells the story (commented on by Time) of a daughter cast adrift at sea for marrying (and conceiving a child by) the Prince of Sicily, a man unacceptable to her father, the King of Thrace. A plague is then visited on the kingdom; a mission is sent to Delphos to find the cause; the message comes back that the King is guilty and will not be cleared till a 'Thracian wonder' appears as a shepherd. At first defiant, the King eventually repents and undertakes a

pilgrimage to search for his daughter and son-in-law. They are now living among Thracian shepherds, unaware of one another's existence. At a shepherds' feast the princess is abducted. The pursuit gets absorbed into a general war between Thrace and Sicily, in which all the characters participate and, recognizing one another, achieve a happy ending. The relevance of this story to both *Cymbeline* and *The Winter's Tale* needs no elaboration.

18. Such figures as Autolycus, Trinculo–Stephano, the Jailor in *Cymbeline*, Boult in *Pericles* are mere shadows of the clown figures of earlier comedies. They are not oppositional figures, given the power of deconstructive commentary, but are absorbed as mere extras into the main story.

19. The often-remarked stretching of time and place in these last plays is used, however, in a different way from that found in the earlier romances. Here the narrative energy is less; the recapitulation of the past in the final moments of presence gives time something of the effect of space (hence, no doubt, G. Wilson Knight's notion of 'spatial form'), as if all the events could finally be seen as a process and yet as simultaneously present.

20. The pattern is clearest here because, where *Pericles* is only the victim of evil, *Cymbeline* only its accidental cause, Leontes is the active destroyer of his family and himself.

21. I have chosen to talk about *The Tempest* in terms of the relation between Prospero and Miranda, not (as commonly in the 1980s) between Prospero and Caliban. The former is more central to the dramatic structure and is the element that links this play to those around it.

22. The Absolved Riddle', *NLH* 17 (1986), 552.

23. The usual discrimination between Shakespeare's and Fletcher's stints gives Fletcher the dominant role in the sub-plot, but also indicates that Fletcher wrote some of the main-plot scenes.

24. (London, 1969), pp. xxix–xxx.

25. Lee Bliss ('Pastiche, Burlesque, Tragicomedy' in *The Cambridge Companion to English Renaissance Drama*, ed. A. R. Braunmuller and Michael Hattaway (Cambridge, 1990)) notes how Beaumont and Fletcher develop Sidney's 'timeless thematic structure, allowing for sharp contrasts between kinds of scenes', that 'replaces plot as the primary organizing principle' and so provides 'a shifting configuration of lovers rather than a true narrative sequence' (p. 249).

26. Cf. Dryden, *Preface to 'Troilus and Cressida, Containing the Grounds of Criticism in Tragedy*': "Tis one of the excellencies of Shakespeare that the manners [*mores, ethos*] of his persons are generally apparent, and you see their bent and inclination. Fletcher comes far short of him in this ... there are but glimmerings of manners in most of his comedies, which run upon adventures ... you know not whether they resemble virtue or vice, and they are either good or bad or indifferent as the present scene requires it' (*Essays of John Dryden*, ed. W. P. Ker (2 vols.; Oxford, 1926), i. 217.

27. The 'modernist' position, to be seen in the criticism of (for example) L. C. Knights, M. C. Bradbrook, T. B. Tomlinson seems to be giving way to a 'postmodernist' one. Two recent anthologies, Nancy K. Maguire's *Renaissance Tragicomedy* (New York, 1987) and Gordon McMullan's *The Politics of Tragicomedy* (London, 1991), show the post-modernist taste for indecidability operating to the advantage of Fletcher and the whole tragicomic genre.

28. And indeed Philip Finkelpearl has been able to mount an argument that Beaumont and Fletcher, far from being royalists, can be counted as dramatists of the opposition. See his *Court and Country Politics in the Plays of Beaumont and Fletcher* (Princeton, 1990).

29. See Dryden, *Essays*, i. 217: 'for the manners can never be evident where the surprise of fortune takes up all the business of the stage; and where the poet is more in pain to tell you what happened to such a man than what he was.'

30. In *The Nice Valour or the Passionate Madman* (c.1615–25) Fletcher sets the extreme (indeed absurd) 'niceness' of a man who cannot bear to live in a world where his honour might be touched against the madness of a man who constantly changes his mind about the standards which require him to fight. Cf. Middleton and Rowley's A Fair *Quarrel* (see pp. 521–2).

31. In the Beaumont and Fletcher canon we see Middletonian figures like Sir Perfidious Oldcraft in *Wit at Several Weapons*, Justice Allgripe in *The Night Walker*, Moorecraft in *The Scornful Lady*, Cacafogo in *Rule a Wife*, all easily converted to comic virtue. Even Dryden complains of the ease with which the usurer in this last case is turned into a boon companion for the prodigal. See the *Essay of Dramatic Poesy* (*Essays*, i. 66).

32. Orie Hatcher (*John Fletcher: A Study in Dramatic Method* (Chicago, 1905)) makes a relevant remark about Fletcher's use of Italian sources for plot and sub-plot. 'As a rule, Fletcher draws upon Bandello for the more serious interest of the main story and upon Boccaccio for the episodes of the comic sub-plot ... [the settings of the *novelle*] were easily adaptable to the romantic coloring at which Fletcher aimed, while the intense passions which they portrayed fascinated the theatric side of his imagination' (p. 43). The emotionally neutral trickery of *The Decameron* then provides a low intensity contrast.

33. As in *Wit Without Money, Love's Pilgrimage, The Nice Valour, The Wild Goose-Chase, The Custom of the Country, The Scornful Lady*.

34. *Cavalier Drama* (New York, 1936), 83.

35. *The Pattern of Tragicomedy*, 85.

36. Sidney Painter (*William Marshall* (Baltimore, 1933)) documents the historical circumstances that support the fiction.

37. *The Critical Works of Thomas Rymer*, ed. Curt Zimansky (New Haven, 1956), 48: 'If the design he wicked, as here the making approaches an incestuous

enjoyment, the audience will naturally loathe and detest it, rather than favour and accompany it with their good wishes.'

38. We might compare the double effect to that, for example, of such an aria as *Come scoglio* in Mozart's *Cosi fan Tutte* where (once again) we wonder how the brilliant emotionalism of the expression can be justified by the farcical 'reality' of the situation.

39. See Lamb's famous explication: 'His [Fletcher's] ideas moved slow; his versification, though sweet, is tedious, it stops every moment; he lays line upon line ... adding image to image so deliberately that we see where they join. Shakespeare mingles everything, runs line into line, embarrasses sentences and metaphors; before one idea has burst its shell, another is hatched and clamorous for disclosure (*The Works of Charles and Mary Lamb*, ed. E. V. Lucas (7 vols.; London, 1903–5), iv. 341).

40. This is what Shakespeare, in the scene of Guiderius' and Arviragus' mourning for the supposed death of Imogen (*Cymbeline*, IV. ii)—the nearest he comes to this mode of rhetoric—calls 'in wench-like words ... protract[ing] with admiration.'

41. We admire the excesses of Arcite refusing to leave prison (*Two Noble Kinsmen*, II. ii–iii), but we do not believe them.

42. Cf. William Cartwright's poem in the 1647 Folio: 'all stand wondering how / The thing will be, until it is.' (sig. d2.)

43. In these moves Middleton is following the lead of Heywood in the second plot of *A Woman Killed with Kindness*.

44. The same device of tragic action suddenly cancelled by the discovery it did not happen appears in the Middleton-Rowley-Massinger *The Old Law* (c.1615–1618; printed 1656) where the law that fathers and mothers over age must face euthanasia is used as a hypothesis to reveal the consequences of youth liberation; but then we learn that the law was never carried out. See also Middleton, *Anything for a Quiet Life* (c.1620–c.1621; printed 1662) where the imperious and spendthrift wife suddenly reveals that she has only been teaching her husband a moral lesson.

45. T.S. Eliot described Webster as 'a very great literary and dramatic genius directed towards chaos' (*Selected Essays* (London, 1932), 117)—that is, as part of 'the movement of progress or deterioration which has culminated in Sir Arthur Pinero and the present regime in Europe'. Webster and Pinero are equally in thrall to 'the aim of realism' (p. 111) and share the need to represent their characters as real people with whom the audience can identify; so they step outside 'the conditions of art'.

ANTHONY B. DAWSON

Giving the Finger: Puns and Transgression in *The Changeling*

My title, potentially transgressive in itself, is not meant to be rude, though the text that I will concentrate on can hardly be said to be very polite. As it is, *The Changeling*'s temerity is characteristic of its principal author, Thomas Middleton. The play's failure to be polite is partly a matter of language and stage action, partly a feature of its ironic relation to earlier Elizabethan texts, especially those of Shakespeare, and partly a result of its clear-eyed exposure of the role the body plays in social and cultural representation. My analysis takes as its point of departure the instability of meaning that is everywhere noticeable in both the language and action of the play, but rather than rest content with deconstructive dalliance, I want to connect slippages of meaning to cultural anxiety and conflict, and, incidentally, I want to pause over various moments when Middleton re-imagines, with unruffled irony, some of the tricks of his greatest precursor. Rather than leaping directly into such turbulent waters, however, I would like to take a run at my subject by glancing first at a pair of Middleton's city comedies. *The Changeling*, I suggest, even though it is a collaborative work, picks up on and brilliantly re-plays patterns of language, thought, and dramatic strategy that are present in some of Middleton's earliest plays.

Let me begin with an ending—that of *A Trick to Catch the Old One*, where Witgood makes a cunning and subversive pun that may serve as a jumping-off point for an investigation of the deconstructive turns that Middleton's language so often takes—dissolving thematic connections and moral hierarchies even as it asserts them. Pacifying the comically disgraced Hoard, whom he has successfully

From *The Elizabethan Theatre XII*, eds. A.L. Magnusson and C.E. McGee. © 1993 by P.D. Meany Company.

saddled with his cast-off mistress (the courtesan who has been masquerading as the widow Medler), Witgood proclaims:

> excepting but my selfe,
> I dare sweare shees a Virgin, and now by marrying your
> Neece I have banisht my selfe for ever from her, she's mine
> Aunt now by my faith, and theres no Medling with mine
> Aunt you know, a sinne against my Nuncle. (5.2.152–56)[1]

That the puns on *aunt* and meddling are part of the texture here is clear from the frequent play on medlar (rotten fruit/punk) in the text and from the underlining of the double meaning of *aunt* in Lucre's speech earlier, where he justifies his cozening of Witgood by asking, "was [the inheritance] not then better bestow'd upon his Uncle, then upon one of his Aunts, I neede not say bawde, for every one knowes what Aunt stands for in the last Translation" (2.1.11–13). Middleton glosses the term here, connecting it to the repeated motif of interlocking family relationships, so that we can hardly miss it when it recurs at the end. Well, not quite the end. The text actually concludes with a passage of primitive tetrameter couplets designed supposedly to confirm Witgood's and the Courtesan's repentance and reformation. The puns and the couplets suggest the possibility of alternate futures, without exactly cancelling each other out. However, the easy moral absolutes of the final speeches and the stage picture of the two kneeling repentant figures are certainly complicated by the reminder that the medlar who is no longer Medler is both Witgood's aunt and not his aunt. The text here makes a strong move toward closure, complete with Calvinistic retreat from the energies that had propelled the comic intrigue, and at the same time keeps those energies afloat through language that escapes from fixed meaning.

In another, exactly contemporary comedy, *A Mad World My Masters*, moral rhetoric again conflicts with ironic interrogation; in fact the ironies so threaten to destabilize the world of that play that the heavy moral absolutes asserted in the conversions of Penitent Brothel and Mistress Harebrain seem to serve as a kind of brake to the threat of deconstruction set in motion by the subversive irony. But such terminology may seem too weighty for this relatively light-hearted play; let's just say that the comedy undoes itself in a kind of effusive overflow. I select one prominent instance—the play-within (known as "The Slip") that comically calls into question the very distinctions and identifications on which the play itself as a theatrical text is based. In a device that recalls the masque in *The Spanish Tragedy* and that Middleton will use again in *Women Beware Women*, "The Slip" plays havoc with onstage audience expectation, Follywit as an "actor" improvising a scene that erases the conventional boundaries between the real and the fictive. For Sir Bounteous and his guests, the play is received as an actual play. For the beleaguered Constable, the action is confusingly real; his "theatrical" persona derives from Dogberry and Elbow (the players, says Sir Bounteous, "put all their fools to the constable's part still"—5.2.93–94)[2] but his "reality" is not actorly at all, not played. And for Follywit, the player-magician, "The Slip," which began as another of his dazzling tricks, becomes a witty translation of life into theatre. As such it makes explicit what has been implicit in many of his exploits throughout the play. The players, says Sir Bounteous when they are first announced, "were never more uncertain in their lives. Now up and now down, they know not when to play, where to play, nor what to play" (5.1.32–35). The very title of the playlet with its multiple meanings points to that wayward uncertainty: the *slip*—a counterfeit coin, an escape or evasion, a slide. The title proclaims not only the slipperiness of Follywit and his cronies, but a semantic slippage, a failure to remain fixed, that the mixed generic status of the piece also makes manifest. The madness of the world alluded to in the title of the larger play turns out to be a madness of meaning. It is characteristic that even Follywit's name is paradoxically double.

The whole episode is itself a kind of extended pun, one that marks the unstable boundaries of theatrical illusion even as it relies on them for comic effect. It is amusingly appropriate then that when Follywit is finally unmasked by the unexpected alarum of his grandfather's watch in his pocket, his comeuppance is marked by a pun that recalls the previous slips: "Have I 'scap'd the constable to be brought in by the watch?" (5.2.281–82).

Follywit, like Hoard in *Trick*, finds himself inadvertently married to a punk, a punishment that for Shakespeare's Lucio is "pressing to death, whipping and hanging"; note that Middleton, urbanizing Shakespeare, marries off his *hero* to the whore. This element, like Follywit's economic reversal, illustrates the familiar comic pattern of the guller gulled. But Hoard, who has been "whored," represents in the pun that marks him, with its sexual and economic overtones, the conflation of normally separated social-hierarchical categories. The verbal slip has powerful social resonance, dealt with comically here but, as I hope to show later on, handled with richer and darker meanings in *The Changeling*. The questionable status of the whore, neither maid, wife nor even widow, is related directly to her role in the social network.[3] She occupies a "low" place (opposite to that of the virgin) while at the same time providing a service that mirrors what happens at a "higher" level—in relation not only to sexual desire but economic exchange as well (virginity, as Parolles knows, is a valuable and "vendible" commodity, a key token in the marriage market). The punk is a focus of both disgust and desire—she may be marginal, but the "socially peripheral is often symbolically central."[4] Marriage to a whore thus ironically confirms the legitimacy of illegitimate desire and questions the differentiation between virgin and whore that is both the sexual and the economic basis of patriarchal marriage-broking.[5] The whore's marriage into the citizen class, into city money, at the end of these plays is an inversion of hierarchy that is not merely satirical. What is at issue is a revealing of contradiction, figured in the pun but extended into the personal and social body. "No absolute borderline can be drawn between body and meaning in the sphere of culture," says V.V. Ivanov, commenting on Bakhtin.[6] The whore's body, bought with the citizen's money and just for that reason a subject of vilification and a site of disease or pollution, becomes the wife's body—a crucial token of legitimate exchange within the social domain. At the end of *Chaste Maid*, to cite a further example, the comedy of Tim's effort to keep the two bodies separate ("*uxor non est meretrix*") only emphasizes the link between them. What I am saying is that the puns in these comedies do not simply undo meaning by creating a deconstructive slip; rather, they contest certain socially sanctioned forms of meaning or, more precisely, make manifest certain hidden relationships in the social network, and in so doing unearth contradictions that underlie the construction of social hierarchies, such as those having to do with the body, sex and money.

"In the beginning was the Pun," wrote Samuel Beckett, himself playing on the hermaphrodite "Word" that has sought through the ages to assert onesidedly its phallogocentric voice. For that initiating word, that originary pun, necessarily carries within itself another, subversive voice, challenging, mocking, undermining the dominant one. It is precisely that other voice that I want to investigate as I turn now to my main subject. In *The Changeling*, doubleness asserts itself most obviously in the double plot, the subplot acting as a kind of carnivalesque parody of the main plot (a theatrical pun), inverting traditional hierarchies like sanity and madness, order and disorder, only to confirm them in the end. But I want to argue further that the derision of the charivari spills over, contesting the main message of the play even as it confirms it. The process is a complex one and requires a close look at the language and meanings of the main plot.[7] The story of Beatrice-Joanna's triangular love-life is full of puns and swerves, full of manifold associations, some of which I want to trace in order to investigate the relationships between slips of meaning, theatricality, and madness on the one hand, and hierarchy, patriarchy, and authority on the other. At the centre of the whole issue is sexual desire and how it is represented.

Patriarchal arrangements in the play are tied to notions of space, especially the castle and the cage, which come to stand for the women who are contained within them and who are the objects of would-be penetration. (In terms of stage space, castle and cage are inevitably linked, often using the same door, and are thus visually and metaphorically identified.) Penetration is in fact a crucial motif. In the subplot, immediately after the murder of Alonso in the castle, Isabella complains of being fettered in a cage and in a series of puns Lollio makes it clear that not only is it his master's pleasure but "'Tis *for* my master's pleasure" (3.3.9; emphasis added)[8] that she is penned, subject only to his penetration. In the main plot, Beatrice's virginity is everywhere at stake. Vermandero, her father, is keeper of the castle—the castle that, as she says in the first scene, Alsemero is "much desirous / To see" (154–55) when they both know it is she herself who is the favoured object of Alsemero's sight. "Our eyes are sentinels unto our judgments" (69), she has earlier declared, but she only has eyes for Alsemero and to her eyes

De Flores is a "basilisk" (111). As it turns out, looks *can* kill; there is a deep and ironic connection between the romantic gaze of Petrarchan devotion and the deadly stare of the basilisk. Here the text ironizes and darkens elements in Shakespearean comedy, *As You Like It* and *A Midsummer Night's Dream* especially, uncovering the potential violence beneath Petrarchan rhetoric. Both those texts play happily with the magic and the fallibility of sight, the romantic force of the devoted gaze, the dazzle of the eye, the mock cruelty of the scornful look. *The Changeling* invokes and inverts such images.

Alsemero has first seen Beatrice in the temple, a fact he takes to be a good omen; but he ignores the turn of the temple's vane (1. 20), and is blithely unaware of the slide of his religious language into Petrarchan images (devotion, temple, saint, etc.), and equally blind to the metaphorical shift from temple to castle to body. The play as a whole dramatizes the failure to arrest that sliding. It makes manifest the difficulty of containing one discourse inside another, and of thus maintaining the binary oppositions, the "violent hierarchies" to cite Jonathan Dollimore's phrase,[9] that sustain social practices.

Vermandero, as I said, is keeper of the castle, an edifice that we are led to associate with Beatrice herself, whom he also keeps. "Our citadels," he reminds Alsemero, "Are plac'd conspicuous to outward view [as Beatrice has been to Alsemero] / On promonts' tops, but within are secrets" (1.1.159–61): Secrets he does not want penetrated by strangers. Much later in the play, when Alsemero has replaced Vermandero as the keeper of the citadel of Beatrice's virginity, he administers a notorious test to her, one that has frequently been scoffed at by commentators; but I would argue that it fits perfectly into the economy of the play. (The fact that Middleton has shifted the source of this test to *The Book of Experiments, / Call'd Secrets in Nature* is not without significance.) The test's function is to penetrate her secret without her knowing it—to know whether she has been known ("This is the strangest trick to know a maid by" [4.2.143], says Jasperino)—that is, to know secretly whether her secret is still intact. Beatrice, having already lost her virginity, has her own knowledge, and so foils Alsemero's venture and guards her own secret.

There is another dimension to all this imagery of spaces, secrets and penetration—murder. "How shall I dare to venture in his castle / When he discharges murderers at the gate?" (1.1.218–19) wonders Alsemero as he follows his future father-in-law out in Act 1. Here the "murderer" (the word means a small cannon) is the news of Beatrice's engagement to Alonso—she is unassailable, already possessed. But the moment that follows Alsemero's lament promises otherwise. In a striking verbal and visual metaphor, Beatrice drops her glove and De Flores retrieves it. She is horrified by his touch—so she strips off her other glove: "There, for t'other's sake I part with this; / Take 'em and draw thine own skin off with 'em" (225-26). Here, as earlier, there are echoes that she cannot control: for the sake of one she parts with the other—Alonso for Alsemero, Alsemero for De Flores. The moment is a powerful example of a theatrical pun, one that doubles or even triples its range of referents. The aggressiveness of her language only excites De Flores, who is a connoisseur of the erotic and the violent: "I know she had rather wear my pelt tann'd / In a pair of dancing pumps, than I should / Thrust my fingers into her sockets here" (228–30). He violates her gloves as he will later violate Alonso's hand and Beatrice's various secrets, most especially her virginity. In Act 3, De Flores returns from the murder to an anxious Beatrice, who, in a reminiscence of impatient Juliet, is waiting for news. He brings with him, as a reminder of one violation and prelude to another, the dead man's finger as a "token" (3.4.26). The ring on the finger, which was "stuck" to it "As if the flesh and it were both one substance" (38–39), had been Beatrice's "first token" (34) to Alonso, one that "my *father* made me send him" (emphasis added). It now returns to her as an ironic sign of all such romantic pledges (the ring plots in *Merchant of Venice*, *All's Well*, and *Cymbeline* come to mind as precursors), and the link between such pledges and the economic and social arrangements of patriarchy. De Flores now offers the ring-encircled finger as a token of his "will" and his meaning, he transforms it from proof of his past "service" (picking up the glove, cutting off the finger) into a sign of his coming penetration of her virginity, a secret about which she is not yet in the know. In *The Merchant of Venice*, to dwell a moment on the Shakespearean parallel, we get Bassanio at his betrothal protesting: "But when this ring / Parts from this finger, then parts life from hence;" and Portia later scolding: "You were to blame ... To part so slightly with your wife's first gift, / A think stuck on with oaths upon your finger, / And so riveted with faith unto your flesh." Bassanio's comic aside is also apposite: "Why, I were best to cut my left hand off, / And swear I lost the ring defending it." There the double meanings function comically, the finger in the ring carrying sanctioned sexual and cultural meanings, any threat of violence and betrayal easily turned aside.

If the scholarly consensus about authorial collaboration is correct, Middleton's first lines in the play are Beatrice's to Jasperino: "Oh, sir, I'm ready now for that fair *service* / Which makes the name of friend sit glorious on you" (2.1.1–2; emphasis added). As Christopher Ricks argued years ago, "service" with its Petrarchan and overtly sexual over-tones is a key term, and a slippery one.[10] It is typical of Beatrice in the first half of the play to display a failure to control her own rhetoric, to speak as if there were no such thing as ambiguity; that "service" is the office of a friend as well as a lover no one would deny, but its links with violence, dismemberment, invasion and madness are more covert. It is De Flores's role to make them emerge. One kind of service, one kind of transgression, slides into another. Again here, Middleton ironically echoes Shakespeare; like her namesake in *Much Ado*, Beatrice wishes she were a man and confers a murderous duty on her servant: "There's horror in my service, blood, and danger" (2.2.119); but, she adds, "Thy reward shall be precious" (130). "The thought ravishes" (132), replies De Flores, capping a series of double meanings that he has invoked in response to her throughout the scene.

That all such language parodies Petrarchan discourse, revealing what the language of romantic devotion usually occludes—lust, dismemberment, social and economic imperatives—goes almost without saying.[11] The point is driven home by the obvious parallelism between this part of the scene (the initial interview between Beatrice and De Flores) and the first part, immediately preceding, in which Alsemero speaks nobly of the honourable service that he could perform to "strike off both [her] fears" (that is, of Alonso and of her father's "command"). As she so often is, Beatrice is behindhand: "Pray let me find you sir; / What might that service be so strangely happy?" (2.2.25–26). But once she finds out it means "valor"—honourable murder—she is quick to extend the definition of manhood and service implied in Alsemero's hollow courtliness by applying it a few moments later to De Flores and *his* desire to serve her.

There is another set of meanings tied to the language of service—the economic one. Words like *recompense, use, precious, reward* ("Never was man dearlier rewarded"—"I do think of that" [2.2.137–38]), link Beatrice's physical body and De Flores's desire for it to the social exchange of money for services. Such language underlines the notion of the body itself as a token of exchange, a cultural element that is implicit in the patriarchal marriage arrangements as the play depicts them (a neat symbol of this is Vermandero pointing to Alsemero in the dumbshow, marking him as the future husband). There is no absolute borderline between the body and meaning in culture.

Thus, as Ricks showed (though with a different purpose in mind), the text plays constantly with double meanings, teasing both audience and characters with the possibility of not being in the know. At the same time, various characters, notably Alonso, Alsemero, and especially Beatrice, talk confidently and recurrently about judgement, understanding, knowledge, a language which is the obverse of that of secrets. Lurking meanings, madness itself, can be a trap for the unknowing who, like Beatrice, may have already articulated such meanings while avoiding or missing recognition of them. We have already noted several instances of this—with her father and Alsemero in the opening scene, with Alsemero and De Flores in Act 2. When, at the end of scene 1, to return to that moment, she strips off her glove to plague De Flores, she is unaware of the erotic component in her hostility, unconscious of the links between the blood of desire and the blood of violence that De Flores later makes concrete in the gift of the finger as sexual token. She calls her revulsion from De Flores her "infirmity," but she fails to see it for what it is—the ironic emotional double of her romantic infatuation with Alsemero (itself an "infirmity") which has been the primary subject of that opening scene. Her reaction to De Flores may remind us again of how Shakespeare's Beatrice, also perhaps unaware of the erotics of hostility, uses witty aggressiveness as a cover for attraction; once again we see Middleton ironizing Shakespeare's romantic patterns.

The marvellous scene that follows De Flores's offering of his token shows him teaching Beatrice his meanings and, beyond that, his way of knowing. The scene recalls similar ones in *Measure for Measure* and *Women Beware Women*, in which sexual blackmail is linked to, or indeed depends on, a power to make and remake meaning. De Flores, like Angelo and Middleton's Duke, displaces his target's confidence in the stability of her own meanings. Beatrice wants to keep their discourse confined to the economic realm, using words like "fee" and "recompense" which De Flores persists in rendering ambiguous. He refuses her gold: "Is anything / Valued too precious for my recompense?" (3.4.68). Her answer, "I understand thee not" (69), is the first in an escalating series of remarks that emphasize her ignorance, her refusal to know: "I'm in a labyrinth" (72), "What's your meaning?" (83), "Heaven, I doubt him" (93), culminating in De Flores's "Justice invites your blood to understand me" and her reply, "I dare not" (101–2). He bluntly forces his meaning upon her, she appeals to her "honor" and her "modesty." But De Flores has an answer for that: "A woman dipp'd in blood and talk of modesty!" (127). Her final appeal is of course to hierarchy, based on "blood" in yet a third sense of the term, but De Flores brushes it aside: "Think but upon the distance that creation / Set 'twixt thy blood and mine and keep thee there" (131–32), she warns. But now she is "the deed's creature" and they are equal: "You must forget your parentage."

Alonso's blood has made her "one with" De Flores. The "act" of murder, as Ricks notes (295), has been equated with the act of love ("Justice invites your blood to understand me"), and so there is a cruel logic to De Flores's demand. He makes manifest in his language what might be termed the play's unconscious, or, to put it in other terms, its delight in meanings that expose the fragility and reversibility of its hierarchical affirmations: for example, the unsublimated desire and impulse toward dismemberment that underlie its Petrarchan images of devotion and service, the sexual "knowledge" that accompanies its preoccupation with understanding and judgement, the blood of murder and desire that surrounds its concern with the blood of caste, and the overt relation between commerce and sex that is latent in the marriage transactions.

De Flores murders Alonso in the castle which has been associated with Beatrice and her virginity. It is a metaphorical rape, confirmed by the cutting and giving of the finger, itself an index of at least two meanings, one already accomplished, the other still to be fulfilled. Alonso's death, as Beatrice realizes too late, is the "murderer of my honor" just as his living presence had been the "murderer" (i.e., cannon) aimed at Alsemero's hopes. De Flores, in a further extension of the pattern, imagines Beatrice's "wanton fingers combing out [his] beard" (2.2.150), while he looks forward to the "banquet" (3.4.18) of his desires, at which "some women are odd feeders" (2.2.155); and then, in the course of his dialogue with Beatrice, he protests (with false innocence) her horror at the offending digit—"A greedy hand thrust in a dish at court ... hath had as much as this" (3.4.32–33). This is a sly comment which, besides giving us a stark glimpse into seventeenth-century table manners, conceals De Flores's pretense that his gestures are accidental, without meaning, when he is then and there engaged in constructing a network of signification.

Still another thread that links murder to deflowering is the insistence on silence—"Do you question / A work of secrecy?" asks De Flores, as he stabs Alonso, "I must silence you. ... I must silence you" (3.2.16–18). And, having won Beatrice to his desire, he suddenly turns tender: "Come, rise and shroud your blushes in my bosom; / Silence is one of pleasure's best receipts. / Thy peace is wrought forever in this yielding" (3.4.167–69). The language recalls the Duke overpowering Bianca in *Women Beware Women*, and in both the woman's silence indicates her sexual capitulation, her defeat. But here the silence not only marks the woman as target of the male gaze and subject to male power (as in both *Women Beware Women* and the end of *Measure for Measure*),[12] but also signals a new awareness of meanings unforeseen. From this point on, Beatrice is much more deeply implicated in multiple meanings and more alert to ambiguity, as well as becoming herself an investigator, a penetrator of others' secrets (Diaphanta's, for example). If in the beginning was the pun, the fall from paradise seems to consist in a responsiveness to the serpentine waywardness of language. A mark of this is Beatrice's public commendation of De Flores after the fire: "A double goodness! / 'Twere well he were rewarded" and De Flores's admiring comment, "Rewarded? Precious, here's a trick beyond me" (5.1.123–24, 126). Now, we might say, she can work hand-in-glove with De Flores.

Beatrice's virginity is as important to De Flores as it is to Alsemero: "And were I not resolv'd in my belief / That thy virginity were perfect in thee, / I should but take my recompense with grudging, / As if I had but half my hopes I agreed for" (3.4.117–20). As much as that promiscuous and insistent finger, her virginity is a token, a sign in a system of social exchanges wherein the meanings constructed by the culture impinge directly and forcefully on the human body. *Violation proclaims ownership.* That is one reason why the finger is such a powerful theatrical symbol, and not just a fortuitous bit of grand guignol. It actually shows a part of the body being handed over, transformed into a social sign, confirmed by the ring as an ironic pledge. We see the meaning of the sign being constructed and understand its association with the secret exchange of a maidenhead. It is thus a symbol of De Flores's and Beatrice's engagement, a fact proclaimed in what may be regarded as a strained pun, though it is one that suits the play's texture: "Nor is it fit we two engag'd so *jointly* / Should part and live asunder" (3.4.89–90; emphasis added).[13] So De Flores's concern with Beatrice's virginity is more than a villainous whim; it is a consistent and necessary part of an extended parody of seventeenth-century love and marriage, revealing the violence and blood usually occluded in pamphlets, homilies, and actual social practice. It is significant, then, that Middleton has changed the source on this point; there, De Flores is unconcerned with virginity and does not sleep with Beatrice until well after her marriage and the onrush of Alsemero's conventionally irrational jealousy.

So far, I have been talking about various kinds of doubleness in the text; but as I said earlier, the most obvious instance of doubleness is the subplot itself, to which I now want to turn. It can, I think, be most fruitfully viewed as an Empsonian "version of pastoral," a trap set up around the main action, a fairy world, signifying an irretrievable step into madness:

> The antimasque at a great wedding [says Empson] ... stood for the insanity of disorder to show marriage as necessary ... [and] ritually mocked the couple. ... [T]he madmen brought in to be mocked form, for [Beatrice] as for Isabella, an appalling chorus of mockers, and assimilate her to themselves. The richness of the thought here does not come from isolated thinking but from a still hearty custom; to an audience which took the feelings about a marriage masque and a changeling for granted the ideas would arise directly from the two plots.[14]

Since Empson wrote we have learned a lot about symbolic inversion (which he invokes in this passage in reference to the antimasque), and we know now that it does not only and necessarily function to support and maintain traditional hierarchies, though it may do so.[15] Empson's notion of the antimasque seems too simple. But that the subplot functions as a kind of carnivalesque parody of the main plot, an extended pun if you wish, seems incontrovertible. I do, however, want to contest the view that it works only to support the hierarchies that it affirms, that there is no "slip." The subplot plays out a series of ludic transgressions that mimic and mock the actions of the main plot. And it does so in the context of a representation of madness as both transgressive in itself (a threat to sanity and reason as well as a further seeing) and a form of play. Madness is "low" but in the symbolic inversion of the text it turns out to be "high"; and it is also a representation, a mimetic sign that proclaims its own connections with theatricality and semiosis through the play-acting of the titular changeling and his rival.

It is interesting that madness, or at least its representation in Jacobean drama, is often associated with mimicry and theatrical imitation: Lear arraigning his daughters, Ophelia repeating snatches of old song, the madmen in *The Duchess of Malfi* and here imitating birds and animals.[16] The comparison with *The Duchess of Malfi* is apt since the dance of madmen in that play is a kind of mock epithalamium, linking love and death through the classic Elizabethan double entendre: "We'll sing like swans, to welcome death, and die in love and rest" (4.2.72–73). So too in *The Changeling* the dance of madmen is a kind of charivari, a mock wedding dance, which takes place exactly as Beatrice's marriage is being consummated—with a substitute. The mockery is apt, since one function of the charivari is to deride incongruous marriages, often through savage imitation. The key issue here is substitution, since both Antonio and Francisco are part of the antimasque, which is presented to them by the manipulative Lollio as an opportunity to destroy each other as rivals, to avert the threat from each one's point of view of the other acting as his substitute. But of course they seek to substitute themselves for Alibius, and Lollio is waiting in the wings as a genial De Flores. Thus the pattern and threat of substitution in the main plot is danced and displaced in the subplot. It is noteworthy that Diaphanta, Beatrice's virginal substitute, recalls a notorious contemporary instance of substitution when Beatrice first approaches her, seeking to penetrate her virginal secrecy: "She will not search me, will she? / Like the forewoman of a female jury?" (4.1.99–100). The reference is probably to the Countess of Essex's divorce trial in 1613, where her virginity was in question and rumour had it that a veiled substitute took her place during the forensic examination. Nor should we forget that that famous case also involved substitution of one lover for another and more crucially a clandestine murder (that of Sir Thomas Overbury) as well. When Lady Frances married the Earl of Somerset a few months after her divorce, she, like Beatrice, wore her hair down as a token of virginity, a flagrant disguising of a more damning loss of innocence than the sexual—murder by proxy.[17] And it is at least interesting that Middleton's lost *Masque of Cupid* was written for that extraordinary wedding.[18]

The charivari traditionally had a double nature, at once upholding and challenging the hierarchical authority that the targeted marriage was seen as disrupting (as Natalie Davis argues).[19] Thus in *The Changeling* the dance of madmen is Beatrice's wedding dance. To recall that earlier metaphor: for the bride who is no bride, De Flores's pelt has indeed been "tann'd / In a pair of dancing pumps" (1.1.228–29). And the moral ending confirms the madness—the last couple at barley-break are left in hell. But at the same time, the derision of the mad dance spills over into De Flores's own derision, and our sense of the intensity of the main characters' experience challenges the platitudes with which they are blandly put in their place.

Another side of the madness-imitation connection is suggested by the fact that so often in Jacobean drama madness is feigned: a state that is represented by a tendency to imitation becomes itself subject to imitation, so that the theatrical propensities inherent within madness are doubled and redoubled. This process is visible in *The Changeling* first in the playing of Antonio and Francisco, themselves imitations of particular categories of lunacy, second in the fact that their pursuit of Isabella mirrors the multiple pursuit of Beatrice in the main plot (with Lollio as a mirror of De Flores), and third by Isabella's entrance into the theatrical fray by the adoption of the guise of madness to pursue Antonio in mockery. The whole game plays out and plays with the fury of love-madness, its links to imitation and rivalry ("mimetic desire" to adopt Girard's phrase[20]), and its ironic connections to the main plot's Petrarchanism. When, as she leaves, Isabella proclaims in mockery, "I came a feigner to return stark mad" (4.3.133), she acknowledges the theatricality but continues the feigning; her stark madness is also a fake, not only because it is a lie, but because it too is an imitation, part of the mad discourse of love, where literal and metaphorical meanings intersect.

Thus theatricality is itself tied up with madness, and the act of playing paradoxically both inverts established meanings and confirms them. As Sir Bounteous said, the players "were never more uncertain in their lives." Their lives *are* uncertainty; in a play that circles through change and changing only to condemn it at the end, the players celebrate it through their associations with madness and their shifts in identity.

In her mimicked madness, Isabella dons the persona of Luna, queen of madness, goddess of chastity in love with Endymion, patroness of inconstancy and change. Earlier, as Luna, she has been said to be responsible for Francisco's lunacy; she is also associated with Titania, a fact that along with the fairy reference in the title, the various lunar associations, the "mimetic desire" of the lovers, and numerous verbal echoes might suggest some linkage with *A Midsummer Night's Dream*, a new quarto of which was published in 1619. Many years ago, Robert Ornstein pointed to the connections between *The Changeling* and *Romeo and Juliet* but no one, as far as I am aware, has pursued its ties with *A Midsummer Night's Dream*, companion piece to *Romeo and Juliet*. Empson, however, has pointed the way with his comments about the frightening fairy world and his naming De Flores as *the changeling*. Ornstein talks about doubling Petrarchan triangles, one lover replacing another[21]—a feature that is treated comically in *A Midsummer Night's Dream*, as madness is as well. Both Petrarchan substitution and madness involve transformation and loss of identity, and both are associated with theatrical mimesis (this is made explicit in the playacting of the clowns and in the physical transformation of Bottom). What is potential in *A Midsummer Night's Dream*, but ultimately sidestepped—that is, an irretrievable change or loss, an exchanged identity, losing the self and becoming the other— is actualized in *The Changeling*. In *A Midsummer Night's Dream* the protective fairy world reinstates what was there before, undoing the madness of transformation (with the interesting exception of Demetrius); in *The Changeling* the fairy world, imaged as Empson says, not as a forest but as a subplot, takes its revenge. The exchange of one lover for another becomes absolute and the image of the circle shifts from the benign ("Two of both kinds makes up four") to the Dantesque: the circle of barley-break, of hell.

This whole paper, if I can reflect back on it now as a way of splicing together some of the strands of my argument, may be seen as an attempt to explore some relations between love and transgression in patriarchal culture. The issue is an apt one for the theatre, since it is involved first of all with acting. Acting in itself is transgressive in that it demands a change of identity, an insertion of instability into what is constructed as stable. Not only that, the Jacobean theatre blurred socially crucial distinctions, mixing meanings and endangering divisions on which value and hierarchy were based. As Jonas Barish has illustrated, one source of antipathy to play-acting and mimesis of any sort was a distrust of boundary-crossing, especially the boundary of gender.[22] This same fear is manifest in a by now well-known text published in 1620, one that was part of the so-called "woman controversy" and that I want to invoke briefly here since it connects in some interesting, if oblique, ways with *The Changeling*. *Hic Mulier* comes out strongly against any kind of gender crossing, emphasizing division as a basis for value and meaning. Boundaries allow for hierarchy, while hermaphroditism is a threat to patriarchal authority. But there is a contradiction in the stance taken by *Hic Mulier* in that it condemns crossdressing both as a blurring of gender distinctions and a form of imitation, and at the same time it proclaims sexual attraction as the main source of power in the fashions it condemns. (A similar contradiction is dramatized in Middleton and Dekker's *The Roaring Girl* [1611].) Women are masculine, but they are also more dangerously attractive. In both guises, they are prone to violence and transgression. At intervals in the text, interestingly, the crimes and yellow ruffs of Lady Frances Howard and her accomplice Mrs. Turner are waved at the reader like flags:

> From the first [Mrs. Turner] you got the false armoury of yellow Starch ..., the folly of imitation, the deceitfulnesse of flatterie, and the grossest basenesse of all basenesse, to do whatsoever a greater power will command you. From the other [the Countess], you have taken the monstrousnesse of your deformitie in apparell, exchanging the modest attire of the comely Hood, Cawle, Coyfe ... to the cloudy Ruffianly broadbrimm'd Hatte and wanton Feather, the modest upper parts of a concealing straight gowne, to the loose, lascivious civill embracement of a French doublet, being all unbutton'd to entice, all of one shape to hide deformitie, and extreme short-wasted to give a most easie way to every luxurious action. ...[23]

The threat is to authority, but it is clearly a sexual one. And thus it can be handled, as in the subplot of *The Changeling*, by a renewal of hierarchy, by an assertion of power over madness that is parallel to power over sexuality: "You need not fear, sir [says Lollio to Alibius]; so long as we are there with our commanding pizzles, they'll [i.e., Antonio, Francisco, and the mad folk] be as tame as the ladies themselves" (4.3.60–61). Restored male sexual authority controls and contains the threat of transgression.

How does all this apply to Beatrice? At the end of the play, she makes a famous speech:

> Oh, come not near me, sir; I shall defile you.
> I am that of your blood was taken from you
> For your better health; look no more upon't
> But cast it to the ground regardlessly.
> Let the common sewer take it from distinction. (5.3.150–54)

She retains the view that she had earlier expressed to De Flores ("Think but upon the distance that creation / Set 'twixt thy blood and mine"), but she reverses its application. Her speech has come in response to her father's bewildered exclamation, "An host of enemies enter'd my citadel / Could not amaze like this" (148–49), and registers her awareness of the dialectical relationship between citadel and sewer. If before she had been the castle or the temple—"high" forms of the "classical body" (Bakhtin's term for what the grotesque body of carnival puts in question), and if before she was a virgin, the sexual form of the same body, there is a binary logic in her now being sewer and whore. A tellingly parallel passage from *Hic Mulier* might be cited as commentary: "[Have] every window closed with a strong Casement and every Loope-hole furnisht with such strong Ordnance, that no unchaste eye may come neere to assayle them; no lascivious tongue wooe a forbidden passage, nor no prophane hand touch reliques so pure and religious" (B4r). This sentence combines the three salient images from *The Changeling*, virginal body, castle, temple; and, in a further parallel, the admonition is to offset the temptation to disguising and imitation, and the threat of change that such boundary-crossing entails.

The point is not to assert direct influence but to suggest that in the social economy represented by the text, Beatrice's playacting guarantees the truth of her fellow-players, while as a sewer she guarantees the purity of the world she has abandoned. Her changes confirm the stability of the patriarchal world smugly maintained by Alsemero at the end: "Here's beauty chang'd / To ugly whoredom" (5.3.198–99). Changing lovers has set her on a destructive course that leads to punishment—an expiation that legitimates patriarchal marriage arrangements and absorbs the "madness" of sexual attraction manifested by Antonio and Francisco toward Isabella. That is one message of the charivari, the masque of transgression that, like the antimasque subplot, actually confirms restitution and "sane" social arrangements.

But, and this is my main point, there is also something derisive here. The failure all the way through the play to keep meanings in their place, the inability of language or representation to contain sexual attraction or keep boundaries from being crossed, undermines the handy restitution of patriarchal values and the legitimation that the end of the play proclaims. The play in a sense undoes what it does, revealing a deep ambivalence about change, boundary-crossing, etc. which are portrayed as dangerous and evil but at the same time revealed as inevitable and engrossing. The whole mix is signalled by the slip of puns, the hermaphroditism of language.

De Flores himself is derisive and unrepentant, proud of having taken Beatrice's "honor's prize" as his "reward". He stabs himself like Othello over the dead body of Desdemona or Juliet over Romeo, reminding us in harshly unromantic language of the token he has so faithfully delivered earlier: "Make haste, Joanna, by that token to thee / Canst not forget so lately put in mind; / I would not go to leave thee far behind" (5.3.176–78). The "token" here is the wound he has given himself—a sign of their bond as the finger was earlier. The slide between murder and love ends with his own self-violation; the two meanings collapse into one, focused on the two merged and bloody bodies that form the centre of the stage picture. In a powerful production of the play at the Toronto Free Theatre in 1985, the staging of this moment illuminated the associations I have been trying to develop. Taking seriously Alsemero's injunction to De Flores when he sends him to her ("Get you in to her, sir. / I'll be your pander now; rehearse again / Your scene of lust" [114–16]), the production treated her murder like an act of love, with climactic sounds and a sudden bursting open of the stage-right door when the couple emerged. The door was liberally daubed with blood, underlining again the connections with violation and virginity, and the spurt of blood from De Flores's neck when he stabbed himself, coupled as it was with an erotic embrace, was again orgasmic. The ending, a deliberate contesting of the restorative patness of the text, was marked by an emphatically formalized rhetoric and an anti-illusionary dance accompanying the epilogue, a kind of nosethumbing reminiscent of the end of the *Marat-Sade*. This was brilliantly parallel to the dance of fools at the end of Act 4, emphasizing derision and making clear how the antimasque can undermine as well as confirm the authoritative values it confronts.

Such derision is appropriate in a play that parodies the love-death motif wrought to the uttermost by Shakespeare in his love tragedies. The tableau at the end of *The Changeling* is clearly and deliberately reminiscent of those at the end of *Othello* and *Romeo and Juliet*. And, although the mocking tone creates a world of difference, there is still a sense of perverse, pained nobility in De Flores's obsessive desire and his refusal to moralize the spectacle. The parallels with *Romeo and Juliet* are extensive—not just the Petrarchan triangles that Ornstein discusses, or the love-death, but also, and equally important, the link between desire and blood, marriage and murder. The killing of Tybalt in Shakespeare's text is tied directly to the sexual love of *Romeo and Juliet*, even though the distribution of the plot elements exonerates Romeo from guilt. Still, the economy is similar: virginity, forced marriage, substitution, killing, sexual consummation. No wonder there is so much talk of mutilation in *Romeo and Juliet* ("when he shall die, / Take him and cut him out in little stars ..."). It seems to me Middleton's irony makes explicit what is implied but romanticized in texts like *Romeo and Juliet* or *Othello*: that at the heart of love in patriarchal culture, or at least in the Elizabethan-Jacobean manifestation thereof, there is a terrible linkage between sex and murder, love and violence.

The final question is why this should be so. Recently, some feminist critics of Shakespeare, working with psychoanalytic theory as their base, have argued that Shakespeare's tragic heroes are characterized by an ambivalence about femininity that manifests itself either as a fear of absorption by the female, or a fear of becoming themselves feminized, or both, leading first of all to feelings of vulnerability and ambivalence, and then, frequently, to a retreat into male bonding and aggressiveness. The most extreme form of this is, paradoxically, the cult of the wound, penetration of the other's body, as in *Coriolanus*. Femininity is associated with the inauthentic, the play-acted, and male rivalry is raised to the peak level of authenticity. In the love tragedies, according to Madelon Sprengnether, sexual passion and the concomitant fear of becoming feminized create "the condition of union in destruction that comprises both the conclusion of the play and the actualization of a basic fantasy about heterosexual relations."[24] So men desire love and resist it—the form of Shakespeare's plays telling the story and dramatizing the disastrous consequences of the conflict.

Middleton settles an ironic gaze on the whole issue, stripping away the pretensions, the powerful delusions and comforts of grand passion and operatic display. But as I have been trying to show, he goes farther than this, seeking to expose not only the underpinnings of the Shakespearean grammar of love but its uncertainties as well, its dependence on unstable language and reversible structures of authority. He thus locates these issues of the body in the realm of social hierarchies; the "classical body," the "inherent *form* of the high official culture,"[25] is indissolubly linked to the mockery of the grotesque, as authority is to transgression, fixed meaning to "the slip." The body, Middleton realizes, is the ultimate locus of social meanings, which is why it costs so much for De Flores to give Beatrice-Joanna the finger.

NOTES

1. The text of *A Trick to Catch the Old One* I have used is that edited by George R. Price (The Hague, 1976).

2. The text of *A Mad World, My Masters* I have used is from *The Selected Plays of Thomas Middleton*, ed. David L. Frost (Cambridge, 1978).

3. I am aware that widows are problematic, even liminal, figures in Jacobean drama and society, but I am thinking here of Escalus's taxonomy in *Measure for Measure*.

4. My analysis here relies partly on Bakhtin's discussion of high and low, "classical" and "grotesque" (in *Rabelais and his World*, trans. Helene Iswolsky [Cambridge, Mass., 1968]) as well as on the notion of inversion developed by symbolic anthropology. The quotation is from Barbara A. Babcock, ed., *The Reversible World: Symbolic Inversion in Art and Society* (Ithaca, N.Y., 1978), 32. Sec Peter Stallybrass and Allon White, *The Politics and Poetics of Transgression* (Ithaca, N.Y., 1986), 1–26, for an excellent discussion of these ideas and their complex relation to social subversiveness.

5. Similarly, at the end of *Your Five Gallants*, Fitzgrave exults that he has the virgin while the gallants are all forced to marry whores.

6. V.V. Ivanov, "The Significance of Bakhtin's Ideas on Sign, Utterance and Dialogue for Modern Semiotics," *Papers on Poetics and Semiotics* 4 (Tel Aviv, 1976),

3; quoted in Stallybrass and White, 21. See also Mary Douglas, *Natural Symbols*, 2nd ed. (London, 1973), chap. 5.

7. Since Middleton probably wrote most of the main plot, and since the contributions of the two authors are so remarkably well integrated (this point has been a mainstay of criticism ever since N.N. Bawcutt's edition of the play for the Revels series in 1958), I have not considered the authorship question at all in this paper. I am interested in the texts rather than their authors, and I see relations between some of Middleton's early texts and *The Changeling* even though I am fully aware that Middleton is not the sole author of the later play.

8. The text of *The Changeling* I have used is the Regents edition, ed. George Walton Williams (Lincoln, Nebr., 1966).

9. In a talk at the Shakespeare Association of America conference in 1987.

10. Christopher Ricks, "The Moral and Poetic Structure of *The Changeling*," *Essays in Criticism* 10 (1960): 296–99.

11. See Nancy J. Vickers, "Diana Described: Scattered Woman and Scattered Rhyme," in *Writing and Sexual Difference*, ed. Elizabeth Abel (Chicago, 1982), 95–109, for an interesting account of the motif of dismemberment implicit in at least one version of Petrarchanism.

12. See my essay *"Women Beware Women* and the Economy of Rape," *Studies in English Literature* 27 (1987): 303–20.

13. The pun may not seem so farfetched if we take note that Middleton puns on a crippled soldier's "unjointed fortunes" in *Father Hubburd's Tales* (*The Works of Thomas Middleton*, ed. A.H. Bullen, 8 vols. [New York, 1964], 8:94) and that Fletcher plays on the word "jointure" in a deliberately rude way in *The Woman's Prize: or, The Tamer Tam'd* (*The Dramatic Works in the Beaumont and Fletcher Canon;*, ed. Fredson Bowers, 7 vols. [Cambridge, 1979], 4:2.1.39–43).

14. William Empson, *Some Versions of Pastoral* ((London, 1950), 51–52. On the double plot, see also Richard Levin, *The Multiple Plot in Renaissance Drama* (Chicago, 1971), 1–20, 34–48.

15. Here I am drawing on Bakhtin, *Rabelais and his World*, Natalie Zemon Davis, *Society and Culture in Early Modern France* (Stanford, 1975), esp. chaps. 4 and 5, Victor W. Turrner, *The Ritual Process: Structure and Anti-Structure* (Chicago, 1969), and Babcock, *Reversible World*.

16. Carol Neely made this point in an unpublished paper, "Madness, Gender and Ritual in Shakespeare," that she kindly sent to me; this essay, much revised, has now appeared as "'Documents in Madness': Reading Madness and Gender in Shakespeare's Tragedies and Early Modern Culture," *Shakespeare Quarterly* 42 (91): 315–38.

17. See Beatrice White, Cast of Ravens: *The Strange Case of Sir Thomas Overbury* (London, 1965) for a full account of this scandalous event; G.P.V. Akrigg, *Jacobean Pageant* (Cambridge, Mass., 1962), chaps. 15 and 16, also

provides a lively account. Anne Lancashire (in "*The Witch*: Stage Flop or Political Mistake?" in K. Friedenreich, ed. *Accompaninge the Players* [New York, 1983], 161–81) and Margot Heinemann (*Puritanism and Theatre: Thomas Middleton and Opposition Drama under the Stuarts* [Cambridge, 1980], 110–11) both discuss Middleton's *The Witch* in the context of the Overbury murder and suggest historical parallels.

18. The masque was performed before the Earl and Countess at the Merchant Taylor's Hall under the auspices of the Lord Mayor and Aldermen. See Alexander Dyce, ed., *The Works of Thomas Middleton*, 5 vols. (London, 1840), 1:xix–xxi.

19. Davis, *Society and Culture in Early Modern France*, 102–3, 122–23, 124–51.

20. Rene Girard, "Myth and Ritual in Shakespeare: *A Midsummer Night's Dream*," *Textual Strategies: Perspectives in Post-Structuralist Criticism*, ed. Josue V. Harari (Ithaca, 1979), 189–212.

21. Robert Ornstein, *The Moral Vision of Jacobean Tragedy* (Madison, 1960), 186–87.

22. Jonas Barish, The Antitheatrical Prejudice (Berkeley, 1981), 80–117.

23. *Hic Mulier* (London, 1620), *STC* 13374, A4r–v. This text is reprinted in Katherine Usher Henderson and Barbara F. McManus, eds. *Half Humankind: Contexts and Texts of the Controversy about Women in England, 1540–1640* (Urbana and Chicago, 1985). See also Linda Woodbridge, *Women and the English Renaissance* (Urbana and Chicago, 1984); she traces the controversy about cross-dressing back to Phillip Stubbes who "characterized the fashion as a deliberate challenge to the immutability of sexual distinctions" (139).

24. Madelon Sprengnether, "Annihilating Intimacy in *Coriolanus*," in Mary Beth Rose, ed., *Women in the Middle Ages and the Renaissance* (Syracuse, 1986), 95.

25. Stallybrass and White, 21. See also Bakhtin's *Rabelais and his World*, 19–25.

Chronology

1553	Mary Tudor becomes Queen; John Lyly is born in Kent.
1554	Sir Philip Sydney is born; Roman Catholicism is restored to England.
1558	Thomas Kyd is born in London; Mary I dies and Elizabeth is proclaimed Queen.
1559	Coronation of Elizabeth I; the Acts of Supremacy and Uniformity are passed, establishing the Elizabethan Religious Settlement.
1560	George Chapman is born in Hitchin, Hertfordshire (date approximate).
1563	The Thirty Nine Articles are issued, establishing the doctrine of the Anglican Church; the Plague returns to London.
1564	Christopher Marlowe and William Shakespeare are born; John Calvin dies in Geneva.
1565	Kyd attends Merchant Taylors school in London.
1566	The future James I is born to Mary, Queen of Scots.
1567	Mary, Queen of Scots is forced to abdicate the crown in favor of her son James, seeking refuge in England where she is later imprisoned.
1568	William of Orange defeats the Spanish force at Heilgerlee, marking the beginning of the Netherlands revolt.
1569	Lyly enters Magdalen College, Oxford; receives his BA in 1573 and MA in 1575.
1570	The Pope excommunicates Queen Elizabeth.

1571	The Royal Exchange is opened; the Treason Act is passed, making it heresy to deny the Supremacy of the Queen.
ca. 1572–1573	Thomas Dekker and Ben Jonson are born in London.
1573	Inigo Jones and John Donne are born; Torquato Tasso writes *Aminta*.
ca. 1574	Chapman attends Oxford, though he does not receive a degree.
1575	Robert Dudley, the Earl of Leicester, entertains Queen Elizabeth at Kenilworth, which allegedly inspires the beginning of Shakespeare's career.
1576	John Marston is born; James Burbage builds the first London playhouse, named the "Theatre."
1577	Sir Francis Drake embarks on a world voyage; Philip Henslowe builds the Curtain Playhouse.
1578	Lyly publishes *Euphues: The Anatomy of Wit*.
1579	John Fletcher is born at Rye in Sussex; Edmund Spenser publishes *The Shepheard's Calendar*.
1580	Lyly publishes *Euphues and his England*; Drake returns to London, having circumnavigated the globe; Christopher Marlowe attends Corpus Christi College, Cambridge; John Webster, John Middleton, and Cyril Tourneur are born.
1582	Shakespeare marries Anne Hathaway.
1583	Philip Massinger is born; The Queen's Men, the first royal liveried theatrical company, is established; the Irish Rebellion is defeated.
ca. 1584	Francis Beaumont is born in Leicestershire.
1584	William of Orange is assassinated; Lyly produces *Campaspe* and *Sappho and Phao* at the Blackfriars Theatre; Sir Walter Raleigh sails to Virginia; Marlowe receives a BA from Cambridge and later an MA after intervention by the Queen's privy council.
1585	The first English colony in America, Roanoke, Virginia, is established; English expedition to the Netherlands results in war with Spain; Kyd writes *The First Part of Hieronimo*.
1586	Shakespeare arrives in London; Mary, Queen of Scots is found to be complicit in the Babington plot to assassinate Elizabeth and is sentenced to death; Marlowe writes *Of Carthage*, possibly with Nashe; John Ford is born.
1587	Mary, Queen of Scots, is executed. Marlowe's *Tamburlaine*, Part One and Part Two are performed by the Lord Admiral's Men; Kyd writes *The Spanish Tragedy*, which is also performed

this year; Philip Henslowe opens the Rose Theatre.

1588	England defeats the Spanish Armada; the Earl of Leicester dies; Thomas Hobbes is born.
1589	Marlowe's *The Jew of Malta* is produced; the three parts of Shakespeare's *Henry VI* are written and produced (ca. 1589–1592).
1590	Edmund Spenser publishes Books I–III of *The Faerie Queene*; Sir Philip Sydney publishes *Arcadia*.
1591	Elizabeth founds Trinity College in Dublin; Sidney publishes *Astrophel and Stella*; Spenser, *Complaints*; and Lyly, *Endymion, the Man in the Moon*.
1592	Plague in London kills 15,000; Lyly publishes *Gallathea* and *Midas*; Kyd is arrested under suspicion of heresy and public libel, claims heretical tract belongs to Marlowe; Marston is matriculated at Brasenose College, Oxford. Marlowe's *Dr. Faustus* is produced; Shakespeare's *Richard III* and *The Comedy of Errors* is produced.
1593	The plague continues and the theaters are temporarily closed; Christopher Marlowe is murdered; his play *Edward II* is published; Dekker begins to write for the Admiral's Men around this time.
1593–94	Publication of Shakespeare's *Venus and Adonis* and *The Rape of Lucrece*—two narrative poems dedicated to Earl of Southampton. Shakespeare joins the Lord Chamberlain's Men, adding to its repertoire *The Taming of the Shrew*, *Titus Andronicus*, and perhaps the first version of *Hamlet*.
1594	Chapman publishes *The Shadow of Night*; Kyd dies.
1595	Chapman publishes *Ovid's Banquet of Sense*; The Swan Theatre is built. Shakespeare's *Richard II*, *Romeo and Juliet*, and *A Midsummer Night's Dream* are produced.
1596	Death of Drake; Blackfriars Theatre opens in London; James Shirley is born in London; Marlowe's translation of Ovid's Elegies is published.
1597	Second Spanish Armada fails; Shakespeare's *The Merchant of Venice* and *Henry IV, Part 1* are written; Lyly publishes *Woman in the Moon*; Jonson writes *The Case is Altered*; the Lord Chamberlain's Men perform at the Curtain Theatre; James Burbage dies.
1598	Shakespeare publishes *Love's Labour's Lost* and writes *Henry IV, Part 2* and *Much Ado About Nothing*; Jonson's *Every Man in his*

Humor is performed with William Shakespeare as the principal actor; Chapman publishes *Achilles Shield* and *Seven Books of the Iliad*, both translations from the Greek; Marston publishes *The Metamorphosis of Pygmalion's Image* and *The Scourge of Villainy*; Marlowe's *Hero and Leander* is published.

1599   Oliver Cromwell is born; the Lord Chamberlain's Men move to the new Globe Theatre; Edmund Spenser dies; Jonson and Dekker collaborate on two now lost plays, *The Page of Plymouth* and *Robert the Second, King of Scots*; Marston writes *Histriomastix*, *Antonio and Melinda*, and *Jack Drum's Entertainment*.

1600   East India Company is established; Shakespeare writes *Hamlet*; the Fortune Theatre built by Alleyn and Henslowe opens in London; Chapman is arrested for debt. Tourneur publishes *The Transformed Metamorphosis*.

1601   Queen Elizabeth delivers her "Golden Speech"; the Earl of Essex is tried for treason and executed after leading a revolt against the Queen. Lyly publishes *Love's Metamorphosis*; The poets' war begins, pitting Dekker and Marston against Jonson; Marston writes *Antonio's Revenge*; Shakespeare writes *The Phoenix and the Turtle*, a narrative poem, as well as *Twelfth Night or What You Will*, *All's Well That Ends Well*, and *Troilus and Cressida*.

1602   Shakespeare's *All's Well That Ends Well* is produced; Massinger enters St. Alban Hall, Oxford; Ford is admitted to the Middle Temple.

1603   Queen Elizabeth I dies; James IV of Scotland becomes King James I of England; Dekker and Middleton collaborate on *The Magnificent Entertainment Given to King James*; the Chamberlain's Men become the King's Men to honor King James I; Jonson's *Sejanus* is performed; *The Malcontent* is written by Marston and performed.

1604   Middleton's *The Phoenix* is performed; Chapman's *All Fools*, *Monsieur d'Olive*, and *Bussy D'Ambois* are performed; Webster and Dekker collaborate on *Westward Ho!* and *Northward Ho!*; the Queen Anne's Men are formed; Shakespeare's *Measure for Measure* and *Othello* are produced.

1605   Chapman's *The Widow's Tears* and *The Tragedy of Caesar and Pompey* are performed; Fletcher writes *Woman's Prize*; Shakespeare's *King Lear* is produced; Jonson's *The Mask of Blackness* is produced, his first collaborative effort with Inigo Jones.

1606	The Virginia Company is granted a charter; Beaumont writes *The Woman Hater*; Tourneur writes *The Revenger's Tragedy* (credited first to Tourneur and later to Middleton); the Act to Restrain Abuses of Players is passed against plays containing profanity and criticism of the establishment; Shakespeare's *Macbeth* and *Antony and Cleopatra* are produced; Jonson's *Volpone, or The Fox* is written.
1607	Jamestown, Virginia is founded; Middleton publishes *The Phoenix, Michaelmas Term, A Trick to Catch the Old One*, and *The Family of Love*; Shakespeare's *Coriolanus, Timon of Athens*, and *Pericles* is written; Dekker and Webster publish *The Famous Historie of Sir Thomas Wyatt*; Beaumont writes *The Knight of the Burning Pestle*.
1608	John Milton is born; Shirley enters Merchant Taylor's school; Chapman's, *The Conspiracy and Tragedy of Charles, Duke of Byron* is published; the King's Men perform at the Blackfriars Theatre in London, taking on a 21 year lease; Fletcher writes *The Faithful Shepherdess*; Middleton and Dekker collaborate on *The Roaring Girl*.
1609	Dekker publishes *Gull's Handbook*; Marston is ordained a priest; Chapman publishes *Twelve Books of the Iliad*; Shakespeare's *Cymbeline* is produced; Jonson's *Epicoene* and *The Masque of Queens* is written; Beaumont and Fletcher write *Philaster and Coxcomb*.
1610	Tourneur writes *The Atheist's Tragedy*; Shakespeare's *Macbeth* is performed at the Globe; Jonson's *The Alchemist* is written; Donne publishes *Pseudo-Martyr*.
1611	James I dissolves Parliament; Beaumont and Fletcher's *A King and No King* is performed; Shakespeare's *The Tempest* is produced; Donne publishes *Ignatius His Conclave* and *The First Anniversarie*; Jonson writes *Catiline His Conspiracy*; Webster's *The White Devil* is written and performed; Chapman's *Revenge of Bussy D'Ambois* is published; Tourneur's missing tragicomedy *The Nobleman* is performed and published; The King James version of The Bible is published.
1612	Shakespeare collaborates with Fletcher on *Henry VIII*; Donne publishes *The Second Anniversarie*.
1613	Beaumont writes the *Inner Temple Masque*. Shakespeare collaborates with Fletcher on *Two Noble Kinsmen*. Middleton's *A Chaste Maid at Cheapside* is performed; Fire destroys the Globe Theatre during a performance of *Henry VIII*.

1614	Middleton's *The Witch* is performed; Jonson writes *Bartholomew Fair*; Webster writes *The Duchess of Malfi*; The Globe Theatre re-opens.
1615	Chapman publishes his complete translation of the *Odyssey*; John Donne is ordained.
1616	Beaumont and Fletcher's *The Scornful Lady* is published. Beaumont and Shakespeare die; Jonson's *The Devil Is an Ass* is produced. Jonson's *Works* is published; Fletcher publishes *Mad Lover* and *Loyal Subject*.
1617	Shirley receives a BA from Cambridge; Middleton collaborates with Rowley on *A Fair Quarrel*; Massinger begins writing for the King's Men; Webster revises *The Duchess of Malfi* for a stage revival.
1618	Massinger, Middleton and Rowley write *The Old Law*.
1619	Middleton's *The Inner Masque* is performed; Webster's *The Devil's Law Case* is written and performed.
1620	The *Mayflower* lands at Plymouth Rock, Massachusetts.
1621	Ford, Dekker and Rowley's *The Witch of Edmonton* is performed; Middleton's *Women Beware Women* is performed. Massinger writes *The Maid of Honor* and *A New Way to Pay Old Debts*.
1622	Middleton and Rowley's *The Changeling* is performed.
1623	Massinger writes *The Duke of Milan* and *The Bondman*; Shakespeare's First Folio Edition is published; the first English settlement in India is formed.
1624	Middleton's *A Game of Chess* is performed; John Donne publishes *Devotions Upon Emergent Occasions*.
1625	James I dies; Charles I assumes the throne; Tourneur, serving as secretary to Sir Edward Cecil, falls ill during the expedition against Cadiz and dies in Kinsale, Ireland. Fletcher dies; Shirley writes for Queen Henrietta's Company for the next eleven years.
1626	Massinger writes *The Roman Actor*; Jonson produces *The Staple of News*.
1627	Middleton dies.
1628	Parliament passes "Petition of Right"; Ford's *The Lover's Melancholy* is performed; Ford writes *'Tis a Pity She's a Whore*; Shirley writes *The Witty Fair One*.
1629	Charles's third Parliament is dissolved—begins 11 years of "personal rule"; Jonson's *Chloridia* is written.

1630	Charles II is born; the Massachusetts Bay Company is founded; John Winthrop founds Boston.
1631	John Donne dies.
1632	Charter for Maryland is issued; Samuel Pepys and John Locke are born; Dekker dies; Massinger writes *The City Madam*; Shirley writes *Hyde Park*.
1633	Massinger writes The Guardian; Ford publishes *'Tis Pity She's A Whore*, *Love's Sacrifice*, and *The Broken Heart*.
1634	Ford publishes *Perkin Warbeck*; Jonson has produced *The New Inn*, *The Magnetic Lady* and re-written *A Tale of a Tub*; Chapman, Marston, and Webster die.
1637	Jonson dies, leaving behind *The Sad Shephard*, his last, unfinished play.
1640	Massinger dies in London.
1641	Shirley writes *The Cardinal*.
1642	Charles I flees London; civil war between Parliament forces and Royalists begins; Parliament closes London theaters.
1645	Oliver Cromwell and the Parliamentary forces defeat the Royalists at the Battle of Naseby.
1646	Charles I and the Parliamentary forces officially surrender; first Civil War ends.
1648	Milton publishes *The Tenure of Kings and Magistrates*.
1649	Charles I is tried for treason and beheaded.
1651	Thomas Hobbes publishes *Leviathan*.
1652	Inigo Jones dies.
1653	Cromwell becomes Lord Protector.
1658	Cromwell dies.
1660	Restoration of Charles II, theaters re-open.
1666	Great Fire of London; Shirley dies.

Contributors

HAROLD BLOOM is Sterling Professor of the Humanities at Yale University and Henry W. and Albert A. Berg Professor of English at the New York University Graduate School. He is the author of over 20 books, including *Shelley's Mythmaking* (1959), *The Visionary Company* (1961), *Blake's Apocalypse* (1963), *Yeats* (1970), *A Map of Misreading* (1975), *Kabbalah and Criticism* (1975), *Agon: Toward a Theory of Revisionism* (1982), *The American Religion* (1992), *The Western Canon* (1994), and *Omens of Millennium: The Gnosis of Angels, Dreams, and Resurrection* (1996). *The Anxiety of Influence* (1973) sets forth Professor Bloom's provocative theory of the literary relationships between the great writers and their predecessors. His most recent books include *Shakespeare: The Invention of the Human* (1998), a 1998 National Book Award finalist, *How to Read and Why* (2000), *Genius: A Mosaic of One Hundred Exemplary Creative Minds* (2002), and *Hamlet: Poem Unlimited* (2003). In 1999, Professor Bloom received the prestigious American Academy of Arts and Letters Gold Medal for Criticism, and in 2002 he received the Catalonia International Prize.

PETER HAPPÉ is the author of multiple works, among them *John Bale*, *Medieval English Drama: A Casebook*, and *English Drama Before Shakespeare*, a volume in the Longman Literature in English series. He has also edited Ben Jonson's *The Magnetic Lady* and *The Devil Is an Ass*, *English Mystery Plays: A Selection*, and, with John N. King, *The Vocacyon of John Bale*.

MARTIN WIGGINS is a Senior Lecturer at the University of Birmingham and author of *Journeymen in Murder* and *Shakespeare and the Drama of his Time*. He also serves as Associate General Editor of English Drama for the Oxford World's Classics series, for which he has edited *Four Jacobean Sex Tragedies*.

EUGENE M. WAITH is Professor Emeritus in English at Yale University. His many books include *Ideas of Greatness: Heroic Drama in England*, *The Heraclean Hero in Marlowe, Chapman, and Shakespeare*, and *Patterns and Perspectives in English Renaissance Drama*, as well as editions of *Macbeth*, *Titus Andronicus*, and *Two Noble Kinsmen*.

MARTHA TUCK ROZETT, Professor of English at the State University of New York at Albany, is the author of *Doctrine of Election and the Emergence of Elizabethan Tragedy*, *Talking Back to Shakespeare*, and *Constructing a World: Shakespeare's England and the New Historical Fiction*.

PATRICK CHENEY is a Professor of English and Comparative Literature at Penn State University. President of the International Spenser Society, his publications include *Spenser's Famous Flight: A Renaissance Idea of a Literary Career*, *Marlowe's Counterfeit Profession: Ovid, Spenser, Counter-Nationhood*, and *Approaches to Teaching Shorter Elizabethan Poetry* (MLA series).

M.C. BRADBROOK, a prolific critic of Elizabethan literature, is the author of *Themes and Conventions of Elizabethan Tragedy*, *The Rise of the Common Player*, *Growth and Structure of Elizabethan Comedy*, and *The Living Monument: Shakespeare and the Theater of His Time*, as well as studies of Marvell, Ibsen, and Malcolm Lowry.

PAUL J. VOSS has written *Elizabethan News Pamphlets: Shakespeare, Spenser, Marlowe & the Birth of Journalism*. He is vice president for academic affairs at Southern Catholic College.

ALVIN B. KERNAN is Avalon University Professor of Humanities (emeritus) at Princeton University. His many books include *The Cankered Muse: Satire of the English Renaissance*, *Playwright as Magician: Shakespeare's Image of the Poet in the English Public Theater*, *The Death of Literature*, *Shakespeare, the King's Playwright: Theater in the Stuart Court, 1603–1613*, and more recently, the memoir *In Plato's Cave* and *Fruited Plain: Fables for a Postmodern Democracy*.

RICHARD DUTTON, Professor of English literature at Lancaster University, has written *Modern Tragicomedy and the British Tradition*, *William Shakespeare: a Literary Life*, *Mastering the Revels: the Regulation and Censorship of English Renaissance Drama*, and *Licensing, Censorship, and Authorship in Early Modern England*. His many edited volumes include *A Midsummer Night's Dream*, *Jacobean Civic Pageants*, *Women Beware Women*, and several works by and about Ben Jonson.

JAMES P. BEDNARZ is Professor of English at the C.W. Post campus of Long Island University. He is the author of *Shakespeare and the Poets' War*, and his articles have appeared in journals such as *ELH, Shakespeare Studies, Renaissance Drama,* and *The Huntington Library Quarterly.*

MATTHEW STEGGLE is a lecturer in English at Sheffield Haddam University. He is the author of *Wars of the Theatres: the Poetics of Personation in the Age of Jonson* and articles in journals such as *Studies in English Literature 1500–1900, Sidney Journal,* and *Review of English Studies.*

JONATHAN DOLLIMORE is a Professor in the University of York's Department of English and Related Literature. His books include *Radical Tragedy: Religions, Ideology, and Power in the Drama of Shakespeare and His Contemporaries, Sexual Dissidence: Augustine to Wilde, Freud to Foucault,* and *Sex, Literature, and Censorship.* He has also edited the *Selected Plays of John Webster* and, with Alan Sinfield, *Political Shakespeare: Essays in Cultural Materialism.*

GAIL KERN PASTER is the Director of the Folger Shakespeare Library and author of *The Body Embarrassed: Drama and the Disciplines of Shame in Early Modern England* and *The Idea of the City in the Age of Shakespeare.* She has also edited texts by Shakespeare and Middleton.

LEAH S. MARCUS is the Edwin Mims Professor of English at Vanderbilt University. Her publications include *Politics of Mirth: Jonson, Herrick, Milton, Marvell, and the Defense of Old Holiday Pastimes, Puzzling Shakespeare: Local Reading and its Discontents,* and *Unediting the Renaissance: Shakespeare, Marlowe, Milton.* Most recently she has edited the works of Elizabeth I.

STEPHEN ORGEL is the Jackson Eli Reynolds Professor of Humanities at Stanford University. His books include *The Jonsonian Masque, The Illusion of Power,* and most recently, *Authentic Shakespeare.* He has also edited Ben Jonson's masques, the poems of Christopher Marlowe, and Shakespeare's *The Tempest.*

G.K. HUNTER, Professor emeritus of English at Yale University, has written *John Lyly, Humanist Courtier, Dramatic Identities and Cultural Tradition: Studies in Shakespeare and His Contemporaries,* and *English Drama 1586–1642: the Age of Shakespeare.* He has also edited a variety of plays by Shakespeare, Lyly, and Marston.

ANTHONY B. DAWSON is a Professor of English at the University of British Columbia. His works include *Indirections: Shakespeare and the Art of Illusion, Watching Shakespeare: A Playgoers' Guide,* and a book-length study of *Hamlet.* He is also co-author, with Paul Yachnin, of *Culture of Playgoing in Shakespeare's England: a Collaborative Debate.*

Bibliography

Barber, C.L. *Creating Elizabethan Tragedy: The Theater of Marlowe and Kyd.* Richard P. Wheeler, ed. Chicago: The University of Chicago Press, 1988.

Bartels, Emily C. *Spectacles of Strangeness: Imperialism, Alienation and Marlowe.* Philadelphia: University of Pennsylvania Press, 1993.

Belsey, Catherine. *The Subject of Tragedy: Identity and Difference in Renaissance Drama.* New York: Methuen, 1985.

Bednarz, James P. *Shakespeare & The Poets' War.* New York: Columbia University Press, 2001.

Bevington, David M. *From Mankind to Marlowe: Growth of Structure in the Popular Drama of Tudor England.* Cambridge: Harvard University Press, 1962.

Bloom, Harold. *Hamlet: Poem Unlimited.* New York: Riverhead Books, 2003.

———. *Shakespeare: The Invention of the Human.* New York: Riverhead Books, 1998.

Boas, Frederick S. *Christopher Marlowe: A Biographical and Critical Study.* Oxford: Clarendon Press, 1940.

———. *Marlowe and His Circle.* Oxford: Oxford University Press, 1931.

Bradbrook, M.C. *The Growth and Structure of Elizabethan Comedy.* Baltimore: Peregrine Books, 1963.

———. *John Webster: Citizen and Dramatist.* New York: Columbia University Press, 1980.

———. *Themes & Conventions.* London: Cambridge University Press, 1969.

Bradley, A.C. *Shakespearean Tragedy.* London: Macmillan, 1915.

Braunmuller, A.R. *Natural Fictions.* Newark: University of Delaware Press, 1992.

Bredbeck, Gregory W. *Sodomy and Interpretation: Marlowe to Milton*. Ithaca: Cornell University Press, 1991.

Butcher, Andrew, ed. *Christopher Marlowe and Canterbury*. London: Faber and Faber, 1988.

Callaghan, Dympna. *Woman and Gender in Renaissance Tragedy*. Great Britain: Humanities Press International, Inc., 1989.

Chambers, E.K. *The Elizabethan Stage*. 4 vols. Oxford: Clarendon Press, 1923.

Cheney, Patrick. *Marlowe's Counterfeit Profession: Ovid, Spenser, Counter-Nationhood*. Toronto: University of Toronto, 1997.

Dabbs, Thomas. *Reforming Marlowe: The Nineteenth-Century Cannonization of a Renaissance Dramatist*. Lewisburg, PA: Bucknell University Press, 1991.

Dawson, Anthony B. "Giving the Finger: Puns and Transgression in *The Changeling*." *The Elizabethan Theatre* XII. Eds. A.L. Magnusson and C.E. McGee. Toronto: P.D. Meany, 1993.

Deats, Sara Munson. *Sex, Gender, and Desire in the Plays of Christopher Marlowe*. Newark: University of Delaware Press, 1997.

Dollimore, Jonathan. *Radical Tragedy: Religion, Ideology and Power in the Drama of Shakespeare and his Contemporaries*. 2d ed. New York: Harvester Wheatsheaf, 1989

Dunn, Ester Cloudman. *The Literature of Shakespeare's England*. New York: Cooper Square Publishers, Inc., 1969.

Dutton, Richard. *Licensing, Censorship and Authorship in Early Modern England*. New York: Palgrave, 2000.

English Literary Renaissance (journal).

Eliot, T.S. "Seneca in Elizabethan Translation." *Essays on Elizabethan Drama*. New York: Harcourt, Brace & World, 1960.

Erne, Lukas. *Beyond* The Spanish Tragedy: *A Study of the Works of Thomas Kyd*. Manchester: Manchester University Press, 2001.

Finkelpearl, Philip J. *Court and Country Politics in the Plays of Beaumont and Fletcher*. Princeton: Princeton University Press, 1990.

———. *John Marston of the Middle Temple: An Elizabethan Dramatist in His Social Setting*. Cambridge: Harvard University Press, 1969.

Friedenreich, Kenneth, Roma Gill and Constance Kuriyama, eds. *"Poet and a filthy Play-Maker": New Essays on Christopher Marlowe*. New York: AMS Press, 1988.

Frye, Northrop. *Anatomy of Criticism*. Princeton: Princeton University Press, 1957.

———*A Natural Perspective: The Development of Shakespearean Comedy and Romance*. New York: Columbia University Press, 1955.

———*The Secular Scripture: A Study of the Structure of Romance*. Cambridge: Harvard University Press, 1976.

Goddard, Harold C. *The Meaning of Shakespeare*. Chicago: The University of Chicago Press, 1951.

Greenblatt, Stephen J. *Renaissance Self-Fashioning: More to Shakespeare*. Chicago: University of Chicago Press, 1980.

Greenfield, Thelma N. *The Induction in Elizabethan Drama*. Eugene: University of Oregon Books, 1969.

Happé, Peter. *English Drama before Shakespeare*. London: Addison Wesley Longman, 1999.

Harrison, G.B. *Shakespeare's Fellows: Being a Brief Chronicle of the Shakespearean Age*. London: John Lane the Bodley Head Ltd., 1923.

Highfill, Jr., Philip H., ed. *Shakespeare's Craft: Eight Lectures*. Carbondale: Southern Illinois University Press, 1982.

Hillman, Richard. *Shakespeare, Marlowe and the Politics of France*. New York: Palgrave, 2002.

———*Intertextuality and Romance in Renaissance Drama: The Staging of Nostalgia*. New York: St. Martin's Press, 1992.

———*Shakespearean Subversions: The Trickster and the Play-Text*. London: Routledge, 1992.

Hoenselaars, A.J. *Images of Englishmen and Foreigners in the Drama of Shakespeare and His Contemporaries: A Study of Stage Characters and National Identity in English Renaissance Drama, 1558–1642*. Rutherford, NJ: Farleigh Dickinson University Press, 1992.

Hopkins, Lisa. *The Female Hero in English Renaissance Tragedy*. New York: Palgrave, 2002.

Hosley, Richard. *Essays on Shakespeare and Elizabethan Drama in Honor of Hardin Craig*. Columbia: University of Missouri Press, 1962.

Hunter, G.K. *English Drama 1586–1642: The Age of Shakespeare*. Oxford History of English Literature VI. Oxford: Clarendon Press, 1997.

———. "Theatrical Politics and Shakespeare's Comedies, 1590–1600." *Elizabethan Theater: Essays in Honor of S. Schoenbaum*. eds R.B. Parker and S.P. Zitner. Newark and London: University of Delaware Press and Associated University Press, 1996. pp. 241–252.

Journal of Renaissance and Medieval Studies.

Kernan, Alvin B. "Shakespeare's and Jonson's View of Public Theatre Audiences." *Jonson and Shakespeare*. Ed. Ian Donaldson. Hong Kong: Australian National University, 1983.

Kernan, Alvin B., ed. *Two Renaissance Mythmakers: Christopher Marlowe and Ben Jonson*. Baltimore: The Johns Hopkins University Press, 1977.

Knight, G. Wilson. *Shakesperian Dimensions*. Totowa, N.J.: Barnes & Noble Books, 1984.

Knights, L.C. *Some Shakespearean Themes*. London: Chattus &Windus, 1959.

Kuriyama, Constance Brown. *Christopher Marlowe: A Renaissance Life*. Ithaca: Cornell University Press, 2002.

Levin, Harry. *The Myth of the Golden Age in the Renaissance*. Bloomington: University of Indiana Press, 1969.

———. *Shakespeare and the Revolution of the Times: Perspectives and Commentaries*. New York: Oxford University Press, 1976.

———. *Scenes From Shakespeare*. Gwynne B. Evans, ed. New York and London: Garland Publishing, Inc., 2000.

Limon, Jerzy. *Dangerous Matter: English Drama and Politics in 1623/24*. Cambridge: Cambridge University Press, 1986.

———. *The Masque of Stuart Culture*. Newark: University of Delaware Press, 1990.

———. Jerzy and Jay L. Halio, eds. *Shakespeare and His Contemporaries: Eastern and Central European Studies*. Newark: University of Delaware Press, 1993.

Lomax, Marion. *Stage Images and Traditions: Shakespeare to Ford*. Cambridge: Cambridge University Press, 1987.

Maquerlot, Jean-Pierre and Michele Willems, eds. *Travel and Drama in Shakespeare's Time*. New York: Cambridge University Press, 1996.

Marcus, Leah S. "Pastimes and the Purging of Theater: *Bartholomew Fair* (1614)." *Staging the Renaissance: Reinterpretations of Elizabethan and Jacobean Drama*. Ed. David Scott Kastan and Peter Stallybrass. New York: Routledge, 1991.

Martin, Matthew R. *Between Theater and Philosophy: Skepticism in the Major City Comedies of Ben Jonson and Thomas Middleton*. Newark: University of Delaware Press, 2001.

Maus, Katharine Eisaman. *Ben Jonson and the Roman Frame of Mind*. Princeton: Princeton University Press, 1984.

McLuskie, Kathleen. *Renaissance Dramatists*. London: Harvester Wheatsheaf, 1989.

Mebane, John S. *Renaissance Magic and the Return of the Golden Age: The Occult Tradition and Marlowe, Jonson, and Shakespeare*. Lincoln: University of Nebraska Press, 1989.

Muir, Kenneth. *Shakespeare: Contrasts and Controversies*. Brighton: The Harvester Press Limited, 1985.

———. *Shakespeare: The Comedies: A Collection of Critical Essays*. Englewood Cliffs, N.J.: Prentice Hall, Inc., 1965.

Murray, Peter B. *Thomas Kyd*. New York: Twayne Publishers, Inc., 1969.

Nuttall, A.D. *A New Mimesis: Shakespeare and the Representation of Reality*. New York: Methuen, 1983.

Orgel, Stephen. *The Illusion of Power: Political Theater in the English Renaissance.* Berkeley: University of California Press, 1975.

Parker, R.B., Zitner, S.P., eds. *Elizabethan Theater: Essays in Honor of S. Schoenbaum.* Newark and London: University of Delaware Press and Associated University Press, 1996.

Paster, Gail Kern. *The Idea of City in the Age of Shakespeare.* Athens: The University of Georgia Press, 1985.

Pinciss, Gerald M. *Forbidden Matters: Religion in the Drama of Shakespeare and His Contemporaries.* Newark: University of Delaware Press, 2000.

Renaissance Drama (journal)

Rozett, Martha Tuck. *The Doctrine of Election and the Emergence of Elizabethan Tragedy.* Princeton: Princeton University Press, 1984.

Schoenbaum, Samuel. *Shakespeare and Others.* Washington: Folger Shakespeare Library; London: Scholar Press, 1985.

Shakespeare Quarterly (journal)

Simkin, Stevie. *A Preface to Marlowe.* New York: Longman, 2000.

Smith, Molly. *Breaking Boundaries: Politics and Play in the Drama of Shakespeare and his Contemporaries.* Brookfield, VT: Ashgate Publishing Company, 1998.

Steggle, Matthew. *The Wars of the Theatres: The Poetics of Personation in the Age of Jonson.* Victoria, B.C.: University of Victoria English Literary Studies, 1990.

Tricomi, Albert H. *Anticourt Drama in England, 1603–1642.* Charlottesville: University Press of Virginia, 1989.

Urry, William. *Christopher Marlowe and Canterbury.* Andrew Butcher, ed. London: Faber and Faber, 1988.

Voss, Paul J. *Elizabethan News Pamphlets.* Pittsburgh: Duquesne University Press, 2001.

Waith, Eugene M. *The Herculean Hero in Marlowe, Chapman, Shakespeare and Dryden.* New York: Columbia University Press, 1962.

Wharton, T.F., ed. *The Drama of John Marston: Critical Revisions.* Cambridge: Cambridge University Press, 2000.

White, Paul Whitfield, ed. *Marlowe, History, and Sexuality: New Critical Essays on Christopher Marlowe.* New York: AMS Press, Inc., 1998.

Wiggins, Martin. *Shakespeare and the Drama of His Time.* New York: Oxford University Press, 2000.

Wilson, Luke. *Theaters of Intention: Drama and the Law in Early Modern England.* Stanford: Stanford University Press, 2000.

Woolland, Brian, Richard Cave, and Elizabeth Schafer, eds. *Ben Jonson and Theatre: Performance, Practice, and Theory.* London; New York: Routledge, 1999.

Acknowledgments

"Theatres and Companies: The Context of the Professional Stage—James Burbage and John Lyly" by Peter Happé. From *English Drama before Shakespeare* by Peter Happé. © 1999 by Addison Wesley Longman Limited. Reprinted by permission.

"New Tragedies for Old" by Martin Wiggins. From *Shakespeare and the Drama of His Time* by Martin Wiggins. © 2000 by Martin Wiggins. Reprinted by permission.

"Marlowe and the Jades of Asia" by Eugene M. Waith. From *Patterns and Perspectives in English Renaissance* by Eugene M. Waith. © 1988 by Associated University Presses, Inc. Reprinted by permission.

"Doctor Faustus" by Martha Tuck Rozett. From *The Doctrine of Election and the Emergence of Elizabethan Tragedy* by Martha Tuck Rozett. © 1984 by Princeton University Press. Reprinted by permission.

'Italian masques by night': Machiavellian Policy and Ovidian Play in *Edward II* by Patrick Cheney. From *Marlowe's Counterfeit Profession* by Patrick Cheney. © 1997 by the University of Toronto Press. Reprinted by permission.

"Artificial Comedy and Popular Comedy: Shakespeare's Inheritance" by M.C. Bradbrook. From *The Growth and Structure of Elizabethan Comedy* by M.C. Bradbrook. © 1955 by Chatto & Windus. Reprinted by permission.

"Marlowe, Shakespeare, Spenser, and the Fictive Navarre" by Paul J. Voss. From *Elizabethan News Pamphlets: Marlowe, Shakespeare, Spenser and the Birth of Journalism* by Paul J. Voss. © 2001 by Duquesne University Press. Reprinted by permission.

"Shakespeare's and Jonson's View of Public Theatre Audiences" by Alvin B. Kernan. From *Jonson and Shakespeare* by Alvin B. Kernan. ©1983 by Australian National University. Reprinted by permission.

"Licensed Fools: the 1598 Watershed" by Richard Dutton. From *Licensing, Censorship, and Authorship in Early Modern England* by Richard Dutton. © 2000 by Richard Dutton. Reprinted by permission.

"The Elizabethan Dramatists as Literary Critics" by James P. Bednarz. From *Shakespeare & the Poets' War* by James P. Bednarz. © 2001 by Columbia University Press. Reprinted by permission.

"Jonson on Shakespeare: Criticism as Self-Creation" by James P. Bednarz. From *Shakespeare & the Poets' War* by James P. Bednarz. © 2001 by Columbia University Press. Reprinted by permission.

"The Other Side of the War: Marston and Dekker" by Matthew Steggle. From *English Literary Studies*, no. 75. © 1998 by Matthew Steggle. Reprinted by permission.

"*The Revenger's Tragedy* (c. 1606): Providence, Parody and Black Camp" by Jonathan Dollimore. From *Radical Tragedy* by Jonathan Dollimore. © 1984, 1989 by the author. Reprinted by permission.

Bussy D'Ambois (c. 1604): A Hero at Court by Jonathan Dollimore. From *Radical Tragedy* by Jonathan Dollimore. © 1984, 1989 by the author. Reprinted by permission.

"Parasites and Sub-parasites: The City as Predator in Jonson and Middleton" by Gail Kern Paster. From *The Idea of the City in the Age of Shakespeare*. © 1985 by the University of Georgia Press. Reprinted by permission.

"Pastimes and the Purging of Theater: *Bartholomew Fair* (1614) by Leah S. Marcus. From *Staging the Renaissance*, ed. David Scott Kastan and Peter Stallybrass. © 1991 by Routledge, Chapman and Hall. Reprinted by permission.

"The Royal Spectacle" by Stephen Orgel. From *The Illusion of Power* by Stephen Orgel. © 1975 by the author. Reprinted by permission.

"Tragicomedy" by G.K. Hunter. From *English Drama 1586–1642: The Age of Shakespeare* by G.K. Hunter. © 1997 by Oxford University Press. Reprinted by permission.

"Giving the Finger: Puns and Transgression in *The Changeling*" by Anthony B. Dawson. From *The Elizabethan Theatre* XII, ed. A.L. Magnusson and C.E. McGee. © 1993 by P.D. Meany Company. Reprinted by permission.

Index

Marlowe, Christopher, 1–3, 7, 35,
       179–180, 202
    his blank verse, 48
    as disreputable, 12
    and experimenter, 79, 160
    as Ovidian poet, 10, 115
    on poetic rivalry, 113–114
    his power as a writer, 65
    his presenters in plays, 69–70
    reinventing tragedy, 57
    his sequels, 52
    his themes, 11
    and turning Navarre into a character,
       152
    use of French history, 154–155
Marston, John, 5, 223–225, 230, 234,
       355–356
Masques
    as analogies, 351
    climatic moment of, 342
    court audience viewed, 352
    essential to Renaissance Court, 341
    expressions of royal, power, 345
    pastoral in, 347
    puritan objection to, 343
    the world of, 346
Masque of Cupid, (Middelton), 391
Massacre at Paris, The, (Marlowe), 57,
       152–153, 168
    changing in, 159
    final scene in, 157–158
    the murders on stage, 156
Massinger, Philip, 371
McDonald, Russ, 258
McMillin, Scott
    and The Massacre at Paris, 155
    on the Queen's Men, 206
Measure for Measure, (Shakespeare),
       313–314, 319, 387
Melville, Herman, 3, 7
Merchant of Venice, The, (Shakespeare),
       12, 72
Mercury Vindicated from the Alchemist
       Court, (Jonson), 350

Merry Devil of Edmonton, 143
Merry Wives of Windsor, The,
       (Shakespeare), 218, 255
Michaelmas Term, (Middleton), 304, 306,
       309, 317
    the city-country contrast in, 321
    unconscious relationships in, 318
Midas, (Lyly), 37, 39 36
    an Ovidian Romance, 137
Middleton, Thomas, 5, 62, 226, 371, 396
    his characters and free space, 317
    and focus on a general scene, 316–317
    as pageant writer, 303
    his urban settings, 310–311, 318
    women in his comedies, 305
Midsummer Night's Dream, A,
       (Shakespeare), 146, 196–197, 200,
       202, 220, 385
    as festive comedy, 254
Milton, John, 3, 7, 18, 274, 343
    his God, 347
Miss Lonelyhearts, (West), 3
'Modern Drama,' 47
Monteverdi, 343
Montrose, Louis, 163
More Dissemblers Besides Women,
       (Middleton), 371
Mother Bombie, (Lyly), 37–38, 137, 139
Mucedorus, (anonymous), 34, 36, 140,
       143–144, 146
Much Ado About Nothing, (Shakespeare),
       386
Mulier, Hic, 393–394
Mullaney, Stephen, 216–217
Munday, Antony, 142
Mutable and Wavering estate of France,
       from the Yeare of our Lord 1460, until
       the Yeare 1595, 178
Mythomystes, (Reynolds), 18

Nashe, Thomas, 68, 120, 144–145, 164
Navarre, 164, 169–170
    attempted assassination of, 153